TRACING YOUR IRISH ANCESTORS: THE COMPLETE GUIDE

Third Edition

TRACING YOUR IRISH ANCESTORS: THE COMPLETE GUIDE

Third Edition

JOHN GRENHAM ~

Genealogical Publishing Co., Inc.

Third edition published in the USA and Canada, 2006, by
Genealogical Publishing Co., Inc.
3600 Clipper Mill Road, Suite 260
Baltimore, Maryland 21211

Published in Ireland by Gill & Macmillan Ltd.
Hume Avenue, Park West
Dublin 12, Ireland

Library of Congress Catalogue Card Number 2005939144
International Standard Book Number 0-8063-1768-X

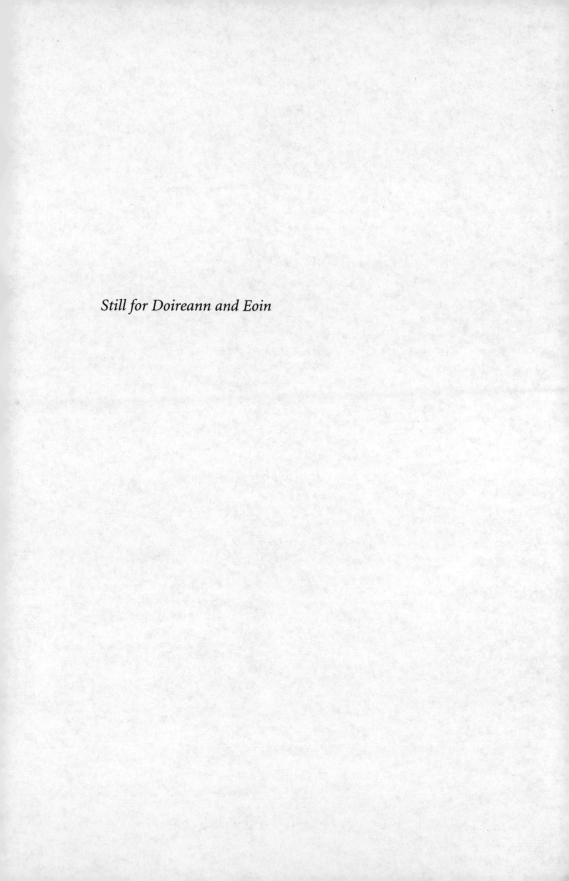

Still for Doireann and Eoin

CONTENTS

ACKNOWLEDGMENTS

My greatest debt is still to Mr Donal Begley, former Chief Herald of Ireland, without whose encouragement and endless patience this work would never have been started. I also owe a great deal to the members and former members of staff at the Genealogical Office, in particular Colette O'Flaherty, Bernard Devaney and the late Willie Buckley, and the Chief Herald, Mr Fergus Gillespie. My colleagues in the Association of Professional Genealogists in Ireland have once again shared their knowledge and experience generously and have contributed very welcome advice and suggestions. I am also grateful to the staff of the National Library of Ireland, the General Register Office, the Public Record Office of Northern Ireland and the National Archives of Ireland for all their help to me over the years. The forbearance and good cheer of the staff of ireland.com were vital, as was Jonathan Hession's unstinting help with rest, recreation and photographs. My deepest thanks to my family, especially to Eoin, who had to suffer months of dark mutterings, wild mood swings and long absences and did so with grace and good humour.

ABBREVIATIONS

AA	Armagh Ancestry
AH	*Analecta Hibernica*
BFA	British Film Area
BIVRI	*British Isles Vital Records Index* (LDS CD-ROM set)
BM	British Museum
C OF I	Church of Ireland
CCAP	Cork City Ancestral Project
CGP	Carlow Genealogy Project
CHGC	Clare Heritage and Genealogical Centre
CHGC	Cavan Heritage and Genealogy Centre
DA	Donegal Ancestry
DCLA	Dublin City Library and Archive
DHG	Dublin Heritage Group
DLGSJ	*Dún Laoghaire Genealogical Society Journal*
DLRHS	Dún Laoghaire-Rathdown Heritage Society
DSHC	Dún na Sí Heritage Centre
EGFHS	East Galway Family History Society Ltd
ENE	Eneclann Ltd
FHP	Fingal Heritage Project
GFHSW	Galway Family History Society West Ltd
GO	Genealogical Office
GPC	Genealogical Publishing Co.
GRO	General Register Office
IA	*The Irish Ancestor*
IFH	*Irish Family History: Journal of the Irish Family History Society*
IG	*The Irish Genealogist*
IGI	International Genealogical Index (LDS)
IGRS	Irish Genealogical Research Society
IMA	Irish Midlands Ancestry
IMC	Irish Manuscripts Commission
Ir.	Irish (National Library of Ireland call number prefix)
IR	*Irish Roots*
IS	*The Irish Sword: the journal of the Military History Society of Ireland*
IUP	Irish University Press

IW	Irish World
J	Joly Collection pamphlet (National Library of Ireland)
JCHAS	*Journal of the Cork Historical & Archaeological Society*
JCLAHS	*Journal of the County Louth Archaeological and Historical Society*
JGAHS	*Journal of the Galway Archaeological and Historical Society*
JKAHS	*Journal of the Kerry Archaeological & Historical Society*
JKAS	*Journal of the Kildare Archaeological Society*
JNMAS	*Journal of the North Munster Archaeological Society*
JPRS	*Journal of the Parish Register Society*
JRSAI	*Journal of the Royal Society of Antiquaries of Ireland*
JWSAS	Journal of the Waterford & Southeast of Ireland Archaeological Society
KA	Kilkenny Ancestry
KCL	Kildare County Library
KGC	Killarney Genealogical Centre
KHGS	Kildare Heritage & Genealogical Society Co. Ltd
LA	Limerick Archives
LC	Local custody
LCL	Leitrim County Library
LDS	Latter-Day Saints (Church of Jesus Christ of)
LEC	Landed Estates Court
LGC	Longford Genealogical Centre
LHC	Leitrim Heritage Centre
LO	Library Office (NLI)
MA	Monaghan Ancestry
MHC	Mallow Heritage Centre
MHC	Meath Heritage Centre
MNFHRC	Mayo North Family History Research Centre
MSFHC	Mayo South Family Heritage Centre
NA (Kew)	The National Archives (England & Wales)
NAI	National Archives of Ireland
NIFHS	North of Ireland Family History Society
NLA	National Library of Australia
NLC	National Library of Canada
NLI	National Library of Ireland
NLNZ	National Library of New Zealand
NLS	National Library of Scotland
O'K	*O'Kief, Coshe Mang etc.* (ed. Albert Casey) NLI Ir. 94145 c 12, LDS film 823801–823809, index 1559438

OS	Ordnance Survey
ph.	Phillimore publication
Pr. Pr.	Privately printed
POS.	Positive (National Library of Ireland microfilm)
PRES	Presbyterian
PRIA	Proceedings of the Royal Irish Academy
PRO	Public Record Office (London)
PRONI	Public Record Office of Northern Ireland
PRS	Parish Register Society Publication
Repr.	Reprinted
RC	Roman Catholic
RCBL	Representative Church Body Library
RDKPRI	Report of the Deputy Keeper of Public Records of Ireland
RHGC	Roscommon Heritage and Genealogy Centre
RIA	Royal Irish Academy
RR	Reading room
SA	*Seanchas Ardmhacha*
SHGC	Sligo Heritage and Genealogical Centre
TCD	Trinity College Dublin
TFHR	Tipperary Family History Research
TGC	The Genealogy Centre, Derry
TNFHF	Tipperary North Family History Foundation
UHF	Ulster Historical Foundation
UHGGN	*Ulster Historical and Genealogical Guild Newsletter*
UJA	*Ulster Journal of Archaeology*
WCHC	West Cork Heritage Centre
WCL	Westmeath County Library
WDCL	Waterford City Library
WFHC	Wicklow Family History Centre
WH	Waterford Heritage Ltd
WSIAHSJ	*Waterford and South East of Ireland Archaeological and Historical Society Journal*

LIST OF ILLUSTRATIONS

PREFACE TO THE THIRD EDITION

In the fourteen years since the first edition of *Tracing your Irish Ancestors* was published, the position of genealogy in Ireland has changed considerably. Then an arcane and eccentric art, practised by and for the blue-rinsed and the tartan-trousered, it has since become a respected and popular area of study. Both the National Library of Ireland and the National Archives of Ireland now have full-time, free genealogy advisory services staffed by professional genealogists—a far cry from the faint condescension meted out to researchers not so long ago. Public libraries all over the country have vastly expanded their holdings and their facilities for genealogists, with database and CD-ROM collections, copies of many LDS Irish microfilms and, in some cases, dedicated research facilities. A highly successful three-year diploma in genealogy is now offered by University College Dublin and attended almost exclusively by Dubliners. Local genealogical conferences are held regularly around the country. Specialist periodicals abound: *Familia, Irish Roots, Irish Family History, The Irish Genealogist, Galway Roots, North Irish Roots*, etc. At the same time, interest in genealogy among the descendants of the Irish emigrants, the Diaspora, has continued to grow.

The single biggest contributory factor to this new state of affairs is information technology and, in particular, the Internet. Although it cannot create new sources for research, the Internet promises to make instantly accessible sources which had previously seemed impossibly fragmented and remote: see, for instance, the Loan Fund Records section in Chapter 2. In Ireland, this promise has not yet been fully realised, but it will be. The most significant change to this current edition of *Tracing your Irish Ancestors* reflects this new dimension: a chapter has been added that deals specifically with the Internet, while a new 'online' subsection has been added to each of the county source lists in Part 3 and, where possible, references have been given throughout for any online versions of the records dealt with. In addition, the Roman Catholic parish maps have been completely revised and redrawn, a guide to variant parish names is supplied and the reference section—Part 3—has been greatly enlarged.

INTRODUCTION

The aim of this book is to provide a comprehensive guide for any person wishing to trace his or her Irish ancestors. As the individual circumstances of each family are unique, the relevant areas of research vary widely from case to case. While some areas will be important for almost all researchers, others are more specialised and are therefore extremely important only in particular cases. This book is structured to reflect that division: Part One examines the basic sources; Part Two details sources with a narrower application; Part Three contains a reference guide to facilitate quick access to a wide range of research materials, including county-by-county source-lists, occupations and Roman Catholic records.

How you use this book depends very much on your individual circumstances. For someone with no experience of genealogical research in Ireland, it would be best to start from this Introduction and work through Part One, leaving Parts Two and Three until the basic materials have been exhausted. For someone who has already covered parish registers, land records, census returns and the State records of births, marriages and deaths, it might be best to start with Part Two. Others may simply want to use the reference guide provided in Part Three as a basis for planning and directing their research. However, as anyone who regularly uses Irish records will know, one of the pleasures of research is the constant discovery of new sources of information and new aspects of familiar sources. The information in this book is the result of many years of such discoveries in the course of full-time professional research, and it is quite possible that even a hardened veteran will find something new in the account of the basic records given in Part One.

WHERE TO START

The first question posed by anyone embarking on ancestral research is: what do I need to know before I start? The answer, rather unhelpfully, is: as much as possible. Although a painstaking examination of original documents can provide much pleasure, in genealogy it is usually better to arrive than to travel in hope. Theoretically, it is possible to start from your own birth and work back through records of births, marriages and deaths, parish records and census records. In practical terms, however, the more that can be gleaned from older family members or from family documents, the better; there is no point combing through decades of parish records to uncover your great-grandmother's maiden name if you could find it out simply by asking Aunt Agatha. Nor does the information you acquire this way need to be absolutely precise. At this point in your research, quantity is superior to quality. Later on, something that at first seemed relatively insignificant—the name of a local parish priest, a story of a contested will, someone's unusual occupation, even a postmark—may well prove to be a vital clue, enabling you to trace the family back further. In any case, whether or not such information eventually turns out to be useful, it will certainly be of interest and will help to flesh out the picture of earlier generations. For most people the spur to starting research is curiosity about their own family, and the kind of anecdotal information provided by the family itself rarely emerges from the official documents.

In order to be able to use the resources fully and successfully, three strands of information are vital: dates, names and places. Dates of emigration, births, marriages and deaths; names of parents, siblings, cousins, aunts, in-laws; addresses, townland names, parishes, towns, counties ... needless to say, not all of this will be essential, and again absolute accuracy is not vital at the beginning. For example, a general location and siblings' names can be used to uncover parents' names and addresses, and their parents' names. One precise name and a date can be used to unlock all the other records. Even the name alone, if it is sufficiently unusual, can sometimes be enough. In general, though, the single most useful piece of information is the precise locality of origin of the family. The county of origin would normally be the minimum information necessary, though in the case of a common surname (of which there are many), even this may not be enough. For the descendants of Irish emigrants, the locality is often one of the most difficult things to discover. There are ways of doing this, however, and the best time to do it is generally before starting your research in Ireland. The most useful Australian, American and British sources for uncovering the locality of origin of Irish emigrants are detailed at the end of this Introduction.

The only cast-iron rule that applies when carrying out research is that you start from what you know and use that to find out more. Each family's circumstances are unique, and where your research leads you will depend very much on the point from which you start. Thus, for example, knowing where a family lived around the beginning of the twentieth century will allow you to uncover a census return with the ages of the individual family members, leading to birth or baptismal records, which will give parents' names and residence, which in turn will lead to early land records, which may permit the identification of generations before the start of parish records. At each stage of such research, the next step should always be determined by what you have just found out: each discovery is a stepping-stone to the next. As a result, it is simply not possible to lay down a routeway that will serve every reader. It is possible, however, to say that there is no point in taking, say, a seventeenth-century pedigree and trying to extend it forward to connect with your family. Although there may very well be a connection, the only way to prove it is by expanding your own family information and then working backwards.

WHAT YOU CAN EXPECT TO FIND
What you will uncover about your family history depends on the quality of the surviving records for the area of origin and, again, on the point from which you

start out. In the majority of cases, that is, for the descendants of Catholic tenant farmers, the limit is generally the starting date of the local Catholic parish records, which varies widely from place to place. However, it would be unusual for records to go back much earlier than the 1780s and for most people the early 1800s is the likeliest limit. In Gaelic culture genealogy was of crucial importance, but the collapse of that culture in the seventeenth century and the subsequent impoverishment and oppression of the native population in the eighteenth century have left a gulf that is almost unbridgeable. That said, exceptions immediately spring to mind. One Australian family, starting with only the name of their great-grandfather, his occupation and the date of his departure from Ireland, uncovered enough information, through parish registers and State records of deaths, marriages and births, to link him incontestably to the Garveys of Mayo, for whom an established pedigree is registered in the Genealogical Office, stretching back to the twelfth century. An American family, knowing only a general location in Ireland and a marriage that took place before emigration, discovered that marriage in the pedigree of the McDermotts of Coolavin, which is factually verified as far back as the eleventh century. Discoveries like this are rare, however, and much likelier in the case of Anglo-Irish families than for those of Gaelic or Scots Presbyterian extraction.

Whatever the outcome, genealogical research offers pleasures and insights that are unique. The desire that drives such an undertaking is simple and undeniable: it is the curiosity of the child who asks, 'Where did I come from?' All history starts from this primary impetus, and genealogy is the most basic form of history— tracing the continual cycle of family growth and demise, unravelling the individual strands of relationship and experience which weave together to form the great patterns of historical change. Reconstructing the details of our own family history is a way of understanding, immediately and personally, the connection between the present and the past: a way of understanding ourselves.

USA SOURCES FOR IDENTIFYING IRISH PLACE OF ORIGIN

Naturalisation Records

These may contain the date and place of birth, occupation, place of residence and name of the ship on which the immigrant arrived in the USA. They are unlikely to give a precise place of origin in Ireland. The records are still found, for the most part, in the courts where the naturalisation proceedings took place, although some records are now held in Federal Record Centres. Pre-1906 Indexes for the states of Maine, Massachusetts, New Hampshire and Rhode Island are available at the National Archives in Washington.

Cemetery and Burial Records

There are two kinds of potentially valuable records: gravestone inscriptions and sextons' records. These vary enormously in usefulness, but can sometimes specify the exact place of origin.

Immigration Records and Passenger Lists

Most of these are now held in the National Archives in Washington. The Customs Passenger Lists, dating from 1820, list only the country of origin, while the Immigration Passenger Lists, dating from 1883, include details of the last place of residence. (See also Chapter 7 for details of other sources, and Chapter 11 for online transcripts.)

Military Records

Depending on place or branch of service, these may specify the place, or at least the county, of origin. See *Guide to Genealogical Records in the National Archives,* by Meredith S. Colket Jr and Frank E. Bridges (1964).

Church Records

In some cases, particularly for the marriages of recently arrived immigrants, these may include details of the Irish place of origin of the persons recorded. Most Catholic records are still held in the individual parishes. The records of other denominations may be held locally, or may be deposited with a variety of institutions, including public libraries, universities and diocesan archives.

Vital Records

Death records, in particular, may be of value because they generally supply parents' names.

CANADIAN SOURCES FOR IDENTIFYING IRISH PLACE OF ORIGIN

National and Provincial Archives

The vast bulk of information of genealogical interest can be found in the National and Provincial Archives of Canada, where the staff members are familiar with the needs of genealogical research and very helpful. The National Archives (395 Wellington Street, Ottawa Ontario K1A 0N3, Tel: 613–995–5138) publishes a useful twenty-page booklet, *Tracing Your Ancestors in Canada,* which is available by mail. Some of the information held in the Provincial Archives, in particular the census records, can also be found in Ottawa, but in general the Provincial Archives has a broader range of information relating to its particular areas. Some of the Provincial Archives also have excellent websites, providing very good immigration information; New Brunswick is an excellent example.

Civil Records

In general, the original registers of births, marriages and deaths, which have widely varying starting dates, are to be found in the offices of the Provincial Registrars General, although microfilm copies of some may also be found in Provincial Archives.

Census Records

Countrywide censuses are available for 1851, 1861, 1871, 1881 and 1891. Many local returns are available for earlier years and record a wide variety of data. The largest such collection is held in the Ottawa National Archives.

Other Sources

Cemetery and burial records, gravestone inscriptions, passenger lists, Church registers and land records may all be of value. The best comprehensive guide is Angus Baxter's *In search of your Canadian roots* (Baltimore, 3rd ed., 1994), which gives details of the wide range of records in the National and Provincial Archives.

AUSTRALIAN SOURCES FOR IDENTIFYING IRISH PLACE OF ORIGIN

Convict Transportation Records

A database index of Dublin Castle's records of those transported from Ireland to Australia was presented to Australia as part of the 1988 Bicentennial celebrations. This index often includes details of the person's conviction and place of residence; see Chapter 7, Emigration, for further information on the records it covers. It is widely available in the Australian State Archives, in the National Archives and on the Internet at *www.nationalarchives.ie*. Many other classes of record, originating both in Australia and in England, also exist and can be found in most Australian repositories.

Assisted Immigration Records

A detailed record was kept of those who availed of assisted passages to Australia: see the New South Wales State Archives' *Guide to Shipping and Free Passenger Lists* and the section, 'Australia', in Chapter 7.

Civil Records

Australian State death records hold a wealth of family detail, in most cases including precise places of origin. Marriage records also supply places of birth and parents' names.

BRITISH SOURCES FOR IDENTIFYING IRISH PLACE OF ORIGIN

England and Wales

Civil registration of births, marriages and deaths began in 1837 and record the same details as those given in Irish records (see Chapter 1). Unfortunately, the marriage records very rarely give exact Irish addresses for parents. But it can sometimes prove worthwhile to extend research into the broader Irish community in a given area because the perennial clannishness of the Irish and the mechanics of chain migration meant that people from a particular area of Ireland tended to gravitate towards each other.

Census records

Seven sets of census returns are available for the period between 1841 and 1901. Those from 1851 to 1901 are available online at various locations, and most allow a search on birthplace. Again, it is rare to find a precise place of birth in Ireland recorded, although the county is sometimes given. As noted before, investigation of the local Irish immigrant populace can yield circumstantial evidence. Both census and civil records are available at the Family Record Centre (1 Myddelton Street, London EC1R 1UW, Tel: +44 181 392 5300, Website: *www.familyrecords.gov.uk*).

Church records

Marriage records for recent immigrants may give the place of origin in Ireland.

Scotland

Civil registration of births, marriages and deaths began in 1855 and recorded substantially more detail than in Ireland or England. In particular, births records show a place and date of marriage, and deaths records supply parents' names.

Scottish census returns are similar to those for England and Wales, and a computerised index for the 1891 census is available.

Civil and census records are available at the General Register Office (New Register House, Princes Street, Edinburgh EH1 3YT). The Scottish Record Office is next door to the GRO and holds a vast array of relevant archive material. Cecil Sinclair's *Tracing Your Scottish Ancestors: a guide to ancestry research in the Scottish Record Office* (Edinburgh, 1990; Revised Edition, 1997) is the standard guide used by researchers. Most relevant records are now searchable online at *www. scotlandspeople.gov.uk*.

The Church of Jesus Christ of Latter-Day Saints

Due to the central importance of the family in its teachings, the Church of Jesus Christ of Latter-day Saints, also known as the Mormon Church, places great emphasis on family history. For many decades the Family History Library in Salt Lake City has been collecting copies of records of genealogical value to aid its members' research. It is now an extraordinary collection, and its Irish section includes virtually all of the General Register Office indexes and registers, a large proportion of church records, the records of the Genealogical Office and the Registry of Deeds, and much more. More detail of the LDS holdings is given in the individual chapters.

If you wish to research these records, it is not necessary to visit the Library in person. Almost every Mormon church has a family history section that is open to non-Church members and that will request copies of any of the microfilms from Salt Lake City on a researcher's behalf—in effect providing a worldwide system of access to copies of the original records. For those for whom a research visit to Ireland is impractical, the LDS Family History Centres are almost as good. To make things even easier, many LDS records are searchable online at *www. familysearch.org*.

Chapter 1 ᕀ

GENERAL REGISTER OFFICE RECORDS

HISTORY AND ACCESS

State registration of non-Roman Catholic marriages in Ireland began in 1845; all births, deaths and marriages have been registered in Ireland since 1864. In order to appreciate what precisely these records comprise, it is necessary to have some idea of how registration began. It was, in fact, an offshoot of the Victorian public health system, in turn based on the Poor Law—an attempt to provide some measure of relief for the most destitute in society. Between 1838 and 1852, 163 workhouses were built throughout the country, each located at the centre of an area known as a Poor Law Union. The workhouse was commonly situated in a large market town and the Poor Law Union comprised the town and its catchment area, with the result that in many cases the Unions ignored the existing boundaries of parish and county. This had consequences for research, which we shall see below.

In the 1850s a large-scale public health system was created, based on the areas covered by the Poor Law Unions. Each Union was divided into Dispensary Districts, with an average of six to seven Districts per Union, and a Medical Officer, normally a doctor, was given responsibility for public health in each District. With the introduction of registration of all births, deaths and marriages in 1864, these Dispensary Districts also became Registrar's Districts, each having a Registrar responsible for collecting the registrations within that particular District. Although not true across the board, in most cases the Medical Officer for the Dispensary District now also acted as the Registrar for the same area. The Registrar's superior was the Superintendent Registrar, responsible for all the Registers within the old Poor Law Union. The returns for the entire Poor Law Union (also known both as the Superintendent Registrar's District and, simply, the Registration District) were indexed and collated centrally, and master indexes for the entire country were produced at the General Register Office (GRO) in Dublin. These are the indexes now used for public research.

The historical origins of the system means that responsibility for registration in the Republic of Ireland still rests with the Department of Health. At present the arrangement is that the local Registrars in each Health Service Executive Area hold the original registers, while the General Register Office public research facility (located at 8–11 Lombard Street, Dublin 2) holds the master indexes to all thirty-two counties up to 1921, and to the twenty-six counties of the Republic of Ireland after 1921. (The administrative headquarters of the GRO is now located at Convent Road, Roscommon.) The General Register Office of Northern Ireland has computerised copies of all the indexes of births, marriages and deaths for the areas now under its jurisdiction. It also holds copies of the birth and death registers. The original marriage registers, up to 1922, are still held by the District Registrars based in the local councils, while database transcriptions of these are held by the Northern Ireland heritage centres (see Chapter 15).

Under the original system, the local registrars forwarded their records to Dublin, where they were copied before being returned to the local office. As well as holding the master indexes for the entire country, the GRO also holds microfilms of all of these copy registers—the only part of the registration system that permits comprehensive public research. These indexes are available to the public on the first floor of 8 Lombard Street at a fee of €1.90 per five years searched, or €15.24 for a general search. It is important to note that only the indexes are open to the public; to obtain the full information contained in the original register entry it is necessary to purchase a printout from the microfilm, at €1.90 per entry. These printouts are supplied for information only and have no legal standing. Full certificates—for use in obtaining passports or in testamentary transactions—currently cost €6.98. Limited research, covering five years of the indexes, is carried out by the staff in response to postal queries only, and for a fee of €1.90.

It is also possible to carry out research in the local registrar's offices around the country. However, this is at the discretion of the local officials, and reforms introduced in the Civil Registration Act 2004 threaten to centralise the local registers and do away with this possibility. This would be a regrettable outcome; in some cases, particularly for common surnames, going through the local offices can be the only way to reconstruct a whole family, since the relevant research is on the original registers rather than on the indexes. Some of the local heritage centres, including Clare, Derry, Mayo and Tipperary South, now have database transcripts of these local registers, but only commissioned research is possible.

Another avenue of access to GRO records is through the Family History Library of the Church of Jesus Christ of Latter-Day Saints (LDS), the Mormons. In the late 1950s and early 1960s the LDS Library carried out a huge microfilming programme on GRO records and it now holds several thousand films of information from both the centralised indexes and the registers. Almost every Mormon temple includes a Family History Centre, which will order copies of any of the LDS microfilms. Unfortunately, the collection is not complete: in particular, the birth registers for the last two decades of the nineteenth century and the marriage and death registers after 1870 are missing, an omission that is now unlikely to be made good. Two Dublin libraries, Dublin City Library and Archive and South Dublin County Library in Tallaght, hold copies of the GRO master indexes on LDS microfilm; details of the full LDS holdings are given below.

LDS **Microfilms of** GRO **records**

BIRTHS

Area	Indexes	Film Reference	Registers	Film Reference
All Ireland	1864–1921	0101041–01001079	1864–1st Q. 1881	0101080–0257861
				1419540–1419541
			1900–1913	0257861–0258168
Republic of Ireland	1922–1958	0101229–0101240, 0231962–0231969	1930–1955	0258169–0258441
Northern Ireland	1922–1959	0231962–0231969	1922–1959	0231970–0259147

MARRIAGES

Area	Indexes	Film Reference	Registers	Film Reference
All Ireland	1845–1921	0101241–0101264	1845–1870	0101265–0101572
Republic of Ireland	1922–1958	0101575–0101581, 0257850–0257852		
Northern Ireland	1922–1959	0232169–0232173	1922–1959	0232174–0232471

DEATHS

Area	Indexes	Film Reference	Registers	Film Reference
All Ireland	1864–1921	0101582–0101608	1864–1870	0101609–0101727
Republic of Ireland	1922–1958	0101735–0101744, 0257853–0257856		
Northern Ireland	1922–1959	0232472–0232478	1922–1959	0232479–0259139

The LDS website, *www.familysearch.org*, includes an index to Irish births for the period 1864–1875 (incl.) as part of its International Genealogical Index. This was originally published as part of the LDS CD-ROM set entitled *British Isles Vital Records Index* (2nd ed., 2001).

All of the Republic of Ireland GRO records have now been computerised, but the system is currently (2005) available only to the Office staff. An internet service is promised and devoutly to be wished, but is likely to take some time. The Scottish GRO, *www.scotlandspeople.gov.uk*, provides a good example of what can be achieved.

INFORMATION GIVEN
One of the peculiarities of the system of registration is that although the local Registrars were responsible for the Registers, the legal obligation to register births and deaths actually rested with the public and was enforced with hefty fines.

Marriage registration, on the other hand, was generally the responsibility of the officiating clergyman. The classes of people required to carry out registration in each of the three categories are given below, along with a detailed account of the information they were required to supply. It should be remembered that not all of this information is relevant to genealogical research.

BIRTHS
Persons required to register births were:
(1)   the parent, or parents;
(2)   in the event of death or inability of the parent or parents, the occupier of the house or tenement in which the child was born; or
(3)   the Nurse; or
(4)   any person present at the birth of the child.

The information they were required to supply was:
(1)   the date and place of birth of the child;
(2)   the name (if any);
(3)   the sex;
(4)   the name, surname and dwelling place of the father;
(5)   the name, surname, maiden surname and dwelling place of the mother;
(6)   the rank, profession, or occupation of the father.

The informant and the Registrar were both required to sign each entry, which was also to include the date of registration, the residence of the informant and his or her 'qualification', for example, 'present at birth'. Notice of the birth was to be given to the Registrar within twenty-one days and full details within three months. It was not obligatory to register a first name for the child. The very small proportion for whom no first name was supplied appear in the indexes as, for example, 'Kelly (male)', or 'Murphy (female)'.

DEATHS
Persons required to register deaths were:
(1)   some person present at death; or
(2)   some person in attendance during the last illness of the deceased; or
(3)   the occupier of the house or tenement where the death took place; or
(4)   someone else residing in the house or tenement where the death took place; or
(5)   any person present at, or having knowledge of the circumstances of, the death.

The information they were required to supply was:
(1)   the date and place of death;
(2)   the name and surname of the deceased;
(3)   the sex of the deceased;

(4)   the condition of the deceased as to marriage;
(5)   the age of the deceased at last birthday;
(6)   the rank, profession, or occupation of the deceased;
(7)   the certified cause of death, and the duration of the final illness.

Again, the informant and the Registrar were both required to sign each entry, which was also to include the date of registration, the residence of the informant and his or her 'qualification', for example, 'present at death'. Notice of the death was to be given to the Registrar within seven days and full details within fourteen days.

MARRIAGES
From 1864 on any person whose marriage was to be celebrated by a Roman Catholic clergyman was required to have the clergyman fill out a certificate containing the information detailed below, and to forward it within three days of the marriage to the Registrar. In practice, as had already been the case for non-Roman Catholic marriages from 1845, the clergyman simply kept blank copies of these certificates, filled them in after the ceremony and forwarded them to the Registrar.
    The information to be supplied was:

(1)   the date of marriage;
(2)   the names and surnames of each of the parties marrying;
(3)   their respective ages;
(4)   their condition (i.e. bachelor, spinster, widow, widower);
(5)   their rank, profession, or occupation;
(6)   their residences at the time of marriage;
(7)   the name and surname of the fathers of each of the parties;
(8)   the rank, profession, or occupation of the fathers of each of the parties.

The certificate also had to state where the ceremony had been performed and had to be signed by the clergyman, the parties marrying and two witnesses.

GENEALOGICAL RELEVANCE
From a genealogical point of view, only the following information is of genuine interest.

Births: the name of the child; the date of birth; the place of birth; the name, surname and dwelling place of the father; the name, surname and dwelling place of the mother; and, occasionally, the name, residence and qualification of the informant.

Marriages: parish in which the marriage took place; names, ages, residences and occupations of the persons marrying; names and occupations of their fathers.

INDEX to BIRTHS REGISTERED in IRELAND in 1866.

District.	Vol.	Page	Name and Registration District.	Vol.	Page	Name and Registra
....	7	411	PELL, John Joseph. Dublin, North	12	584	PERCY, Robert Henry Car
....	13	328	PELLETT, Anna Maria. Dublin, South	12	656	—— William. Antrim ....
....	20	286	PELLICAN, John. Listowel	10	500	PERDUE, John. Callan ...
....	6	991	PELLY, Catherine. Ballinasloe	19	37	—— Mary Anne. Tipper
elin. Lisburn .	1	659	—— Catherine Evangiline. Dublin, South ...	2	745	PERIL, Patrick. Gort ....
....	17	715	—— John Joseph. Dublin, South	2	737	PERKINS, Cornelius. Thu
....	11	893	—— Mary. Portumna	14	946	—— Joseph John. Dubli
th..................	7	572	PEMBERTON, Marian Sydney. Dublin, North .	17	527	—— Patrick. Naas ....
....	5	140	—— (female). Dublin, South	7	811	—— Robert Henry. Dubl
....	11	222	PEMBROKE, Ellen. Tralee..........	20	627	—— Thomas. Oughterar
....	20	104	—— Ellen. Tralee..........	15	596	—— (female). Ballina
....	11	782	—— Margaret. Kilkenny	8	603	PERKINSON, Barkly. Abb
....	7	937	—— Mary. Dingle	15	207	PERKISSON, Briget. Thur
....	7	732	—— Mary Eliza. Kilkenny	3	609	PERRILL, Patrick. Cliffden
....	3	447	—— Patrick. Listowel	10	501	PERRIN Ellen. Dublin, N
erick	20	432	PENDER, Anne. Enniscorthy	14	725	—— Henrietta. Rathdow
....	19	500	—— Bernard. Carrick-on-Shannon	18	65	—— William Alexander.
....	14	82	—— Bridget. Enniscorthy	4	814	—— (female). Cavan ...
....	14	476	—— Bridget. Enniscorthy	9	753	PERROT, Catherine. Dubl
....	10	128	—— Daniel. Gorey	7	876	—— Sarah. Clonakilty ...
....	6	178	—— Daniel. Gorey	7	877	PERROTT, Margaret. Ban
forth..........	7	549	—— Elizabeth. Nenagh	3	651	—— Robert. Cork ....
....	15	394	—— Elizabeth. Carlow	13	447	—— William Cooke Colli
....	20	154	—— Ellen. Ballymoney	6	194	—— William Thomas. C
....	10	735	—— Ellen. Rathdown	12	920	PERRY, Agnes. Belfast ...
....	2	728	—— Ellen. Enniscorthy	19	764	—— Agnes. Lisburn ...
....	11	112	—— James. Waterford	9	951	—— Angelina Margaret.
....	6	613	—— John. Carlow	8	507	—— Ann. Downpatrick
....	14	376	—— John. Enniscorthy	14	722	—— Ann Jane. Ballymea
....	1	173	—— John. Mullingar	13	317	—— Anthony. Enniscort
thdown	17	889	—— Joseph. Athy	13	406	—— Catherine. Baltingl
....	5	232	—— Laurance. Carlow	13	436	—— Eliza. Ballymahon
... .	1	264	—— Mary. Wexford	14	911	—— Eliza. Naas ....
f. Parsonstown	18	599	—— Mary Anne. Carlow	3	505	—— Eliza. Belfast ....
atrick..........	11	531	—— Mary Catherine. Carlow	18	427	—— Elizabeth. Ballyme
....	11	834	—— Mathew. Wexford	14	910	—— Elizabeth. Larne ..
....	2	463	—— Michael. Carlow	3	494	—— Ellen. Ballymena ..
....	17	386	—— Peter. Rathdrum	2	1061	—— Etheld Letitia. Mul
....	7	653	—— Thomas. Ballinasloe	19	31	—— Hannah. Larne....
blin, South ...	17	622	—— William. Waterford	19	925	—— Helena Jane. Londo
....	10	665	—— (female). Limerick	10	454	—— Henry. Newry ....
louth	7	672	PENDERGAST, Anne. Roscommon	18	333	—— James. Dundalk ...
....	16	281	—— Bridget. Tulla	19	606	—— James. Dublin, Nor
....	12	892	—— Catherine. Swineford	4	579	—— James. Baltinglass
....	2	750	—— Ellen. Castlereagh	19	161	—— Jane. Banbridge ...
....	15	244	—— Margaret. Castlereagh	19	162	—— Jane Eleanor. Belf
....	20	179	—— Margaret. Killarney	5	400	—— John. Lisburn ....
....	14	905	—— Mary. Bawnboy	3	51	—— John. Naas ....
....	9	950	—— Mary. Castlebar	19	133	—— Joseph. Ballymena.
... .	12	655	—— Myles. Wexford	19	955	—— Letitia Anne. Dubl
....	9	370	—— Pat. Ballinrobe	4	51	—— Martin. Newtownar
th..................	7	571	—— Patrick. Rathdown	17	891	—— Mary. Ballymahon
....	11	82	—— Patrick. Monaghan	8	330	—— Mary Anne. Banbr
outh	7	813	PENDERGAST, Anne. New Ross	4	969	—— Rebecca. Ballymen
....	1	757	—— Ellen. Killarney	15	315	—— Robinson Gale. R
n, North	2	690	—— Michael. Killarney	15	316	—— Sarah. Downpatric
agh	11	82	PENDERS, Mary. Nenagh	13	584	—— Sarah. Newtownar
....	8	503	PENDLETON, Essie. Lurgan	16	673	—— Sarah. Ballymena.
....	17	38	PENGELLY, Michael James. Cork	20	193	—— Susanna. Downpat
n, North	2	630	PENNAFATHER, (male). Rathkeale	10	621	—— Thomas. Trim ....
forth	12	547	PENNAMEN, Mary Jane Fraser. Belfast	11	277	—— Thomas. Belfast ..
....	...	838	PENNEFATHER, John Thomas. Dublin, North .	2	608	—— Thomas Shanklin.
....	...	...	—— Richard Dymock. Cashel	3	331	—— William. Tipperar
....	16	768	PENNELL, (male). Cork	15	101	—— William Gardiner.
....	11	43	PENNINGTON, Charles. Banbridge	16	229	—— William Richard Vic
....	9	871	PENNY, John. Ballymena..........	11	113	—— William Robinson.
....	5	175	—— (male). Wexford	14	922	—— (male). Clonmel ..
....	11	98	PENNYCOOK, Janet. Athy	8	459	—— (male). Armagh ..

General Register Office births index

(Courtesy of the National Library of Ireland)

Deaths: place of death; age at death; and, occasionally, the name, residence and qualification of the informant.

Of these three categories the most useful is certainly the marriage entry, both because it provides fathers' names, thus giving a direct link to the preceding generation, and because it is the easiest to identify from the indexes, as we shall see below. Birth entries are much more difficult to identify correctly from the indexes without having precise information about date and place, and even with such information the high concentrations of people of the same surname within particular localities of the country can make it difficult to be sure that a particular birth registration is the relevant one. Unlike many other countries, death records in Ireland are not very useful for genealogical purposes because there was no obligation to record family information and the 'age at death' is often imprecise. That said, these records can sometimes be of value. The 'person present at death' was often a family member and the relationship is sometimes specified in the register entry. Even the age recorded may be useful, since it at least gives an indication of how old the deceased was thought to be by family or neighbours.

A general word of warning about civil registration is necessary here: a certain proportion of all three categories simply went unregistered. It is impossible to be sure how much is missing, since the thoroughness of local registration depended very much on local conditions and on the individuals responsible, but experience in cross-checking from other sources, such as parish and census records, suggests that as much as 10–15 per cent of marriages and births simply do not appear in the registers.

RESEARCH IN THE INDEXES

When carrying out research in all three areas a large dose of scepticism is necessary with regard to the dates of births, marriages and deaths reported by family members before 1900. This is especially true for births; the ages given in census returns, for example, are almost always inaccurate and round figures—50, 60, 70, etc.—must be treated with particular caution. The actual date of birth is almost always well before that reported, sometimes by as much as fifteen years. Why this should be so is a matter for speculation, but vanity and mendacity are probably not to blame. It seems more likely that until quite recently very few people actually knew their precise date of birth. And as most people don't feel their age, after middle age at least, a guess will usually produce an underestimate. Whatever the explanation, charitable or otherwise, it is always wiser to search a range of the indexes before the reported date, rather than after it.

From 1864 to 1877 the indexes consist of a single yearly volume in each of the three categories—births, marriages and deaths—which covers the entire country and records all names in a straightforward alphabetical arrangement. The same arrangement applies to the non-Roman Catholic marriages registered from April 1845. From 1878 the yearly volume is divided into four quarters, with each quarter covering three months and indexed separately. This means that a search for a name in, for example, the 1877 births index requires looking in one place in the index, but checking four different places in the 1878 index—one in each of the four quarters. From 1903, in the case of births only, the indexes once again cover the entire year, and from this year on the mother's maiden surname is also supplied. In all three categories each index entry lists surname, first name, Registration District, volume and page number. The deaths indexes also list the reported age at death. The 'volume and page number' simply make up the reference for the original register entry, necessary in order to identify it and, in the GRO research room, to obtain a photocopy of the full information given in that entry. The remaining three items— surname, first name and Registration District—are dealt with in detail below.

Surname

While the order followed in the indexes is strictly alphabetical, it is always necessary to keep possible variants of the surname in mind. In the late nineteenth century, when the majority of the population was illiterate, the precise spelling of surnames was a matter of indifference to most people. As a result, members of the same family may be registered as, for example, Kilfoyle, Gilfoyle and Guilfoile. The question of variants is particularly important for names beginning with 'O', or 'Mac'. Until the start of the Gaelic revival, at the end of the last century, these pre-fixes were often treated as entirely optional and, particularly in the case of 'O', more often omitted than included. For instance, until well into the twentieth century a large number of O'Briens were recorded under 'Brien', or 'Bryan'. Accordingly, before starting a search in the indexes it is essential to have as clear an idea as possible of the variants that must also be checked. Otherwise it may be necessary to review the same period as many as three or four times.

First name

The range of first names in use in the nineteenth century was severely limited among the vast majority of the population. Apart from some localised names— Cornelius in south Munster, Crohan in the Caherdaniel area of the Iveragh Peninsula, Sabina in the east Galway/north Roscommon area—the anglicisation of older Gaelic names was restrictive and unimaginative. In all parts of the country John, Patrick, Michael, Mary and Bridget occur with almost unbelievable frequency. Combined with the intensely localised nature of surnames, which reflected the earlier tribal divisions of the country, this trend can present great difficulties for those using the indexes. For example, a single quarter of 1881, from January to March, might contain twenty or more John (O')Reilly or Riley regis-trations within a single County Cavan Registration District. A further difficulty is the fact that it is very rare for more than one first name to be registered. Therefore a person known to the family as John James (O')Reilly will almost certainly appear in the index simply as John.

It is, of course, possible to examine all of the original register entries, but unless some other piece of information can be used to cross-check, such as the parents' names or the townland address, it will almost certainly not be possible to identify which, if any, of the original register entries is the relevant one. This uncertainty is compounded still further by the persistent inaccuracies regarding ages and dates of birth, which mean that over the seven- or eight-year period when the relevant birth might have taken place, there might be fifty or sixty births of the same name in the one county. Where the precise district is known, one way to overcome this problem is to examine the original registers in order to build a picture of every family in which the relevant name occurs. As already mentioned, the original registers are kept in the local registrar's offices. Although the situation varies from district to district, people visiting the offices in person are usually allowed to examine the original books. The relevant addresses can be found in local telephone directories, under the Health Service Executive. Despite all of these problems there is a number of ways in which the countrywide births indexes can be used successfully by narrowing the area and period to be searched with information obtained from other sources. We shall examine this solution presently.

Registration District

As a result of the original arrangements for administering the system, the Registration Districts were, and still are, largely identical with the old Poor Law Unions. As these were based on natural catchment areas—normally a large market town and its rural hinterland—rather than on the existing administrative divisions of townland, parish and county, Registration Districts for births, marriages and deaths cut right across these earlier boundaries, a fact that can be very significant for researchers. For example, Waterford Registration District, which centres on the town of Waterford, also takes in a large part of rural south Co. Kilkenny. The only comprehensive guide to the towns and townlands contained in each Registration District is a series of pamphlets produced in the nineteenth century by the Registrar-General's Office for the use of local registrars. This information has now been reproduced in George B. Handran's *Townlands in poor law unions: a reprint of poor law union pamphlets of the general registrar's office with an introduction, and six appendices relating to Irish genealogical research* (Salem, Massachusetts: Higginson Book, 1997, 616 p. NLI Ir. 9291 h 5.).This is particularly useful when a problem arises in identifying a variant version of a townland name given in the original register entry for a marriage, birth, or death. By scanning the lists of townlands in the relevant district in which the entry is recorded, it is almost always possible to identify the standard version of the name and, from this, to progress to census, parish and land records.

To go in the other direction, that is, to find out which Registration District a particular town or townland lies within, the standard source is the *Alphabetical Index to the Towns, Townlands and Parishes of Ireland*. Three editions of this index were published, based on the census returns for 1851, 1871 and 1901, respectively. In the first two editions the Registration District is recorded as the Poor Law Union; in the 1901 index it does not appear in the body of the work but is presented as an appendix. Copies of these editions can be found on open access in NLI, NAI, the GRO, or in any public library. The 1851 index is by far the most widely available and can be accessed online at *www.seanruad.com* and at *scripts.ire-land.com/ancestor/placenames*. If the original townland or address of the family being researched is known and the search thus narrowed to a single Registration District, then at least some of the problems in identifying the relevant entry, particularly in the birth indexes, can be significantly reduced.

RESEARCH TECHNIQUES

Births
As highlighted above, it is important to approach the birth indexes with as much information as possible from other sources. If the birth took place between 1864 and 1880, the family was Roman Catholic and the relevant area is known, it may be best in the first instance to try to identify a baptism from parish records. If information rather than a certificate is the aim of the research, then in many cases the parish record will suffice. If the area is known but not the date, it may be useful to search the 1901 and 1911 census returns to obtain at least an approximate age and, hence, date of birth. If the names of siblings and the order of their birth are known but the area and date are not, it may be necessary to search a wide range of years in the indexes, noting all births registered under those names which occur in the family, and from that try to work out which births of the relevant names occur in the right order in the same Registration District. If the name is unusual, of course, none of this may be necessary. In Ireland, however, few of us are lucky enough to have an ancestor called Horace Freke-Blood, or Euphemia Thackaberry.

Marriages
As long as care is taken over the question of surname variants, and the names of both parties are known, research in the marriage indexes is straightforward. If two people married each other, then obviously the Registration District, volume and page number references for them in the indexes must be the same. Therefore it is only necessary to cross-check the two names in the indexes, working back from the approximate date of birth of the eldest child, if this is known, until two entries are found in which all three references correspond. Marriage records are especially important in the early years of civil registration because they record the names of the fathers of people born c.1820–c.1840 as well as their approximate ages, thus providing evidence that can be used to establish earlier generations in parish records. For non-Roman Catholic families the value of these records is even greater, as the records of non-Roman Catholic marriages start in 1845.

Deaths
As in the case of births, it is essential to uncover as much information as possible from other sources before starting a search of the death indexes. If a date of birth is gleaned from parish or other records, then the 'age at death' given in the index along with the Registration District provides at least a rough guide as to whether

or not the death recorded is the relevant one. If the location of a family farm is known, the approximate date of death can often be worked out from the changes in occupier recorded in the Valuation Books of the Land Valuation Office (see Chapter 4). Similarly, if the family had property, the Will Calendars of the National Archives post-1858 (see Chapter 8) can be the easiest way to pinpoint the precise date of death. Armed with such information, it is usually a simple matter to pick out the relevant entry from the indexes. Information from a marriage entry may also be useful on occasion; along with the names of the fathers of the parties marrying, the register entry might also specify that one or both of the fathers is deceased. There is no rule about this, however. The fact that a father is recorded as, say, 'John Murphy, labourer', does not necessarily mean that he was alive at the time of the marriage. If an individual is recorded as 'deceased', this at least provides an end-point for any search for his death entry. As already pointed out, however, death records give no information on preceding generations and only occasionally name a surviving family member.

LIVING RELATIVES

It is very difficult to use the records of the GRO to trace descendants, rather than forebears, of a particular family. From 1902, as already noted, the birth indexes do record the mother's maiden name, as well as the name and surname of the child, so it can be a straightforward matter to trace all the births of a particular family from that date forward. Uncovering the subsequent marriages of those children without knowing the names of their spouses is a much harder proposition, however. To take one example, the likely range of years of marriage for a Michael O'Brien born in 1905 would be 1925–1940, but there are hundreds of marriages recorded in the indexes under that name. One could, of course, purchase copies of all of the original register entries in the hope that one entry might show the relevant address and father's name and then investigate births of that marriage, but in most cases the work involved in such an undertaking makes the task impractical. But there are other ways to track descendants: through land, census, voters' and, sometimes, parish records (see Chapters 2, 3 and 4).

LATE REGISTRATIONS, ARMY RECORDS, etc.

Late Registrations

A significant proportion of all births, marriages and deaths were not registered. When the individuals concerned, or their relatives, later needed a certificate for official purposes, it then became necessary to register the event. The index references for these late registrations are included in the volume for the year in which the event took place. Thus, for example, the index reference for someone born in 1880 but whose birth was not registered until 1900 is to be found in the index for 1880. In the case of births and deaths, these references are indexed separately from the main body of the index, at the back of the volume. For marriages, late registrations are written in by hand at the relevant point in the main body of the index. Although the chance of finding a missing registration among these is quite slim, it is still necessary to include them in any thorough search of the indexes.

Maritime records
Since 1864 the General Register Office has maintained a separate Marine Register of births and deaths of Irish subjects which took place at sea. For the years since 1886 a printed index to this register is bound into the back of the birth and death for each year. For earlier registers, the indexes must be specifically requested from the staff in the GRO. The LDS copy is on Film 101765. No separate register was kept for marriages which took place at sea.

Army records
The Births, Deaths and Marriages (Army) Act 1879 required these events to be registered with the Office of the Registrar-General in Dublin where they affected Irish subjects serving abroad with the British Army. Separate indexes, bound into the back of the main, yearly indexes, start from 1888 and continue until 1930 for birth and until 1931 for marriages and deaths. The death index for 1902 also contains an index to 'Deaths of Irish Subjects pertaining to the South African War (1898–1902)'. There is also a separate register for deaths of Irish soldiers in the First World War (1914–1918).

The Foreign Register
From 1864 the GRO was required to keep a separate register of births of Irish subjects abroad, where such births were notified to the relevant British consul. There is no index to this register, which is small, and it is not available in the public research room; it may be requested from the staff of the Office.

The Schulze Register
The GRO also holds the 'General Index to Baptisms and Marriages purported to have been celebrated by the Rev J.G.F. Schulze 1806–1837'. Schulze was one of a group of eleven Dublin clergymen known, with characteristic Dublin bluntness, as 'couple-beggars'. Between 1799 and 1844 Schulze and his ilk specialised in clandestine marriages. The records of the other ten men were destroyed in the fire in the Public Record Office in 1922, but a court challenge in the 1870s resulted in Schulze's marriages being declared legally sound and two volumes of his records were acquired by the GRO. These record fifty-five baptisms and c.6,000 marriages. Most of the marriages, which were celebrated at the German Lutheran Church in Poolbeg Street, Dublin, occurred in the years 1825–1837 and record only the names of the contracting parties. The LDS copy is on Film 101771.

USING CIVIL RECORDS WITH OTHER SOURCES
We have already examined some of the areas in which information from other sources may be used to simplify research in civil records. What follows is an

expanded guide to the ways in which civil records can supplement, or be supplemented by, those other sources.

Births
Ages recorded in the 1901 and 1911 census returns (see Chapter 2) can be used to narrow the range of years to be searched. If the birth registration is uncovered first, it records the precise residence of the parents, which can then lead to the relevant census returns, which in turn can provide more comprehensive information on other family members.

Marriages
The 1911 census records the number of years each couple has been married, the number of children born and the number of those children still living. This information is obviously very useful in narrowing the range of years to be searched for a particular marriage. In the case of names common in a particular area, the father's name given in the marriage record is often the only firm evidence to allow identification of the relevant baptismal record in the parish registers. Once a marriage has been located in civil records, thus showing the relevant parish, it is always worthwhile to check the church record of that marriage. As church marriage registers were standardised from the 1860s on, they became more informative and in many cases names, addresses and occupations of both the mother and father of the parties marrying are supplied. In the case of most Dublin Roman Catholic parishes, this information is recorded from around 1856.

Deaths
The records of the Valuation Office (Chapter 4), or the testamentary records of the National Archives (Chapter 8) can be used to pinpoint the year of death, thus making a successful search more likely. The place of death given, if it is not the home of the deceased person, may be the home of a relative. This can be investigated first through land records (Chapter 4), and subsequently through parish and census records, which may provide further information on other branches of the family.

Chapter 2 ⌒

CENSUS RECORDS

OFFICIAL CENSUSES IN IRELAND

Full government censuses of the whole island were taken in 1821, 1831, 1841, 1851, 1861, 1871, 1881, 1891, 1901 and 1911. The first four—1821, 1831, 1841, 1851— were largely destroyed in the fire at the Public Record Office in 1922; surviving fragments are detailed below. Those for 1861, 1871, 1881 and 1891 were completely destroyed prior to 1922, by order of the government. This means that the earliest surviving comprehensive returns are for 1901 and 1911. Because of this, the normal rule that census returns should not be available to the public for 100 years has been suspended in the Republic of Ireland and microfilm copies of the census for 1901 and 1911 can be consulted in the NAI. Microfilm copies are also available via the LDS Family History Library in Salt Lake City, America. Indexes, published or online, are available for the 1901 returns of some counties; these are noted under the relevant county in Chapter 13. Copies of the 1901 returns for the six counties now in Northern Ireland are available at the Public Record Office of Northern Ireland.

1901 AND 1911

Information given

Although these returns are very late and therefore of limited value for most research purposes, the information they contain can still be extremely useful. The 1901 returns record:

- name;
- relationship to the head of the household;
- religion;
- literacy;
- occupation;
- age;
- marital status;
- county of birth;
- ability to speak English or Irish.

The returns also record details of the dwelling house, listing the number of rooms, outhouses and windows and the roof type. Family members not present when the census was taken are not given. The same information was collected again in 1911, with one important addition: married women were required to state the number of years they had been married, the number of children born alive and the number of children still living. Unfortunately, widows were not required to give this information, although a good number obliged in any case. Only the initials, not the full names, of policemen and inmates of mental hospitals were recorded.

Uses

(i) Age
The most obviously useful information given in 1901 and 1911 is age; unfortunately, this is also the information that needs to be treated with the most caution. Precious few of the ages given in the two sets of returns match precisely. Indeed, in the decade between the two censuses most people appear to have aged significantly more than ten years. Of the two, 1901 seems to be the less accurate, with widespread underestimation of age. Nonetheless, if used with caution, the returns do provide a rough guide to age, which can help to narrow the range of years to be searched in earlier civil records of births, marriages and deaths, or in parish records.

(ii) Location
When the names of all or most of the family are known and the general area, although not the precise locality, it is possible to search all of the returns for that area to pinpoint the relevant family. This can be particularly useful when the surname is very common; the likelihood of two families of Murphy in the same area naming their children identically is slight.

(iii) Cross-checking
In some instances, again when a name is common, it is impossible to be certain from information uncovered in civil or parish records that a particular family is the relevant one. In such cases, where details of the subsequent history of the family are known—dates of death or emigration, or siblings' names, for instance—a check of the 1901 or 1911 census for the family can provide useful circumstantial evidence. More often than not any certainties produced will be negative, but the elimination of false trails is a vital part of any research. An example will illustrate why: Peter Barry, born in Co. Cork, c.1880, parents unknown, emigrated to the USA in 1897. A search of civil birth records turns up four cases of 'Peter Barry' recorded in the county between 1876 and 1882, with no way of distinguishing which, if any, is the relevant one. A search of the 1901 census returns for the addresses given in the four birth entries shows two of the four to be still living there. These can now be safely eliminated and research concentrated on the other two families.

CENSUS OF IRELAND, 1901.

(Two Examples of the mode of filling up this Table are given on the other side).

FORM A.

No. on Form B. 3

RETURN of the MEMBERS of this FAMILY and their VISITORS, BOARDERS, SERVANTS, &c., who slept or abode in this House on the night of SUNDAY, the 31st of MARCH, 1901.

No.	NAME and SURNAME	RELATION to Head of Family	RELIGIOUS PROFESSION	EDUCATION	AGE (Males / Females)	SEX	RANK, PROFESSION, OR OCCUPATION	MARRIAGE	WHERE BORN	IRISH LANGUAGE	If Deaf and Dumb; Dumb only; Blind; Imbecile or Idiot; or Lunatic
1	Bernard McEnret	Head of Family	Roman Catholic	Read & Write	50	M	Farmer	Married	Co. Cavan	Irish & English	—
2	Mary McEnret	Wife	do. Catholic	Read & Write	48	F	Farmers Wife	Married	Co. Cavan	Irish & English	—
3	Marie McEnret	Daughter	do. Catholic	Read & Write	23	F	Farmers Daughter	not married	Co. Cavan	English	—
4	Ellen McEnret	Daughter	do. Catholic	Read & Write	19	F	Farmers Daughter	not married	Co. Cavan	English	—
5	John McEnret	Nephew	do. Catholic	Read & Write	6	M	Scholar	not married	Co. Cavan	English	—
6											
7											
8											
9											
10											
11											
12											
13											
14											
15											

I hereby certify, as required by the Act 63 Vic., cap. 6, s. 6 (1), that the foregoing Return is correct, according to the best of my knowledge and belief.

Michael Gillen (Signature of Enumerator.)

I believe the foregoing to be a true Return.

Bernard McEnret (Signature of Head of Family).

Form A, 1901 Census (NAI: Cen 1901/Cavan/89/2/3)
(Courtesy of the National Archives of Ireland)

CENSUS OF IRELAND, 1911.

Two Examples of the mode of filling up this Table are given on the other side.

FORM A.

RETURN of the MEMBERS of this FAMILY and their VISITORS, BOARDERS, SERVANTS, &c., who slept or abode in this House on the night of SUNDAY, the 2nd of APRIL, 1911.

No. on Form B. ....

Name and Surname		Relation to Head of Family	Religious Profession	Education	Age (last Birthday) and Sex		Rank, Profession, or Occupation	Particulars as to Marriage					Where Born	Irish Language	If Deaf and Dumb; Dumb only; Blind; Imbecile or Idiot; or Lunatic.
Christian Name	Surname				Ages of Males	Ages of Females		Whether "Married," "Widower," "Widow," or "Single."	Completed years the present Marriage has lasted.	Total Children born alive.	Children still living.				
1	2	3	4	5	6	7	8	9	10	11	12		13	14	15
Patrick	Hird	Head of Family	Roman Catholic	Read and Write	68		Tenant?	Widower		9			County Cavan	Irish and English	
Patrick	Hird	Son	Roman Catholic	Read and Write	23		Farmer's Son	Single					County Cavan	English	
Alice	Hird	Daughter	Catholic	Read and Write		21		Single					County Cavan	English	
Mary Agnes	Hird	Daughter	Catholic	Read and Write		18	Scholar	Single					County Cavan	English	
John	Hird	Son	Catholic	Read and Write	12		Scholar	Single					County Cavan	English	
James	Hird	Son	Catholic	Read and Write	10		Scholar	Single					Co. Cavan	English	

I hereby certify, as required by the Act 10 Edw. VII., and 1 Geo. V., cap. 11, that the foregoing Return is correct, according to the best of my knowledge and belief.

_____ Signature of Examiner.

I believe the foregoing to be a true Return.

Patrick Hird .... Signature of Head of Family.

Form A, 1911 Census (NAI: C 1911/Cavan/89/1/21)
(Courtesy of the National Archives of Ireland)

(iv) Marriages

The requirement in the 1911 census for married women to supply the number of years of marriage is obviously a very useful aid when subsequently searching civil records for a marriage entry. In the case of the 1901 census, the age of the eldest child recorded can give a rough guide to the latest date at which a marriage is likely to have taken place.

(v) Living Relatives

Children recorded in 1901 and 1911 are the grandparents of people still living. Their ages—generally more accurate than those given for older family members—can be useful in trying to uncover later marriages in civil records. When used together with Valuation Office records (see Chapter 4), or the voters' lists at the NAI, they can provide an accurate picture of the passing of property from one generation to another. Fortunately, the Irish attitude to land means that it is quite unusual for rural property to pass out of a family altogether.

Research techniques

The basic geographical unit used in carrying out both the 1901 and 1911 censuses was the District Electoral Division (D.E.D.), a county subdivision created, as the name implies, for electoral purposes. To search the returns successfully, ideally the relevant street or townland name should be known. The 1901 *Townlands Index* (LDS Film 865092), which is based on the census returns, supplies the name and number of the D.E.D. in which the townland is situated. County-by-county volumes, found on open shelves in the NAI Reading Room, go through the D.E.D for both 1901 and 1911 in numerical order, giving the name and number of each of the townlands contained therein. To order the returns for a specific townland, it is necessary to supply the name of the county, the number of the D.E.D. and the number of the townland, as given in these volumes. For the cities of Belfast, Cork, Dublin and Limerick separate street indexes have been compiled, and are also on open shelves in the NAI Reading Room (LDS Fiches 6035493/4/5). Again, each street or part of a street is numbered, and these numbers must be supplied when ordering specific returns. Between 1901 and 1911 some changes took place in the District Electoral Divisions, and their numbering therefore differs in some cases. There is no separate townlands index for 1911, but the changes are minor, so a D.E.D. numbered 100 in 1901 may be 103 in 1911, for instance, and can be found simply by checking the D.E.D.s above and below 100 in the 1911 volume for the relevant county.

All the returns for a townland or street are grouped together and preceded by an enumerator's abstract that gives the details of the houses and lists the names of the heads of households. These lists can be very useful where the precise townland or street name is not known and it is therefore necessary to search a large area, checking all households of a particular surname—though such a procedure is, of course, less precise than a check of each of the returns. One problem that can arise when searching a large area is the difficulty of translating from the earlier geographical division of a parish, for instance, to the relevant District Electoral Divisions, since the latter cut across the earlier boundaries. The most straightforward, though cumbersome, way to cover a large area is to take all the townlands in a particular civil parish and check their D.E.D.s in the 1901 *Townlands Index*. The 1841 *Townlands Index*, also known as *Addenda to the 1841 Census* and available on request from the NAI Reading Room staff or in the National Library (Ir. 310 c 1), organises townlands alphabetically within civil parishes.

NINETEENTH-CENTURY CENSUS FRAGMENTS

1821
This census, organised by townland, civil parish, barony and county, took place on 28 May 1821 and aimed to cover the entire population. It recorded:

* name;
* age;
* occupation;
* relationship to the head of the household;
* acreage of landholding;
* number of storeys of house.

Almost all of the original returns were destroyed in 1922, with only a few volumes surviving for parts of Counties Cavan, Fermanagh, Galway, Meath and Offaly (King's County). These are now in the NAI, and full details of call numbers and areas covered are provided in Chapter 13, under the relevant county. The overall reliability of the population figures produced by the 1821 census has been questioned, but there is no doubt as to the genealogical value of the returns. Once again, however, the ages listed need to be treated with scepticism.

1831
Organised by townland, civil parish, barony and county, this census recorded:

* name;
* age;
* occupation;
* relationship to the head of the household;
* acreage of landholding;
* religion.

Very little of this census survives, with most of the remaining fragments relating to Co. Derry. Details of locations and call numbers are provided in Chapter 13, under the relevant county.

No. 38 Townland of *Affalion*		in the Parish of *Castlerahan*		B

N. B.—In Counties where Plowlands or other denominations or sub-denominations are in use, the word " Townlands" is to be

Col. 1. No. of House.	Col. 2. No. of Stories	Column 3. NAMES OF INHABITANTS.	Col. 4. AGE.	Column 5. OCCUPATION.	Col. 6. No. of Acres.
		Eliza Fitzsimmons Daughter	15	Spinner	
8	1	Garrett Fitzsimmons	60	Farmer	12
		Cath Fitzsimmons his Wife	57	Spinner	
		Patrick Fitzsimmons his Son	32	Labourer	
		Thos Fitzsimmons Do	27	Labourer	
		John Fitzsimmons Do	23	Labourer	
		Mary Smyth	20	House Servt	
9	1	John Gilroy	37	Farmer	16
		Mary Gilroy his Wife	33	Spinner	
		Patrick Gilroy his Son	10		
		Owen Gilroy his Son	1		
		Mary Gilroy Daughter	15	Spinner	
		Mary Gilroy Do	13	Same	
		Bridget Gilroy Do	7		
		Anne Gilroy Do	5		
10	1	Peter Lynch	64	Farmer	15
		Eliza Lynch his Wife	61	Spinner	
		Hugh Lynch his Son	32	Labourer	
		Law Lynch his Son	16	Labourer	
		Anne Lynch Daughter	25	Spinner	
		Mary Lynch Daughter	23	Spinner	
		John Lynch his Nephew	1		
11	1	John Flood	33	Farmer	4½
		Anne Flood his Wife	30	Spinner	
		John Flood his Son	8		
		Mary Flood Daughter	10		
		Cath Flood Do	6		
		Anne Flood Do	3		
12	1	John Smyth	55	Mason	
		Peter Smyth his Son	25	Labourer	
		James Smyth his Son	22	Labourer	
		Cath Smyth Do	15	Labourer	

1821 Census return (NAI: Cen 1821/3)

(Courtesy of the National Archives of Ireland)

1841

Unlike the two earlier censuses, the householders themselves filled out the returns in 1841, rather than government enumerators. The information supplied was:

- name;
- age;
- occupation;
- relationship to the head of the household;
- date of marriage;
- literacy;
- absent family members;
- family members who died since 1831.

Only one set of original returns survived the fire in 1922, that for the parish of Killeshandra in Co. Cavan. There are, however, a number of transcripts of original returns extant. The 1841 census was the earliest to be used when State old age pensions were introduced in the early twentieth century: copies of the household returns from 1841 and 1851 were occasionally used as proof of age. The forms detailing the results of searches in the original returns to establish age have survived and are found in the NAI for areas in the Republic of Ireland, and in the Public Record Office of Northern Ireland for areas now in its jurisdiction. Copies of the Northern Ireland returns are also available at the LDS Library. County-by-county indexes to the areas covered, giving the names of the individuals concerned, are found on open shelves in the NAI Reading Room. A number of other miscellaneous copies are also available, some related to the Old Age Pension, most relating to Northern counties. These are detailed (though not indexed) in the pre-1901 census catalogue at the NAI, also found on open shelves in the Reading Room. For the counties with significant numbers of these copies, details are provided in Chapter 13, under the relevant county.

As well as these copies, there are also a number of researchers' transcripts and abstracts which were compiled from the original returns prior to their destruction and then donated to public institutions after 1922 in an attempt to replace some of the lost records. Since the researchers in question were usually interested in particular families rather than whole areas, these transcripts are generally of limited value. The most significant collections are the Walsh-Kelly notebooks, which also abstract parts of the 1821, 1831 and 1851 returns and relate particularly to south Kilkenny, and the Thrift Abstracts, held in the NAI. Details of dates, areas covered and locations for the Walsh-Kelly notebooks are provided under the Co. Kilkenny heading in Chapter 13. The Thrift Abstracts are listed in detail in the NAI pre-1901 census catalogue under 'miscellaneous copies'. Counties for which significant numbers exist are given in Chapter 13, under the relevant county.

1851
This census recorded:

- name;
- age;
- occupation;
- relationship to the head of the household;
- date of marriage;
- literacy;
- absent family members;
- family members who died since 1841;
- religion.

Most of the surviving returns relate to parishes in Co. Antrim, and details are provided in Chapter 13. An online transcript, albeit of doubtful accuracy, is also available. The above comments on transcripts and abstracts of the 1841 census also apply to the 1851 census.

1861, 1871, 1881, 1891
The officially sanctioned destruction of the returns for these years was commendably thorough: virtually nothing survives. The only transcripts extant are contained in the Catholic registers of Enniscorthy, Co. Wexford (1861), and Drumcondra and Loughbraclen, Co. Meath (1871); details are provided in Chapter 13.

CENSUS SUBSTITUTES
Almost any document which records more than a single name can be called a census substitute, at least for genealogical purposes. What follows is a listing, chronological where possible, of the principal substitutes. It is intended as a gloss on some of the sources provided county-by-county under 'Census Returns and Substitutes' in Chapter 13, and as a supplement to include those sources which do not fit the county-by-county format. Any material given in the source-lists in Chapter 13 that is self-explanatory is not dealt with here.

Sixteenth and seventeenth centuries

1521–1603: Fiants
The Irish fiants of the Tudor sovereigns during the reigns of Henry VIII, Edward VI, Philip & Mary, and Elizabeth I (4 vols, Dublin, Edmund Burke, 1994), NLI Ir. 94105 i 1. These documents, unique to Ireland, were created to facilitate the issuing of royal grants and were originally published in the late nineteenth century as a series of appendices to the *Reports of the Deputy Keeper of Public Records in Ireland*. For many of those Irish chieftains who submitted to English authority under the policy of surrender and re-grant, the fiants provide long lists of extended family members and followers.

1612–1613, 'Undertakers'

The Historical Manuscripts Commission Report 4 (Hastings Mss) lists English and Scottish large landlords who were granted land in the northern Counties of Cavan, Donegal and Fermanagh.

1630, Muster Rolls

These are lists of large landlords in Ulster and the names of those able-bodied men that the landlords could assemble to fight, if the need arose. The lists are arranged by county, and by district within each county. The Armagh County Museum copy is available in NLI (Pos. 206). Published lists are noted under the relevant county in Chapter 13, along with later lists from 1642/3 in PRONI.

1641, Books of Survey and Distribution

After the wars of the mid-seventeenth century the English government needed solid information on land-ownership throughout Ireland in order to carry out its policy of land redistribution. The Books of Survey and Distribution record ownership before the Cromwellian and Williamite confiscations, c.1641, and after, c.1666–1668. The Books for Clare, Galway, Mayo and Roscommon have been published by the Irish Manuscripts Commission; for other counties manuscript copies are available at the NLI. Details are provided under the relevant counties in Chapter 13.

1654–1656, The Civil Survey

This too was a record of land-ownership in 1640, compiled between 1655 and 1667, and more comprehensive than the Books of Survey and Distribution. It contains a great deal of topographical and descriptive information, as well as details of wills and deeds relating to land title. The Survey has survived for only twelve counties: Cork, Derry, Donegal, Dublin, Kildare, Kilkenny, Limerick, Meath, Tipperary, Tyrone, Waterford and Wexford; all twelve have been published by the Irish Manuscripts Commission. Details are provided under the relevant counties in Chapter 13.

1659, Pender's 'Census'

This was compiled by Sir William Petty, also responsible for the Civil Survey, and records the names of persons with title to land ('tituladoes'), the total number of English and Irish people living in each townland and the principal Irish names in each barony. Five counties are not covered: Cavan, Galway, Mayo, Tyrone and Wicklow. The work was edited by Seamus Pender and published in 1939 (NLI I 6551, Dublin).

1662–1666, Subsidy Rolls

These list the nobility, clergy and laity who paid a grant in aid to the King. Names and parishes are supplied, and sometimes also amount paid and occupation. They relate principally to the counties located in the province of Ulster.

1664–1666, Hearth Money Rolls
The Hearth Tax was levied on the basis of the number of hearths in each house; these Rolls list the householders' names, as well as this number. They seem to be quite comprehensive. Details of surviving lists will be found under the relevant counties in Chapter 13. For the copies of the Hearth Money Rolls listed in the Public Record Office of Northern Ireland under 'T.307', an index is available on the Public Search Room shelves.

Various Dates, Cess Tax Accounts
'Cess' (an abbreviation of 'assessment') was a very elastic term and could be applied to taxes levied for a variety of reasons. In Ireland, it very often related to taxes collected to support a military garrison. The accounts generally consist of lists of householders' names, along with amounts due.

Eighteenth and nineteenth centuries

1703–1838, Converts
The Convert Rolls (ed. Eileen O'Byrne, IMC, 1981, 308 p.) NLI Ir. 2741 c 25. A list of those converting from Catholicism to the Church of Ireland. The bulk of the entries date from 1760 to 1790.

1740, Protestant householders
Relating to parts of Counties Antrim, Armagh, Derry, Donegal and Tyrone and arranged by barony and parish, this listing gives names only. Sections of the list are held at the Public Record Office of Northern Ireland, at the Genealogical Office, at the NLI and at the Representative Church Body Library. Details will be found under the relevant counties in Chapter 13.

1749, Elphin Diocesan Census
Arranged by townland and parish, this census lists householders, their religion, the numbers, sex and religion of their children, and the numbers, sex and religion of their servants. Elphin diocese includes parts of Counties Galway, Roscommon and Sligo. Details of the parishes covered and any indexes or transcripts will be found under the relevant counties in Chapter 13.

1766, Census
In March and April of 1766, on the instructions of the government, Church of Ireland rectors were requested to compile complete returns for all householders in their parishes, recording their religion and giving an account of any Catholic clergy active in their area. The result was extraordinarily inconsistent, with some rectors producing only numerical totals of population, some drawing up partial lists, while the most conscientious detailed all householders and their addresses individually. All of the original returns were lost in 1922, but extensive transcripts survive for some areas and are deposited with various institutions. The only full

listing of all surviving transcripts and abstracts is held in the NAI Reading Room, on the open shelves. However, this listing does not differentiate between those returns which supply names and those which merely give numerical totals. The details given under the relevant counties in Chapter 13 refer only to those parishes for which names are supplied.

1790–1880, Official Papers, Petitions

The 'Official Papers' form part of the incoming correspondence records of the Office of the Chief Secretary to the Lord Lieutenant of Ireland, usually known simply as the Chief Secretary's Office—the primary organ of central administration in Ireland for the period. Two main series exist in NAI, 1790–1831 and 1832–1880, the former calendared and classified by year and subject, the latter covered by card indexes. As well as records of the administration of justice (see Chapter 12), they also include a long series of petitions to the Lord Lieutenant from around the country, generally described as 'memorials', that very often include long lists of names or signatures. The mother of all memorials is the William Smith O'Brien petition of 1848/9, a plea for clemency for the main instigator of an abortive rising in 1848, the so-called Battle of Widow McCormack's Cabbage Patch. It includes almost 90,000 names from all over Ireland and from Irish people living in England. Ruth Lawler's transcription has been published on CD-ROM by Eneclann (# CD2) and is searchable online, for a fee, at *www.origins network.com*.

Many smaller petitions also exist, ranging from pleas for relief from distress among weavers to an appeal for a road to be built from Kanturk to Cork City. The largest numbers relate to changes made in the arrangements for local court sittings ('Quarter Sessions') in 1837–1838. Bids to host the courts poured in from all over the country; the economic spin-offs must have been considerable. At least forty of these smaller petitions have been identified and are listed under the relevant county in Chapter 13, with estimates of the number of names they contain. No doubt there are many more.

1795–1862, Charleton Trust Fund marriage certificates

As an encouragement to Protestant population growth, the Charlton Trust Fund offered a small marriage gratuity to members of the Protestant labouring classes. To qualify, a marriage certificate—recording both partners' occupations and fathers' names and signed by the local Church of Ireland clergyman—had to be submitted, and these certificates are now held in the NAI. They are particularly useful for the years before the start of registration of non-Catholic marriages in 1845. The areas covered by the Fund are mainly in Counties Meath and Longford, but a few certificates exist for parts of Counties Cavan, Offaly (King's County), Louth and Westmeath, as well as for Dublin City. They are indexed in NAI Accessions Vol. 37.

No.   No. in Receipt.

CHARLETON'S CHARITABLE FUND.

County of LONGFORD, To Wit.

WE, the Undersigned, Minister and Church Wardens of the Parish of *Ardagh* in the County of Longford, DO CERTIFY, that *James Burtley* of *Slenagh Gr* in the Parish of *Kilcommock* in said County, was duly married to *Elizabeth Young* otherwise *Burtley* on the *Twenty fifth* day of *January* 18*13 thirteen* in our presence, and that the said Marriage was solemnized with the consent of the parents of the said *several parties* who were also present and expressed their approbation thereof; AND WE DO FURTHER CERTIFY, that *William Burton* the father of the said *James Burton* was at the time of said Marriage, and for *31* years previous thereto, a resident day labourer of the said County of Longford, and that *Henry Young*, the father of the said *Elizabeth Young* was also at the time of the said marriage, and for *many* years previous thereto, a resident day labourer of the said County of Longford, and that we know the said *James Burtley* to have been aged more than fifteen years and less than thirty years at the time of the said marriage, and that we know the said *Elizabeth Young* to have been aged more than fifteen years and less than forty years at the time of the said marriage.

Given under our hands this *Eleventh* day of *April* 1838

Rich. Thos. Hearn } Minister of the Parish of *Ardagh for the time then being* in the County of Longford.

John Morris }

{ Church Wardens of the said Parish.

There is only one Church Warden at present in this Parish. Matthew Hamshedd

Charleton Marriage Fund (NAI: Charleton Funds, Longford A–K)
(Courtesy of the National Archives of Ireland)

1796, Spinning-Wheel Premium Entitlement Lists
As part of a government scheme to encourage the linen trade, free spinning-wheels, or looms, were granted to individuals who planted a prescribed area of land with flax. The lists of those entitled to the awards, covering almost 60,000 individuals, were published in 1796. These record only the name of the individual and the civil parish in which he lived. As might be expected, the majority—over 64 per cent of the total—were in Ulster, but some names appear from every county except Dublin and Wicklow. Only those counties with significant numbers have a reference in the county-by-county source-lists. A microfiche index to the lists is available in the NAI and PRONI offices, and online at *www.failteromhat.com*.

1798, Persons who Suffered Losses in the 1798 Rebellion
This comprises a list of claims for compensation from the government for property destroyed by the rebels during the insurrection of 1798, and is particularly useful in relation to the property-owning classes of Counties Wexford, Carlow, Dublin, Kildare and Wicklow. Where significant numbers are recorded, these are supplied in the county source-lists in Chapter 13. (NLI I 94107.)

1803, Agricultural censuses of Antrim and Down
As part of the preparations for a possible French invasion in the aftermath of the abortive rebellion of 1803, plans were drawn up for the evacuation of coastal areas. A survey of livestock, crops, wagons and horses was ordered, but appears to have been carried out only in Counties Antrim and Down. In most cases occupiers' names are also recorded. Eleven parishes in Antrim are covered (see Chapter 13) in NAI Official Papers (OP 153/103/1–16), with a copy also lodged in PRONI. The County Down survey survived as part of the papers of the First Marquess of Londonderry and is available at PRONI. It covers fifty Down parishes, with returns for thirty including at least some occupiers' names. Ian Maxwell's *Researching Down Ancestors* (UHF, 2004) provides a parish-by-parish description.

1822–1854, Loan Fund records
In the mid-nineteenth century, when the practice was at its peak, hundreds of local loan funds took deposits and made loans to the poorest classes in Ireland. One estimate puts the number of loans at 500,000 per year in the early 1840s, affecting almost 20 per cent of the households in the country. The system originated in 1822 when a severe but localised famine became a focus of attention in England and a London-based committee, established 'for the relief of the distressed Irish', collected over £300,000 for the famine victims. More than £55,000 of this remained after the famine abated, and the committee decided to establish a 'Reproductive Loan Fund' to make available small loans to the 'industrious poor' of the ten most needy counties. The Fund was reproductive in the sense that the loan would, in theory at least, finance the purchase of an asset from which an income would be derived to pay the instalments. Legislation was passed in 1823, 1836 and 1838 to encourage such funds and to establish a regulatory body: the

Loan Fund Board. By 1843 some 300 local funds were registered with the Board, over and above the 50–100 funds created by the Reproductive Institution, which were administered from London and exempt. In 1843, at the prompting of the commercial banks, yet more legislation was passed to reduce sharply the interest rates the Funds could charge. The effect was an immediate increase in closures of Funds and a corresponding sharp drop in the number of loans paid out. The Great Famine took hold in 1845, magnifying further the destructive effects of the new legislation. A large number of Funds failed and closed.

Records of the Loan Funds: virtually no detailed records survive from the institutions administered by the Loan Fund Board. The only exceptions currently known are the Tanderagee Estate Fund—preserved in PRONI as part of the more general Tanderagee estate records, D1248/LF/3—and the Shirley Estate Loan Book—in Carrickmacross Library, Co. Monaghan. However, the records produced by the original Reproductive Institution have survived almost entire. After lending ceased at the end of 1848, all of the records were eventually returned to the Institution's headquarters in London, and are now kept in the National Archives (Kew), series T/91. As well as the notes of security for the loans, there are loan ledgers, repayment books and defaulters' books for the local associations and the county committees. The minimum information supplied is name and address, but often much additional detail is provided in the local association records, including notes on health, occupation, family circumstances and emigration. The local records generally run from the late 1830s to the mid-1840s and are available for the following associations:

Clare: County Account Book and Minutes.
Cork: Baltimore, Castletown, Castle Townsend, Cloyne, Creagh, Kilmoe and Crookhaven, Schull.
Galway: Ahascragh, Ballygar, Castle Hackett, Clifden, Kilconickny, Outerard, Galway town.
Limerick: a single Association covered the entire county.
Mayo: Ballina or Carramore, Ballindine, Ballinrobe, Castlebar, Claremorris, Kilmore, Swineford.
Roscommon: Aughnasurn, Ballinlough, Ballymoe, Clonfinlough, Elphin, Mosshill, Rockville, Tybohan.
Sligo: Templehouse.
Tipperary: Tipperary town.

A large obstacle to researching and using these records is the fact that they are extremely extensive, unindexed and inaccessible to researchers outside London. However, a subsidiary website of the National Archives, *www.movinghere.org.uk*, scanned and indexed part of the records in 2003 to make them more widely available. The records chosen for scanning were the Returns to the Clerk of the Peace of each county, created as part of the process of winding up the Funds. For each local Fund, these returns generally consist of two parts:

1. An overall account, usually dated 1846–1848, showing the names and addresses of the borrower and of his/her two sureties, or guarantors, along with amounts outstanding.
2. A more detailed townland-by-townland listing, organised by constabulary sub-district and carried out by the local RIC in 1853–1854, recording details of deaths, economic circumstances and emigration.

No Return to the Clerk of the Peace appears to survive for Clare, and the Return for Sligo was not scanned. For Counties Cork, Galway, Limerick, Mayo, Roscommon and Tipperary almost 40,000 names are indexed. While the indexing is imperfect, the organisation of the records confusing and a broadband connection essential, for those areas they cover the records are superb, in many cases providing a before-and-after survey of the effect of the Great Famine on a particular locality. To take one example: Philip Ebzery of Doonscardeen townland, in Robertstown parish, in Limerick, is recorded in the overall account (T/91/180/0060) as borrowing £4 from the Limerick Fund on 23 November 1846, with the entire amount still outstanding in 1848. His sureties were John Ebzery and Michael Ryan, both also of Doonscardeen. In the 1853 constabulary account (T/91/180/0448), Ebzery is recorded as being resident in Doonscardeen in 1846, 'a farmer, was poor, died about 4 years ago, family all emigrated'. The two sureties are there also: John Ebzery 'was a farmer, went to Australia about four years since with his mother and sisters'; Michael Ryan was 'a poor labourer, supporting his mother and sisters, emigrated to America with his family in 1847'.

1824–1838, Tithe Applotment Books
See Chapter 4, Property and Valuation Records.

1831–1921, National School Records
In 1831 a countrywide system of primary education was established under the authority of the Board of Commissioners for National Education. The most useful records produced under this system are the school registers themselves, which record the age of the pupil, religion, father's address and occupation and general observations. In the Republic of Ireland very little effort has been made to centralise these records; most remain in the custody of local schools or churches. The NAI has c.145 of these registers, most dating from the 1870s and 1880s. The PRONI has a collection of over 1,500 registers for schools in the six counties of Northern Ireland. The administrative records of the Board of Commissioners are held by the NAI in Dublin and include teachers' salary books, which can be very useful if an ancestor was a teacher. (See also Chapter 12).

1838– Workhouse Records
The 130 Poor Law Unions established in 1838, which had risen to 163 by 1852, were responsible for administering what little public relief was available. They dealt with huge numbers during the Great Famine (1845–1849). Unfortunately, most of

the records of interest to family historians, in particular the workhouse admissions registers, do not appear to have survived, and what is available to us is scattered and somewhat piecemeal. There is no comprehensive guide. The best source available is *Records of the Irish Famine, a guide to local archives, 1840–1855*, by Deirdre Lindsay and David Fitzpatrick (Dublin Irish Famine Network, 1993). See also *The Workhouses of Ireland* by John O'Connor (Dublin, Anvil Books,1995). The best single collection is held by the PRONI and covers the twenty-seven Poor Law Unions which were established in the counties of Northern Ireland. An excellent guide to the history of workhouses throughout the British Isles can be found at *users.ox.ac.uk/~peter/workhouse*.

1848–1864, Griffith's Valuation
See Chapter 4, Property and Valuation Records.

1876, Landowners
Landowners in Ireland: Return of owners of land of one acre and upwards (London: Her Majesty's Stationery Office, 1876. [Reissued by GPC Baltimore, 1988]). This records 32,614 owners of land in Ireland in 1876, identifying them by province and county. The entries list the owner's address, along with the extent and valuation of the property. This has limited application because a minority of the population owned the land they occupied, but when researching a person who did own land, this record is invaluable.

Various dates

Freeholders
Freehold property is held either by fee simple, meaning one has absolute freedom to dispose of it, or by fee tail, meaning the disposition is restricted to a particular line of heirs, or by a life tenure. From the early eighteenth century freeholders' lists were regularly drawn up, usually in connection with the right to vote, which went with freeholds over a certain value. It follows that such lists are of genealogical interest for a minority of the population. Details of surviving lists will be found under the relevant counties in Chapter 13.

Voters' Lists and Poll Books
Voters' lists cover a slightly larger proportion of the population than freeholders' lists because freehold property was not the only determinant of the franchise. In particular, freemen of the various corporation towns and cities had a right to vote in at least some elections. Since membership of a trade guild carried with it admission as a freeman and this right was hereditary, a wider range of social classes is covered here. Details of surviving lists will be found under the relevant counties in Chapter 13.

Poll books record the votes actually cast in elections.

Electoral Records

We do not have a complete collection of the electoral lists used in the elections of the twentieth century. This is unfortunate because they can be very helpful in tracing living relatives, listing, as they do, all eligible voters by townland and household. The largest single collection of surviving electoral registers is to be found in the NAI, but the coverage of the various areas is still quite skimpy. An excellent collection of Dublin City voters' lists is held by Dublin City Library and Archive.

Valuations

Local valuations and re-valuations of property were carried out with increasing frequency from the end of the eighteenth century, usually for electoral reasons. The best of these record all householders. Again, details are given under the relevant counties in Chapter 13.

Chapter 3 ～

CHURCH RECORDS

THE PARISH SYSTEM

After the coming of the Reformation to Ireland in the sixteenth century, the parish structures of the Roman Catholic Church and the Anglican Church of Ireland diverged. The Church of Ireland retained the medieval parochial divisions and became the State Church—in effect, an arm of the government. The secular authorities used its parish framework for administrative purposes. Consequently, civil parishes—the geographical basis of early censuses, tax records and land surveys—are almost identical to Church of Ireland parishes. The Roman Catholic Church, on the other hand, weakened by the confiscation of its assets and the restrictions imposed on its clergy, was forced to create larger and less convenient parishes. In some ways this weakness produced more flexibility, allowing parishes to be centred on new, burgeoning population centres and permitting the creation of new parishes in the nineteenth century to accommodate this growth in population.

The differences in the parish structures of the two Churches are reflected in their records. Even allowing for the fact that Church of Ireland members almost always formed a small minority of the total population, the records of each parish are proportionally less extensive than Roman Catholic records, covering smaller areas and thus relatively easy to search in detail. Catholic records, by contrast, cover the majority of the population and a much larger geographical area and so can be very time-consuming to search in detail. The creation of new Catholic parishes in the nineteenth century can also mean that the registers relevant to a particular area may be split between two parishes. Both Roman Catholic and Church of Ireland parishes are organised on the diocesan basis first laid out in the Synod of Kells in the Middle Ages, and remain almost identical, although the Catholic system has amalgamated some of the smaller medieval dioceses.

ROMAN CATHOLIC RECORDS

Dates

Prior to the introduction of comprehensive civil registration in 1864, virtually the only direct sources of family information for the vast majority of the population are local parish records. The intense hostility shown by the State towards the

Roman Catholic Church from the sixteenth to the nineteenth centuries made efficient record-keeping an understandably low priority, and as a result very few registers survive from before the latter half of the eighteenth century. The earliest Roman Catholic parish records in the country appear to be the fragments for Waterford and Galway cities, dating from the 1680s, and for Wexford town, dating from 1671. Generally speaking, early records tend to come from the more prosperous, anglicised areas, in particular the towns and cities on the eastern half of the island. In the poorest and most densely populated rural parishes of the west and north—those which saw most emigration—the parish registers very often do not start until the mid- or late nineteenth century. The majority of Catholic registers, however, begin in the first decades of the nineteenth century. Where a local tradition of Gaelic scholarship survived, records were often kept from an even earlier date, even in poor areas.

The list given in Chapter 14 reflects the state of knowledge of the dates of Roman Catholic registers at the time of writing (mid-2005). No listing can ever be absolutely definitive, however. The number of parishes covered by the local heritage centres will continue to grow, the National Library microfilming programme will carry on to completion, online transcripts will continue to appear and there are almost certainly some unrecorded registers awaiting discovery in sacristies around the country.

Nature of the Records

Roman Catholic registers consist primarily of baptismal and marriage records. The keeping of burial records was much less thorough than in the Church of Ireland, with fewer than half the parishes in the country having a register of burials before 1900; even where they do exist, the records were generally kept intermittently and are patchy, at best. For some reason almost all extant Roman Catholic burial registers relate to the northern half of the island.

Baptisms and marriages, on the other hand, were more thoroughly preserved and were recorded in either Latin or English, never in Irish. Generally, parishes in the more prosperous areas, where English was more common, tended to use English, while in Irish-speaking parishes Latin was used, but there is no absolute consistency. The Latin entries present very few problems, since only first names were translated, not surnames or place names, while the English equivalents are almost always self-evident. The only difficulties or ambiguities are the following: *Carolus* (Charles); *Demetrius* (Jeremiah, Jerome, Darby, Dermot); *Gulielmus* (William); *Eugenius* (Owen or Eugene); *Jacobus* (James); *Ioannes* or *Joannes* (John); *Honoria* (Hannah, Nora). Apart from names, the only other Latin words requiring explanation are those used in recording marriage dispensations. These were necessary when the couple was related, *consanguinati*, with the relationship being given in terms of degrees—siblings were first degree, first cousins were second degree and second cousins were third degree. Thus a couple recorded as *consanguinati in tertio grado* are second cousins, a piece of information that can be of value when attempting to disentangle earlier generations. A less frequent Latin comment, *affinitatus*, records an earlier relationship by marriage between the families of the two parties.

Baptisms

Roman Catholic baptismal registers almost invariably contain the following information:

- date;
- child's name;
- father's name;
- mother's maiden name;
- names of sponsors (godparents).

Most registers also record the residence of the parents. A typical Latin entry in its full form would read as follows:

> *Baptisavi Johannem, filium legitimum Michaeli Sheehan et Mariae Sullivan de Lisquill.*
> *Sponsoribus, Danielus Quirk, Johanna Donoghue.*

Much more often the entry is abbreviated to:

> *Bapt. Johannem, f.l. Michaeli Sheehan et Mariae Sullivan, Lisquill,*
> *Sp: Daniel Quirk, Johanna Donoghue.*

This translates as: I baptised John, legitimate son of Michael Sheehan and Mary Sullivan of Lisquill, with godparents Daniel Quirk and Johanna Donoghue. In many cases even the abbreviations are omitted and the entries simply consist of dates, names and places.

Marriages

The information given in marriage records is more variable, but always includes at least the following:

- date;
- names of persons marrying;
- names of witnesses.

Other information that may also be supplied includes: residences (of all four people); ages; occupations; and fathers' names. In some rare cases the relationships of the witnesses to the people marrying are also specified. Some Dublin City registers from the mid-nineteenth century record the full names and addresses of the parents of both bride and groom, a wonderful innovation. A typical Latin marriage entry would read:

> *In matrimonium coniunxi sunt Danielum McCarthy et Brigidam Kelliher, de Ballyboher.*
> *Testimonii: Cornelius Buckley, Margarita Hennessy.*

Abbreviated, the entry reads:

Mat. con. Danielum McCarthy et Brigidam Kelliher, Ballyboher.
Test: Cornelius Buckley, Margarita Hennessy.

Translated this means: Daniel McCarthy and Brigid Kelliher, of Ballyboher, are joined in matrimony; witnesses, Cornelius Buckley, Margaret Hennessy.

Locations
In the 1950s and early 1960s the National Library of Ireland carried out a project to microfilm the surviving Roman Catholic parish registers of the entire island. Out of 1,153 sets of registers, this project covered 1,066. Among the parishes whose records are not included are: Rathlin Island (Co. Antrim); Crossgar (Co. Down); Kilmeen, Clonfert, Fahy, Clonbern (Co. Galway); Killorglin (Co. Kerry); Kilmeena (Co. Mayo); Rathcore and Rathmolyon (Co. Meath); and the Dublin county parishes of Clontarf, Naul and Santry. Almost all of these parishes appear to have registers earlier than 1880 in local custody. In addition, the parishes of St John's (Sligo town), Cappawhite (Co. Tipperary) and Waterford City have locally held registers that are more comprehensive than those microfilmed by the NLI. Not all of the microfilmed registers in the Library are available to the public—for parishes in the dioceses of Cloyne and Kerry permission is required before the Library can allow access to the records. Permission is normally granted over the telephone. In addition, at the time of writing (2005) no records for the diocese of Cashel and Emly are available for research as the Archbishop has closed them in order to oblige researchers to go through Tipperary Family History, who carry out commissioned research on indexes produced in the 1970s and 1980s under State-funded job-creation schemes.

A separate microfilming project was carried out by PRONI for the six counties under its jurisdiction. The results are generally identical to the NLI copies, although in some cases PRONI has used a later cut-off date; see Chapter 14 for details.

The Church of Jesus Christ of the Latter-Day Saints also holds an extensive collection of Roman Catholic parish register microfilms, made up partly of copies of some of the NLI microfilms and partly of material microfilmed by the Church itself. Of the 1,153 parishes in the country, the LDS Library has records of 398; see Chapter 14 for details. The volunteer transcripts and extracts appearing on the internet are almost invariably taken from these LDS microfilms.

Apart from research in the original records, or microfilm copies, one other route exists to the information in parish registers. This is through the network of local heritage centres that has come into being throughout the country since c.1980. The centres are engaged in transcribing and computerising all of the surviving parish records for the country, as part of the Irish Genealogical Project. At the time of writing c.90 per cent of all Roman Catholic records have been transcribed. These records are not directly accessible to the public; it is necessary to commission research from the centre. Full details of the Project and the heritage centres are given in Chapter 14.

It is inevitable that these records will eventually be searchable online, probably for a fee. For the moment, only the Ulster Historical Foundation, covering Counties Antrim and Down, has made its records available, at *www.ancestry ireland.co.uk*. In addition, Irish Genealogy Ltd, an umbrella body supporting Irish genealogy, has a signposting index based on a limited subset of some of the centres' records at *www.irishgenealogy.ie*. The aim is to direct researchers to the relevant centre rather than to allow direct research on the records, but some useful information could still be gleaned.

Research in Roman Catholic Records

As the records are so extensive and there are so many parishes, the first step in any research must be to try to identify the relevant parish. In the ideal case, where a precise town or townland is known, this is a relatively simple exercise. The Townland Indexes from 1851, 1871, or 1901 will show the relevant civil parish and there are then a number of ways to uncover the corresponding Roman Catholic parish. Lewis' *Topographical Dictionary of Ireland* (1837), available on open access at most libraries, gives an account, in alphabetical order, of all of the civil parishes in Ireland and specifies the corresponding Roman Catholic parish. Brian Mitchell's *Guide to Irish Parish Records* (GPC, Baltimore, 1987) contains a county-by-county alphabetical reference guide to the civil parishes of Ireland and the Roman Catholic parishes in which they lie. The National Library's 'Index of Surnames' (or 'Householders Index') includes a map of the civil parishes in each county and a key, loosely based on Lewis, to the corresponding Roman Catholic parishes. A guide that is less reliable, though useful if the exact location of the church is required, is *Locations of Churches in the Irish Provinces*, produced by the LDS (NLI Ir. 7265 i 8). For Dublin City the procedure is slightly different. Where the address is known, the relevant civil parish can be found in the street-by-street listings of the Dublin directories, Pettigrew and Oulton's *Dublin Almanac and General Register of Ireland* (yearly from 1834 to 1849) and Thom's *Irish Almanac and Official Directory* (yearly from 1844). More details of these will be found in Chapter 10. Once the civil parish has been thus located, the corresponding Roman Catholic parish can then be found in Mitchell's Guide, or in James Ryan's *Tracing your Dublin Ancestors* (Flyleaf Press, 1988).

Unfortunately, in most cases a precise address is not known. How this obstacle is overcome depends on what other information is known. Where a birth, death or marriage took place in the family in Ireland after the start of civil registration in 1864, State records are the first place to look. Where the occupation is known, records relating to this may supply the vital link (see Chapter 12). For emigrants, the clue to the relevant area might lie in passenger and immigration lists, naturalisation papers, burial or death records, or even the postmarks on old family letters. In general, unless the surname is quite rare, the minimum information necessary to research parish records with any prospect of success is the county of origin.

When the county is known, the areas to be searched in the registers can then be narrowed down with the help of the early and mid-nineteenth-century land records, the Tithe Books (c.1830) and Griffith's Valuation (c.1855) (see Chapter 4). The National Library's 'Index of Surnames' provides a guide, on a county basis, to the surnames occurring in these records in the different civil parishes, giving at least an indication of the areas in which a particular surname was most common. A similar online service is available at *www.ireland.com/ancestor*. The CD-ROM and online versions of Griffith's Valuation can also be very helpful in narrowing the area of research.

The creation of new Roman Catholic parishes in the nineteenth century means the apparent starting dates of many Roman Catholic registers can be deceptive. Quite often, earlier records for the same area can be found in the registers of what is now an adjoining parish. To take an example: the Roman Catholic parish of Abbeyleix, in Co. Laois (Queen's County), has records listed in the NLI catalogue as starting in 1824. In fact, the parish was only created in that year and its earlier records will be found in Ballinakill parish, which has records dating from 1794. Therefore, where surviving records appear to be too late to be of interest, it is always advisable to check the surrounding parishes for earlier registers. The maps of Roman Catholic parishes accompanying Chapter 14 are intended to simplify this task. These maps are not intended to be geographically precise, rather their purpose is to show the locations of Roman Catholic parishes relative to one other. Since the only published source of information on nineteenth-century Roman Catholic parishes is Lewis' *Topographical Dictionary of Ireland*, which was published in 1837, and the influence and public presence of the Church increased greatly after Emancipation in 1829, some caution is necessary when identifying which sets of records are relevant to a particular area.

At first sight, parish registers, particularly those stored on microfilm, can appear quite daunting. The mass of spidery, abbreviated Latin, complete with blots and alterations and crosshatched with the scratches of a well-worn microfilm, can strike terror into the heart of even the most seasoned researcher. Some registers are a pleasure to use, with decade after decade of carefully laid out copper-plate handwriting; many more, unfortunately, appear to have been intended by local clergymen as revenge on posterity. The thing to remember is that it is neither possible nor desirable to read every single word on every page. Your aim should be to extract efficiently any relevant information. The way to do this is to scan the pages rather than actually read them. In general, each parish adopts a particular format and sticks to it. The important point is to identify this format and where the relevant information appears within it. For most purposes the family surname is the crucial item, so that in the baptismal example given earlier, the best procedure would be to scan fathers' surnames, stopping to read fully, or note, only those with the relevant surname. For other formats, such as,

John Maguire of Patrick and Mary Reilly
Sp. Thos McKiernan, Rose Smith,

where the family surname is supplied with the child's name rather than with the father's name, it is the child's surname which must be scanned. However, even with very efficient scanning there are registers which can only be deciphered line by line, which change format every page or two, or which are simply so huge that nothing but laborious hours of eye-strain can extract any information. The most notorious of these are the registers for St Catherine's in Dublin, for Cork City, Clonmel in Co. Tipperary and Clifden in Co. Galway.

When searching parish records—as for census returns and State records of births, marriages and deaths—a large measure of scepticism must be applied to all reported ages. In general, a five-year span around the reported date is the minimum that can be expected to yield results, and ten years is better, time permitting, with emphasis on the years before the reported date. An open mind is also necessary in relation to surname variants: widespread illiteracy made consistency and exactness of spelling extremely rare. It is essential, especially if searching more than one parish, to keep a written note of the precise period searched; even the best memory blurs after a few hours in front of a microfilm screen and it is perfectly, horribly possible to have to search the same records twice. This kind of frustrating duplication is an endemic hazard of genealogy, since the nature of the research is such that the relevance of particular pieces of evidence often only emerges with hindsight; this is especially true of research in parish records. To take an example: a search in parish records for Ellen, daughter of John O'Brien, born c.1840. The search starts in 1842 and moves back through the baptismal registers. There are many baptisms recording John O'Brien as the father, but no Ellen is recorded until 1834. If it is then necessary to check the names of her siblings, much of what has already been researched will have to be covered again. The only way to guard against being forced to duplicate work in this way is to note all the baptisms recording John O'Brien as father, even though there is a possibility (in most cases a probability) that ultimately none of them will turn out to be relevant.

Apart from the obvious family information they record, Roman Catholic parish registers may also include a wide variety of incidental information—details of famine relief, parish building accounts, marriage dispensations, local censuses, even personal letters. Anything of immediate genealogical interest is noted under the relevant county in Chapter 13.

CHURCH OF IRELAND RECORDS

Dates
Records of the Established Church, the Church of Ireland, generally start much earlier than those kept by the Roman Catholic Church. From as early as 1634 local parishes were required to keep records of christenings and burials in registers supplied by the Church authorities. As a result, a significant number of parishes, especially urban parishes, have registers dating from the mid-seventeenth century. The majority, however, start in the years between 1770 and 1820. The only countrywide listing of all Church of Ireland parish records that gives full details of

dates is the National Archives of Ireland catalogue, a copy of which can also be found at the NLI. In addition, the Irish Family History Society has published *A Table of Church of Ireland Parochial Records* (ed. Noel Reid, IFHS, 1994; 2nd ed., 2002), while the *Guide to Church Records: Public Record Office of Northern Ireland* (PRONI, 1994) gives details of PRONI's holdings.

The nature of the records

Burials
Unlike their Roman Catholic counterparts, the majority of Church of Ireland clergymen recorded burials as well as baptisms and marriages. These burial registers are often of interest for families of other denominations; the sectarian divide appears to have narrowed a little after death. The information given for burials rarely consists of more than the name, age and townland, making it difficult to establish definite family connections. However, since early burials generally record the deaths of those born well before the start of the register, they can sometimes be the only evidence on which to base a picture of preceding generations, and are particularly valuable because of this.

Baptisms
Church of Ireland baptismal records almost always supply only:

* the child's name;
* the father's name;
* the mother's Christian name;
* the name of the officiating clergyman.

Quite often the address is also given, but this is by no means as frequent as in the case of Roman Catholic registers. The omission of the mother's maiden name can be an obstacle to further research. From about 1820 the father's occupation is supplied in many entries.

Marriages
As the Church of Ireland was the Established Church, only those marriages performed under its aegis were legally valid—in theory, at least. In practice, of course, *de facto* recognition was given to marriages validated by other denominations. Nonetheless, the legal standing of the Church of Ireland meant that many marriages, particularly those of members of other Protestant Churches, were recorded in Church of Ireland registers. The information given is not extensive, usually consisting of no more than the names of the parties marrying and the name of the officiating clergyman. Even addresses are not usual, unless one of the parties is from a different parish. More comprehensive material is included in records of marriage banns, where these exist; although it was obligatory for notification of the intention to marry to be given in church on three

consecutive Sundays, written records of these are relatively rare. After 1845, when non-Roman Catholic marriages began to be registered by the State, the marriage registers record all the information contained in State records, including occupations, addresses and fathers' names.

Ballymodan Church of Ireland baptismal register (NAI: MFCI *Reel 30*)
(Courtesy of the National Archives of Ireland)

Marriage Licence Bonds

As an alternative to marriage banns, members of the Church of Ireland could take out a Marriage Licence Bond. The parties lodged a sum of money with the diocese to indemnify the Church against there being an obstacle to the marriage: in effect, this system allowed the well-off to purchase privacy. The original Bonds were all destroyed in the fire of 1922, but the original indexes are available at the NAI and on LDS microfilm. Some transcriptions have also appeared online—see Chapter 13. The Dublin diocesan index was published as part of the *Index to Dublin Will and Grant Books*, RDKPRI 26, 1895 (1270–1800) and RDKPRI 30 1899 (1800–1858). The Genealogical Office holds abstracts of Prerogative Marriage Licence Bonds from 1630 to 1858 (GO 605–607), as well as Marriages recorded in Prerogative Wills (GO 255–6). For an explanation of the Prerogative Court see Chapter 5.

Other

As well as straightforward information on baptisms, marriages and burials, Church of Ireland parish records very often include vestry books. These contain the minutes of the vestry meetings of the local parish, which can supply detailed information on the part played by individuals in the life of the parish. It should be kept in mind that since the Church of Ireland was, in effect, an arm of government, matters concerning non-Anglicans, such as poor relief, were also treated in these vestry books. The books are not generally included with the parish registers in the NAI, but PRONI and the Representative Church Body Library (RCBL) in Dublin hold extensive collections.

Locations

After the Church of Ireland ceased to be the Established Church, in 1870, its pre-1845 marriage records and pre-1871 baptismal and burial records were declared to be the property of the State, i.e. public records. Unless the local clergyman was in a position to demonstrate that he could house the records safely, he was required to deposit them in the Public Record Office. By 1922 the original registers of nearly 1,000 parishes—more than half the total for the country—were stored at the Public Record Office: all of these were destroyed in the fire at the Office on 28 June of that year.

Fortunately, 637 registers had been kept locally in secure storage, and in many cases local rectors had made a transcript before surrendering the originals. In addition, local historians and genealogists using the Office before 1922 had amassed collections of extracts from the registers. All of these factors mitigated, to some extent, the loss of this invaluable collection. Unfortunately, it also means that surviving registers, transcripts and extracts are held in a variety of locations. The Appendix to *The 28th Report of the Deputy Keeper of Public Records in Ireland* lists the Church of Ireland parish records for the entire island, giving full details of the years covered and specifying those which were in the Public Record Office at the time of its destruction. No information on locations is included. A more comprehensive account is supplied by the NAI catalogue of Church of Ireland records, available in the NAI Reading Room, at the National Library and in *A Table of Church of Ireland Parochial Records* (ed. Noel Reid, IFHS, 1994; 2nd ed., 2002). The NAI copy is the only one that is always fully up-to-date. As well as the dates of the registers, this catalogue also supplies some details of locations, but only when the Archives hold the originals, a microfilm copy, a transcript or abstracts on open access, or when the RCBL in Dublin holds original registers for dates which make them public records, or when they are still held in the parish. The catalogue does not indicate when microfilm copies are held by the RCBL, PRONI or NLI, only specifying 'local custody'. This is accurate in that the originals are indeed held locally, but it is unhelpful to researchers.

The Representative Church Body Library in Dublin is the Church of Ireland's own repository for its archives and manuscripts, and it holds the original records of some 830 parishes—not all of genealogical interest. Except where the originals are too fragile, all these records are open for public research. Again, *A Table of Church of Ireland Parochial Records* is the only comprehensive published guide.

For the Ulster counties of Antrim, Armagh, Cavan, Derry, Donegal, Down, Fermanagh, Leitrim, Louth, Monaghan and Tyrone, surviving registers have been microfilmed by PRONI and are available to the public at its Belfast office. The *Guide to Church Records: Public Record Office of Northern Ireland* (PRONI, 1994), also available online, gives full details of this collection. For those counties that are now in the Republic of Ireland—Cavan, Donegal, Leitrim, Louth and Monaghan—copies of the PRONI microfilms are available to the public at the RCBL. For parishes further away from the border it is worth checking directly with the RCBL as it is pursuing an active archival programme to house all of the surviving records. If the surviving records are only available locally, the current *Church of Ireland Directory* will supply the relevant name and address.

PRESBYTERIAN RECORDS

Dates
In general, Presbyterian registers start much later than those of the Church of Ireland and early records of Presbyterian baptisms, marriages and deaths are often to be found in the registers of the local Church of Ireland parish. There are exceptions, however. In areas that had a large Presbyterian population from an early date, particularly in the northeast, some registers date from the late seventeenth and early eighteenth centuries. The only published listing remains that included in Margaret Falley's *Irish and Scotch-Irish Ancestral Research* (repr. GPC, 1988). However, this gives a very incomplete and out-of-date picture of the extent and location of the records. For the six counties of Northern Ireland and for many of the adjoining counties, the PRONI *Guide to Church Records* provides a good guide to the dates of surviving registers. The copy of the list held in PRONI includes a listing of Registers in Local Custody, which covers all of Ireland but is much less comprehensive for the South than for the North.

The nature of the records
Presbyterian registers record the same information as is supplied in the registers of the Church of Ireland (see above). It should be remembered that after 1845 all non-Roman Catholic marriages, including those of Presbyterians, were registered by the State. Therefore, from that year on Presbyterian marriage registers contain all the detailed information given in State records.

Locations
Presbyterian registers are held in three main locations: in local custody, in PRONI and at the Presbyterian Historical Society in Belfast. PRONI also has microfilm copies of almost all registers in Northern Ireland that have remained in local custody, and also lists those records held by the Presbyterian Historical Society. For the rest of Ireland, almost all of the records are in local custody. It can be very difficult to locate these, however, because many congregations in the South have moved, amalgamated, or simply disappeared over the last sixty years. The congregational basis of Presbyterianism complicates matters further, since it means that Presbyterian records do not cover a definite geographical area: the same town often had two or more Presbyterian churches, drawing worshippers from the same community but keeping distinct records. In the early nineteenth century especially, controversy within the Church fractured the records, with seceding and non-seceding congregations in the same area, often in violent opposition to each other.

Apart from the PRONI listing, the only guide is *History of Congregations* (Belfast, PHS, 1982, NLI Ir. 274108 p.11), which gives a brief outline of the history of each congregation. Lewis' *Topographical Dictionary of Ireland* (1837) records the existence of Presbyterian congregations within each civil parish, and Pettigrew and Oulton's *Dublin Almanac and General Register of Ireland* (1835) includes a list of all Presbyterian ministers in the country, along with the names and locations of their congregations. Brian Mitchell's *A new Genealogical Atlas of Ireland* (Baltimore, GPC, 2nd ed., 2002, NLI RR 9292 m 36) maps the locations of historic Presbyterian congregations in the nine counties of Ulster. A brief bibliography of histories of Presbyterianism is given in the section 'Clergymen' in Chapter 12.

METHODIST RECORDS
Despite the hostility of many Church of Ireland clergy, the Methodist movement remained part of the Established Church from 1747, when John Wesley first came to Ireland and founded the movement, until 1816, when it split. Between 1747 and 1816 records of Methodist baptisms, marriages and burials are found in the registers of the Church of Ireland. The split in 1816 was occasioned by the issue of whether Methodist ministers had the authority to administer Sacraments and it resulted in the 'Primitive Methodists' remaining within the Church of Ireland, and the 'Wesleyan Methodists' authorising their ministers to perform baptisms and communions. (In theory at least, until 1844 only marriages carried out by a minister of the Church of Ireland were legally valid.) The split continued until 1878, when the two sides were reunited, outside the jurisdiction of the Church of

Ireland. What this means for researchers is that the earliest surviving registers that are specifically Methodist date from 1815/1816 and relate only to the Wesleyan Methodists. The information recorded in these registers is identical to that given in the Church of Ireland registers.

There are a number of problems in locating Methodist records specific to that Church. First, the origins of Methodism as a movement, rather than as a Church, gave its members a great deal of latitude in their attitude to Church membership, so that records of the baptisms, marriages and burials of Methodists may also be found in Quaker and Presbyterian registers, as well as the registers of the Church of Ireland. In addition, the ministers of the Church were preachers on a circuit rather than administrators of a particular area, and moved frequently from one circuit to another. Quite often, the records moved with them. Tracking the ministers' movements is often the only way of locating the relevant records: *An Alphabetical Arrangement of all the Wesleyan Methodist Preachers and Missionaries (Ministers, Missionaries & Preachers on Trial), etc*, Bradford T. Inkersley (originally by William Hill, and republished twenty-one times between 1819 and 1927) tracks all ministers in the British Isles.

For the nine historic counties of Ulster, PRONI has produced a county-by-county listing of the surviving registers, their dates and locations. This listing is appended to their Parish Register Index. Unfortunately, no such listing exists for the rest of the country. Again, Pettigrew and Oulton's *Dublin Almanac and General Register of Ireland* (1835 and subsequent years) provides a list of Methodist preachers and their stations, which gives an indication of the relevant localities. The next step is to identify the closest surviving Methodist centre and enquire about surviving records. Many of the local county heritage centres also hold database copies of surviving Methodist records (see Chapter 15).

QUAKER RECORDS

From the time of their first arrival in Ireland in the seventeenth century, the Society of Friends, or Quakers, kept rational and systematic records of the births, marriages and deaths of all of their members, and in most cases these continue without a break up to the present. Parish registers as such were not kept. Instead, each of the local weekly meetings reported any births, marriages or deaths to a larger Monthly Meeting, which then entered them in a register. Monthly Meetings were held in the following areas: Antrim, Ballyhagan, Carlow, Cootehill, Cork, Dublin, Edenderry, Grange, Lisburn, Limerick, Lurgan, Moate, Mountmellick, Richhill, Tipperary, Waterford, Wexford and Wicklow. For all but Antrim and Cootehill registers have survived from an early date, and are detailed below.

The entries for births, marriages and deaths do not contain information other than the names and addresses of the immediate parties involved, but the centralisation of the records and the self-contained nature of the Quaker community make it a relatively simple matter to establish familial connections; many of the local records are given in the form of family lists, in any case.

There are two main repositories for Quaker records, Libraries of the Society of

Friends in Dublin and Lisburn. The LDS Library in Salt Lake City has microfilm copies of the records of the Dublin Friends' library, while PRONI has microfilm copies of records from the province of Ulster. As well as the records outlined below, these also include considerable collections of letters, wills and family papers, as well as detailed accounts of the discrimination suffered by the Quakers in their early years.

BIRTHS, MARRIAGES AND BURIALS

Ballyhagan Marriages, Library of the Society of Friends, Lisburn. Also NLI Pos. 4127 & PRONI.

Bandon 1672–1713, in Casey A. (ed.), *O'K*, Vol. 1.

Carlow births, marriages and deaths up to 1859, Library of the Society of Friends, Dublin. Also NLI Pos. 1021.

Cork, births, marriages and deaths up to 1859, Library of the Society of Friends, Dublin (NLI Pos. 1021). See also Cork (seventeenth to nineteenth centuries), NLI Pos. 5530.

Dublin, births, marriages and deaths up to 1859, Library of the Society of Friends, Dublin. Also NLI Pos. 1021 (births and marriages) and 1022 (burials).

Edenderry, births, marriages and deaths up to 1859, Library of the Society of Friends, Dublin. Also NLI Pos. 1022, 1612–1814 (in the form of family lists) and NLI Pos. 5531.

Grange, births, marriages and deaths up to 1859, Library of the Society of Friends, Dublin. Also NLI Pos. 1022.

Lisburn, births, marriages and deaths up to 1859, Library of the Society of Friends, Dublin. Also NLI Pos. 1022 and PRONI.

Limerick, births, marriages and deaths up to 1859, Library of the Society of Friends, Dublin. Also NLI Pos. 1022.

Lurgan, births, marriages and deaths up to 1859, Library of the Society of Friends, Dublin (NLI Pos. 1022). See also Lurgan Marriage Certificates, Library of the Society of Friends, Lisburn (NLI Pos. 4126). Also PRONI.

Moate, births, marriages and deaths up to 1859, Library of the Society of Friends, Dublin. Also NLI Pos. 1022.

Mountmellick, births, marriages and deaths up to 1859, Library of the Society of Friends, Dublin. Also NLI Pos. 1023. Also NLI Pos. 5530.

Mountrath, Library of the Society of Friends, Dublin. Also NLI Pos. 5530.

Richhill, births, marriages and deaths up to 1859, Library of the Society of Friends, Dublin. Also NLI Pos. 1023.

Tipperary, births, marriages and deaths up to 1859, Library of the Society of Friends, Dublin. Also NLI Pos. 1024.

Waterford, births, marriages and deaths up to 1859, Library of the Society of Friends, Dublin. Also NLI Pos. 1024.

Wexford, births, marriages and deaths up to 1859, Library of the Society of Friends, Dublin. Also NLI Pos. 1024.

Wicklow, births, marriages and deaths up to 1859, Library of the Society of Friends, Dublin. Also NLI Pos. 1024.

Youghal, births, marriages and deaths up to 1859, Library of the Society of Friends, Dublin. Also NLI Pos. 1024.

Births, Marriages and Deaths throughout Ireland 1859–1949, Library of the Society of Friends, Dublin. Also NLI Pos. 1024.

Also

Leinster Province, births, marriages and deaths, seventeenth century, Library of the Society of Friends, Dublin (NLI Pos. 5530).

Munster Province, births, marriages and deaths 1650–1839, Library of the Society of Friends, Dublin (NLI Pos. 5531).

Ulster Province Meeting Books, 1673–1691. Library of the Society of Friends, Lisburn. (Also PRONI & NLI Pos. 3747.)

Ulster Province Meetings Minute Books to 1782. Library of the Society of Friends, Lisburn. (Also PRONI & NLI Pos. 4124 & 4125.)

OTHER RECORDS
(1) Published

Butler, David M., *Quaker Meeting Houses of Ireland*, Historical Committee of Friends in Ireland, Dublin: 2004, 256p.

Eustace, P.B. & Goodbody O., *Quaker Records, Dublin, Abstracts of Wills* (2 vols, 1704–1785), IMC, 1954–8, 136p., NLI Ir. 289 e 6.

Goodbody, Olive, *Guide to Irish Quaker Records 1654–1860, with contribution on Northern Ireland records by B.G. Hutton*, IMC, 1967, 237 p. NLI Ir. 2896 g 4.

Grubb, Isabel, *Quakers in Ireland*, London: The Swarthmore Press, 1927. 128 p. NLI Ir. 2896 g 3.

Harrison, Richard S., *Cork City Quakers 1655–1939: a brief history*, The author, 1991, NLI, Ir. 289.h.3.

Harrison, Richard S., *A Biographical Dictionary of Irish Quakers*, Dublin: Four Courts Press, 1999, NLI, 123 p.

Impey, E.J.A., *A Roberts Family, quondam Quakers of Queen's Co.*, Frome, London: Butler and Tanner Ltd, 1939, NLI, Ir. 9292 r 3.

Leadbetter, *Biographical Notices of the Society of Friends*, NLI J 2896.

Lunham, T.A., *Early Quakers in Cork: and Cork topographical notes*, Cork: Guy, 1904, NLI, Large Pamphlets LP 2.

Myers, A.C., *Immigration of Irish Quakers into Pennsylvania*, Baltimore: GPC, 1969 (repr. of 1902 ed.) NLI Ir. 2896 m 2 & 4.

(2) Manuscript

Manuscript records of the Quaker library (see *Guide* above): Quaker House, Stocking Lane, Rathfarnham, Dublin 16 Tel: +353 (0)1 4950021, ext. 222. Open Thursday, 11.00am-1.00pm.

Quaker Pedigrees. Library of the Society of Friends, Dublin. Also NLI Pos. 5382, 5383, 5384, 5385.

Quaker Wills and Inventories: Library of the Society of Friends, Lisburn. Also NLI Pos. 4127.

Chapter 4 ❧

PROPERTY AND VALUATION RECORDS

IRISH PLACE NAMES

The smallest official division used in Ireland is the townland. Loosely related to the ancient Gaelic '*Bally betagh*' and to other medieval land divisions, such as ploughlands and 'quarters', townlands can vary enormously in size from a single acre or less to several thousand acres. There are more than 64,000 townlands in Ireland. They were used as the smallest geographical unit in official records from the mid-eighteenth century on, were standardised after the Ordnance Survey in the 1830s and are still in use today. Standardisation resulted in the loss of a large number of traditional names, later referred to as 'sub-denominational'. A guide to sources useful in identifying townlands is provided in the introduction to Chapter 13.

Anything from five to thirty townlands may be grouped together to form a civil parish. These parishes are a legacy of the Middle Ages, pre-dating the formation of counties and generally co-extensive with the parishes of the Established Church, the Church of Ireland. (They should not be confused with Catholic parishes, which are usually much larger.) Civil parishes are collected together in baronies. Originally related to the tribal divisions, or the *tuatha*, of Celtic Ireland, these baronies were multiplied and subdivided over the centuries until their standardisation in the 1500s. As a result, the current names represent a mixture of Gaelic, Anglo-Norman and English influences. A number of baronies—from five in Co. Leitrim to twenty-two in Co. Cork—together make up the modern county. Today, baronies and civil parishes are no longer in use as administrative units.

These geographical units formed the basis of the only two nineteenth-century Irish property surveys to cover the entire country. These surveys, the Tithe Applotment Books of c.1823–1838 and Griffith's Valuation of 1847–1864 have acquired a somewhat unnatural level of importance because of the destruction of early century census returns.

TOWNLANDS AND LAND-LORDS.	OCCUPIERS.	1st Quality.			2ND.			3RD.			4TH.		
		A.	R.	P.	A.	R.	P.	A.	R.	P.	A.	R.	P.	A.
Aghlion	Forwarded	52	1	20	73	2	25	10	0	05	4	0	00	~
"	Peter Lynch &c.	4	2	~	5	~	~	2	2	~	~	~	~
"	J. B. & I. Lynch	10	~	~	17	~	~	5	~	~	~	~	~
"	J. & P. Keogan	3	~	~	24	1	~	4	~	~	~	~	~
"	J. Kilroy & Brady	4	~	~	12	~	~	3	~	~	7	2	~
"	Garret Fitzsimons	3	~	~	7	~	~	1	1	15	~	~	~
"	Jn.º Fitzsimons	4	~	~	7	~	~	~	2	15	~	~	~
"	John Brady	~	~	1	~	~	~	~	~	~	~	~	~
"	Luke Magnis	1	0	30	4	~	~	~	~	~	1	~	~
"	Richd. Glannon	1	~	~	1	~	~	~	~	~	~	~	~
		83	1	10	150	3	25	26	1	35	12	2	~

Tithe Applotment Book, Aghalion, Co. Cavan
(Courtesy of the National Archives of Ireland)

TITHE APPLOTMENT BOOKS

The Composition Act 1823 specified that tithes due to the Established Church, the Church of Ireland, which had hitherto been payable in kind, should now be paid in money. As a result, it was necessary to carry out a valuation of the entire country, civil parish by civil parish, in order to determine how much would be payable by each landholder. This was done over the course of the next fifteen years, up to the suspension of tithe payments in 1838. Not surprisingly, those who were not members of the Church of Ireland fiercely resented the tithes, all the more because the tax was not payable on all land. The exemptions which were granted produced spectacular inequalities. In Munster, for instance, tithes were payable on potato patches but not on grassland, with the result that the poorest had to pay the most. The exemptions also have an impact on research because the Tithe Books are not comprehensive: apart from the fact that they omit entirely anyone not in occupation of land, certain categories of land, varying from area to area, are simply passed over in silence. They do not record a full list of house-holders. Nonetheless, they do constitute the only countrywide survey for the period, and are valuable precisely because the heaviest burden of tithes fell on the poorest, for whom few other records survive.

Microfilm copies of the Tithe Books for all of Ireland are available in the NAI, DCLA, and via the LDS Family History Library. Those for the nine counties of Ulster are available in PRONI. From a genealogical point of view, the information recorded in the Tithe Books is quite basic, typically consisting of townland name, landholder's name, area of land and tithes payable. In addition, many Books also record the landlord's name and an assessment of the economic productivity of the land. The tax payable was based on the average price of wheat and oats over the seven years up to 1823, and was levied at a different rate depending on the quality of the land.

The usefulness of the Tithe Books varies enormously, depending on the nature of the research. Since only a name is given, with no indication of family relationships, any conclusions drawn are inevitably somewhat speculative. However, for parishes where registers do not begin until after 1850, they are often the only surviving early records. They can provide valuable circumstantial evidence, especially where a holding passed from father to son in the period between the Tithe survey and Griffith's Valuation. The surnames in the Books have been roughly indexed in the NLI's 'Index of Surnames', described more fully below.

In 1831 an organised campaign of resistance to the payment of Tithes, the so-called Tithe War, culminated in large-scale refusals to pay the tax. In order to apply for compensation for the resultant loss of income, local Church of Ireland clergy-men were required to produce lists of those liable for tithes who had not paid, known as 'Tithe Defaulters'. These lists can provide a fuller picture of tithe-payers than the original Tithe Book, and can be useful to cross-check against the Book, especially where it dates from before 1831. One hundred and twenty-seven of these lists survive and are held in the NAI Chief Secretary's Office as part of the Official Papers series. They relate principally to Counties Kilkenny and Tipperary, with some coverage also of Counties Carlow, Cork, Kerry, Laois, Limerick, Louth, Meath, Offaly, Waterford and Wexford. A full list was published in *The Irish Genealogist* (Vol. 8, No. 1, 1990). A CD-ROM index has been produced by Data Tree Publishing (*www.alphalink.com.au/~ datatree*).

GRIFFITH'S VALUATION

From the 1820s to the 1840s a complex process of reform attempted to standard-ise the basis of local taxation in Ireland. The first steps taken were to map and fix administrative boundaries through the Ordnance Survey and the associated Boundary Commission. The next step was to assess in a thoroughly uniform way the productive capacity of all property in the country. Richard Griffith, an English geologist based in Dublin, became Boundary Commissioner in 1825 and Commissioner of Valuation in 1830. The results of his massive survey, the Primary Valuation of Ireland, were published between 1847 and 1864. The Valuation is arranged by county, barony, Poor Law Union, civil parish and townland, and it lists every landholder and every householder in Ireland. Apart from townland address and householder's name, the particulars given are:

• name of the person from whom the property was leased ('immediate lessor');
• description of the property;
• acreage;
• valuation.

The only directly useful family information supplied is in areas where a surname was particularly common. The surveyors often adopted the Gaelic practice of using the father's first name to distinguish between individuals of the same name, so that 'John Reilly (James)' is the son of James, while 'John Reilly (Michael)' is the son of Michael. For similar reasons, occupations are also sometimes used to distinguish, for example, 'John Ryan (weaver)' from 'John Ryan (farmer)'. Copies of the Valuation are widely available in major libraries and record offices, both on microfiche and in their original published form. The dates of first publication are given under the individual counties in Chapter 13.

The Valuation was never intended as a census substitute; if the 1851 census had survived, it would have little genealogical significance. As things stand, however, it is the only detailed guide to where people lived in mid-nineteenth century Ireland and what property they occupied. In addition, a huge quantity of material was produced both prior to publication and in subsequent revisions, making it possible in many cases to identify occupiers before the publication date and to trace living descendants of those originally listed by Griffith (see 'Valuation Office Records', below).

INDEXES TO GRIFFITH'S AND TITHE BOOKS

In the early 1960s the NLI undertook to part-index the surnames occurring in Griffith's Valuation and the Tithe Books, which produced the county-by-county series known as the Index of Surnames, or the Householders' Index. This records the occurrence of households of a particular surname in each of the civil parishes of a given county, supplying the exact number of households in the case of Griffith's, as well as providing a summary of the total numbers in each barony of the county. Since it is not a true index—providing only an indication of the presence or absence of a surname in the Tithe Books and the numbers of householders bearing the surname in Griffith's—its usefulness is limited. In any case, Griffith's is now well-indexed elsewhere. For names that are relatively uncommon it can still have a role to play, but is of little help for a county in which a particular surname occurs frequently. The county volumes include outline maps of the civil parishes covered and a guide to the corresponding Catholic parishes. Full sets of the Index of Surnames can be found in the NAI, NLI, PRONI and the LDS Library.

Valuation of Tenements.

ACTS 15 & 16 VIC., CAP. 63, & 17 VIC., CAP. 8.

COUNTY OF CAVAN.

BARONY OF CASTLERAHAN.

UNION OF OLDCASTLE.

PARISH OF CASTLERAHAN.

No. and Letters of Reference to Map.		Names.		Description of Tenement.	Area.			Rateable Annual Valuation.		Total Annual Valuation of Rateable Property.
		Townlands and Occupiers.	Immediate Lessors.					Land.	Buildings.	
					A.	R.	P.	£ s. d.	£ s. d.	£ s. d.
		AGHALION. (Ord. S. 39.)								
1	a	John Lynch,	C. T. Nesbit,	House, offices, and land,	14	2	28	6 5 0	0 10 0	6 15 0
–	b	C. T. Nesbit,	In fee,	Land,	0	3	30	0 5 0	—	0 5 0
2	a	Bryan M'Donald,	C. T. Nesbit,	Herd's house & land,	19	3	22	4 0 0	1 5 0	5 5 0
		John Fitzsimon,		Land,				4 0 0	—	4 0 0
3		John Fitzsimon,	Same,	House, offices, and land,	6	1	34	2 0 0	1 0 0	3 0 0
4		John Fitzsimon,	Same,	Land,	4	1	34	2 0 0	—	2 0 0
–	a	Rose Fitzsimon,	Same,	House,				—	0 10 0	0 10 0
5	a	John Fitzsimon, jun.,	Same,	House, offices, and land,	8	1	35	4 0 0	1 0 0	5 0 0
–	b	John Fitzsimon,	Same,	Land,	0	2	15	0 5 0	—	0 5 0
	c	John Fitzsimon,	Same,	Land (gardens),	0	1	24	0 5 0	—	0 5 0
6		John Flood,	Same,	House, offices, and land,	17	2	8	8 0 0	1 15 0	9 15 0
7				House, offices, and land,	31	0	12	10 0 0	1 5 0	14 0 0
8		Michael Cogan,	Same,	Land,	7	2	16	2 15 0	—	
				House, offices, and land,	5	0	22	1 18 0	0 10 0	2 15 0
9	a	Peter Lynch,	Same,	Bog,	7	0	17	6 7 0	—	0 10 0
	b	Joseph Brady,	Same,	Ho., off., & sm. garden,				—	0 10 0	0 10 0
10				Land,	1	1	33	0 10 0	—	0 10 0
11		Catherine Fitzsimon,	Same,	House and land,	2	0	4	0 10 0	0 5 0	0 15 0
12		Matthew Cogan,	Same,	House, office, and land,	13	0	9	4 10 0	0 10 0	5 0 0
13				Land,	11	0	24	4 0 0	—	
14		Patrick Cogan,	Same,	House, offices, and land,	23	3	18	12 0 0	1 5 0	22 5 0
15				Land,	8	2	21	4 0 0	—	
16				Land,	1	2	2	1 0 0	—	
				Land,	0	1	24	0 4 0	—	0 4 0
17	a	John Lynch,	Same,	House, offices, and land,	38	0	30	15 0 0	1 0 0	16 0 0
	a	Terence & Patk. Cogan,	Same,	House,				—	0 5 0	0 5 0
	b	Vacant,	Terence & Patk. Cogan,	House,				0 10 0	—	0 10 0
	c	Vacant,	Same,	House,				—	0 15 0	0 15 0
18		Michael Brady,	C. T. Nesbit,	House, office, and land,	9	2	30	4 0 0	0 15 0	4 15 0
19	a	James Bennett,	Same,	House, offices, and land,	34	2	18	17 10 0	1 5 0	18 15 0
	b	Margaret Gilroy,	James Bennett,	House,				—	0 10 0	0 10 0
	c	Anne Timmon,	Same,	House,				—	0 5 0	0 5 0
	d	Peter Lynch,	C. T. Nesbit,	Land,	0	0	20	0 1 0	—	0 1 0
	e	Joseph Brady,	Same,	Land,	0	0	20	0 1 0	—	0 1 0
20		Anthony Brady,	Same,	House, offices, and land,	12	0	14	5 15 0	1 0 0	6 15 0
21		John Lynch,	Same,	House, offices, and land,	12	1	18	6 5 0	1 0 0	7 5 0
22		Edward Fitzsimons,	Same,	House, office, and land,	6	2	16	3 0 0	0 10 0	3 10 0
23	a	Michael Brady,	Same,	Herd's house and land,	14	3	13	7 10 0	0 10 0	8 0 0
	b	Terence & Patk. Cogan,	Same,	Land,	0	1	24	0 5 0	—	0 5 0
24		Peter Brady,	Same,	Land,	7	0	31	3 0 0	—	3 0 0
25		John Brady,	Same,	Herd's house and land,	34	3	2	16 0 0	0 5 0	16 5 0
26		Patrick Brady,	Same,	House, offices, and land,	18	1	17	8 15 0	1 15 0	10 10 0
27		C. T. Nesbit,	In fee,	Land,	14	0	13	0 15 0	—	0 15 0

B

Griffith's Valuation, Aghalion, Co. Cavan
(Courtesy of the Genealogical Office)

For the Tithe Books, the Index of Surnames remains the sole countywide guide. A CD-ROM index to the Tithe Books of the six counties of Northern Ireland, *International Land Records: Tithe Applotment Books, 1823–38,* was published by FamilyTreeMaker in 1999 and is now available to subscribers at *www.genealogy. com.* Various volunteer transcripts from the LDS microfilms are also online—see Chapter 13.

The situation with Griffith's is entirely different. There are at least three comprehensive online transcripts or indexes:

- Origins, at *www.originsnetwork.com,* has the most comprehensive version: scanned, indexed and related to the accompanying Ordnance Survey maps.
- John Hayes, a*t www.failteromhat.com,* has an index to householders that is free, but flawed.
- Irish Ancestors, at *www.ireland.com/ancestor,* reproduces the functionality of the Index of Surnames, giving counts of householders by county (free) and by parish (fee).

In addition, many volunteer transcripts of individual parishes are available online—see Chapter 13.

VALUATION OFFICE RECORDS

Pre-publication records
The account given above of the creation of Griffith's Valuation is actually a serious over-simplification. In fact, three separate valuation methods were used prior to publication, each producing its own distinct set of records. First, the initial Townland Valuation Act 1826 allowed for a complete assessment of every parcel of land and tenement (building) in Ireland, with the aim of identifying an equitable replacement for the unevenly applied local cess taxes. However, after Griffith began surveying in Londonderry in 1831, it soon became apparent that this plan was far too ambitious for the resources available. A lower threshold of a £3 valuation was adopted for buildings to be assessed, which excluded the large majority of householders but still covered a significant number of dwellings and commercial premises, especially in towns. The Valuation continued on this basis for the next seven years, covering eight of the nine northern counties. But by 1838 it was clear that even with the revised £3 threshold the surveying would last for a very long time indeed. In that year the threshold was raised to £5, so now only the most substantial buildings were covered.

17

Surname			Barony	Surname			Barony
Fitzgerald	G2		Loughtee L.	Flood	G21	T	Loughtee U.
Fitzgerald	G	T	Loughtee U.	Flood	G18	T	Tullygarvey
Fitzgerald		T	Tullygarvey	Flood	G4	T	Clankee
Fitzgerald	G2	T	Clankee	Flood	G14	T	Clanmahon
Fitzgerald	G2		Clanmahon	Flood	G29	T	Castlerahan
Fitzmaurice	G		Tullyhunco	Floody	G3	T	Tullygarvey
Fitzpatrick	G25	T	Tullyhaw	Floyd	G2	T	Loughtee U.
Fitzpatrick	G114	T	Loughtee L.	Flynn	G13	T	Tullyhaw
Fitzpatrick	G24	T	Tullyhunco	Flynn	G6	T	Loughtee L.
Fitzpatrick	G73	T	Loughtee U.	Flynn	G		Tullyhunco
Fitzpatrick	G30	T	Tullygarvey	Flynn	G3	T	Loughtee U.
Fitzpatrick	G9	T	Clankee	Flynn		T	Tullygarvey
Fitzpatrick	G33	T	Clanmahon	Flynn	G		Clankee
Fitzpatrick	G10	T	Castlerahan	Flynn	G9	T	Clanmahon
Fitzsimmons		T	Tullyhunco	Flynn	G20	T	Castlerahan
Fitzsimmons	G	T	Loughtee U.	Foghlan	G		Tullyhaw
Fitzsimmons	G	T	Clanmahon	Folbus		T	Tullyhunco
Fitzsimon	G	T	Tullyhunco	Foley	G2		Tullygarvey
Fitzsimon	G2	T	Loughtee U.	Follett	G		Loughtee U.
Fitzsimon	G7	T	Tullygarvey	Fonor		T	Castlerahan
Fitzsimon	G	T	Clankee	Forbes	G	T	Tullyhunco
Fitzsimon	G		Clanmahon	Forbes	G	T	Clankee
Fitzsimon	G5	T	Castlerahan	Ford	G		Tullyhaw
Fitzsimon	G39	T	Castlerahan	Ford	G		Loughtee U.
Fitzsimons	G	T	Tullyhaw	Ford	G2	T	Tullygarvey
Fitzsimons	G6	T	Loughtee L.	Ford	G		Clankee
Fitzsimons	G12	T	Loughtee U.	Forde	G	T	Tullyhaw
Fitzsimons	G8	T	Tullygarvey	Foreman	G6	T	Clankee
Fitzsimons	G7	T	Clankee	Forest		T	Loughtee U.
Fitzsimons	G14	T	Clanmahon	Forster		T	Loughtee U.
Fitzsimons	G6	T	Castlerahan	Forster	G10	T	Clanmahon
Flack		T	Tullyhunco	Forsyth	G3	T	Castlerahan
Flack	G2	T	Tullygarvey	Foreythe	G3	T	Clanmahon
Fleck	G3	T	Clankee	Fosqua		T	Tullygarvey
Flaherty		T	Loughtee L.	Foster	G	T	Tullyhaw
Flanagan	G14	T	Tullyhaw	Foster	G6	T	Loughtee U.
Flanagan	G3	T	Loughtee L.	Foster	G5		Tullygarvey
Flanagan	G		Tullyhunco	Foster	G9	T	Clanmahon
Flanagan	G20	T	Loughtee U.	Foster	G3	T	Castlerahan
Flanagan	G	T	Tullygarvey	Fotton		T	Tullygarvey
Flanagan	G4	T	Clankee	Fottrell	G		Clankee
Flanagan	G3	T	Clanmahon	Fox	G2	T	Tullyhaw
Flanagan	G14	T	Castlerahan	Fox	G2	T	Tullyhunco
Flanigan	G2	T	Tullyhaw	Fox		T	Loughtee U.
Flanigan	G		Loughtee L.	Fox	G4	T	Tullygarvey
Flanigan		T	Loughtee U.	Fox	G15	T	Clankee
Flannagan	G		Loughtee L.	Fox	G2	T	Clanmahon
Flannery	G		Loughtee U.	Fox	G36	T	Castlerahan
Fleming	G		Tullyhaw	Foy	G3	T	Loughtee L.
Fleming	G	T	Loughtee L.	Foy	G2	T	Loughtee U.
Fleming	G3	T	Tullyhunco	Foy	G26	T	Tullygarvey
Fleming	G8	T	Loughtee U.	Foy	G5	T	Clankee
Fleming	G	T	Tullygarvey	Foy	G	T	Clanmahon
Fleming	G	T	Clankee	Foy		T	Castlerahan
Fleming	G9	T	Clanmahon	Foy		T	Tullygarvey
Fleming	G7	T	Castlerahan	Foyragh			
Fletcher	G		Loughtee U.	Francen	G	T	Clankee
Fleuker	G	T	Clankee	Francey	G3		Clankee
Flewker	G2	T	Clankee	Francis		T	Loughtee L.
Flinn		T	Clankee	Fraser	G3	T	Tullyhaw
Flinn	G	T	Clanmahon	Frazer	G		Tullyhaw
Flood	G	T	Tullyhaw	Frazer	G		Loughtee U.
Flood	G8	T	Loughtee L.	Frazer		T	Tullyhunco
Flood	G3	T	Tullyhunco	Freeland	G	T	Castlerahan
				Freeman	G2	T	Tullygarvey

'Index of Surnames', Co. Cavan
(Courtesy of the Genealogical Office)

The year 1838 also saw the introduction of the Irish Poor Law, a system of relief for the destitute. The funding of this system—based on property assessments carried out on behalf of the local Board of Guardians in each of the 138 Poor Law Unions—soon turned into a source of contention, with widespread accusations of bias in the valuations. It became obvious fairly quickly that it made no sense to have two separate systems of local taxation, each based on a different valuation of the same property. Therefore in 1844, when so-called townland valuations had been completed for twenty-seven of the thirty-two counties, Griffith was told to change the basis of assessment by dropping the £5 threshold and covering *all* properties in the outstanding counties, which were all in Munster. The aim of this revision was to establish whether a uniform basis could be created to unify Poor Law Rates and the cess tax. The experiment was an almost unqualifed success and the 1852 Tenement Valuation Act authorised Griffith to extend the system throughout Ireland, a procedure he had in fact already begun. The results were published between 1847 and 1864, generally with the southern counties published earlier and the northern counties later.

In the course of this long-drawn-out administrative saga, large quantities of manuscript records were produced. First, the pre-1838 valuation of the northern counties, based on the £3 building threshold, created local valuers' 'house books' and 'field books'—the former including the names of occupiers, the latter concerned purely with soil quality. The originals are in the NAI and PRONI, with microfilm copies in the LDS Family History Library. These are particularly useful for urban or semi-urban areas in northern counties before 1838.

After the change in the basis of assessment in 1844 the main categories of valuers' notebooks continued to be known as 'house books' and 'field books', but the distinction became more than a little blurred, with information on occupiers appearing in both. To add to the merriment, other classes of notebook were also created:

- Tenure books, showing landlord and lease information;
- Rent books, showing rents paid, as an aid to valuation;
- Quarto books, covering towns;
- Perambulation books, recording valuers' visits; and
- Mill books.

There are far fewer of these types of books than of the 'house' and 'field' books. Copies of all of them are available at the NAI, the LDS Library, though not in PRONI, with some still held in the Valuation Office.

A number of points need to be kept in mind here. First, pre-publication manuscript valuation records do not survive for all parishes. The only way to find out if something is there is to check the NAI, LDS, PRONI or Valuation Office catalogues. Secondly, the categories into which the records are sorted were somewhat hazy to begin with and have only become hazier over the years. Accordingly, check under every category and investigate anything that survives for an area you are interested in. And you should remember that Griffith's Valuation, far from being the record of a settled population, is in fact a snapshot of the aftermath of a catastrophe, the Great Famine of 1845–1849. In many areas, enormous changes took place in the interim period between the original and the published valuations.

Post-publication records

The 1852 Act envisaged annual revisions to the valuations to record any changes in occupier, lessor, size or value of holding. In practice, revisions were relatively rare until well into the 1860s. From then until the 1970s a system of handwritten amendments was employed, coded by colour for each year, with a new manuscript book created when the number of alterations threatened legibility. These are the 'Cancelled Land Books', still available at the Valuation Office, which is currently based in the Irish Life Centre, Abbey Street, Dublin 1, but due for decentralisation to Youghal, Co. Cork, in the near future.

The Books can be very useful in pinpointing a possible date of death or emigration, or in identifying a living relative. A large majority of those who were in occupation of a holding by the 1890s, when the Land Acts began to subsidise the purchase of the land by its tenant-farmers, have descendants or relatives still living in the same area. The Cancelled Land Books for Northern Ireland are now in PRONI.

ESTATE RECORDS

In the eighteenth and nineteenth centuries the vast majority of the Irish population lived as small tenant-farmers on large estates owned for the most part by English or Anglo-Irish landlords. The administration of these estates inevitably produced large quantities of records, maps, tenants' lists, rentals, account books, lease books, etc. During the twentieth century many of the estates were broken up and sold off, and many record collections found their way into public repositories. They constitute a largely unexplored source of genealogical information.

There are good reasons for their being unexplored. First, it was quite rare for a large landowner to have individual rental or lease agreements with the huge numbers of small tenants on his land. Instead, he would let a significant area to a middleman, who would then sublet to others, who might in turn rent out parts to the smallest tenants. It is very rare for estate records to document the smallest landholders, since most of these had little or no right of tenure in any case.

Secondly, there is the related problem of access. The estate records in the two major Dublin repositories—the NAI and NLI—are not catalogued in detail. The only comprehensive guide is that given in Richard Hayes' *Manuscript Sources for the Study of Irish Civilisation* and its supplements, copies of which can be found in the NLI and NAI. This catalogues the records by landlord's name and by county, with entries such as: 'NL Ms. 3185. Rent Roll of Lord Cremorne's estate in Co. Armagh, 1797'. Hayes gives no more detail of the areas of the county covered, and it can be difficult to ascertain from the Tithe Books or Griffith's just who the landlord was; Griffith's supplies only the name of the immediate lessor. In addition, some of the collections in the NLI have still not been catalogued at all. The holdings of PRONI are catalogued more comprehensively, but they still do not relate the papers to the precise areas covered. Again, it is necessary to know the landlord's name.

There are a number of ways to overcome, or at least to partially overcome, this obstacle. Common sense often makes it possible to identify the landlord by examining Griffith's for the surrounding areas: the largest lessor is the likeliest candidate. If the immediate lessor in Griffith's is not the landlord but a middleman, then it can be useful to try to find this middleman's own holding or residence and check from whom he was leasing. Two publications may also be of assistance: O.H. Hussey de Burgh's *The Landowners of Ireland* provides a guide to the major landowners, the size of their holdings and where in the country they were situated; *Landowners in Ireland: Return of owners of land of one acre and upwards ...* (London: 1876) is comprehensive to a fault and is organised alphabetically within the county, a rather awkward system of organisation.

The largest single collection of estate records, now held in the NAI, is the Landed Estate Court Records, also known as the Encumbered Estate Courts, which is not catalogued in Hayes. The Court was set up to facilitate the sale of estates whose owners could not invest enough to make them productive. Between 1849 and 1857 it oversaw the sale of more than 3,000 Irish estates. Its records contain many rentals and maps drawn up for the sales, but are so close in time to Griffith's as to make them of limited use, except in very particular circumstances. The NAI also has an index to the townlands covered by the records.

Despite all the problems, research in estate records can be very rewarding, especially for the period before the major nineteenth-century surveys. To take one example, the rent rolls of the estate of Charles O'Hara in Counties Sligo and Leitrim, which date from c.1775, record a large number of leases to smaller tenants and supply the lives named in the leases, often specifying family relationships. It must be emphasised, however, that information of this quality is rare; the majority of the extant rentals and tenants' lists only give details of major tenants.

A more detailed guide to the dates and areas covered and the class of tenants recorded in the estate papers of the NLI and NAI is currently being prepared by the NLI, in association with the Irish Genealogical Society of Minnesota. To date, Counties Armagh, Carlow, Cavan, Clare, Cork, Donegal, Fermanagh, Kerry, Kildare, Leitrim, Limerick, Longford, Galway, Mayo, Monaghan, Roscommon, Sligo, Tyrone, Waterford, Westmeath and Wicklow have been covered; a brief outline of the results is given in Chapter 13 under these counties.

Chapter 5 ∾

WILLS

PART 1: BACKGROUND

In Ireland, as elsewhere, wills have always been an extremely important source of genealogical information on the property-owning classes. They provide a clear picture of a family at a particular point in time and can often supply enough details of a much larger network of relationships—cousins, nephews, in-laws and others—to produce quite a substantial family tree. Apart from their genealogical significance, wills can also vividly evoke the way of life of those whose final wishes they record.

Information supplied
The minimum information found in a will is:

- the name, address and occupation of the testator;
- the names of the beneficiaries;
- the name(s) of the executor(s);
- the names of the witnesses;
- the date the will was made;
- the date of probate of the will.

Specific properties are usually mentioned, though not always. The two dates provided, that of the will and that of its probate, indicate the period during which the testator died. Up to the nineteenth century most wills were made close to the date of death, and witnesses were normally related to the person making the will. As well as the minimum information, of course, many wills also contain much more, including addresses and occupations of beneficiaries, witnesses and executors, and details of family relationships, quarrels along with affection.

Testamentary Authority pre-1857
Before 1857 the Church of Ireland, as the Established Church, had charge of all testamentary affairs. Consistorial Courts in each diocese were responsible for granting probate, that is, for legally authenticating a will and conferring on the executors the power to administer the estate. The Courts also had the power to issue letters of administration to the next-of-kin or to the main creditor on the

estates of those who died intestate. Each Court was responsible for wills and administrations within its own diocese. However, when the estate included property in another diocese that was worth more than £5, responsibility for the will or administration passed to the Prerogative Court, under the authority of the Archbishop of Armagh.

Consistorial Wills and Administrations

The wills and administration records of the Consistorial Courts were held locally in each diocese until the abolition of the testamentary authority of the Church of Ireland in 1857. After that date the Public Record Office began the lengthy process of collecting the original records and transcribing them into Will and Grant Books. The PRO then indexed the wills and Administration Bonds—the sureties administrators had to produce as a guarantee that the estate would be administered properly. None of the Consistorial Courts had comprehensive records of all of the wills and administrations they had dealt with. There was very little information earlier than the seventeenth century, and the majority of the Courts appear to have had serious gaps in their records before the mid-eighteenth century.

The entire collection of original wills and administrations held in the PRO was destroyed in 1922, along with almost all of the Will and Grant Books into which they had been transcribed. The only exceptions are the Will Books for Down (1850–1858) and Connor (1853–1858), and the Grant Books for Cashel (1840–1845), Derry and Raphoe (1818–1821), and Ossory (1848–1858).

The indexes to wills and administration bonds were not destroyed, although a number were badly damaged in the blaze. These are now available in the Reading Room of the NAI. The wills indexes are alphabetical and normally give the testator's address and the year of probate, occasionally specifying his occupation. The administration bonds indexes are not fully alphabetical, being arranged year by year under the initial letter of the surname of the deceased person. They give the year of the bond, the full name and usually the address of the deceased and sometimes his occupation. Some of the wills indexes have been published, details of which are provided at the end of this chapter.

Prerogative Wills and Administrations

To recap: if an estate held property worth more than £5 in a second diocese, it was dealt with by the Prerogative Court, rather than the Consistorial Court. Accordingly, Prerogative wills and administrations tend to cover the wealthier classes, for example, merchants with dealings in more than one area, or those who lived close to diocesan borders. Up to 1816 the Prerogative Court was not housed in a single place, with hearings generally held in the residence of the presiding judge. From 1816 on the King's Inns building in Henrietta Street in Dublin provided a permanent home for the Court. For this reason the records of the Court before 1816 cannot be taken as complete. After 1857 all of these records were transferred to the PRO, where the original wills and grants of administration were transcribed into Prerogative Will and Grant Books and then indexed. The indexes survived 1922, but all of the original wills and grants and almost all of the Will and Grant Books were destroyed. Details of the surviving Books are given at the end of this chapter.

The loss of the original Prerogative wills is mitigated to a large extent by a project carried out in the early decades of the nineteenth century by Sir William Betham, Ulster King of Arms. As well as preparing the first index of testators, recording up to 1810, Betham also made abstracts of the family information contained in almost all of the wills before 1800. The original notebooks in which he recorded the information are now in the NAI and the Genealogical Office has his Sketch Pedigrees based on these abstracts and including later additions and amendments. PRONI has a copy of the Genealogical Office series, minus the additions and amendments, made by a successor of Betham's, Sir John Burke (T/559). Betham also made a large number of abstracts from Prerogative Grants up to 1802. The original notebooks for these are also in the NAI. The Genealogical Office transcript copy (GO 257–260) is fully alphabetical, unlike the notebooks.

The first index to Prerogative wills, up to 1810, was published in 1897 by Sir Arthur Vicars, Burke's successor as Ulster King of Arms, and can be used as a guide to Betham's abstracts and Sketch Pedigrees, with the proviso that wills from the decade 1800–1810 are not covered by Betham. The manuscript index for the period from 1811 to 1857 is in the NAI Reading Room. As with the consistorial administration bonds indexes, the Prerogative Grants indexes are not fully alphabetical, being arranged year by year under the initial letter of the surname of the deceased person.

Testamentary Authority post-1857

The Probate Act of 1857 did away with the testamentary authority of the Church of Ireland. Instead of the Consistorial Courts and the Prerogative Court, power to grant probate and issue letters of administration was now vested in a Principal Registry in Dublin, and in eleven District Registries. Rules similar to those governing the geographical jurisdiction of the ecclesiastical courts applied to the Registries, with the Principal Registry taking the place of the Prerogative Court and covering Dublin and a large area around it. Transcripts of the wills proved and administrations granted were made in the District Registries and the originals forwarded to the Principal Registry. Almost all of the records of the Principal Registry were destroyed in 1922; the few surviving Will and Grant Books are detailed below. The Will Book transcripts made by the District Registries did survive, however. The records of those Districts covering areas now in the Republic of Ireland—Ballina, Cavan, Cork, Kilkenny, Limerick, Mullingar, Tuam and Waterford—are held in the NAI. For districts now in Northern Ireland—Armagh, Belfast and Derry—the Will Books are held in PRONI.

Fortunately, from 1858 a new system of indexing and organising wills and administrations had been used. A printed, alphabetically ordered 'Calendar of Wills and Administrations' was produced for every year, and copies of all of these have survived. For each will or administration they record:

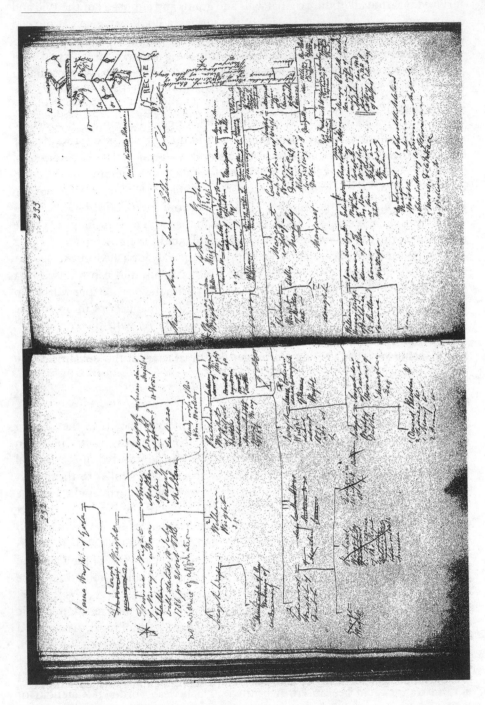

Betham's 'Sketch Pedigrees from Will Abstracts'
(Courtesy of the Genealogical Office)

- the name, address and occupation of the deceased person;
- the place and date of death;
- the value of the estate;
- the name and address of the person or persons to whom probate or administration was granted.

In many cases the relationship of the executor is also specified. This means that, despite the loss of so much original post-1857 testamentary material, at least some information is available on all wills or administrations from this period. Very often, much that is of genealogical value can be gleaned from the Calendars, including such information as exact dates of death, places of residence and indications of economic status. A consolidated index covers the period between 1858 and 1877, making it unnecessary to search each yearly Calendar. The Calendars are on open access in the NAI Reading Room, with a copy also available in PRONI.

Abstracts and Transcripts

As well as the original Consistorial and Prerogative wills and grants and the transcripts made of them in the Will and Grant Books, a wide number of other sources exist, particularly for material pre-1857. The most important of these is the NAI collection, gathered after 1922 in an attempt to replace some of what had been lost. As well as original wills from private legal records and individual families, this ever-expanding collection also includes pre-1922 researchers' abstracts and transcripts. It is covered by a card index in the Reading Room, which also gives details of those wills and grants in the surviving pre-1857 Will and Grant Books. The card index has been published on CD-ROM by Eneclann. Separate card indexes cover the Thrift, Jennings and Crossley collections of abstracts and the records of Charitable Donations and Bequests. PRONI has made similar efforts and the copies it holds are indexed in the Pre-1858 Wills Index, part of the Subject Index in the Public Search Room.

Inland Revenue Records

The Inland Revenue in London kept a series of annual Indexes to Irish Will Registers and Indexes to Irish Administration Registers from 1828 to 1879, which are now in the NAI. These give the name and address of both the deceased and the executor or administrator. As well as the Indexes, the Archives also hold a set of the actual Inland Revenue Irish Will Registers and Irish Administration Registers for the years 1828–1839, complete apart from the Wills Register covering January–June 1834. Although the Will Registers are not exact transcripts of the original wills, they do supply a good deal of detailed information, including the precise date of death, the principal beneficiaries and legacies and a brief inventory of the estate. The Administration Registers are less informative, but still include details of the date of death, the administrator and the estate.

Estate Duty Office Records

Between 1812 and 1857 copies of all wills liable for Estate Duty proved in English Prerogative and Diocesan Courts of testators with an Irish address—almost 3,000 in total—were sent to the Estate Duty Office in London. There they remained until after 1922, at which time 1,370 of them, dating from 1821 to 1857, were transferred to PRONI. They are indexed in the Pre-1858 Wills Index and concern testators from the entire island of Ireland.

Land Commission Records

Under the provisions of the Land Purchase Acts, which subsidised the purchase of smallholdings by their tenant occupiers, it was necessary for those wishing to sell their land to produce evidence of their ownership to the Irish Land Commission. As a result, over 10,000 wills were deposited with the Commission, the majority dating from the nineteenth century but many earlier still. The NLI and PRONI hold a card index to the testators, but the original documents remain unavailable to the public. They are housed in the office of the Land Commission, on the ground floor of the NAI.

The Registry of Deeds

The registration of wills was normally carried out when the executor(s) anticipated a legal problem arising in the provisions—almost inevitably the exclusion of parties who would feel they had some rights over the estate. Because of this, wills held at the Registry cannot be taken as providing a complete picture of the family. Abstracts of all wills registered from 1708—the date of foundation of the Registry—to 1832 were published in three volumes by the Irish Manuscripts Commission between 1954 and 1986. These are available on open shelves at the NLI and NAI. Although the abstracts record and index all the persons named—testators, beneficiaries and witnesses—they do not show the full provisions of the wills. These can be found in the original memorials in the Registry.

The Genealogical Office

Most of the will abstracts held by the Genealogical Office are covered by the Office's own index, GO Ms. 429, which was published in *Analecta Hibernica*, No. 17 (1949) (NLI Ir. 941 a 10). The manuscript index has since been added to, but is still not entirely comprehensive as it excludes all of the Betham material and many of the collections relating to individual families. A guide to the major collections is included at the end of this chapter.

English records

If a testator held property in both Ireland and England or Wales, then a grant of probate was made both in England and in Ireland. Almost all wills proved before the Prerogative Court of Canterbury are now available online at *www. nationalarchives.gov.uk/documentsonline*. Many of the Society of Genealogists' indexes to other English and Welsh wills are available, for a fee, via Origins at *www.originsnet work.com*.

270 WILLS AND ADMINISTRATIONS. 1871.

HORGAN Daniel.

[191]   Effects under £200.

20 March.   Letters of Administration of the personal estate of Daniel Horgan late of Great George's-street **Cork** Builder deceased who died 21 February 1870 at same place were granted at **Cork** to Michael Joseph Horgan of the South Mall in said City Solicitor the Nephew of said deceased for the benefit of Catherine Horgan Widow John Horgan the Reverend David Horgan Ellen Gillman Mary Daly and Margaret Horgan only next of kin of said deceased.

HORNE Christopher.

[67]   Effects under £100.

7 March.   Letters of Administration of the personal estate of Christopher Horne late of Ballinasloe County **Galway** Gentleman a Widower deceased who died 21 March 1867 at same place were granted at the **Principal Registry** to Patrick Horne of Ballinasloe aforesaid M.D. the only Brother of said deceased.

HORNER Isabella.

[17]   Effects under £100.

29 April.   Letters of Administration of the personal estate of Isabella Horner late of Rahaghy County **Tyrone** Widow deceased who died 13 April 1871 at same place were granted at **Armagh** to James Horner of Rahaghy (Aughnacloy) aforesaid Farmer the Son and one of the next of kin of said deceased.

HORNIDGE John Isaiah.

[79]   Effects under £450.

8 June.   Letters of Administration (with the Will annexed) of the personal estate of John Isaiah Hornidge late of the South Dublin Union Workhouse **Dublin** Master of said Workhouse a Widower deceased who died 22 April 1871 at same place were granted at the **Principal Registry** to James Seymour Longstaff of Stephen's-green Dublin Merchant and William Thomas Orpin of George's-terrace George's-avenue Blackrock County Dublin Accountant the Guardians during minority only of the Daughter and only next of kin of deceased.

HOUSTON Eliza.

[337]   Effects under £200.

22 September.   Letters of Administration of the personal estate of Eliza Houston late of Gortin County **Donegal** Spinster deceased who

Calendar of Wills and Administrations, 1871
(Courtesy of the National Archives of Ireland)

Other Sources

There are many other collections of will abstracts and transcripts in public repositories, such as the NLI, the RCBL, the RIA, PRONI and Trinity College Library. There are no separate indexes to these testamentary collections. Where a significant group of abstracts or transcripts exists, this is noted in the reference guide given below.

PART 2: A REFERENCE GUIDE

What follows is an attempt to provide a series of checklists and guides to the various testamentary sources available. Because of the changes in testamentary jurisdiction in 1858, it is divided into two sections to deal with records before and after that date. Section One examines the pre-1858 period and includes: (1) a general checklist of surviving indexes; (2) a list of surviving Will and Grant Books; (3) a list of major collections of abstracts and transcripts divided into (i) general collections, (ii) those relating to particular surnames and (iii) those relating to particular diocesan jurisdictions; (4) a detailed list of surviving consistorial wills and administrations indexes, both published and held in the NAI. Section Two examines the post-1858 period and covers: (1) the yearly calendars; (2) original wills and transcripts.

SECTION ONE: PRE–1858

1. General Indexes

1. Card Indexes, NAI Search Room, published on CD-ROM by Eneclann, *Irish Records Index Vol. 1: Index of Irish Wills 1484–1858*, Dublin: 1999.
2. Pre-1858 Wills Index, PRONI Reading Room.
3. Indexes to Consistorial Wills and Administrations, diocese by diocese; see below for details.
4. Indexes to Prerogative Wills:
    (a) Sir Arthur Vicars, *Index to the Prerogative Wills of Ireland 1536–1810* (1897);
    (b) Ms. Index, 1811–1858, NAI, PRONI.
5. Index to Prerogative Grants, NAI, PRONI.
6. Index to Wills in the Records of the Land Commission, NLI.

2. Surviving Will and Grant Books

1. Prerogative Will Books: 1664–1684, 1706–1708 (A–W), 1726–1728 (A–W), 1728–1729 (A–W), 1777 (A–L), 1813 (K–Z), 1834 (A–E), NAI, included in Card Index.
2. Prerogative Administrations: Grants 1684–1688, 1748–1751, 1839; Day Books, 1784–1788, NAI.
3. Consistorial Will Books: Connor (1853–1858); Down (1850–1858), NAI.
4. Consistorial Grant Books: Cashel (1840–1845); Derry & Raphoe (1812–1821); Ossory (1848–1858), NAI.

3. Abstracts and Transcripts

(i) General Collections

1. Betham abstracts from Prerogative Wills, to c.1800, NAI (notebooks); GO and PRONI (Sketch Pedigrees). See Vicars, above.
2. Betham abstracts from Prerogative Administrations, to c.1800, NAI (notebooks); GO (alphabetical listing).
3. Indexes to Irish Will Registers, 1828–1879 (Inland Revenue), NAI. See Testamentary Catalogue.
4. Irish Will Registers, 1828–1839 (Inland Revenue), NAI. See Testamentary Catalogue.
5. Indexes to Irish Administration Registers, 1828–1879 (Inland Revenue), NAI. See Testamentary Catalogue.
6. Irish Administration Registers, 1828–1839 (Inland Revenue), NAI. See Testamentary Catalogue.
7. Index to Will Abstracts at the Genealogical Office. *Analecta Hibernica*, 17; GO Ms. 429.
8. P.B. Phair & E. Ellis, *Abstracts of Wills at the Registry of Deeds (1708–1832)*, IMC: 1954–1988.
9. Abstracts of wills of Irish testators registered at the Prerogative Court of Canterbury 1639–1698, NLI Ms. 1397.
10. Abstracts of miscellaneous eighteenth-century wills made by the Protestant clergy and their families, RCBL (for the years 1828–1839, see also NLI Ms. 2599).
11. Leslie Collection, 981 wills, NLI Ms. 1774. See also NLI Pos. 799.
12. Ainsley Will Abstracts, GO 535 & 631.
13. Wilson Collection, NLI Pos. 1990.
14. Welply Collection, 1,500 wills, 100 administrations, RCBL, Indexed in *The Irish Genealogist*, 1985/86.
15. Richey Collection, NLI Mss 8315–6.
16. Upton Collection, RIA. Also NLI Pos. 1997. Principally families in Co. Westmeath, with some from Counties Cavan and Longford.
17. MacSwiney Papers, RIA, mainly Counties Cork and Kerry.
18. Westropp Manuscripts, RIA, mainly Counties Clare and Limerick.

(ii) By Surname

Burke: GO Ms. 707.

Butler: Wallace Clare, *The Testamentary Records of the Butler Family*, 1932, NLI Ir. 9292 b 11.

Dawson: almost all eighteenth-century Dawson wills, NLI Mss 5644/5.

Domville: NLI Mss 9384–6.

Drought: Crossley Abstracts, NAI. Also GO 417/8.

Gordon: GO Ms. 702, abstracts of most Irish Gordon wills.

Griffith: NLI Ms. 8392.

Greene: see NAI Card Index.

Hamilton, Co. Down: PRONI T.702A.

Hill: GO Mss 691–2.
Kelly: GO Ms. 415.
Manley: NLI D.7075–86, the Manley family of Dublin and Offaly.
Mathews: Prerogative wills and administrations, PRONI T.681.
O'Loghlen, Co. Clare: NLI Pos. 2543.
Skerrett: *The Irish Ancestor*, Vol. 5, No. 2 (1975).
Young: NLI Pos. 1276.

(iii) By Diocese

A word of warning is necessary: the identification of a collection of abstracts or transcripts under a particular diocese does not necessarily mean that all of the wills it covers belong to that diocese. In the case of the larger collections especially, it is just not possible to be absolutely precise about the areas covered.

Armagh

Four Wills of old English merchants of Drogheda, 1654–1717, *JCLAS*, Vol. XX, 2 (1982).
Alphabetical list of the prerogative wills of residents of Co. Louth up to 1810, NLI
    Ms. 7314.
Index to the wills of Dundalk residents, *JCLAS*, Vol. X, No. 2, 113–115 (1942).

Cashel and Emly

White, J.D., 'Extracts from original wills, formerly in the consistorial office Cashel, later moved to Waterford Probate Court', *Kilkenny & South of Ire. Arch. Soc. Jnl.*, Ser. 2, Vol. 2, Pt 2 (1859); Vol. IV (1862).

Clogher

Swanzy Collection, NAI T.1746. Copies also held at the Genealogical Office (GO 420, indexed in 429), and at the RCBL. Abstracts from Clogher and Kilmore Will Books, Marriage Licence Bonds, Administrations, militia lists. Principal names include: Beatty, Nixon, Armstrong, Young, Veitch, Jackson, Mee, Noble and Fiddes.

Clonfert

GO 707: numerous abstracts, mainly relating to wills mentioning Burke families.

Cloyne

Welply Abstracts (4 vols), RCBL, indexed IG, 1985/1986.
Index to Will Abstracts at the Genealogical Office, *AH*, 17; GO Ms. 429.

Connor

Connor Will Book, 1818–1820, 1853–1858, NAI.
Stewart-Kennedy notebooks: will abstracts, many from Down & Connor. Principal families include Stewart, Clarke, Cunningham, Kennedy and Wade. Trinity College Library and PRONI. See also NLI Pos. 4066.

PUBLIC RECORD OFFICE OF IRELAND.

Class.—TESTAMENTARY. *Diocese - Cork & Ross* Sub-Class.—WILLS.

District Registry — Cork.

Testator's Name.		Year of Probate.	Day.	Tray.	Number.
O'Coghlane	Donell Reige *Crookhaven*	1620	13	31	
O'Comon	Connor *Tuamore*	1675			
O'Conohan	Teige *Cork*	1664			
O'Connor	Joshua *Cork*	1796			
"	Patrick	1851			
O'Crouly	Teige *Behegallane*	1683			
O'Crowly	Rev. Jas. Patrick *Ballinrishig*	1829			
"	Timothy P.P. *Killmocomoy*	1789			
O'Daniel	Theophilus *Cork*	1736			
O'Dea als Walsh	Beale	1649			
O'Donnell	James *Ballyaurrig*	1781			
"	Mary *Cork*	1845			
O'Donoghue	Elizabeth *Cork*	1809			

Diocesan Wills Index, Cork and Ross
(Courtesy of the National Archives of Ireland)

Cork and Ross
Welply Abstracts (4 vols), RCBL, indexed in IG, 1985/1986.
Caulfield transcripts: mainly sixteenth century, RCBL. See also *JCHAS* (1903/1904).
Notes from wills of Cork Diocese, 1660–1700, NA M. 2760.

Derry
Young, Amy, *300 Years in Inishowen* (NLI Ir. 9292 y 1), contains forty-six Donegal wills.

Down
Down Will Book, 1850–1858, NAI and PRONI.
Stewart-Kennedy notebooks: see Connor, above.

Dublin and Glendalough
Lane-Poole papers: NLI Ms. 5359 (abstracts).
Abstracts of wills proved in Dublin Diocesan Court 1560–1710, A–E only, GO Ms. 290.

Elphin
Wills & Deeds from Co. Sligo, 1605–1632, NLI Ms. 2164.

Kildare
Betham Collection, NAI: abstracts of almost all Kildare wills up to 1827. Also NLI
    Pos. 1784–5.

Killaloe and Kilfenora
O'Loghlen wills from Co. Clare, NLI Pos. 2543.
Wills and Administrations from Counties Clare and Limerick: Westropp manu-
    script volume, 3A 39, RIA.

Kilmore
Swanzy Collection, NAI. See Clogher, above.

Leighlin
Carrigan Collection: NL. Pos. 903 (952 wills, mainly Ossory & Leighlin), indexed
    in *The Irish Genealogist* (1970).
Abstracts from Ossory & Leighlin Admons., *The Irish Genealogist* (1972).

Limerick
Hayes, R., 'Some Old Limerick Wills', *JNMAS*, Vol. I, 163–168; Vol. II, 71–75.
Wills and Administrations from Counties Clare and Limerick: Westropp manu-
    script volume, 3A 39, RIA.

Meath
Rice, G., 'Extracts from Meath priests' wills 1658–1782', *Riocht na Midhe*, Vol. IV,
    No. 1, 68–71 (1967).

Ossory

Carrigan Collection: NL. Pos. 903 (952 wills, mainly Ossory & Leighlin), indexed in *The Irish Genealogist* (1970).

Abstracts from Ossory & Leighlin Admons., *The Irish Genealogist* (1972).

Sadlier, T.U., Abstracts from Ossory Admons., 1738–1884, NAI.

Calendar of Administrations, Ossory. NAI T.7425.

GO 683–6, Walsh-Kelly notebooks: will abstracts, mainly from Ossory.

Raphoe

Young, Amy, *300 Years in Inishowen* (NLI Ir. 9292 y 1), contains forty-six Donegal wills.

Tuam

GO 707: numerous abstracts, mainly relating to wills mentioning Burke families, 1784–1820.

Waterford and Lismore

Wills relating to Waterford: *Decies* 16, 17, 19, 20, 22, 23; Jennings Collection, NAI & *Decies* (above); 166 Waterford Wills and Administrations, NLI D. 9248–9413.

4. Consistorial Wills and Administration Bonds Indexes, Published and in the NAI

Diocese	*Wills*	*Admon. Bonds*
Ardagh	1695–1858 (also *IA*, 1970)	1697–1850
Ardfert and Aghadoe	1690–1858 (*Ph.*: 1690–1800; *o'k*, Vol. 5, 1690–1858)	1782–1858 (*o'k*, Vol. 5, 1782–1858)
Armagh	1666–1837 (A–L) Drogheda District 1691–1846	1677–1858 (M–Y)
Cashel and Emly	1618–1858 (*Ph*: 1618–1800)	1644–1858
Clogher	1661–1858	1660–1858
Clonfert	1663–1857 (*IA*, 1970)	1771–1857 (*IA*, 1970)
Cloyne	1621–1858 (*Ph.*: 1621–1800 *o'k.*, Vol. 8, 1547–1858)	1630–1857 (*o'k.*, Vol. 6)
Connor	1680–1846 (A–L) 1636–1857 (M–Y)	1636–1858
Cork and Ross	1548–1858 (*Ph.* & *o'k.*, Vol. 8, 1548–1800; *JCHAS*, 1895–8, 1548–1833)	1612–1858 (*o'k.*, Vol. 5)
Derry	1612–1858 (*Ph.*)	1698–1857
Down	1646–1858	1635–1858

Diocese	Wills	Admon. Bonds
Dromore	1678–1858 with Newry & Mourne, 1727–1858 (*ph.*)	1742–1858 with Newry & Mourne 1811–45 (*IA*, 1969: Newry & Mourne)
Dublin and Glendalough	1536–1858 (*RDKPRI*, Nos 26 & 30)	1636–1858 (*RDKPRI*, Nos 26 & 30)
Elphin	1650–1858 (fragments)	1726–1857
Ferns	1601–1858 (fragments) 1603–1838 (F–V) 1615–1842 (unproved, W only) (*ph.*: 1601–1800)	1765–1833
Kildare	1661–1858 (*ph.*: 1661–1800; *JKAS*, 1905: 1661–1858)	1770–1848 (*JKAS*, 1907: 1770–1858)
Killala and Achonry	1756–1831 (fragments)	1779–1858 (*IA*, 1975)
Killaloe and Kilfenora	1653–1858 (fragments) (*ph.*: 1653–1800)	1779–1858 (*IA*, 1975)
Kilmore	1682–1858 (damaged)	1728–1858
Leighlin	1642–1858 (*ph.*: 1642–1800)	1694–1845 (*IA*, 1972)
Limerick	1615–1858 (*ph.*: 1615–1800)	1789–1858
Meath	1572–1858 (fragments partial transcript 1635–1838)	1663–1857
Ossory	1536–1858 (fragments) (*ph.*: 1536–1800)	1660–1857
Raphoe	1684–1858 (damaged) (*ph.*)	1684–1858
Tuam	1648–1858 (damaged)	1692–1857
Waterford and Lismore	1648–1858 (damaged) (*ph.*: 1648–1800)	1661–1857

SECTION TWO: POST–1857

1. Yearly Calendars of Wills & Administrations, 1858–present

Provide: name, address and occupation of the deceased; place and exact date of death; names and addresses of grantees of probate or administration, and relationship; exact date of probate; value of the estate. Available on open access in the Search Room of NAI and PRONI; the consolidated index, 1858–1877, is only available in NAI.

2. Original Wills or Transcripts

(a) Card Index, NAI *Search Room.*

(b) Surviving Will and Grant Books in NAI, *as follows:*
  (i)   Principal Registry Wills: 1874, G–M
        Principal Registry Wills: 1878, A–Z
        Principal Registry Wills: 1891, G–M
        Principal Registry Wills: 1896, A–F
        Principal Registry Wills, Dublin District: 1869, G–M
        Principal Registry Wills, Dublin District: 1891, M–P
        Principal Registry Wills, Dublin District: 1901, A–F

  (ii) Principal Registry Grants: 1878, 1883, 1891, 1893

  (iii) District Registry Will Books:
        Ballina: 1865–present
        Cavan: 1858–1909
        Cork: 1858–1932
        Kilkenny: 1858–1911
        Limerick: 1858–1899
        Mullingar: 1858–1901
        Tuam: 1858–1929,
        Waterford: 1858–1902

(c) District Registry Will Books in PRONI:
        Armagh: 1858–1900 (MIC 15C)
        Belfast: 1858–1900 (MIC 15C)
        Londonderry: 1858–1900 (MIC 15C).

Chapter 6

THE GENEALOGICAL OFFICE

The Genealogical Office is the successor to the Office of Ulster King of Arms, also known as the Office of Arms, which was created in 1552 when Edward VI designated Bartholomew Butler the chief heraldic authority in Ireland, with the title of 'Ulster'. The reasons for the choice of 'Ulster' rather 'Ireland' are somewhat unclear; it is likely that the older title of 'Ireland King of Arms' was already in use amongst the heralds at the College of Arms in London. Whatever the reason, Ulster King of Arms acquired full jurisdiction over arms in Ireland and retained it for almost 400 years until 1943, when the Office became the Genealogical Office and Ulster became Chief Herald of Ireland, with substantially the same powers as his predecessor. The Office is now a department of NLI.

At the outset the authority of Ulster was limited to those areas of the country under English authority; as a feudal practice, heraldry was in any case quite alien to Gaelic culture. Up to the end of the seventeenth century the functions of the Office remained purely heraldic: ascertaining and recording which arms were in use and by what right families used them. From the late seventeenth century, Ulster began to acquire other duties as an officer of the Crown intimately linked to the government. These duties were largely ceremonial, such as deciding and arranging precedence on State occasions, introducing new peers to the Irish House of Lords and recording peerage successions. In essence, these two areas— the heraldic and the ceremonial—remained the principal functions of the Office over the succeeding three centuries, with Ulster becoming registrar of the chivalric Order of St Patrick, instituted in 1783, and continuing to have responsibility for the ceremonial aspects of State occasions at the Court of the Viceroy.

The functioning of the Office depended to an inordinate degree on the personal qualities of Ulster, and an unfortunate number of the title-holders, especially in the eighteenth century, appear to have regarded it as a sinecure, paying little attention to the keeping of records and treating the manuscript collection as their personal property. It was only with the arrival of Sir William Betham in the early nineteenth century that the business of the Office was placed on a sound footing and serious attention was given to the collection and care of manuscripts. As a consequence, although a number of the official records date from much earlier, the vast majority of the Office's holdings do not pre-date the nineteenth century.

In the course of carrying out its heraldic functions, the Office inevitably acquired a large amount of material of genealogical interest, as the right to bear arms is strictly hereditary. Nonetheless, the new title given to the Office in 1943, the Genealogical Office, was somewhat inaccurate because its principal function continues to be heraldic: the granting and confirmation of official achievements to individuals and corporate bodies. Up to the 1980s the Office also carried out commissioned research into family history, but this service has been discontinued.

An excellent account of the history of the Office is given in Susan Hood's *Royal roots—republican inheritance: the survival of the office of Arms,* Dublin: Woodfield Press, 2002.

GENEALOGICAL OFFICE RECORDS

Manuscripts

The manuscripts of the Genealogical Office are numbered in a single series from 1 to 822. They are, however, of a very mixed nature—reflecting the Office's changing functions over the centuries—and are best dealt with in categories based on those functions. The following account divides them into: (1) Official Records, (2) Administrative Records and Reference Works and (3) Research Material.

(1) Official Records

A number of sets of manuscripts are direct products of the official functions of the Office and may therefore be termed official records. On the heraldic side, the principal records are the Visitations (GO 47–9), the Funeral Entries (GO 64–79), the official grants and confirmations of arms (GO 103–111g) and the Registered Pedigrees (GO 156–182). In addition to these, four other manuscript groups reflect duties acquired by Ulster's Office over the centuries: the Lords Entries (GO 183–188), Royal Warrants for Changes of Name (GO 26 & 149–154A), Baronets' Records (GO 112–4) and Gaelic Chieftains (GO 610 & 627).

The Visitations were an attempt to carry out heraldic visitations in Ireland along the lines of those employed by the College of Arms in England for almost a century to control the bearing of arms. The results were meagre, confined to areas close to Dublin and almost certainly incomplete, even for those areas. The following places were covered: Dublin and parts of Co. Louth, 1568–1570; Drogheda and Ardee, 1570; Swords, 1572; Cork, 1574; Limerick, 1574; Dublin City, 1607; Dublin County, 1610; and Wexford, 1610. These are indexed in GO 117.

The Funeral Entries, covering the period 1588–1691, make up some of the deficiencies of the Visitations. Their aim was to record the name, wife and issue of deceased nobility and gentry, along with their arms. In addition, many of the Entries include very beautiful illustrations of the arms and armorial devices used at the funeral, as well as notes on the ordering of the funeral processions and ceremonies. An index to the Entries is found in GO 386.

One of the later effects of the lack of Visitations was that it was difficult for Ulster to verify from his own records that a particular family had a right to its arms. This gave rise to the practice, peculiar to Ireland, of issuing 'confirmations' of arms, which were taken as official registrations and were dependent on an applicant being able to show that the arms in question had been in use in his family for three generations, or 100 years. The records of these confirmations, and of actual grants of arms, are found in GO 103–111g, dating from 1698 and still current. Earlier grants and confirmations are scattered throughout the manuscript collection; a complete index to all arms officially recorded in the Office is located in GO 422–3. Hayes' *Manuscript Sources for the Study of Irish Civilisation* reproduces this and includes a summary of any genealogical information.

As the right to bear arms is hereditary, the authentication of arms required the collection of a large amount of genealogical material. This was undoubtedly the origin of the Registered Pedigrees, GO 156–182, but the series very quickly acquired a life of its own and the majority of entries are now purely genealogical. It is particularly important for the collection of eighteenth-century pedigrees of Irish *emigrés* to France. These were produced in response to the need to prove membership of the nobility, admission to which carried very substantial privileges. The various proofs required included the signature of Ulster. The series continues up to the present and is indexed in GO 469, as well as Hayes' *Manuscript Sources*.

Partly stemming from the issues concerning the status of lords who had supported James II, one of the duties of Ulster from 1698 was to maintain an official list of Irish peers, known as 'Ulster's Roll'. In theory, all of those entitled, whether by creation of a new peerage or by succession, to sit in the Irish House of Lords were obliged to inform Ulster before they could be officially introduced to the House. In practice, the vast bulk of information collected relates to successions, with the heirs supplying the date of death and place of burial, arms, marriages and issue. The series covers the period from 1698 to 1939, and is indexed in GO 470.

In order to regulate the assumption of arms and titles it was made compulsory, after 1784, to obtain a warrant from the king for a change of name and arms. From 1795 the Irish House of Lords made it obligatory to register such a warrant in Ulster's Office. The result is the manuscript series known officially as 'Royal Warrants for changes of name and licences for changes of name'. Most of the nineteenth-century changes came about as a result of wills, with an inheritance made conditional on a change of name. Hayes' *Manuscript Sources* indexes this series.

A similar need to regulate the improper assumption of titles produced the Baronets' Records (GO 112–4). A royal warrant of 1789 for 'correcting and preventing abuses in the order of baronets' made compulsory the registration of arms and pedigrees with Ulster. The volumes are indexed in GO 470.

The records of Gaelic Chieftains in GO 610 and 627 are the consequence of a revival instituted in the 1940s by Dr Edward MacLysaght, the first Chief Herald of Ireland. He attempted to trace the senior lineal descendants in the male line of the last recorded Gaelic 'Chief of the Name', who was then officially recognised as the contemporary holder of the title. The practice has met with mixed success. Problems arise from the collapse of Gaelic culture in the seventeenth century and the fact that originally chieftainships were not passed on by primogeniture but by election within the extended kin-group. Nonetheless, more than twenty Chiefs were recognised and the records of the research that established their right to the title are extremely interesting. However, following a controversy over the recognition of MacCarthy Mór in the 1990s, the practice was discontinued.

(2) Administrative Records and Reference Works

Many of the documents now part of the general manuscript series derive from the routine paperwork necessary to run an office. These include cash books, receipts, Ulster's Diaries, letter books, day books and records of fees due for the various functions carried out by Ulster. Of these, the most interesting from a genealogical point of view are the letter books (GO 361–378), which contain copies of all letters sent out from the Office between 1789 and 1853 and also contain the Betham letters (GO 580–604), a collection of the letters received by Sir William Betham between c.1810 and 1830 and purchased by the Genealogical Office in 1943. The former are indexed volume by volume. The latter are of more potential value. The only index, however, appears in the original catalogue of the sale of the letters, dated 1936, a copy of which is held at the GO, though not numbered among the manuscripts. The catalogue lists the letters alphabetically by addressor and a supplementary surnames index provides a guide to the families dealt with. Another eight volumes of the series, unindexed, are held in NAI (M.744–751).

As well as documents produced by the day-to-day running of the office, a large number of manuscripts exist relating to the ceremonial functions performed by Ulster. These include official orders relating to changes of insignia, papers dealing with precedence and protocol, records of official functions at the Viceregal Court and the records of the Order of St Patrick. There is little of genealogical interest in these.

In the course of their heraldic and genealogical work, Ulster and his officers accumulated a large series of manuscripts for use as reference works. These include manuscript armories, ordinaries of arms, treatises on heraldry and precedence, a series of English Visitations and blazons of arms of English and Scottish peers. The bulk of the material is heraldic, but there is a good deal of incidental genealogical information, particularly in the seventeenth-century ordinaries of arms.

(3) Research Material

The most useful manuscripts in the Genealogical Office collection are those acquired and created to provide sources for genealogical research. This policy, instigated in the early nineteenth century by Sir William Betham and adopted by all of his successors, has produced a wide range of material, much of it based on records that were destroyed in the PRO fire in 1922. It may be divided into three broad categories: (i) Betham's own compilations; (ii) the collections of later genealogists; (iii) other records. The sheer diversity of these documents makes a complete account impractical, instead a broad outline is provided below.

The greatest single work produced by Betham is a collection of abstracts of family information from prerogative wills. These are divided into a number of series: GO 223–226 ('Old Series', Vols I–IV) covers wills before 1700; GO 227–254 ('New Series', Vols 1–31) covers wills from 1700 to c.1800. The series are roughly alphabetical, with each volume containing its own index. Sir Arthur Vicars' *Index to the Prerogative Wills of Ireland 1536–1810* provides a guide to the wills covered. Many of the Sketch Pedigrees include later amendments and additions from other sources. The GO 255–256 index lists all the marriage alliances recorded in the wills. Another series, GO 203–214 ('Will Pedigrees', Vols I–XII) represents an unfinished attempt to rearrange all of these Sketch Pedigrees into strictly alphabetical order. Betham also produced a large number of Sketch Pedigrees based on other sources and collected as 'Ancient Anglo-Irish Families', Vols I–VI (GO 215–219), 'Milesian Families', Vols I–III (GO 220–222), and the '1st series', Vols I–XVI (GO 261–276) and the '2nd series', Vols I–VII (GO 292–298). All of these are indexed in GO 470.

As well as the Sketch Pedigrees and the letters (covered above under 'Administrative Records'), there are two other sources in the collection which owe their origin to Betham. The first of these, genealogical and historical excerpts from the plea rolls and patent rolls from Henry III to Edward VI (GO 189–193), constitutes the single most important source of information on Anglo-Norman genealogy in Ireland. Betham's transcript of Roger O'Ferrall's *Linea Antiqua*, a collation of earlier genealogies compiled in 1709, is the GO's most extensive work on Gaelic, as opposed to Anglo-Irish, genealogy. This copy (in three volumes, GO 145–147, with an index to the complete work in GO 147) also contains Betham's interpolations and additions, unfortunately unsourced. It records the arms of many of the Gaelic families covered, without giving any authority for them, and is the source of most of the arms illustrated in Dr Edward MacLysaght's *Irish Families*.

Pedigrees and research notes produced by later amateur and professional genealogists make up a large part of the Office's manuscript collection. Among those who have contributed to these are Sir Edmund Bewley, Denis O'Callaghan Fisher, Tenison Groves, Alfred Moloney, T.U. Sadleir and Rev. H.B. Swanzy. For the most part, their records concern either particular groups of families or particular geographical areas. Some have their own indexes, some are covered by GO 470 and GO 117, while others have will abstracts indexed only in GO 429. As well as these, some of the results of Ulster's Office own research in the late nineteenth and early twentieth century are classed as manuscripts, GO 800–822. These constitute no more than a fraction of the total research information produced by the Office, and are indexed in Hayes' *Manuscript Sources*.

A final class of records comprises extremely diverse documents, having in common only their potential genealogical usefulness. It includes such items as freeholders' lists from different counties, extracts from parish registers, transcripts of the Dublin City roll of freemen, of returns from the 1766 census, of City directories from various periods, militia lists and much more. The most useful of these materials are referenced in the county source-lists in Chapter 13.

ARCHIVES
As well as the manuscripts series, now closed, the GO also has extremely extensive archive records of the commissioned research it carried out up to the 1980s. For the closing decades of the nineteenth century and the early decades of the twentieth century, these records are still largely concerned with the Anglo-Irish class. Manuscripts 800–822 cover perhaps 5 per cent of this material, while the remainder is sorted in roughly alphabetical order and stored in cardboard boxes along one wall of the GO strong room.

After the creation of The Genealogical Office in 1943, the focus of the commissioned research shifted and most work was now carried out on behalf of the descendants of emigrants to Australia and North America. There are over 20,000 research files giving details of the results of these commissioned searches.

RESEARCH IN GENEALOGICAL OFFICE MANUSCRIPTS
The biggest single obstacle to research in GO manuscripts is the lack of a single, comprehensive index, though this has been mitigated to some extent by the recent work of Ms V.W. McAnlis (see below). Many attempts have been made over the centuries of the Office's existence to produce a complete index. The result has been a proliferation of partial indexes, each covering some of the collection, none covering all of it; these partial indexes are dealt with below. In addition, the policy applied to the creation of manuscripts appears to have become somewhat inconsistent after the 1940s. Before then, only the earliest and most heterogeneous manuscripts were numbered in a single series, with each of the other groups acquiring its own volume numbers, for example, Lords' Entries Vol. II, or Registered Pedigrees Vol. 12. The laudable attempt to produce a consistent numbering system, starting at GO 1 and moving through the entire collection, seems to have given rise to the piecemeal addition of material that is more properly the preserve of the NLI. The subsequent transfers to the NLI and the retrospective renumbering of remaining material has adversely affected the system in the upper numbers: no manuscripts exist for many of the numbers between 600 and 800. The numerical list of manuscripts at the end of this article reflects the current situation, with titles in brackets indicating those manuscripts no longer held in the Office.

In recent years Virginia Wade McAnlis has taken on the task of creating a consolidated index for GO manuscripts, working from the microfilm copies available through the Family History Centres of the Church of Jesus Christ of the Latter-Day Saints. This work, in four volumes, is available at the NLI, Ir. 9291 c 11/1. It brings together the references from the indexes numbered as GO Mss 117, 148, 255–260, 386, 422–423 and 470, details of which are found below. In addition to the page references included in these indexes, Ms McAnlis also includes microfilm references for the LDS collection.

INDEXES

GO 59: This is a detailed calendar of manuscripts 1–58, particularly useful since many of these consist of very early heterogeneous material bound together for preservation.

GO 115: Indexes the following: Arms A–C; Grants & Confirmations, A & B; Visitations; British Families; Funeral Entries; Registered Pedigrees Vols 1–10. Only the Visitations (GO 47–49) and British Families (GO 44–46) are not indexed more fully elsewhere.

GO 116: An unfinished index.

GO 117: Duplicates much of the material indexed in GO 422, GO 470 and Hayes' *Manuscript Sources*. Only the following are not covered elsewhere: Antrim Families (GO 213); Fisher Mss (GO 280–285); Irish Arms at the College of Heralds (GO 37); Irish Coats of Arms (Fota) (GO 526); Heraldic Sketches (GO 125); Betham Letter Books (GO 362–378); Ecclesiatical Visitations (GO 198–199); Reynell Mss (GO 445).

GO 148: Index to *Linea Antiqua*. The version at the end of GO 147, *Linea Antiqua* Vol. III, is more complete.

GO 255–6: Index to Alliances in Prerogative Wills (Betham).

GO 386: Index to the Funeral Entries.

GO 422–3: Index to arms registered at the Office.

GO 429: Eustace Index to Will Abstracts at the Genealogical Office. The published version in *Analecta Hibernica*, Vol. 17, is less extensive than the manuscript copy.

GO 469: Index to Registered Pedigrees. This appears to be less complete than the version included in Hayes' *Manuscript Sources*. Attached to it is a typescript copy of the index to the Genealogical Office collection of pedigree rolls.

GO 470: Index to Unregistered Pedigrees. This is the single most useful index in the Office, covering the Lords' Entries, the Betham Pedigrees and many of the genealogists' Pedigree collections. It is divided into three separate parts, and gives the descriptive titles in use before the adoption of the single GO numbering system. The flyleaf lists the manuscripts covered.

GO 476: Numerical listing of GO manuscripts. Dating from the 1950s, and now inaccurate for the higher numbers.

See also Hayes' *Manuscript Sources for the Study of Irish Civilisation*, which indexes the following: Registered Pedigrees, GO 800–822, Fisher Mss (GO 280–285).

Access

Access to the Genealogical Office Collection is via the Manuscript Reading Room of the NLI, at 2 Kildare Street in Dublin—the same building which houses the GO. For the most valuable manuscripts—in general those in the lower numbers—only microfilm copies are available to the public and these can be consulted in the NLI Microfilm Reading Room. The microfilms are as follows:

NLI Pos. 8286:	GO Mss 47, 48, 49, 64, 65
NLI Pos. 8287:	GO Mss 66, 67, 68, 69
NLI Pos. 8288:	GO Mss 70, 71, 72, 73
NLI Pos. 8289:	GO Mss 74, 75, 76, 77, 78
NLI Pos. 8290:	GO Mss 79, 103, 104, 105, 106
NLI Pos. 8290A:	GO Mss 93, 94, 95
NLI Pos. 8291:	GO Mss 107, 108, 109
NLI Pos. 8292:	GO Mss 110, 111, 111A to p.95
NLI Pos. 8293:	GO Mss 111A from p.96, 111B, 111C
NLI Pos. 8294:	GO Mss 111D, 111E, 111F
NLI Pos. 8295:	GO Ms 112
NLI Pos. 8295A:	GO Ms 113
NLI Pos. 8295B:	GO Ms 141
NLI Pos. 8296:	GO Mss 145, 146, 147 to p.42
NLI Pos. 8297:	GO Mss 147 from p.43, 148, 149, 150 to p. 319
NLI Pos. 8298:	GO Mss 150 from p.319, 151, 152
NLI Pos. 8299:	GO Mss 153, 154
NLI Pos. 8300:	GO Mss 154A, 155, 156, 157, 158, 159 to p.109
NLI Pos. 8301:	GO Mss 159 from p.110, 160, 161, 162, 163, 164
NLI Pos. 8302:	GO Mss 165, 166, 167, 168
NLI Pos. 8303:	GO Mss 169, 170
NLI Pos. 8304:	GO Mss 171, 172, 173
NLI Pos. 8305:	GO Mss 174, 175
NLI Pos. 8306:	GO Mss 176
NLI Pos. 8307:	GO Mss 177, 178
NLI Pos. 8308:	GO Mss 179, 180
NLI Pos. 8309:	GO Mss 181, 182
NLI Pos. 8310:	GO Mss 182A, 183, 184
NLI Pos. 8311:	GO Mss 185, 186, 187
NLI Pos. 8312:	GO Mss 188

Chapter 7 ∽

EMIGRATION AND THE
IRISH ABROAD

EMIGRATION RECORDS

For the descendants of emigrants from Ireland, it seems natural to first seek out emigration records held in Ireland. Unfortunately, there are almost no such records. For North America, in particular, where ships' passenger lists were kept, most records appear to have been deposited at the port of arrival rather than the port of departure. In general, the authorities were more concerned with recording those entering the country rather than those leaving. As a result, the most comprehensive records for the USA are the Customs Passenger Lists, dating from 1820, and the Immigration Passenger Lists, dating from 1883, both held in the US National Archives in Washington. Unfortunately, the earlier lists are not very informative, giving only the country of origin of the emigrant. The US National Archives has collected the records for the most important immigrant ports: Boston, New York, Baltimore, and Philadelphia, as well as Mobile, New Bedford and New Orleans. Microfilm copies of the lists for New York and Boston are available at the NLI, but no index is available, making them very difficult to use if a relatively precise date of arrival is not known. A good guide is at *www.genealogybranches.com/irishpassengerlists*.

As well as these, there are many less comprehensive lists, published and unpublished, which record intending and actual emigrants and ships' passengers to North America. A number of attempts have been made to systematise access to these. The most important are: the *Passenger and Immigration Lists Index* (14 vols, including supplements), edited by P. William Filby and Mary K. Meyer, Detroit: Gale, 1981–2001 (NL RR 387 p 7), a consolidated index to a wide variety of lists relating to North American immigration from all over the world; and *The Famine Immigrants* (7 vols; indexed), Baltimore: The Genealogical Publishing Company, 1988 (NLI Ir. 942 g 12), which records more than half-a-million Irish arrivals in New York between 1846 and 1851. Even these, however, cover only a fraction of the material of potential value. A brief bibliography is given in the section 'North America, Passenger lists' in the latter half of this chapter.

For emigrants to Australia and New Zealand, the situation is somewhat better. Given the distance involved very few emigrants could afford the journey and most, whether assisted free settlers or transported convicts, are therefore quite well documented. Transportation from Ireland, or for crimes committed in Ireland, lasted from 1791 to 1853, ending some fifteen years earlier than transportation from England. The only mass transportation later than 1853 was of sixty-three Fenians sent to Western Australia in 1868 aboard the last convict ship from England to Australia. The records of the Chief Secretary's Office, which had responsibility for the Penal system, are the major Irish source of information on transportees. Not all of the relevant records have survived, particularly for the period before 1836, but what does exist can provide a wealth of information. The records were formerly housed in the State Paper Office in Dublin Castle, which is now part of NAI. The principal classes of relevant records are as follows:

1. **Prisoners' Petitions and Cases, 1788–1836:** these consist of petitions to the Lord Lieutenant for commutation or remission of sentence, and record the crime, trial, sentence, place of origin and family circumstances.
2. **State Prisoners' Petitions:** these specifically concern those arrested for participation in the 1798 rebellion, and record the same information as the main series of petitions.
3. **Convict Reference Files, from 1836:** these continue the earlier petitions series and can include a wide range of additional material.
4. **Transportation Registers, from 1836:** these record all the names of those sentenced to death or transportation, giving the name, age, date and county of trial, crime and sentence. Other details, including the name of the transport ship or the place of detention, are sometimes given as well.
5. **Male Convict Register, 1842–1847:** in addition to the information supplied by the Transportation Registers, this volume also gives physical descriptions of the convicts.
6. **Register of Convicts on Convict Ships, 1851–1853:** this gives the names, dates and counties of trial of those transported to Van Diemen's Land and Western Australia for the period covered.
7. **Free Settlers' Papers, 1828–1852:** after serving a minimum of four years, male convicts had the right to request a free passage for their wife and family to join them. The Papers contain lists of those making such a request, along with transportation details and the names and addresses of the wives. A number of petitions from husbands and wives, and prisoners' letters, are also included.

To celebrate the Australian Bicentenary in 1988, all of these records were microfilmed and a database of the surnames contained therein was created. Copies of the microfilms and the database were presented to the Australian government and can now be found in many State archives. The NAI retains copies and the database, in particular, can save a great deal of time and effort for the researcher. It supplies enough details from the originals to identify the relevant record, and is available online at *www.nationalarchives.ie*. Early convict arrivals records, making up some of the gaps in the NAI material, are also online at *www.pcug.org.au/~ ppmay/convicts.htm* (Irish Convicts to Australia 1791–1815).

For obvious reasons, the records relating to free settlers are more scattered and less easily researched. The single most useful source for early settlers, and also invaluable for convict settlers, is the 1828 census of New South Wales, published by the Library of Australian History in 1980. Although the precise place of origin is not recorded, the details given include age, occupation, marital status and household. For later settlers the University of Woolongong has produced, on microfiche, a complete index and transcript of all information concerning immigrants of Irish origin recorded on ships' passenger lists between 1848 and 1867. The later lists, in particular, are extremely useful, often recording the exact place of origin as well as parents' names. The Public Record Office of Victoria has good online databases of settlers at *www.prov.vic.gov.au.*

Other than these, the principal records likely to be of relevance are held in the Colonial Office Papers of the United Kingdom Public Record Office at Kew, class reference CO 201. This class contains a wide variety of records, including petitions for assisted passages, emigrants' lists, records of emigrants on board ship, petitions from settlers for financial assistance and much more besides. A number of these have been published in David T. Hawkings' *Bound for Australia,* Sussex: Phillimore & Co., 1987. The Society of Australian Genealogists provides excellent guidance on its website, *www.sag.org.au.*

The remainder of this chapter is an attempt to present a systematic guide to published material covering Irish emigrants abroad. The passenger lists, which were given separately in earlier editions, are now included under the general area of arrival. Lists relating to emigrants from specific localities are shown in the county source-lists in Chapter 13.

THE IRISH ABROAD

AFRICA

South Africa
Akenson, D.H., *Occasional papers on the Irish in South Africa,* Grahamstown: Institute
of Social and Economic Research, Rhodes University, 1991, NLI Ir. 942 a 15, 101 p.
Blake, J.Y.F., *A West Pointer with the Boers,* Boston, Irish in the Boer War.
Davitt, Michael, *The Boer Fight for Freedom,* USA, Irish in the Boer War.
Dickason, G.D., *Irish settlers to the Cape: history of the Clanwilliam 1820 settlers
from Cork Harbour,* Cape Town: A. A. Balkema, 1973, NLI Ir. 968 d 7, 113 p.
Irish Republican Association of South Africa, *The Irish in South Africa, 1920–1921,*
Cape Town: Die Nasionale Pers Beperk, 1921, NLI Ir. 968 i 2, 183 p.
Liggett, Neville D., *The Longbottom family: Dublin to South Africa, c. 1781 to 1994,*
Beacon Bay, South Africa: N.D. Liggett, 1995., LOC, 39 p.
McCracken, D.P, 'The Irish Transvaal Brigades', IS (Winter 1974).
McCracken, D.P. (ed.), 'The Irish in Southern Africa, 1795–1910', *Southern African-
Irish Studies,* Vol. 2, 1991.

McCracken, D.P. (ed.), 'Irish Settlement and Identity in South Africa before 1910', *Southern African-Irish Studies,* Vol. 1 (1991).

McCracken, D.P., 'Odd man out: the South African experience' in Bielenberg, Andy (ed.), *The Irish Diaspora,* England: Harlow; New York: Longman, 2000, NLI, 368 p.

McCracken, D.P., *The Irish Pro-Boers, 1877–1902,* Johannesburg: Perskor, 1989.

McCracken, J.L., *New Light at the Cape of Good Hope: William Porter, the Father of Cape Liberalism,* Belfast: UHF, 1993, NLI Ir. 92 p. 201, 160 p.

Naidoo, Indren, *The Irish diaspora and its impact on the Eastern and Western Cape in the colonial era [microform],* 1994, NLSA, MF.1163, 6 microfiches. Originally presented as: M.A. thesis, University of Durban-Westville, 1994.

Vincent, John, 'A new Era for the Irish in South Africa', *IR,* No. 4 (1994), 13.

AUSTRALASIA

Australia

The Ulster Link, Magazine of the Northern Irish In Australia & New Zealand, NLI Ir. 994 u 1.

The Australian Journal of Irish studies, Perth, W.A.: Centre for Irish Studies, Murdoch University, 2001–, NLI.

The Irish link: the Irish family history magazine, South Melbourne, Victoria: 1984–, NLI Ir. 9292 i 2.

Akenson, D.H., 'Reading the texts of rural immigrants: Letters from the Irish in Australia, New Zealand and America', *Canadian papers in Rural History,* VII 1990, Gananoque, Ontario: Langdale Press, c.1978–c.1996, NLC.

Adam-Smith, Patsy, *Heart of exile: Ireland, 1848, and the seven patriots banished, their adventures, loneliness, and loves in three continents as they search for refuge,* Melbourne: Nelson, 1986, NLI Ir. 94108 a 5, 369 p.

Amos, Keith, *The Fenians in Australia: 1865–1880,* Kensington, N.S.W.: New South Wales University Press, 1988, NLI Ir. 994 a 18, 330 p.

Bull, Philip (co-eds., Francis Devlin-Glass and Helen Doyle), *Ireland and Australia, 1798–1998: studies in culture, identity and migration,* Sydney: Crossing Press, 2000, NLA, 367 p.

Campbell, Malcolm, 'A comparative study of Irish rural settlement in nineteenth-century Minnesota and New South Wales', in Bielenberg, *The Irish Diaspora.* See McCracken, in 'Africa'.

Cleary, P.J.S., *Australia's Debt to Ireland's Nation-builders,* Sydney: Angus & Robertson Limited, 1933, NLI Ir. 994 c 6, 280 p.

Clinton, Brian Hankard, *Clinton our name, from Erin we came,* Wamberal, NSW, Australia. B.H. Clinton, 1995, LOC, 201 p. 'Patrick and Charles Clinton who came from Ireland to Australia in 1877'.

Coffey, Hubert W., *Irish Families in Australia and New Zealand 1788–1979,* Melbourne: H.W. Coffey, 1979–1994, NLI Ir. 942 c 14, 4-vol. biographical dictionary. Co-author Marjorie Jean Morgan.

Costello, Con, *Botany Bay*, Cork: Mercier Press, c.1987, NLI Ir. 942 c 27, 172 p.

Curry, C.H., *The Irish at Eureka*, Sydney: 1954, NLI Ir. 993 c 7.

Davis, Richard, *Ireland & Tasmania 1848: sesquicentenary papers*, Sydney: Crossing Press, 1998, NLI Ir. 990 d 23, 152 p. (eds., Richard Davis and Stefan Petrow).

Donohoe, James Hugh, *The bibliography of the convict transports*, Sydney: the author, 1988, NLI 016 p 5(3).

Donohoe, H., *The convicts and exiles transported from Ireland 1791–1820*, Sydney: the author, 1992, NLI Ir. 942 p 17(3).

Evans, A.G., *Fanatic heart, a life of John Boyle O'Reilly 1844–1890*, Boston: Northeastern University Press, 1999, NLI Ir. 92 o 529, 280 p.

Fitzpatrick, David, *Home or Away? Immigrants in Colonial Australia*, Canberra: Australian National University, 1992, NLA 130 p.

Fitzpatrick, David, *Oceans of Consolation*, Cork: Cork University Press, 1994, NLI Ir. 942 f 12, personal accounts of Irish migration to Australia.

Forth, G.J., *A biographical register and annotated bibliography of Ango-Irish colonists in Australia*, Warrnambool: Deakin University, 1992, NLI Ir. 942 b 23, 85pp.

Gleeson, Damian John, *Carlon's town: a history of the Carolan/Carlon sept and related Irish pioneer families in New South Wales*, Sydney: Damian John Gleeson, 1998, NLI Ir. 9292 g 38, 100 p.

Graham, John, *Far from Owenreagh: memories of John Graham (1899–1893)*, Draperstown: Moyola Books, 1990, NLI Ir. 92 p 172(2), 36 p.

Greiner, Alyson Lee, *British and Irish immigration to rural nineteenth-century Australia [microform]: sources and destinations*, 1996, NLA, 318 p. Presented as Ph.D. thesis: University of Texas at Austin, 1996.

Grimes, Seamus, *The Irish-Australia Connection*, Galway: Irish Academic Press, 1989, NLI Ir. 999 g 20, 159 p. Irish-Australian Bicentenary Conference. Co-ed., Gearoid O'Tuathaigh.

Hall, Barbara, *A desperate set of villains: the convicts of the Marquis Cornwallis, Ireland to Botany Bay, 1796*, Barbara Hall, 2000, NLI, 287 p.

Hall, Barbara, *A nimble fingered tribe: the convicts of the Sugar Cane, Ireland to Botany Bay, 1793*, Barbara Hall, 2002, NLI.

Hall, Barbara, *Of infamous character: the convicts of the Boddingtons, Ireland to Botany Bay, 1793*, Sydney: Hall, 2004, NLI 242 p.

Hawkings, David T., *Bound for Australia*, Sussex: Phillimore, 1987.

Hogan, J., *The Irish in Australia*, Melbourne: G. Robertson, 1888, NLI Ir. 9940.

Hughes, Robert, *The Fatal Shore*, London: Collins Harvill, 1988, NLI 993 h 11.

Kiernan, T.J., *The Irish exiles in Australia*, Dublin: Clonmore & Reynolds, 1954, NLI Ir. 994 k 1, 196 p. Irish exiles of 1848.

Langmead, Donald, *Accidental architect*, Sydney: The Crossing Press, 1994, NLI 92 K n 13, 280 p. George Strickland Kingston, 1807–1880.

Larkin, David A., *Memorials to the Irish in Queensland*, Brisbane, Genealogical Society of Queensland, 1988, NLA, 143 p.

Larkin, David A., *Here lyeth O'Flaherty: some notable Irish buried in Brisbane,* Brisbane: O'Lorcan, David Austin, 1991, NLA 63 p.

Larkin, David A., *Irish research compendium: guide and directory of sources available in Australia,* Burpengary, Qld.: D. Larkin, c.1999, NLA, 236 p.

Larkin, David A., *Pushing up shamrocks: index to biographies,* Burpengary, Qld.: Larkin Clan Association, 1998, NLA, 158 p. Irish in Queensland.

Maher, Brian, *Planting the Celtic cross: foundations of the Catholic Archdiocese of Canberra and Goulburn,* Canberra: B. Maher, 1997, NLA, 379 p.

McClaughlin, Trevor, *Barefoot and Pregnant: Irish Famine Orphans in Australia,* Melbourne: GSV, 1991, NLI Ir. 942 b 20, 256 p.

McClaughlin, Trevor, *Irish women in colonial Australia,* St Leonards NSW: Allen & Unwin, 1998, NLI Ir. 990 i 47, 229 p.

McClaughlin, Trevor, *From shamrock to wattle: digging up your Irish ancestors,* Melbourne: Genealogical Society of Victoria, 1990, NLA, 158 p. 2nd ed.

McConville, Chris, *Croppies, Celts & Catholics: the Irish in Australia,* Caulfield East, Vic.: Edward Arnold, 1987, NLA, 167 p.

McDonagh & Mandle, *Australia and Ireland, 1788–1988,* Dublin, 1988, NLI Ir. 942 a 9.

McDonagh & Mandle, *Ireland & Irish-Australians,* Sydney, 1982, NLI Ir. 942 i 12.

Mitchell, Brian, *Australia—the early years: from reports in the Derry Journal,* Derry, Northern Ireland: Genealogy Centre, 1988, NLA, 68 p.

Neary, Bernard, *Irish Lives: the Irish in Western Australia,* Dublin: Lenhar Publications, 1989, NLI Ir. 92001 p 8(1).

Ó Luing, Seán, *Fremantle mission,* Tralee: Tralee Anvil Books, 1965, NLI Ir. 993 o 11, 183 p.

O'Brien, John (ed.), *The Irish Emigrant Experience in Australia,* Dublin: Poolbeg Press, 1991, NLI Ir. 942 i 25, 279 p. Co-ed., Pauric Travers.

O'Farrell, Patrick, *The Irish in Australia,* Cork: Cork University Press, 2001, NLI Ir. 942 o 29/1A 3224; Revised edition.

O'Farrell, Patrick, *Letters from Irish Australia,* NSW: New South Wales University Press, 1984, NLI Ir. 942 o 31, co-ed., Brian Trainer, co-publisher, UHF.

O'Farrell, Patrick, *The Catholic Church in Australia: a short history, 1788–1967,* London: Chapman, 1969, NLI 282099 o 2, 294 p.

O'Farrell, Patrick, *Through Irish eyes: Australian and New Zealand images of the Irish 1788–1948,* Richmond, Victoria: Aurora Books, 1994, NLI Ir. 942 o 43, 131 p.

O'Farrell, Patrick, *Vanished kingdoms Irish in Australia and New Zealand: a personal excursion,* Kensington, NSW: New South Wales University Press, 1990, NLI Ir. 942 o 34, 310 p.

O'Hearn, D., *Erin Go Bragh—Advance Australia Fair,* Melbourne: Celtic Club, 1990, 86 p. History of the Celtic Club, Melbourne.

O'Leary, J., *A Catholic miscellany: containing items of interest to Queenslanders, Irishmen and Irish Australians,* South Brisbane: Father O'Leary, 1914, NLA, 207 p.

O'Mahoney, Dr C., *Poverty to promise: the Monteagle emigrants 1838–58,* Australia: The Crossing Press, 1994, NLI Ir. 993 o 40, co-author, Valerie Thompson.

O'Sullivan, Margaret Mary Kathleen, *A cause of trouble? Irish nuns and English clerics*, Sydney: The Crossing Press, 1995, NLI Ir. 994 o 51.

Patrick, Ross, *Exiles undaunted: the Irish rebels, Kevin and Eva O'Doherty*, St Lucia, Qld.: University of Queensland Press, 1989, NLA, 293 p. 1848 exiles.

Pawsey, Margaret M., *The Popish plot: culture clashes in Victoria 1860–1863*, Manly, NSW: Catholic Theological Faculty, St Patrick's College, 1983, NLA, 211 p.

Press, Kate, *West Limerick families abroad*, Melbourne: Kate Press, 2001, NLA, 217 p., co-author, Valerie Thompson.

Reece, Bob, *Exiles from Erin: Convict Life in Ireland and Australia*, Basingstoke: Macmillan, 1991, NLI Ir. 994 r 16, 336 p.

Reece, Bob, *Irish convicts the origins of convicts transported to Australia*, Dublin: Dept. of History, University College Dublin, 1989, NLI Ir. 942 r 9, 191 p.

Reece, Bob, *The origins of Irish convict transportation to New South Wales: mixture of breeds*, Basingstoke: Macmillan, 2000, NLI Ir. 942 r 22, 392 p.

Reece, Bob, *Irish convict lives*, Sydney: The Crossing Press, 1993, NLI Ir. 942 i 35, 266 p.

Reid, Richard, *The Irish Australians*, Sydney: Society of Australian Genealogists, 1984, NLI, 56 p., co-publisher, UHF, co-ed., Keith Johnson.

Reid, Richard, *A decent set of girls...: the Irish Famine Orphans of the Thomas Arbuthnot, 1849–1850*, Yass, Australia: Yass Heritage Project, 1996, NLI Ir. 942 r 17, 130 p.

Richards, Eric, *Visible Immigrants: Neglected Sources for the History of Australian Immigrants*, Canberra: ANU, 1989, NLI, co-authors, Richard Reid and David Fitzpatrick.

Richards, Eric (ed.), *Poor Australian Immigrants in the Nineteenth Century*, Canberra: ANU, 1991, NLI.

Robinson, P., *The Hatch and Brood of Time: Australians 1788–1828*, Oxford: Oxford University Press, 1985, NLI Ir. 993 r 5.

Robson, L.L., *The Convict Settlers of Australia*, Melbourne: Melbourne University Press, 1965, NLI 325 r 2, 257 p.

Ronayne, Jarlath, *The Irish in Australia: rogues and reformers: First fleet to federation*, Camberwell, Vic.: Viking/Penguin, c.2003, NLA, 252 p. Previously published as *First fleet to federation*, Dublin: Trinity College Dublin Press, 2002.

Sheedy, Kieran, *The Tellicherry Five: the transportation of Michael Dwyer & the Wicklow rebels*, Dublin: Woodfield Press, 1997, NLI Ir. 92 d 268, 182 p.

Simons, P. Frazer, *Tenants no more: Voices from an Irish Townland 1811-1901 and the Great Migration to Australia and America*, Richmond, Australia: Prowling Tiger Press, 1996, NLI Ir. 994 s 32, 288 p. Clay family from Gurteen, Offaly (King's), Methodist migrants to the US and Australia.

Trainor, Brian, *Researching Irish Australians: directory of research*, Belfast: UHF, 1998, NLA, 87 p.

Whitaker, Anee-Marie, 'Armagh convicts in Australia, 1800–1806', SA, 16 No. 1 (1994) 100–102.

Whitaker, Anee-Marie, *Unfinished revolution: United Irishmen in New South Wales 1800–1810*, Darlinghurst, NSW: The Crossing Press, 1994, NLI Ir. 993 w 15, 275 p.

India

Holmes, Michael, 'The Irish and India: imperialism, nationalism and internationalism', in Bielenberg, *The Irish Diaspora*. See McCracken, in 'Africa'.

New Zealand

'Family Migration to New Zealand: the Bassett Family of Ballygawley, Downpatrick, Co. Down', *Familia: Ulster Genealogical Review*, Vol. 2, No. 5 (1989).

Akenson, D.H., 'Reading the texts of rural immigrants: Letters from the Irish in Australia, New Zealand and America', *Canadian papers in Rural History*, VII 1990, Gananoque, Ontario: Langdale Press, c.1978–c.1996, NLC.

Akenson, D.H., 'The Irish in New Zealand', *Familia: Ulster Genealogical Review*, 2, 5 (1989).

Akenson, D.H., *Half the world from home: perspectives on the Irish in New Zealand, 1860–1950*, Wellington (NZ): Victoria University Press, 1990, NLI Ir. 942 a 14, 250 p.

Akenson, D.H., *Small differences, Irish Catholics and Irish Protestants, 1815–1922: an international perspective*, Dublin: Gill and Macmillan, 1991, NLI Ir. 94108 a 7, 236 p.

Bellam, Michael, 'The Irish in New Zealand', *Familia: Ulster Genealogical Review*, 2, 1 (1985).

Boyd, Murray A., *From Donegal to Blackguard's Corner*, Kaikoura (New Zealand): Rangiora Printing Services, 1992, NLI 2C 9 [sic], 448 p.

Coffey, Hubert W., *Irish Families in Australia and New Zealand 1788–1979*, Melbourne: H.W. Coffey, 1979–1994, NLI Ir. 942 c 14, 4-vol. biographical dictionary. Co-author, Marjorie Jean Morgan.

Davis, Richard, *The Whistling Irish bushrangers: Tasmania & South Australia, 1848–1863*, Sandy Bay, Tasmania: Sassafras Books, c.2002, NLI 3A 150, 40 p.

Davis, Richard, *Irish issues in New Zealand politics, 1868–1922*, Dunedin, NZ: University of Otago Press, 1974, NLI Ir. 942 d 15, 248 p.

Eccleston, Norman, *Irish Kiwi*, Levin, NZ: Levin Chronicle for Palmerston North Newspapers, 1977, NLNZ, 112 p.

Fraser, Lyndon, *To Tara via Holyhead: Irish Catholic immigrants in nineteenth-century Christchurch*, Auckland: Auckland University Press, 1997, NLI Ir. 990 f 16, 208 p.

Fraser, Lyndon, *A distant shore: Irish migration & New Zealand settlement*, Dunedin, NZ: University of Otago Press, 2000, NLNZ, 196 p.

Golden, John, *Some old Waikato days*, Dunedin [NZ]: NZ Tablet Printing and Publishing Co., 1922, NLNZ, 57 p.

Gray, Arthur J., *An Ulster plantation, the story of the Katikati settlement*, Wellington: A. H. & A. W. Reed, 1950, NLI Ir. 970.g17, 154 p.

Graydon, E., *People of Irish descent: biographical notes on New Zealanders of Irish descent*, Tauranga (NZ): E.M. Graydon, 1992, NLNZ.

King, Michael, *God's farthest outpost: a history of Catholics in New [sic] New Zealand*, Auckland, NZ: Penguin, 1997, NLNZ, 208 p.

McCann, Patrick D., *In quest of roots: the Dooney family of County Kildare in Ireland and Hawke's Bay District in New Zealand*, Dublin: de la Salle

Provincialate, 1977, NLI GO 475, 62 p.

McCarthy, Angela, 'The desired haven? Impressions of New Zealand in letters to and from Ireland, 1840–1925', in Bielenberg, *The Irish Diaspora*. See McCracken, in 'Africa'.

McGill, David, *The lion and the wolfhound: the Irish rebellion on the New Zealand goldfields*, Wellington, NZ: Grantham House, 1990, NLI Ir. 994 m 49, 178 p.

McGuire, Hugh, A brief family account of Laurence & Anne 1865–1990, first compiled by Elizabeth Coombes and Leonie Flower, Auckland [s.n.]: 1999, NLI Ir. 9292 m 85, 95 p. Rev. ed., Hugh McGuire.

O'Farrell, Patrick, *Through Irish eyes: Australian and New Zealand images of the Irish 1788–1948*, Richmond, Victoria: Aurora Books, 1994, NLI Ir. 942 o 43, 131 p.

O'Farrell, Patrick, *Vanished kingdoms: Irish in Australia and New Zealand: a personal excursion*, Kensington, NSW: New South Wales University Press, 1990, NLI Ir. 942 o 34, 310 p.

Patterson, Brad, *The Irish in New Zealand: historical contexts and perspectives*, Wellington, NZ: Stout Research Centre University of Wellington, 2002, NLNZ, 212 p.

Reiher, Gwen, Irish Interest Group, NZSG newsletter supplement, Auckland, NZ: Irish Interest Group, 1998–2002, NLNZ.

Reiher, Gwen, 'Suggestions for research in Ireland', Auckland, NZ: Irish Interest Group, New Zealand Society of Genealogists, 1999, NLNZ, 28 p.

Rogers, Anna, *A lucky landing: the story of the Irish in New Zealand*, Auckland/London: Random House, 1996, NLI Ir. 300 r 22, 246 p.

Rombouts, Michael, 'A register of Irish settlers to Otago-Southland', Dunedin, NZ: M.J. Rombouts, 2002, NLNZ, 518 p.

Sharp, C.A., *The Dillon letters: the letters of the Hon. Constantine Dillon, 1842–1853*, Wellington, NZ: A.H. & A.W. Reed, 1954, NLI, 174 p.

Shaw, M. Noeline, *The history of the McKay family of Wyndham*, Waikanae, NZ: Heritage Press, 1986, NLI GO 110, 295 p.

Stewart, George Vesey, *Notes on the origin and prospects of the Stewart special settlement, Kati-Kati, New Zealand, and on New Zealand as a field for emigration*, Omagh [Northern Ireland]: N. Carson, 1877, NLNZ, 128 p.

The Irish link: the Irish family history magazine, South Melbourne, Victoria: *The Irish Link*, 1984–, NLI Ir. 9292 i 2.

Went, A. E. J., 'William Spotswood Green', *The Scientific proceedings of the Royal Dublin Society*. Series B, Vol. 2, No. 3 (1967), 17–35, Dublin: Royal Dublin Society, NLI Ir. 506 r 12.

Wily, Henry E.R.L., *Robert Maunsell: a New Zealand pioneer, his life and times*, Dunedin: A.H. & A.W. Reed, 1938, NLI Ir. 92 m 191, 189 p., co-author, Herbert Maunsell.

See also

List of New Zealand's Irish immigrants, available online at *www.geocities.com/ Heartland/Prairie/7271/immlist.htm*

The Irish in New Zealand, available online at *www.teara.govt.nz*

EUROPE

General

O'Connor, Thomas, *The Irish in Europe, 1580–1815*, Dublin; Portland, Oregon, Four Courts Press, 2001, NLI, 219 p.

Austria

Walsh, V. Hussey, 'The Austrian branches of the family of Walsh', *The Genealogist*, N.S. XVIII (1901), 79–88.

France

General

(-), 'A Maguire family in France', *Clogher Record*, V (1a), 222–6.

(-), 'An O'Brien family in France', *IG*, 8, No. 2 (1994), 207–209.

Boyle, Patrick, *The Irish college in Paris from 1578 to 1901, with a brief account of the other Irish colleges in France: viz., Bordeaux, Toulouse, Nantes, Poitiers, Douai, and Sille*, London: Art and Book Co., 1901, NLI Ir. 28207 b 1, 236 p. Also New York: Benziger Bros.

Barnwell, Stephen B., 'Some Irish Nuns in 18th-century France', *IG*, 8, No. 2 (1994), 213.

Forgues, E., *Histoire d'un sept irlandais: Les Macnamara*, Paris: Bureaux de la Revue Britannique, 1901, NLI Ir. 9292 m 22, 54 p.

Griffin, G. T, *The wild geese: pen portraits of famous Irish exiles*, London: Jarrolds, limited, 1938, NLI Ir. 920041 g 5, 288 p.

Hayes, Richard, *Ireland and Irishmen in the French Revolution*, Dublin: Phoenix Pub. Co., 1932, NLI Ir. 94404 h 1, 314 p.

Hayes, Richard, *Irish Swordsmen of France*, Dublin: M.H. Gill & son, 1934, NLI Ir. 94404 h 3, 307 p. Dillon, O'Moran, Lally, Kilmaine, Warren.

Hayes, Richard, *Biographical Dictionary of Irishmen in France*, Dublin: M.H. Gill & Son, 1949, NLI Ir. 9440 h 16, 332 p.

Hayes, Richard, *Old Irish Links with France, some echoes of exiled Ireland*, Dublin: NLI Ir. 944 h 11, 230 p.

Hennessy, Maurice, *The wild geese; the Irish soldier in exile*, London: Sidgwick & Jackson, 1973, NLI Ir. 942 h 10, 227 p.

Holohan, Renagh, *The Irish Chateaux—in search of descendants of the Wild Geese*, Dublin: Lilliput Press, 1989, NLI Ir. 942 h 21, 187 p. Co-author, Jeremy Williams.

Jones, Paul, *The Irish Brigade*, Washington: R.B. Luce, 1969, NLI Ir. 942 j 3.

Lee, G.A., *Irish Chevaliers in the Service of France*, NLI Ir. 340 l 3.

McDonnel, Hector, *The Wild Geese of the Antrim McDonnells*, Blackrock: Irish Academic Press, 1996, NLI Ir. 942 m 46.

McLaughlin, Mark G., *The Wild Geese: the Irish brigades of France and Spain*, London: Osprey, 1980, NLI Ir. 358 m 20, 40 p.

O'Callaghan, J.C., *History of the Irish Brigades*, New York: P. O'Shea, 1874, NLI Ir. 944 o 13, 649 p.

O'Connell, M.J., *The Last Colonel of the Irish Brigade, Count O'Connell, 1745–1833*, London: Truboner & Co., 1892, NLI Ir. 92027 (2 vols).

O'Connor, Thomas H., *An Irish theologian in Enlightenment France Luke Joseph Hooke 1714–96*, Dublin: Four Courts Press, 1995, NLI Ir. 92 h 171, 218 p.

Ó hAnnracháin, Eoghan, 'Irish veterans in the *invalides*: the Tipperary contingent', *Tipperary Historical Journal (Irisleabhar staire Thiobraid Arann)* (1998).

O'Reilly, Andrew, *Reminiscences of an emigrant Milesian. The Irish abroad and at home; in the camp; at the court. With souvenirs of "the Brigade"*, London: R. Bentley, 1853, NLI Ir. 94107 o 6, 358 p. Also New York: D. Appleton and co., 1856.

Swords, Liam, *The Irish-French connection: 1578–1978*, Paris: The Irish College, 1978, NLI Ir. 942 i 6, 177 p.

Terry, James, *Pedigrees and Papers*, NLI Ir. 9292 T.7. Part of the collection of pedigrees taken to France by Terry in the early eighteenth century.

Walsh, V. Hussey, 'The French branches of the family of Walsh', *The Genealogist*, N.S. XVII 1900–1901, 36–43, 90–99, 153–158.

Bordeaux

Clark de Dromentin, Patrick, *Les oies sauvages: mémoires d'une famille irlandaise réfugiée en France, Nantes, Martinique, Bordeaux: 1691–1914*, Bordeaux: Presses Universitaires de Bordeaux, 1995, NLI Ir. 942 c 37.

Hayes, Richard, *Les Irlandais en Aquitaine*, Bordeaux: Héritiers E.-F. Miailhe, 1971, NLI 3B 811, 61 p. Co-authors, Christopher Preston and Colonel J. Weygand.

Walsh, T.J., *The Irish continental college movement: the colleges at Bordeaux, Toulouse, and Lille*, Dublin: Golden Eagle Books, 1973, NLI Ir. 271 w 8, 202 p.

Brittany

Dagier, Patricia, *Les réfugiés Irlandais au 17ème siècle en Finistère*, Quimper: Genealogie Cornouaille, 1999, NLI Ir. 944 d 21, 357, p.

Brive

[-], *La colonie Irlandaise de Brive (Corrèze) 1662 et 1762–1792: d'après le fonds Pataki aux A.D. Lot* (30J)., Noisy le Grand, 1994, NLI 1B 793, 15 p.

Grenoble

Barnwell, Stephen B., 'Some Irish in Grenoble, France, 1694–1771', *IG*, 8, No. 2 (1994), 210–2.

Lille

Walsh, T.J., *The Irish continental college movement: the colleges at Bordeaux, Toulouse, and Lille*, Dublin: Golden Eagle Books, 1973, NLI Ir. 271 w 8, 202 p.

Nantes

Clark de Dromentin, see 'Bordeaux'.

Mathorez, J., *Les irlandais nobles ou notables a Nantes aux XVIIe et XVIIIe siecles*, NLI Ir. 941, p 20.

Toulouse

Walsh, T.J., *The Irish continental college movement: the colleges at Bordeaux, Toulouse, and Lille*, Dublin: Golden Eagle Books, 1973, NLI Ir. 271 w 8, 202 p.

Great Britain

General

Connolly, Tracey, 'Emigration from Ireland to Britain during the Second World War', in Bielenberg, *The Irish Diaspora*. See McCracken, in 'Africa'.

Clancy, Mary, *The emigrant experience: papers presented at the second annual Mary Murray Weekend seminar, Galway, 30 Mar.–1 Apr. 1990*, Galway: Galway Labour History Group, 1991, NLI Ir. 942.i.26, 142 p.

Davis, Graham, 'The Irish in Britain, 1815–1939', in Bielenberg, *The Irish Diaspora*. See McCracken, in 'Africa'.

Davis, Graham, *The Irish in Britain 1815–1914*, Dublin: Gill and Macmillan.

Vaughan, W.E., *A New History of Ireland, Vol. V, Ireland under the Union*, Oxford.

Durham

Duffy, G., 'County Monaghan immigrants in the Consett area of County Durham, England, 1842–1855', *Clogher Record*, Vol. 16, No. 1 (1997), 37–45.

Liverpool

Brady, L.W., *T.P. O'Connor and the Liverpool Irish*, London: Royal Historical Society, 1983, NLI Ir. 92 o 340, 304 p.

Gallman, J. Matthew, *Receiving Erin's children: Philadelphia, Liverpool, and the Irish famine migration, 1845–1855*, Chapel Hill: University of North Carolina Press, c.2000, NLI A 3A 2106, 306 p.

Kelly, Michael, *Liverpool: the Irish connection: the story of some notable Irish people who helped create the great city of Liverpool*, Southport: the author, 2003, NLI 148 p.

Neal, Frank, *Sectarian violence: the Liverpool experience, 1819–1914: an aspect of Anglo-Irish history*, Manchester, UK: Manchester University Press, 1988, NLI Ir. 942 n 7, 272 p.

Scotland

Aspinwall, Bernard, 'A long journey: the Irish in Scotland', in O'Sullivan, Patrick (ed.), *Religion and identity*, London: Leicester University Press, 1996, 146–182, Irish worldwide series. History, heritage, identity: v.5.

Devine, T.M., *Irish immigrants and Scottish society in the nineteenth and twentieth centuries: proceedings of the Scottish Historical Studies Seminar, University of Strathclyde 1989–90*, Edinburgh: John Donald, c.1991, NLI Ir. 942 i 34, 141 p.

Dickson, David, *Ireland and Scotland: Nation, Region, Identity*, Dublin: The Centre for Irish-Scottish Studies, 2001, NLI 113 pp. Co-eds., Seán Duffy, Cathal Ó Háinle, Ian Campbell Ross.

Gallagher, Tom, *Glasgow: the uneasy peace: religious tension in modern Scotland, 1819–1914*, Manchester: Manchester University Press, c.1987, NLI G 305 g 2, 383 p.

McCready, Richard B., 'Revising the Irish in Scotland: the Irish in nineteenth- and early twentieth-century Scotland', in Bielenberg, *The Irish Diaspora*. See McCracken, in 'Africa'.

McFarland, E.W., *Protestants first: Orangeism in nineteenth-century Scotland*, Edinburgh: Edinburgh University Press, c.1990, NLI 941508 m 15, 255 p.

McFarland, E.W., *Ireland and Scotland in the age of revolution: planting the green bough*, Edinburgh: Edinburgh University Press, c.1994, NLI Ir. 94107 m 24, 272 p.

Mitchell, Martin J., *The Irish in the west of Scotland 1797–1848 trade unions, strikes and political movements*, Edinburgh: John Donald, 1998, NLI Ir. 942 m 57, 286 p.

Sloan, William, 'Employment opportunities & migrant group assimilation: Highlanders & Irish in Glasgow, 1840–1860', in Cummings, A.J.G. (ed.), *Industry, business and society in Scotland since 1700*, Edinburgh: c.1994, 197–217, co-editor, T.M. Devine.

Tyneside

Barrington, Mary A., *The Irish independence movement on Tyneside 1919–1921*, Dun Laoghaire, Co. Dublin: Dun Laoghaire Genealogical Society, 1999, NLI, 40 p.

York

Clancy, Mary, *The emigrant experience: papers presented at the second annual Mary Murray Weekend seminar, Galway, 30 Mar.–1 Apr. 1990*, Galway: Galway Labour History Group, 1991, NLI Ir. 942.i.26, 142 p.

Portugal

Notas e documentos genealogicos a'cerca de familia O'Neill, Lisboa: Imprensa Minerva, 1893, NLI GO 480, 22 p. The O'Neills in Portugal.

Spain

General

Fannin, Samuel, 'Carew, Langton and Power, an Irish trading company in 18th-century Spain', *IG*, 11, 1 (2002), 53–59.

Henry, Gráinne, *The Irish Military Community in Spanish Flanders 1586–1621*, Dublin: Irish Academic Press, 1992, NLI Ir. 942 h 23.

MacSwiney de Mashanaglass, Patrice, Marquis, *Notes on the early services of "Irlanda el famoso": with reference to a recent paper on the Irish regiments in the service of Spain*, Dublin: printed at Mahon's Printing Works, Yarnhall Street, 1930, NLI Ir. 94107 m 4, 12 p.

McDonnel, Hector, *The Wild Geese of the Antrim McDonnells*, Blackrock: Irish Academic Press, 1996, NLI Ir. 942 m 46.

McLaughlin, Mark G., *The Wild Geese: the Irish brigades of France and Spain*, London: Osprey, 1980, NLI Ir. 358 m 20, 40 p. Colour plates by Chris Warner.

O'Ryan, W.D., 'The family of O'Mulryan in Spain', *IG*, III (1961), 195–7.

O'Ryan, W.D., 'O'Ryan of Mallorca', *IG*, III (1962), 266–9.

Santiago, Mark, *The red captain: the life of Hugo O'Conor, commandant inspector of the interior provinces of New Spain,* Tucson, Arizona: Arizona Historical Society, 1994, NLI A 2A 217, 127 p.

Schüller, Karin, *Die Beziehungen zwischen Spanien und Irland im 16. und 17. Jahrhundert: Diplomatie, Handel und die soziale Integration katholischer Exulanten,* Münster: Aschendorff, 1999, NLI Ir. 946 s 43, 280 p.

Stradling, R.A., *The Spanish Monarchy and Irish Mercenaries: the Wild Geese in Spain 1618–68,* Dublin: Irish Academic Press, 1994, NLI Ir. 94106 s 13.

Terry, Kevin, 'The Ryan and Terry families in Spain', *IG*, 10, 2 (1999), 245–9.

Terry, Kevin, 'Some Spanish Terrys of Irish origin', *IG*, 10, 1 (2000), 372–3.

Walsh, Micheline, *An Exile of Ireland, Hugh O'Neill,* Dublin: Four Courts Press, 1996, NLI Ir. 92 o 491, 154 p.

Walsh, Micheline, *Spanish knights of Irish origin; documents from continental archives,* Dublin: IMC, 1960, NLI Ir. 946 w 3.

Bilbao

Aceves, Amaia Bilbao, *The Irish Community in the Basque Country 1700–1800,* Dublin: Geography Publications, 2003, NLI 114 p.

NORTH AMERICA

General

(-) 'Sources for the Identification of Emigrants from Ireland to North America in the 19th Century', *Ulster Historical and Genealogical Guild Newsletter* (1979), Vol. 1, Nos. 2 & 3, Belfast, UHF, NLI Ir. 9292 u 3.

Adams, William Forbes, *Ireland and Irish Immigration to the New World: From 1815 to the Famine,* Baltimore: GPC 1980 NLI Ir. 3252 a 6.

Akenson, D.H., *Being had: historians, evidence, and the Irish in North America,* Port Credit, Ont., Canada: P.D. Meany, 1985, NLI Ir. 973 a 10, 243 p.

Akenson, D.H., 'Irish migration to North America, 1800–1920', in Bielenberg, *The Irish Diaspora.* See McCracken, in 'Africa'.

Blake, J.W. (ed.), *The Ulster-American Connection,* New University of Ulster, NLI Ir. 942 u 3.

Bolton, C.K., *Scotch Irish pioneers in Ulster and America,* Baltimore: Genealogical Publishing, 1986, NLI Ir. 973 b 14, 398 p.

Bradley, A.K., *History of the Irish in America,* Chartwell, 1986, NLI Ir. 942 b 19.

Concannon & Cull, *Irish-American Who's Who,* New York: The Irish American's Who's Who, 1984, 981 p. NLI Ir. 942 i 13.

Dickson, R.J., *Ulster Emigration to Colonial America, 1718–75,* Belfast, UHF, 1988, 320 p., NLI Ir. 9411 d 22.

Dobson, David, 'Scottish Emigration to Colonial America: An Overview', *Familia: Ulster Genealogical Review,* No. 18 (2002).

Dobson, David, *Irish emigrants in North America*, Baltimore: reprinted for Clearfield Co. by Genealogical Pub. Co., 1997–2000, LOC; originally published in 5 vols: Fife, Scotland: St Andrews, 1994–1999.

Dobson, David, *Ships from Ireland to early America, 1623–1850*, Baltimore: GPC, c.1999, LOC, 153 p.

Doyle, D. & Edwards (eds.), *America and Ireland 1776–1976*, Westport, Connecticut: Greenwood Press, 1980, NLI Ir. 973 a 5. The proceedings of the United States Bicentennial conference of Cumann Merriman, Ennis, August 1976.

Drudy, P.J., *The Irish in America: emigration, assimilation, and impact*, Cambridge, New York: Cambridge University Press, 1985, NLI Ir. 942 i 9, 359 p.

Glasgow, M., *Scotch-Irish in Northern Ireland and the American Colonies*, New York: 1936, NLI Ir. 973 g 16.

Glazier, Michael, *The encyclopedia of the Irish in America*, Notre Dame: University of Notre Dame Press, 1999, NLI RR 970 e 11, 988 p.

Green, E.R.R., *Essays in Scotch-Irish History*, Belfast: UHF, 1992, 110 p. NLI Ir. 942 p 14(2).

Griffin, William D., *The Irish in America, 550–1972; a chronology & fact book*, Dobbs Ferry, NY: Oceana Publications, 1973, NLI Ir. 942 g 5, 154 p.

Harris, Ruth-Ann, *The Search for Missing Friends: Vols. 1–4, 1831–1860*, Boston: New England Historic Genealogical Society (1989–1993), NLI Ir. 942 s 22. Irish immigrant advertisements placed in *The Boston Pilot*; co-editors, D.M. Jacobs and B.E. O'Keeffe. Available online at *www.infowanted.bc.ed*.

Hotten, J.C., *Original Lists of Persons of Quality emigrating to America, 1600–1700*, London: 1874, NLI 'emigrants; religious exiles; political rebels; serving men sold for a term of years; apprentices; children stolen; maidens pressed; and others who went from Great Britain to the American plantations, 1600–1700; with their ages, the localities where they formerly lived in the mother country, the names of the ships in which they embarked, and other interesting particulars, from mss. preserved in the state paper department of Her Majesty's public record office', Reprint GPC, 1968 and 2003.

King, Joseph A., *The uncounted Irish in Canada and the United States*, Toronto: P.D. Meany, c.1990, NLI GR 192, co-author, Margaret E. Fitzgerald.

Knowles, Charles, *The Petition to Governor Shute in 1718; Scotch-Irish Pioneers in Ulster and America*, NLI.

Laxton, Edward, *The famine ships the Irish exodus to America 1846–51*, London: Bloomsbury, 1997, NLI Ir. 94108 L 22, 250 p.

Linehan, John C., *Irish Schoolmasters in the American Colonies, 1640–1775*, Washington, DC: American-Irish Historical Society (1898), NLI Ir. 942 r 9, 31 p. [with a continuation of the subject during and after the War of the Revolution].

Lockhart, Audrey, *Some aspects of emigration from Ireland to the North American colonies between 1660 and 1775*, New York: Arno Press, 1976, NLI Ir. 973 l 5, 243 p.

Maguire, John, *The Irish in America*, London: Longmans, Green, and Co., 1868, 653 p. NLI Ir. 973 m 3.

Marshall, W.F., *Ulster Sails West*, Baltimore, Md: GPC, 1996, NLI Ir. 973 m 59.

McDonnell, Frances, *Emigrants from Ireland to America 1735–1743*, Baltimore: GPC, 1992, NLI Ir. 94107 e 10, 134 p. (A transcription of the report of the Irish House of Commons into enforced emigration to America.)

McGee, Thomas D'Arcy, *A history of the Irish settlers in North America: from the earliest period to the census of 1850*, New York: 1852, NLI Ir. 970 m 1; Reprint, Baltimore: GPC, 2003.

Metress, Seamus P., *The Irish in North America: a regional bibliography*, Toronto: P.D. Meany Publishers, c.1999, NLI GR 2602, 227 p. Co-author, Donna M. Hardy-Johnston.

Metress, Seamus P., *The Irish-American experience: a guide to the literature*, Washington, DC: University Press of America, c.1981, NLI Ir. 942 m 21, 220 p.

Miller, K.A., *Exiles and Emigrants*, Oxford: 1985, NLI Ir. 942 m 26.

Miller, K.A., *Irish immigrants in the land of Canaan: letters and memoirs from colonial and revolutionary America, 1675–1815*, Oxford, New York: Oxford University Press, 2003, 788 p.

Miller, K.A., *Out of Ireland: the story of Irish emigration to America*, Washington DC: Elliott & Clark Pub., c.1994, LOC, 132 p. Co-author, Paul Wagner.

Miller, K.A., '"Scotch-Irish" myths and "Irish" identities in eighteenth- and nineteenth-century America', in Fanning, *New perspectives* ... see 'USA, General'.

Miller, K.A. '"Scotch-Irish", "Black Irish" and "Real Irish": emigrants and identities in the old South', in Bielenberg, *The Irish Diaspora*. See McCracken, in 'Africa'.

Mitchell, Brian, *Irish Emigration Lists 1833–39*, Baltimore: GPC, 1989, Antrim and Derry.

O'Brien, M.J., *Irish Settlers in America: A consolidation of articles from the journal of the American-Irish Society*, Baltimore: GPC, 1979, NLI Ir. 942 o 23.

Quinn, David B., *Ireland and America their early associations, 1500–1640*, Liverpool: Liverpool University Press, 1991, NLI Ir. 942 p 14(1), 57 p.

Schrier, Arnold, *Ireland and the American emigration, 1850–1900*, Chester Springs, PA: Dufour, 1997, NLI Ir. 94108 s 31, 210 p.

Shannon, W.V., *The American Irish*, New York: Macmillan, 1963, NLI Ir. 973 s 3, 458 p.

Shaw, J., *The Scotch-Irish in History*, Springfield: 1899, NLI Ir. 942 s 13.

Weaver, Jack W., *Migrants from Great Britain and Ireland: a guide to archival and manuscript sources in North America compiled*, Westport, Connecticut: Greenwood Press, 1986, NLI Ir. 016 w 2, co-editor, DeeGee Lester, 129 p.

Wokeck, Marianne S., *Trade in strangers: the beginnings of mass migration to North America*, University Park, Penn: Pennsylvania State University Press, 1999, NLI Ir. 324 w 6, 319 p.

Passenger lists

Adams, Raymond D., *An Alphabetical Index to Ulster Emigrants to Philadelphia, 1803–1850*, Baltimore: GPC, 1992. Family Archive CD 7257. From PRONI records.

Begley, D.F., *Handbook on Irish Genealogy*, Dublin: Heraldic Artists, 1984 (6th ed.), 101–110, 115, 1803/4.

Coldham, Peter Wilson, *The Complete Book of Emigrants in Bondage, 1614–1775*, Baltimore: GPC, 1988 (& supplements) 600 p., NLI Ir. 973 c 47.

Dept. of State, *Passengers Arriving in the U.S., 1821–1823*, Baltimore: Magna Carta Book Co., 1969, 427 p. NLI G 3251 u 1.

Filby, P. William & Meyer, Mary K. (eds.), *Passenger and immigration lists bibliography, 1538–1900: being a guide to published lists of arrivals in the United States and Canada* (14 Vols. Revision of Lancour, below). Gale, Detroit: 1981–2001. NLI RR, 387 p.

Glazier, Ira A. (ed.), *The Famine immigrants: lists of Irish immigrants arriving at the port of New York, 1846–1851*, Baltimore: GPC 7 Vols (associate editor, Michael Tepper), NLI Ir. 942 g 12.

Hackett, J. Dominick and Early, Charles M., *Passenger Lists from Ireland*, Baltimore: GPC, 1998 (1811, 1815–16, from *Journal of the American Irish Historical Society*, Vols 28 and 29).

Lancour, Harold, *A bibliography of ship passenger lists, 1538–1825; being a guide to published lists of early immigrants to North America*, New York: New York Public Library, 1963, 137 p. (3rd ed. revised by Richard J. Wolfe), NLI G 387 L 14.

Maher, James P., *Returning Home, Transatlantic Migration from North America to Britain & Ireland 1858–1870*, Dublin: Eneclann, #CD10, 2005. British Isles incoming passenger lists.

McDonnell, Frances, *Emigrants from Ireland to America 1735–1743*, Baltimore: GPC, 1992. Family Archive CD 7257. Records the names of almost 2,000 convict transportees.

Mitchell, Brian, *Irish Emigration Lists, 1833–1839*, Baltimore: GPC, 1989/Family Archive CD 7257. From Antrim/Derry OS letters.

Mitchell, Brian, *Irish Passenger Lists, 1847–1871*, Baltimore: GPC, 1989/Family Archive CD 7257. Londonderry, Cooke & McCorkell shipping.

Mitchell, Brian, *Irish Passenger Lists, 1803–1806*, Baltimore: GPC, 1995/Family Archive CD 7257. Departure lists, Dublin, Belfast, Newry, Londonderry.

Schlegel, Donald M. *Passengers from Ireland: lists of passengers arriving at American ports between 1811 and 1817*, Baltimore: GPC, 1980/Family Archive CD 7257 (transcribed from the Shamrock or Hibernian chronicle).

Tepper, Michael, *New England Passengers to America*, Baltimore: GPC, 1986, 554. NLI 387 p. 6.

Tepper, Michael, *Passenger arrivals at the Port of Philadelphia, 1800–1819: the Philadelphia baggage lists/general editor*, Baltimore: GPC, 1986, 913. NLI Ir. 970 p. 12.

See also

The Immigrant Ships Transcribers Guild, at *www.immigrantships. net.*

The Irish Passenger Lists Research Guide, at *www.genealogybranches.com/irish-passengerlists.*

Ellis Island, at *www.ellisisland.org.*

Castle Garden, at *www.castlegarden.org*

CANADA

General

(-) Typed transcripts of Canadian newspaper notices querying the whereabouts of emigrants, 1984, PRONI, D/3000/82, mainly the *New Brunswick Courier* (1830–1846) and the *Toronto Irish-Canadian* (1859).

Cowan, Helen I., *British emigration to British North America, 1773–1837*, Toronto: University of Toronto Library, 1928, NLC, 275 p.

Davin, N.F., *The Irishman in Canada*, Shannon, NLI Ir. 971 d 1.

Elliott, B.S., *Irish Migrants in the Canadas: A New Approach*, McGill: McGill-Queen's University Press, 2002, NLI Ir. 942 e 7, 408 p. Irish Protestants from North Tipperary especially.

Fromers, V., *Irish Emigrants to Canada in Sussex Archives 1839–47*, IA, 1979, 31–42.

Houston, Cecil J., *Irish Emigration and Canadian Settlement: Patterns, Links and Letters*, Canada: University of Toronto Press, 1990, NLI Ir. 942 h 20, 370 p. Co-author, William J. Smyth; co-publisher, UHF.

MacKay, Donald, *Flight from famine: the coming of the Irish to Canada*, Toronto London: McClelland & Stewart, 1992, NLI Ir. 942 m 45, 368 p.

Mannion, John J., *Irish settlements in eastern Canada; a study of cultural transfer and adaptation*, Toronto: University of Toronto Press, c.1974, NLI Ir. 971 m 11, 219 p.

O'Driscoll & Reynolds, R. & L. (eds.), *The Untold Story: the Irish in Canada* (2 Vols), Toronto: Celtic Arts of Canada, 1988, NLI Ir. 971 o 67.

New Brunswick

Cook, Jane L., 'Scots & Irish in the lower St John River Valley, 1815–1851', in *Coalescence of styles: the ethnic heritage of St John River Valley regional furniture, 1763–1851*, Montreal: McGill-Queen's Studies in Ethnic History, 2000, 112–150, NLS.

Cushing, J.E., *Irish Immigration to St John, New Brunswick, 1847*, St John: The New Brunswick Museum, 1979, NLI Ir. 942 c 16.

Daley, Caroline, *Middle Island: before and after the tragedy*, Miramichi, NB: Middle Island Irish Historical Park, 2002, NLI, co-author, Anna Springer.

Jack, D.R., *Centennial Prize Essay on the History of the City and County of St John*, St John NB: J. & A. McMillan, 1883.

Johnson, Daniel F., *Irish emigration to New England through the port of Saint John, New Brunswick, Canada 1841 to 1849*, Baltimore, Md: Clearfield, 1997, NLI Ir. 274 j 4, 284 p.

King, Joseph A., *Ireland to North America: emigrants from West Cork*, Lafayette, California: K & K Publications, 1994, NLI Ir. 942 k 7, 124 p. Also Toronto: P.D. Meany. Schull to Miramichi River Region, NB.

King, Joseph A., *The uncounted* … see 'North America, General'.

McDevitt, Mary Kilfoil, *We Hardly Knew Ye: St. Mary's Cemetary, An Enduring Presence*, St John, New Brunswick: Irish Canadian Cultural Association, 1990,

NLI Ir. 942 p 16(4), 140 p.

McGahan, Elizabeth, *The Port in the City: Saint John N.B. (1867–1911) and the Process of Integration*, unpublished Ph.D. thesis: University of New Brunswick.

Murphy, Peter, *Together in Exile, Nova Scotia, 1991, Carlingford emigrants to St John's, New Brunswick*, St John, P. Murphy, 1990, NLC, 283 p.

Murphy, Peter, *Poor, ignorant children: Irish famine orphans in Saint John, New Brunswick*, Halifax, NS: D'Arcy McGee Chair of Irish Studies, St Mary's University, 1999, NLI Ir. 942 m 63, 83 p.

Power, Thomas P., *The Irish in Atlantic Canada, 1780–1900*, New Brunswick: New Ireland Press, 1979, NLI Ir. 942 p 15, 210 p.

Rees, Ronald, *Some other place– than here: St. Andrews and the Irish emigrant*, Fredericton, NB: New Ireland Press, c.2000, NLI, 81 p.

Rees, J., *Surplus people: the Fitzwilliam clearances, 1847–1856*, Doughcloyne, WIlton, Cork: Collins Press, 2000, NLI 156 p.

Rogers, Ralph W. Jr, *The Rogers family of Northampton Parish, New Brunswick, and some descendants*, Homosassa, FL: R.W. Rogers, 1989, LOC, 65 p.

See, Scott W., *Riots in New Brunswick Orange nativism and social violence in the 1840s*, London Toronto, London: 1993, NLI Ir. 942 s 28, 266 p.

Toner, P.M., *New Ireland Remembered: historical essays on the Irish in New Brunswick*, New Brunswick, 1988.

Toner, P.M., *The green fields of Canada: Irish immigration and New Brunswick settlement, 1815–1850*, Fredericton: Provincial Archives of New Brunswick, c.1991, NLI.

Toner, P.M., *An index to Irish immigrants in the New Brunswick census of 1851*, Fredericton: Provincial Archives of New Brunswick, c.1991, NLI Ir. 942 t 2, 378 p.

Newfoundland

Clancy, Mary, *The emigrant experience*—see 'Great Britain, General'.

Greene, John Carrick, *Of fish and family: family trees and family histories of Tilting, set against the background of historical developments in the Newfoundland fisheries, 1700–1940*, St John's, NF: Triumphant Explorations, 2002, NLC, 731 p.

Mannion, John J., 'Kilkennymen in Newfoundland', *Old Kilkenny Review* (1987), 358.

McCarthy, Michael, *The Irish in Newfoundland 1600–1900: their trials, tribulations & triumphs*, St John's, Nfld: Creative, 1999, NLI GR 515, 216 p.

Nova Scotia

Blois, Ralph S., *The Joshua Smith family of Ireland and Hants County, NS*, Woodburn, OR, R.S. Blois, 1994, LOC, 224 p.

MacKenzie, A.A., *The Irish in Cape Breton*, Antigonish, NS: Formac Pub. Co, 1988, NLI Ir. 942 m 20, 129 p.

Punch, T.M., *Some Sons of Erin in Nova Scotia*, Halifax, NS: Petheric Press, 1980, NLI Ir. 971 p 10. 127 p.

Punch, T.M., *Irish Halifax: the immigrant generation, 1815–1859*, Halifax, NS: International Education Centre, Saint Mary's University, 1981, NLI Ir. 942 p 11, 86 p.

Stewart, H.L., *The Irish in Nova Scotia: annals of the Charitable Irish Society of Halifax (1736–1836)*, Kentville, NS: Kentville Pub. Co., 1949, NLI Ir. 971 s 2, 199 p.

Ontario

Akenson, D.H., *The Irish in Ontario, a study in rural history*, Kingston: McGill, 1985, 404 p. NLI Ir. 971 a 8.

Heald, Carolyn A., *The Irish Palatines in Ontario: Religion, Ethnicity and Rural Migration*, Garanoque, Ontario: Langdale Press.

McCuaig, Carol Bennett, *The Kerry chain: the Limerick link*, Renfrew, Ontario: Juniper Books, c.2003, NLI 178 p.

Prince Edward Island

O'Grady, Brendan, *Exiles and Islanders: The Irish Settlers of Prince Edward Island*, Montreal: McGill-Queen's Studies in Ethnic History, 2004, NLI, 313 p.

Quebec

Dagneau, G.-H., *Révélations sur les trois frères O'Leary de Québec*, Québec: Société historique de Québec, 1998, NLC, 117 p.

Grace, Robert J., *The Irish in Quebec: an introduction to the historiography*, Québec: Institut québécois de recherche sur la culture, 1993, NLC, 265 p. Followed by *An annotated bibliography on the Irish in Quebec*/Fernand Harvey.

Guerin, T., *The Gael in New France*, Montreal: 1946, 134 p. NLI Ir. 971 g 4.

O'Farrell, John, *Irish Families in Ancient Quebec Records*, Montreal: 1908.

O'Gallagher, M., *St Patrick's & St Brigid's, Quebec*, Quebec: Carraig Books, 1981, NLI Ir. 942 o 29, 124 p.

O'Gallagher, M., *The shamrock trail: tracing the Irish in Quebec City*, Ste. Foy. QC: Livrès Carraig Books, 1998, NLC, 35 p.

Redmond, P.M., *Irish Life in Rural Quebec*, Duquesne: 1983, NLI Ir. 942 r 6.

Rees, J., *Surplus people*—see 'New Brunswick'.

Sheehy, Réjeanne, *L'alliance irlandaise Sheehy au Québec*, Chicoutimi, Québec: Editions Entreprises, c.2000, LOC, 118 p.

Timbers, Wayne, *Britannique et irlandaise; l'identite ethnique et demographique des Irlandais protestants et la formation d'une communaute a Montreal, 1834–1860*, c.2001, NLC, 107 leaves; McGill, Thesis (M.A.).

Trigger, Rosalyn, *The role of the parish in fostering Irish-Catholic identity in nineteenth-century Montreal*, c.1997, NLC, McGill, Thesis (M.A.).

Saskatchewan

Coughlin, Jack, *The Irish colony of Saskatchewan*, Scarborough, Ontario: Lochleven Publishers, c.1995, NLC, 108 p.

CENTRAL AMERICA

Mexico

Davis, Graham, *Land!: Irish pioneers in Mexican and revolutionary Texas,* College Station: Texas A&M University Press, 2002, NLI, 304 p.

Hogan, Michael, *Los soldardos Irlandeses de México,* Guadalajara, Mexico: Fondo Editorial Universitario, 1999, NLI, 268 p.

Santiago, Mark, *The red captain: the life of Hugo O'Conor, commandant inspector of the interior provinces of New Spain,* Tucson, Arizona: Arizona Historical Society, 1994, NLI, 127 p.

USA

General

History of the Friendly Sons of St. Patrick and of the Hibernian Society for the Relief of Emigrants from Ireland: March 17, 1771–March 17, 1892, NLI Ir. 973 c 1.

The Irish-American Genealogist, Torrance, California: Irish Genealogy & Research Committee of the Augustan Society, 1973 to date, NLI Ir. 9291 i 3.

Journal of the American-Irish Historical Society, NLI Ir. 973 a 1.

(-) 'Early Irish Emigrants to America, 1803, 1806', *The Recorder,* 1926, June, New York: American Irish Historical Society (1901), NLI Ir. 973 r 1.

Akenson, D.H., *The United States and Ireland,* Cambridge, Massachusetts: Harvard University Press, 1973, NLI Ir. 941 a 15.

Beller, Susan Provost, *Never were men so brave: the Irish Brigade during the Civil War,* New York: Margaret K. McElderry Books, 1998, NLI Ir. 9737 b 25, 98 p.

Blessing, Patrick J., *The Irish in America: a guide to the literature and the manuscript collections,* Washington DC: Catholic University of America Press, 1992, NLI Ir. 016 b 9, 347 p.

Bradley, A.K., *History of the Irish in America,* Chartwell: 1986, NLI Ir. 942 b 19.

Bric, Maurice J., 'Patterns of Irish emigration to America, 1783–1800', *Éire-Ireland: a journal of Irish studies,* 36, 1–2 (2001).

Byron, Reginald, *Irish America,* Oxford, New York: Oxford University Press, 1999, NLI Ir. 973 b 30, 317 p.

Cobb, Irwin, *The lost tribes of the Irish in the South,* New York: 1917, LOC, 2 p.

D'Arcy, William, *The Fenian movement in the United States: 1858–1886,* Washington DC: Catholic Univ. of America Press, 1947, NLI Ir. 94108 d 15, 453 p.

Dezell, Maureen, *Irish America: coming into clover: the evolution of a people and a culture,* New York: Doubleday, 2000, LOC, 259 p.

Diner, Hasia R., *Erin's daughters in America: Irish immigrant women in the nineteenth century,* Baltimore: Johns Hopkins University Press, c.1983, NLI Ir. 942 d 14, 192 p.

Doerries, Reinhard R., *Iren und Deutsche in der Neuen Welt: Akkulturationsprozesse in der amerikanischen Gesellschaft im späten neunzehnten Jahrhundert,* Stuttgart: F. Steiner, 1986, NLI 3A 117, 363 p.

Donohoe, H., *The Irish Catholic Benevolent Union*, NLI Ir. 973 d 6.

Doyle, D., *Ireland, Irishmen, and Revolutionary America*, Dublin: Mercier Press, 1981, NLI Ir. 942 d 12, 257 p.

Drudy, P.J., *The Irish in America: emigration, assimilation, and impact*, Cambridge, New York: Cambridge University Press, 1985, NLI Ir. 942 i 9, 359 p.

Duff, John B., *The Irish in the United States*, Belmont, California: Wadsworth Pub. Co., 1971, LOC.

Dunne, Robert, *Antebellum Irish immigration and emerging ideologies of "America": a Protestant backlash*, Lewiston, NY: Edwin Mellen Press, c.2002, LOC, 148 p.

Durney, James, *The Mob/ The history of Irish gangsters in America*, Naas, Kildare, Ireland: *Leinster Leader* [n.d.], NLI Ir. 330 D 32, 208 p.

Fanning, Charles (ed.), *New perspectives on the Irish diaspora*, Carbondale: Southern Illinois University Press, c.2000, NLI, 329 p.

Fallows, Marjorie R., *Irish Americans: Identity and Assimilations*, New Jersey: Prentice-Hall, 1979, NLI Ir. 942 f 2, 158 p.

Femminella, Francis X., *Italians and Irish in America: proceedings of the Sixteenth Annual Conference of the American Italian Historical Association*, Staten Island, NY: The Association, 1985, NLI Ir. 973 f 7, 308 p.

Foy, R.H., *Dear Uncle: immigrant letters to Antrim from the U.S.A.—the Kerr letters [...]*, Antrim: Antrim & District Historical Society, 1991, NLI Ir. 842 f 9, 117 p.

Funchion, M.F., *Irish American voluntary organizations*, Westport, Connecticut: Greenwood Press, 1983, NAI Ir. 942 i 10, 323 p.

Gleeson, Ed, *Erin go gray!: an Irish rebel trilogy*, Carmel, Indiana: Guild Press of Indiana, 1997, NLI GR 1476, 148 p.

Golway, Terry, *The Irish in America*, New York: Hyperion, c.1997, LOC, 272 p.

Goodwin, Donn, *Look Back Upon Erin*, Milwaukee: Woodland Books, c.1980, LOC, 171 p.

Greeley, Andrew M., *The Irish Americans: the rise to money and power*, New York: Harper & Row, c.1981, NLI Ir. 942 g 11, 215 p.

Gribben, Arthur, *The great famine and the Irish diaspora in America*, University of Massachusetts Press London Eurospan, 1999, NLI Ir. 970 g 30, 268 p.

Griffin, William D., *A Portrait of the Irish in America*, Dublin: Academy Press, 1981, NLI 2B 785, 260 p.

Hartigan, J., *The Irish in the American Revolution*, Washington: 1908, NLI Ir. 973 h 8.

Hayden, Tom, *Irish on the inside: in search of the soul of Irish America*, London and New York: Verso, 2001, NLI, 312 p.

Johnson, James E., *The Irish in America*, Minneapolis: Lerner Publications, 1978, NLI Ir. 973.j4, 80 p.

Kennedy, John. F., *A Nation of Immigrants*, London: Hamish Hamilton.

Kenny, Kevin, *The American Irish: a history*, Harlow, England: Longman, 2000, NLI Ir. 973 k 16, 328 p.

Kenny, Kevin, *New directions in Irish-American history*, Madison, Wisconsin: University of Wisconsin Press, c.2003, LOC, 334 p.

Knobel, Dale T., *Paddy and the republic: ethnicity and nationality in antebellum America*, Middletown, Connecticut: Wesleyan University Press, 1986, NLI Ir. 942 k 5, 251 p.

Linehan, John C., *The Irish Scots and the "Scotch-Irish"*, Bowie, Md: Heritage Books, Inc., 1997, LOC, 138 p.

Lynch, Mary C., *O'Sullivan Burke, Fenian*, Carrigadrohid, Co. Cork, Ireland: Ebony Jane Press, 1999, NLI, 247 p. Co-author, Seamus O'Donoghue.

McCaffrey, Lawrence J., *The Irish Catholic diaspora in America*, Washington DC: Catholic University of America Press, 1997, NLI Ir. 973 m 55, 253 p.

McCaffrey, Lawrence J., *Textures of Irish America*, Syracuse, NY: Syracuse University Press, 1992, NLI Ir. 970 m 40, 236 p.

McCaffrey, Lawrence J., *The Irish diaspora in America*, Bloomington: Indiana University Press, c.1976, NLI Ir. 973 m 13.

McGrath, Thomas F., *A history of the Ancient Order of Hibernians*, NLI 1B 3243, 180 p.

McKenna, Erin, *A student's guide to Irish American genealogy*, Phoenix, Arizona: Oryx Press, 1996, NLI Ir. 9291 m 25, 168 p.

Meagher, T.J., *From Paddy to Studs: Irish-American communities in the turn of the century era, 1880 to 1920*, Westport, Connecticut: Greenwood Press, 1986, NLI Ir. 942 f 8, 202 p.

Mullin, James V., *The Irish Americans*, Evanston, Illinois: Nextext, c.2001, LOC, 224 p, 'A historical reader'.

O'Brien, M.J., *A Hidden Phase of American History*, Baltimore: 1973, NLI Ir. 9733 o. 25, Irishmen in the American Revolution.

O'Carroll, Ide, *Models for Movers*, Dublin: Attic Press, 1990, NLI Ir. 942032, 156 p. Focuses on women emigrants.

O'Dea, John, *History of the Ancient Order of Hibernians and Ladies' Auxiliary*, Notre Dame: University of Notre Dame Press, 1994, NLI Ir. 942 o 6, 3 vols.

O'Donovan, Jeremiah, *Irish immigration in the United States; immigrant interviews*, New York: Arno Press, *New York Times*, 1969, NLI Ir. 942.033, 382 p.

O'Grady, Joseph P., *How the Irish became Americans*, New York: Twayne Publishers, 1973, NLI Ir. 973 o 15, 190 p.

O'Hanlon, John, *Irish-American history of the United States*, Bristol: Thoemmes, 2003, NLI 2 v. (798 p.).

Padden, Michael, *May the road rise to meet you: everything you need to know about Irish American history*, New York, NY: Plume, c.1999, NLI Ir. 942 p 21, 332 p. Co-author, Robert Sullivan.

Potter, G., *To the Golden Door: the story of the Irish in Ireland and America*, Boston: Little, Brown, 1960, 631 p. NLI Ir. 973 p 4.

Reynolds, F., *Ireland's Important & Heroic Part…*, Chicago: Daleiden, 322 p., NLI Ir. 973 r 3, Irish in the American Revolution.

Ridge, John T., *Erin's Sons in America*, New York: 1986, NLI Ir. 973 r 7, the Ancient Order of Hibernians.

Roberts, E.F., *Ireland in America*, New York and London: G.P. Putnam's Sons, 1931, NLI Ir. 973 r 2, 218 p.

Rose, Walter R., *A bibliography of the Irish in the United States*, Afton, NY: Tristram Shanty Publications, 1969, LOC, 18 leaves.

Sawyer, Kem Knapp, *Irish Americans*, Carlisle, Massachusetts: Discovery Enterprises, 1998, NLI Ir. 973 i 48, 64 p. Sources.

Seagrave, Pia Seija, *The history of the Irish Brigade: a collection of historical essays*, Fredericksburg, Vancouver: Sergeant Kirkland's Museum and Historical Society, 1997, NLI GR 261, 225 p.

Simons, *Tenants no more* —see 'Australia'.

Spalding, J.L., *The religious mission of the Irish people and Catholic colonization*, New York: Christian Press Association, c.1900, NLI Ir. 942.s18, 339 p.

Tucker, Phillip Thomas, *The history of the Irish Brigade: a collection of historical essays*, Fredericksburg, Vancouver: Sergeant Kirkland's Museum and Historical Society, c.1995, LOC, 223 p.

Wakin, Edward, *Enter the Irish-American*, New York: Crowell, c.1976, NLI Ir. 973 w 9, 189 p.

Walsh, James P., *Ethnic militancy: an Irish Catholic prototype*, San Francisco: R & E Research Associates, 1972, NLI GR 308, 145 p.

Walsh, James D., *The Irish: America's political class*, New York: Arno Press, 1976, NLI Ir. 973 w 8, 350 p.

Wells, Ronald A., *Ulster migration to America: letters from three Irish families*, New York: P. Lang, c.1991, LOC, 170 p. 'Irish studies, vol. 2'.

Werkin, E., *Enter the Irish-American*, New York: Crowell, 1976, 189 p. NLI Ir. 973 w 9.

Williams, Richard, *Hierarchical structures and social value: the creation of Black and Irish identities in the United States*, Cambridge, New York: Cambridge University Press, 1990, LOC, 190 p.

Wilson, David A., *United Irishmen, United States: immigrant radicals in the early republic*, Dublin: Four Courts Press, 1998, NLI Ir. 973 w 21, 223 p.

Wittke, C., *The Irish in America*, Baton Rouge: Louisiana State University Press, 1956, 319 p. NLI Ir. 973 w 2.

Regional

The South

Gleeson, David T., *The Irish in the South, 1815–1877*, Chapel Hill: University of North Carolina Press, 2001, NLI A 2A 1609, 278 p.

McCullough, Eileen, *More than blarney: the Irish influence in Appalachia*, Old Fort, NC: Wolfhound Press, c.1997, LOC, 165 p.

The West

Maume, Patrick, *19th-century Irish and Irish-Americans on the Western frontier*, Ft. Lauderdale, FL: Department of Liberal Arts, Nova Southeastern University, c.2000, LOC, 18 p. Co-author, Marguerite Quintelli-Neary.

Quigly, Hugh, *The Irish Race in California and on the Pacific Coast*, San Francisco: A. Roman & Co., 1878, NLI Ir. 973 q 1, 548 p.

O'Laughlin, M., *Irish settlers on the American frontier*, Kansas City, MO: Irish Genealogical Foundation, 1984, LOC.

Sarbaugh, Timothy J., *The Irish in the West*, Manhattan, Kansas: Sunflower University Press, c.1993, LOC, 116 p. Co-editor, James P. Walsh.

New England

(-) *New England Irish Guide 1987*, Boston, Mass.: Quinlin Campbell Publishers, 1987, NLI Ir. 973 n 6, 171 p. .

(-) *Scotch-Irish Heritage Festival*, Winthrop: 1981, NLI Ir. 942 s 15.

Cahill, Robert Ellis, *The old Irish of New England*, Peabody, MA: Chandler-Smith, c.1985, NLI GR 3019, 48 p.

Johnson, Daniel F., *Irish emigration*—see 'New Brunswick'.

O'Brien, M.J., *Pioneer Irish in New England*, Baltimore, MD: Genealogical Publishing Company, 1998, NLI Ir. 974 o 66, 325 p.

O'Connor, Thomas H., *The Irish in New England*, Boston: New England Historic Genealogical Soc., 1985, NLI Ir. 9292 p 25(5), The Irish in New England/Sources of Irish-American Genealogy/The Kennedys of Massachussetts.

Midwest

Benson, James K., *Irish and German families and the economic development of Midwestern cities, 1860–1895*, New York: Garland, 1990, LOC, 418 p.

Herr, Cheryl Temple, *Critical regionalism and cultural studies: from Ireland to the American Midwest*, Gainesville: University Press of Florida, c.1996, LOC, 233 p.

Wyman, Mark, *Immigrants in the Valley: Irish, Germans, and Americans in the upper Mississippi country, 1830–1860*, Chicago: Nelson-Hall, c.1984, LOC, 258 p.

Arkansas

Rees, J., *A farewell to famine*, Arklow: Arklow Enterprise Centre, 1994, NLI Ir. 94138 r 6, 174 p.

California

Burchell, R.A., *San Francisco Irish, 1848–1880*, Manchester: Manchester University Press, 1979, NLI Ir. 973 b 12, 227 p.

Calhoon, F. D., *49er Irish: one Irish family in the California mines*, Hicksville, NY: Exposition Press, c.1977, LOC, 194 p. McGuire family.

Dillon, Richard H., *Iron men: California's industrial pioneers, Peter, James, and Michael Donahue*, Point Richmond, California: Candela Press, c.1984, LOC, 334 p., San Francisco.

Dowling, Patrick J., *Irish Californians: historic, benevolent, romantic*, San Francisco: Scottwall Associates, 1998, NLI Ir. 973 d 25, 515 p.

Dowling, Patrick J., *California, the Irish dream*, San Francisco, CA: Golden Gate Publishers, 1988, NLI GR 2938, 429 p.

Fox, John, *Macnamara's Irish colony and the United States taking of California in 1846*, Jefferson, NC: McFarland, c.2000, NLI Ir. 973 f 19, 230 p.

Hickey, Anne O'Brien, *Ballroom of romance: the K.R.B. revisited: a collection of memoirs*, San Francisco, CA: California Pub. Co., c.2000, LOC, 306 p. An account of the social life of Irish Americans in San Francisco centered around the K.R.B. (Knights of the Red Branch) Hall, 1133 Mission Street.

Prendergast, T.F., *Forgotten Pioneers: Irish Leaders in Early California*, San Francisco: Trade Pressroom, 1942, NLI Ir. 942 p 13, 278 p.

Sarbaugh, Timothy J., *Post Civil War fever and adjustment: Fenianism in the Californian context, 1858–1872*, Boston, MA: Northeastern University, c.1992, LOC, 30 leaves.

Shaw, Eva, *The sun never sets: the influence of the British on early Southern California: contributions of the English, Irish, Scottish, Welsh, and Canadians*, Irvine, California: Dickens Press, 2001, LOC, 177 p.

Walsh, James P., *The San Francisco Irish, 1850–1976*, San Francisco: The Society, 1978, LOC, 150 p.

Connecticut

Hogan, Neil, *The cry of the famishing: Ireland, Connecticut and the potato famine*, East Haven, Connecticut: Connecticut Irish-American Historical Society, 1998, NLI GR 1736, 201 p.

Hogan, Neil, *The wearin' o' the green: St. Patrick's Day in New Haven, Connecticut, 1842–1992*, [New Haven?], Connecticut Irish-American Historical Society (1992), NLI GR 1758, 234 p.

Stone, Frank Andrews, *Scots & Scotch Irish in Connecticut: a history*, Storrs, CT: University of Connecticut, 1978, NLI Ir. 929 p 5, 69 p.

Stone, Frank Andrews, *The Irish—in their homeland, in America, in Connecticut: a curriculum guide*, Storrs, CT: School of Education, University of Connecticut, c.1975, LOC, 113 p.

Toole, Arthur T., 'Roll of the 2nd Connecticut Volunteer Heavy Infantry 1862–1865', IG, 9, 4 (1997), 530–565.

Delaware

Purcell, R.J., 'Irish Settlers in early Delaware', *Pennsylvania History* (1947), April, NLI Ir. 973 p 2.

Mulrooney, Margaret M., *Black powder, white lace: the du Pont Irish and cultural identity in nineteenth-century America*, Hanover: University Press of New England, c.2002, LOC, 296 p. Brandywine Creek Valley (Pa. and Del.).

Wokeck, Marianne S., 'Family and Servants: Critical Links in the 18th-Century Immigration Chain to the Delaware Valley', *Familia: Ulster Genealogical Review*, No. 18 (2002).

Georgia

(-) *Constitution of the Hibernian Society of the City of Savannah*, 1812, Philadephia: F. McManus, Jr. & Co., 1887, NLI LO p 341, 61 p.

Callahan, Dave, *The Callihans of Fannin County, Georgia, 1843 to 2003*, Leesburg, Vancouver: Dave Callahan, 2003, LOC, 632 p.

Fogarty, William L., *The days we've celebrated: St. Patrick's Day in Savannah*, Savannah: Printcraft Press, c.1980, NLI GR 1746, 206 p.

Illinois

Barry, P.T., *The first Irish in Illinois; reminiscent of old Kaskaskia days*, Chicago: Chicago Newspaper Union, 1902, LOC, 16 p.

Columb, Frank, *Chicago May: queen of the blackmailers*, Cambridge: Evod Academic Publishing Co., 1999, NLI Ir. 92 c 400, 195 p.

Curtin, Paul J., *West Limerick Roots: the Laurence Curtin family of Knockbrack, Co. Limerick*, Austin TX: P.J. Curtin, 1995, NLI Ir. 9292 c 47, 424 p. Christian County (Ill.).

Fanning, Charles, *Mr Dooley and the Chicago Irish*, New York: 1976, NLI Ir. 973 d 10.

Fanning, Charles, *Nineteenth century Chicago Irish: a social and political portrait*, Chicago, Illinois: Center for Urban Policy, Loyola University of Chicago, 1980, LOC, 46 p. Co-authors, Ellen Skerrett and John Corrigan.

Funchion, M.F., *The Irish in Chicago*, Chicago: 1987, NLI Ir. 970 i 15.

Funchion, M.F., *Chicago's Irish Nationalists 1881–1890*, New York: Arno Press, 1976, NLI Ir. 973 f 1, 160 p.

Hilton, Dolores, *Cemetery inscriptions, records, early history, and biographies of St. Patrick's Irish Grove, Rock Run Township, Stephenson County, Illinois*, Pecatonica, Illinois: D. Hilton, c.1981, LOC, 83 p.

Koos, Greg, *Irish immigrants in McLean County, Illinois*, Bloomington, Illinois: McLean County Historical Society, c.2000, LOC, 81 p.

McCaffrey, Lawrence J., *The Irish in Chicago*, Urbana: University of Illinois Press, c.1987, NLI Ir. 970 i 15, 171 p.

McMahon, Eileen M., *What parish are you from? a Chicago Irish community and race relations*, Lexington: University Press of Kentucky, 1995, NLI Ir. 300 m 37, 226 p.

Metress, Seamus P., *The Irish in the Great Lakes region: a bibliographic survey*, Toledo, Ohio: 1990, NLI GRP 47, 52 p. Co-author, Kathleen R. Annable.

Skerrett, Ellen, *At the crossroads: Old Saint Patrick's and the Chicago Irish*, Chicago: Wild Onion Books, c.1997, LOC, 171 p.

Skerrett Ellen, 'The Irish of Chicago's Hull-House neighborhood', in Fanning (ed.), *New perspectives* - see 'USA, General'.

Walsh, James B., 'J.R. Walsh of Chicago', in *The Irish: America's political class*, New York: Arno Press, 1976, NLI Ir. 973 w 8, 350 p.

Wyman—see 'Midwest'.

Indiana

Burr, David, *The Irish War*, Fort Wayne, 1953, LOC, 8 p.

Driscoll, Allen W., *Driscolls and more Driscolls: from County Cork (Ireland) to Township York (Noble County, IN)*, Wawaka, IN: the author, c.1998, LOC, 436 p.

Iowa

Costello, Timon, *Shining emeralds,* Fond du Lac, WI: T. Costello, c.1994, LOC, 302 p., McGalloway family.

Mullaley, Robert C., *History of the Mullaleys: a twelve hundred year journey from County Galway to Iowa,* Los Altos, California: R.C. Mullaley, c.1993, LOC, 214 p.

Naughton, Michael L., *A genealogical history of the Naughton family: from Ireland to Iowa and beyond,* Aurora, Colorado: M.L. Naughton, 1989, NLI GO 593, 108 leaves.

Tierney, Evelyn Sinclair, *But of course they were Irish,* Moravia, Iowa: E. Sinclair Tierney, c.1984, LOC, 491 p. Melrose, Iowa.

Wallace, Gene, *Emeralds of the heartland: a story of Irish Catholic immigrants of the nineteenth century, based on the family history stories of John M. Sheehan,* Santa Paula, California: Wallace Pub., c.1994, LOC, 275 p. Iowa, Adair County.

Ward, Leo R., *Holding up the hills, the biography of a neighborhood,* New York: Sheed & Ward, 1941, LOC, 202 p.

Wyman—see 'Midwest'.

Kansas

Gillespie, LaRoux K., *The Iretons of Kansas and Oklahoma,* Kansas City, MO: Family History and Genealogy Center, c.1985, NLI GO 37, 296 p.

Kentucky

Crews, Clyde F., *Mike Barry and the Kentucky Irish American: an anthology,* Lexington, KY: University Press of Kentucky, c.1995, LOC, 167 p.

Fitzgerald, 'Early Irish Settlers in Kentucky', *Journal of the American-Irish Historical Society,* 2 (1899), 139–44, NLI Ir. 973 a 1.

Kelly, Mary Ann, *My old Kentucky home, good-night,* Hicksville, NY: Exposition Press, c.1979, LOC, 310 p. Ludlow, Kentucky.

Kendall, Margaret M.G., *Irish in the 1850 Mason County, Ky. federal census,* Maysville, KY: M.M.G. Kendall, 1980, LOC, 30 leaves.

Linehan, John C., 'Irish Pioneers and Builders of Kentucky', *Journal of the American-Irish Historical Society,* 3 (1900), 78–88, NLI Ir. 973 a 1.

Louisiana

Finn, John, *New Orleans Irish: famine exiles,* Luling, LA: Holy Family Church, 1997, LOC, 683 p.

Niehaus, E.F., *The Irish in New Orleans 1800–1860,* Baton Rouge: Louisiana State University Press, 1965, NLI Ir. 973 n 3, 194 p.

Walsh, Terence G., *James Joseph Walsh: a chronicle of his life and that of Mary Ann McConochie,* Dallas, TX: T.G. Walsh, 1988, NLI B 2B 535, 89 p. Orleans Parish (La.).

Maine

Mundy, James H., *Hard times, hard men: Maine and the Irish, 1830–1860,* Scarborough, ME: Harp Publications, 1990, NLI Ir. 942 m 12, 209 p.

Thibadeau, W.J., *The Irishman a factor in the development of Houlton: A history of the Parish of St. Mary's, Augusta*, Maine: O'Ceallaigh Publications, 1992, NLI Ir. 970 t 1, 109 p.

Maryland
(-) *A salute to the Maryland Irish: a Bicentennial publication of the Ladies' Auxiliary to the Ancient Order of Hibernians*, Baltimore: Uptown Press, 1976, LOC, 63 p.

Athy Jr, Lawrence F., *Captain George Athy (of Galway and Maryland) and his descendants: a guide to the first six generations of the Athy, Athey, Atha, Athon family in America*, Houston, TX: L.F. Athy, 1987, LOC, 140 p.

Hoffman, Ronald, *Princes of Ireland, planters of Maryland: a Carroll saga, 1500–1782*, Chapel Hill, Virginia: University of North Carolina Press, 2000, NLI Ir. 9292 c 59, 429 p.

Moore-Colyer, Richard, 'The Moores of Londonderry and Baltimore: a Study in Scotch-Irish Eighteenth-Century Emigration', *Familia: Ulster Genealogical Review*, 19 (2003), 11–40.

O'Brien, M.J., 'Irish Pioneers in Maryland', *Journal of the American-Irish Historical Society*, 14 (1915), 207–19, NLI Ir. 973 a 1.

O'Brien, M.J., 'The Irish in Montgomery and Washington Counties, Maryland in 1778', *Journal of the American-Irish Historical Society*, 24 (1925), 157–61, NLI Ir. 973 a 1.

Riley, Robert Shean, *The colonial Riley families of the Tidewater frontier*, Utica, KY: McDowell Publications, c.1999, NLI G 9292 r 23, 2 vols, 'A history of several Riley families of Maryland and Virginia'.

Williams, H.A., *History of the Hibernian Society of Baltimore 1803–1951*, Baltimore: 1951, NLI Ir. 942 w 1.

Massachussetts
Calvary Cemetery, Boston, Mass.: New England Historic Genealogical Society, c.2000, NLI Ir. 9291 p 19, 246 p.

Powers, Vincent Edward, *Invisible immigrants: the pre-famine Irish community in Worcester, Massachusetts, from 1826 to 1860*, New York: Garland Pub., 1989, LOC, 549 p.

Riley, George R., *Reilly to Riley, Galway to Quincy: Book of Rileys*, Boston, Mass.: Recollections Bound, c.1986, NLI GR 659, 342 leaves.

Ryan, D.P., *Beyond the Ballot Box: Boston Irish 1845–1917*, London: 1983, NLI Ir. 973 r 4, 173 p.

Ryan, Michael, *The Irish in Boston*, Boston: Boston 200, c.1975, NLI Ir. 800 p 33, 31 p.

Samito, Christian G., *Commanding Boston's Irish Ninth: the Civil War letters of Colonel Patrick R. Guiney, Ninth Massachusetts Volunteer Infantry*, New York: Fordham University Press, 1998, NLI GR 382, 280 p.

Walsh, Louis S., *The early Irish Catholic schools of Lowell*, Boston: Press of T.A. Whalen & co., 1901, LOC, 20 p.

Wood, S.G., *Ulster Scots & Blandford Scouts*, West Medway, Mass.: Wood, 1928, 438 p. NLI Ir. 973 W 1.

Michigan

Doby, J., *The last full measure of devotion*, Raleigh, NC: Pentland Press, c.1996, NLI GR 2967, 216 p., 15th Michigan Infantry Regiment (1862–1865).

Duncan, Mary Lou Straith, *Passage to America, 1851–1869: the records of Richard Elliott, passenger agent, Detroit, Michigan*, Detroit: Detroit Society for Genealogical Research, 1999, LOC, 194 p.

Marman, Ed, *Modern journeys: the Irish in Detroit*, Detroit: United Irish Societies, 2001, NLI A 2A 973, 237 p.

McGee, John Whalen, *The passing of the Gael: [our Irish ancestors, their history & exodus]*, Grand Rapids: Wolverine Print. Co., c.1975, LOC, 332 p. Kent County.

Metress—see 'Illinois'.

Vinyard, JoEllen, *The Irish on the urban frontier: Nineteenth-century Detroit, 1850–1880*, New York: Arno Press, 1976, NLI Ir. 973 V 1, 446 p.

Minnesota

Campbell, Malcolm, 'A comparative study of Irish rural settlement in nineteenth-century Minnesota and New South Wales', in Bielenberg, *The Irish Diaspora*. See McCracken, in 'Africa'.

Connelly, Bridget, *Forgetting Ireland*, St Paul, MN: Borealis Books, c.2003, LOC, 263 p. Graceville.

Donahue, Deborah Bozell, *The light of the future: the O'Donoghue story*, Ormond Beach, Fla: Donahue Pub., c.2000, LOC, 184 p.

Johnston, Patricia Condon, *Minnesota's Irish*, Afton, Minn: Johnston Pub. Inc., c.1984, NLI GR 1959, 92 p.

Metress—see 'Illinois'.

Regan, Ann, *Irish in Minnesota*, St Paul, MN: Minnesota Historical Society Press, c.2002, NLI B 3B 853, 89 p.

Rogers, Jr, Ralph W., *The Rogers family of Northampton Parish, New Brunswick, and some descendants*, Homosassa, FL: R.W. Rogers, 1989, LOC, 65 p.

Shannon, James P., *Catholic colonization on the western frontier*, New York: Arno Press, 1976, NLI G 2820973 S 1, 302 p.

Smith, Alice E., *The Sweetman Irish colony-*, LOC.

Wingerd, Mary Lethert, *Claiming the city: politics, faith, and the power of place in St. Paul*, Ithaca: Cornell University Press, 2001, LOC, 326 p. (20th century).

Wyman—see 'The Midwest'.

Missouri

(-), 'Passenger list of Ticonderoga', 1850 (New Wexford, Missouri), *The Past (Journal of the Ui Cinsealaigh Historical Society)*, 12 (1978), 49–52, NLI Ir. 941382 p 1.

Cochran, Alice Lida, *The saga of an Irish immigrant family: the descendants of John Mullanphy*, New York: Arno Press, 1976, NLI Ir. 973 C 12, 270 p. St Louis.

Faherty, William B., *The St. Louis Irish: an unmatched Celtic community*, Saint Louis, Missouri: Historical Society Press, c.2001, NLI A 3A 467, 270 p.

O'Leary, Cornelius F., 'The Irish in the Early Days of St Louis', *Journal of the American-Irish Historical Society*, 9 (1910), 206–13, NLI Ir. 973 a 1.

O'Neill, Pat, *From the bottom up: the story of the Irish in Kansas City*, Kansas City, MO: Seat O' The Pants Pub., c.2000, LOC, 244 p.

Montana

Emmons, David A., *The Butte Irish: an American Mining Town 1875–1925*, Chicago: University of Illinois Press, 1998, NLI Ir. 942 e 8, 443 p.

Sullivan, Mary Connelly, *A Montana saga: "our yesterdays"*, Great Falls, Montana: H.S. Pannell, c.1984, LOC, 112 p., "with Helena Sullivan Pannell's story".

Nebraska

DeVries, Ellen M., *Irish and Scotch-Irish who made a declaration of intention to naturalize from Cass, Douglas, Lancaster, Nemaha, Otoe, Richardson, Sarpy, and York counties in Nebraska, 1855–1940+*, Lincoln, Nebraska: Nebraskans of Irish and Scotch-Irish Ancestry, c.1997, LOC, 152 p. Co-author, Raymond D. De Vries.

New Hampshire

Brennan, James F., *The Irish settlers of southern New Hampshire*, Peterborough?: 1910, LOC 11 p.

O'Brien, M.J., *Irish pioneers in New Hampshire, Historical papers: reprinted from The Journal of the American Irish Historical Society* (1926), NLI GR 2240, Vol. xxv.

New Jersey

Quinn, Dermot, *The Irish in New Jersey: four centuries of American life*, New Brunswick, NJ: Rutgers University Press, c.2004, 226 p. NLI.

Shaw, Douglas V., *The making of an immigrant city: ethnic and cultural conflict in Jersey City, New Jersey, 1850–1877*, New York: Arno Press, 1976, NLI G 32373 s 8, 273 p.

New York

New York Irish History Roundtable: newsletter (Spring 1998), NLI Ir. 970 n 14.

New York Irish History: Journal of the New York Irish History Roundtable, New York, New York: 1986–, NLI Ir. 973 n 13.

Emigrant Savings Bank Records (New York), New York: New York Public Library, NLI Pos. 9179–87, 1850–1877. Indexed, 9 microfilm reels. See Rich, below. Also DCLA.

Almeida, Linda Dowling, *Irish immigrants in New York City, 1945–1995*, Bloomington: Indiana University Press, c.2001, NLI GR 2832, 211 p.

Bannan, Theresa, *Pioneer Irish of Onondaga (about 1776–1847)*, New York and London: G.P. Putnam's sons, 1911, NLI Ir. 971 b 2, 333 p.

Bayor, Ronald H., *Neighbors in conflict: the Irish, Germans, Jews, and Italians of New York City, 1929–1941*, Baltimore: Johns Hopkins University Press, c.1978, NLI c.1978, 232 p.

Bayor, Ronald H., *The New York Irish*, Baltimore and London: Johns Hopkins University Press, 1996, NLI Ir. 937 n 2, 743 p. Co-editor, Timothy J. Meagher.

Beadles, John Asa, *The Syracuse Irish, 1812–1928: immigration, Catholicism, socio-economic status, politics, and Irish nationalism*, Syracuse, NY: Beadles, 1974, NLI Pos. 8719, 501 leaves.

Bennett, Brian A., *The beau ideal of a soldier and a gentleman: the life of Col. Patrick Henry O'Rorke from Ireland to Gettysburg*, Wheatland, NY: Triphammer Pub., c.1996, LOC, 196 p. Rochester, NY.

Bigelow, Bruce, *Ethnic separation in a pedestrian city: a social geography of Syracuse, New York in 1860*, Syracuse, NY: Dept. of Geography, Syracuse University, 1987, LOC.

Bilby, Joseph G., *Remember Fontenoy!: the 69th New York and the Irish Brigade in the Civil War*, Hightstown, NJ: Longstreet House, 1997, NLI GR 1478, 270 p. Irish in the Army of the Potomac.

Buckley, John Patrick, *The New York Irish, their view of American foreign policy, 1914–1921*, New York: Arno Press, 1976, NLI G 327973 b 9, 395 p.

Carmack, Sharon DeBartolo, *My wild Irish rose: the life of Rose (Norris) (O'Connor) Fitzhugh and her mother Delia (Gordon) Norris*, Boston, MA: Newbury Street Press, 2001, LOC, 84 p.; 'a study in the lives of Irish immigrant women in America with a summary of matrilineal generations'.

Dolan, Jay P., *The immigrant church: New York's Irish and German Catholics, 1815–1865*, Baltimore: Johns Hopkins University Press, 1975, NLI G 2820973 d 1, 221 p.

Dunkak, Harry M., *Freedom, culture, labor: the Irish of early Westchester County, New York*, New Rochelle, NY: Iona College Press, 1994, NLI GR 1737, 145 p.

English, T. J., *The Westies: inside the Hell's Kitchen Irish mob*, New York: Putnam, 1990, NLI GR 1927, 384 p.

Gibson, Florence Elizabeth, *The attitudes of the New York Irish toward state and national affairs, 1848–1892*, New York: Columbia University Press, 1951, LOC 480 p.

Glasco, Laurence Admiral, *Ethnicity and social structure: Irish, Germans, and native-born of Buffalo, N.Y., 1850–*, New York: Arno Press, 1980, LOC, 366 p.

Gordon, Michael A., *The Orange riots: Irish political violence in New York City, 1870 and 1871*, Ithaca: London, Cornell University Press, 1993, NLI Ir. 942 g 21, 263 p.

Henderson, Thomas M., *Tammany Hall and the new immigrants: the progressive years*, New York: Arno Press, 1976, NLI Ir. 973 h 12, 314 p.

Lizzi, Dominick C., *Governor Martin H. Glynn: forgotten hero*, Valatie, NY: Valatie Press, c.1994, LOC, 122 p.

Mann, A.P., 'The Irish in New York in the Early 1860s', *Irish Historical Studies*, 7 (1950), 87–108.

McDonald, Brian, *My father's gun: one family, three badges, one hundred years in the NYPD*, New York: Dutton, 1999, LOC, 309 p.

O'Brien, M.J., *In Old New York: Irish Dead in Trinity & St Paul's Churchyards*, New York: 1928, NLI Ir. 973 o 8.

Raghallaigh, Eibhilín, *St Paul's Roman Catholic Church, Brooklyn, New York: the Irish parish. Baptism and marriage registers, 6 September 1857–30 December 1900*, Floral Park, NY: Delia Publications, LLC, 2001, LOC, 440 leaves.

Raghallaigh, Eibhilín, *St Paul's Roman Catholic Church, Court Street, Brooklyn, New York. Baptism register July 22, 1839–July 12, 1857; marriage register August 7, 1839–August 18, 1857*, Salt Lake City: Redmond Press, 1996, LOC, 282 p.

Rich, Kevin J., *Irish immigrants of the Emigrant Industrial Savings Bank. Vol. I, 1850–1853*, New York: Broadway-Manhattan Co., 2001?, NLI B 3B 1134, 285 p.

Ridge, John T., *Sligo in New York: the Irish from County Sligo, 1849–1991*, New York: County Sligo Social & Benevolent Association, c.1991, NLI Ir. 947 r 21, 157 p.

Ridge, John T., *The Flatbush Irish*, Brooklyn, NY: Division 35 Ancient Order of Hibernians, c.1983, NLI 3B 900, 44 p.

Ridge, John T., *The St. Patrick's Day Parade in New York*, New York: Patrick's Day Parade Committee, 1988, NLI Ir. 973 r 12, 204 p.

Rowley, William E., 'The Irish Aristocracy of Albany, 1798–1878', *New York History*, 52 (1971), 275–304.

Ruddock, George, *Linen threads and broom twines: an Irish and American album and directory of the people of the Dunbarton Mill, Greenwich, New York, 1879–1952*, Bowie, Md: Heritage Books, 1997, NLI Ir. 9292 r 27, 2 vols.

Shea, Ann M., *The Irish experience in New York City: a select bibliography*, New York, New York: Irish History Roundtable, c.1995, NLI 130 p. Co-author, Marion R. Casey.

Silinonte, Joseph M., *Tombstones of the Irish born: cemetery of the Holy Cross, Flatbush, Brooklyn*, Bowie, Md: Heritage Books, 1994, NLI Ir. 9292 s 29, 112 p.

Smith, Dennis, *A song for Mary: an Irish-American memory*, New York: Warner Books, 1999, NLI GR 2466, 369 p.

Stevenson, Lenore Blake, *From Cavan to the Catskills: an informal history of the Conerty, Finigan and Smith families of upstate New York*, Baltimore: Gateway Press, 1989, NLI GR 2767, 230 p.

Toole, Arthur T., 'Roll of the 10th NY Volunteer Infantry, 1861–1865', *IG*, 9, 2 (1995), 238–281.

Trimble, Richard M., *Brothers 'til death: the Civil War letters of William, Thomas, and Maggie Jones, 1861-1865: Irish soldiers in the 48th New York volunteer regiment*, Macon, GA: Mercer University Press, 2000, LOC, 173 p.

Waters, Maureen, *Crossing Highbridge: a memoir of Irish America*, Syracuse, NY: Syracuse University Press, 2001, NLI 2A 192, 149 p.

North Carolina

[-], 'Irish Builders in North Carolina', *Journal of the American-Irish Historical Society*, 10 (1911), 258–61, NLI Ir. 973 a 1.

Deans, Frances Lynch, *The Lynches, from Ireland to eastern North Carolina: in the counties of Craven, Johnston, Bobbs, Wayne,* Goldsboro, NC: F.L. Deans, c.1989, LOC, 577 p.

McGinn, Brian, 'The Irish on Roanoake Island', *IR*, 3 (1993), 21, NLI.

O'Brien, M.J., 'North Carolina. Some Early MacCarthys, McGuires, [...]', *Journal of the American-Irish Historical Society,* 12 (1913) 161–67, NLI Ir. 973 a 1.

Ohio

Callahan, Nelson J., *Irish-Americans and their Communities of Cleveland,* Cleveland: Cleveland State University, 1978, NLI Ir. 942 c 23, 254 p.

Wolf, Donna M., *The Irish in central Ohio: baptisms and marriages, 1852–1861, St. Patrick Roman Catholic Church, Columbus, Ohio,* Columbus, Ohio: D.M. Wolf, 1991?, LOC, 71 p.

Wolf, Donna M., *Irish immigrants in nineteenth century Ohio: naturalizations: selected years,* Apollo, PA: Closson Press, 1999, LOC, 166 p.

Wolf, Donna M., *Irish immigrants in nineteenth century Ohio: a database,* Apollo, PA: Closson Press, c.1998, LOC, 216 p.

Oklahoma

Blessing, Patrick J., *The British and Irish in Oklahoma,* Norman: University of Oklahoma Press, c.1980, NLI GR 1748, 57 p.

Gillespie—see 'Kansas'.

Oregon

(-) 'The Irish of Morrow County, Oregon', *Historical Quarterly* (June 1968).

Ó Longaigh, David, *We Irish in Oregon: a historical account of the Irish in Oregon from the pioneer times to the present day,* Portland, Oregon: All-Ireland Cultural Society of Oregon, 1998, NLI Ir. 942 w 22, 103 p.

Pennsylvania

List of members of the Hibernian Society for the Relief of Emigrants from Ireland, together with the list of members of the Friendly Sons of St Patrick, 1771–1884, Philadelphia, Pub. by Authority of the Society, 1884, NLI GR 2945, 42 p.

Adams, E. & O'Keeffe, B.B., *Catholic Trails West: The Founding Catholic Families of Pennsylvania,* Baltimore: Genealogical Publishing Company, 1988, Vol. 1, St Joseph's Church, Philadelphia.

Armor, William C., *Scotch-Irish Bibliography of Pennsylvania,* Nashville: Barbee & Smith, 1896.

Brauer, Carl M., *The man who built Washington: a life of John McShain,* Wilmington, Delaware: Hagley Museum and Library, c.1996, NLI Ir. 92 m 582, 298 p.

Burstein, Alan Nathan, *Residential distribution and mobility of Irish and German immigrants in Philadelphia, 1850–1880,* 1975, NLI Pos. 7838, microfilm, 355 leaves.

Campbell, John H., *History of the Friendly Sons of St. Patrick and of the Hibernian Society for the Relief of Emigrants from Ireland: March 17, 1771–March 17, 1892*, Philadelphia: Hibernian Society, 1892, NLI Ir. 973 c 1, 570 p.

Chambers, George, *A tribute to the principles, virtues, habits and public usefulness of the Irish and Scotch early settlers of Pennsylvania / by a descendant.*, Chambersburg, PA: printed by M. Kieffer & Co., 1856, LOC, 171 p.

Clark, Dennis, *The Irish relations: trials of an immigrant tradition*, Rutherford: Fairleigh Dickinson University Press, 1982, NLI Ir. 973 c 26, Irish-Americans in Philadelphia, 255 p.

Clark, Dennis, *The Irish in Philadelphia: ten generations of urban experience*, Philadelphia: Temple University Press, 1973, NLI Ir. 973 c 11, 246 p.

Clark, Dennis, *Erin's heirs: Irish bonds of community*, Lexington, KY: University Press of Kentucky, c.1991, LOC, 238 p. Irish American families in Philadelphia.

Clark, Dennis, *The Irish in Pennsylvania: a people share a commonwealth*, University Park: Pennsylvania Historical Association, 1991, NLI GR 3017, 56 p.

Clark, Dennis, *A history of the Society of the Friendly Sons of St. Patrick for the Relief of Emigrants from Ireland in Philadelphia, 1951–1981*, Philadelphia: The Society, c.1982, NLI Ir. 973 c 22.

Coleman, J. Walter, *The Molly Maguire riots industrial conflict in the Pennsylvania coal region*, Richmond, VA: Garrett & Massie, 1936, NLI Ir. 3318.c.49, 189 p.

Cummings, H.M., *Scots Breed*, Pittsburgh: 1964, NLI Ir. 942 c 17 (Scotch-Irish in Pennsylvania).

Dougherty, Daniel J., *History of the Society of the Friendly Sons of St. Patrick for the Relief of Emigrants from Ireland of Philadelphia: March 17, 1771–March 17, 1892*, Philadelphia: Friendly Sons of St Patrick, 1952, NLI Ir. 973 c 24 448 p.

Dunaway, W., *Scotch-Irish of Colonial Pennsylvania*, Baltimore: Genealogical Publishing Company, 1985, NLI Ir. 974 d 16.

Gallman, J. Matthew, *Receiving Erin's children: Philadelphia, Liverpool, and the Irish famine migration, 1845–1855*, Chapel Hill: University of North Carolina Press, c.2000, NLI, 306 p.

Gudelunas Jr, William A., *Before the Molly Maguires: the emergence of the ethno-religious factor in the politics of the lower anthracite region, 1844–1872*, New York: Arno Press, 1976, NLI Ir. 973 g 7. Co-author, William G. Shade. 165 p. Schuylkill County.

Hackett, Dominic J., 'Philadelphia Irish', *Journal of the American-Irish Historical Society*, 30 (1932), 103–17, NLI Ir. 973 a 1.

Hood, Samuel, *A brief account of the Society of the friendly sons of St. Patrick*, Philadelphia: By order of the Hibernian society, 1844, LOC, 112 p.

Kenny, Kevin, *Making sense of the Molly Maguires*, New York and Oxford: Oxford University Press, 1998, NLI Ir. 300 k 16, 336 p.

Laughlin, Ledlie Irwin, *Joseph Ledlie and William Moody, early Pittsburgh residents: their background and some of their descendants*, Pittsburgh: University of Pittsburgh Press, 1961, NLI GO 147, 208 p.

Light, Dale B., *Class, ethnicity, and the urban ecology in a nineteenth-century city:*

Philadelphia's Irish, 1840–1890, 1979, NLI Fiche 199(3), Microfiche. 246 leaves.

Lynott, William J., *The Lynotts of Ireland and Scranton the story of Peter Lynott and his descendants,* Scranton: William J. Lynott, 1996, NLI Ir. 9292 L 23, 43 p.

Mahony, M.E., *Fág an bealach: the Irish contribution to America and in particular to Western Pennsylvania,* Pittsburgh: United Irish Societies Bicentennial Committee of Western Pennsylvania, 1977, NLI Ir. 973 m 16, 132 p. Allegheny and Washington counties.

McMaster, Richard K., 'James Fullton: A Philadelphia Merchant and his Customers', *Familia: Ulster Genealogical Review,* No. 17 (2001), 23–4.

Mulholland, St Clair A., *The story of the 116th regiment Pennsylvania Volunteers in the War of the Rebellion,* New York: Fordham University Press, 1996, NLI G 9737 m 11, edited, with an introduction by Lawrence Frederick Kohl [480 p.].

Mulrooney—see 'Delaware'.

O'Brien, M.J. 'Irish Pioneers in Berks County, Pennsylvania', *Journal of the American-Irish Historical Society,* 27 (1928), 39–45, NLI Ir. 973 a 1.

Searight, James A., *A record of the Searight family,* Uniontown, Penn: 1893, NLI LO 5287, 'Londonderry, ... to Lancaster County, Pennsylvania, about 1740' [228 p.].

Silcox, Harry C., *Philadelphia politics from the bottom up: the life of Irishman William McMullen, 1824–1901,* London and Cranbury, NJ: Associated University Presses, c.1989, NLI GR 2249, 175 p.

Rhode Island

(-) 'A Seed Drops on a Distant Land: The Emigration of Patrick McMahon', *IG,* 9, No. 2 (1995), 188–94.

Conley, Patrick T., *The Irish in Rhode Island: a historical appreciation,* Providence: Rhode Island Heritage Commission: Rhode Island Publications Society, 1986, NLI GRP 87, 46 p.

McCarron, E.T., 'Altered states: Tyrone migration to Providence, Rhode Island during the nineteenth century', *Clogher Record,* Vol. 16, No. 1 (1997), 145–161.

McMahon, Timothy E., *The McMahon chronicles: the story of an Irish-American family in Rhode Island, 1870–1995,* Pawtucket, RI: Taurus House Publications, 1995, LOC, 88 p.

Murray, Thomas Hamilton, *The Irish vanguard of Rhode Island,* Boston: 1904, LOC, 27 p.

South Carolina

Motes, Margaret Peckham, *Irish Found in South Carolina—1850 Census,* Baltimore: GPC, 2003, LOC, 209 pp.

O'Brien, M.J., 'The Irish in Charleston, South Carolina', *Historical papers: reprinted from The Journal of the American Irish Historical Society* (1926), NLI GR 2240, Vol. xxv.

O'Brien, M.J., 'Lymerick Plantation', Berkeley County, South Carolina, *Historical papers: reprinted from The Journal of the American Irish Historical Society* (1926), NLI GR 2240, Vol. xxv.

O'Connor, M.P., *The life and letters of M. P. O'Connor*, New York: Dempsey & Carroll, 1893, LOC, 561 p.

Stephenson, Jean, *Scotch-Irish Migration to South Carolina*, Strasburg, VA: the author, 1971. Includes methodology on connecting families in South Carolina and Ireland using newspapers, records and other sources.

South Dakota

Kemp, David, *The Irish in Dakota*, Sioux Falls, SD: Mariah Press, 1995, NLI GR 2555, 158 p.

McDonald, Bill, *The Nunda Irish, a story of Irish immigrants: the joys and sorrows of their life in America and Dakota*, Stillwater, Minn: Farmstead Publishing, 1990, NLI Ir. 942 m 41, 237 p.

Tennessee

Gleeson, Ed, *Rebel sons of Erin: a Civil War unit history of the Tenth Tennessee Infantry Regiment (Irish) Confederate States volunteers*, Indianapolis, IN: Guild Press of Indiana, c.1993, LOC, 429 p.

Gleeson, Ed, 'Tennessee Irishmen in Confederate service', in, D. O'Hearn (ed.), *Erin Go Bragh—Advance Australia Fair*, Melbourne: Celtic Club, 1990, 86 p. History of the Celtic Club, Melbourne.

Taylor, Carol Sue, *The arrow & the shillelagh*, Knoxville, TN: Tennessee Valley Pub., c.1996, LOC, 74 p. Edward Henry & Jeanette McCarthy.

Texas

Davis—see 'Mexico'.

Flannery, J.B., *The Irish Texans*, San Antonio: University of Texas, Institute of Texan Cultures at San Antonio, 1980, NLI Ir. 973 f 4, 173 p.

Hébert, Rachel Bluntzer, *The forgotten colony: San Patricio de Hibernia: the history, the people, and the legends of the Irish colony of McMullen-McGloin*, Burnet, TX: Eakin Press, c.1981, NLI GR 1383, 459 p.

Linehan, John C., 'The Irish Pioneers of Texas', *Journal of the American-Irish Historical Society*, 2 (1899), 120–38, NLI Ir. 973 a 1.

Oberste, W.H., *Texas Irish empresarios and their colonies: Power & Hewetson, McMullen & McGloin. Refugio–San Patricio*, Austin: Von Boeckmann-Jones Co., 1953, NLI Ir. 973 o 10, 310 p.

Oberste, W.H., *Knights of Columbus in Texas, 1902–1952*, Austin: Von Boeckmann-Jones Co., 1952, LOC, 298 p.

Rice, Bernardine, 'The Irish in Texas', *Journal of the American-Irish Historical Society*, 30 (1932), 60–70, NLI Ir. 973 a 1.

Roche, Richard, *The Texas connection [the story of the Wexford colony in Refugio]*, Wexford: Wexford Heritage Committee, 1989, NLI Ir. 942 r 10, 59 p.

Santiago, Mark, *The red captain: the life of Hugo O'Conor, commandant inspector of the interior provinces of New Spain*, Tucson, Arizona: Arizona Historical Society, 1994, NLI A 2A 217, 127 p.

Vermont

Murphy, Ronald Chase, *Irish famine immigrants in the state of Vermont: gravestone inscriptions,* Baltimore, Md.: Clearfield, c.2000, LOC, 723 p. Co-author, Janice Church Murphy.

Virginia

[-], 'Grantees of Land in Virginia', *Journal of the American-Irish Historical Society,* 13, NLI Ir. 973 a 1.

[-], 'Irish Settlers on the Opequan', *Journal of the American-Irish Historical Society,* 6 (1906), 71–4, NLI Ir. 973 a 1.

Chalkey, Lyman, *The Scotch-Irish Settlement in Virginia* (Vols 1–3), Baltimore: Genealogical Publishing Company, 1989, Reprint. Exhaustive compendium.

Jamieson, Jean, *Jamieson and O'Callaghan ancestors,* United States,—1978, LOC, 124 p.

Lawless, Joseph T., 'Some Irish Settlers in Virginia', *Journal of the American-Irish Historical Society,* 2 (1899), 161–66, NLI Ir. 973 a 1.

Linehan, John C., 'Early Irish Settlements in Virginia', *Journal of the American-Irish Historical Society,* 4 (1904), 30–42, NLI Ir. 973 a 1.

McGinn, Brian, 'Virginia's Lost Irish Colonists', *IR,* No. 4 (1994), 21–24, NLI.

O'Brien, M.J., 'Pioneer Irish families in Virginia, the Meades and Sullivans', *Historical papers: reprinted from The Journal of the American Irish Historical Society* (1926), NLI GR 2240, Vol. xxv.

O'Grady, Kelly J., *Clear the Confederate way!: the Irish in the army of Northern Virginia,* Mason City, IA: Savas, c.2000, NLI, 348 p.

Riley, Robert Shean, *The colonial Riley families of the Tidewater frontier,* Utica, KY: McDowell Publications, c.1999, NLI, G 9292 r 23, 2 vols, 'A history of several Riley families of Maryland and Virginia'.

West Virginia

Cook, Samuel R., *Monacans and miners: Native American and coal mining communities in Appalachia,* Lincoln: University of Nebraska Press, c.2000, LOC, 329 p. Wyoming county.

Maloney, Charles R., *Devoted to Sunday: the meaning of the name Maloney: a West Virginia genealogy,* Charleston, W. VA: C.R. Maloney, 1988, LOC, 127 leaves.

Wisconsin

Irish genealogical quarterly, Irish Genealogical Society of Wisconsin, NLI 1K 120.

Barlow, Carol Doran, *Descendants of the Walsh-Dorans of Ireland and Rock County, Wisconsin,* Roseville, California: Roseville Printing Co., c.2000, LOC, 315 p.

Barlow, Carol Doran, *Chronicles of the Smith-Crowleys of Ireland and Iowa County, Wisconsin,* Roseville, California: Roseville Printing Co., 1999, LOC.

Beaudot, William J.K., *An Irishman in the Iron Brigade the civil war memoirs of James P. Sullivan, Sergt., company K, 6th Wisconsin volunteers,* New York: Fordham University Press, 1993, NLI GR 1694, 189 p. Co-editor, Lance J. Herdegen.

Childs, Blanche Reardon, *A Reardon family history,* Evanston: the author, 1991, NLI
    Ir. 9292 r 16. Tipperary to St Croix, Wisconsin.

Conzen, Kathleen Neils, *Immigrant Milwaukee, 1836–1860: accommodation and
    community in a frontier city,* Cambridge, MA: Harvard University Press, 1976,
    NLI G 977 c 18, 300 p.

Costello, Timon, *Shining emeralds*—see 'Iowa'.

Costello, Timon, *Transplanted Shamrocks: the story of Daniel and Ann Claugher
    Costello coming to Byron, Wisconsin from County Sligo, Ireland in 1859,*
    Appleton, Wis: St Patrick Press, c.1989, LOC, 265 p.

Gorman, Elizabeth Joyce, *Edmund and Elizabeth (Patterson) Greany and their
    descendants from Ireland, 1848, to Wisconsin, 1856,* Janesville, Wis: J. Gorman,
    1989, LOC, 1989, 128 p.

Holmes, David G., *Irish in Wisconsin,* Madison: Wisconsin Historical Society
    Press, 2004, LOC, 86 p.

Kennedy, Genieve C., *The descendants of Charles Flynn and Margaret Faherty,
    County Longford, Ireland, and Crawford County, Wisconsin, 1850–1998,* Chula
    Vista, California: G.C. Kennedy, 1998, LOC, 239 p.

Kinney, Thomas P., *Irish settlers of Fitchburg, Wisconsin 1840–1860,* Fitchburg:
    Fitchburg Historical Society, 1993, NLI Ir. 942 k 10, 111 p.

MacDonald, M. Justille, *History of the Irish in Wisconsin in the Nineteenth Century,*
    Washington: Holic University of America Press, 1954, NLI Ir. 973 m 9, 324 p.

Metress—see 'Illinois'.

Michaels, Bernard L., *A bit of the old sod: the account of the Byron-Lima settlement,*
    Wisconsin, BL: Michaels, c.1999, LOC, 163 p.

Ryan, Carol Ward, *Descendants of two Irish families: Ryan and Moore, from Ireland
    to Wisconsin, 1780's–1979,* Green Bay, Wis: C.W. Ryan, 1979, LOC, 162 p.

Sheahan, Thomas J., *All those folks from Saint Patrick's: the Irish community of
    rural Maple Grove, Wisconsin,* Reedsville, WI: Friends of St Patrick's, c.2001,
    LOC, 125 p.

Thibaudeau, May Murphy, *I shall not die, I shall live on in you,* South Milwaukee,
    Wis: Ramur Pub., c.1990, LOC, 167 p. Calvy and Green families.

U'Ren, William, *The Albany vindicator index: Green Co., WI, 1911–1925,* Wisconsin:
    Rock Co. Genealogical Society, 2000, LOC.

Wyoming
Ward, Harry Arundel, *Register: the story of Casper's Irish colony,* Illinois: Bantry
    Publications, 2002, NLI A 2A 2777 and online at *www.geocities.com/reenacoppal.*

WEST INDIES

General

Coldham, Peter Wilson, *The Complete Book of Emigrants in Bondage, 1614–1775*, GPC, 1988 (& supplements) 600 p. NLI Ir. 973 c 47.

Gwynn, A., 'Documents relating to the Irish in the West Indies, with accounts of Irish Settlements, 1612–1752', *AH*, Vol. 4, 140–286.

Kirby, Peadar, *Ireland and Latin America*, Dublin: Trocaire, Gill and Macmillan, 1992, NLI.

MacInery, M.H., *Irish slaves in the West Indies*, Dublin: Sealy, Bryers & Walker, 1909, NLI Ir. 3269 m 1, 52 p.

Oliver, Vere Langford, *Caribbeana: Miscellaneous Papers Relating to the History, Topograhy, Genealogy and Antiquities of the British West Indies*, London: 1900–1919, NLI 9729 o 1, 6 vols.

Oliver, Vere Langford, *The Monumental inscriptions in the churches and church-yards of the island of Barbados, British West Indies*, London: Mitchell Hughes and Clarke, 1915, BL, Repr. 1988 by Sidewinder Press, Glendale, California.

Antigua

Oliver, Vere Langford, *The History of the island of Antigua ... from the first settlement in 1635 to the present time*, London: Mitchell and Hughes, 1894–1899, BL, 3 vols.

Barbados

O'Callaghan, Sean, *To Hell or Barbados: The Ethnic Cleansing of Ireland*, Dingle: Brandon Books, 2000, NLI, 240 p.

Williams, Joseph J., *Whence the "black Irish" of Jamaica?*, New York: L. MacVeagh, Dial Press Inc., 1932, NLI Ir. 94106 w 3, 97 p.

Jamaica

Williams—see 'Barbados'.

Martinique

Clark de Dromentin—see 'France, Bordeaux'.

Montserrat

Akenson, D.H., *If the Irish ran the world: Montserrat, 1630–1730*, Liverpool: Liverpool University Press, 1997, NLI Ir. 94106 a 5, 372 p.

McGinn, Brian, 'How Irish is Monserrat?', *IR*, Nos. 1 & 2, 1994, 21–3; 15–17, NLI.

Clancy, Mary, *The Emigrant Experience*—see 'Great Britain, General'.

SOUTH AMERICA

General

Cayol, Rafael, *El Baron de Ballenary*, Buenos Aires: 1989, Ambrose O'Higgins.

de Courcy Ireland, John, 'Irish Soldiers and Seamen in Latin America', *IS*, Vol. 1, No. 4 (1952–3), 296–303.

Kirby, Peadar, *Ireland and Latin America*, Dublin: Trocaire, Gill and Macmillan, 1992, NLI.

Lambert, Eric, *Voluntarios Britanicos e Irlandeses en la Gesta Bolivariana*, Caracas: Dirección de Artes Graficas del Ministerio de la Defensa, 1993, NLI Ir. 942 L 14, 3 vols.

Lambert, Eric, 'Irish soldiers in South America, 1818–1830', *IS*, XVI, No. 62 (Summer 1984), pp. 22–35.

MacErlean, John, 'Irish Jesuits in Foreign Missions from 1574 to 1773', *The Irish Jesuit directory and year book* (1930), 127–138, NLI Ir. 2715 i 1.

MacLoughlin, Guillermo, 'The Irish in South America', in M.D. Evans (ed.), *Aspects of Irish Genealogy: proceedings of the ... Irish Genealogical Congress*, pp. 170–177, Dublin: Irish Genealogical Congress Committee, 1993, NLI Ir. 9291 a 3. Co-editor, Eileen Ó Dúill.

Marshall, Oliver, *European Immigration and Ethnicity in Latin America: A Bibliography*, London: Institute of Latin American Studies, 1991.

McGinn, Brian, 'The South American Irish', *IR*, Nos. 25–28, 1998, NLI.

Mulhall, Marion MacMurrough, 'Erin in South America', *The Irish Rosary*, Vol. XII, No. 11 (November 1908), 810–819, NLI Ir. 05 i 21.

Mulhall, Michael G., *The English in South America*, Buenos Aires: Standard Office, 1878, LOC, F2239.B8 M9 1977, Reprint New York: Arno Press, 1977.

Read, Jan, *The New Conquistadors*, London: Evans Brothers Limited, 1980. Foreign officers in South America.

Ready, William B., 'The Irish and South America', *Éire-Ireland; a journal of Irish studies*, Vol. 1, No. 1 (1966), 50–63.

Vicuna Mackenna, Benjamin, *Vida del General D. Juan Mackenna*, Santiago: Imprenta del Ferrocarrill, 1856.

Vila, Manuel Perez, *Vida de Daniel Florencio O'Leary: Primer Edecan del Libertador*, Caracas: Imprenta Nacional, 1957, LOC, F2235.5.O5 P4, 619 p.

Williams, W. J., 'Bolivar and his Irish Legionaires', *Studies: an Irish quarterly review*, Vol. 18 (1929), 619–632, NLI Ir. 05 s 7.

Argentina

The Southern Cross, Buenos Aires, 1875–

(-) 'The Lynch family of Argentina', *IR*, No. 2, 1993, 11–14, NLI.

Belgrano, Mario, *Repatriacion de los restos del general Juan O'Brien, Guerrero de la Independencia Sud Americana*, Buenos Aires: Guillermo Kraft Ltda, 1938.

Brabazon, John, *Andanzas de un Irlandés en el Campo Porteño (1845–1864)*, Buenos Aires: Ediciones Culturales Argentinas, Secretaria de Estado de Cultura, 1981,

NLI GO 441, 207 p. Traducción del inglés de Eduardo A. Coghlan, con notas del autor y del traductor.

Brown, Guillermo, *Memorias del Almirante Brown*, Buenos Aires: Academia Nacional de la Historia, 1957.

Bulfin, William, *Rambles in Eirinn*, London: Sphere, 1981, NLI Ir. 9141 b 128, 2 vols (repr.).

Coghlan, Eduardo, *Los Irlandeses en Argentina*, Buenos Aires: 1987, NLI LO 5273, 963 p.

Coghlan, Eduardo, *El Aporte de los Irlandeses a la formacion de la nacion Argentina*, Buenos Aires: Libreria Alberto Casares, 1982.

de Courcy Ireland, John, 'Admiral William Brown', *IS*, Vol. VI, No. 23 (1962), 119–121.

de Courcy Ireland, John, *The admiral from Mayo: a life of Almirante William Brown of Foxford,...*, Dublin: E. Burke, c.1995, NLI Ir. 92 b 472. 159 p.

Fleming de Cornejo, Margarita, *Detrás de los retratos, Salta*, Argentina: M. Fleming de Cornejo, 2000, LOC, 259 p. Fleming family.

Gaynor, John, *The History of St. Patrick's College in Mercedes*, Buenos Aires: The Southern Cross, 1958.

Graham-Yooll, Andrew, *The Forgotten Colony: A History of the English Speaking Communities in Argentina*, London: Hutchinson, 1981, NLI G 982 g 3, 317 p.

Gwynn, A., 'The First Irish Priests in the New World', *Studies: an Irish quarterly review*, Vol. XXI, No. 82 (June 1932), 213–228, NLI Ir. 05 s 7.

Harrington, Isabel H., *Un criollo irlandes*, Buenos Aires: 1976, LOC, 99 p. Life of Alfredo Harrington, Argentinian polo player.

Hayes, Séan S., 'Hurling in Argentina', *A Century of Service*, pp. 80–82, Dublin: Cumann Luthchleas Gael, 1984, NLI Ir. 396 g 18.

Julianello, Maria Theresa, 'The Story of Camilla O'Gorman', *IR*, No. 3 (1996), pp. 18–19, NLI.

King, Seamus J., 'Hurling in Argentina', in *The Clash of the Ash in Foreign Fields: Hurling Abroad*, Boherclough, Cashel, Co. Tipperary: King, 1998, NLI.

Korol, Juan Carlos, *Cómo fue la inmigración irlandesa en la Argentina*, Buenos Aires: Plus Ultra, 1981, NLI Ir. 942 k 4, 213 p.

Landaburu, Roberto E., *Irlandeses; Eduardo Casey, vida y obra*, Venado Tuerto, Sta. Fe, Argentina: Fondo Editorial Mutual Venado Tuerto, 1995, LOC, 1995, 220 p. Founder of the city of Venado Tuerto.

MacLoughlin, Guillermo, 'Argentina: The Forgotten People', *IR*, 4 (1993), 6–7, NLI.

MacLoughlin, Guillermo, 'Casey and the One-Eyed Deer', *IR*, No. 3 (1994), 20, NLI.

MacLoughlin, Guillermo, 'The Hibernian-Argentinian', *IG*, 9, No. 4 (1997) 423–7.

McKenna, Patrick, 'Irish emigration to Argentina: a different model', in Bielenberg, *The Irish Diaspora*. See McCracken, in 'Africa'.

Mulhall, Marion MacMurrough, *Between the Amazon and the Andes; or, Ten years of a lady's travels in the pampas, Gran Chaco, Paraguay and Matto Grosso*, London: E. Stanford, 1881, LOC, F2217.M95, 340 p.

Murray, Thomas, *The story of the Irish in Argentina*, New York: P.J. Kenedy & Sons, 1919, NLI Ir. 982 m 8, 512 p.

Murray, John, 'The Irish and Others in Argentina', *Studies: an Irish quarterly review*, No. 38 (1949), 377–388, NLI Ir. 05 s 7.

Nally, Pat, 'Los Irlandeses en la Argentina', *Familia: Ulster Genealogical Review*, Vol. 2, No. 8 (1992), 69–77.

O'Sullivan, Patrick, 'Irish migration to Argentina', in *Patterns of migration*, Leicester: Leicester University Press, 1992, NLI Ir. 324 o 8 Vol. 1, 231 p.

Platt, D.C.M., 'British Agricultural Colonization in Latin America', *Inter-American Economic Affairs*, XVIII, No. 3 (Winter 1964), 3–38.

Pyne, Peter, *The invasions of Buenos Aires, 1806–1807 the Irish dimension*, Liverpool: University of Liverpool, Institute of Latin American Studies, 1996, NLI Ir. 982 p 20, 102 p.

Pyne, Peter, 'A Soldier under Two Flags. Lieutenant-Colonel James Florence Burke: Officer, Adventurer and Spy', *Etudes irlandaises* (Spring 1996), Villaneuve-d'Ascq, France, C.E.R.I.U.L., NLI Ir. 05 e 7.

Rodriguez, Horacio, *King*, Buenos Aires: Instituto Browniano, 1995. Argentine Naval hero Don Juan (John) King from Westport, Co. Mayo.

Saez-Germain, Alejandro, 'Siempre al frente. Los Lynch: casi mil anos de historia', *Noticias Magazine* (20 March, 1994), 44–51, Buenos Aires.

Share, Bernard, 'Tan gaucho como los Gauchos: The Irish in Argentina', *CARA*, Vol. 16, No. 5 (Sept/Oct 1983), 42–66.

Ussher, Santiago M., *Padre Fahy, biografía de Antonio Domingo Fahy, O.P., misionero irlandés en la Argentina 1805–1871*, Buenos Aires, 1952, NLI Ir. 92 f 84, 219 p.

Ussher, Santiago M., *Los capellanes irlandeses en la collectividad hiberno-argentina durante el siglo XIX*, Buenos Aires, 1954.

Ussher, Santiago M., *Las Hermanas de la Miseracordia (1856–1956)*, Buenos Aires: 1956.

Ussher, Santiago M., 'Irish immigrants in Argentina', *The Irish ecclesiastical record*, 5th Ser., Vol. 70, 385–392, NLI Ir. 282 i 4.

Walsh, Micheline, 'Unpublished Admiral Brown Documents in Madrid', *IS*, Vol. III, No. 10 (1957), 17–19.

White, Arden C., 'Irish Immigration to Argentina: An Historical Focus', *The Irish at Home and Abroad*, Vol. 4, No. 3 (3rd Quarter) (1997), 133–134, Salt Lake City, Utah, 1993–2001, NLI Ir. 9292 i 6.

White, Arden C., 'Researching the Irish in Argentina', *The Irish at Home and Abroad*, Vol. 5, No. 1 (1st Q) (1998), 26–30, Salt Lake City, Utah, 1993–2001, NLI Ir. 9292 i 6.

Bolivia
(-) 'Francis Burdett O'Connor', *IS*, XIII, No. 51 (Winter 1977), 128–33.

Burdett O'Connor, Francis, *Un Irlandes con Bolivar*, Caracas: El Cid Editor, 1977.

Brazil

ABEI Newsletter (Brazilian Association for Irish Studies), University of Sao Paulo

de Araujo Neto, Miguel Alexandre, 'An Anglo-Irish Newspaper in Nineteenth Century Brazil: The Anglo-Brazilian Times, 1865–84', *ABEI Newsletter* (Brazilian Association for Irish Studies), No. 8 (1994), 11–13, University of Sao Paulo.

Basto, Fernando Lázaro de Barros, *Ex-combatentes irlandeses em Taperoá*, Rio de Janeiro: Editorial Vozes, 1971, NLI Ir. 360 p 13, 52 p.

Gwynn, A., 'Father Thomas Field, S.J.' Dublin: *The Irish Messenger*, 1924.

Gwynn, A., 'An Irish Settlement on the Amazon', *Proceedings of the Royal Irish Academy*, Vol. XLI, Section C, No. 1 (1932), 1–54, NLI Ir. 7941 o 3 (27).

Lauth, Aloisius Carlos, *A Colonia Principe Dom Pedro: um caso de politica imigratoria no Brasil Imperio*, Brusque, Brazil: Museo Arquidiocesano Dom Joaquim, 1987.

Lorimer, Joyce, *English and Irish settlement on the River Amazon, 1550–1646*, London: Hakluyt Society, 1989, NLI G 325 L 6, 499 p.

McCann, William, *Two Thousand Miles' Ride through the Argentine Provinces*, London: 1853, 2 vols (Repr. New York: AMS Press, 1971).

McGinn, Brian, 'The Irish in Brazil', *IR*, No. 22 (1997), 25–26, NLI.

Mulhall—see 'Argentina'.

O Maidin, Padraig, 'An Irish Mutiny in Brazil and a betrayal', *The Cork Examiner*, 21 May, 1981.

von Allendorfer, Frederic, 'An Irish regiment in Brazil', 1826–28, *IS*, III, No. 10 (1957), 18–31.

Chile

Clissold, Stephen, *Bernardo O'Higgins and the Independence of Chile*, London: Hart-Davis, 1968, NLI G 983 o 4, 254 p.

Figueroa, Pedro Pablo, *Vida del General Don Juan O'Brien, Heroe de la Independencia Sud Americana, Irlandes de nacimiento, chileno de adopcion*, Santiago, Chile: Imprente Mejia, de A. Poblete Garin, 1904.

Figueroa, Pedro Pablo, *Historia del popular escritor Don Benjamin Vicuna Mackenna, su vida, su caracter i sus obras*, Santiago, Chile: Impr. Barcelona, 1903.

Vicuna Mackenna, Benjamin, *Vida de O'Higgins. La corona del heroe*, Santiago, Chile: Universidad de Chile, 1936, Bernardo O'Higgins.

Yanez, Raul Tellez, *El General Juan MacKenna*, Santiago: Editorial Francisco de Aguirre, SA, 1976.

Colombia

Puyana, Edmundo Harker, *Bucaramanga y los Puyana: mi pueblo y mi gente*, Bucaramanga, Colombia: Editorial Camara de Comercio de Bucaramanga, 1984, LOC, F2291.B77 H36 1984, 160 p. How Francis O'Farrell founded the Puyana family.

Ecuador

de Courcy Ireland, John, 'Thomas Charles Wright: Soldier of Bolivar; Founder of the Ecuadorian Navy', *IS*, Vol. VI, No. 25 (Winter 1964), 271–275.

Lambert, Eric, 'Arthur Sandes of Kerry', *IS*, Vol. XII, No. 47 (Winter 1975), 139–46.

Paraguay

(-), 'The First Irish Priests in the New World', *Studies: an Irish quarterly review*, Vol. XXI, No. 82 (June 1932), 213–228, NLI Ir. 05 s 7.

Brodsky, Alyn, *Madame Lynch & friend: the true account of an Irish adventuress and the dictator of Paraguay who destroyed that American nation*, London: Cassell, 1976, NLI Ir. 92 L 7.3, 312 p.

Caraman, Philip, *The Lost Paradise: an account of the Jesuits in Paraguay, 1607–1768*, London: Sidgwick and Jackson, 1975.

Gwynn, A., 'Father Thomas Field, S.J.' Dublin: *The Irish Messenger*, 1924.

Mulhall—see 'Argentina'.

Peru

McGinn, Brian, 'Saint Patrick's Day in Peru', *IR*, No. 1 (1995), 26–27, NLI.

Venezuela

(-) 'General O'Leary and South America', *IS*, Vol. XI. No. 43 (Winter 1973), 57–74.

McGinn, Brian, 'Venezuela's Irish Legacy', *Irish America Magazine* (November 1991), 34–37.

Lambert, Eric, *Carabobo*, Caracas: Fundación John Boulton, 1974, NLI G 987 l 2. Vital battle for Venezuela's independence in 1821; includes Irish participants.

Vila, Manuel Perez, *Vida de Daniel Florencio O'Leary: Primer Edecan del Libertador*, Caracas: Imprenta Nacional, 1957, LOC, 619 p.

Chapter 8 ∾

THE REGISTRY OF DEEDS

THE SCOPE OF THE RECORDS

As research in the Registry of Deeds can be very laborious and time-consuming, it is prudent to be aware of the limitations of its records before starting work there. The Registry was set up by the Irish Parliament in 1708 to help regularise the massive transfer of land-ownership from the Roman Catholic, Anglo-Norman and Gaelic populations to the Protestant Anglo-Irish, which had taken place during the preceding century. The registration of deeds was not obligatory. The function of the Registry was simply to provide evidence of legal title in the event of a dispute. These two facts—the voluntary nature of registration and the general aim of copperfastening the Cromwellian and Williamite confiscations—determine the nature of the records held by the Registry. The overwhelming majority deal with property-owning members of the Church of Ireland, and a disproportionate number of these relate to transactions that carried some risk of legal dispute. In other words, the deeds registered are generally of interest for a minority of the population, and constitute only a fraction of the total number of property transactions carried out in the country.

The implications of these facts are worth spelling out in detail. During the most useful period covered by the Registry's records, the non-Roman Catholic population of Ireland comprised, at most, 20 per cent of the total. A high proportion were dissenting Presbyterians, largely concentrated in the north and suffering restrictions on their property rights similar to, though not as severe as, those imposed on Catholics; very few deeds made by dissenting Protestants are registered. Of the remaining non-Roman Catholics, the majority were small farmers, tradesmen or artisans, usually in a position of economic dependence on those with whom they might have had property transactions and thus in no position to dispute the terms of a deed. The Registry's records therefore cover only a small number of the non-Roman Catholic minority. There are exceptions, of course, for example, large landlords who made and registered great numbers of leases with their smaller tenants, marriage settlements between families of relatively modest means, the business transactions of the small Catholic merchant classes, the registration of the holdings of the few surviving Catholic landowners after the relaxation of the Penal laws in the 1780s. These are definitely exceptions, however, and for the vast bulk of the population—Catholic tenant farmers—the possibility of a registered deed can almost certainly be discounted as they owned virtually nothing and had tenuous legal rights to the properties they occupied.

A further limit to the scope of the records is the scant use made of the Registry before the mid-eighteenth century. It was only from about the 1750s that registration became even relatively widespread, and its major genealogical usefulness is for the century or so from then until the 1850s, when it is generally superseded by other sources.

With these *caveats* in mind, it should now be said that for those who did make and register deeds, the records of the Registry can often provide superb information. The inclination to register deeds appears to have run in families: a single document can name two or three generations, as well as leading back to a chain of related records that can draw a picture of the family's evolving fortunes and the network of its collateral relationships.

REGISTRATION

Registration worked in the following way. After a deed had been signed and witnessed, one of the parties to it had a copy made, known as a 'memorial', signed it and had it in turn witnessed by two people, at least one of whom had to have witnessed the original, too. The memorial was then sworn before a Justice of the Peace as a faithful copy of the original and sent to the Registry. Here it was transcribed into a large manuscript volume and indexed. The original memorial was retained and stored; all of them are still preserved in the vaults of the Registry. For research purposes, however, the large manuscript volumes containing the transcripts of the memorials are the source to be consulted. Registration of a deed normally took place fairly soon after its execution, within a month or two in most cases, although delays of up to two years were quite common. If the gap between the execution and the registration of a deed is much longer, this may be significant: it indicates an impending need for one of the parties to the deed, or their heirs, to be able to show legal proof of its execution. The most common reason for such a necessity would have been the death of one of the parties.

THE INDEXES

The indexing system used by the Registry is complicated and incomplete. There are two sets of indexes: one by grantor's name (i.e. the name of the party disposing of the asset); the other by the name of the townland in which the property was located. The Grantors' Index is fully alphabetical and divided into a number of sets, covering different initial letters and periods. Between 1708 and 1833 the Grantors' Index records the name of the grantor, the surname of the first grantee and the volume, page and deed number. No indication is given of the location of the property concerned—an omission that can make a search for references to a family with a common surname very tedious indeed. After 1833 the index is more comprehensive, listing the county in which the property was located. In general the index is remarkably accurate, but there are some mistakes, particularly in the volume and page references. In such instances the deed number can be used to trace the transcript; several transcribers worked simultaneously on different volumes, and the volume numbers were sometimes transposed. If, for example, Volume 380 is not the correct reference, Volumes 378–382 may contain the transcript. Within each volume the transcripts are numerically consecutive.

The Lands Index is subdivided by county and is roughly alphabetical within each county, with townland names grouped together under their initial letter. This means that a search for deeds relating to, say, Ballyboy, Co. Roscommon involves a search through all of the references to Co. Roscommon townlands that start with the letter 'B'. The information given in the index is brief, recording only the surnames of two of the parties along with the volume, page and deed numbers. As with the Grantors' index, the index is divided into a number of sets, covering different periods. After 1828 the index further subdivides the townlands into baronies, making research a good deal more efficient. Alongside the county volumes, there are separate indexes for corporation towns and cities. The subdivisions within these are somewhat eccentric, particularly in the case of Dublin, making it necessary to search even more widely than in the rural indexes. It should be pointed out that the Registry does not make it possible to trace the history of all of the transactions in which a property was involved because inevitably some of the deeds recording the transactions have not been registered.

In general, of the Registry's two sets of indexes, the Grantors' Index is the most genealogically useful because it is strictly alphabetical and lists transactions by person rather than by property. The single greatest omission in the Registry is that of an index to the grantees; given the distribution of wealth in the country, the social range covered would be enhanced greatly by the production of such an index. Microfilm copies of both the Lands Index and the Grantors' Index, amounting to more than 400 reels, are available at the NLI, PRONI and the LDS Family History Library. Volume 1 of Margaret Falley's *Irish and Scotch-Irish Ancestral Research*, available on open shelves in the NLI Reading Room, gives a complete breakdown of the locations and microfilm numbers of the NLI indexes up to 1850 (pp. 71–90).

THE NATURE OF THE RECORDS

The archaic and legalistic terminology used in deeds can make it extremely difficult to work out what precisely the parties to a deed intended it to do. This is particularly true in cases where earlier agreements are referred to, but not recited in full. However, from a genealogical point of view the precise nature of the transaction recorded is not always vital, and with a little practice it becomes relatively easy to pare down the document to the essentials of dates, place names and personal names. It should be kept in mind that all personal names—buyers, sellers, trustees, mortgagees, witnesses—may be important and should be noted. There are, however, numerous cases in which the nature of the deed is of interest, and some advance knowledge will speed up the process of interpretation. So what follows here is an attempt to clarify some of the less familiar terms and to describe the most common or useful documents likely to be encountered.

The most important part of most deeds is the opening and it follows an almost invariable pattern. After the phrase, 'A memorial of', which indicates that the transcript is of a copy rather than the original, the following are stated: (1) the nature of the deed; (2) the date on which the original was made; (3) the names of the parties to the deed. It must be remembered that a number of people could constitute a single party for the purposes of a legal transaction. A typical opening would then read:

> 'A memorial of an indented deed of agreement dated October 13th 1793 between John O'Hara of Oak Park, Co. Meath, farmer, and George O'Hara of Balltown, Co. Meath, farmer, his eldest son of the first part, William Coakley of Navan, Co. Meath, merchant, of the second part, and Christopher French of Navan, gentleman, of the third part, in which ...'

Often it is necessary to read no more than this to know whether or not a deed is relevant; if, for example, the research is on the O'Haras of Sligo, it is evident at a glance that the above document has no direct relevance. But as happens so often in genealogy, the significance of information in a deed may only become clear retrospectively, in the light of something uncovered later. When carrying out a search for a particular family it is therefore a good idea to note briefly the important points in all deeds examined—names, addresses and occupations—whether or not they seem immediately relevant. This way, if it subsequently emerges that, for example, the O'Haras of Sligo and Meath are in fact related, then the relevant deeds can be readily identified.

Categorising the kinds of deeds that appear in the Registry can be difficult, since many of them are not what they appear to be. The most common misleading description in the opening of the memorial is the 'deed of lease and release', which may in fact be a conveyance or sale, a mortgage, a marriage settlement, or a rent charge. 'Lease and Release' was a legal device whereby the obligation to record a conveyance publicly could be avoided; it was not obligatory to record a transaction to a tenant or lessee already in occupation, and it was not obligatory to record a lease for one year only. Accordingly, a lease for one year was first granted and then the true transaction, conveyance, mortgage, marriage settlement, or other was carried out. It remained popular as a method of conveyance until 1845, when the Statute of Uses, which had made it possible, was repealed.

Despite the difficulties created by such disguises as 'lease and release', the underlying transactions fall into a number of broad classes.

1. Leases
By far the most common of the records in the Registry, leases could run for any term between one and 999 years, or could depend on the lives of a number of persons named in the document, or could be a mixture of the two, lasting three lives or sixty years, whichever was the longer. Only leases for more than three years could be registered. The most genealogically useful information in such

leases is the lives they mention. The choice of lives generally rested with the lessee or grantee, and in most cases those chosen were related. Often the names and ages of the grantee's children appear—an extremely valuable addition for families in the eighteenth century. Leases for 900 years, or for lives renewable in perpetuity, were much more common in Ireland than elsewhere and amounted to a permanent transfer of the property, although the grantor remained the nominal owner. As might be imagined, such leases provided a rich source of legal disputes.

2. Marriage Settlements

Any form of pre-nuptial property agreement between the families of the prospective bride and groom was known as a 'marriage settlement', or 'marriage articles'. A variety of transactions can therefore be classed in this way. What they have in common is that they aim to provide security, to women in particular; since married women could hold no property in their own right, it was common practice for the dowry to be granted to trustees rather than directly to the future husband, which allowed her some degree of independence. It was also common for the family of the prospective husband, or the husband himself, to grant an annuity out of the income of his land to his future wife and children, should he predecease them. The information given in settlements varies, but in general it should at least include the names, addresses and occupations of the bride, groom and bride's father. Other relatives—brothers, uncles, etc.—may also put in an appearance. For obvious reasons, marriage settlements are among the most useful of the records held in the Registry. The period for which they were most commonly registered appears to have been the three decades from 1790 to 1820. When searching the Grantors' Indexes for these records, it should be remembered that they are not always indicated as such and that the formal grantor may be a member of either family, which means it is necessary to search under both surnames.

3. Mortgages

In the eighteenth and nineteenth centuries mortgages were very commonly used as a form of investment, on the one hand, and as a way of raising short-term cash, on the other. Generally they do not provide a great deal of family information, but as they were an endless source of legal disputes they form a disproportionate number of the deeds registered. It was quite common for mortgages to be passed on to third or fourth parties, each hoping to make money, so the resulting deeds can be very complicated.

4. Bills of Discovery

Under the Penal laws, Catholics were not allowed to possess more than a very limited amount of land, and a Protestant who discovered a Catholic in possession of more than the permitted amount could file a Bill of Discovery to claim it. In practice, most Bills appear to have been filed by Protestant friends of Catholic landowners to pre-empt hostile Discovery, and as a means of allowing them to remain in effective possession. Registered Bills are not common, but they are extremely interesting, both genealogically and historically.

5. Wills

Only those wills likely to be contested legally were registered, in other words those which omitted someone, almost certainly a family member who might have a legitimate claim. Abstracts of the personal and geographical information in all of the wills registered between 1708 and 1832 have been published in P.B. Phair and E. Ellis (eds.), *Abstracts of Wills at The Registry of Deeds* (3 vols), Irish Manuscripts Commission, 1954–1988. The full provisions of the wills are only to be found in the original memorials.

6. Rent Charges

These were annual charges of a fixed sum payable from the revenue generated by nominated lands. They were used to provide for family members in straitened circumstances, or to pay off debts or mortgages in instalments. Once made, they could be transferred to others and were valuable assets in their own right. Depending on the terms, they can provide useful insights into family relationships and family fortunes.

Other, miscellaneous classes of deed also appear in the Registry Office's files. As outlined above, the only common feature is that they record a property transaction of some description; any family information they may contain is a matter of luck.

Chapter 9 ∽

NEWSPAPERS

Newspapers are the one of the most enjoyable and one of the most difficult of genealogical sources. Faced with so much of the everyday particularity of the past, it is virtually impossible to confine oneself to biographical data; again and again research is sidetracked by curiosity. In addition to this, the endemic imprecision of family information means that it is almost always necessary to search a wide range of dates. As a result, a sustained search for genealogical information in original newspapers is extremely time-consuming. If the efficient use of research time is a priority, newspapers are certainly not the place to start.

This proviso notwithstanding, the destruction of so many Irish records in 1922 has lent a disproportionate importance to Irish newspapers, and when they do throw up information it can be extremely rewarding. Events are reported virtually as they happen, within a few weeks at most, and the reports have an authority and accuracy that is hard to match—even making all necessary allowances for journalistic errors. And it is no longer necessary in every case to search the original papers themselves, as we shall see.

INFORMATION GIVEN
There are two principal formats in which useful information appears: biographical notices and, in the early papers, advertisements. Up to the 1850s the former consist largely of marriage announcements and obituaries; birth announcements tend to be sparse, relate only to the wealthiest classes and often give no more than the father's name, taking the form: 'on the 12th, the lady of George Gratton Esq., of a son'. After the mid-nineteenth century the number of birth notices rises sharply, but they remain relatively uninformative.

Marriage announcements contain a much broader range of information, from the bare minimum of the names of the two parties to comprehensive accounts of the addresses, occupations and fathers' names. In the majority of cases the name of the bride's father and his address are supplied, in a form such as: 'married on Tuesday last Michael Thomson Esq. to Miss Neville eldest daughter of James Neville of Bandon Esq.'. For many eighteenth-century marriages, a newspaper announcement may be the only surviving record, particularly where the relevant Church of Ireland register has not survived.

Obituaries are by far the most numerous newspaper announcements and cover a much broader social spectrum than either births or marriages. Again, the kind of information given can vary widely, from the barest, 'died at Tullamore Mr Michael Cusack', to the most elaborate, giving occupation, exact age, and family relationships: 'died at the house of her uncle Mr Patrick Swan in George's St in the 35th year of her age Mrs Burgess, relict of Henry Burgess Esq., late of Limerick.' This level of information is rare, however; most announcements confine themselves to name, address, occupation and place of death. Because of the paucity of Catholic burial records, newspaper obituaries are the most comprehensive surviving records of the deaths of the majority of the Catholic middle classes. From about the 1840s the numbers of both obituaries and marriage announcements rose sharply; unfortunately, by then these events are usually more easily traceable in parish or civil records.

Advertisements, especially in the early newspapers, were more often paid announcements than true advertisements in the modern sense, and an extraordinary variety of information can be gleaned from them. The most useful types are as follows:

(i)   **Elopements:** a husband would announce that his wife had absconded and disclaim all responsibility for any debts she might contract. Usually his address and her maiden surname are given.
(ii) **Business announcements:** the most useful are those which record the place and nature of the business, which announce a change of address or ownership for the business, or which record the succession of a son to a business after his father's death.
(iii) **Bankruptcies:** these usually request creditors to gather at a specified time and place. They can be useful in narrowing the focus of a search for relevant transactions in the Registry of Deeds.

As well as advertisements and biographical notices, newspapers naturally reported the news of the day, concentrating on the details of court cases with particular relish. For an ancestor who was a convict, these hold great interest, since much of the evidence was reported *verbatim* and may provide vital clues for further research. However, uncovering the relevant report depends very much on knowing the date of conviction with some degree of accuracy, as well as the area in which the trial is likely to have taken place.

PERSONS COVERED
Apart from reports of trials, the genealogical information to be gleaned from newspapers relates primarily to fairly well defined social groups. First, the doings of the nobility were of general interest, and their births, marriages and deaths are extensively covered. Next in terms of coverage are the merchant and professional classes of the towns in which the newspapers were published. These would include barristers and solicitors, doctors, masters of schools, military officers and

clergy, as well as the more prosperous businesspeople. It should be remembered that from about the 1770s this would include the growing Catholic merchant class. Next are the farming gentry from the surrounding areas. After them come the less well-off traders, traceable largely through advertisements. Finally, the provincial papers also cover the inhabitants of neighbouring towns in these same classes, albeit sparsely at times. No information is to be found concerning anyone at or below middling farmer level, in other words the great bulk of the population. This remains true even from the third and fourth decades of the nineteenth century, when the number of announcements rose markedly and the social classes covered broadened somewhat.

DATES AND AREAS

The earliest Irish newspapers were published in Dublin at the end of the seventeenth century. However, it was not until the mid-eighteenth century that they became widespread and began to carry information of genealogical value. The period of their prime usefulness is from about this time, c.1750, to around the mid-nineteenth century, at which point other sources become more accessible and thorough. Obviously not all areas of the country were equally well served, particularly at the start of this period. Publications tended to be concentrated in particular regions, as follows:

(i) **Dublin:** the most important eighteenth-century publications were the *Dublin Evening Post*, started in 1719, *Faulkner's Dublin Journal*, from 1725, *The Freeman's Journal*, from 1763, and the *Dublin Hibernian Journal*, from 1771. As well as carrying plentiful marriage and obituary notices relating to Dublin and surrounding areas from about the mid-century, these papers also reproduced notices that had first appeared in provincial papers, something that should be kept in mind in cases where the original local newspapers have not survived. From the early nineteenth century a great proliferation of publications began to appear, but unfortunately the custom of publishing family notices fell into disuse in the first decades of the century and did not resume until well into the 1820s.

(ii) **Cork:** after Dublin, Cork was the area of the country best served by newspapers, with many publications following the lead of the *Corke Journal*, which began in 1753. As well as publishing notices relating specifically to Cork City and County, these papers also carried much of interest for other Munster counties, notably Co. Kerry, and also, like the Dublin papers, republished notices relating to Munster which had originally appeared in other publications. An index exists to newspaper biographical notices relating to Counties Cork and Kerry between 1756 and 1827, details of which will be found below.

(iii) **Limerick/Clare:** there was a great deal of overlap between the earliest Clare newspapers, the *Clare Journal* from 1787 and the *Ennis Chronicle* from 1788, and those of Limerick, where the first publications were the *Munster Journal*

(1749) and the *Limerick Chronicle*. As well as Clare and Limerick, both groups of papers carried extensive coverage of Co. Tipperary, and in the case of the Limerick publications this coverage also extended to Counties Kerry and Galway. The Molony manuscripts series in the Genealogical Office (see Chapter 6) includes extensive abstracts from the Clare papers. Details of a more accessible and far-ranging set of abstracts will be found below.

(iv) **Carlow/Kilkenny:** this area was covered by a single publication, *Finn's Leinster Journal*, which began in 1768. Although the advertisements are useful, early biographical notices are sparse. The earliest have been published in *The Irish Genealogist* (1987/88).

(v) **Waterford:** the earliest newspapers here were the *Waterford Chronicle* (1770), the *Waterford Herald (1791)* and the *Waterford Mirror* (1804). Few of the earliest issues appear to have survived. For surviving issues before 1800, *The Irish Genealogist* has published the biographical notices (1974, and 1976–1980 incl.). Notices to 1821 are included with the abstracts for Clare/Limerick.

(vi) **Belfast and Ulster:** the single most important newspaper in this area was the *Belfast Newsletter*, which began publication in 1737. It had a wider geographical range than any of the Dublin papers, covering virtually all of east Ulster. Outside Belfast the most significant publications were the *Londonderry Journal*, from 1772, which also covered a good area of Donegal and Tyrone, and the *Newry Journal* and *Strabane Journal*, of which very few, if any, early issues survive.

LOCATIONS

The best single repository for Irish newspapers is the British Library. After 1826 the Library was obliged to hold a copy of all Irish publications and from that date its collection is virtually complete. It also has an extensive, though patchy, collection before that date. Within Ireland the largest collection is held by the NLI, though this is by no means comprehensive. Many unique copies are held in local libraries and other repositories. The *Report of the NEWSPLAN Project in Ireland* (NLI, 2nd edition, 1998 and *www.nli.ie*) lists all known hard-copy and microfilm holdings of Irish newspapers.

INDEXES

A number of indexes exist to the biographical material to be found in newspapers, which can greatly alleviate the burden of research. The following list orders them by date.

1730–1740	*Pue's Occurrences and the Dublin Gazette* (marriages and deaths) NLI Ms. 3197
1737–1800	*Belfast Newsletter* (biographical material), online at *www.ucs.louisiana.edu/bnl/*.
1756–1827	Rosemary ffolliott's 'Index to Biographical Notices Collected from Newspapers, Principally Relating to Cork and Kerry, 1756–1827'

transcribes all the notices from eleven Cork newspapers, as well as relevant notices from a further eight Dublin and Leinster publications. Her 'Index to Biographical Notices in the Newspapers of Limerick, Ennis, Clonmel and Waterford, 1758–1821' covers eleven provincial and five Dublin newspapers Between the two works almost all of the surviving eighteenth-century notices for the southern half of the country are extracted. Copies are available in DCLA local libraries, NLI and in the library of the Society of Australian Genealogists.

1771–1818	*Hibernian Chronicle* (1771–1802), *Cork Mercantile Chronicle* (1803–1818) – biographical notices. IGRS, London.
1772–1784	Schlegel, Donald M., *Irish Genealogical Abstracts from the Londonderry Journal 1772–1784* (Baltimore: 1990, repr. 2001) 190 p.
1772–1812	Farrar, Henry, *Biographical Notices in Walker's Hibernian Magazine 1772–1812*, (Dublin: 1889), online at *www.celticcousins.net*
1792–1964	*The Northern Star* (1792–1797), *The Northern Herald* (1833–1836), *The Downpatrick Recorder* (1836–1886), *The Co. Down Spectator* (1904–1964), *The Mourne Observer* (1949–1980), *The Newtownards Chronicle* (1871–1873), Southern Education and Library Board (Northern Ireland).
1828–1864	Vol. 6 of Albert Casey's *O'Kief, Coshe Mang*, etc. reprints the biographical notices from the *Kerry Evening Post* from 1828 to 1864, and includes them in the general index at the back of the volume.

In addition, the website of Irish Newspaper Archives Ltd *(www.irishnewspaperarchives.com)* promises to enhance the importance of newspapers as a genealogical source. At the time of writing (June 2005) the site has not yet been launched, but it appears to include *The Freeman's Journal* from 1763 with a full-text search and anticipates incorporating most of the historic Irish newspapers currently stored on microfilm.

Chapter 10

DIRECTORIES

For those areas and classes which they cover Irish directories are an excellent source, often supplying information not readily available elsewhere. Their most obvious and practical use is to find out where precisely a family lived in one of the larger towns. However, for members of the gentry and the professional, merchant and trading classes they can detail much more, providing indirect evidence of reversals of fortune or growing prosperity, of death and emigration. In many cases, in fact, directory entries are the only precise indication of occupation. In terms of coverage, the only classes totally excluded from all directories are, once again, the most disadvantaged: small tenant farmers, landless labourers and servants. Virtually all classes other than these are at least partly included, in some of the nineteenth-century directories in particular. One point to keep in mind when using any directory is that every entry is at least six months out of date by the time of publication.

The account that follows divides directories into: 1. Dublin directories, 2. countrywide directories and 3. provincial directories, in each case supplying the dates, locations and information included, followed by a chronological checklist for the Dublin and countrywide directories.

DUBLIN DIRECTORIES

The Gentleman's and Citizen's Almanack, produced by John Watson, began publication in Dublin in 1736 and continued until 1844. But the first true trade directories in Ireland were those published by Peter Wilson for Dublin City, starting in 1751 and continuing until 1837, with a break from 1754 to 1759. From the outset these were regarded as supplements to Watson's *Almanack* and were regularly bound with it. In 1787 the two publications were put together with the *English Court Registry*, and until it ceased publication in 1837 the whole was known as *The Treble Almanack*.

Initially the information supplied in Wilson's *Directory* consisted purely of alphabetical lists of merchants and traders, supplying name, address and occupation. In the early years these were quite scanty, but they grew steadily over the decades from less than 1,000 names in the 1752 edition to almost 5,000 in 1816. As well as merchants and traders, the last decades of the eighteenth century also saw the inclusion of separate lists of those who might now be termed 'The

Establishment'—officers of the city guilds and of Trinity College, State officials, those involved in the administration of medicine and the law, Church of Ireland clergy, etc. The range of people covered expanded markedly, if a little eccentrically, in the early nineteenth century. The most permanent addition was a new section, added in 1815, which covered the nobility and gentry. As well as this, a number of other listings of potential use to readers were added, though some appear only intermittently. Persons covered by these lists include pawnbrokers, bankers, apothecaries, police, dentists, physicians, militia officers and ships' captains.

The most significant difference between *The Treble Almanack* and Pettigrew and Oulton's *Dublin Almanac and General Register of Ireland*, which began annual publication in 1834, is the inclusion in the latter of a street-by-street listing, initially encompassing the inhabitants of Dublin proper but enlarged year by year to include the suburbs. From 1835 this listing was supplemented by an alphabetical list of the individuals recorded. In theory, at least, the combination of the two listings should now make it possible to track the movements of individuals around the city—an important feature as changes of address were very frequent in the nineteenth century when the common practice was to rent rather than purchase. Unfortunately, in practice the alphabetical list is much less comprehensive than the street list.

Pettigrew and Oulton extended even further the range of persons covered. The officers of virtually every Dublin institution, club and society are recorded, as well as clergy of all denominations. Another significant difference from the earlier *Treble Almanack* is the extension of the coverage beyond the Dublin area. Under the rubric 'Official Authorities of Counties and Towns', Pettigrew and Oulton record the names of many of the rural gentry and more prosperous inhabitants of the large towns in their guise as local administrators. This is particularly useful for areas which were not served by a local directory, or for which none has survived. Similarly, the officials of many of the better-known institutions and societies in the larger country towns are also recorded, as well as the more important provincial clergy.

The successor to Pettigrew and Oulton was Alexander Thom's *Irish Almanac and Official Directory*, which began in 1844 and has continued publication up to the present. As the name implies, it continued the extension of coverage beyond Dublin. To take one year as an example, the 1870 edition includes, along with the alphabetical and street listings for Dublin, alphabetical lists of the following for the entire country: army officers; attorneys, solicitors and barristers; bankers; Catholic, Church of Ireland and Presbyterian clergy; coast guard officers; doctors; MPs; magistrates; members of the Irish Privy Council; navy and marine officers; officers of counties and towns; and peers. Although Thom's is generally regarded as a Dublin directory, its usefulness goes well beyond Dublin.

As well as these annual directories, Dublin was also included in the country-wide publications of Pigot and Slater, which were issued at intervals during the nineteenth century. The only significant difference is the arrangement of the individuals listed under their trades, making it possible to identify all of those engaged in the same occupation, a factor that is important considering many occupations were handed down from one generation to the next. These directories are dealt with more fully below.

1866	DUBLIN STREET DIRECTORY.	

1 N.—Bessborough-avenue.
Off North-strand-road.

1 Boyd, Mrs.	8*l.*
2 Flanagan, Mr. Thomas	
3 Preest, Mr. Patrick,	9*l.*
4 M'Carthy, Mr. Patk. J. G.P.O.	7*l.*
5 Hutchin, Mrs.	7*l.*
6 Purcell, Mr. Thomas,	10*l.*
7 Conroy, Mr. John,	10*l.*
8 Hatchell, Geo. master mariner,	8*l.*
9 Harbron, Mr. Wm. J.	9*l.*
10 Bell, Mr. Peter,	9*l.*
11 Keane, Alphons., photographer, and 9½ North-strand,	9*l.*
12 Byrne, Mr. Joseph,	8*l.*
13 Goulding, Daniel, carpenter,	7*l.*
14 O'Kelly, Mr. Alexander,	7*l.*
15 Curtis, Mrs.	8*l.*
16 O'Callaghan, Mrs.	8*l.*
Link Line	
19 Frazer, Mr. James,	7*l.*
20 Reynolds, Mr. Thomas,	6*l.*
21 Robinson, Mr. Charles,	6*l.*
22 Armstrong, Mr. Andrew,	6*l.*
Link Line.	
24 Wren, Mr. James,	6*l.*
25 Carroll, Mr. Patrick,	7*l.*
26 Byrne, Mr. Patrick,	7*l.*
27 M'Cauley, Mr. Peter,	7*l.*
28 Gregan, Mr. Hugh,	
Drumcondra Link Line Railway	
32 Tomlinson, Mr. William,	12*l.*
33 Halliday, Mr. Thomas,	9*l.*
34 Grimes, James, engineer,	9*l.*
35 Wilcocks, Mr. Joseph,	9*l.*
36 Dillon, Mr. Andrew,	9*l.*
37 Lacy, Mr. James,	9*l.*
38 Scott, Mr. William,	9*l.*
39 Lambert, Mr. Thomas	7*l.*
40 Mooney, Mr. Mathew,	7*l.*
41 Hayden, Mr. John,	7*l.*
42 Smith, Mrs.	7*l.*
43 Hendry, Mr. William,	7*l.*
44 Sweny, Mr. Herbert Sidney,	7*l.*
45 Tuites, Mr. R.	7*l.*
46 Griffith, John,	7*l.*
47 Homan, Mr. Thomas,	4*l.* 10*s.*
48 Kennedy, Mrs.	4*l.* 10*s.*
49 Murphy, Mrs.,	6*l.*
50 Holmes, Mr. William,	6*l.*
51 Langan, Mr. John	

Bethesda-place.
Upper Dorset-street.
Three small cottages

3 S.—Bishop-street.

22½ Dunne, J. fishmonger,	7*l.*
23 Tenements,	16*l.*
24 Hayden, Mrs. board & lodging,	16*l.*
here Redmond's-hill & Peter's-row inters.	
25 Kelly, James, grocer, wine and spirit dealer, & 13 Peter's-row,	58*l.*
26, 27, 27A, 28 to 39 Jacob, W. R. & Co. (limited)	
40, 41 & 42 Tonge and Taggart, *South City* foundry and iron works,	37*l.*, 17*l.*
43 to 45 Tenements,	14*l.* to 17*l.*
46 Jacob, W. R. and Co. (limited) stores,	20*l.* 9*l.*, 17*l.*
.........*here Bishop-court intersects*........	
47 to 49 Tenements,	20*l.* 9*l.*
50 Jacob, W. R. and Co. stores,	30*l.*
51 Tenements,	26*l.*
52 & 53 Tenements,	21*l.*, 24*l.*
54 & 55 Tenements,	17*l.*, 16*l.*
56 Leigh, P. provision merchant,	21*l.*

Black-street.
Infirmary-road.
Twenty small houses — Artizan's Dwellings company.

3 N.—Blackhall-parade.
From Blackhall-street to King-street, Nth.
P. St. Paul.—Arran-quay W.

1 Bourke, Mr. James,	9*l.*
2 Duffy, Mrs. lodgings,	9*l.*
3 Murphy, Mrs. M.	13*l.*
4 & 5 Condron, J. horseshoer and farrier,	8*l.*
6 & 7 Chew T. C. & Co. wool merchants, with 55 and 56 Queen-street, and 27 Island-street	
8 Dardis, Mr. M.	17*l.*
9 Clarke, Joseph, watch maker,	14*l.*
10 Tenements,	14*l.*
11 Duignan, Mrs.	14*l.*

3 N.—Blackhall-place.
From Ellis's-quay to Stoneybatter.
P. St. Paul.—Arran-quay W.

KING's, OR BLUE COAT HOSPITAL—George R. Armstrong, esq. agent and registrar; Rev. T. P. Richards, M.A. chaplain & head master

1 and 2 Menton, Denis, dairy, and 17 King-street, north,	59*l.*
3 and 4 Losty, Mr. M. J.	30*l.* 34*l.*
5 Young, Mr. William	
6 and 7 Paul and Vincent, farming implement manufs. millwrights, and iron founders, chemical ma-	

30 McKeever, Mr. J.	
34 Dixon, Mrs.	
35 King, Mrs. M.	
36 Kirk, Mr. B.	
37 Muldoon, Mr. T.	
38 Behan, Mr. P.	
39 Donovan, Mr. Henry,	
40 *Dublin Prison Gate Mission* Laundry workroom, and *dormitories*—J. C. Wilkinson, secretary.	

3 N.—Blackhall-street
From Queen-street to Blackhall-pl.
P. St. Paul.—Arran-quay W.

1 Gorman, Mrs.	
2 Hopkins, Mr. Robert,	
.......*here Blackhall-parade intersec*	
3 Gordon, Samuel, wholesale manufacturer,	
4 *The National Hotel*—John We proprietor,	
5 Baird, Mrs.	
6 Clancy, Mrs. Mary,	
„ Doyle, Mr. T. M.	
„ Montgomery, Mr. James	
7 Dillon, Mr. John,	
8 Lemass, Mr. Joseph,	
9 Nurses' Training Institu Miss Tierney Superintende	
10 Mooney, Mrs.	
11 and 12 Ruins,	
13 Keogh, Mrs. J.	
14 Vacant,	
15 Tenements,	
.......*here Blackhall-place interse*	
16 to 18 Fitzgerald, P. corn an stores,	10*l.* 1
19 & 20 Hickey & Co. stores offi	
21 & 22 *Cairn's Memorial Home*,	
23 Correll, Mr. J.	
24 Doran, Mr. C. J.	
25 Leahy, Mr. W. J.	
26 Doheney, Mr. Joseph	
27 Eivers & Rispin, cattle sales	
„ Curtis, T. H. forage contrac	
28 Ralph, Mrs.,	
29 Hickey, Paul, & Co. cattle s corn, hay, and wool facto	
30 Scott, Mr. John F.	
31 Byrne, Mr. P. J.	
32 Cobbe, Mrs.	

3 S.—Blackpitt
From New-row, South, to Grea
P. St. Nicholas Without, east sid
Luke, west.—Merchants'-qu
...... LETTER BOX, oppo*

Thom's Directory, 1901
(Courtesy of the Genealogical Office)

Checklist

1751–1837: *Wilson's Directory*, published from 1787 and issued as part of *The Treble Almanack.*

1834–1849: Pettigrew and Oulton's *Dublin Almanac and General Register of Ireland.*

1844–present: Thom's *Irish Almanac and Official Directory.*

See also Pigot and Slater's countrywide Directories from 1820.

The NLI, NAI and Dublin City Library and Archive hold the most comprehensive collections of these directories. Copies can be requested directly at the Reading Room counter in the Library and are on open access in the Archives. Archive CD Books Ireland (*www.archivecdbooks.ie*) began the process of republishing early directories on CD-ROM in early 2005, and will include some of the Dublin directories in due course.

COUNTRYWIDE DIRECTORIES

Until the productions of Pigot and Co. in the early nineteenth century, very little exists which covers the entire country. Although not true directories in the sense of the Dublin publications, four works may be used in a similar manner—at least as far as the country gentry are concerned. The earliest of these is George Taylor's and Andrew Skinner's *Road Maps of Ireland* (1778), which prints maps of the principal routes from Dublin to the country towns, including the major country houses and the surnames of their occupants, and an alphabetical index to these surnames. The aim of William Wilson's *The Post-Chaise Companion* (1786) is similar, providing a discursive description of what might be seen on various journeys through the countryside. These descriptions include the names of the country houses and, again, their owners' surnames. There is no index. The next publications were the two editions, in 1812 and 1814, of Ambrose Leet's *Directory*. This contains an alphabetical listing of placenames in an arbitrary mix—towns, villages, country houses, townlands—showing the county, the nearest post town and, in the case of the houses, the full name of the occupant. These names are then indexed at the back of the volume.

The earliest countrywide directory covering more than the gentry was Pigot's *Commercial Directory of Ireland*, published in 1820. This goes through the towns of Ireland alphabetically, supplying the names of nobility and gentry living in or close to the town and arranging the traders of each town according to their trade. Pigot published a subsequent edition in 1824 and his successor, Slater, issued expanded versions in 1846, 1856, 1870, 1881 and 1894. These followed the same basic format, dividing the country into four provinces and then dealing with towns and villages alphabetically within each province. With each edition the scope of the directory was steadily enlarged, including ever more towns and villages. 'Guide to Irish Directories', Chapter 4 of *Irish Genealogy: A Record Finder* (ed., Donal Begley, Dublin: Heraldic Artists, 1981), includes a detailed county-by-county listing of the towns and villages covered in each edition. Otherwise, the most important differences between the various editions are as follows:

1824: includes a countrywide alphabetical index to all the clergy, gentry and nobility listed in the entries for individual towns; omitted in subsequent issues.

From 1824: separate alphabetical listings are given for the clergy, gentry and nobility of Dublin and most of the larger urban centres.

1846: includes the names of schoolteachers for the towns treated, a practice continued in subsequent editions.

1881: this supplies the names of the principal farmers near each of the towns treated, giving the relevant parish. This feature was continued in the 1894 edition.

The best single collection of these directories is in the NLI, where most of the early editions have now been transferred to microfiche.

Checklist

1778: George Taylor and Andrew Skinner, *Road Maps of Ireland* (reprint IUP: 1969), NLI Ir. 9141 t 1 (Repub. Archive CD Books Ireland, CD-ROM #IET0027, 2005).

1786: William Wilson's *The Post-Chaise Companion*, NLI J 9141 w 13.

1812: Ambrose Leet, *A List of [...] noted places*, NLI Ir. 9141 l 10, LDS film 990023 Item 2.

1814: Ambrose Leet, *A Directory to the Market Towns, Villages, Gentlemen's Seats and other noted places in Ireland*, NLI Ir. 9141 l 10.

1820: J. Pigot, *Commercial Directory of Ireland*, NLI Ir. 9141 c 25.

1824: J. Pigot, *City of Dublin and Hibernian Provincial Directory*, NLI Ir. 9141 p 75 (Repub. Archive CD Books Ireland, CD-ROM #IET0005, 2005).

1846: Slater's *National Commercial Directory of Ireland*, NLI Ir. 9141 s 30.

1856: Slater's *Royal National Commercial Directory of Ireland*.

1870: Slater's *Royal National Commercial Directory of Ireland*.

1881: Slater's *Royal National Commercial Directory of Ireland*.

1894: Slater's *Royal National Commercial Directory of Ireland*.

See also Dublin directories from 1834.

PROVINCIAL DIRECTORIES

John Ferrar's *Directory of Limerick*, published in 1769, was the first directory to deal specifically with a provincial town, and the practice spread throughout Munster in the remaining decades of the eighteenth century, with Cork particularly well covered. In the nineteenth century local directories were produced in abundance, especially in areas with a strong commercial identity, such as Belfast, the northeast and Munster. The quality and coverage of these varies widely, from the street-by-street listings in Martin's 1839 *Belfast Directory* to the barest of commercial lists. A guide to the principal local directories is included in the county source-lists in Chapter 13. These lists cannot be regarded as complete, however; many small, local publications, especially from the first half of the nineteenth century, are now quite rare, with only one or two surviving copies. Locating these can be extremely difficult. Some guides are:

Carty, James, *Bibliography of Irish history, 1870–1911*, Dublin: NLI, 1940, 319 p. NLI RR.

Evans, Edward, *Historical and Bibliographical Account of Almanacks, Directories etc., in Ireland from the Sixteenth Century*, Dublin: 1897, 149 p. (Repr. Blackrock: Carraig Books, 1976), NLI Ir. 9410016 e 3.

Keen, M.E. *A Bibliography of Trade Directories of the British Isles in the Victoria and Albert Museum*, London: V&A Museum, 1979, 121 p. NLI G 01742 v 1.

Chapter 11 ∾

THE INTERNET

G enealogy and computers were made for one another, and the internet holds the promise of transforming genealogical research. For many areas outside Ireland, that promise is already coming good: witness the Scottish General Register Office's website at *www.scotlandspeople.gov.uk*, or the 1901 census for England and Wales at *www.census.pro.gov.uk*. Unfortunately, in the case of Irish research the change has been slow and piecemeal. Few of the record-holding institutions have begun the process of making records available online, and what records are available vary greatly in quality. Nonetheless, the huge interest in Irish genealogy, particularly in North America, has produced a profusion of resources for anyone with Irish ancestors. The survey that follows presumes familiarity with the basics of web browsers and e-mail.

STARTING POINTS

Research guides
* Good, basic guides can be found on the NAI website, *www.national archives.ie/genealogy.html*, and on the NLI site, *www.nli.ie/pdfs/famili.pdf*. A more detailed treatment can be found on a site in which I have a personal involvement, Irish Ancestors, part of *The Irish Times*' ireland.com site, at *www.ireland.com/ancestor*. The 'Browse' section gives detailed accounts of all the record sources used in Irish research.

Other, brief guides include:
* Sean Murphy's Beginner's Guide, *homepage.eircom.net/~seanjmurphy/dir/guide.htm*.
* The Fianna Homepage at *www.rootsweb.com/~fianna*, which presumes research is being carried out via the Family History Centres of the Church of Jesus Christ of Latter-Day Saints.

Listings sites
There are numerous listings that provide links to Irish genealogy sites. Since many of these sites consist largely of listings, a frustrating amount of travelling in circles is inevitable. The sites listed below are the largest and most stable. For a

more detailed treatment of the structure of the first two, in particular, see Peter Christian's *The Genealogist's Internet* (Public Record Office, 2001), by far the most comprehensive publication on genealogy and the internet. By definition, all of these sites suffer from a certain amount of link-rot.

- The mother of all genealogy site lists is Cyndi Howell's *www.cyndislist.com*, which categorises and cross-references online genealogical resources. The Irish section is at *www.cyndislist.com/ireland.htm*. With over 175,000 links in total, the sheer scale of the enterprise is very impressive, but also means it can be almost as difficult to track something down on Cyndi's List as it is on the internet itself.
- A more discriminating guide can be found at Genuki, *www.genuki.org.uk/indexes/IRLcontents.html*, where a good attempt is made to give a comprehensive overview of the relevant records, with links listed where there are matching online resources.
- The WorldGenWeb project is a volunteer-run survey of sources relating to particular localities. The county-by-county listings for the twenty-six counties now in the Republic of Ireland can be found at *www.irelandgenweb.com*, while those for the six counties of Northern Ireland are at *www.rootsweb.com/~nir-wgw*. The quality of the listings depends very much on the enthusiasm and discrimination of the individuals responsible; some counties are superb.
- Ireland Genealogy Projects at *irelandgenealogyprojects.rootsweb.com* is the original home of the IrelandGenWeb project. Again, some of the county pages are excellent, some not so excellent.
- The Irish Ancestors listings at *scripts.ireland.com/ancestor/browse/links* attempts to present a county-by-county listing of available online source materials, as well as passenger lists and family sites.

Other sites with valuable listings include:
- *www.genealogylinks.net/uk/ireland*: a good listing, despite the identification of Ireland as a region of the UK.
- *www.tiara.ie/links.html*: another well-maintained and comprehensive site is that of the Irish Ancestral Research Association.
- *www.doras.ie*: the Irish telecom company, Eircom, has a very large directory of Irish sites, which includes a large listing of Irish surname and family sites as well as many Irish genealogy sites. Unusually, a rating system is used to try to give some idea of the quality of the sites listed. Unfortunately, no categorisation other than 'genealogy' is used, which can make it difficult to pin down specifics.

Online sources
As already outlined, there are very few sites offering comprehensive searches of Irish sources. But for particular areas and records there are some very good sites, giving a tantalising glimpse of the way things should be.

MAJOR SOURCES

General Register Office Records
The Republic GRO website is at *www.groireland.ie* and the Northern Ireland office is at *www.groni.gov.uk*—neither has any online search facility. Although an Irish government computerisation project has been ongoing for some years, it is focused primarily on facilitating the work of the Irish legal, health and welfare systems, with historical use well down the list of priorities. However, the nineteenth-century records will certainly be searchable online at some point, and it is worth keeping an eye on the GRO website for updates. In any case, the fact that the LDS Church has microfilm copies of most of the records has allowed a certain amount of piecemeal transcription to happen. It should be remembered that the microfilm copies they transcribe are themselves transcriptions of local registrations, with the inevitable additional layer of human error.

* *www.familysearch.org*: the LDS site includes transcripts of the first eleven years of birth registrations, 1864–1875, as part of the International Genealogical Index.
* *www.waterfordcountylibrary.ie*: Waterford County Library has made local death registrations from 1864 to 1901 available and freely searchable.
* *www.clarelibrary.ie/eolas/coclare/genealogy/deaths_in_the_liscannor_area.htm*: Clare County Library has a list of deaths in the Liscannor area.
* *www.sci.net.au/userpages/mgrogan/cork/*: partial transcripts for Co. Cork are available on Margaret Grogan's site.
* There are quite a few sites that invite users to submit records they have transcribed themselves; one of the best organised is *www.cmcrp.net*. The problems are self-evident: accuracy is always doubtful and, in most cases, it is not clear what proportion of the records is included.

Census records
As a result of the destruction of most of the nineteenth-century records, the earliest complete censuses of Ireland, dating from 1901 and 1911, have been available for public research for more than thirty years, with LDS microfilm copies of the 1901 census widely available. However, to date no systematic attempt has been made to make either census searchable online, although NAI is exploring the possibility. Again, the availability of the microfilms has allowed transcriptions for particular areas. Only the most extensive transcripts are listed below.

* For county-by county listings, see *www.census-online.com/links/Ireland/*, *www.censusfinder.com/ireland.htm* and *scripts.ireland.com/ancestor/browse/links/counties.htm*, as well as *www.cyndislist.com/ireland.htm*.
* *www.leitrim-roscommon.com*: the best site for Irish census returns, indeed possibly the single best Irish research site on the internet, is the Leitrim–Roscommon Genealogy website. As well as an almost complete database of

the 1901 returns for Counties Leitrim and Roscommon, the site contains large numbers of transcripts from Counties Mayo, Sligo, Westmeath and Wexford. Unlike many other sites there is a systematic account of which records are complete and which are still to be added. The quality of the transcripts is consistently good.

- *www.clarelibrary.ie*: Clare County Library has a full transcript of the 1901 census for the county.
- *www.sci.net.au/userpages/mgrogan/cork*: Margaret Grogan's site has a large number of transcripts for Cork, for both 1901 and 1911, submitted by volunteers.
- *freepages.genealogy.rootsweb.com/~donegal/census.htm*: volunteer transcripts for 1901 and 1911 for parts of Donegal.
- *www.caora.net/find.php*: an index to the heads of household for Co. Down in 1901.

Parish records
Despite the fact that virtually all Irish parish records have been transcribed in database format, no systematic attempt has been made to make them searchable online. Anything available online is once again largely a result of the availability of LDS microfilms to volunteer transcribers.

- County-by-county listings can be found at *scripts.ireland.com/ancestor/ browse/links/counties.htm* and a general listing is at *www.cyndislist.com/ireland.htm*.
- *www.familysearch.org*: the LDS website includes the records of twelve Roman Catholic parishes in Kerry and northwest Cork, which were published by Albert Casey in *O'Kief, Coshe Mang* (16 vols, Pr. Pr. 1964–1972). As transcripts of transcripts, they need to be approached with caution. A number of other parishes, mainly in Galway, Roscommon and Sligo, are also included in the IGI. Most were originally published on the second edition of the LDS CD-ROM *British Isles Vital Records Index* (2002).
- *www.rootsweb.com/~irllog/churchrecs.htm*: the records of five Longford Roman Catholic parishes.
- *www.irishgenealogy.ie*: Irish Genealogy Ltd is a company set up to promote Irish genealogy. It currently offers a signposting database using the records of eleven local heritage centres, Armagh, Cavan, Derry, Donegal, Fermanagh, Leitrim, Limerick, Mayo, Sligo, Tyrone and Wexford, which allows users to identify if records matching their search criteria are held by a particular centre. To access fuller details, a commissioned search is then necessary.
- *www.ancestryireland.co.uk*: the UHF has made an index to its parish record collection searchable online.

Property Records
Because of the lack of nineteenth-century census material the two property surveys, Griffith's Valuation (1847–1864) and the Tithe Applotment Books

(1823–1838) have acquired unusual importance. The former, Griffith's, is the single most widely available online source.

*   *scripts.ireland.com/ancestor/surname/index.cfm*: has a count of the number of Griffith's householders of a particular surname by county (free) and parish (fee).
*   *www.leitrim-roscommon.com*: has transcripts for twenty-two parishes in Roscommon, twenty-four in Limerick and ten in Galway.
*   *www.irishorigins.com*: a pay-per-view version of Griffith's, including the associated Ordnance Survey maps, was launched in 2003 in association with the NLI and Eneclann.

The Tithe Books are less well served:

*   *www.caora.net*: has an index to the Tithe Books of Co. Down.
*   Otherwise *scripts.ireland.com/ancestor/browse/links/counties.htm* and *www. genealogylinks.net/uk/ireland* have county-by-county listings for individual parishes.

OTHER SOURCES

Migration records
The vast majority of these records relate to North America and Australia.

*   *www.immigrantships.net*: the major site for ships' lists, copied by volunteers.
*   *www.ellisisland.org*: the Ellis Island site has New York arrivals records from 1892 to 1924.
*   *www.genealogybranches.com/irishpassengerlists*: the Irish Passenger Lists Research Guide gives a good overview of the available records.
*   *scripts.ireland.com/ancestor/browse/links/passship-a.htm*: has a selection of links to ships' lists.
*   *www.nationalarchives.ie/search1.html*: has an extensive but incomplete database of transportation records from Ireland to Australia up to 1868.
*   *www.pcug.org.au/~ppmay/convicts.htm*: has details of convict arrivals in Australia for 1791–1820, a period for which the National Archives transportation registers have not survived.
*   *www.castlegarden.org*: New York arrivals, 1830–1892.

Gravestone inscriptions
*   *interment.net/Ireland*: provides web-space for volunteers to submit transcriptions and compilations. The site is well-organised, but very few of the transcripts are complete.
*   *www.fermanagh.org.uk*: Fermanagh Gold has a good collection of Fermanagh gravestone inscriptions, as well as other information about the county.
*   *www.webone.com.au/~sgrieves/cemetries__ireland.htm*: has a good selection, mostly from Tipperary.

- *www.historyfromheadstones.com:* the UHF and Irish World have made their collection of headstone transcripts for the six counties of Northern Ireland searchable online, for a fee.

Military and Police records
- *www.ancestry.com:* has the Royal Irish Constabulary List, an index to the LDS microfilms of the original service registers. As of May 2005, the index is about 70 per cent complete.
- *www.cwgc.org:* the Commonwealth War Graves Commission is probably the best online military database.
- *www.greatwar.ie:* the Royal Dublin Fusiliers Association has excellent information on the Irish in the First World War.
- *www.nationalarchives.gov.uk/documentsonline:* has a complete listing of Royal Navy seamen from 1853.

Loan Fund records
- *www.movinghere.org.uk:* a subsidiary site of the National Archives (Kew) has scanned and indexed a large proportion of the Reproductive Loan Fund records, c.1838–1852. The indexing is peculiar and the layout of the site confusing, but it is worth persevering. See Chapter 2, and the county source-lists for Cork, Galway, Limerick, Mayo, Roscommon and Tipperary.

Newspapers
- *www.ucs.louisiana.edu/bnl/*: the *Belfast Newsletter*—biographical material.
- *www.irishnewspaperarchives.com:* promises to allow full-text searches of a number of eighteenth- and nineteenth-century Irish newspapers, but has yet to launch at the time of writing (June 2005).

Discussion groups

Usenet
Discussion or news groups were one of the first uses of the internet and can still be extremely interesting. Most browsers now provide a newsreader, but the simplest means of access is through *groups.google.com.* The Irish group is soc.genealogy.ireland, which was set up in August 1997—messages before that date will be in soc.genealogy.uk+ireland. Access is also provided by *www.irishinbritain.com.* A less widely used newsgroup, also available as above, is soc.genealogy.surnames.ireland.

Mailing lists
These send a copy of every message submitted to the group to all subscribed members. They can be useful for unusual surnames, or for specific research issues. However, be sure to keep the initial instructions on how to unsubscribe, or you may find yourself swamped. By far the largest and most venerable collection of lists is at *lists.rootsweb.com.* A full Irish list can be found at *www.rootsweb.*

com/~jfuller/gen_mail_country-unk-irl.html. Yahoo has forty-six Irish genealogy lists at *groups.yahoo.com*.

Geography
A specific townland address of origin is the key to most Irish sources. *The General Alphabetical Index to the Townlands and Towns, Parishes and Baronies of Ireland* (repr. GPC GPC, 1981), first published in 1861 and based on the 1851 census, is the standard source. It is freely searchable on two sites:

- *www.seanruad.com*: has a straightforward interface and includes information on acreage and barony.
- *scripts.ireland.com/ancestor/placenames*: allows wildcard searches and complete listings for individual parishes.

Surname sites
Many researchers who have done a good deal of research will publish it on a website, partly through straightforward altruism, partly through enlightened self-interest—the more people publish, the greater the chance that someone from a related branch of the family will see the information and be able to add to it. The information provided ranges from superb to abysmal. There are now millions of personal family history sites, and tracking down any relevant ones can be difficult.

- *www.cyndislist.com*: has an enormous list, indexed alphabetically.
- *freepages.rootsweb.com*: is the largest provider of free genealogy pages.
- *www.genealogy.com*: also gives users free web pages and allows searches.
- *www.google.com*: a straightforward search—for example, 'Murphy Family History'—on a site such as Google or Yahoo can often be surprisingly rewarding.

Archives and libraries
Web addresses are given in Chapter 15.

Commercial sites
- *www.originsnetwork.com*: the Irish section of the site includes Griffith's Valuation (see above), as well as many of the sources published on CD-ROM by Eneclann. These include the William Smith O'Brien Petition (see Chapter 2), the index to the Dublin City census of 1851 and the NAI Wills Index.
- *www.ancestry.com*: the biggest commercial genealogy site has so far added little of direct Irish interest. Apart from the RIC index (see above), the main resource is the collection of US passenger and immigration lists.
- *www.ancestryireland.co.uk*: the UHF has a wide range of sources relating to Ulster, including indexes to its databases, transcripts of Down and Antrim church records, as well as some with wider relevance, such as the Irish Will Calendars 1858–1878.

- *www.ireland.com/ancestor*: provides personalised guidance on relevant sources. Most of the site is free to view, including civil and Roman Catholic parish maps.

COMMISSIONING RESEARCH

- The NLI, NAI and NA (Kew) websites include lists of researchers willing to carry out commissioned research, purely as a convenience.
- *www.apgi.ie*: the home site of the Association of Professional Genealogists in Ireland.
- *www.irish-roots.net*: the home of the Irish Family History Foundation, the umbrella body of the network for most of local heritage centres in Ireland.

Finally, a perennial problem with online information is that websites, especially small, personal sites with family or record details, are very perishable. The Internet Archive Project at *web.archive.org* is a brave attempt to store the web. Their 'Wayback Machine' holds copies of virtually all sites that have appeared (and disappeared) since 1998 and is readily searchable.

Chapter 12 ❧

OCCUPATIONAL RECORDS

ARMY, LAWYERS, MEDICS, CLERGY, TEACHERS, POLICE

Army

Identifying which records are relevant depends on whether your ancestor was a soldier or an officer, and on the period in which they served. Almost all of the records are in the English National Archives.

Soldiers

From the late eighteenth century on a very large proportion of the rank-and-file of the British Army consisted of Irishmen: one estimate for the mid-nineteenth century is 40 per cent of the total men serving. You should remember that these men served throughout the Army, not exclusively in the Irish regiments.

Soldiers' Documents (Discharges)

WO97 contains records of discharges from the Army between 1760 and 1913 and can often provide details of place of birth, age and appearance and, after 1882, next-of-kin. The records up to 1882 only cover those soldiers discharged to pension; after that year all discharges are recorded. Before 1873 the records are organised by regiment, but a name index exists for the period 1760–1854. Between 1854 and 1873 you must know the regiment to use the records. From 1873 to 1882 they are organised under the collective headings 'Artillery', 'Cavalry', 'Corps' and 'Infantry', and then alphabetically within these headings. From 1883 they are alphabetical. Many of the early discharge papers are summarised in the online National Archives catalogue at *www.catalogue.nationalarchives.gov.uk*. It can be worthwhile to enter the name of the individual, or the county militia, in the catalogue search page and see what emerges.

A minority of soldiers were discharged to pension; if your soldier does not appear in the Soldiers' Documents, you many find him in one of the sources below.

Pension Records

In Ireland, if a soldier was discharged to pension or discharged as medically unfit before 1823, detailed information will be found in the Registers of the Royal Hospital Kilmainham, wo119, containing the Certificates of Service. These are organised by regimental number, which you can trace through wo118, Kilmainham Admission Books. In-pensioners' records—for those actually resident in the institution—go from 1704 to 1922 and are also in wo118. Irish out-pensioners—those receiving a pension but not actually resident—were administered from the Royal Hospital Chelsea after 1822 (wo 116/117). Regimental Registers of Admissions to Pension also exist, indexed from 1806 to 1836; otherwise, each regimental volume includes an index. The NAI also holds microfilm copies of the Kilmainham records.

You should remember that:

1. It was quite common for Irishmen to be discharged outside Ireland, in which case pension papers would be in the Chelsea records, even between 1760 and 1822.
2. Only a minority of those who served are covered.

Pay Lists and Musters

From the early eighteenth century to 1878 each regiment made a quarterly return of all personnel. From the 1860s these included details of wives and children living in married quarters. These are obviously much more comprehensive than the pensions and discharge records and can supply fascinating detail about individuals. The date of enlistment can be used to search the relevant muster, which should give birthplace, age and former occupation. The records are in wo10–wo13. However, it is necessary to know the regiment before using these records, a prerequisite which can prove a serious obstacle.

Other Records

Casualties and deserters: soldiers who died on active service are recorded in the regimental returns of casualties from 1795 to 1875, in wo25, which are indexed. Additional material, such as wills, lists of effects or details of next-of-kin, may also be found. The same series also includes details of absentees and registers of deserters for the first half of the nineteenth century. There is also an incomplete card index of army deserters (1689–1830).

Description Books: also in wo25 are the regimental description books, the earliest dating from 1756, the latest from 1900, which give physical details as well as service history. They are not comprehensive and do not cover the entire period.

Regimental Registers of Births, 1761–1924: the index to regimental registers of births, 1761–1924, gives the regiment and place of birth of children born to the wives of serving soldiers, if they were attached to the regiment. The index is available at NA (kew), but the records are held by the Family Records Centre and are not on open access.

Finding the Regiment
For most of the pre-1873 records, knowing the regiment is vital, but can be quite difficult to ascertain.

1. Uniforms: try *www.regiments.org*, or D.J. Barnes' 'Identification and Dating: Military Uniforms', in *Family History in Focus*, D.J. Steel and L. Taylor (eds.) (Guildford: 1984), or the National Army Museum (*www.national-army-museum. ac.uk*).
2. The Regimental Registers of Births (see above) can help if you have some idea of the names of children, or the areas in which a soldier served.
3. Wills of soldiers dying overseas were proved at the Prerogative Court of Canterbury (PROB 11). There are various published indexes. The registers of next-of-kin in wo25 may also be useful.
4. If you have an idea where a soldier was stationed, and approximately when, J.M. Kitzmiller's *In Search of the Forlorn Hope: a Comprehensive Guide to Locating British Regiments and their Records* (Salt Lake City: 1988) will help you to identify which regiments were stationed where.

Later Records

The Irish Soldiers' & Sailors' Fund
This Fund was set up to provide cottages for Irishmen who had served in the armed forces during the First World War and over 4,000 cottages were built up to the 1930s. In Northern Ireland cottages were built up until 1952. The records are organised by place; there is no name index. The tenancy files are in AP 7.

Boer War
The Family Record Centre has separate indexes to the deaths of Army personnel in the South African ('Boer') war from 1899 to 1902. The GRO in Dublin also has an index to 'Deaths of Irish Subjects pertaining to the South African War (1898–1902)' in the deaths index for 1902. Certified copies of the original entries include regiment and rank.

First World War
Of the 6.5 million records of servicemen in the First World War originally held at the War Office Record Store, more than four million were destroyed during the Second World War. Those that survived were charred or suffered water damage and consequently are unavailable for research. A microfilming project to make the records (generally known as the 'burnt documents') publicly accessible was completed in the summer of 2002, and the films are now available at NA (Kew) and via the LDS Family History Centres. More than two million individuals are

covered, with a variety of records. Among the most common are attestation papers, which give information regarding name, address, date of birth and next-of-kin.

Ireland's Memorial Records (Dublin, 1923) is an eight-volume commemorative publication listing the Irishmen and women killed during the war and those of other nationalities who died while serving with Irish regiments. It also supplies the place of origin. (Eneclann CD-ROM #CD11, 2004.)

The Commonwealth War Graves Commission

The Commission maintains graves in more than 150 countries, covering more than 925,000 individuals who were members of the forces of the Commonwealth killed in the two World Wars. Their website, at www.cwgc.org, includes extensive details on the individuals whose graves they look after.

Officers

Lists

The official Army List was published at least annually from 1740 and records all officers. Hart's Army List was published from 1839 to 1915 and supplies more information about individual's army careers. Both publications are available at NA (Kew). Annotated copies, sometimes including supplementary details, are in wo65 (1754–1879) and wo66 (1879–1900).

Commissions

Records concerning the purchase and sale of the commissions of Irish officers from 1768 to 1871 can be found in HO123. Correspondence relating generally to commissions between 1793 and 1871 is in wo31. These records are arranged chronologically, can be extremely informative and are relatively simple to use as the date of commission is supplied by the Army List.

Service records

These records, in wo25, are not comprehensive, consisting of a series of surveys carried out every fifteen to twenty years between 1809 and 1872. The early returns concentrate on military service, with some biographical detail supplied in the later ones. The records are covered by an alphabetical card index on open access, which also takes in wo75, an episodic series of regimental service returns between 1755 and 1954.

Pensions

Up to 1871, if an officer did not sell his commission on retirement, he went on half-pay—a retainer that meant he was theoretically available for service. Records of these payments, as well as widows' and dependants' pensions, can provide detailed biographical information. The half-pay ledgers of payment from 1737 to 1921 are in PMG 4, arranged by regiment up to 1841 and thereafter alphabetically. wo25 also contains much detail on pensions and dependants.

Other

Many officers' original baptismal certificates are included in War Office records for 1777–1868 in w032/8903–w032/8920 (code 21A) and for 1755–1908 in w042. Both are indexed.

Attornies and Barristers

Up to 1867 it was necessary to be admitted to the King's Inns Society in order to become either a barrister or an attorney (solicitor); Roman Catholics were excluded until 1794. To gain admission to the Society as either an apprentice (to become a solicitor), or as a student (to become a barrister), one had to submit a good deal of family information. The earlier papers relating to admission are incomplete, but what survives has been published in *King's Inns admission papers, 1607–1867*, Edward Keane, P. Beryl Phair and Thomas U. Sadlier (eds.) (Dublin: Stationery Office for the Irish Manuscripts Commission, 1982). To research the later careers of lawyers, directories, in particular Dublin directories, are the major source.

Clergymen

Roman Catholic

Since Roman Catholic priests did not marry, their usefulness for genealogical research is limited, but their relative prominence means they left records that can lead the researcher to other members of their families. Obituaries are relatively common from the latter half of the nineteenth century, while the information in seminary records can lead to a precise place of origin.

Until the 1790s all Irish Catholic clergy were educated in continental Europe because of the legal restrictions laid down by the Penal laws. When these restrictions were lifted, two seminaries were founded in short order: St Patrick's in Carlow and St Patrick's in Maynooth. Some of their records have been published:

* *Maynooth students and ordinations index, 1795–1895* (Patrick J. Hamell Birr, Co. Offaly: P.J. Hamell, 1992).
* *Carlow College 1793–1993 the ordained students and the teaching staff of St. Patrick's College, Carlow* (J. McEvoy, Carlow: St Patrick's College, 1993).

The *Irish Catholic Directory* was published annually from 1836 and lists priests by diocese and parish.

Church of Ireland

Biographical details of Church of Ireland clergy can be found in the Leslie Biographical Index, a far-reaching compendium originated by the Rev. James Leslie and held at the RCBL in Dublin. Additional information is also available in Leslie's Succession Lists—chronological accounts arranged by diocese and parish. The succession lists for thirteen dioceses have been published. The RCBL has these and the remaining dioceses in typescript. Church of Ireland Directories were also published, intermittently but frequently, in the first half of the nineteenth century, and annually from 1862.

Methodist

The key work for Methodist clergy is *An Alphabetical Arrangement of all the Wesleyan Methodist Preachers and Missionaries (Ministers, Missionaries & Preachers on Trial), etc* (Bradford T. Inkersley), originally by William Hill but republished twenty-one times between 1819 and 1927. It covers all clergy in the British Isles, giving locations and year of service. C.H. Crookshank's *History of Methodism in Ireland, 1740–1860* (3 vols, Belfast: 1885–1888) records brief biographical details of preachers. It is continued in H. Lee Cole's *History of Methodism in Ireland, 1860–1960* (Belfast: 1961).

Presbyterian

Two works cover almost all ministers: the Rev. James McConnell's *Fasti of the Irish Presbyterian Church 1613–1840* (Belfast: 1938) covers the early years of the Synod of Ulster; John M. Barkly's *Fasti of the General Assembly of the Presbyterian Church in Ireland 1840–1910* (3 vols, Presbyterian Historical Society: 1986–1987) takes things up to 1910. Other useful sources are listed below.

- *McComb's Presbyterian Almanack, Belfast*, W. M'Comb, 1841–1886?, NLI, Ir. 285 m 1.
- *New Plan for Education in Ireland 1838* (Part 1 pp (27.8) 200–205) (Names of Presbyterian Clergymen and their congregations in Cos Antrim, Armagh, Down, Donegal, Fermanagh, Tyrone, Cork, Dublin, King's, Louth, Westmeath, Mayo, 1837) NLI.
- *History of Congregations*, NLI, Ir. 285 h 8.
- Smith's *Belfast Almanack*, 1820 (see Chapter 13, 'Antrim').
- Ferguson, Rev. S., *Brief Biographical Notices of some Irish Covenanting Ministers who laboured during the latter half of the eighteenth century*, Londonderry: J. Montgomery, 1897, NLI, Ir. 285 f 1.
- Irwin, C.H., *A History of Presbyterians in Dublin and the South and West of Ireland*, Dublin: Mecredy & Kyle 1890, NLI, Ir. 285 i 1.
- Latimer, W.T., *History of the Irish Presbyterians*, Belfast: J. Cleeland, 1902, NLI, Ir. 285 l 1.
- Marshall, W.F., *Ulster Sails West*, Baltimore: GPC, 1996, NLI, Ir. 973 m 59.
- McConnell, J., *Fasti of the Irish Presbyterian Church*, Belfast: 1938, NLI, Ir. 285 m 14.
- Reid, James Seiton, *History of the Presbyterian Church, London, 1853*, NLI, Ir. 285 r 2.
- Stewart, Rev. D., *The Seceders in Ireland, With Annals of Their Congregations*, Belfast: Presbyterian Historical Society, 1950, NLI, Ir. 285 s 5.
- Witherow, Thomas, *Historical and Literary Memorials of Presbyterianism in Ireland 1731–1800*, London: W. Mullan, 1880, NLI Ir. 285 w 1.

Doctors

As medical practice was only partly regulated before the mid-nineteenth century, early records of medical education are patchy. The major Irish institutions were the Dublin Guild of Barber-Surgeons (from 1576), the Royal College of Physicians of Ireland (from 1667), the Royal College of Surgeons in Ireland (from 1784) and Apothecaries' Hall (from 1747). In addition, Dublin University (Trinity College) had a School of Physic (Medicine) from 1711. Many Irish medical men also trained in Britain or on the Continent.

The Dublin Guild of Barber-Surgeons records are held in Trinity College (Ms. 1447), and the Royal College of Physicians of Ireland has registers from the seventeenth century. However, both sources are difficult to access and use and in most cases Dublin Directories or Freeman's Lists are just as informative and easier to use. The records of Apothecaries' Hall from 1747 to 1833 are on microfilm in the NLI (Pos. 929). *Alumni Dublinenses* (George D. Burtchaell and Thomas U. Sadleir (eds.), Dublin: 1935) contains detailed records of Trinity College students up to 1860.

To trace the careers of medical practitioners, the major sources are Dublin Directories, which list physicians and surgeons from 1761 and apothecaries from 1751, local (generally later) Directories (see Chapter 10) and Irish Medical Directories, published intermittently between 1843 and the end of the nineteenth century.

Another, less conventional source is the 'Biographical file on Irish medics', compiled by T.P.C. Kirkpatrick and comprising a compendium of biographical material on Irish medics up to 1954. It is held in the Royal College of Physicians. The College and the NLI both hold a copy of the index.

A bibliography of published works will be found in the checklist in Part 2.

Policemen

From the late eighteenth century a police force was in operation in Dublin City, with a part-time, *ad hoc* constabulary serving the rest of the country. In 1814 an armed Peace Preservation Force was created, followed by the full-time County Constabulary in 1822. These two were amalgamated in 1836 as the Irish Constabulary, renamed the Royal Irish Constabulary in 1867 (better known as the RIC). The separate Dublin force remained in existence and was known as the Dublin Metropolitan Police (DMP). When the Irish Free State came into being in 1922, the RIC was disbanded and responsibility for policing passed to An Garda Síochána in the twenty-six counties, and to the newly formed Royal Ulster Constabulary (RUC) in the six counties of Northern Ireland.

Excellent personnel records were kept from 1816. The General Register from that date to 1922 is now in NA (Kew) (HO 184), with microfilm copies in the NAI, the LDS Family History Library and PRONI. For each recruit it includes a brief service record, date of marriage and wife's native county, and the name of the individual who recommended him. This can be important in helping to identify an exact place of origin, since the recommendations usually came from local clergymen or magistrates who knew the recruit personally. Thom's Directories (see Chapter 10) can be used to pinpoint addresses. HO 184 also includes a separate Officers' Register.

The partly alphabetical index to the Registers included in HO 184 has now been superseded by Jim Herlihy's *The Royal Irish Constabulary: a complete alphabetical list of officers and men, 1816–1922* (Dublin: Four Courts, 1999), which supplies the Service Number needed to use the Registers quickly and easily.

A further source, available only at Kew, is PMG 48: 'Pensions and allowances to officers, men and staff of the Royal Irish Constabulary and to their widows and children'. This dates from the 1870s and usually gives the address of the recipient.

The DMP Register is held by the Garda Archives at Dublin Castle, but is more readily available on microfilm at the NAI. It does not give marriage details but does supply a parish of origin.

Teachers

Irish education was relatively informal until quite recently and up to the last quarter of the nineteenth century a large majority of teachers in Ireland had received no formal training. The Society for Promoting the Education of the Poor of Ireland, better known as the Kildare Place Society, made the first attempt to provide systematic, non-denominational primary education. Founded in 1811, it trained several thousand teachers and supported schools throughout the country. Its personnel records from 1814 to 1854 are now held by the Church of Ireland College of Education at Upper Rathmines Road, Dublin 6 *(www.cice.ie)*.

Appendix 22 of the *Irish Education Enquiry, 1826, 2nd Report* (4 vols) lists all parochial schools in Ireland in 1824, including names of teachers and other details. It is indexed in *Schoolmasters and schoolmistresses in Ireland, 1826–1827* (1982), by Dorothy Rines Dingfelder (NLI Ir. 372 d 38).

The Enquiry itself was set up in response to objections from the Roman Catholic hierarchy to the Kildare Place schools. Its outcome was the establishment of the Board of National Education in 1831, which ended State support for the Kildare Place schools and placed control of elementary education in the hands of the local clergy in the form of National Schools, a system still in place today.

The principal source for teachers in the National Schools is the series of Teachers Salary Books from 1834 to 1855, held by the NAI. These are not particularly informative from a genealogical point of view, but sometimes include comments that can be of interest. They are organised by school, so it is necessary to know where your teacher was working. See also the bibliography of published sources in Part 2.

CHECKLIST OF SOURCES

Apothecaries

(a) GO Ms. 648 *Apothecaries, apprentices, journeymen and prosecutions, 1791–1829.*

(b) List of Licensed Apothecaries of Ireland 1872, NLI Ir. 61501 i 1.

(c) *Admissions to the guilds of Dublin, 1792–1837, Reports from Committees,* Parliamentary Papers, 1837, Vol 11 (ii).

(d) NLI Report on Private Collections No. 208.

(e) Records of Apothecaries Hall, Dublin, 1747–1833. NLI Pos. 929.

(f) McWalter, James Charles, A *history of the Worshipful Company of Apothecaries of the City of Dublin,* Dublin: E. Ponsonby, 1916, 166 p. NLI Ir. 615 m 1.

Architects

Loeber, Rolf, *A biographical dictionary of architects in Ireland, 1600–1720,* London: John Murray, 1981, 127 p. NLI Ir. 9291 L 2.

Aristocracy and Gentry

(a) *A Visitation of Seats and Arms of the Noblemen and Gentlemen of Great Britain and Ireland* (1852–1853), see Hugh Montgomery-Massinberd's *Burke's Family Index,* Burke's: 1976, for a composite index; also covers d), e), f) and g) below.

(b) Bence-Jones, Mark, *Burke's Guide to Country Houses, Vol 1, Ireland,* Burke's: 1978. A clear guide to which families owned particular houses.

(c) *Burke's Commoners of Great Britain and Ireland* (3 vols), 1837.

(d) *Burke's Extinct Peerages ...* (1831), five subsequent editions.

(e) *Burke's Peerage and Baronetage of the United Kingdom ...* (1826), 106 subsequent editions.

(f) *Burke's Landed Gentry of Great Britain and Ireland* (4 vols), subsequent editions in 1858, 1863, 1871, 1879, 1886, 1894, 1898, 1937; (Irish supplement).

(g) *Burke's Landed Gentry of Ireland,* 1904, 1912, 1958.

(h) *Debrett's Peerage, Baronetage, Knightage and Companionage (1852),* many subsequent editions.

(i) Leet, Ambrose, *A Directory to the Market Towns, Villages, Gentlemen's Seats and other Noted Places in Ireland,* 1812, 1814 NLI Ir. 9141 l 10. Shows country houses and their owners.

(j) Taylor and Skinner, *Road Maps of Ireland* (1778, Repr. IUP: 1969). NLI Ir. 9414 t 1. Shows homes of gentlemen along the major routes through the country; the surnames are alphabetically indexed.

(k) *The Post-Chaise Companion through Ireland* (1783). Descriptions of journeys along the main coach roads, including the names of country houses and their owners' surnames, NLI.

(l) Walford, E., *The County Families of the United Kingdom,* Britain: Chatto & Windus, 1877. Subsequent editions annually.

Artists
(a) Artists of Ireland (1796), Williams. NLI Ir. 9275 w 3.
(b) Breeze, George, *Society of Artists in Ireland: index of exhibits, 1765–1780*, Dublin: National Gallery of Ireland, 1985, 57 p. NLI Ir. 708 b 1.
(c) Stewart, Ann M., *Royal Hibernian Academy of Arts: index of exhibitors and their works 1826–1979*, Dublin: Manton, 1986 (3 vols.). NLI Ir. 921 r 2.
(d) Crookshank, Ann and Glin, Knight of, *The painters of Ireland, c.1660–1920*, London: Barrie and Jenkins, 1978. NLI Ir. 750 c 2.
(e) Murray, Peter, *Cork artists in the 19th century*, Cork: 1991. NLI Ir. 708 c 7. (Catalogue of Crawford Gallery exhibition.)
(f) Strickland, Walter, *A Dictionary of Irish Artists*, Dublin: IUP, 1969, 2 vols. Repr. of 1913 ed., DCLA.

Bakers
(a) Admissions to the guilds of Dublin, 1792–1837, *Reports from Committees, Parliamentary Papers, 1837*, Vol. 11 (ii).
(b) *Freemen's Rolls of the city of Dublin 1468–1485 & 1575–1774* in (i) GO 490–493 (Thrift Abstracts), (ii) DCLA (Original Registers), (iii) NLI Mss 76–79.

Barbers and Surgeons
(a) *Admissions to the guilds of Dublin, 1792–1837, Reports from Committees*, Parliamentary Papers, 1837, Vol. 11 (ii).
(b) *Freemen's Rolls of the city of Dublin 1468–1485 & 1575–1774* in (i) GO 490–493 (Thrift Abstracts), and (ii) DCLA (Original Registers).

Board of Ordnance employees
Mainly concerned with the upkeep of fortifications and harbours, with some of the principal locations being Buncrana, Enniskillen, Ballincollig, Cobh, Spike Island. *IG*, 1985.

Booksellers and Printers
(a) *Dictionary of Printers & Booksellers, 1668–1775*, E.R. McC. Dix, NLI 6551 b 1, 6551 b 4. See also under 'Dix' in NLI Author Catalogue for various provincial centres.
(b) Kirkpatrick, T.P.C., *Notes on Dublin Printers in the Seventeenth Century*, Dublin: University Press, 1929. NLI Ir. 65510941 k 1.
(c) *Irish Booksellers & English Authors*, R.C. Cole, Dublin: 1954.
(d) Pollard, A.W., *A short title catalogue of books printed in England, Scotland and Ireland … 1475–1640*, Bibliographical Society: 1986–1991, co-editor, G.R. Redgrave; 3 vols; Vol. 3 includes an index of printers and publishers.

Brewers
Old Kilkenny Review, 1988, p. 583.

Bricklayers
Records of the Bricklayers' and Stonemasons' Guild, from 1830. NAI Acc. 1097.
Dún Laoghaire Genealogical Society Journal, 'Dublin City Tradesmen employed by
    Board of Works', Vol. 4 (2) (1995).
See also 'Barbers and Surgeons', above.

Carpenters
'The Dublin Guild of Carpenters, 1656', IG 8, No. 3 (1992), 333–335.
Dún Laoghaire Genealogical Society Journal, 'Dublin City Tradesmen employed by
    Board of Works', Vol. 4 (2) (1995).
See also 'Barbers and Surgeons', above.

Clockmakers
(a)   National Museum Ms, List of Watch & Clockmakers in Ireland, 1687–1844.
      NLI Pos. 204.
(b)   Fennell, Geraldine, *A List of Irish Watch- and Clockmakers,* Dublin: The
      Stationery Office, 1963. 42 p. NLI Ir. 681 f 10.

Coachbuilders
Cooke, Jim, *Ireland's premier coachbuilder, John Hutton & Sons, Summerhill,
    Dublin 1779–1925,* Dublin: 1993. NLI Ir. 670 p. 33(2).

Coastguard
(a)   See Navy.
(b)   *www.coastguardsofyesteryear.org.*

Convicts

Eighteenth-and early nineteenth-century: Prisoners' Petitions. NLI.

1796	Return of prisoners who were discharged out of the Four Courts Marshalsea by virtue of the Acts of Insolvency from the 9th day of February 1796 to the 10th day of January, 1798, 160 names. NAI OP 52/16.
1800	List of boys sent to New Geneva Prison Feb. 13, 1800. 19 names. NAI OP 87/3.
1806	List of debtors confined in the Marshalsea of Clonmel. Calendar of Prisoners found guilty and executed – together with those tried and found guilty and now confined in the Gaol of Clonmel, 30 Dec. 1806. 51 names. NAI OP 245/1.
1808	List of persons in Limerick Gaol admitted to bail: charged by L. Burke [sic] 10 Dec 1808. NAI OP 267/19.
1809	Calendars of prisoners in Waterford Goal detained for trial at the next assizes, 29 Jan 1809. 21 names. NAI OP 267/2.

1810   Calendars of Prisoners not tried and confined in the Gaols of Limerick city and county, Waterford and Clonmel. 148 names. NAI OP 308/15b, c, d, e.

1810   Prisoners for trial, Co. Kilkenny, Dec. 4 1810. 6 names. NAI OP 308/15a.

1810   Lists of Prisoners: Croom, Kilross, Rathkeale and Kilfinnane Bridewells Co. Limerick, Dec. 17 1810. NAI OP 308/16a & b.

1811   Calendar of prisoners in Limerick Gaol, Jan. 1811. NAI OP 347/1.

1812   Quarterly reports of the Governors of the House of Industry on Dublin Penitentiaries: James' St Smithfield and Kilmainham, July 5 1812. Listing all prisoners, with detailed notes and including prisoners convicted outside Dublin. NAI OP 373/15.

1814–23   *Parliamentary Papers Vol. 22* (1824) Convictions 1814–23, Limerick City Assizes & Quarter sessions; All persons committed for trial under the Insurrection Act, 1823–24 in Cos Clare, Cork, Kerry, Kildare, Kilkenny, King's, Limerick, Tipperary. NLI.

1815   Return of boys committed to Smithfield Penitentiary. Jan. 1815–Jan 1821. NAI OP 538/1.

1815   Return of Convicts (with name, age, crime, etc.) sentenced to death or transportation at spring and summer assizes 1815: Antrim, Armagh, Cavan, Donegal, Down, Drogheda, Fermanagh, Leitrim, Longford, Louth, Meath, Monaghan, Tyrone, Tipperary. July–Aug. 1815. Part only – 102 names. NAI OP 439/15.

1816   List of Prisoners in Roscommon Gaol who solicit that their sentences may be speedily put in execution. Nov. 8 1816. NAI OP 462/20.

1817   Calendars of prisoners confined in various gaols, Dec. 31 1817. NAI OP 488/50.

1817   Convictions at Downpatrick Assizes, Mar. 31 1817. NAI OP 488/36.

1818   Lists of Convicts under sentence of Death or Transportation in the Gaol of Newgate. Mar. 5 1818. NAI OP 515/2.

1818   Lists of Convicts under sentence of Death or Transportation in the several Gaols of Ireland (names, ages, crimes, etc), Feb. 1818. NAI OP 515/1.

1832   Register of persons convicted at the Assizes and Petty Sessions in Co. Kerry, 1832–99. NLI Ms. 906.

1842–3   Prosecutions at Spring Assizes, 1842–43. *Parliamentary Papers*, 1843, Vol. 50, pp (619) 34 & ff.

1798–   Original Prison Registers for more than 40 individual prisons in many cases giving details of prisoners' families; unindexed, in chronological order. Most date from the 1840s, but some start much earlier, for example, Kilmainham (1798), Cork City Gaol (1822), Limerick Gaol (1830), Sligo Gaol (1836) and Trim Gaol (1837). NAI.

See also NAI Registered Papers, Indexes and Calendars.

Cooks and Vintners
See 'Barbers and Surgeons', above.

Doctors
See Part 1 of this chapter.

Cameron, Charles A., *History of the Royal College of Surgeons in Ireland, and of the Irish schools of medicine; including numerous biographical sketches, also a medical bibliograph*, Dublin: Fannin 1916, NLI Ir. 6107 c 1.

Doolin, W., *Dublin's surgeon-anatomists and other essays: a centenary tribute*, Dublin Dept. of History of Medicine, RCSI 1987, NLI Ir. 610 d 8.

Fleetwood, John F., *The history of medicine in Ireland*, Dublin: Skellig Press, 1983, NLI Ir. 610 f 3, 373 p.

Lyons, J.B., *A pride of professors: the professors of medicine at the Royal College of Surgeons in Ireland, 1813–1985*, Dublin: A&A Farmar, 1999, NLI Ir. 610 L 3.

Lyons, J.B., *Brief lives of Irish doctors*, Dublin: Blackwater, c.1978, NLI Ir. 921 L 1, 182 p.

Lyons, J.B., *The quality of Mercer's: the story of Mercer's Hospital, 1734–1991*, Dun Laoghaire: Glendale, 1991, NLI Ir. 362 L 2, 215 p.

Lyons, J.B., *St. Michael's Hospital, Dun Laoghaire, 1876–1976*, Dalkey: Systems Printing, 1976, NLI Ir. 610 L 1, 47 p.

Sheppard, Julia, *Guide to the Contemporary Medical Archives Centre in the Wellcome Institute for the History of Medicine*, The Institute: 1971, BL YK.1991.a.10735.

Wallis, P.J., *Eighteenth century medics: subscriptions, licenses, apprenticeships*, Newcastle-upon-Tyne Project for Historical Bio-bibliography, 1985, NLI Ir. 610 w [sic], by P.J. and R.V. Wallis with the assistance of T.D. Whittet.

Widdess, J.D.H, *A history of the Royal College of Physicians of Ireland, 1654–1963*, Edinburgh: E. & S. Livingstone, 1963, NLI Ir. 6107 w 2.

Widdess, J.D.H, *The Richmond, Whitworth & Hardwicke Hospitals: St. Laurence's Dublin, 1772–1972*, 1972, NLI Ir. 362 w 2.

Widdess, J.D.H, *The Royal College of Surgeons in Ireland and its medical school, 1784–1984*, Dublin: The College, 1984, NLI Ir. 61709 w 2.

Widdess, J.D.H, *The Charitable Infirmary, Jervis Street, Dublin, 1718–1968*, Dublin: H. Thom, 1968, NLI 1B 2988, 68 p.

Engineers
Loeber, Rolf, 'Biographical dictionary of engineers in Ireland, 1600–1730', *The Irish Sword: the journal of the Military History Society of Ireland*, Vol. xiii, No. 52 (1978–1979), 230–55. NLI Ir. 355 i 6.

Goldsmiths

(a)   GO 665: LDS British Film 100213, item 9. Dublin Goldsmiths 1675–1810.
(b)   Assay Office. Registrations of gold- and silversmiths (1637–). See also NLI Pos. 6851 (1637–1702); Pos. 6785 (1704–1855, with some gaps); Pos. 6782 Freemen, 1637–1779; Pos. 6784, 6788, 6851: Apprentices.
(c)   NAI M.465: Notes and pamphlets relating to goldsmiths and silversmiths in Cork, Dublin and Galway.
(d)   *JCHAS*, Ser. 2, Vol. VIII (1902).

Linenworkers/Weavers

(a)   Workers & Manufacturers in Linen, in *The Stephenson Reports* 1755–84, NLI Ir. 6551 Dublin.
(b)   1796 Linen Board premiums for growing flax. NLI Ir. 633411 i 7. Online: Hayes.

Masons

Dún Laoghaire Genealogical Society Journal, 'Dublin City Tradesmen employed by Board of Works', Vol. 4 (2) (1995).
See 'Barbers and Surgeons', above.

Members of Parliament

NLI Mss 184 and 2098. Details of Irish Members of Parliament.
Johnston-Liik, Edith Mary, *History of the Irish Parliament 1692–1800: commons, constituencies and statutes,* Belfast: UHF, 2002. NLI RR 94107 j 7.
See also local history source-lists under the relevant county.

Merchants

(a)   See 'Barbers and Surgeons', above.
(b)   See also local directories under county source-lists.

Militia

The English National Archives has more than 800 muster books and pay lists of Irish county militia and volunteer regiments, WO13/2574–3370, dating from the end of the eighteenth century to the late nineteenth century: a seriously under-explored source. Musters may also show enrolment and discharge information. GO Ms. 608 has 1761 militia Lists for Counties Cork, Derry, Donegal, Down, Dublin, Kerry, Limerick, Louth, Monaghan, Roscommon, Tyrone and Wicklow. The Militia Attestations Index (1872–1915) covers over 12,500 militiamen in the Royal Garrison Artillery (present-day Royal Artillery) in Ireland. Online source available at *www.originsnetwork.com.*

Millers

(a)   See 'Barbers and Surgeons', above.
(b)   Hogg, William E., *The Millers and Mills of Ireland ... of about 1859,* Dublin: 1997. NLI Ir. 620 h 2.

Navy

(a)   The Navy List, 1814, 1819, 1827–79, 1885 *et seq.*, 35905 NLI, Top floor [sic] (Seniority and disposition lists of all commissioned officers, masters, pursers, surgeons, chaplains, yard officers, coastguards, revenue cruisers, packets.)

(b)   Records of the Public Record Office, Kew. See Rodger, N.A.M., *Naval Records for Genealogists*, HMSO: 1984.

(c)   O'Byrne, W.R., *A Naval Biographical Dictionary* (London: J. Murray, 1849) 3 vols. NLI 9235 0 1/ 3B 2676–8.

(c)   Royal Navy Seamen (1853–1923): *nationalarchives.gov.uk/documentsonline*.

Papermakers

Muir, Alison, 'The Eighteenth-century Paper-makers of the north of Ireland', *Familia: Ulster Genealogical Review*, 7 No. 2 (2005), 37–73.

Plumbers

Dún Laoghaire Genealogical Society Journal, 'Dublin City Tradesmen employed by Board of Works', Vol. 4 (2) (1995).
See 'Barbers and Surgeons', above.

Post Office employees

Correspondence and reports to 1835: subsection in pre-1831 Calendars of Official Papers, NAI.
Dún Laoghaire Genealogical Society Journal, 'Dublin City Tradesmen employed by Board of Works', Vol. 4 (2) (1995).
Records of the Post Office, reports, minutes and pensions, 1686–1920 (all Ireland), 1920–present (N.I.). The British Postal Museum & Archive.

Prison Warders

General Prison Board applications for employment, NAI. From 1847.

Publicans

Excise Licences in premises valued under £10, 1832–1838; Reports from Committees, Parliamentary Papers 1837–38, Vol. 13 (2), 558–601 and 602–607.

Railway Workers

(a)   (1870s–1950s) Irish Transport Genealogical Archives, Irish Railway Record Society, Heuston Station, Dublin, *www.irrs.ie*.

(b)   Lecky, Joseph, *Records of the Irish Transport Genealogical Museum*, IRRS. NLI Ir. 385 L 8.

Revenue Officers

Employees of the Irish Revenue Service in 1709: *www.from-ireland.net/lists/ revenue officers ireland 1709.htm*.

Seamen
(a) 'In Pursuit of Seafaring Ancestors', Frank Murphy, *Decies* 16. NLI Ir. 9414 d 5.
(b) Agreements and Crew Lists series in NA, Kew.
(c) Cox, N.G., 'The Records of the Registrar General of Shipping and Seamen', *Maritime History*, Vol. 2 (1972).
(d) Deceased Seamen 1887–1949, NLI, 31242 d. Names (and other information) for seamen whose deaths were reported to the GRO.
(e) Agreements and Crew Lists series, NAI.

Silversmiths
See 'Goldsmiths' above.

Smiths
See 'Barbers and Surgeons', above.
Dún Laoghaire Genealogical Society Journal, 'Dublin City Tradesmen employed by Board of Works', Vol. 4 (2) (1995).

Stonemasons
See 'Bricklayers', above.

Teachers
Akenson, D.H., *The Irish Education Experiment,* London: Routledge & K. Paul, 1970. NLI Ir. 372 a 4.
Brennan, M., *Schools of Kildare and Leighlin, 1775–1835,* Dublin: M.H. Gill and Son, 1935. NLI Ir. 37094135 b 4, 616 p.
Corcoran, T.S., *Some lists of Catholic lay teachers and their illegal schools in the later Penal times,* Dublin: M.H. Gill and son, 1932. NLI Ir. 370941 c 12.
Ffolliott, R., 'Some schoolmasters in the diocese of Killaloe, 1808', *JNMAS,* Vol. XI, 1968.
Linehan, John C., 'Irish school-masters in the American colonies', *The Catholic Bulletin,* Vol. XXIX, 784–788. NLI Ir. 942 l 9.
'Some Early Schools of Kilkenny', *Old Kilkenny Review,* 1960, 3.
'Teachers of Cashel & Emly 1750–60', *The Catholic Bulletin,* Vol. XXIX, 784–788.
'The Irish Society's Bible Teachers 1818–1827', *Eigse, A Journal of Irish Studies,* Vol. 18, Nos 1 & 2. NLI Ir. 8916205 e 4.

Vintners
See 'Barbers and Surgeons', above.

Watchmakers
See 'Clockmakers', above.

Weavers
See 'Linenworkers', above.

Chapter 13 ～

COUNTY SOURCE-LISTS

EXPLANATORY

The source-lists included here are intended primarily as working research tools, with references as specific as possible and very little explanation given of the records. An outline of some of the categories used is thus necessary here.

CENSUS RETURNS AND SUBSTITUTES

Where no indication of the nature of the record is given, a description should be found in Chapter 2. Griffith's Valuation and the Tithe Books are dealt with in Chapter 4. Locations are given in the text for all records mentioned, with exact reference numbers where possible. NLI call numbers for published works should be found in the 'Local History' or 'Local Journal' sections. The absence of a LDS reference does not mean that the work is not in the Library.

THE INTERNET

References are generally given only to the home page of the relevant website, unless the records are especially well hidden. To preserve clarity, cross-references from the main record categories use only the title of the website rather than the full online address (URL); the URL can be found in the 'Online' section. Only those websites referred to directly in the census, parish, or other county listings are given here. Other, more general sites are dealt with in Chapter 11.

LOCAL HISTORY

The bibliographies given are by no means exhaustive and the works cited vary enormously in their usefulness. I have tried, where possible, to give a sample location and reference number for each work. NLI entries given without a reference were in cataloguing at the time of writing. The lists also include some unpublished material, where this is relevant.

LOCAL JOURNALS

The journals noted are those originating in, or covering part of the particular county. Where possible, NLI call numbers are given. The absence of the number means that the journal started publication relatively recently and, at the time of writing, had not yet been assigned a number.

GRAVESTONE INSCRIPTIONS

Many of the largest collections of indexed transcripts of gravestone inscriptions are now held by local heritage centres. For counties where this is the case, the name of the relevant centre is supplied. Further details will be found in Chapter 15. This section does not cover the transcripts published in the *Journal of the Association for the Preservation of the Memorials of the Dead*, since the records are not treated in a geographically consistent way. Nonetheless, over the forty-seven years of its existence, between 1888 and 1934, the *Journal* published a huge number of inscriptions, many of which have since been destroyed. A composite index to surnames and places for the first twenty years of publication was published in 1910; the remaining volumes have their own indexes. Again, NLI call numbers for the local history journals or local histories will be found in the sections dealing specifically with the journals and histories. Online listings for gravestones transcripts are not comprehensive. Although many partial transcripts submitted by users are available on sites such as *interment.net,* listing them all would be impossible.

ESTATE RECORDS

A summary is provided of relevant, catalogued records in the NAI and NLI for Counties Armagh, Carlow, Cavan, Clare, Cork, Donegal, Fermanagh, Galway, Kerry, Kildare, Leitrim, Limerick, Longford, Mayo, Monaghan, Roscommon, Sligo, Tyrone, Waterford and Westmeath. It should be kept in mind that these lists omit other repositories. A great deal of material, covering all areas of Ireland, survives in county libraries, in private collections, in the English national and local archives and above all in PRONI. Some of the larger collections in PRONI are briefly referenced here, and a more detailed account of the nature of these records is given at the end of Chapter 4.

PLACE NAMES

References previously given in these lists to works dealing with place names on a county basis are now incorporated into the local history section. Material of more general use in identifying Irish place names for the entire island is as follows:

- **Townlands Indexes:** produced on the basis of the returns of the 1851, 1871 and 1901 censuses, these list all the townlands in the country in strict alphabetical order. The full 1851 Townlands Index is now available online at *www.ireland.com/ancestor* and at *www.leitrim-roscommon.com.*
- **Addenda to the 1841 Census:** also known as the 1841 Townlands Index, this too is based on the census returns but organises townlands on a different basis. They are grouped alphabetically within civil parishes, which are then grouped alphabetically within baronies, which are in turn grouped by county. This method of organisation is very useful in tracking down variant townland spellings; once it is known that a particular townland is to be found in a particular area, but the later Townlands Indexes do not record it, the general

area can be searched in the 1841 *Addenda* for names which are close enough to be possible variants. NLI Ir. 310 c 1.

- **Townlands in Poor-Law Unions:** produced by the Office of the Registrar General for use by local registration officers, this lists townlands in each Registration District, or Poor-Law Union (see Chapter 1). It is useful in attempting to identify place names given in civil records. (NLI Ir. 9141 b 35.) It has been reprinted as *Townlands and Poor-Law Unions* (ed., Handran, Salem MA: Higginson, 1997).

- *Topographical Dictionary of Ireland*, Samuel Lewis, 1837: this goes through civil parishes in alphabetical order, giving a brief history, an economic and social description and the names and residences of the 'principal inhabitants'. It also records the corresponding Catholic parish and the locations of Presbyterian congregations. The accompanying *Atlas* is useful in determining the precise relative positions of the parishes.

- **Ordnance Survey:** there are two main OS sources of value when tracking down the many unapproved or 'sub-denominational' place names that escaped standardisation in the 1830s:

  1) Manuscript indexes to place names on the original OS 6" maps include many sub-townland names not found elsewhere. Microfilm copies in NLI are:
     - Pos. 4621: Cork, Clare, Kerry.
     - Pos. 4622: Tipperary, Galway, Leitrim, Mayo.
     - Pos. 4623: Sligo, Antrim, Armagh, Cavan, Donegal, Roscommon, Waterford, Limerick.
     - Pos. 4624: Kildare, Carlow, Down, Dublin, Fermanagh, Kilkenny, Offaly, Longford, Louth, Meath, Monaghan.
     - Pos. 4625: Laois, Tyrone, Westmeath, Wexford, Wicklow and Derry/Londonderry.

  2) Ordnance Survey Name Books, compiled by John O'Donovan in the course of the Survey, record local naming practices and traditions. Microfilm copies are at NLI, with microfilms for Ulster held at Queen's University, Belfast.

Other works of general interest include Yann Goblet's *Index to Townlands in the Civil Survey 1654–6* (Irish Manuscripts Commission: 1954); *Locations of Churches in the Irish Provinces* (Church of Jesus Christ of Latter-Day Saints: 1978), NLI Ir. 7265 i 8; *The Parliamentary Gazetteer of Ireland* (1846), NLI Ir. 9141 p 30.

ANTRIM

Census returns and substitutes

1614/5	Carrickfergus merchants and ships' captains, *Carrickfergus and District Historical Society Journal*, Vol. 2 (1986)
1630	Muster Roll of Ulster; Armagh Co. Library and PRONI D.1759/3C/1; T. 808/15164; NLI Pos. 206
1642	Muster Roll. PRONI T.3726/2
1642–1643	Muster Roll, Shankill. PRONI T.2736/1
1659	Pender's 'Census'
1666	Hearth Money Roll. NLI Pos. 207. Also PRONI T/307
1666	Subsidy Roll. PRONI T/808/14889
1669	Hearth Money Roll. NLI Ms. 9584, PRONI T.30
1720	Down and Antrim landed gentry RIA 24 k 19
1734	Religious census of the barony of Cary. *The Glynns* 1993, 1994. Supplies householders' names
1740	Protestant Householders in the parishes of Ahoghill, Armoy, Ballintoy, Ballymoney, Ballywillin, Billy, Drummaul, Duneane, Dunluce, Finvoy, Kilraghts, Kirkinriola, Loughguile, Ramoan, Rasharkin, Rathlin Island. PRONI T808/15258. GO 539
1766	Ahoghill parish; NAI M.2476(1) also RCBL and NLI Ms. 4173
1766	Ballintoy parish. Also GO 536 and NLI Ms. 4173. PRONI T808/15264
1776	'Deputy Court Cheque Book' (votes cast). PRONI D1364/L/1. Online: Freeholders
1779	Map of Glenarm, including tenants' names. *The Glynns*, No.9, 1981
1796	Spinning-Wheel Premium List. 1125 names for Co. Antrim. Online: Hayes
1798	Persons who suffered losses in the 1798 rebellion. Propertied classes only. NLI I 94107. C. 140 names
1799–1800	Militia Pay Lists and Muster Rolls. PRONI T.1115/1A & B
1803	Ballintoy inhabitants. C of I registers. PRONI T.679/68–69; MIC.1/111 p
1803	Agricultural survey recording householders, occupations and agricultural possessions. Covers Armoy, Ballymoney, Ballyrashane, Billy, Culfeightrin, Derrykeighan, Dunluce, Kilraghts, Loughguile, Ramoan, Rathlin Island. NAI OP 153/103/1–16. Also PRONI. Part online: Ballymoney, Rathlin, Ulsterancestry (Armoy district)
1804–1810	Ballymoney inhabitants listed by street. *North Antrim Roots*, Vol. 2 (3) (1989)
1813	Census of Ballyeaston Presbyterian Congregation in Ballycor, Donagore, Glenwhirry, Grange of Doagh, Kilbride and Rashee, Co. Antrim. LDS Fiche 6026299, LDS Film 100173
1820	Lisburn householders. PRONI T679/107–112
1821	Various fragments. NAI Thrift Abstracts
1823	Parishioners' list, C of I parish of Layd, Co. Antrim. PRONI T.679/359–363

1823–1838   Tithe Books

1833–1839   Emigrants from Antrim. *Irish Emigration Lists 1833–39,* Baltimore: Genealogical Publishing Co., 1989

1834   Carrickfergus freeholders, leaseholders and householders. From Court of Quarter Sessions, LDS Film 990408

1837   House Book for Belfast. House-by-house valuation, giving house-holders' names. Date not completely certain. NAI OL 70001 VO Quarto book

1837–1838   Memorials from inhabitants of for Quarter sessions. (1837: Lisburn c. 70 names, Ballycastle c.100 names, Glenarm c.65 names; 1838: Ballynure, Ballylinny Ballycorr, Rashee (commonly called Ballyeaston) and the Grange of Doagh, c.350 names). Many with occupations NAI OP 1837/10

1837   Valuation of towns returning M.P.s (occupants and property values), Lisburn. *Parliamentary Papers 1837, Reports from Committees*

1839–1848   Workhouse records: some material, including admissions registers and relief registers, survives for all of the unions of Co. Antrim. PRONI. LDS hold microfilm copies of Ballymena (259181-5), Belfast (259177), Ballymoney (259174-5), Ballycastle (259173), Lurgan (259166–72)

1851   Partial: Ahoghill—Craigs townland only; Aghagallon—'M' to 'T' only; Ballymoney—Garryduff only; Killead—'A' to 'C' only; Rasharkin—'K' to 'T' only; PRONI MIC. 5A/11-26. Also NAI. Online: 1851

1856–1857   Voters. NLI ILB 324

1856   Census of united parishes of Glenavy, Camlin and Tullyrusk, Co. Antrim, taken in 1856-7, revised in 1858–9 and 1873; with Glenavy C of I registers. PRONI MIC.1/43–4, 44A, 74; C.R.1/53; T.679/1, 74

1861–1862   Griffith's Valuation. Indexed online: Hayes

1870   Parishioners' list, Carnmoney, Co. Antrim; with C of I parish registers. PRONI T.679/325–9, 332, D.852/8, 48, 85, 91, 105, 122, 125

1901   Census

1911   Census

1912   The Ulster Covenant. Almost half-a-million original signatures and addresses of those who signed. Online: Covenant

Online

1851	*home.iprimus.com.au/s_steffensen/*	1851 census extracts
Ballymoney	*www.ballymoneyancestry.com*	Wide range of Ballymoney sources
Bann Valley	*www.4qd.org/bann/*	Records from the Antrim/Derry border
Covenant	*www.proni.gov.uk/ulstercovenant*	
Freeholders	*www.proni.gov.uk/freeholders*	
Hayes, John	*www.failteromhat.com*	

Headstones	www.historyfromheadstones.com	Comprehensive collection of inscriptions
History	www.antrimhistory.net	Glens of Antrim Historical Society
Newsletter	www.ucs.louisiana.edu/bnl/	*Belfast Newsletter* Index 1737–1800
Rathlin	rathlin.info	Extraordinary collection of Rathlin sources
UHF	www.ancestryireland.co.uk	Parish record indexes online
Ulster-ancestry	www.ulsterancestry.com	Many transcribed early sources

Publications

Local histories
— *Listing Mid-Antrim Presbyterians in 1864*, Ballymena, Mid-Antrim Historical Group, 1996, NLI [96 p.]
Castlereagh: some local sources, Ballynahinch, South Eastern Education and Library Service, 1980, NLI Ir. 914115 p 15, 27 p.
— *Presbyterians in Glenarm*, 'The Glynns', Vol. 9, 1981
Allen, Andrew W., *Old Ballyclug*, Ballymena, Ballymena Borough Council, 1994, NLI Ir. 9295 p[sic], 17 p.
Allen, Andrew W., *Skerry burying ground*, Ballymena, Ballymena Borough Council, NLI, 4B 1704, 4 p.
Akenson, D.H., *Between two revolutions: Islandmagee, County Antrim, 1798–1920*, Port Credit, Ont.: P. D. Meany, 1979, NLI Ir. 94111 a 3, 221 p.
Akenson, D.H., *Local poets and social history: James Orr, bard of Ballycarry*, Belfast: PRONI, 1977, NLI Ir. 82189 o 107, 130 p.
Barr, W.N., *The oldest register of Derryaghy, Co. Antrim 1696–1772*, NLI Ir. 9293 b 3
Bassett, G.H., *The Book of Antrim*, 1888
Benn, George, *A History of the Town of Belfast*, London, 1877–80
Boyd, H.A., *A History of the Church of Ireland in Ramoan Parish*, Belfast: R. Carswell, 1930, NLI Ir. 2741 b 9, 232 p.
Carmody, V. Rev. W.P., *Lisburn Cathedral and its Past Rectors*, Belfast: R. Carswell & Son, 1926, NLI Ir. 27411 c 2, 190 p.
Cassidy, William, *Gravestone inscriptions in Lambeg churchyard*, PRONI
Clarke, Harry Jessop St John, *Thirty centuries in south-east Antrim: The parish of Coole or Carnmoney*. Belfast: Quota Press, 1938, NLI Ir. 274111 c 3, 319 p.
Cox, John H.R., *Cromwellian Settlement of the parish of Kilbride*, 1959
Day, Angelique & McWilliams, Patrick (eds.), *Ordnance Survey Memoirs of Ireland series*, Belfast: Inst. of Irish Studies/RIA, 1990–7

Vol. 2: *Co. Antrim I*: (1990) Ballymartin, Ballyrobert, Ballywalter, Carnmoney, Mallusk. NLI Ir. 914111 o 11

Vol. 8: *Co. Antrim II* (1991) Blaris, (Lisburn), Derryaghy, Drumbeg, Lambeg. NLI Ir. 9141 o 80

Vol. 10: *Co. Antrim III* (1991) Carncastle and Killyglen, Island Magee, Kilwaughter, Larne

Vol. 13: *Co. Antrim IV* (1992) Ardclinis, Dunaghy, Dundermot, Layd, Inispollan, Loughguile, Newton Crommelin, Racavan, Skerry, Tickmacrevan. NLI Ir. 914111 o 11

Vol. 16. *Co. Antrim V* (1992) Ballymoney, Ballyrashane, Ballywillin, Billy, Derrykeighan, Drumtullagh, Dunluce, Kilraughts. NLI Ir. 914111 o 11

Vol. 19: *Co. Antrim VI* (1993) Ballyscullion, Connor, Cranfield, Drummaul, Duneane, Shilvodan. NLI Ir. 9141 o 84

Vol. 21: *Co. Antrim VII* (1993) Aghagallon, Aghalee, Ballinderry, Camlin, Glenavy, Lough Neagh, Magheragall, Magheramesk, Tullyrusk. NLI Ir. 9141 o 83

Vol. 23: *Co. Antrim VIII* (1993) Ahoghill, Ballyclug, Finvoy, Killagan, Kirkinriola, Rasharkin. NLI Ir. 9141 o 80

Vol. 24: *Co. Antrim IX* (1994) Armoy, Ballintoy, Culfeightrin, Ramoan, Rathlin Island. NLI Ir. 9141 o 80

Vol. 26: *Co. Antrim X* (1994) Glynn, Inver, Kilroot, Templecorran. NLI Ir. 94111 o 7

Vol. 29: *Co. Antrim XI* (1995) Antrim, Doagh, Donegore, Kilbride. NLI Ir. 9141 o 80

Vol. 32: *Co. Antrim XII* (1995) Ballycor, Ballylinny, Ballynure, Glenwhirry, Raloo, Rashee. NLI Ir. 9141 o 80

Vol. 35: *Co. Antrim XIII* (1996) Carmavy, Killead, Muckamore, Nilteen, Templepatrick, Umgall. NLI Ir. 9141 o 80

Vol. 37: *Co. Antrim XIV* (1996) Carrickfergus. NLI Ir. 9141 o 80

Dunlop, Bill, *Ahoghill Part 1: Buick's Ahoghill a filial account (1910) of seceders [ ]*, Ballymena: Mid-Antrim Historical Group, 1987, NLI Ir. 94111 a (1), 113 p.

Dunlop, Bill, *Ahoghill Part 2: Ahoghill folk photographs of people of the Fourtowns and round about,* Ballymena: Mid-Antrim Historical Group, 1989, NLI Ir. 94111 a (2), 96 p.

Dunlop, Bill, *Ahoghill Part 3: Around Ahoghill further photographs and other ...,* Ballymena: Mid-Antrim Historical Group, 1990, NLI Ir. 94111 p 5(8), 96 p.

Dunlop, Eull, *McIlmoyle of Dervock pastor of two,* Ballymena: Mid-Antrim Historical Group, 1991, NLI Ir. 92 m 505, 180 p.

Dunlop, Eull, *Round "Kells & Conyer" [Part 1],* Ballyclare: Kells & Connor Luncheon Club, 1989, NLI Ir. 94111 d 8, 101 p.

Dunlop, Eull, *Mid-Antrim Part 2 further articles on Ballymena & district,* Ballymena: Mid-Antrim Historical Group, 1991, NLI Ir. 94111 d 9, 208 p.

Fulton, Eileen, *A history of the Parish of St. Jospeh's Hannahstown, Co. Antrim 1826–1993 Detailing the Names of the Graves (...),* Ulster Journals Ltd.: 1993

Gaston, Stephen, *Inscriptions in first & second Killymurris Presbyterian burying-grounds*, Ballymena: Ballymena Borough Council, 1996, NLI Ir. 285 p [sic], 45 p.

Gillespie, Raymond, *Irish Historic Towns Atlas 12: Belfast, part 1, 1840*, Dublin: RIA, 2002, NLI

IGRS, *Tombstone inscriptions Vol. 1*, Dublin: IGRS Tombstone Committee, 2001, NLI, 850 p.

Joy, Henry, *Historical Collections relative to the town of Belfast*, Belfast, 1817

Lee, Rev. W.H.A., *St Colmanell, Aghoghill: A History of its Parish*, Belfast: Newton Publishing Co., 1939, LHL, BPB1939.11

Liggett, Michael, *A district called Ardoyne: a brief history of a Belfast: Community*, Belfast: Glenravel Publications, 1994, NLI Ir. 9411 P 41(3)

Marshall, Rev. H.C., *The Parish of Lambeg*, Lisburn: Victor McMurray, 1933, NLI Ir. 27411 m 2, 127 p.

McConnell, Charles, *The witches of islandmagee*, Antrim: Carmac, 2000, NLI Ir. 9411 m 45, 78 p.

McNeill, Hugh, *The annals of the Parish of Derrykeighan from A.D. 453 to A.D. 1890 compiled by Hugh McNeill*, Ballymena: Mid-Antrim Historical Group, 1993, NLI, 81 p.

McSkimin, Samuel, *The History and Antiquities of the Town of Carrickfergus 1318–1839*, Belfast: 1909

M'Meekin, D., *Memories of '59: or the revival movement as manifested itself at Ahoghill, Grange, Longstone, New Ferry, Ballymena, Broughshane, Cullybackey, Teeshan, and Whiteside's Corner*, Hull: M. Harland, 1908, LHL, U.28/MACM

Millin, S.S., *Sidelights on Belfast History*, 1932

Mullin, Julia, *A history of Dunluce Presbyterian church*, 1995, NLI Ir. 285 m 37

NIFHS, *These Hallowed Grounds—Lisburn, Kilrush & St. Patrick's Cemeteries*, Belfast: NIFHS, 2001, Linen Hall Library, I/929.5041619

NIFHS, *Carved in stone: a record of memorials in the ancient graveyard around the Church (...)*, Belfast: NIFHS, 1994, NLI

NIFHS, *Mallusk Memorials*, Belfast: NIFHS, 1997, NLI Ir. 9295 m 4, 108 p.

Observer, The, Ballymena, *Old Ballymena: a history of Ballymena during the 1798 Rebellion*, 1857

Owen, D.J., *History of Belfast*, Belfast: W. & G. Baird, 1921, NLI Ir. 94111 o 1, 459 p.

Rankin, Kathleen, *The linen houses of the Lagan Valley: the story of their families*, Belfast: UHF, 2002, NLI, 221 p.

Robinson, Philip, *Irish Historic Towns Atlas 2: Carrickfergus*, Dublin: Royal Irish Academy, 1986, NLI, ILB 941 i 3(2)

Robinson, Rev. Aston, *The presbytery of Ballymena 1745–1945*, Ballymena: Mid-Antrim Historical group, 1949, NLI

Rutherford, George, *Gravestone Inscriptions, Co. Antrim, Vol. 1*, Belfast: UHF, 1977, NLI Ir. 9295 c 1

Rutherford, George, *Gravestone Inscriptions County Antrim, Volume 4: Old Families of Larne & District from Gravestone Inscriptions, Wills and Biographical Notes*, Belfast: UHF, 2004, NLI, 224 p.

Rutherford, George, *Gravestone Inscriptions, Co. Antrim, Vol. 2*, Belfast: UHF, 1980, NLI Ir. 94111 c 4

Sharpe, Robert, *'By the light of the hurricane lamp': (growing up in Glenariffe in the thirties)*, NI: author, 2004, NLI, 119 p.

Shaw, William, *Cullybackey, the Story of an Ulster Village*, Edinburgh: Macdonald, 1913, NLI Ir. 91411 s 1, 201 p.

Smyth, Alastair, *The story of Antrim*, Antrim: Antrim Borough Council, 1984, NLI Ir. 94111 s 9, [116 p.]

St John Clarke, H.J., *Thirty centuries in south-east Antrim: the Parish of Coole or Carnmoney*, Belfast: 1938, NLI Ir. 27411 c 3

Walker, B.M., *Sentry Hill: an Ulster farm and family*, Dundonald: Blackstaff Press, 1981, NLI Ir. 9292 w 19, 167 p.

Watson, Charles, *The Story of the United Parishes of Glenavy, Camlin and Tullyrusk ...*, Belfast: McCaw, Stevenson & Orr, 1892, NLI Ir. 94111 w 1, 63 p.; Repr. 1982

Young, Robert M., *Historical Notices of Old Belfast and its Vicinity*, 1896

Young, Robert M., *The Town Book of the Corporation of Belfast, 1613–1816*, 1892, LDS, SLC Film 0990294. Includes freemen 1635–1796

Local Journals
Carrickfergus and District Historical Society Journal, NLI Ir. 9411 c 5
Down & Connor Historical Society Magazine
East Belfast Historical Society Journal
Historic Belfast Magazine
Irish Family Links, NLI Ir. 9292 f 19
Lisburn Historical Society Journal, LHL
North Antrim Roots
North Irish Roots (Journal of the North of Ireland Family History Society), NLI Ir. 92905 n 4
North Belfast Historical Society Magazine, NLI Ir. 94111 n 1
South Belfast Historical Society Journal
The Glynns, NLI Ir. 94111 g 2
Ulster Journal of Archaeology, NLI Ir. 794105 u 1

Directories

1807/8	Joseph Smith, *Belfast Directories*: Repr. as J.R.R. Adams (ed.), *Merchants in Plenty*, Belfast: UHF, 1992, NLI Ir. 914111.s.27
1811	*Holden's annual London and country directory of the United Kingdoms & Wales, in three volumes, for ... 1811*. (3 vols. Facsimile repr. Norwich: M. Winton, 1996) NLI G 942 h 23, LDS Film 258722 Item 2
1820	*Belfast Almanack* NLI JP 5331
1820	J. Pigot, *Commercial Directory of Ireland* PRONI, NLI Ir. 9141 p 107, LDS Film 962702 Item 1
1831–1832	Donaldson's *Belfast Directory*, LDS Film 258724 Item 2
1835	Matier's *Belfast directory*, PRONI, NLI Ir. 9141111 m 5, LDS Film 258724,

(Repub. Archive CD Books Ireland, CD ROM #IET0018, 2005)

1839   Martin, *Belfast Directory*, PRONI, NLI Ir. 9141111 m 4

1841   Martin, *Belfast Directory* (repr. Ballymena: Mid-Antrim Historical Group, 1992) PRONI, NLI Ir. 914111 m 24, LDS Film 258724/5

1843–1852 Henderson's *Belfast and Province of Ulster Directory*, PRONI, NLI Dix Belfast (1852), LDS Film 908816 Item 1

1846   Slater's *National Commercial Directory of Ireland*

1854–   *Belfast and Province of Ulster Directory*. Also 1856, 1858, 1861, 1863, 1865, 1868, 1870, 1877, 1880, 1884, 1887, 1890, 1894, 1900, PRONI. LDS (various years)

1856   Slater's *Royal National Commercial Directory of Ireland*, NLI, LDS Film 1472360 Item 1

1860   Hugh Adair, *Belfast Directory*. NLI Dix Belfast 1860, LDS Film 990275 Item 4

1865   R. Wynne, *Business Directory of Belfast*, NLI Ir. 91411 b 2

1870   Slater's *Directory of Ireland*, NLI

1881   Slater's *Royal National Commercial Directory of Ireland*, NLI

1887   *Derry Almanac and Directory* (Portrush only)

1888   George Henry Bassctt, *The Book of Antrim*, Repr. Belfast: Friar's Bush, 1989, NLI Ir. 94116 b 29

1894   Slater's *Royal Commercial Directory of Ireland*, NLI

Gravestone Inscriptions

The UHF has transcripts for 151 graveyards in Antrim and Belfast. Irish World has transcripts of thirty-two graveyards and these are now searchable online, for a fee, at *www.historyfromheadstones.com*. Published or publicly available transcripts are given below. Full publication details are in the publications list above.

Ardclinis: Carrivemurphy, RC, *The Glynns*, Vol. 4
Blaris: Lisburn town, Carmody, *Lisburn*
Ballyclug: Ballymarlagh (Ballyclug), Allen, *Old Ballyclug*
Camlin: Ballydonagh, NIFHS, *These Hallowed Grounds*
Carnmoney: Carnmoney, NIFHS, *Carved in stone*
Culfeightrin: Cross, IA, Vol. 2, No. 2
Culfeightrin: Bonamargy, IGRS, *Tombstones 1*
Drumbeg: C of I, Clarke, *Down*, Vol. 3
Glynn: Glynn, Rutherford, *Antrim*, Vol. 2
Islandmagee: Ballyprior More, Rutherford, *Antrim*, Vol. 1
Islandmagee: Ballykeel, Rutherford, *Antrim*, Vol. 1,
Kilroot: Rutherford, *Antrim*, Vol. 2
Lambeg: Lambeg North, C of I, Cassidy, *Inscriptions*
Larne: St Macnissi's, Rutherford, *Antrim*, Vol. 4
Layd: Kilmore, *The Glynns*, Vol. 4
Layd: Layd, *Survey of Layde Graveyard*, Glens of Antrim Historical Soc., 1991. NLI Ir. 9295 s 2

Magheragall: Magheragall, C of I, *Family Links*, Vol. 1, Nos 2 and 3, 1981

Muckamore (Grange of): Muckamore, *Carved in stone: a record of memorials in the ancient graveyard around the Church (...)*, NIFHS, 1994

Newton Cromlin: Skerry East, Allen, *Old Ballyclug*

Raloo: Ballyvallagh, Rutherford, *Antrim*, Vol. 2

Rasharkin: Dromore/Killymurris?, Gaston, *Inscriptions*

Templecorran: Forthill (Ballycarry?), C of I, Rutherford, *Antrim*, Vol. 2

Templepatrick: Grange of Molusk, *Mallusk Memorials*, NIFHS, 1997

Shankill: St Jospeh's, Hannahstown, RC, in Fulton, *[...]St. Jospeh's, Hannahstown, [...]*, 1993

Clifton Street, Clarke, R.S.J., *Gravestone Inscriptions, Belfast Vol. 4 (Old Belfast Families and the New Burying Ground)*, UHF 1991 NLI Ir. 9295 0 1

Milltown, RC, Clarke, R.S.J., *Gravestone Inscriptions, Belfast Vol. 2*, UHF, 1986

Friar's Bush, RC, Clarke, R.S.J., *Gravestone Inscriptions, Belfast Vol. 2*, UHF, 1986

St George's interior, C of I, Clarke, R.S.J., *Gravestone Inscriptions, Belfast Vol. 1*, UHF, 1982

Christ Church interior, C of I, Clarke, R.S.J., *Gravestone Inscriptions, Belfast Vol. 1*

Shankill, Clarke, R.S.J., *Gravestone Inscriptions, Belfast Vol. 1*

Estate records

Antrim, Earls of: Rentals 1603–1900, PRONI D/2977, covering areas in: Ahoghill; Antrim; Ardclinis; Armoy; Ballintoy; Ballymartin; Ballyrashane; Ballywillin; Billy; Carncastle; Culfeightrin; Derrykeighan; Dunaghy; Duneane; Dunluce; Finvoy; Grange of Drumtullagh; Grange of Killyglen; Island Magee; Killagan; Kilraghts; Kilwaughter; Larne; Layd; Loughguile; Newton Cromlin; Ramoan; Rasharkin; Rathlin; Skerry; Tickmacrevan. May cover further parishes. Also a rent roll. All tenants 1779–1781, NAI M524. Similar area.

Foster/Massereene: Rentals, 1830, PRONI D/1739, covering areas in: Aghnamullen; Antrim; Connor; Killead; Muckamore (Grange of). May cover further parishes.

ARMAGH

Census returns and substitutes

1625–1627	Leet Court Rolls. Jurors and litigants in Armagh Manor; Arboe, Ardtrea, Donaghmore (Tyrone); Termonfeckin (Louth) SA, Vol. 11, No. 9, 1957 pp 295–322
1630	Muster Roll of Ulster; Armagh Co. Library and PRONI D.1759/3C/1; T. 808/15164; NLI Pos. 206
1631	Muster Roll of Armagh SA Vol. 5, No. 2, 1970
1634	Subsidy roll. Portadown area NAI M. 2471, 2475. Shankill and Seagoe PRONI T/808/14950
1654–1656	Civil Survey. *Civil Survey*, NLI Ir. 31041 c 4
1659	Pender's 'Census'. Repr. GPC, 1997, IMC, 2002. LDS Film 924648
1660	Poll Tax Returns, Co. Armagh. PRONI MIC/15A/76

1661	Books of Survey and Distribution. PRONI T370/A & D.1854/1/8
1664	Hearth Money Roll. *Archivium Hibernicum*, 1936. NLI Ms. 9586; PRONI T.604
1670/1	Armagh diocese gentry, clergy and parishioners supporting the Franciscans. SA Vol. 15, No. 1, 1992 186–216
1689	Protestants attainted by James II. PRONI T808/14985. List of names only
1737	Tithe-payers, Drumcree. NLI I 920041 p 1
1738	Freeholders. NLI Pos. 206. Also Armagh Co. Library
1740	Protestant householders: Creggan, Derrynoose, Loughgall, Mullaghbrack, Shankill, Tynan, NAI. Also GO 539; PRONI T808/15258, LDS Film 258517; Portadown, LDS Film 1279357, item 8 & SA Vol. 18, 2 2001
1753	Poll Book. NAI M. 4878. Also GO 443; PRONI T808/14936; LDS Film 1279237. Online: Freeholders
1766	Creggan parish. NAI Parl. Ret. 657. Also GO 537; PRONI T808/14936; LDS Film 100173; *JCLAS* 8, (2); Transcripts for parts of Armagh, Ballymore, Creggan, Drumcree, Kilmore, Loughgall, Tartaraghan. PRONI T/808/15265–7, T/3709 Lurgan NAI M2476, RCBL Ms. 23
1770	Armagh City householders. NLI Ms. 7370. Also PRONI T808/14977; LDS Film 258621
1793–1908	Armagh Militia Records. NLI Pos. 1014. Also Armagh Co. Library
1796	Spinning-Wheel Premium List. 3,100 names for Co. Armagh. Online: Hayes
1796	Catholics Emigrating from Ulster to Mayo. SA, 1958, pp 17–50. See also "Petition of Armagh migrants in the Westport area", *Cathair na Mart*, Vol. 2, No. 1 (Appendix)
1799–1800	Militia Pay Lists and Muster Rolls. PRONI T.1115/A–C
1803–1831	Armagh Freeholders and Poll Books PRONI ARM 5/2/1–17, D 1928. Also NLI Ir. 94116 a 1, Ir. 352 p 2 (baronies of Tiranny, Lower Fews & Upper Fews 1821–31). Online: Freeholders
1821	Kilmore parish. PRONI T. 450. Portadown PRONI T/281/7 Also LDS Films 258511/258621
1821	Various fragments. NAI Thrift Abstracts
1823–1838	Tithe Books. NAI, PRONI, LDS
1831	Memorial of the Inhabitants of part of Cos Down & Armagh praying for relief. April 21 1831. More than 1300 names, 'more particularly in the neighbourhood of Shane Hill'– Knocknashane, Shankill parish? NAI OP 974/122
1834–1837	Valuation of Armagh town (heads of households). *Parliamentary Papers 1837, Reports from Committees*, Vol. II (1), Appendix G
1836	Memorial from inhabitants of Moyntaghe and Seagoe parishes, 'on behalf of Mr Handcock'. More than 1,000 names NAI OP 1836/20
1837	Marksmen (i.e. illiterate voters), Armagh Borough. *Parliamentary Papers 1837, Reports from Committees*, Vol. II (1), Appendix A

1838	Memorial from inhabitants of Portadown for Quarter sessions. c.90 signatures NAI OP 1837/10
1839	Valuation of Co. Armagh. NLI Pos. 99. Also Armagh Co. Library
1840	Ratepayers for the Union of Armagh PRONI D/1670/13/6
1840–1855	Emigrants from Derrynoose to the US and Scotland; with parish registers. PRONI MIC.1/158
1840–	Workhouse records: Armagh Union PRONI. BG/2, LDS Film 259166–72; Castleblayney Union, MA
1843	Armagh voters. NAI 1842/85
1851–1873	Persons entitled to vote; Armagh County Museum, D7; also LDS Film 1279325
1851	Various fragments. NAI Thrift Abstracts
1864	Tynan parish c.1864. *The History of Charlemont Fort and Borough,* 1921
1864	Griffith's Valuation. Indexed online: Hayes
1868	Census of the C of I parish of Shankill, Cos Armagh & Down. With the local clergyman
1871	Creggan Upper. *Archivium Hibernicum,* Vol. 3
1901	Census. Lurgan district online: Lurgan
1911	Census
1912	The Ulster Covenant. Almost half-a-million original signatures and addresses of those who signed. Online: Covenant

Online

Armagh History   *www.asaz58.dsl.pipex.com*

Covenant	*www.proni.gov.uk/ulstercovenant*	PRONI transcription of the Covenant
Freeholders	*www.proni.gov.uk/freeholders*	74 freeholders/voters' lists for Armagh, 1712–1832
Hayes, John	*www.failteromhat.com*	Large compendium of transcribed records
Headstones	*www.historyfromheadstones.com*	Comprehensive collection of inscriptions
Lurgan	*www.lurganancestry.net*	Wide range of Lurgan sources

Publications

Local histories
Armagh Road Presbyterian Church, Portadown (1868–1968), NLI Ir. 2741 p 25
Armagh Royal School: Prizes & prizemen 1854, NLI, p. 439
Balleer School: Copy-book of letters, 1827–29, NLI Ir. 300 p 106
Mullaghbrack from the tithepayers list of 1834, NLI, I 920041 p 1
Historical sketches of various parishes, NLI Ir. 27411 l 4 & 5

'Provisional list of pre-1900 School Registers in the Public Record Office of Northern Ireland', UHGGN, 9, 1986, 60–71

'Life and Times of Fr. Edmund Murphy, Killeavy, 1680', JCLAHS, 7 (3), 1931, 336–81. Lists Catholic residents

Blaney, Roger, 'Blaney of Lurgan', Co. Armagh, IG, III, 1, 1971, 32–9

Canavan, T., Frontier town: an illustrated history of Newry, Belfast: Blackstaff Press, 1989

Coffey, Hubert W., A history of Milltown Parish, the Birches, North-West Armagh, Portadown, 1950?, NLI Ir. 283 p 5, 86 p. Jackson family (Stonewall Jackson)

Coyle, Michael F., Genealogy of the Smyths of Carrickaduff in the Parish of Derrynoose, Carnagh, Keady, Co. Armagh, Dunleer, Co. Louth: the author, 1980, NLI, GO 613, 22 leaves

Day, Angelique, Ordnance Survey Memoirs of Ireland: Volume 1: Parishes of County Armagh 1835–8, Belfast: Institute of Irish Studies, 1990, NLI Ir. 914116 o 10, 144pp. Co-editor, Patrick McWilliams. All of Armagh, except the city

Donaldson, John, A Historical and Statistical Account of the Barony of Upper Fews

Ferrar, Major M. L., Register of the Royal School, Armagh, Belfast, 1933, NLI Ir. 37941 f 5, 235 p.

Galogly, John, The History of St Patrick's Parish, Armagh, 1880

Gwynn, A., The medieval province of Armagh, Dundalk, 1946, NLI Ir. 27411 g 1

Hogg, Rev. M.B., Keady Parish: A Short History of its Church and People, 1928

Lockington, John W., A history of the Mall Presbyterian Church, Armagh: 1837–1987, Belfast: Ulster Services, 1987, NLI, 56 p.

Marshall, J.J., History of the parish of Tynan in the County of Armagh: with notices of the O'Neill, Hovenden, Stronge and other families connected with the district, Dungannon: Tyrone Printing Co., 1932, NLI Ir. 94116 m 1, 83 p. O'Neill, Ecklund, Hovenden and Strong families

Marshall, J.J., The History of Charlemont Fort and Borough ..., Dungannon: Tyrone Printing Co., 1921

McCorry, F.X., Lurgan: an Irish Provincial Town, Inglewood Press, 1993

McGleenon, C.F., '17th and 18th century patterns of settlement in the Catholic parishes of Ballymore and Mullaghbrack', SA, 15, No. 2, 1993, 51–83

Moore, Rev. H.H., Three hundred years of congregational life: the story of the First Presbyterian Church, Markethill, Co. Armagh. Established A.D. 1609, Armagh, R. P. M'Watters, 1909, NLI, LO 5327, 65 p.

Murray, Rev. Lawrence P., History of the Parish of Creggan in the Seventeenth and Eighteenth Centuries, Dundalk, 1940

Nelson, Simon, History of the Parish of Creggan in Cos Armagh and Louth from 1611 to 1840, Belfast: PRONI, 1974, NLI Ir. 941 p 43, 37 p. 'Copied from the original mss. ... with a new introduction ... by Rev. Tomas O'Fiaich'

Patterson, T., Armagh Manor Court Rolls, 1625–7 & incidental notes on 17th century sources for Irish surnames in Co. Armagh, 1957, SA, 295–322

Richardson, James N., The Quakri at Lurgan / by two of themselves, Ireland, 1899, NLI Ir. 82189 Irish r 7, 160 p. Richardson family and the Society of Friends, Lurgan

Stewart, James, *Historical Memoirs of the City of Armagh*, Dublin, 1900, Ambrose Coleman (ed.)

Swayne, John, *The register of John Swayne, Archbishop of Armagh, and Primate of Ireland*, Belfast: 1939, NLI Ir. 2741153

Atkinson, Edward D., *Dromore, an Ulster Diocese*, Dundalk: W. Tempest, 1925, NLI Ir. 274116 a 1, 317 p.

Local Journals

Craigavon Historical Society Review, LHL

Irish Family Links, NLI Ir. 9292 f 19

Mullaghbawn Historical & Folk-Lore Society, NLI Ir. 800 p 50

North Irish Roots (Journal of the North of Ireland Family History Society), NLI Ir. 92905 n 4

Old Newry Journal

Seanchas Ardmhacha, NLI Ir. 27411 s 4

Seanchas Dhroim Mor (Journal of the Dromore Diocesan Historical Society), NLI Ir. 94115 s 3

Ulster Journal of Archaeology, NLI Ir. 794105 u 1

Directories

1819   Thomas Bradshaw's *General directory of Newry, Armagh, and the towns of Dungannon, Portadown, Tandragee, Lurgan, Waringstown, Banbridge, Warrenpoint, Rosstrevor, Kilkeel, Rathfriland, 1820*. PRONI, NLI Ir. 91411 b 18, LDS Film 258723. Online: Armagh History (Armagh city)

1820   J. Pigot, *Commercial Directory of Ireland*, PRONI, NLI Ir. 9141 p 107, LDS Film 962702 Item 1

1824   J. Pigot and Co., *City of Dublin and Hibernian Provincial Directory*, NLI, LDS Film 451787. Online: Armagh History

1839   Martin, *Belfast Directory*, PRONI, NLI Ir. 9141111 m 4

1846   Slater's *National Commercial Directory of Ireland*, PRONI, NLI LO, LDS Film 1696703 Item 3

1843–1852 Henderson's *Belfast and Province of Ulster Directory*, PRONI, NLI Dix Belfast (1852), LDS Film 908816 Item 1

1854–   *Belfast and Province of Ulster Directory*. Also 1856, 1858, 1861, 1863, 1865, 1868, 1870, 1877, 1880, 1884, 1887, 1890, 1894, 1900. PRONI. LDS (various years)

1856   Slater, *Royal National Commercial Directory of Ireland*, NLI, LDS Film 1472360 Item 1

1865   R. Wynne, *Business Directory of Belfast*, NLI Ir. 91411 b 2

1870   Slater, *Directory of Ireland*, NLI

1881   Slater, *Royal National Commercial Directory of Ireland*, NLI

1883   S. Farrell, *County Armagh Directory and Almanac*

1888   George Henry Bassett, *The Book of Armagh*, Repr. Belfast: Friar's Bush, 1989 NLI Ir. 94116 b 3

1894   Slater, *Royal Commercial Directory of Ireland*, NLI

Gravestone Inscriptions

The UHF has transcripts for 135 graveyards in Armagh. Heritage World has transcripts for fifty-four graveyards. These are searchable online, for a fee, at *www. historyfromheadstones.com*. Published or publicly available transcripts are given below.

Armagh: Sandy Hill, SA, Vol. 11, 2, 1985
Creggan: Creggan Bane Glebe, C of I, SA, Vol. 4, 1976
Kilclooney: LDS Film 1279354
Mullaghbrack: LDS Film 1279384

Estate Records

Anglesea: Tenants list, 1856. Most tenants. Covering: Newry–Crobane; Derryleckagh; Desert; Sheeptown in the civil parish of Newry. *JCLAHS*, 12 (2) (1950), 151–3.

Armagh Diocesan Registry: Rentals 1628–1878, PRONI D/848, covering areas in the civil parishes of: Armagh; Ballymore; Drumcree; Eglish; Kilmore; Lisnadill; Loughgall; Mullaghbrack; Shankill; Tynan. May cover further parishes.

Charlemont: Freeholders list, 1820. NLI Ms. 3784. Rentals, 1798–1802. NLI Ms. 2702. Major tenants only. Covering areas in the civil parishes of: Eglish; Forkill; Grange; Keady; Kilclooney; Killevy; Lisnadill; Loughgall; Loughgilly; Mullaghbrack; Tartaraghan.

Charlemont: Partial rentals, 1798–1802. Major tenants only, NLI Ms. 2702. Covering areas in the civil parishes of: Clonfeacle; Donaghmore; Eglish; Forkill; Grange; Keady; Kilclooney; Killevy; Lisnadill; Loughgall; Loughgilly; Mullaghbrack; Tartaraghan.

Commissioners of Education: Rentals, 1846–1854. NLI Ms. 16924. All tenants. Covering areas in the civil parish of Loughgilly.

Dawson: Rent rolls, 1787 (NLI Ms. 3183, 3283), 1797 (NLI Ms. 3185), 1812 (NLI Ms. 3188), 1838–1839 (NLI Ms. 3189) 1846 (NLI Ms. 1648), 1852–1853 (NLI Ms. 5674). All tenants. Covering areas in the civil parish of Clonfeacle.

Gosford, Earls of: Rentals, 1787–1824, PRONI D/1606. Covering areas in the civil parishes of: Kilclooney; Kilmore; Lisnadill; Loughgilly; Mullaghbrack; Tynan. May cover further parishes.

Johnston: Rentals, 1791–1802, 1853 (with observations) NAI M.3508. All tenants. Covering areas in the civil parish of Eglish.

Kilmorey, Viscounts: Rental, 1816, PRONI D/2638. Covering areas in the civil parishes of: Kilkeel; Magheralin; Newry. May cover further parishes.

Moore: Rentals, 1848. NAI M.2977. All tenants. Covering areas in the civil parish of Seagoe.

Obins: Rent roll, 1753 (Major tenants only). 1770 (All tenants). NLI Ms. 4736. Covering areas in the civil parish of Drumcree.

Verner/Wingfield: Rental, PRONI D/2538, 1830. Covering areas in the civil parishes of Killyman; Kilmore; Lisnadill; Tartaraghan. May cover further parishes.

[No landlord given]: Tenants list, 1714. NLI Ms. 3922. All tenants. Covering areas in the civil parishes of: Armagh; Clonfeacle; Derrynoose; Drumcree; Killyman; Kilmore; Tynan.

CARLOW

Census returns and substitutes

1641	Book of Survey and Distribution. NLI Ms. 971
1659	Pender's 'Census'. Repr. GPC, 1997, IMC, 2002. LDS Film 924648
1669	Carlow parish householders, *JKAS*, 10, 1918–2, 255–57
1767	Co. Carlow Freeholders. *IG*, 1980
1797	Chief Catholic inhabitants, Parishes of Graiguenamanagh and Knocktopher. *IA*, 1978
1798	Persons who suffered losses in the 1798 rebellion. Propertied classes only. c.300 names. NLI I 94107
1817	Emigrants from counties Carlow and Wexford to Canada. *Wexford: History and Society.* Online: Emigrants
1823–1838	Tithe Books. NAI LDS
1832–1837	Voters registered in Carlow borough. *Parliamentary Papers 1837, Reports from Committees,* Vol. II (2), 193–6
1835	List of electors; with addresses. NLI Ms. 16899
1837	Marksmen (illiterate voters) in parliamentary boroughs: Carlow. *Parliamentary Papers 1837, Reports from Committees,* Vol. II (1), Appendix A
1843	Co. Carlow voters. NAI 1843/55
1852–1853	Griffith's Valuation. Indexed online: Hayes
1901	Census, Carlow & Graiguecullen. Indexed online: Rootsweb Carlow
1911	Census

Online

Emigrants	*www.rootsweb.com/~irish/igsi_published/wextocan.htm*	
Hayes, John	*www.failteromhat.com*	Large compendium of transcribed records
Rootsweb Carlow	*www.rootsweb.com/~irlcar2*	

Publications

Local histories
Carlow Parliamentary Roll 1872, NLI Ir. 94138 m 1
Vigors papers (Burgage, Co. Carlow), *AH*, XX, 302–10
Kavanagh papers (Borris, Co. Carlow), *AH*, XXV, 15–30
Blackall, Sir Henry, 'The Blackneys of Ballyellin, Co. Carlow', *IG*, III, 1957–8, 44–5, 116
Brennan, M., *Schools of Kildare and Leighlin, 1775–1835,* Dublin, M.H. Gill and Son, 1935, NLI Ir. 37094135 b 4, 616 p.

Brophy, M., *Carlow past and present: a brochure containing short historical notes and miscellaneous gleanings of the town and county of Carlow*, Carlow: Printed at the Nationalist and Leinster Times Office, 1888, NLI Ir. 94138 b 1, 138 p.

Coleman, James, *Bibliography of the counties Carlow, Kilkenny and Wexford*, Waterford and South-east of Ireland Archaeological Society Journal, ll, 1907, NLI, 794105 W 1

Coyle, James, *The Antiquities of Leighlin*, Dublin, Browne and Nolan, n.d., NLI Ir. 94138 c 1

Farrell, Noel, *Exploring Family Origins in Carlow Town*, Longford: Noel Farrell, 2004?, 48 p.

Gallwey, Hubert, 'Tobin of Caherlesk and Tobinstown', *IG*, V, 1979, 760–62

Hood, Susan, 'Marriage in Ireland before the famine: case study of Rathvilly parish', *Journal of the West Wicklow Historical Society*, 3, 1989, 33–40

Hore, H.F., *The Social State of the Southern and Eastern Counties of Ireland in the Sixteenth Century*, Dublin, 1870, NLI Ir. 794105 r 2, 'being the presentments of the gentlemen, commonalty, and citizens of Carlow, Cork, Kilkenny, Tipperary, Waterford, and Wexford, made in the reigns of Henry VIII and Elizabeth. / Printed from the originals in the Public Record Office, London'. Edited by the late Herbert J. [i.e. F.] Hore, ... and the Rev. James Graves

IGRS, *Tombstone inscriptions Vol. 1*, Dublin: IGRS Tombstone Committee, 2001, NLI, 850 p.

Joyce, John, *Graiguenamanagh a town and its people: an historical and social account of Graiguenamanagh & Tinnahinch*, Graiguenamanagh [Co. Kilkenny]: Graigue Publications, 1993, NLI Ir. 94139 j 2, 198 p.

Joyce, John, *Graiguenamanagh and the South Carlow–Kilkenny area in 1798*, Graignamanagh Historical Society, 1998, NLI, 1A 337, [20] p.

King, Thomas, *Carlow the manor and town, 1674–1721*, Dublin: Irish Academic Press, 1997, NLI Ir. 94138 k 5, 72 p. Maynooth studies in Irish local history No. 12

Mac Suibhne, Peadar, *Ballon and Rathoe*, Carlow: Nationalist & Leinster Times, 1980, NLI, 117 p.

Mac Suibhne, Peadar, *Clonegal Parish*, Carlow: Newark Printers, 1975, NLI Ir. 2741 m 14, 190 p.

Morris, Andrew, *Dunleckney Headstone Inscriptions*, Morris, 1987, NLI, GS, 66 p.

Muintir na Tire, *Co. Carlow Tombstone Inscriptions*, St Mullin's, Ireland: St Mullin's Muintir na Tire, 1985, NLI Ir. 9295 c 3

O'Toole, Edward, *The Parish of Ballon, Co. Carlow*, Dublin: Thom, 1933, NLI Ir. 94138 o 3

Quane, Michael, *D'Israeli School, Rathvilly*, Dublin: Royal Society of Antiquaries, 1948, NLI, 23 p.

Ryan, John, *The history and antiquities of the County Carlow*, Dublin: R.M. Times, 1833, NLI Ir. 94138 r 1 388 p.

Veale, T., *Richard Lucas 1788: directory extract for south east of Ireland*, Dublin: Veale, 1995 NLI Ir. 9414 v

Veale, T., *Index of Surnames in 'The New Commercial Directory for the cities of Waterford and Kilkenny and the towns of Clonmel, Carrick-on-Suir, New Ross and Carlow'*, Dublin: Veale, 1996 NLI Ir. 9414 p.

White, W.D., *Heirs to a heritage: a story of the people and places of the Clonegal area of Clonegal Parish*, Clonegal: Co. Carlow, s.n., 1992, NLI Ir. 941 p 132(2), 72 p.

Local Journals
Carloviana, NLI Ir. 94138 c 2
Carlow Past and Present, NLI Ir. 94138 c 3
The Carlovian, NLI Ir. 379 c 29

Directories

1788	Richard Lucas, *General Directory of the Kingdom of Ireland*, NLI Pos. 3729. Repr. in Veale, *Lucas*, IG 1965, 1966, 1967, 1968. Online: Rootsweb Carlow
1820	J. Pigot, *Commercial Directory of Ireland*, PRONI, NLI Ir. 9141 p 107, LDS Film 962702 Item 1
1824	J. Pigot and Co., *City of Dublin and Hibernian Provincial Directory*, NLI, LDS Film 451787
1839	T. Shearman, *New Commercial Directory for the cities of Waterford and Kilkenny, Towns of Clonmel, Carrick-on-Suir, New Ross and Carlow*. Indexed in Veale, *Index*
1840	*New Trienniel Commercial Directory for 1840, 1841, 1842* (Carlow town)
1846	Slater's *National Commercial Directory of Ireland*, PRONI, NLI LO, LDS Film 1696703 Item 3
1856	Slater, *Royal National Commercial Directory of Ireland*, NLI, LDS Film 1472360 Item 1
1870	Slater, *Directory of Ireland*, NLI
1881	Slater, *Royal National Commercial Directory of Ireland*, NLI
1894	Slater, *Royal Commercial Directory of Ireland*, NLI

Gravestone Inscriptions

Aghade: in Ryan, *History and Antiquities*. Online: Rootsweb Carlow
Ballyellin: Ballyellin and Tomdarragh, Muintir na Tire, *Inscriptions*, Vol. 4
Clonygoose: Borris, Muintir na Tire, *Inscriptions*, Vol. 2
Clonygoose: Ballycoppigan, New, Muintir na Tire, *Inscriptions*, Vol. 2
Clonygoose: Muintir na Tire, *Inscriptions*, Vol. 2,
Dunleckny: Morris, *Dunleckney*
Killerrig, IGRS, *Vol.1*
Kiltennell: Rathanna, RC, Muintir na Tire, *Inscriptions*, Vol. 3
Kiltennell: Killedmond, C of I, Muintir na Tire, *Inscriptions*, Vol. 3
Kiltennell: Ballinvalley and Kiltennell, Muintir na Tire, *Inscriptions*, Vol. 2
Rathvilly: Kellymount (Mountkelly), Muintir na Tire, *Inscriptions*, Vol. 4
St Mullins: C of I, Muintir na Tire, *Inscriptions*, Vol. 1

St Mullins: Ballymurphy, RC, Muintir na Tire, *Inscriptions*, Vol. 3
Tullowmagimma: Linkardstown, IGRS, *Vol.1*
Wells: Muintir na Tire, *Inscriptions*, Vol. 4

Estate records

Bindon, Lady Henrietta: Rental and accounts, 1705–1709, NLI Ms. 3071. Principally major tenants. Covering areas in the civil parishes of: Aghade, Ballinacarrig, Carlow, Clonmelsh, Killerrig.

Cuffe, Sir Wheeler: Map and survey, 1807, NLI Ms. 2148. All tenants. Covering areas in the civil parish of Moyacomb.

Dawson: Rental, map, 1852, NLI Ms. 8391. Coverage unclear. Covering areas in the civil parish of Killerrig.

Farnham: Rentals 1818–1830, NLI Mss. 3133, 3502. All tenants. Covering areas in the civil parish of Barragh.

Fishbourne, William: Rental, 1830, NLI Ms. 10,078 (5). Most tenants. Covering areas in the civil parish of Carlow.

Hamilton, James Hans: Rentals and accounts, 1822–1833, NLI Mss.6000, 5885. All tenants. Covering areas in the civil parish of Carlow.

Kavanagh, Thomas: Map 1738–1758, NLI Pos. 576; Rent ledger, 1755–1810, NLI Pos. 7155; Map and rent ledger, 1736–1768, NLI Pos. 4645. Major tenants only. Covering areas in the civil parishes of Ballyellin; Clonygoose; Kiltennell; St Mullin's; Ullard.

Kavanagh: Tithe book, 1829, NLI Pos. 7156. Principally major tenants. Covering areas in the civil parish of St Mullin's.

[No landlord given]: Survey, 1170–1623, NLI Pos. 1707 [Lambeth Palace Library Ms. 635 (extracts)]. Coverage unclear. Covering areas in the civil parishes of: Agha; Ballyellin; Clonygoose; Cloydagh; Dunleckny; Fennagh; Killinane; Kiltennell; Lorum; Myshall; Nurney; Oldleighlin; Sliguff; Tullowcreen; Ullard; Wells.

O'Brien: Rentals, 1690–1690, NLI Pos. 4769. Principally major tenants. Covering areas in all civil parishes.

Ormond, Duke of: Survey, 1690–1690, NLI Ms. 10, 469. Major tenants only. Covering areas in the civil parishes of Ardristan; Ballon; Ballyellin; Barragh; Fennagh; Gilbertstown; Kellistown; Myshall; Templepeter; Tullowmagimma. Rent rolls 1690–1691, 1689–1704, 1703–1728, 1706, NLI Mss. 2562, 2561, 23,790, 23,789. Major tenants only. Covering areas in the civil parishes of: Agha: Aghade: Ardristan: Ballinacarrig: Ballon; Barragh; Carlow; Clonmore; Clonygoose; Cloydagh; Fennagh; Gilbertstown; Kellistown; Killerrig; Kiltennell; Kineagh; Rahill; Rathvilly; Sliguff; St Mullins; Tullowcreen; Tullowphelim; Urglin.

Paul, Sir. R.J.: Map, 1843, NLI Ms. 21.F.136. Most tenants. Covering areas in the civil parish of Tullowphelim.

Vigors: Account book, 1826, NLI Pos. 7629. Most tenants. Covering areas in the civil parish of Oldleighlin.

CAVAN

Census returns and substitutes

1612–1613	'Survey of Undertakers Planted in Co. Cavan'. *Historical Manuscripts Commission Report,* No. 4 (Hastings Mss), 1947. pp 159–82
1630	Muster Roll of Ulster; Armagh Co. Library and PRONI D.1759/3C/1; T. 808/15164; NLI Pos. 206
1660–1834	Belturbet Corporation records: Annual lists of court cases, commons grazing payments, charitable payments. Some gaps. NAI MFP 4.1
1664	Hearth Money Roll, parishes of Killeshandara, Kildallan, Killenagh, Templeport, Tomregan. PRONI 184
1703–1704	Tenants in Kildallan and Killeshandara. *IA,* 8 (2), 86–7
1761	Poll Book. PRONI T 1522. Online: Freeholders
1766	Protestants in parishes of Kinawley, Lavey, Lurgan, Munterconnaught. NAI m 2476(e). Also RCBL; GO Ms. 536/7; LDS Film 258517, 100173
1796	Spinning-Wheel Premium List. 2,400 names for Co. Cavan
1802	Protestants in Enniskeen parish. *IA,* 1973 (Vol. 8 (2), 86–7)
1813–1821	Freeholders, NLI Ir. 94119 c 2
1814	Youthful Protestants in the parishes of Drung & Larah. *IA,* 1978
1821	Parishes of Annagelliff, Ballymachugh, Castlerahan, Castleterra, Crosserlough, Denn, Drumlumman, Drung, Kilbride, Kilm ore, Kinawley, Larah, Lavey, Lurgan, Mullagh, Munterconnaught. NAI, LDS Films 597154–8; CGHP. Crosserlough online: Cmcrp (Cavan)
1823–1838	Tithe Books
1833	Arms registered with the Clerk of the Peace, April. Over 1,500 names. NLI ILB 04 p 12
1838	Householders, Mullinanalaghta RC parish—Contributors to new church, *Teathbha* 1 (3), 1978, 244–51
1841	Part of Killashandra parish only. Also some certified copies of census returns for use in claims for old age pensions. NAI
1843	Voters list NAI 1843/71
1845–1913	Enniskillen Union Workhouse records. PRONI BG/14. Also LDS Films 25914–53
1851	'List of inhabitants of Castlerahan barony'. c.1851. With Killinkere parish registers. NLI Pos. 5349
1851	Some certified copies of census returns for use in claims for old age pensions. NAI
1856–1857	Griffith's Valuation. Indexed online: Hayes
1901	Census
1911	Census
1912	The Ulster Covenant. Almost half-a-million original signatures and addresses of those who signed. Online: Covenant

Online

Beagan, Al	*members.tripod.com/~Al_Beagan /tcavan.htm*	
Clogher	*www.clogherhistoricalsoc.com*	Clogher Historical Society
Cmcrp (Cavan)	*www.cmcrp.net/OtherCty/ Cavan1821–1.htm*	Researcher-transcribed extracts
Covenant	*www.proni.gov.uk/ulstercovenant*	PRONI transcription of the Covenant
Freeholders	*www.proni.gov.uk/freeholders*	
Genweb Cavan	*www.irelandgenweb.com/~cavan*	
Hayes, John	*www.failteromhat.com*	Large compendium of transcribed records
Killeshandra	*homepages.iol.ie/~galwill/*	
Townland Maps	*freepages.genealogy.rootsweb.com/ ~colin/Ireland/CAV/Maps/*	

Publications

Local histories

'As time goes by—' compiled by Kingspan and Kingscourt Community Council Vol. 1, Kingscourt: The Council, 1994, NLI Ir. 94119 a 1, 100 p.

Cavan Freeholders since 1813, NLI Ir. 94119 c 2

'The Volunteer Companies of Ulster 1778–1793', lll, Cavan, *IS*, 7, 1906, 308–0

'Nugent papers (Mount Nugent, Co. Cavan)', *AH*, XX, 126–215

Brady, J., *A short history of the parishes of the diocese of Meath, 1867–1944*, NLI Ir. 94132 b 2

Cavan County Library, *Guide to Local Studies Dept.*, NLI Ir. 0179 p 6

Clarke, Desmond, *List of subscribers to Kilmore Academy Co. Cavan 1839*, Dublin: the compiler, 1999, NLI Ir. 260 L 6

Cullen, Sara, *Castlerahan*, Cavan: Printed by The Anglo-Celt Ltd, 1981, NLI Ir. 94119 g 3, 58 p.

Cunningham, T.P., *The Ecclesiastical History of Larah Parish*, Larah, Co. Cavan: Rev. Michael Canon O'Reilly, 1984, NLI Ir. 27412 c 2, 84 p.

Day, Angelique, *Ordnance Survey Memoirs of Ireland: Volume 40 Counties of South Ulster, 1834–8, Cavan, Leitrim, Louth, Monaghan and Sligo*, Belfast: Institute of Irish Studies, 1997, NLI Ir. 9141 o 80, 216pp. Co-editor, Patrick McWilliams. Co. Cavan: Drumgoon; Drumloman; Drung; Enniskeen; Killdrumsherdan; Laragh

Farrell, Noel, *Exploring Family origins in Cavan*, Longford: Self, 1993, NLI Ir. 941 p 118(1), 47p.

Flood, Cathal, *Greaghrahan National School 1871–2001: a history*, Greaghrahan: Greaghrahan National School Committee, 2001, NLI, 2A 2123, 157 p.

Gillespie, Raymond, *Cavan: Essays on the History of an Irish County*, Dublin: Irish Academic Press, 1995, NLI Ir. 94119 c 4, 240 p.

Hall, Juanita Arundell, *The John Hall family from Cootehill, Cavan County, Ireland*, Baltimore, Md.: Gateway Press, 1990, NLI Ir. 9292 h 21, 482 p.

Keogh, Marie, *Crosserlough, Co. Cavan 1821 census*, Dun Laoghaire: Genealogical Society of Ireland, 2000, NLI Ir. 9291 g 7, 298 p.

Kernan, John Devereux, *The Utica Kernans, descendants of Bryan Kernan, gent, ... of the townland of Ned in the parish of Killeshandra, barony of Tullyhunco, county of Cavan*, Hamden, Conn.: Kernan Enterprises, 1969, NLI Ir. 9292 k 7, 101 p.

Kernan, John Devereux, *Supplement to The Utica Kernans: descendants of Bryan Kernan*, United States: J.D. Kernan, 1993, NLI, GO 36, 107 p.

MacNamee, James J., *History of the Diocese of Ardagh*, Dublin: Browne and Nolan, 1954, NLI Ir. 274131 m 5, 858 p.

Masterson, Josephine, *A transcription and index of the 1841 census for Killeshandra parish, County Cavan, Ireland*, Indianapolis, Ind.: Masterson. Also FamilyTreeMaker CD ROM 7275. 1990, NLI

McCullam, R., *Sketches of the Highlands of Cavan, and of Shirley Castle, in Farney, taken during the Irish famine / by a Looker-On*, Belfast: J. Reed, 1856, NLI, Dix Belfast 1856, 316 p.

McGuinn, James, *Staghall a history*, Belturbet, Co. Cavan: Staghall Church Committee, 1995, NLI Ir. 94119 s 4, 451 p.

Monahan, Rev. J., *Records Relating to the Diocese of Ardagh and Clonmacnoise*, Dublin: M.H. Gill and son, 1886, NLI Ir. 27413 m 3, 400 p.

Mullagh Historical Committee, *Portrait of a Parish: Mullagh, Co Cavan*, Mullagh: Mullagh Historical Committee, 1988, NLI, 1, 396 p.

O'Brien, Hugh B., *St. Michael's, Cootehill a brief history of the Church, its buildings, its people*, Cootehill, Co. Cavan: St Michael's Church, 1993, NLI Ir. 282 o 16, 124 p.

O'Connell, Philip, *The Diocese of Kilmore: its History and Antiquities*, Dublin: Browne and Nolan, 1937, NLI Ir. 274119 o 3, 579 p.

Smyth, T.S., *A civic history of the town of Cavan*, Cavan, 1934, NLI Ir. 94119 s 1

Stewart, Herbert, *Billis school revisited: a history of Billis school 1826–2002*, 2002, NLI, 4A 1775, 66 p.

Sullivan, Tom, *Drumkilly: from Ardkill Mountain to Kilderry Hill*, Drumkilly: History Committee, 2001, NLI Ir. 94119 d 4, 503 p.

Swanzy, Rev. H.B., 'Some account of the family of French of Belturbet', *UJA*, 2nd Ser. VIII, 1902, 155–60

Local Journals
Ardagh & Clonmacnoise Historical Society Journal, NLI Ir. 794105
Breifne: journal of Cumann Seanchais Bhreifne, NLI Ir. 94119 b 2
Heart of Breifny, NLI Ir. 94119 h 1
The Drumlin: a Journal of Cavan, Leitrim and Monaghan, NLI Ir. 05 d 345

Directories

1820   J. Pigot, *Commercial Directory of Ireland*, PRONI, NLI Ir. 9141 p 107, LDS Film 962702 Item 1

1824   J. Pigot and Co., *City of Dublin and Hibernian Provincial Directory*, NLI, LDS Film 451787

1846   Slater's *National Commercial Directory of Ireland*, PRONI, NLI LO, LDS Film 1696703 Item 3

1852   *Belfast and Province of Ulster Directory*. Also 1856, 1858, 1861, 1863, 1865, 1868, 1870, 1877, 1880, 1884, 1887, 1890, 1894, 1900. PRONI, LDS (various years), NLI Dix Belfast 1852

1856   Slater, *Royal National Commercial Directory of Ireland*, NLI, LDS Film 1472360 Item 1

1870   Slater, *Directory of Ireland*, NLI

1881   Slater, *Royal National Commercial Directory of Ireland*, NLI

1894   Slater, *Royal Commercial Directory of Ireland*, NLI

Gravestone Inscriptions

Annagh: Clonosey, CHGC

—— Killoughter, CHGC

Ballintemple: Ballintemple, C of I, CHGC

—— Pottahee (Brusky?), RC, CHGC

Castlerahan: Castlerahan, C of I, *Breifne*, 1925/6. Also CHGC

Castleterra: RC, CHGC

Crosserlough: Kill, *Breifne*, 1976. Also CHGC

—— Crosserlough, RC, CHGC

Denn: Denn Glebe, C of I, *Breifne*, 1924

Drumgoon: Drumgoon, CHGC

Drumlane: Drumlane, *Breifne*, 1979

Drung: Magherintemple, *Breifne*, 1963

—— Drung, CHGC

Kilbride: Gallonreagh (Kilbride?), CHGC

Killeshandra (Old): Online: Killeshandra

Killinagh: Termon (Killinagh Old?), C of I, CHGC

Killinkere: Gallon, CHGC

Kilmore: Trinity Island (St Mogue's?), CHGC

Larah: CHGC

Lavey: C of I, GO. Also CHGC

Lurgan: *Breifne*, 1961. Also CHGC

Mullagh: Mullagh (Raffoney?), C of I, CHGC

Munterconnaught: Knockatemple, RC, *Breifne*, 1927/8. Also CHGC

Scrabby: Cloone, C of I, SA, Vol. 10, No. 1, 1980–1981

Templeport: Port, *Breifne*, 1971

Urney: Cavan, Church Lane, *Breifne*, 1986

Estate Records

Annesley: Maps, with tenants' names, 1805–1817, NLI Ms. 2730. Coverage unclear. Covering areas in the civil parishes of: Annagh; Denn; Drumlumman; Drung; Kilmore; Larah; Lavey; Templeport; Urney.

Commissioners of Education: Rentals, 1818–1845, NLI Ms. 16920(5), 1837–1842, NLI Ms. 16926. All tenants. Covering areas in the civil parish of Annagelliff.

Craigies, Robert: Tenants list, 1703–1704, IA, 1978. Coverage unclear. Covering areas in the civil parishes of Kildallan and Killashandra.

Crofton: Rent rolls, 1792, NLI Ms. 4530, 1796–1831, NLI Ms. 8150. Major tenants only. Covering areas in the civil parish of Kinawley.

Farnham, Earl of: Rent rolls etc., 1718–1790, NLI Ms. 11491. Major tenants only. Rentals, 1820, NLI Ms. 350; 1841–1848, NLI Ms. 5012–13; 1842–1843, NLI Ms. 18624. All tenants. Covering areas in the civil parishes of: Ballintemple; Ballymachugh; Castlerahan; Crosserlough; Denn; Drumlane; Drumlumman; Kilbride; Kildallan; Killashandra; Killinkere; Kilmore; Lurgan and Urney.

Fingall, Earl of: Rent rolls, 1750, NLI Ms. 8024. Major tenants only. Covering areas in the civil parishes of: Loughan or Castlekeeran; Lurgan; Mullagh; Munterconnaught.

Garvagh, Lord: Rentals, 1829–1848, NAI M5535. All tenants. Covering areas in the civil parishes of: Drumgoon; Knockbride and Larah.

Gosford, Earls of: Rentals, 1787–1824, PRONI D/1606. Covering areas in the civil parishes of: Ballintemple; Killashandra; Scrabby. May cover further parishes.

Greville, William: Rentals, surveys etc., 1810–1848, NAI M6178 (1–89). All tenants. Covering areas in the civil parishes of: Drumgoon and Knockbride.

Groome, Edward: Rentals, with observations, 1822, NAI M5559. All tenants. Covering areas in the civil parishes of: Bailieborough; Knockbride; and Moybolgue.

Hamilton: Rentals, with observations, 1851, NAI M5571 (1–39). All tenants. Covering areas in the civil parishes of: Kildallan; Killashandra; and Kilmore.

Hodson: Rentals, 1811–1824, NLI Ms.16397–8. All tenants. Covering areas in the civil parishes of: Bailieborough; and Knockbride.

Mayne, Robert: Map, 1780. NAI M1853. All tenants. Map of Begleive and Killcross in Knockbride parish.

O'Reilly, James: Rentals, 1815–1816, NAI M.6962. All tenants. Covering areas in the civil parishes of: Annagelliff; Castlerahan; Crosserlough; Denn; and Kilbride.

Pratt: Rentals, 1837–1863, NLI Ms. 3021, 1837–1855, NLI Ms. 3284. All tenants. Covering areas in the civil parish of Enniskeen.

Saunderson: Rent roll, 1779, NLI Ms. 13340. Major tenants only. Covering areas in the civil parishes of: Annagelliff; Killinker; Lavey.

Tennison: Rentals, 1846–1854, NLI Ms. 1400–1409. All tenants. Covering areas in the civil parish of Annagelliff.

CLARE

Census returns and substitutes

1641	*Book of Survey and Distribution,* Dublin: Irish Manuscripts Commission, 1947. Also NLI Ms. 963. Transcribed online: Clare Co. Library
1659	Pender's 'Census'. Repr. GPC, 1997, IMC, 2002. LDS Film 924648
1745	Voters. TCD Ms. 2059
1778	Militia volunteers in Ennis. *JNMAS* 6 (4), 1952, 143–151
1821	Part of Ennis. NAI: See pre-1901 census catalogue
1823–1838	Tithe Books. Transcribed online: Clare Co. Library
1829	Freeholders. NLI P.5556
1837	Marksmen (illiterate voters) in parliamentary boroughs: Ennis. *Parliamentary Papers 1837, Reports from Committees,* Vol. II (i), Appendix A
1843	Clare voters. NAI 1843/68
1848–1849	Smith O'Brien Petition ENE #CD2. Almost 4,000 names for Ennis/Tulla. See Chapter 2 'Official Papers, Petitions'
1849	Evictions in Kilrush Union. Online: Clare Co. Library
1850	Deaths in Kilrush & Ennistymon workhouses, hospitals, infirmaries, 25/3/1850–25/3/1851. *Accounts & Papers (Parliamentary Papers), 1851,* Vol. 49 pp (484) 1–47
1855	Griffith's Valuation. Indexed online: Hayes & Clare Co. Library
1866	Kilfenora. NLI Pos. 2440
1901	Census. Transcribed online: Clare Co. Library
1911	Census

Online

Celtic cousins	*www.celticcousins.net*	Assorted records for Clare and Galway
Clare Co. Library	*www.clarelibrary.ie*	Clare sources
Connors	*www.connorsgenealogy.com*	
Hayes, John	*www.failteromhat.com*	Large compendium of transcribed records
Rootsweb Clare	*www.rootsweb.com/~irlcla*	

Publications

Local histories

Visions of Famine in West Clare "vultures in the wild bogs": pictures of yesterday, words of today, [Clare?], Westwords, 199?, NLI, 40 p.

Páirtín 1885–1985 Parteen centenary book, Parteen: the Club, 1985, NLI Ir. 396 p. 56(1), 176 p.

A Guide to Ennistymon Union 1839–1850, Ennistymon: North Clare Historical Society, 1992, NLI Ir. 360 g, 47 p.

'Businessmen of Ennis early in the Napoleonic wars', *IA*, 16 (1), 1984, 6–8

Ainsworth, J.F., *The Inchiquin Manuscripts*, Dublin: 1960, NLI Ir. 091 a 1

Bourke, Freddie, *Kiltenanlea Parish Church and its community, Clonara, Co. Clare 1782–1992*, Clonlara, Co. Clare: Clonlara Development Association, 1992, NLI Ir. 941 p 116(4), 36 p.

Brew, Frank, *The parish of Kilkeedy a local history compiled*, Tubber: Frank Brew, 1998, NLI Ir. 94143 b 10, 310 p.

Clancy, John, Rev. Canon, 'Gleanings in 17th century Kilrush', *North Munster Antiquarian Society Journal*, 1942–1943

Clancy, John, Rev. Canon, *Short History of the Parish of Killanena or Upper Feakle*, Ennis: Clare Champion, 1954, NLI Ir. 941 p 27

Coffey, Thomas, *The Parish of Inchicronan (Crusheen)*, Mountshannon: Ballinakella Press, 1993, NLI Ir. 94143 c 10

Coleman, James, 'Limerick and Clare Bibliography', *Limerick Field Club Journal* No. 32, 1907

Comber, Maureen (ed.), *Poverty before the famine County Clare 1835: first report from His Majesty's Commissioners into the Condition of the Poorer Classes in Ireland*, Ennis: CLASP Press, 1995, NLI Ir. 94143 p 2, 170 p.

Cotter, Maura, *Parish of Kilmihil: Historical cultural and sporting achievements*, 1975?, NLI Ir. 94143 c 6, 264 p.

Dwyer, Philip, *A handbook to Lisdoonvarna and its vicinity: giving a detailed account of its curative waters, and tours to the principal places of interest in the County Clare*, Dublin: Hodges, Foster, 1876, NLI Ir. 914143 l 4, 86 p.

Dwyer, Philip, *The Diocese of Killaloe, from the Reformation to the Close of the Eighteenth Century*, Dublin: Hodges, Foster, and Figgis, 1878, NLI Ir. 94143 d 11, 602 p. Reprint: Newmarket-on-Fergus: O'Brien Book Publications, 1997

Edward, Thomas, *An Irish commune: the experiment at Ralahine, County Clare, 1831–1833*, Dublin: Irish Academic Press, c 1983, NLI Ir. 630941 c 38, 208 p.

Flanagan, John, *Kilfenora a history*, Lahinch, Co. Clare: John Flanagan, 1991, NLI Ir. 94143.f.7, 141 p.

Frost, James, *The history & topography of Co. Clare from the earliest times to the beginning of the eighteenth century*, Dublin: 1893, NLI Ir. 94143 f 3. Repr. Newmarket-on-Fergus: O'Brien Book Publications, 1997

Gwynn, A., *A history of the diocese of Killaloe*, Dublin: M.H. Gill and Son, 1962, NLI Ir. 27414.g.3, 566 p.

Hayes McCoy, G.A., *Index to 'The Compossicion Booke of Connoght, 1585'*, Dublin: Irish Manuscripts Commission, 1945, NLI Ir. 9412 c 1, 179 p.

Herbert, Robert, *Worthies of Thomond: a compendium of short lives of the most famous men and women of Limerick and Clare*, Limerick: Printed by the 'Limerick Leader' Ltd., and published by the author, 1946, NLI, 3 parts

Holohan, Pat, *Cill Mhuire na nGall a history of Kilmurry 1891–1991 written by the people of Kilmurry*, Kilmurry, Co. Clare: Kilmurray Centenary Committee,

1991, NLI Ir. 94143.k.7, 172 p.

IGRS, *Tombstone inscriptions Vol. 1*, Dublin: IGRS Tombstone Committee, 2001, NLI, 850 p.

Jones, Anne, *The scattering: images of emigrants from an Irish county*, Dublin: A. & A. Farmar, 2000, NLI, 256 p. Text by Ray Conway

Kelly, John S., *The Bodyke evictions*, Scariff, Co. Clare: Fossabeg Press, 1987, NLI Ir. 94143 k 6, 184 p.

Kierse, Sean, *The famine years in the parish of Killaloe 1845*, Killaloe, Clare: Boru Books, 1984, NLI Ir. 94143 k 5, 86 p.

Kierse, Sean, *Priests and religious of Killaloe parish, Co. Clare*, Killaloe, Co. Clare: Boru Books, 2000, NLI, 3B 961, 54 p.

Kierse, Sean, *Historic Killaloe: a guide to its antiquities*, Killaloe, Co. Clare: Boru Books, 1983, NLI Ir. 941 p 77, 46 p.

Lane, Michael, *Church of St. Sena, Clonlara: parish of Doonass and Truagh*, Clonara, Clare: M. Lane, 1984, NLI Ir. 270 p 15, 36 p.

Lee, David, *Ralahine land war and the co-operative*, Limerick: Bottom Dog in association with Co-op Books, 1981, NLI Ir. 333 p 52, 56 p.

Lloyd, A.R., *Lloyd's tour of Clare, 1780: (from Henn's exact reprint of 1893)*, Whitegate, Co. Clare: Ballinakella, c. 1986, NLI Ir. 914143 L 15, 60 p.

Mac Mathúna, Seosamh, *Kilfarboy: a history of a west Clare parish*, Milltown Malbay: S. Mac Mathúna, 1976?

Madden, Gerard, *Holy Island, jewel of the Lough. A history*, Tuamgraney, Co. Clare: East Clare Heritage Centre, 1990, NLI Ir. 941 p 102(1), 39 p.

Madden, Gerard, *For God or King: the history of Mountshannon, Co. Clare 1742–1992*, Tuamgraney, Co. Clare: East Clare Heritage, 1993, NLI Ir. 94143 f 8, 204 p.

Madden, Gerard, *A history of Tuamgraney and Scariff: since earliest times*, Tuamgraney, Co. Clare: East Clare Heritage, 2000, NLI Ir. 94143 m 19, 208 p.

Markham, Paul, *Kilmurry McMahon and Killofin remembered: an accurate and detailed account—past and present—of a rural parish in the barony of Clonderlaw, Co. Clare*, Ireland: s.n., NLI Ir. 94143 m 18, 236 p.

McAuliffe, E.J., *Notes on the parishes of Kilmurry McMahon and Killofin, Co. Clare and tombstone inscriptions from Kilrush*, Dublin: McAulliffe, 1989, NLI Ir. 941 p. 137(4), 31 p.

McCarthy, Daniel, *Ireland's banner county: Clare from the fall of Parnell to the great war, 1890–1918*, Ennis: Saipan Press, 2002, NLI, 213 p.

McGuane, James T., *Kilrush from olden times*, Inverin, Galway: Clódoiri Lurgan, 1984, NLI Ir. 94143 m 11, 114 p.

Murphy, Ignatius, *Father Michael Meehan and the Ark of Kilbaha*, Ennis: Rev. Michael Greene, 1980, NLI Ir. 920041 p. 7, 16 p.

Murphy, Ignatius, *The Diocese of Killaloe 1800–1850*, Dublin: Four Courts Press, 1992, NLI Ir. 27414 m 7, 488 p.

Murphy, Ignatius, *Before the Famine struck: life in West Clare, 1834–1845*, Blackrock, Co. Dublin: Irish Academic Press, 1996, NLI Ir. 94143 m 16, 105 p.

Murphy, Ignatius, *A People Starved—Life and Death in West Clare 1845–1851*, Dublin: Irish Academic Press, 1995, NLI Ir. 94143 m 15, 113 p.

Murphy, Ignatius, *The Diocese of Killaloe 1850–1904*, Dublin: Four Courts Press, 1995, NLI Ir. 27414 m 9, 527 p.

Murphy, Ignatius, *The diocese of Killaloe in the eighteenth century*, Dublin: Four Courts Press, 1991, NLI Ir. 27414 m 8, 373 p.

Murphy, Paul, *Cuchulain's Leap: a history of the parishes of Carrigaholt and Cross*, Carrigaholt, Co. Clare: Carrigaholt and Cross Heritage Group, 1992, NLI Ir. 94143 m 12, 288 p.

Ó Conchúir, M.F., *O Conor Corcomroe a bilingual history*, –, M.F. Ó Conchuir, 1996, NLI Ir. 9292 o 68, 293 p.

Ó Dálaigh, Brian, *Corporation book of Ennis 1660–1810*, Dublin: Irish Academic Press, 1990, NLI Ir. 94143 c 8, 455 p.

Ó Dálaigh, Brian, *Ennis in the 18th century: portrait of an urban community*, Dublin: Irish Academic Press, 1995, NLI Ir. 94143 o 9, 62 p. Maynooth studies in local history; No. 3

Ó Murchadha, Ciarán, *County Clare studies: essays in memory of Gerald O'Connell, Seán Ó Murchadha, Thomas Coffey and Pat Flynn*, Ennis: Clare Archaeological and Historical Society, 2000, NLI, 271 p.

O'Brien, Grania Rachel, *These my friends and forebears: the O'Briens at Dromoland Castle*, Whitegate: Ballinakella Press, 1991, NLI Ir. 9292 o 54, 259 p.

O'Cillin, Sean P., *Travellers in Co. Clare, 1459–1843*, Galway: S.P. O'Cillin and P.F. Brannick, 1977, NLI Ir. 914143 o 16, 55 p.

O'Donovan, John, *The antiquities of County Clare ... collected during the progress of the Ordnance survey in 1839; & letters and extracts relative to ancient territories in Thomond, 1841*, Ennis: CLASP Press, 1997, NLI Ir. 94143 o 10, 323 p. John O'Donovan & Eugene Curry ; [edited and indexed by Maureen Comber]

O'Gorman, Michael, *A pride of paper tigers: a history of the Great Hunger in the Scariff Workhouse Union from 1839 to 1853*, Tuamgraney, Co. Clare: East Clare Heritage, 1994, NLI Ir. 94143 o 8, 82 p.

O'Mahoney, Dr C., 'Emigration from Kilrush Workhouse, 1848–1859', *The Other Clare*, 1983

Power, Joseph, *A history of Clare Castle and its environs*, Ennis: Power, 2004, NLI, 4B 1621, 646 p.

Shiely Jr, James F., *The Shealys (Shielys) of Kilrush, County Clare, Ireland, and Minnesota, U.S.A.*, Prescott, WI: J.F. Shiely, Jr, 1998, NLI Ir. 94143 s 14

Simington, Robert C., *The transplantation to Connacht, 1654–58*, Shannon: Irish University Press for the Irish Manuscripts Commission, 1970, NLI Ir. 94106 s 9, 306 p.

Spellisy, Seán, *The merchants of Ennis*, Blarney, Co. Cork: On Stream Publications for Ennis Chamber of Commerce, 1996, NLI Ir. 380 s 10, 200 p.

Spellisy, Seán, *A history of County Clare*, Dublin: Gill & Macmillan, 2003, NLI, 156 p.

Starkie, Virginia, *Indexed abtracts from Co. Clare civil records 1864–1880*, Vienna, VA: the author, 1990, LDS Family History Library, Film 1696528

Swinfen, Averin, *Forgotten stones ancient church sites of the Burren & environs*, Dublin: Lilliput Press, 1992, NLI Ir. 726 s 19, 151 p.

Weir, H., *Historical genealogical architectural notes on some houses of Clare*, Whitegate (Co. Clare): Ballinakella Press, 1999, NLI Ir. 728 w 12, 285 p.

Westropp, Thomas J., *Westropp Manuscripts, Royal Irish Academy*, Will abstracts mainly for Counties Clare and Limerick

White, Rev. P, *History of Clare and the Dalcassian Clans of Tipperary, Limerick and Galway*, Dublin: 1893, NLI Ir. 94143 w 4, 398 p. Repr. Newmarket-on-Fergus: O'Brien Book Publications, 1997

Local Journals

Dál gCais, NLI Ir. 94143 d 5

Journal of the North Munster Archaeological Society, NLI Ir. 794105 n 1

Shannonside Annual (1956–1960), NLI Ir. 94146 s 2

Sliabh Aughty: E. Clare Heritage Journal, NLI Ir. 94133.s [sic]

The Other Clare (Journal of the Shannon Archaeological & Historical Society), NLI Ir. 9141 p 71

Directories

1788	Richard Lucas, *General Directory of the Kingdom of Ireland*, NLI Pos. 3729. Repr. in Veale, *Lucas*, IG, 1965, 1966, 1967, 1968
1820	J. Pigot, *Commercial Directory of Ireland*, PRONI, NLI Ir. 9141 p. 107, LDS Film 962702 Item 1
1824	J. Pigot and Co., *City of Dublin and Hibernian Provincial Directory*, NLI, LDS Film 451787
1842	*A directory of Kilkee*, NLI Ir. 61312 k 1
1846	Slater's *National Commercial Directory of Ireland*, PRONI, NLI LO, LDS Film 1696703 Item 3
1856	Slater, *Royal National Commercial Directory of Ireland*, NLI, LDS Film 1472360 Item 1
1866	George Henry Bassett, *Directory of the City and County of Limerick, and of the Principal Towns in the Cos. of Tipperary and Clare*, NLI Ir. 914144 b 5
1870	Slater, *Directory of Ireland*, NLI
1881	Slater, *Royal National Commercial Directory of Ireland*, NLI
1886	Francis Guy, *Postal Directory of Munster*, NLI Ir. 91414 g 8, LDS Film 1559399 Item 8
1893	Francis Guy, *Directory of Munster*, NLI Ir. 91414 g 8
1894	Slater, *Royal Commercial Directory of Ireland*, NLI

Gravestone Inscriptions

The Clare Genealogy Centre has transcripts for eight graveyards in the county. Contact details will be found in Chapter 15. Clare entries from the *Journal of the Association for the Preservation of the Memorials of the Dead, Ireland 1888–1916* are online (Clare Co. Library). Published or publicly available transcripts are given below.

Clooney: Clooney South, IGRS, GO,
—— Killeinagh, IGRS, GO,
Drumcreehy: Ballyvaghan, IGRS, GO,
Inchicronan: Kilvoydan South, IGRS, GO,
Kilfarboy: Kilcorcoran, IGRS, GO,
—— Kildeema South, IGRS, GO,
—— Kilfarboy, IGRS, GO,
—— Milltown Malbay, Mullagh Road, C of I, IGRS, GO,
Kilfenora: Kilfenora, Well Lane, C of I, IGRS, GO,
Killinaboy: Coad, IGRS, GO,
—— Corrofin town, Church Street, C of I, IGRS, GO,
Killinaboy: Killinaboy, IGRS, GO,
Kilmacrehy: Dough, IGRS, GO,
Kilmurry: Killernan, IGRS, GO,
—— Kilmurry town, IGRS, GO,
Kilrush: Kilrush, Grace Street, C of I, IGRS, *Vol. 1*, also McAuliffe, *Notes*
Kilshanny: Ballyalla, GO 622 pp79/80, GO,
—— Kilshanny, IGRS, GO,
Kiltenanlea: Doonass Demesne, IGRS, GO,
Noughaval: Glebe, IGRS, GO,
Rath: Rath, IGRS, GO,

Estate Records

Arthur, Thomas: Map, 1823. Major tenants only, NLI Ms. 21 f 75 (3). Covering areas in the civil parishes of: Kilballyowen; Moyarta.

Brown, John: Rental 1828–1832, NLI Ms. 8990. Principally major tenants. Covering areas in the civil parishes of: Killaloe; Killilagh; Kiltenanlea; Templemaley.

Buckingham, Duke of: Estate sale & map, 1848. NLI Ms. 14.A.20. All tenants. Covering areas in the civil parishes of: Drumcreehy; Killinaboy; Rathborney.

Burton, Edward William: Rental, 1828 NLI Ms. 8683. All tenants. Covering areas in the civil parishes of: Feakle; Kilballyowen; Kilfenora; Killinaboy; Kilmurry; Kiltoraght.

Butler: Rentals, undated (late nineteenth century), NAI M. 3703 (179) & (180). All tenants. Covering areas in the civil parishes of: Clondagad; Doon; Inchicronan; Mungret.

Inchiquin: Rentals, 1840–1860 NLI Ms. 14355 &ff. All tenants. Full; approximate dates. Covering areas in the civil parish of Kilnasoolagh.

O'Brien, Sir Donat: Rent rolls, 1688–1717, NLI Mss. 14353–14410. Principally major tenants. Covering areas in the civil parishes of: Clonloghan; Doora; Drumline; Kilfintinan; Kilnasoolagh; Kilseily; Quin; Templemaley; Tomfinlough; Tulla.

O'Brien, Sir Lucius: Map; 1768–1781, NLI Maps 21 f 138. Major tenants only. Covering areas in the civil parishes of: Clareabbey; Killinaboy; Kilnasoolagh; Tomfinlough.

O'Callaghan-Westropp estate rentals: barony of Tulla Upper. NLI Ms. 867.

Roxton estate rentals: Inchiquin barony, Co. Clare, 1834. NAI M 5764.

Stacpoole Kenny: Rental, 1824–1826, NLI Ms. 18910. Most tenants. Clonloghan; 1851–1853, NLI Ms. 18913. Covering areas in the civil parish of Killaspuglonane.

Studdert (1830s?): Tenants, 'List of persons who are in want of immediate employment in the different townlands in the parish of Kilballyowen'; Tenants' names; number in each family; number able to work; observations. NLI Ms. 20640.

Westby, Nicholas: Survey 1842, NLI Ms. map 21 f 85. Major tenants only. Ennis town.

Westropp: Map 1844–1895, NLI Ms. maps 21 f126. Most tenants. Covering areas in the civil parishes of: Clareabbey; Doora; Kilmacduane; Kilmihil; Kilnoe; Quin.

Vandeleur: note on the Leconfield estate papers at the NAI, Accession No. 1074. (Vandeleur leases, Kilrush, 1816–1929, Lord Leconfield rentals, 1846–1917, including comments on age, health, poverty, etc.) *North Munster Antiquarian Journal*, Vol. XXIII (1981).

CORK

Census returns and substitutes

1500–1650	The Pipe Roll of Cloyne. *JCHAS*, 1918
1641	Book of Survey and Distribution. Proprietors in 1641, grantees in 1666–8. NLI Ms. 966–7
1641	Survey of Houses in Cork City, listing tenants and possessors. NAI Quit Rent Office Papers
1654	Civil Survey. *Civil Survey*, Vol. VI
1659	Pender's 'Census'. Repr. GPC, 1997, IMC, 2002. LDS Film 924648
1662–1667	Subsidy rolls. Extracts for Condons and Clangibbons baronies. NAI M.4968, M.2636
1700–1752	Freemen of Cork city. NAI M. 4693
1761	Militia list of Co. Cork, NAI
1753	Householders St Nicholas' parish Cork City. Also later years. NAI MFCI 23, 24, 25; M 6047
1766	Aghabulloge, Aghada, Ardagh, Ballintemple, Ballyhay, Ballynoe, Carrigdownane, Carrigrohanebeg, Castlelyons, Castletownroche, Churchtown, Clenor, Clondrohid, Clondulane, Clonfert, Clonmeen, Clonmult, Clonpriest, Cloyne, Coole, Farahy, Garrycloyne, Glanworth, Grenagh, Ightermurragh, Imphrick, Inishcarra, Kildorrery, Kilmahon, Kilnamartry, Kilshannig, Kilworth, Knockmourne, Lisgoold, Litter, Macroney, Macroom, Magourney, Mallow, Marshalstown, Matehy, Middleton, Mogeely, Mourneabbey, Roskeen, Shandrum, St Nathlash,

Templemolaga, Whitechurch, Youghal, M5036a; Rathbarry, Ringrone, NAI; Parl. Ret, 773, 774 Dunbulloge *JCHAS*, Vol. 51; Kilmichael, Vol. 26. Part online: Prendergast, Swanton

1783 Freemen & freeholders, Cork City. NLI p. 2054

1792 Kinsale Loyalty Petition. Online: Hall #2

1793 Householders in the parish of St Anne's, Shandon. Also includes householders of additional houses built up to 1853. *JCHAS*, Vol. 47, pp. 87–111

1796 Spinning-Wheel Premium List. 1,170 names for Co. Cork

1814 Jurors, Co. Cork. NAI M2637, Grove-White Abstracts

1817 Freemen, Cork City. NLI P 722

1821 18 townlands in Inchigeelagh. Online: Grogan

1823–1838 Tithe Books. Part online: Prendergast

1830 House-owners, St Mary's, Shandon. *JCHAS*, Vol. 49

1831 Memorial of inhabitants of Kanturk for Kanturk to Mallow–Cork road, Jul. 12, 1831 (128 names) NAI OP 974/132

1830–1837 Registered householders, Cork City (alphabetical). *Parliamentary Papers 1837, Reports from Committees, 1837/8*, Vol. 13 (2), pp. 554–7

1832–1837 Voters, Cork City. *Parliamentary Papers 1837, Reports from Committees*, 1837/8, Vol. 13 (1), pp. 320/1

1834 Protestant families Magourney parish; with C of I Registers. NAI M 5118

1834 Protestant parishioners: Bandon town (Ballymodan only). NLI Ms. 675

1834–1837 Valuation of Bandonbridge, Kinsale, Youghal towns (£5 householders). *Parliamentary Papers 1837, Reports from Committees*, Vol. II (1), Appendix G

1836 Memorials for Quarter sessions at: Kanturk (c.120 signatures); Middleton (c.40 names); Mitchelstown (c.100 signatures, with addresses); Mallow (c.85 signatures). NAI OP OP 1836/130

1836–1852 Kingwilliamstown Crown estate censuses, 1836, 1849, 1852. LDS Film 101767

1837 Marksmen (i.e. illiterate voters), Bandonbridge, Kinsale, Youghal Boroughs. *Parliamentary Papers 1837, Reports from Committees*, 1837, Vol. II (1), Appendix A

1837 Lists of waste and poor Cork City parishes. *Parliamentary Papers 1837, Reports from Committees*, 1837/8. Vol. 13 (1), pp 324–334

1838–1848 Reproductive Loan Fund records. Parishes of Ballinadee, Brigown, Castlehaven, Cloyne, Durrus, Inch, Kilcaskan, Kilcatherine, Kilfaughnabeg, Killaconenagh, Kilmacabea, Kilmeen (East Carbery), Kilmocomoge, Kilmoe, Kinsale, Marshalstown, Ringcurran, Ross, Skull, Tullagh. 5,000+ names, with accounts of deaths and emigration. NA (Kew). T 91. Partly online: Moving Here

1841–1851 Extensive extracts for Kilcrumper, Leitrim and Kilworth parishes NAI M4685. Also abstracts used in application for old age pensions. See Masterson (local history)

1842	Cork voters. West 1842/26, East 1842/23
1843–1850	Records of Easter and Christmas dues. Catholic parish of Ballyclogh: includes names of parishioners, with children. NLI Pos. 5717. NLI Pos. 5717
1848	Memorial from inhabitants of Cork City for additional Quarter sessions. c.80 names. NAI OP 1836/130
1851	Extracts for Kilcrumper, Kilworth, Leitrim, and Macroney. Online: Swanton
1851–1853	Griffith's Valuation. Transcribed online: Hayes
1901	Census. Part online: Grogan
1911	Census. Part online: Grogan

Online

Grogan, Margaret	www.sci.net.au/userpages/mgrogan	Volunteer-transcribed Cork records
Hall #2, Brendan	homepage.tinet.ie/~jbhall	
Hayes, John	www.failteromhat.com	Compendium of Irish records, esp.Clonakilty
Moving Here	www.movinghere.org.uk/search/	
Prendergast, Jean	homepage.eircom.net/~ridgway	Assorted records for most areas of Cork
Swanton, Ginni	www.ginnisw.com/corkmain.html	Assorted records for most areas of Cork
Turner, Paul	www.paulturner.ca	Ballymoney/Kinneigh/ Bandon

Publications

Local histories, etc.

Cil na Martra, Muscrai, Co. Chorcaí, Kilnamartyra: Coiste Forbartha, Cill na Martra, 1995, NLI Ir. 94145 c 28, 151 p.

A vision fulfilled 1846–1996: a Skibbereen school, Skibbereen: St Fachtna's de la Salle, Past Pupils Union, 1996, NLI Ir. 373 v 1, 92 p.

Ahern, Madge, *Inniscarra looks back through the avenues of time,* Cork: St Coleman's, 1995, NLI Ir. 94145 a 1, 97 p.

Allen, D.H., *Ath trasna: a history of Newmarket, county Cork,* Cork: Cork Historical Guides Committee, 1973, NLI, 104 p.

Aubane Historical Society, *A Millstreet medley,* Millstreet: Aubane Historical Society, 2001, NLI, 1B 388, 47 p.

Aubane Historical Society, *Aubane notes on a townland,* Aubane: Aubane Historical Society, 1996, NLI, 51 p.: this is the text of a talk in Aubane School on 26 August 1996

Aubane Historical Society, *Aubane school and its roll books, 1913–1974,* Aubane: Aubane Historical Society, 1998, NLI, 2B 667, 50 p.

Aubane Historical Society, *250 years of the butter road,* Millstreet: Aubane Historical Society, 1997, NLI, 1B 482, 50 p.

Ballynoe Cemetery Committee, *Ballynoe Cemetery, a guide and brief history,* Ballynoe, Co. Cork: 1993, NLI Ir. 9295 p. 3(1)

Ballynoe National School, *Ballynoe national schools 1850–1990,* Ballynoe, Co. Cork: Ballynoe National School, 1990, NLI Ir. 372.b.66, 160 p.

Ballyvongane Committee, *Ballyvongane N.S. 1845–1995 Beal Atha Na Marbh Aghinagh: a rural community,* Ballyvongane: 150th Anniversary Committee, 1995, NLI, Ir. 94145 b 18, 239 p.

Barry, E., *Barrymore: the records of the Barrys of Co. Cork,* Cork: Guy, 1902, 214 p. NLI Ir. 9292 b 19

Barry, J.M., *Old Glory at Queenstown: American maritime activity in the Queenstown era 1800–1922,* Cork: Sidney Publishing, 1999, NLI Ir. 94145 b 21, 206 p.

Barry, J.M., *Queenstown for orders: contributions to the maritime history of Queenstown Harbour, the Cove of Cork,* Cork: Sidney Pub, 1999, NLI, 185 p.

Barry, J.M., *The Victoria Hospital, Cork a history,* Cork: the author?, 1992, NLI Ir. 362 b 8, 310 p.

Bennett, G., *The history of Bandon & the principal towns of the West Riding of Cork,* Cork: Francis Guy, 1869, NLI Ir. 94145 b 1, 572 p. Online: Turner

Bolster, Evelyn, *A history of the Diocese of Cork: from the Reformation to the Penal Era,* Cork: Tower Books, 1982, NLI, 355 p.

Bolster, Evelyn, *A history of the Diocese of Cork: from the earliest times to the Reformation,* Shannon: Irish University Press, 1972, NLI Ir. 27414 b 6, 548 p.

Bowen, Elizabeth, *Bowen's Court,* London: 1944, NLI Ir. 9292 b 18

Brady, W. Maziere, *Clerical and Parochial Records of Cork, Cloyne and Ross (3 vols.),* Dublin: Printed for the author by A. Thom, 1864, NLI Ir. 27414 b 4

Broderick, Mary, *A History of Cobh,* Cobh, Co. Cork: Mary Broderick, 1989, NLI Ir. 94145 p 7(3), 169 p.

Cadogan, Tim, *Tracing your Cork Ancestors,* Dublin: Flyleaf Press, 1998, NLI, 123 p.; co-editor, Tony McCarthy

Casey, Albert, *O'Kief, Cosh Mang, Slieve Lougher, and Upper Blackwater in Ireland.* Privately printed, 1962–74, NLI Ir. 94145 c 12, Massive, multivolume compendium of information on the Slieve Luachra/Blackwater Valley area on the Cork/Kerry border

Caulfield, R., *Council Book of the Corporation of Kinsale,* Guildford: Printed by J. Billing and sons, 1879, NLI Ir. 94145 c 3, 447 p.

Caulfield, R., *Council Book of the Corporation of Youghal (1610–1659 1666–87 and 1690–1800),* Guildford: Printed by J. Billing and sons, 1878, NLI Ir. 94145 c 4, 637 p.

Caulfield, R. (ed.), *Annals of the cathedral of St. Coleman-Cloyne,* Cork: Purcell, 1882, NLI Ir. 7266 c 2, 59 p.

Caulfield, R. (ed.), *The pipe roll of Cloyne,* Cork, Guy, 1918, NLI Ir. 94145 c 1, ('From the original, formerly preserved in the registry of the ancient cathedral church of Cloyne, now in the Public Record Office, Dublin') Latin transcribed, by

Dr. Caulfield ; English version by Rev. Canon O'Riordan, P.P.; annotated by James Coleman

Cole, Rev. J.H., *Church and Parish Records of the United Dioceses of Cork Cloyne and Ross*, Cork: Guy and Co., 1903, NLI Ir. 274145 c 1, 347 p: Supplements Brady

Connolly, Sean, *The Bandon River from source to sea*, S.I., S.N., 1993, NLI Ir. 94145 p 6(5), 100 p.

Coombes, James, *A history of Timoleague and Barryroe*, Timoleague: Muintir na Tire (Friary Preservation Committee), 1969, NLI Ir. 941 p. 134(3), 89 p.

Cork Archives Institute, *The poor law records of County Cork*, Cork: Archives Institute, 1995, NLI Ir. 94145 c 30, 80 p. A list of the records of County Cork Poor Law Unions transferred from St Finbar's Hospital Cork to the Cork Archives Institute

Courtney, Sean, *Memories of Kilcorney and Rathcoole*, Mallow: Kilcorney–Rathcoole Historical Society, 1998, NLI Ir. 94145 c 37, 152 p.

Cox, Richard, *Description of the County and City of Cork: between the years 1680 and 1690*, Dublin: Printed at the University Press by Ponsonby and Gibbs, 1903, NLI Ir. 94145 c 6, 23 p: edited, with notes, by T.A. Lunham

Cronin, Maura, *Country, class or crafl?: the politicisation of the skilled artisan in nineteenth-century Cork*, Cork: Cork University Press, 1994, NLI Ir. 94145 c 27, 294 p.

Cusack, Mary F., *A History of the City and County of Cork*, Dublin: McGlashan and Gill, 1875, NLI Ir. 94145 c 8, 586 p.

d'Alton, Ian, *Protestant society and politics in Cork, 1812–1844*, Cork: Cork University Press, 1980, NLI Ir. 94145 d 4, 264 p.

Darling, John, *St Multose Church Kinsale*, Cork: 1895

Dennehy, The Ven. Archdeacon, *History of Queenstown*, Cork: 1923

Denny, H.L.L., *The family of Limrick, of Schull, Co. Cork*, 1907, NLI, GO 413, 8 p.

Donnelly Jr, James S., *The land and the people of nineteenth-century Cork: the rural economy and the land question*, London; Boston: Routledge and Kegan Paul, 1975, NLI Ir. 333 d 14, 440 p.

Duhallow Heritage Project, *Newmarket Court (1725–1994)*, Newmarket: Duhallow Heritage Project, 1994, NLI Ir. 720 n 10, 88 p.

Ellis, Éilis, *Emigrants from Ireland 1847–52*, Baltimore: Genealogical Publishing Co., 1977, NLI Ir. 325 e 5

Falvey, Jeremiah, *The chronicles of Midleton 1700–1900*, Cloyne, Co. Cork: Sira Publications, 1998, NLI Ir. 94145 f 4, 356 p.

Farrell, Noel, *Youghal family roots: exploring family origins in Youghal*, Longford: Noel Farrell, 2001, NLI, 48 p.

Farrell, Noel, *Kinsale family roots: exploring family origins in Kinsale*, Longford: Noel Farrell, 2001, NLI, 48 p.

FÁS Community Training, *Buttevant Co. Cork a short history*, Buttevant: Buttevant Community Council, 1991, NLI Ir. 941 p 134(2), 48

Fisher, William A., *Appeal for improvements at 'The church of the poor near Crookhaven'* [n.pub.], 1851, NLI, JP 4271. Includes list of subscribers

Fitzgerald, Séamus, *Mackerel and the making of Baltimore, County Cork, 1879–1913*, Dublin; Portland, OR: Irish Academic Press, 1999, NLI Ir. 94145 f 5, 64 p.: Maynooth studies in Irish local history; no. 22

Foley, Con, *A history of Douglas*, Douglas: Con Foley, 1991, NLI Ir. 94145 f 2, 185 p.

Gaughan, Rev. J.A., *Doneraile*, Dublin: Kamac Publications, 1970, NLI Ir. 94145 g 1, 171 p.

Gibson, C.B., *The history of the county and city of Cork*, London: 1861, NLI, J 94145

Grove-White, Col. James, *History of Kilbryne, Doneraile, Cork.* Cork

Grove-White, Col. James, *Historical and Topographical Notes etc. on Buttevant, Castletownroche, Doneraile, Mallow and places in their vicinity*, Cork: Guy and Co., Ltd, 1905–16, NLI Ir. 94145 w 1

Hajba, Anna-Maria, *Historical genealogical architectural notes on some houses of Cork, Vol. 1, North Cork*, Whitegate, Co. Clare: Ballinakella Press, 2002, NLI, 414 p.

Harrison, Richard S., *Béara and Bantry Bay: history of Rossmacowen*, Bantry: Rossmacowen Historical Society, 1990, NLI Ir. 94145.h.5, 236 p.

Harrison, Richard S., *Cork City Quakers 1655–193: a brief history*, The author, 1991, NLI Ir. 289.h.3, 91 p.

Harrison, Richard S., *Bantry in olden days*, Bantry: the author, 1992, NLI Ir. 94145 p 7(4), 62 p.

Hawke, Siobhán, *A social and economic history of Bere Island: 1900–1920*, Castletownbere, Beara, Co. Cork: The Shell, 2004, NLI, 81 p.

Hayman, S., *The handbook for Youghal*, Youghal: J.W. Lindsay, 1852, NLI, Dix Youghal 1852, 96 p. 'containing an account of St Mary's Collegiate Church, (including memorials of the Boyles;) the College, Sir Walter Raleigh's house, the Franciscan and Dominican Friaries, the Templar's house at Rhincrew, and the Monastery of St John's; with the historical annals of the town'

Hayman, Samuel, *The Handbook for Youghal*, Youghal: John Lindsay, 1858, NLI, Dix Youghal 1858, 76 p.

Healy, Dan, *Cork national school registers*, Cork: Cork Genealogical Society, 2000, NLI, 62 p.

Hickey, Nora M., *St. Peter's, Ballymodan, Bandon, Co. Cork Gravestone Inscriptions*, Bandon: Droichead na Banndan Community Co-operative Society Ltd, 1986, NLI Ir. 9295 p 3(3), 45 p.

Hickey, Nora M., *Kilbrogan, Roman Catholic, Bandon, Co. Cork Gravestone Inscriptions*, Bandon: Droichead na Banndan Community Co-operative Society Ltd., 1985, NLI Ir. 9295 p 3(4), 44 p.

Holland, Rev. W., *History of West Cork and the Diocese of Ross*, Skibbereen: Southern Star, 1949, NLI Ir. 94145 h 3, 427 p.

Hore, H.F., *The Social State of the Southern and Eastern Counties of Ireland in the Sixteenth Century*, Dublin, 1870, NLI Ir. 794105 r 2 [see Carlow]

Hurley, Frank, *St Joseph's Convent of Mercy, Kinsale a celebration of 150 years 1844–1944*, Kinsale: St Joseph's Convent of Mercy, 1994, NLI Ir. 270 s 20, 156 p.

Hurley, Mícheál, *Home from the sea: the story of Courtmacsherry lifeboat 1825–1995*, Courtmacsharry: Mícheál Hurley, 1995, NLI Ir. 363 h 10, 133 p.

Hyde S.J., Fr John, *Ballycotton long 'go by*, Ballycotton: Margaret Hyde, 1990, NLI Ir. 941 p 110(3), 63 p.

IGRS, *Tombstone inscriptions Vol. 1*, Dublin: IGRS Tombstone Committee, 2001, NLI, 850 p.

Jephson, M.D., *An Anglo-Irish Miscellany: some records of the Jephsons of Mallow*, Dublin: Allen Figgis, 1964, NLI Ir. 9292 j 2, 434 p.

Jordan, Kieran, *Kilworth & Moore Park British Army camps from 1896 to 1922*, Fermoy, Co. Cork: Strawhall Press, 2004, NLI, 126 p.; Kilworth Ranges Historical Project

Keane Jr, Leonard M., *Ancestors and descendants of John Keane and Elizabeth Leader of Keale, Milistreet, County Cork, Ireland and related female lines*, Wakefield, Mass.: L.M. Keane, c.1984, LOC

Kelleher, B. J., *Kelleher family, of Knockraheen, Carriganimma, Macroom, Co. Cork, Ireland and Australia and U.S.A.*, Chadstone, Australia: Kelleher, 1970, NLI, GO 443, 42 leaves

Kelleher, George D., *The gunpowder mill at Ballincollig an extract from Gunpowder to guided missiles, ...*, Inniscarra, Co. Cork: John F. Kelleher, 1993, NLI Ir. 3380 p. 42(5), 89 p.

Killavullen Community Council, *The History of Killavullen*, Killavullen: Killavullen Community Council, 1986, NLI, 16 p.

King, Joseph A., *Ireland to North America: emigrants from West Cork*, Lafayette, Calif: K & K Publications, 1994, NLI Ir. 942 k 7, 124 p. Also Toronto: P.D. Meany. Schull to Miramichi River Region, N.B.

Kingston, W.J., *The story of West Carbery*, Waterford: Friendly Press, 1985, NLI Ir. 94145 k 2, 133 p.

Lane, Fintan, *In search of Thomas Sheahan: radical politics in Cork, 1824–36*, Dublin; Portland, OR: Irish Academic Press, 2001, NLI, 69 p.: Maynooth studies in Irish local history ; no. 37

Lannin, Joseph, *The Wilcox family of Ardravinna, Goleen, Co. Cork*, Dublin: Joseph Lannin, 1995, NLI Ir. 9292 w, 54 p.

Lannin, Joseph, *The Lannin family of Gubbeen, Schull, Co. Cork*, Dublin: The author, 1994, NLI Ir. 941 p 140(5), 181 p.

Leland, Mary, *That endless adventure: a history of the Cork Harbour Commissioners*, Cork: Port of Cork Company, 2001, NLI, 272 p.

Lindsay, John W., *An account of the present state of Youghal Church [ ]*, Youghal, John W. Lindsay, 1850, NLI Ir. 94145 d 1, 52 p. Edited by John Gough Nichols

Lomasney, Michael, *Ballynoe Cemetery, a guide and brief history*, Ballynoe, Co. Cork: Ballynoe Cemetery Committee, 1993, NLI Ir. 9295 p.(3(1)

Mac Suibhne, Maire, *Famine in Muskerry: an drochshaol: an outline of conditions in the sixteen parishes of Macroom Poor Law Union, Co. Cork, during the Great Famine, 1845–'51*, Macroom, Co. Cork: Cuilin Greine Press, 1997, NLI Ir. 94145 m 10, 160 p.

MacCarthy, John George, *The history of Cork*, Cork: Miros Press, 1974, NLI Ir. 94145 m 5, 47 p. Reprint of the 3rd ed. published in 1870 by F. Guy, Cork.

MacSwiney, *Unpublished manuscripts; Royal Irish Academy. Historical notes and will abstracts, mainly from Cos. Cork and Kerry,* Royal Irish Academy. Historical notes and will abstracts, mainly from Counties Cork and Kerry

Masterson, Josephine, *County Cork, Ireland: a collection of 1841/1851 census records,* Indianapolis, IN: Masterson. Also FamilyTreeMaker CD ROM 7275. 1993. NLI Ir. 94145 m 11

Mercer, J. Douglas, *Record of the North Cork Regiment of Militia, with sketches extracted from history of the times in which its services were required, from 1793 to 1880,* Dublin: Printed by Sealy, Bryers & Walker, 1886, 128 p. NLI Ir. 355942 m 4

McCarthaigh, David, *The Gurranabraher story: a history of the place and its people,* Cork: printed by Cork Office Supplies, 1997, NLI, 69 p.

McCarthy, M., *Kinsale inscriptions (Church of Ireland),* Kinsale: the author

Mooney, Canice, *The friars of Broad Lane: the story of a Franciscan friary in Cork, 1229–1977,* Cork: Tower Books, 1977, NLI Ir. 27414 m 4, 101 p.: revised and extended by Bartholomew Egan

Murphy, Ina, *Speaking of Lyre 1844–1994,* Lyre: Lyre Community Association, 1994, NLI Ir. 372 m 136, 175 p.

Murphy, John A., *The College a history of Queen's/University College, Cork, 1845–1995,* Cork: Cork University Press, 1996, NLI Ir. 37841 m 24, 469 p.

Murphy, Pat, *The magic of west Cork,* Dublin: Mercier Press, 1978, 94p. Crookhaven, Social life and customs

Myers, Declan, *My own place Ballyphelane,* Ballyphelane: the author, 1995, NLI Ir. 94145 m 9, 202 p.

Ó Coindealbháin, Seán, *The story of Iveleary: the history, antiquities and legends of Uibh-Laoghaire,* Dundalk: Dundalgan, 1921, NLI, 54 p.

O Mahony, Colman, *In the shadows: life in Cork 1750–1930,* Ballincollig: Tower Books, 1997, NLI, Ir. 94145 o 19, 396 p.

Ó Ríordáin, John J., *Where Araglen so gently flows,* Tralee: Kerryman Ltd, 1989, NLI Ir. 94145 o 16, 304 p.

O'Brien, Brigid, *From Ilen to Roaring Water Bay: reminiscences from the Parish of Aughadown,* [S.l.], Aughadown: Guild of the ICA, 2000, NLI, 2A 2753, 160 p.; edited by Brigid O'Brien and Mary Whooley.

O'Brien, Susan, *A history of Bessborough House and the Pike family,* Cork: Quality Print, n.d., 52 p.: with Karan Mullan.

O'Connor, W.R., *The New Cork Guide. ... names and dwelling of ... physicians, lawyers, merchants, bankers, teachers, shopkeepers, architects, mechanics, publicans, &c., (satire in verse),* Cork, 1803, NLI, Dix Cork [1803?] [P 4.], 10 p.

O'Donovan, Derry, *Ballinspittle and De Courcy country: historical landscapes,* Bray, Co. Wicklow: Wordwell, 2003, NLI, 276 p.

O'Dwyer, Riobárd, *Who Were my Ancestors? Family Trees of Eyeries Parish,* Astoria, Illinois: K.K. Stevens Publishing Co., 1976, NLI

O'Dwyer, Riobárd, *Who Were my Ancestors? Family Trees of Allihies Parish,* Astoria, Illinois: K.K. Stevens Publishing Co., 1988, 307 p. NLI Ir. 9292 o 60

O'Dwyer, Riobárd, *Who Were my Ancestors? Family Trees of Castletownbere and Bere Island Parishes*, Astoria, Illinois: K.K. Stevens Publishing Co., 1989 292 p. NLI Ir. 9292 o 61 & 62

O'Flanagan & Buttimer, *Cork History and Society*, Dublin: Geography Publications, 1994, NLI Ir. 94145 c 25, 1000 p.

O'Flanagan, Patrick, *Irish Historic Towns Atlas 3: Bandon*, Dublin: Royal Irish Academy, 1988, NLI, ILB 941 p 13 (1)

O'Mahony, Frank, *Kilcrohane the holy ground. Book 1. O'Mahony—the diary of Frank. Book 2 Frank O'Mahony*, Dromkeal: Frank O'Mahony, 1990, NLI Ir. 9292 o 57, 148 p.

O'Mahony, Jeremiah, *West Cork and its story*, Tralee: Kerryman, 1961, NLI, 288 p.

O'Mahony, Jeremiah, *West Cork parish histories and place-names*, Tralee: Kerryman, 1959, NLI Ir. 94145 o 12

O'Murchadha, D., *Family Names of Co. Cork*, Dublin: Glendale Press, 1985, NLI Ir. 9291 o 11

O'Rahilly, Ronan, *A history of the Cork Medical School, 1849–1949*, Cork: Cork University Press, 1949, NLI Ir. 6109 o 1, 69 p.

O'Sullivan, Florence, *The History of Kinsale*, Dublin: 1916

O'Sullivan, John L., *By Carraigdonn and Owenabue*, Ballinhassig: Ballyheeda Press, 1990, NLI Ir. 94145.0.15, 442 p.

O'Sullivan, John L., *The Cork City Gaol*, Ballinhassig, Co. Cork: Ballyheeda Press, 1996, NLI, Ir. 366 o [sic], 169 p.

O'Sullivan, Ted, *Bere Island a short history*, Cork: Inisgragy Books, 1992, NLI Ir. 94145 p 8(1), 128 p.

Pettit, S.F., *This city of Cork 1700–1900*, Cork: Studio Publications, 1977, NLI Ir. 94145 p 1, 304 p.

Power, Bill, *From the Danes to Dairygold a history of Mitchelstown*, Mitchelstown: Mount Cashell Books, 1996, NLI Ir. 94145 p 10, 150 p.

Power, Bill, *White knights, dark earls: the rise and fall of an Anglo-Irish dynasty*, Doughcloyne, Wilton, Cork: Collins Press, 2000, NLI, 303 p. King family, earls of Kingston

Power, Bill, *Mitchelstown through seven centuries: being a concise history of Mitchelstown, County Cork*, Fermoy, Co. Cork: Éigse Books, c.1987, NLI Ir. 94145 p 4, 138 p.

Power, V. Rev. P., *Waterford and Lismore: A Compendious History of the Dioceses*, Dublin: Cork University Press, 1937, NLI Ir. 274141 p 1, 402 p.

Pratt, John, *Pratt Family Records: an account of the Pratts of Youghal and Castlemartyr and their Descendants*, Millom: P.C. Dickinson & Sons, 1931, NLI Ir. 9292 p 15, 82 p.

Pratt, John, *The Family of Pratt of Gawsworth, Carrigrohane, Co.Cork*, Millom: 1925, NLI Ir. 9292 p 3

Prentice, Sydney, *Bear and forbear: a genealogical study of the Prentice, Barnard and related families in Great Britain, Ireland and Australia*, Taringa, Qld.: S.A and M. Prentice, 1984, NLI Ir. 9292 p 32, 285 p. Bandon

Quane, Michael, *Midleton School, Co. Cork*, Dublin: Royal Society of Antiquaries, 1952, NLI, 27 p.

Quinlan, P., *Old Mitchelstown and the Kingston family*, Kilworth: the author, 1980, NLI Ir. 941 p 66, 21 p.

Reedy, Rev. Donal A., *The diocese of Kerry (formerly Ardfert)*, Killarney: Catholic Truth Society, 1937, NLI, 46 p.

Robinson, A.C., *St. Fin Barre's Cathedral, Cork: historical and descriptive*, Cork: Guy and Co., 1897, Cork City Library, 87 p.

Roche, Christy, *The Ford of the apples: a history of Ballyhooly*, Fermoy: Eigse, 1988, NLI Ir. 91414 r 5

Ryan, Eileen, *Mohera National School a history 1847–1996*, [S.l.], [s.n.], 1996, NLI, Ir. 94145 r 3, 157 p.

Rynne, Colin, *At the sign of the cow: the Cork Butter Market, 1770–1924*, Cork: Collins Press, 1998, NLI, 118 p.

Smith, Charles, *The ancient and present state of the county and city of Cork*, Dublin: 1750, NLI Ir. 94145 s 1, Reprint: Cork, Guy & co., Ltd., 1893–94.

St James', Durrus, *St. James', Durrus a parish history: published for the bi-centenary of the Church 1992*, Cloghroe, Co. Cork: Forum Publications, 1992, NLI, 80 p.

St Leger, Alicia, *Silver, sails and silk: Huguenots in Cork 1685–1850*, Cork: Cork Civic Trust, 1991, NLI Ir. 283 s 2, 71 p.

Sullivan, T.D., *Bantry, Berehaven and the O'Sullivan sept and The O'Dalys Muintiravara: the story of a bardic family / by D.D.*, Cork: Tower Books of Cork, 1978, NLI Ir. 94145 s 4, 119 p. (The O'Dalys Muintiravara by Dominick Daly, originally published 1821)

Swanzy, Rev. H.B., *The family of Nixon of Nixon Hall, Co. Fermanagh, and Nixon Lodge, Co. Cavan: with a short account of the families of Erskine of Cavan and Allin of Youghal, by a descendant*, Dublin: Thom, 1899, NLI, GO 513, 45 p.

Tangney, Denis, *St. Anna's Church, Millstreet a history*, Millstreet: Millstreet Museum Society, 1995, NLI, 1A 1222, 56 p.

Thompson, Francis, *Families of the Catholic Parish of Carrigaline–Crosshaven 1826–1880*, 1986, LDS Film 1441035

Troy, Bartholemew, *Ballycotton wrecks and rescues: 1800–1855*, Ireland, s.n., NLI, 3A 1457, 43 p.

Troy, Bartholemew, *The cemetery, Church of Our Lady of the Most Holy Rosary, Midleton, Co. Cork: gravestone inscriptions*, Midleton: Troy, 1994. NLI Ir. 9295 t 1 224 p.

Tuckey, Francis, *The County and City of Cork Remembered*, Cork: O. Savage and son, 1837, NLI, Dix Cork 1837, 352 p.

Veale, T., *Richard Lucas 1788: directory extract for south east of Ireland*, Dublin: Veale, 1995 NLI Ir. 9414 v

W., T.J., *The parish of Blackrock, a retrospect*, Cork: St Michael's Parish, 1962, NLI, 1A 347, 27 p.

Wain, H., *Eochoill: the history of Youghal*, Cork: Cork Historical Guides Committee, 1965, NLI Ir. 94145 w 8, 72 p.

Walshe, Denis, *Bishops, priests and religious of Cloyne Parish, County Cork,* Cloyne:
  Co. Cork, s.n., 1994, NLI, 1A 1223
West, Trevor, *Midleton College, 1696–1996 a tercentenary history,* Midleton, Co.
  Cork: Midleton College, 1996, NLI Ir. 379 w 4, 57 p.
West, W., *Directory & picture of Cork,* 1810, NLI, J 914145
Williams, R. Allan, *The Berehaven Copper Mines, Allihies, Co. Cork,* Sheffield:
  Northern Mine Research Soc., 1991, NLI Ir. 621 w 5,228 p. Puxley family
Windele, J., *Cork: historical & descriptive notices ... to the middle of the 19th century,*
  Cork: 1910, NLI Ir. 94145 w 3

Local Journals
Bandon Historical Journal, NLI Ir. 794105 c 1
Bantry Historical and Archaeological Society journal, NLI Ir. 94145 b 27
Canovee an historical society magazine, 1986–, NLI Ir. 914145 c 35
Donoughmore remembers: journal of times past, Vol. 1 ([2004])-, NLI 1 F 233
Harbour lights: journal of the Great Island Historical Society, 1988–, NLI Ir. 94145 h 6
Journal of the Ballincollig Community School Local History Society, NLI Ir. 94145 b 15
Journal of the Cork Genealogical Society, NLI
Journal of the Cork Historical & Archaeological Society, NLI Ir. 794105 c 1
Kinsale Historical Journal, Annual from 1986, NLI Ir. 95145 k 5
Mizen journal, 1995–, NLI Ir. 794105 m 1
Ogham magazine: Ballindangan and district review, 1 issue, NLI Ir. 94145 o 22
Old Blarney: journal of the Blarney and District Historical Society, 1989–, NLI
  1H 359
Seanchas Chairbre, NLI Ir. 94145 s 6
Seanchas Duthala (Duhallow magazine), NLI Ir. 94145 s 3

Directories
1787   Richard Lucas, *Cork Directory,* NLI JCHAS 1967
1788   Richard Lucas, *General Directory of the Kingdom of Ireland,* NLI Pos.
          3729. Repr. in Veale, *Lucas,* IG 1965, 1966, 1967, 1968
1797   John Nixon, *Cork Almanack,* NLI Pos. 3985
1809   Holden's *Annual London and country directory of the United Kingdoms
          & Wales, in three volumes, for ... 1811* (3 vols. Facsimile repr. Norwich M.
          Winton, 1996) NLI G 942 h 23, LDS Film 258722 Item 2
1810   William West, *Directory of Cork,* NLI Pos. 3985
1812   John Connor, *Cork Directory.* Also 1817, 1826, 1828. NLI Pos. 3985
1820   J. Pigot, *Commercial Directory of Ireland,* PRONI, NLI Ir. 9141 p 107, LDS
          Film 962702 Item 1
1824   J. Pigot and Co., *City of Dublin and Hibernian Provincial Directory,* NLI,
          LDS Film 451787
1846   Slater's *National Commercial Directory of Ireland,* PRONI, NLI LO, LDS
          Film 1696703 Item 3
1856   Slater, *Royal National Commercial Directory of Ireland,* NLI LDS Film
          1472360 Item 1

1870   Slater, *Directory of Ireland*, NLI
1875   Francis Guy, *City and County Cork Almanack and Directory*, NLI Ir. 91414
          g 9
1881   Slater, *Royal National Commercial Directory of Ireland*, NLI
1886   Francis Guy, *Postal Directory of Munster*, NLI Ir. 91414 g 8, LDS Film
          1559399 Item 8
1889   Francis Guy, *City and County Cork Almanack and Directory*. Annually
          from this year
1894   Slater, *Royal Commercial Directory of Ireland*, NLI

Gravestone Inscriptions

Aghadown: Glebe, C of I, IGRS, *Vol. 1*
Aghinagh: Caum, JCHAS, No. 216 1967. Also O'K, Vol. 8
—— Ballaghboy IGRS, GO. Also Cork County Library
Ballyclogh: Village of Ballyclogh, Main St, O'K, Vol. 8
Ballycurrany: Ballycurrany West, JCHAS, No. 237 1978
—— Ballydesmond, O'K, Vol. 6
—— Ballyhoolahan East, O'K, Vol. 6
Ballymartle: Mill-land, C of I, JCHAS, 235, 1989
Ballymodan: Clogheenavodig (Kilbeg?), WCHC
Ballymodan: Knockanreagh, RC?, WCHC
Ballymodan: Knockaveale, Hickey, *St Peter's*
—— Ballynakilla, Castletown Berehaven, IGRS, GO,
—— Ballynamona, O'K, Vol. 11
Ballynoe: *Ballynoe Cemetery*
Ballyvourney: Glebe, C of I, O'K, Vol. 6
Brinny: C of I, WCHC,
Buttevant: Templemary, O'K, Vol. 11
Caheragh: Caheragh, RC, IGRS, *Vol. 1*
—— Cappyaughna, RC, IGRS, *Vol. 1*
Carrigrohanebeg: JCHAS, No. 218 1968
—— Castle-land (Buttevant?), C of I, O'K, Vol. 11
Castlemagner: O'K, Vol. 6
Churchtown: Village of Churchtown, Georges St, O'K, Vol. 11
Clondrohid: O'K, Vol. 6
—— Clonfert, O'K, Vol. 6
Clonfert: Newmarket, Main Street, C of I, O'K, Vol. 6
Clonmeen: Clonmeen North, C of I, O'K, Vol. 7
Clonmult: Ballyeightragh, JCHAS, No.223/4/5 1976/7
—— Cloonaghlin West (Killaconenagh?), Cork County Library,
—— Cooranuller, C of I, IGRS, GO
Creagh: Skibbereen IGRS, GO
Cullen: Cullen, O'K, Vol. 6
—— Curradonohoe, Bere Island, IGRS, GO

Dangandonovan: Kilcounty, *JCHAS*, No. 229 1974
Desertmore: Kilcrea, *JCHAS*, No. 219 1969
Doneraile: Oldcourt (Donraile), *O'K*, Vol. 11
Drishane: Millstreet, *O'K*, Vol. 6
—— Dromtariff, *O'K*, Vol. 6
Dromtarriff: Garraveasoge or Dromagh, *O'K*, Vol. 8
Dunderrow: Horsehill More North, *JCHAS*, No. 224 1971
Fermoy: Carrignagroghera, *IS*, Nos 51/3 1977/9 (Military only)
—— Inchigeelagh interior, *O'K*, Vol. 6
—— Inchigeelagh New, *O'K*, Vol. 6
Inchigeelagh: Glebe, C of I, *O'K*, Vol. 6
Kilbrin: Castlecor Demesne (Kilbrin?), *O'K*, Vol. 8
Kilbrogan: Kilbrogan, RC C of I, Hickey, *Kilbrogan*
KIlcaskan: Adrigole, C of I, *IGRS*, *Vol. 1*. Also Cork County Library
Kilcatherine: Gortgarriff *IGRS*, *Vol. 1*,
Kilcoe: *IGRS*, *Vol. 1*
Kilcorney: *O'K*, Vol. 7
—— Kilcrea Friary, *JCHAS*, No. 226 1972
Kilgrogan: *O'K*, Vol. 11
Killaconenagh: Clanlaurence, Cork County Library
Ballynakilla, Castletown Berehaven *IGRS*, *Vol. 1*
Curradonohoe, Bere Island, *IGRS*, *Vol. 1*
Cloonaghlin West (Killaconenagh?), *IGRS*, *Vol. 1*
Killeagh: Town of Killeagh, Main Street, C of I, *JCHAS*, No. 226 1972
Kilmeen: Glebe (Boherbue?), C of I, *O'K*, Vol. 6
Kilmocomoge: Bantry (St Finbarr's) *IGRS*, *Vol. 1*
Kilmonoge: Coolnagaug (Kilmonoge?), *JCHAS*, 251, 1987
Kilnaglory: Kilnaglory, *JCHAS*, No. 220 1969
Kilnamanagh: Cloan (Kilnamanagh?), Cork County Library, *IGRS*, *Vol. 1*
Kilnamartry: Glebe, *O'K*, Vol. 6
Kinsale: Kinsale, Church Street, C of I, McCarthy, *Kinsale inscriptions*
—— Kishkeam, *O'K*, Vol. 6
Liscarroll: Village of Liscarroll, Main Street, *O'K*, Vol. 11
Lisgoold: Lisgoold East, C of I, *JCHAS*, No. 237 1978
Macloneigh: *O'K*, Vol. 8
Macroom: Castle Street, C of I, *O'K*, Vol. 8
Magourney: Coachford, *O'K*, Vol. 11
—— Mallow, Main Street, C of I, *O'K*,
Mallow: Mallow, Main Street, RC, *O'K*, Vol. 8
Midleton: Midleton, RC, Troy, *The cemetery*
—— Millstreet (Old), *O'K*, Vol. 6
Mourneabbey: Kilquane (Mourneabbey?), *O'K*, Vol. 11
—— Nohaval Lower, *O'K*, Vol. 8
Nohavaldaly: Knocknagree, *O'K*, Vol. 6

Rathgoggan: Charleville, Main Street, C of I, O'K, Vol. 11
—— Rodeen IGRS, GO
—— Rossmackowen, Cork County Library
Shandrum: Dromina, O'K, Vol. 11
St Finbars: Curraghconway, C of I, St Finbarr's Cathedral, 1897
St Peter's: Duncan Street, JCHAS, 252, 1988
Timoleague: Castle Lower, C of I, GO
Tisaxon: Tisaxon Beg, JCHAS, No. 222 1970
Titeskin: JCHAS, No. 221 1970
Tullylease: Tulllylease, O'K, Vol. 8
Youghal: Nelson Place, Hayman, The Handbook for Youghal

Estate Records

Arden, Lord: Rentals 1824–1830, NLI Ms. 8652. All tenants. Covering townlands in the civil parishes of: Bregoge; Buttevant; Castlemagner; Clonfert; Dromtarriff; and Dungourney.

Bantry, Earl of: Rentals, 1829, NLI Ms. 3273. All tenants. Covering townlands in the civil parishes of: Kilcaskan; Kilcatherine; and Killaconenagh.

(Barrymore barony): 'Tenant Farmers on the Barrymore Estate', JCHAS, Vol. 51, 31–40.

Bennett: Rental of the Bennett estate 1770 (mainly Cork City and surrounding areas). NLI Pos. 288.

Benn-Walsh, Sir John: Donnelly, J.S., The journals of Sir John Benn-Walsh relating to the management of his Irish estates (1823–64)', JCHAS, Vol. LXXXI (1975).

Bishop of Cork: Rentals 1807–1831, NAI M6087. Major tenants only. Townlands in the civil parishes of: Aghadown; Ardfield; Fanlobbus; Kilbrogan; Kilmocomoge; Kilsillagh; Ross; St Finbarr's; Skull.

Boyle/Cavendish: The Lismore Papers. Rentals, valuations, lease books, account books for the estates of the Earls of Cork and the Dukes of Devonshire, 1570–1870, NLI Mss. 6136–6898. Generally covering only major tenants. A detailed listing is given in NLI Special List 15. Covering townlands in the civil parishes of: Ahern; Ardagh; Ballymodan; Ballynoe; Brinny; Clonmult; Clonpriest; Ightermurragh; Kilbrogan; Killeagh; Killowen; Kinneigh; Knockmourne; Lismore; Mogeely; Murragh; St Finbarr's; Youghal.

Cox, Richard: NAI Gordon Presentation 214; rentals 1839. Major tenants only. Townlands in the civil parishes of: Aghinagh; Clondrohid; Desertserges; Fanlobbus; Kilcaskan; Kilmeen; Kilmichael; Kilnamartery; Macloneigh.

Doneraile, Lord: Rent roll 1777: NLI Ms. 10933 'of the right honble Lord Donneralle's Estate at Ballyhooly'.

Earbery estates: Rentals 1788–1815, NLI Ms. 7403. Principally major tenants. NLI Ms. 5257, Full tenants list, 1800. Townlands in the civil parishes of: Aghabulloge; Clondrohid; Donoghmore; Kilmurry.

Eyre, Robert Hodges: Rentals, 1833 and 1835, of the Bere Island estate. NLI Mss. 3273, 3274. All tenants. Civil parish of: Killaconenagh.

Graham, James: Rentals c.1763. NAI M. 2329. Major tenants only. Covering townlands in the civil parish of Killathy.

Lombard, Rev. Edmund: Rentals, 1795, NLI Ms. 2985. Major tenants only. Covering townlands in the civil parishes of: Kilmacdonagh; Kilshannig.

Newenham?: Rentals, c.1825, NLI Ms. 4123. All tenants. Covering townlands in the civil parishes of: Kilcrumper; Kilworth; Leitrim; Macroney.

Neville, Richard: Rentals of lands in Counties Cork, Kildare and Waterford. NLI Ms. 3733. Principally major tenants. Covering townlands in the civil parishes of: Aglishdrinagh; and Cooliney.

O'Murchadha, D.: 'Diary of Gen. Richard O'Donovan 1819–23', JCHAS (1986) (Lands in West Cork).

Perceval, Lord Egmont: Rentals, 1688–1750. Major tenants only. NLI Pos. 1355 (1688); NLI Pos. 4674 (1701–12, 1713–14); NLI Pos. 4675 (1714–19); NLI Pos. 4676 (1720–24, 1725–27); NLI Pos. 4677 (1728–33); NLI Pos. 4678 (1734–38); NLI Pos. 4679 (1739–41, 1742–46); NLI Pos. 4680 (1747–50). Covering townlands in the civil parishes of: Aglishdrinagh; Ballyclogh; Bregoge; Brigown; Britway; Buttevant; Castlemagner; Churchtown; Clonfert; Cullin; Dromtarriff; Hackmys; Imphrick; Kilbrin; Kilbrogan; Kilbroney; Kilcaskan; Kilgrogan; Kilmichael; Kilroe; Liscarroll; Rathbarry.

Putland, George: NLI Mss. 1814–1827. Eleven rentals of land in Counties Cork, Carlow, Kilkenny, Tipperary and Wicklow. Principally major tenants. Covering townlands in the civil parishes of: Garrycloyne; Matehy; and Templeusque.

Ronayne, Thomas: NLI Ms. 1721. Rentals 1755–1777. Major tenants only. Covering townlands in the civil parishes of: Carrigaline; Clonmel; Killanully; Kilquane; Midleton; and Templerobin.

Sarsfield: Rentals, 1817–1823, NLI Ms. 3638. Major tenants only. Covering townlands in the civil parishes of: Kilmoney; Kinsale; St Finbars; Templerobin.

Shuldam: NLI Ms. 3025. Estate map 1801–1803, with some tenants' names given. Covering townlands in the civil parishes of: Dreenagh; Fanlobbus; Iveleary; and Kilmichael.

(No landlord given): NLI Ms. 13018. Rental, c.1835–1837. Major tenants only. Covering townlands in the civil parishes of: Castlelyons; Gortroe; Knockmourne; and Rathcormack.

(No landlord given): NLI Ms. 3273. Rentals, 1821, covering all tenants. Townlands in the civil parish of Kilmocomoge.

DERRY/LONDONDERRY

Census returns and substitutes

1618	Survey of Derry city & county. TCD Ms. 864 (F.I.9.)
1620–1622	Muster Roll. PRONI T510/2
1630	Muster Roll of Ulster; Armagh Co. Library and PRONI D.1759/3C/2; NLI Pos. 206.

1654–1656 Civil Survey. *Civil Survey,* Vol. lll (NLI I 6551 Dublin)

1659   Pender's 'Census'. Repr. GPC, 1997, IMC, 2002. LDS Film 924648

1660   Poll Tax Returns PRONI MIC/15A/82

1661   Books of Survey and Distribution. PRONI D.1854/1/23 & T370/C

1663   Hearth Money Roll. PRONI T307. Also NLI Ms. 9584 (indexed in Ms. 9585)

1670–1671 Armagh diocese gentry, clergy and parishioners supporting the Franciscans SA 15, No. 1 1992 186–216

1740   Protestant Householders Aghadowey, Aghanloo, Artrea, Ballinderry, Ballyaghran, Ballynascreen, Ballyrashane, Ballyscullion, Ballywillin, Balteagh, Banagher, Bovevagh, Clondermot, Coleraine, Cumber Lower, Cumber Upper, Derryloran, Desertlyn, Desertmartin, Desertoghill, Drumachose, Dunboe, Dungiven, Errigal, Faughanvale, Kilcronaghan, Killelagh, Killowen, Kilrea, Lissan, Macosquin, Maghera, Magherafelt, Tamlaght, Tamlaght Finlagan, Tamlaght O'Crilly, Templemore, Termoneeny, PRONI T808/15258. Also GO 539, LDS Films 100182, 1279327. Magherafelt NAI M2809

1752–1930 Tenants' lists Ballylifford (Ballinderry parish) Ballyheifer Ballymilligan (Ballymoghan?) & Aghaskin (Magherafelt parish) only. 1752, 1795, 1812, 1825, 1845, 1859, 1900, 1930 *South Derry Historical Society Journal 2,* 1991/2

1766   Artrea, Desertlyn, Magherafelt, NAI Parl. Ret. 650, 659, 674; Boveagh, Comber, Drumachose, Inch NAI 2476; Protestants in Ballynascreen, Banagher, Donaghedy, Dungiven, Leck. NAI M2476 Desertmartin (all) RCB M23. Also PRONI T808/15264–7

1775   Arboe parish census. With C of I registers PRONI. T679/111, 115–119; D.1278

1796   Census of Garvagh 1st Presbyterian congregation, also 1840, 1850. PRONI, MIC.1P/257

1796   Spinning-Wheel Premium List. 4,900 names for Co. Derry/ Londonerry. Online: Hayes

1797–1804 Yeomanry muster rolls. PRONI T1021/3. Also LDS Film 993910

1803   Faughanvale Local census; with C of I registers PRONI MIC.1/7B. Also The Genealogy Centre (database), and UHGGN 1 (10), 1984, pp 324–332

1808–1813 Freeholders. NAI M.6199

1808   Memorial from the mayor and inhabitants of Coleraine to the Privy Council on the scarcity of provisions May 5 1808, 51 names, NAI OP 268/7

1813   Freeholders (A–L). PRONI T2123. Online: Freeholders

1823–1838 Tithe Books

1829   Census of Protestants, Chapel of the Woods parish. PRONI T308

1830   Census of Drumachose parish; with C of I Registers. PRONI T.679/3, 394. 396–7, 416–7

1831   Aghadowey, Aghanloo, Agivey, Arboe, Artrea, Ballinderry, Balteagh, Banagher, Ballyaughran, Ballymoney, Ballynascreen, Ballyrashane,

Ballyscullion, Ballywillin, Boveagh, Clondermot, Coleraine, Cumber, Desertlyn, Derryloran, Desertmartin, Desertoghill, Drumachose, Dunboe, Dungiven, Errigal, Faughanvale, Kilcrea, Kilcunaghan, Killeagh, Killowen, Lissane, Maghera, Magherafelt, Macosquin, Tamlaght, Tamlaght Finlagan, Tamlaght O'Crilly, Tamlaghtard, Templemore, Termoneny, Killdollagh (Glendermot). NAI; PRONI MIC5A/6–9; The Genealogy Centre (database). Dunboe online: Genweb, Derry

1831–1832	Derry Youth *First Valuation*. LDS Fiche 6342808. Also NAI
1832	Voters, Londonderry city. PRONI T1048/1–4. Online: Freeholders; Coleraine NAI Outrage papers 1832/2188
1833–1834	Emigrants to the US. Martin, *Historical gleanings*
1833–1839	Emigrants list. Mitchell, *Emigration Lists*. Originals in PRONI, MIC.6. Part online
1837	Marksmen (illiterate voters) in parliamentary boroughs: Londonderry and Coleraine. *Parliamentary Papers 1837, Reports from Committees*, Vol. II (i), Appendix A
1837	Aldermen, Burgesses and Freemen of Coleraine. *Parliamentary Papers 1837, Reports from Committees*, Vol. II (2), Appendix B
1837	Memorial of c.50 individuals (mainly from Buncrana & Derry) to have Quarter Sessions at Buncrana NAI OP 1851/79
1840	Freeholders. PRONI D834/1
1842–1899	Magherafelt Workhouse records. PRONI. Also LDS Film 259179–80
1850	Census of Magilligan Presbyterian congregation, c.1850, PRONI MIC 1P/215
1858–1859	Griffith's Valuation. Indexed online: Hayes
1864–1927	Limavady Workhouse records. PRONI. Also LDS Film 259176
1868	Voters list. PRONI D1935/6, NLI JP 733
1888	Ballinascreen local census; with C of I registers. PRONI t.679/45. 206–208, 227
1901	Census
1911	Census
1912	The Ulster Covenant. Almost half-a-million original signatures and addresses of those who signed. Online: Covenant

Online

Bann Valley	*www.4qd.org/bann/*	Records from the Antrim/Derry border
Covenant	*www.proni.gov.uk/ulstercovenant*	
Freeholders	*www.proni.gov.uk/freeholders*	5 freeeholders/voters lists, 1813–1840
Genweb, Derry	*www.rootsweb.com/~nirldy*	Aghadowey & Dunboe records
Grieves	*members.iinet.net.au/~sgrieves/*	Gravestones

Hayes, John	*www.failteromhat.com*	
Headstones	*www.historyfromheadstones.com*	Comprehensive collection of inscriptions
Lavey	*www.lmi.utvinternet.com*	Lavey (Termoneeny) RC parish
Ulster-ancestry	*www.ulsterancestry.com*	Many transcribed sources

Publications

Local histories, etc.

A Register of Trees for Co. Londonderry, 1768–1911, Belfast: PRONI, 1984, including names of tenant planters

Bernard, Nicholas (ed.), *The Whole Proceedings of the Siege of Drogheda [&] Londonderry*, Dublin: 1736

Boyle, E.M.F-G., *Records of the town of Limavady, –1808*, Londonderry: 1912, NLI Ir. 94112 b 2

Boyle, E.M.F-G., *Genealogical Memoranda relating to the family of Boyle of Limavady*, Londonderry: Sentinel, 1903, NLI Ir. 9292 b 8

Campbell, Barry L., *The Campbell´s [sic].. from Tamlaght O´Crilly (Ireland) to Tallygaroopna (Victoria, Australia)*, Turramurra, NSW:, B.L. Campbell, c.1999, LOC, CS2009–C35 1999, 'a history of the Campbell, Weston, Caldwell, Killough, McInnes, Sandilands, Wilson, Winnett, Pollock, Pavey & Thompson families'

Canning, Bernard J., *By Columb's footsteps trod—the long tower's holy dead: 1784–1984*, Ballyshannon: Donegal Democrat, 198–, NLI Ir. 27411 c 8

Carson, W.R.H., *A bibliography of printed material relating to the county & county borough of Londonderry*, 1969, NLI Ir. 914112 c 8

Day, Angelique, & McWilliams, Patrick (eds.), *Ordnance Survey Memoirs of Ireland series*, Belfast: Inst. of Irish Studies/RIA, 1990–7

Vol. 6: Co. Londonderry I (1990), Arboe, Artrea, Ballinderry, Ballyscullion, Magherafelt, Termoneeny. NLI Ir. 914111 o 15

Vol. 9: Co. Londonderry II (1991), Balteagh, Drumachose (Newtownlimavady). NLI Ir. 9141 o 15

Vol. 11: Co. Londonderry III (1991), Aghanloo, Dunboe, Magilligan (Tamlaghtard).

Vol. 15: Co. Londonderry IV (1992), Dungiven NLI Ir. 914111 o 15

Vol. 18. Co. Londonderry V (1992), Maghera & Tamlaght O'Crilly, NLI Ir. 914111 o 15

Vol. 22: Co. Londonderry VI (1993), Aghadowey, Agivey, Ballyrashane, Kildollagh, Macosquin NLI Ir. 9141 o 85

Vol. 25: Co. Londonderry VII (1993), Bovevagh, Tamlaght Finlagan NLI Ir. 9141 o 80

Vol. 27: Co. Londonderry VIII (1993), Desertoghill, Errigal, Killelagh, Kilrea NLI Ir. 9141 o 86

Vol. 28: Co. Londonderry IX (1994), Cumber (Upper and Lower)NLI Ir. 9141 o 80

Vol. 30: Co. Londonderry X (1994), Banagher NLI Ir. 94111 o 6

Vol. 31: Co. Londonderry XI (1995), Londonderry, Ballynascreen, Desertlyn, Desertmartin, Kilcronaghan, Lissan NLI Ir. 9141 o 80

Vol. 33: Co. Londonderry XII (1995), Ballyaghran, Ballywillin, Coleraine, Killowen NLI Ir. 9141 o 80

Vol. 34: Co. Londonderry XIII (1996), Clondermot & the Waterside NLI Ir. 9141 o 80

Vol. 36: Co. Londonderry XIV (1996), Faughanvale NLI Ir. 9141 o 80

Derry Youth & Community Workshop, *First Valuation of the City of Derry, parish of Templemore 1832*, Derry: Derry Youth & Community Workshop, 1984. LDS Fiche 6342808. Also NAI

Ewart, L.M., *Handbook to the dioceses of Down, Connor & Dromore*

Ferguson, Rev. S., *Some items of Historic Interest about Waterside, Londonderry, 1902, with tables of householders in Glendermot parish, 1663, 1740*

Graham, John, *Far from Owenreagh: memories of John Graham (1899–1893)*, Draperstown: Moyola Books, 1990, NLI Ir. 92 p 172(2), 36 p.

Graham, Rev. John, *Derriana, a History of the Siege of Derry and the Defence of Enniskillen in 1688 and 1689, with Biographical Notes*, Londonderry, pr. for the author, by William M'Corkell, 1823, NLI, J 94112, 64 p.

Henry, Samuel, *The Story of St Patrick's Church, Coleraine*, Coleraine: The Coleraine Chronicle, 1941, NLI Ir. 7265 h 3, 108 p.

Hughes, Samuel, *City on the Foyle*, Londonderry: 1984

Innes, R., *Natural History of Magiligan Parish in 1725*

Kernohan, J.W., *The County of Londonderry in Three Centuries*, Belfast: 1921

King, R.G.S., *A particular of the houses and families in Londonderry, 15/5/1628*, Londonderry: Sentinel Office, 1936, NLI Ir. 94112 l 1. Also LDS Films 1363860 & 990087

MacRory, Patrick, *Days that are gone, Limavady*, County Londonderry: North-West Books, 1983, NLI Ir. 92 m 346, 167 p. Also Pottinger family

Martin, Samuel, *Historical gleanings from Co. Derry, and some from Co. Fermanagh*, Dublin: 1955, NLI Ir. 94112 m 2

McMahon, Kevin, *Guide to Creggan Church and Graveyard*, Creggan: 1988, Creggan Historical Society, NLI Ir. 9295 p 3(2) 48 p.

Mitchell, Brian, *Derry, A City Invincible*, Eglinton: 1990

Mitchell, Brian, *Irish Emigration Lists 1833–39*, Baltimore: GPC, 1988

Mitchell, Brian, *Derry—Sources for Family History*, Derry: The Genealogy Centre, 1992

Moody, T.W., *The Londonderry plantation, 1609–41*, Belfast: Genealogical Publishing Co., 1989, Belfast, 1939, NLI Ir. 94112 m 2

Mullin, T.H., *Ulster's Historic City*, Derry, Londonderry, Coleraine, 1986

Mullin, T.H., *Families of Ballyrashane: a district in Northern Ireland*, Belfast: News Letter Print Co., 1969, 386 p. NLI Ir. 9292 m 33

Mullin, T.H., *Aghadowey*, Coleraine, Mullin, 1971 255 p. NLI Ir. 94112 m 8

Mullin, T.H. & J., *The Ulster clans: O'Mullan, O'Kane and O'Mellan*, Limavady: North-West Books, 1984, 249 p. NLI Ir. 9292 m 54

Mullin, Julia, *The Presbytery of Limavady*, Limavady: 1989

Murphy, Desmond, *Derry, Donegal, and modern Ulster, 1790–1921*, Londonderry: Aileach Press, 1981, NLI Ir. 94112 m 11, 294 p.

O'Laverty, Rev. James, *An Historical Account of the Dioceses of Down and Connor*, Dublin: 1878–89, 4 Vols

Phillips, Sir Thomas, *Londonderry and the London Companies*, Belfast: PRONI, 1928

Reeves, William, *Ecclesiastical Antiquities of Down*, Connor and Dromore: 1847

Simpson, Robert, *The Annals of Derry*, Londonderry: 1847

Witherow, Thomas, *A True Relation of the Twenty Week Siege* ... London: 1649

Witherow, Thomas, *Derry and Enniskillen, in the year 1689*, 1873, 1885, Belfast: W. Mullen & Son, 1895, NLI Ir. 94112 w 8, 419 p.

Local Journals

Benbradagh (Dungiven parish magazine)

Derriana: The journal of the Derry Diocesan Historical Society

Down & Connor Historical Society Magazine

Irish Family Links, NLI Ir. 9292 f 19

North Irish Roots (Journal of the North of Ireland Family History Society), NLI Ir. 92905 n 4

Seanchas Ardmhacha, NLI Ir. 27411 s 4

South Derry Historical Society Journal

Ulster Journal of Archaeology, NLI Ir. 794105 u 1

Directories

1820	J. Pigot, *Commercial Directory of Ireland*, PRONI, NLI Ir. 9141 p 107, LDS Film 962702 Item 1
1824	J. Pigot and Co., *City of Dublin and Hibernian Provincial Directory*, NLI, LDS Film 451787
1835	William T. Matier, *Belfast Directory*
1839	Mathew Martin, *Belfast Directory*. Also 1841, 1842
1846	Slater's *National Commercial Directory of Ireland*, PRONI, NLI LO, LDS Film 1696703 Item 3
1852	James A. Henderson, *Belfast and Province of Ulster Directory*. Issued also in 1854, 1856, 1858, 1861, 1863, 1865, 1868, 1870, 1877, 1880, 1884, 1887, 1890, 1894, 1900, PRONI. LDS (various years)
1856	Slater, *Royal National Commercial Directory of Ireland*, NLI, LDS Film 1472360 Item 1
1865	R. Wynne, *Business Directory of Belfast*, NLI Ir. 91411 b 2
1870	Slater, *Directory of Ireland*, NLI
1881	Slater, *Royal National Commercial Directory of Ireland*, NLI
1887	*Derry Almanac and Directory* NLI Ir. 914112 d 1
1888	George Henry Bassett, *The Book of Antrim*. Repr. Belfast: Friar's Bush, 1989 NLI Ir. 94116 b 29 (Portglenone only)
1894	Slater, *Royal Commercial Directory of Ireland*, NLI

Gravestone Inscriptions

The UHF has transcripts for seventy-six graveyards in Derry. Heritage World has transcripts of forty-two graveyards. These are searchable online, for a fee, at *www.historyfromheadstones.com*. Published or publicly available transcripts are given below.

Aghanloo: Rathfad (Aghanloo Old?), *Irish Family Links* 1985 2 (3)
—— Derramore, Presbyterian, *Irish Family Links*, 2 (4), 1985
—— Drumbane, C of I, *Irish Family Links*, 1985 2 (3)
Artrea: Ballyeglish Old, *South Derry Historical Society Journal*, 1981/2
Ballinderry: Ballinderry, Methodist, *South Derry Historical Society Journal*, 1982/3
Balteagh: Lislane, Presbyterian, *Irish Family Links*, 2 (4), 1985
Carrick: Largy, Presbyterian, *Irish Family Links*, 2 (5), 1985
Clondermot: Glendermot Old. Online: Grieves
Coleraine: Coleraine, Church Street, C of I, Henry, *[...] St Patrick's Church, Coleraine*, n.d.
Drumachose: Limavady, First, Presbyterian, *Irish Family Links*, 2 (5), 1985
—— Rathbrady More, Presbyterian, *Irish Family Links*, 2 (5), 1985
—— Limavady, Myroe, Presbyterian, *Irish Family Links*, 2 (5), 1985
—— Limavady, RC, *Irish Family Links*, 2 (5), 1985
—— Drummond (Drumachose Old?), *Irish Family Links*, 2 (4), 1985
Magherafelt: Magherafelt, Castledawson Street, C of I, *South Derry Historical Society Journal*, 1980/1
Magilligan: Tamlaght, RC, *Irish Family Links*, 2 (5), 1985
—— Magilligan, Presbyterian, *Irish Family Links*, 2 (5), 1985
Tamlaght Finlagan: Ballykelly town, *Irish Family Links*
—— Oghill, RC, *Irish Family Links*, 2 (5), 1985
—— Ballykelly town, Presbyterian, *Irish Family Links*
Templemore: Creggan, McMahon, *Guide to Creggan*
Templemore: Derry, Glendermot, C of I, NAI

Estate Records

Desertmartin Estate Rentals: *Derriana*, 1981–1982
Londonderry, Marquis of: PRONI D/654. Rentals, 1750–1940. Covering townlands in the civil parishes of: Faughanvale; and Magherafelt. May cover further parishes.
The Salters' Company Co. Londonderry: PRONI D/4108. Rentals, 1750–1950. Covering townlands in the civil parishes of: Artrea; Ballinderry; Ballyscullion; Desertlyn; Magherafelt; Tamlaght. May cover further parishes.
[No landlord given]: Tenants' lists, Magherafelt & Ballinderry parishes (Aghaskin, Ballyheifer, Ballylifford, Ballymilligan) 1752–1930. *South Derry Historical Society Journal* 1 (2).

DONEGAL

Census returns and substitutes

1612–1613   'Survey of Undertakers Planted in Co. Donegal', *Historical Manuscripts Commission Report,* No. 4 (Hastings Mss.), 1947, pp 159–82

1630   Muster Roll of Ulster; Armagh Co. Library and PRONI D.1759/3C/1; T. 808/15164; NLI Pos. 206

1641   Book of Survey and Distribution. NLI Ms. 968

1654   Civil Survey. *Civil Survey,* Vol. lll NLI I 6551 Dublin

1659   Pender's 'Census'. Repr. GPC, 1997, IMC, 2002. LDS Film 924648

1665   Hearth Money Roll. PRONI T.307/D. Also GO 538; NLI Ms. 9583. Part online: Ulster Ancestry, Buckley

1669   Subsidy Roll, covering baronies of Kilmacrenan, Raphoe, Tirhugh, Taughboyne. PRONI T 307. Also LDS Film 258502

1740   Protestant Householders: parishes of Clonmany, Culdaff, Desertegny, Donagh, Fawne, Moville, Templemore: GO 539. LDS Film 100182

1761–1775   Freeholders. PRONI T.808/14999. Also GO 442; NLI P.975. LDS Film 100181. Online: Freeholders

1766   Diocesan census Donoghmore parish. NAI 207/8; Protestants in Leck and Raphoe. NAI M2476.

1770   Freeholders entitled to vote. NLI Mss. 787–788

1782   Persons in Culdaff. Young, *300 Years in Inishowen*

1796   Spinning-Wheel Premium List. 7,525 names for Co. Donegal. Online: Hayes

1796   Clondevaddock local census; with C of I registers, PRONI MIC.1/164

1799   Protestant Householders, Templecrone parish. *IA,* 1984

1802–1803   Protestants in part of Culdaff parish. *300 Years in Inishowen*

1823–1838   Tithe Books

1836–1844   Memorials from the inhabitants of the towns of Ballyshannon, Pettigo & Bundoran (1836, c.70 names), Buncrana & Derry (1837 c.50 names) and Leterkenny (1844 c.130 names) NAI OP 1851/79

1843   Voters NAI OP 1843/56

1857   Griffith's Valuation. Indexed online: Hayes

1860–1867   Emigrants to North America from Inver; with C of I registers. PRONI MIC.1/158

1862–1883   Strabane Union Workhouse records. PRONI BG/27. Also LDS Film 259164–5

1901   Census. Part online: Buckley

1911   Census. Part online: Buckley

1912   The Ulster Covenant. Almost half-a-million original signatures and addresses of those who signed. Online: Covenant

Online

Buckley, Lindel	*freepages.genealogy.rootsweb.com/~donegal/*	Large collection, mainly north-west
Covenant	*www.proni.gov.uk/ulstercovenant*	
Freeholders	*www.proni.gov.uk/freeholders*	
Hayes, John	*www.failteromhat.com*	
Palmer, Ben	*www.benpalmer.co.uk/movillerecords.htm*	
Ulster-ancestry	*www.ulsterancestry.com*	

Publications

Local histories, etc.

Historical notes of Raphoe, Vol.; 3 Finn Valley, Lifford and Twin towns, Stranorlar: Knights of Columbanus, 1991 NLI Ir. 94113 b 8

Ordnance Survey Memoirs of Ireland: Volume 38: Parishes of County Donegal I, 1833–5, North-East Donegal, Belfast: Institute of Irish Studies, 1997, NLI Ir. 9141 0 80, 168pp. Clondavaddog, Clonmany, Culdaff, Desertegney, Donagh, Killygarvan, Kilmacrenan, Mevagh, Mintiaghs (Bar of Inch), Moville, Muff, Tullyaughnish, Lough Swilly (with Burt and Inch)

A golden jubilee story and index to contents of fifty annuals County Donegal historical society, Donegal: County Donegal Historical Society, 1995, NLI Ir. 94113 d 14, 76 p.

Aalen, F.H., *Gola: the life and last days of an island community,* Cork: Mercier Press, 1969, 127 p. NLI Ir. 914113 a 2

Allingham, Hugh, *Ballyshannon: its history and antiquities (with some account of the surrounding neighbourhood),* Londonderry: 1879. Repr. Ballyshannon 1937. 112 p. NLI Ir. 94113 p. 2(3)

Beattie, Seán, *The book of Inistrahull,* Carndonagh: Lighthouse, 1992. 24 p. NLI Ir. 941 p 115(4)

Bonner, Brian, *Where Aileach guards a millennium of Gaelic civilisation,* Pallaskenry: Salesian Press Trust, 1986?, NLI Ir. 94113 b 7, 150 p.

Briody, Liam, *Glenties and Iniskeel,* Ballyshannon: Donegal Democrat, 1986. 320 p. NLI

Campbell, Patrick, *Memories of Dungloe,* New Jersey: the author, 1993, NLI Ir. 92 c 360, 149 p.

Campbell, Patrick, *Death in Templecrone, an account of the Famine years in northwest Donegal, 1845–1850,* New Jersey: P.H. Campbell, 1995, NLI Ir. 94113 c 7, 193 p.

Carville, Geraldine, *Assaroe abbey of the morning star,* Abbey Mill Wheel Trust, 1989, NLI Ir. 27411 c 9, 63 p.

Conaghan, Charles, *History and antiquities of Killybegs,* Ballyshannon: Donegal Democrat, 1975

Conaghan, Pat, *The Zulu Fishermen: Forgotten Pioneers of Donegal's First Fishing Industry,* Aghayeevoge, Co. Donegal: Bygones Enterprise, 2003, NLI, 3A 3994, 340 p.

Conaghan, Pat, *Bygones: New Horizons on the History of Killybegs*, Killybegs: the author, 1989, NLI Ir. 94113 c 6, 399 p.

Conaghan, Pat, *The great famine in South-West Donegal, 1845–1850*, Aghayeevoge, Co. Donegal: Bygones Enterprise, 1997, NLI, 280 p.

Day, Angelique, & McWilliams, Patrick (eds.), *Ordnance Survey Memoirs of Ireland: Volume 39: Parishes of County Donegal II, 1835–6, Mid, West & South Donegal*, Belfast: Institute of Irish Studies, 1997, NLI Ir. 9141 o 80, 216pp. Clonleigh, Convoy, Conwal, Donaghmore, Donegal, Drumhome, Glencolmbcille, Inishkeel, Kilbarron, KIllea and Taughboyne, Killymard, Kilteevoge, Leck, Raphoe, Raymoghy, Taughboyne, Templecarn, Tullaghobegley, Urney

Devitt, James W., *Boyds of Loughros Point, The Rosses, America, Australia, and New Zealand*, US: J.W. Devitt, –, 1994, LOC, 1994

Doherty, William J., *The abbey of Fahan in Inishowen, Co. Donegal*, Dublin: P. Traynor, 1881

Doherty, William J., *Inis-Owen and Tirconnel: being some account of the antiquities ... of Donegal*, Dublin: 1895, NLI Ir. 94113 d 1

Duffy, Godfrey F., *A guide to tracing your Donegal ancestors*, Dublin: Flyleaf Press, 1996, NLI Ir. 941 d 9, 94 p.

Egan, Bernard, *Drumhome*, Ballyshannon: Donegal Democrat, 1986, NLI 93 p.

Farrell, Noel, *Exploring family origins in Ballyshannon*, Longford: Noel Farrell, 1998, NLI, 48 p.

Farrell, Noel, *Exploring Family origins in Ballybofey/Stranorlar & Killygordon*, Longford: Self, 1994, NLI, 48 p.

Farrell, Noel, *Exploring Family origins in Letterkenny*, Longford: Self, 1997, NLI, 47 p.

Farrell, Noel, *Exploring family origins in Mountcharles, Inver & Donegal town*, Longford: Noel Farrell, 1997, NLI, 48 p.

Fleming, Sam, *Letterkenny: past and present*, Ballyshannon: Donegal Democrat, 197–. 88 p. NLI Ir. 94113 f 1

Fox, Robin, *The Tory islanders, a people of the celtic fringe*, Notre Dame/London: University of Notre Dame Press, 1995, NLI Ir. 914111 f 10, 210 p.

Friel, Deirdra, *St. Mary's Church, the Lagg 1829–1961*, Milford: Deirdra Friel, 1996, NLI, 31 p.

Gallagher, Barney, *Arranmore Links: the families of Arranmore*, Dublin: Aiden Gallagher, 1986, NLI Ir. 94109 g 18

Harkin, M., *Inishowen: its history, traditions, and antiquities ... / by Maghtochair*, Carndonagh, County Donegal: M. Harkin, 1935, NLI Ir. 94113 h 1, 227 p.

Harvey, G.H., *The Harvey families of Inishowen, Co. Donegal, and Maen, Cornwall*, Folkestone: F. Weatherhead, 1927, NLI Ir. 9292 h 3, 178 p.

Hill, Rev. George, *Facts from Gweedore*, Dublin: 1854, NLI, p. 1191 (10), 64 p.

IGRS, *Tombstone inscriptions Vol. 1*, Dublin: IGRS Tombstone Committee, 2001, NLI, 850 p.

Jensen, Marjorie Molloy, *The family of Big Jimmy McLaughlin of Dreenagh, Malin Head, Donegal, Ireland*, Golden, CO: M.M. Jansen, 1999, LOC

Knights of St Columbanus C.K. 56., *Ballybofey and Stranorlar historical notes*, Stranorlar: 1987, NLI Ir. 94113 b 8

Lawrenson, Leslie Robert, *The parish of Conwall, Aughanunshin, and Leck*, Letterkenny: the parish, 1944, NLI Ir. 2741 p 41, 36 p.

Leiball, Abigail Cone, *The Coane family of Ballyshannon, Donegal*, Stamford, Connecticut: the author, 2002, NLI

Lucas, Leslie W., *Mevagh Down the Years*, Portlaw; Volturna, 1972. 214 p. NLI Ir. 94113 l 1

Lucas, Leslie W., *More about Mevagh*, Belfast: Appletree Press, 1982, 93 p. NLI Ir. 941 p. 22

MacDonagh, J.C.T., *Bibliography of Co. Donegal*, Donegal Historical Society Journal, 1947–50, pp 217–30

Maguire, Edward, *Letterkenny past and present*, Letterkenny: McKinney & O'Callaghan, 192–

Maguire, Edward, *Ballyshannon past and present*, Bundoran: Stepless, 193–

Maguire, V. Rev. Canon, *The History of the Diocese of Raphoe*, Dublin: Browne and Nolan, 1920, NLI Ir. 274113 m 1, 2 vols

Manning, Aidan, *Glencolumbkille 3000 B.C.–1985 A.D.*, Ballyshannon: Donegal Democrat, 1985

McCarron, Edward, *Life in Donegal: 1850–1900*, Dublin: Mercier Press, c.1981, NLI Ir. 92 m 321, 140 p.

McClintock, May, *The heart of the Laggan the history of Raymoghy & Ray National School*, Letterkenny, Co. Donegal: An Taisce, 1990, NLI Ir. 372.m.109, 93 p.

McClintock, May, *After the battering ram: the trail of the dispossessed from Derryveagh, 1861*, Letterkenny: An Taisce, 1991, NLI Ir. 941 p 102(3), 20 p.

McCreadie, John, *Glenwar & Oughterlin*, Carndonagh: Foyle Press, 198–

McGarrigle, Joe, *Donegal Past and present*, Donegal: McGarrigle family, 1995, NLI, Ir. 94113 m 11, 195 p.

McLaughlin, Gerry, *Cloughaneely: myth and fact*, Johnswood Press, 2002, NLI, 304 p.

McLaughlin, John A., *Carrowmenagh: history of a Donegal village and townland*, Letterkenny: JAML, 2001, NLI, 118 p.

Montgomery, H.H., *A history of Moville and its neighbourhood by Rt. Rev. Bishop Henry Montgomery*, Crawford Norris and C. Doherty, 1992, NLI, Ir. 94113 p. 2(2), 52 p.

Mullin, T.H., *The kirk and lands of Convoy since the Scottish settlement*, Belfast: Belfast Newsletter, 1960

Murphy, Desmond, *Derry, Donegal, and modern Ulster, 1790–1921*, Londonderry: Aileach Press, 1981, NLI Ir. 94112 m 11, 294 p.

Nolan, W., *Donegal History and Society*, Dublin: Geography Publications, 1995, NLI Ir. 94113 d 12, 920 p. Co-editors Liam Ronayne, Mairead Dunlevy

Ó Ceallaigh, Seosamh, *Aspects of our rich inheritance: [Cloughaneely]*, Ireland: Dulra, 2000, NLI Ir. 94113 c 8, 240 p.

O Gallachair, P., *Where Erne and Drowes meet the sea. Fragments from a Patrician parish*, Ballyshannon: Donegal Democrat, 1961, 118 p.

O Gallachair, P., *The history of landlordism in Donegal*, Ballyshannon: Donegal Democrat, 1962, NLI Ir. 94113 o 5, 192 p.

Ó Searcaigh, Cathal, *Tulach Beaglaoich inné agus inniú (Tullaghobegley past and present)*, Fál Carrach: Glór na nGael, 1993, NLI Ir. 27411 o, 68 p.

O'Carroll, Declan, *Rockhill House, Letterkenny, Co. Donegal: a history*, Ballyshannon: Donegal Democrat, 1984

O'Donnell, Ben, *History of the parish of Templecrone*, Donegal: 1999, Donegal County Library, 941.693, Photocopy

O'Donnell, Ben, *The Story of The Rosses*, Lifford: Caoran Publ., 1999, Donegal County Library, 441p. Much detail on local families

O'Donnell, Vincent, *Ardaghey Church and people*, Ardaghey: St Naul's Church, 1995, NLI Ir. 94113 a 5, 146 p.

Parke, W.K., *The parish of Inishmacsaint*, Fermanagh: 1982, NLI Ir. 27411 p 6, 73 p.

Patterson, W.J., *Rossnowlagh remembered*, Ballyshannon: Donegal Democrat, 1992, NLI Ir. 94113 p.

Ronayne, Liam, *The battle of Scariffhollis 1650*, Letterkenny: Eagráin Dhún na nGall, 2001, NLI, 72 p.

Smeaton, Brian, *The parish of Kilmacrennan now and then with a history of the Parish Church of Saint Finian and Saint Mark 1846–1996*, 1995, NLI Ir. 9411 p, 40 p.

Strong, Dale G., *The descendants of John Strong (1770–1837) and Martha Watson (1772–1851) of Drumhome Parish, Co. Donegal, Ireland*, Cassatt, SC, Mr. & Mrs. D.G. Strong, 1983, LOC, CS71.S923 1983a, 98 leaves

Swan, H.P., *The Book of Inishowen*, Buncrana: 1938. 192 p. NLI Ir. 94113 s 1

Trimble, H., *Killymard ancient & modern*, Killymard, s.n., 2001, NLI, 240 p.

Trimble, T.H., *The legacy that is Laughey Community and Church*, Letterkenny: printed by Browne Printers, 2000, NLI, 160 p.

Young, Amy, *300 Years in Inishowen*, Belfast: M'Caw, Stevenson & Orr, 1929, NLI Ir. 9292 y 1. 357 p.

Local Journals
Journal of the Donegal Historical Society, NLI Ir. 94113 d 3
Clogher Record, NLI Ir. 94114 c 2
Donegal Annual
Ulster Journal of Archaeology, NLI Ir. 794105 u 1

Directories

1824	J. Pigot and Co., *City of Dublin and Hibernian Provincial Directory*, NLI, LDS Film 451787
1839	*Directory of the Towns of Sligo, Enniskillen, Ballyshannon, Donegal [...]*
1846	Slater's *National Commercial Directory of Ireland*. PRONI, NLI LO, LDS Film 1696703 Item 3
1852	James A. Henderson, *Belfast and Province of Ulster Directory*. Issued also in 1854, 1856, 1858, 1861, 1863, 1865, 1868, 1870, 1877, 1880, 1884, 1887, 1890, 1894, 1900, PRONI. LDS (various years)

1856	Slater, *Royal National Commercial Directory of Ireland*, NLI, LDS Film 1472360 Item 1
1870	Slater, *Directory of Ireland*, NLI
1881	Slater, *Royal National Commercial Directory of Ireland*, NLI
1887	*Derry Almanac and Directory*, NLI Ir. 914112 d 1
1894	Slater, *Royal Commercial Directory of Ireland*, NLI

Gravestone Inscriptions

Aghanunshin: Kiltoy, DA
—— Killydonnell, DA
Aughnish: Tullyaughnish, DA
Fahan Lower: Buncrana town, C of I, HW
Gartan: Churchtown (Gartan?), DA
Inishmacsaint: Assaroe Abbey. Online: Ulsterancestry
Ballyshannon town (Assaroe?), RC, DA
—— Finner. O Gallachair, *Where Erne*
Inver: Cranny Lower (Old Inver?), C of I, DA
—— Cranny Lower (Old Inver?), C of I *IGRS, Vol. 1*
Kilbarron: Ballyshannon, Church Lane, C of I, *Donegal Annual*, Vol. 12, No. 2
Killaghtee: Beaugreen Glebe (Old Killaghtee?), IGRS Collection, GO. Also DA
Killybegs Lower: Kilrean Upper, IGRS Collection, GO
Killybegs Upper: St Catherine's, DA
Kilmacrenan: Kilmacrenan town, DA
Leck: Leck, DA
Muff: Muff, Scared Heart, RC, HW
Taughboyne: St Johnstown town, Presbyterian, HW
Tullaghobegly: Magheragallan, DA
—— Ballintemple (Tullaghobegly?), Ó Searcaigh, *Tulach beaglaoich*, Vol. 8

Estate Records

Abercorn, Earls of: Tenants' list, 1799 in Lecky, *The Laggan*. Covering townlands in the civil parishes of: Clonleigh; Taughboyne; Urney.

Connolly: Rent rolls, 1724–1831. NLI Ms. 17302. Major tenants only. Rent rolls, 1772–1793. NAI M. 6917 (1–17). Major tenants only. Rent rolls, 1848. NAI M. 6917 (18). Major tenants only. Covering areas in the civil parishes of: Drumhome; Glencolumbkille; Inishkeel; Inishmacsaint; Kilbarron; Kilcar; Killybegs Upper; Killymard.

Connolly: Rent rolls, 1724–1831, intermittent. NLI Ms. 17302. NAI M. 6917 (1–17) Major tenants only. Covering areas in the civil parishes of: Drumhome; Glencolumbkille; Inishkeel; Inishmacsaint; Kilbarron; Kilcar; Killybegs Upper; Killymard.

Ferguson, Andrew: Maps, with names, 1790. NLI Ms. 5023. Major tenants only. Rentals, 1838–1842. NLI Ms. 8410 (2). All tenants. Tenants list, 1840. NLI Ms. 8410 (3). All tenants. Covering areas in the civil parish of Donagh.

William Forward: Valuation and survey, 1727. NLI Ms. 4247. Major tenants only. Maps, with tenants, 1727. NLI Ms. 2614. All tenants. Covering areas in the civil parishes of: Allsaints; Burt.

Hart: Rentals, 1757–1767. NLI Ms. 7885. All tenants. Covering areas in the civil parishes of: Clonca; Muff.

Leslie: Rentals, 1819–1837. NLI Ms. 5811–2. All tenants. Covering areas in the civil parish of Templecarn.

Leslie: Valuation, with names and observations, 1833. NLI Ms. 5813. All tenants. Rental, 1846. NLI Ms. 5813. All tenants. Covering areas in the civil parish of Templecarn.

Maxwell: Valuation, with names, 1807. NLI Ms. 5357. All tenants. Covering areas in the civil parishes of: Clonleigh; Fahan Upper.

Stewart: Rentals, 1813–1853. NAI BR DON 21/1/1-3. All tenants. Covering areas in the civil parishes of: Clondahorky; Clonmany; Raymunterdoney; Tullyfern.

Stuart-Murray: Rentals, 1842–1850. NLI Ms. 5465–70. All tenants. Rentals, 1849. NLI Ms. 3084. All tenants. Rentals, 1851–1859. NLI Ms. 5472–67, 5892–96. Covering areas in the civil parishes of: Inishkeel Kilcar; Killaghtee; Killea; Killybegs Lower; and Killymard.

Sir Charles Styles: Valuation and survey, 1773. NLI Ms. 402. Major tenants only. Covering areas in the civil parish of Kilteevoge.

Lord Wicklow: Rent roll, with leaseholders, 1780. NLI Ms. 9582. Major tenants only. Covering areas in the civil parishes of: Allsaints; Burt; Raymoghy; Taughboyne.

[No landlord given]: Visiting book, with observations, 1842–1843. NLI Ms. 7938. Coverage unclear. Covering areas in the civil parish of Inishkeel.

DOWN

Census returns and substitutes

1642–1643	Muster Roll. PRONI T.563/1
1642	Muster Roll, Donaghadee. PRONI T.3726/1
1659	Pender's 'Census'. Repr. GPC, 1997, IMC, 2002. LDS Film 924648
1661	Books of Survey and Distribution. PRONI T.370/A & D.1854/1/18
1660	Poll Tax Returns Co. Down. PRONI MIC/15A/76 LDS Film 993164
1663	Subsidy Roll. NAI M. 2745. Also NLI Pos. 206; PRONI T.307; LDS Film 1279356
1669	Newry & Mourne Poll Tax Returns. PRONI T1046
1708	Householders in Downpatrick town. *The City of Downe*, R.E. Parkinson
1720	Down and Antrim landed gentry, RIA 24 k 19
1722–1970	Records of Southwell Charity School Downpatrick. PRONI D/2664.
1740	Protestant Householders (Partial). PRONI T.808/15258
1746–1789	'Deputy Court Cheque Book'—freeholders A–G only PRONI D.654/A3/1B. Online: Freeholders
1766	Kilbroney, Seapatrick, Inch, Shankill. NLI Ms. 4173

1789	'Deputy Court Cheque Book' (votes cast). PRONI D.654/A3/1B. Online: Freeholders
1775	Dissenters' petitions. Presbyterians in Ballee, Comber, Donacloney, Dundonald, Dromore, Dromara, Drumballyroney, Drumgooland, Killyleagh, Newry, Rathfriland, Seapatrick, Tullylish. PRONI T/808/14977, NLI Ms. 4173
1777–1795	Freeholders Registers PRONI DOW 5/3/1 & 2 (1777, 1780, 1795), Lecale barony only, c.1790 PRONI T.393/1
1796	Spinning-Wheel Premium List. 2,975 names for Co. Down
1798	Persons who suffered losses in the 1798 rebellion. Propertied classes only, c.180 names. NLI I 94107
1799–1800	Militia Pay Lists and Muster Rolls. PRONI T.1115/4A C
1803	Agricultural survey recording householders, occupations and agricultural possessions. Covers parts at least of thirty parishes. See Maxwell (*Down Ancestors*) for details. More than 11,000 names. PRONI D/654/A2/1–37A–C
1813–1821	Freeholders. PRONI T.761/19, LDS Film 258701. Online: Freeholders
1815–1846	Downpatrick electors. NLI Ms. 7235
1820	Lisburn householders PRONI T679/107–112
1821	Some extracts. NAI Thrift Abstracts
1823–1838	Tithe Books. Online index: Caora
1824	Freeholders. PRONI T.761/20. Online: Freeholders
1831	Memorial of the Inhabitants of part of Counties Down & Armagh praying for relief. April 21 1831. More than 1,300 names, 'more particularly in the neighbourhood of Shane Hill'—Knocknashane, Shankill parish? NAI OP 974/122
1837	Valuation of Newry town (heads of households). *Parliamentary Papers 1837, Reports from Committees,* Vol. II (1), Appendix G
1837	Marksmen (illiterate voters) in parliamentary boroughs: Newry and Downpatrick. *Parliamentary Papers 1837, Reports from Committees,* Vol. II (i), Appendix A
1837	Memorial from inhabitants of Lisburn, NAI OP 1837/10
1839–1948	Some material, including admissions registers and relief registers, survives for all of the unions of Co. Down. PRONI. LDS hold microfilm copies of Lurgan (259166–72) and Downpatrick (993164 part, 259159–61)
1841–1861	Religious censuses: Aghaderg. RCBL Ms. 65
1842	Voters OP 1842/113
1851	Some extracts. NAI Thrift Abstracts
1851	Presbyterians only: Loughinisland, *Family Links,* Vol. 1 Nos 5 & 7, 1982/83
1851	Inhabitants of Scarva. Also Church of Ireland parishioners 1858, 1860, 1861 RCBL Ms. 65
1852	Poll Book (votes cast). Incomplete. PRONI D.671/02/5 6 D.671/02/7 8; LDS Film 993158

1861	Loughinisland Presbyterians only. *Family Links,* Vol. 1 Nos 5 & 7, 1982/83
1863–1864	Griffith's Valuation. Indexed online: Hayes, Caora
1868	Census of the C of I parish of Shankill, Counties Armagh & Down. Local clergyman
1873	Census of the congregation of the C of I parish of Knockbreda, Co. Down. Also 1875; with C of I registers
1901	Census. Indexed online: Caora
1911	Census
1912	The Ulster Covenant. Almost half-a-million original signatures and addresses of those who signed. Online: Covenant

Online

Caora	www.caora.net	Tithes, Griffith's, 1901 indexed
Covenant	www.proni.gov.uk/ulstercovenant	
Freeholders	www.proni.gov.uk/freeholders	34 Freeholders/voters lists for Down, 1746–1831
Hayes, John	www.failteromhat.com	
Headstones	www.historyfromheadstones.com	Comprehensive collection of inscriptions
UHF	www.ancestryireland.co.uk	Parish records online

Publications

Local histories, etc.

Donaghadee: a local history list, Ballynahinch: South Eastern Education and Library Service, 1981, NLI Ir. 9411 s 12, 38 p.

Killyleagh & Crossegar: a local history list, Ballynahinch: South Eastern Education and Library Service, 1981, NLI Ir. 914115 p 15, 18 p.

Clandeboye: a reading guide, Ballynahinch: South Eastern Education and Library Service, 1981, NLI Ir. 914115 p. 15, Blackwood family bibliography

Atkinson, Edward D., *An Ulster Parish: Being a History of Donaghcloney,* Dublin: Hodges, Figgis, 1898, NLI Ir. 94115 a 1, Waringstown, Co. Down. Jenny and Warren families

Atkinson, Edward D., *Dromore, an Ulster Diocese,* Dundalk: W. Tempest, 1925, NLI Ir. 274116 a 1, 317 p.

Barry, J., *Hillsborough: a parish in the Ulster Plantation,* Belfast: W. Mullan, 1982, NLI Ir. 94115 b 3, 129 p. Ed. Wm. Mullin

Bowsie, George A., *Carryduff 2000: a chronological record of events in the life and development of Carryduff, past and present and memoirs of the district from bygone days,* Northern Ireland, 2000, NLI Ir. 94115 b 8, 90 p. Co-author, Graham Murphy

Buchanan, R.H., *Irish Historic Towns Atlas 8: Downpatrick*, Dublin: Royal Irish Academy, 1997, NLI

Buchanan, Rev. James, *An historical sketch of the Reformed Presbyterian Church of Rathfriland*, Newry: Newry Telegraph, 1908, NLI, LO P 560 23 p.

Canavan, T., *Frontier town: an illustrated history of Newry*, Belfast: Blackstaff Press, 1989

Carr, P., *The most unpretending of places: a history of Dundonald*, Belfast: White Row Press, 1987, NLI Ir. 94115 c 13, 252 p.

Carr, P., *Portavo, an Irish townland and its peoples: part one, earliest times to 1844*, Belfast: White Row Press, 2003, NLI, 339 p.

Clarke, R.S.J., *Gravestone Inscriptions, Co. Down Vols. 1–20*, Belfast: UHF, 1971–1989, NLI Ir. 9292 c 43, See Gravestone Inscriptions, below

Cowan, J. Davison, *An Ancient Parish, Past and Present; being the Parish of Donaghmore, County Down*, London: D. Nutt, 1914, NLI Ir. 94115 c 1, 402 p.

Crossle, Francis, *Local Jottings of Newry Collected and Transcribed, Vols 1–34*, Newry: 1890–1910

Crowther, J.A. Claire, *The Cloughley family of Loughans, Co. Down, Ireland*, Ireland: Claire Crowther, 1985, NLI, GO 573

Day, Angelique & McWilliams, Patrick (eds.), *Ordnance Survey Memoirs of Ireland series*, Belfast: Inst. of Irish Studies/RIA, 1990–7

> *Vol. 3: Co. Down I* (1990), Clonallan, Clonduff, Donaghmore, Drumballyroney, Drumgath, Drumgooland, Kilbroney, Kilcoo, Kilkeel, Kilmegan, Newry, Warrenpoint. NLI Ir. 914111 o 12

> *Vol. 7: Co. Down II* (1991), Ardkeen, Ardquin, Ballyhalbert (Saint Andrew's), Ballyphilip, Ballytrustan, Ballywalter, Bangor, Castleboy, Comber, Donaghadee, Drumbeg, Drumbo, Dundonald, Grey Abbey, Holywood, Inishargy, Kilinchy, Kilmood, Knockbreda, Newtownards, Saintfield, Slanes, Tullynakill, Witter. NLI Ir. 9141 o 80

> *Vol. 12: Co. Down III* (1993), Aghaderg, Annaclone, Annahilt, Blaris, Donaghcloney, Dromara, Dromore, Garvaghy, Hillsborough, Magheralin, Magherally, Moira, Seapatrick, Shankill, Tullylish. NLI *Ir.* 914115 o 12

> *Vol. 17: Co. Down IV* (1992), Ardglass, Ballee, Ballyculter, Ballykinler, Bright, Down, Dunsfort, Inch, Kilclief, Killyleagh, Kilmore, Loughinisland, Magheradrool, Rathmullan, Saul NLI Ir. 914111 o 12

Ewart, L.M., *Handbook to the dioceses of Down, Connor & Dromore*

Haddock, Josiah, *A Parish Miscellany, Donaghcloney*

Hill, Rev. George, *Montgomery Manuscripts, 1603–1706*, Belfast: 1869

Irwin, David, *Tide and Times in the Port: a narrative history of the Co. Down village of Groomsport*, Groomsport: Groomsport Presbyterian Church, 1993

James, W.V., *Strangford: The Forgotten Past of Strangford Village*, Belfast: The Northern Whig, 1994

Keenan, Padraic, *Historical Sketch of the Parish of Clonduff*, Newry: 1941

Keenan, Padraic, 'Clonallon Parish; its Annals and Antiquities', NLI, JCLAS Vol. X

Kelly, Charles, *The Kelly's of County Down: a record of ...the Kelly's of County*

Down, with particular reference to Newtownards and surrounding parishes, Ayr, C. Kelly, 1999?, NLI, GO 112, 132, p.

Knox, Alexander, *History of the County Down*, Dublin: 1875, NLI Ir. 94115 k 2, 724 p. Repr. Davidson Books, 1982

Lamont, J.A., *Presbyterianism in Holywood: Bangor Road Congregation*, Bangor: 1967, NLI, 50 p.

Linn, Capt. Richard, *A history of Banbridge*, Belfast: 1935, ed. W.S., Kerr; Including Tullylish

Lockington, John W., *Robert Blair of Bangor*, Belfast: Presbyterian Historical Society of Ireland, Biographical portrait of Robert Blair, 1593–1666, Minister in Ulster and Scotland

Lowrie, T.K., *The Hamilton Mss: settlement of Clandeboye, Great Ardes, and Dufferin..., by Sir James Hamilton, Knight (Viscount Claneboye) ... reigns of James I and Charles I: (with his family)*, Belfast: Archer & Sons, 1867, NLI Ir. 94115 h 1, 166 p.

McCavery, T., *Newtown: a history of Newtownards*, Belfast: White Row Press, 1994, NLI Ir. 94115 m 6, 221 p.

McCavery, T., *A covenant community: a history of Newtownards Reformed Presbyterian Church*, Newtownards, 1997, NLI Ir. 285 m 40, 186 p.

McCullogh, S., *Ballynahinch, Centre of Down*, Ballynahinch: Chamber of Commerce, 1968

Monroe, Horace, *Foulis Castle and the Monroes of Lower Iveagh*, London: Mitchell, Hughes and Clarke, 1929, NLI Ir. 9292 m 10, 83 p.

Nangle, F.R. & J.F.T., *A short account of the Nangle family of Downpatrick*, Great Britain: F. Nangle, 1986, NLI Ir. 9292 n 8, 46 p.

O'Laverty, Rev. James, *An Historical Account of the Dioceses of Down and Connor*, Dublin: 1878–89, 4 Vols

Parkinson, Edward, *The City of Down from its earliest days*, Bangor, County Down: Donard Publishing Co., 1977, NLI, Ir. 94115 p 1, 162 p. Repr. of 1928 edition.

Patton, W.D., *A short history of First Dromore Presbyterian Church: 1660–1981*, Banbridge, Co. Down: Review Press, 1982, NLI, 55 p.

Pilson, A., *Downpatrick & its Parish Church*, 1852, NLI, P 1938, including lists of clergy & churchwardens

Pooler, L.A., *Down and its Parishes*, 1907

Rankin, Kathleen, *The linen houses of the Lagan Valley: the story of their families*, Belfast: UHF, 2002, NLI, 221 p.

Redpath, Beverly J., *The Monk family from Bally William, Co Down Ireland: across the world, a family history*, Avoca, Vic.: B. and A. Redpath, 1989, LOC

Reeves, William, *Ecclesiastical Antiquities of Down, Connor and Dromore*, 1847

Reilly, E.J.S., *A genealogical history of the family of Montgomery, comprising the lines of Eglinton and Braidstane in Scotland, and Mount-Alexander and Grey-Abbey in Ireland*, 1942, NLI Ir. 9292 m 24, 84 p.

Reside, S.W., *St Mary's Church, Newry, its History*, 1933

Roden, Clodagh Rose Jocelyn Countess of, *Kilcoo Parish Church, Bryansford*, 1971, NLI, 31 p.

Rudnitzky, Honor, *Killinchy Parish Church: [written] to celebrate the 150th anniversary of the consecration of the present church*, Killinchy, 1980, NLI, 19

Schmidt, Joanne C. Fisher, *Tombstones of Ireland: counties Down & Roscommon*, Bowie, MD: Heritage Books, c.2000., LOC, 110 p.

Shearman, Hugh, *Ulster*, London, 1949, NLI Ir. 91422 s 3, 426 p. (incl. bibliographies)

Smith, Charles, *The Ancient and Present State of the County of Down*, Dublin: 1744, NLI, I 94115 h 2, co-author, Walter Harris. Reprint Ballynahinch, County Down: Davidson Books, 1977

Smith, K., 'Bangor Reading List', NLI, *Journal of the Bangor Historical Society*

Wilson, A.M., *Saint Patrick's town: a history of Downpatrick and the Barony of Lecal*, Belfast: Isabella Press, 1995, NLI Ir. 94115 w 5, 243 p.

Local Journals
12 Miles of Mourne: journal of the Mourne Local Studies Group, NLI Ir. 94115 T 1
Craigavon Historical Society Review, LHL
Down & Connor Historical Society Magazine
Irish Family Links, NLI Ir. 9292 f 19
Journal of the Bangor Historical Society
Lecale Miscellany
Lisburn Historical Society Journal
North Irish Roots (Journal of the North of Ireland Family History Society), NLI Ir. 92905 n 4
Old Newry Journal
Saintfield Heritage
Seanchas Dhroim Mor (Journal of the Dromore Diocesan Historical Society), NLI Ir. 94115 s 3
Ulster Journal of Archaeology, NLI Ir. 794105 u 1

Directories
1807/8   Joseph Smith, *Belfast Directories*: Repr. as J.R.R. Adams (ed.), *Merchants in Plenty*, Belfast: UHF, 1992. NLI Ir. 914111.s.27

1811   Holden's *Annual London and country directory of the United Kingdoms & Wales, in three volumes, for ... 1811.* (3 vols. Facsimile repr. Norwich M. Winton, 1996) NLI G 942 h 23, LDS Film 258722 Item 2

1819   Thomas Bradshaw's *General directory of Newry, Armagh, and the towns of Dungannon, Portadown, Tandragee, Lurgan, Waringstown, Banbridge, Warrenpoint, Rosstrevor, Kilkeel, Rathfriland, 1820.* PRONI, NLI Ir. 91411 b 18, LDS Film 258723

1820   Joseph Smyth, *Directory of Belfast and its Vicinity*

1820   J. Pigot, *Commercial Directory of Ireland* PRONI, NLI Ir. 9141 p 107, LDS Film 962702 Item 1

1824   J. Pigot and Co., *City of Dublin and Hibernian Provincial Directory*, NLI, LDS Film 451787

1835   Matier's *Belfast Directory* PRONI, NLI Ir. 9141111 m 5, LDS Film 258724

1839   Martin, *Belfast Directory* PRONI, NLI Ir. 9141111 m 4. Also 1841, 1842

1846   Slater's *National Commercial Directory of Ireland*. PRONI, NLI LO, LDS Film 1696703 Item 3

1843–1852 Henderson's *Belfast and Province of Ulster Directory*. PRONI, NLI Dix Belfast (1852), LDS Film 908816 Item 1

1854   James A. Henderson, *Belfast and Province of Ulster Directory*. Issued also in 1854, 1856, 1858, 1861, 1863, 1865, 1868, 1870, 1877, 1880, 1884, 1887, 1890, 1894, 1900

1856   Slater, *Royal National Commercial Directory of Ireland*, NLI, LDS Film 1472360 Item 1

1865   R. Wynne, *Business Directory of Belfast*, NLI Ir. 91411 b 2

1870   Slater, *Directory of Ireland*, NLI

1881   Slater, *Royal National Commercial Directory of Ireland*, NLI

1883   Farrell, *County Armagh Directory and Almanac* (Newry)

1888   George Henry Bassett, *The Book of Antrim*. Repr. Belfast: Friar's Bush, 1989 NLI Ir. 94116 b 29 (Lisburn & Dromara)

1888   George Henry Bassett, *The Book of Armagh*, (Donaghcloney, Moira, Waringstown)

1894   Slater, *Royal Commercial Directory of Ireland*, NLI

Gravestone Inscriptions

The UHF has transcripts for 128 graveyards in Down. Heritage World has transcripts for fifty-six graveyards. These are searchable online, for a fee, at *www.historyfromheadstones.com*. Published or publicly available transcripts are given below, ordered by civil parish.

Gravestone Inscriptions, Co. Down
Vols 1–20, R.S.J. Clarke, 1966–81. NLI Ir. 9295 c 1

Annaclone: Ballydown, Pres. Vol. 20
Annahilt: Cargacreevy, Pres. Vol. 18
Cargygary (Loughaghery), Pres. Vol. 18
—— Glebe (Annahilt), C of I. Vol. 18
Ardglass: Ardglass town, C of I. Vol. 8
Ardkeen: Ardkeen, Vol. 13
—— Kirkistown, C of I. Vol. 13
—— Ballycran Beg, RC (1 inscription), Vol. 13
—— Lisbane, RC. Vol. 13
Ardquin: Ardquin, C of I. Vol. 13
Ballee: Church Ballee, C of I. Vol. 8
—— Church Ballee, Pres., (N.S.)/Unitarian. Vol. 8

Ballyculter: Ballyculter Upper, C of I. Vol. 8
—— Strangford Lower, C of I. Vol. 8
Ballykinler: Ballykinler Upper, RC. Vol. 16
—— Ballykinler Upper, RC. Vol. 9
Ballyphilip: Portaferry town (Ballyphilip), Vol. 13
—— Ballygalget, RC. Vol. 13
Ballytrustan: Ballytrustan, RC. Vol. 13
Ballywalter: Whitechurch, Vol. 15
Bangor: Castle Park, Bangor, 1 inscription. Vol. 17
—— Conlig town, Pres. Vol. 17
—— Groomsport, Pres. Vol. 17
—— Groomsport, C of I. Vol. 17
—— Ballyleidy (Clandeboye House), Family graveyard. Vol. 17
—— Bangor Church, C of I, interior. Vol. 17
—— Bangor Abbey, Vol. 17
—— Ballygilbert Church, Pres. (1 inscription). Vol. 17
—— Copeland Island, Vol. 16
—— Bangor, Pres. (1st). Vol. 17
Blaris: Maze, Pres. Vol. 18
—— Blaris, Vol. 5
—— Eglantine, C of I. Vol. 18
—— Eglantine, C of I. Vol. 18
Bright: Bright, C of I /Mixed. Vol. 8
Castleboy: Cloghy/Clough, Pres. Vol. 14
Comber: Comber, The Square, C of I. Vol. 5
—— Gransha, Pres. Vol. 1
—— Moneyreagh, Pres. N.S. (Unitarian). Vol. 1
Donaghadee: Templepatrick, Vol. 14
—— Ballymacruise (Millisle), Pres. Vol. 16
—— Ballycopeland, Pres. Vol. 16
—— Donaghadee, Church Lane, C of I. Vol. 16
—— Ballyrawer, C of I. Vol. 14
Donaghcloney: Donaghcloney, Vol. 19
—— Waringstown town, C of I. Vol. 19
Down: Downpatrick, Church Lane, C of I. Vol. 7
—— Downpatrick, Fountain Street, Pres. Vol. 7
—— Downpatrick, Stream Street, RC. Vol. 7
—— Downpatrick, Stream Street, Unitarian (N.S. Pres.). Vol. 7
—— Downpatrick, English Street, C of I. Vol. 7
Dromara: Finnis, RC. Vol. 19.
—— Drumgavlin, Magherahamlet, Vol. 9
—— Dromara, C of I. Vol. 19
—— Drumgavlin, Magherahamlet Pres. Vol. 9
Dromore: Dromore, Church Street, C of I. Vol. 19

—— Drumlough, Vol. 19

Drumbeg: Drennan, Pres. (Baileysmill). Vol. 2

—— Drumbeg, C of I. Vol. 3

Drumbo: Ballycarn, Pres. Vol. 1

Knockbreckan, Pres. (reformed). Vol. 1

—— Edenderry House, Dunlop family. Vol. 3

—— Carrickmaddyroe, Pres. Vol. 2

—— Drumbo, Pres. Vol. 4

—— Carryduff, Pres. Vol. 1

—— Ballelessan, C of I. Vol. 1

—— Legacurry, Pres. Vol. 2

—— Ballelessan, C of I. Vol. 18

—— Carryduff, Pres. Vol. 18

Dundonald: Dundonald town, C of I. Vol. 2

Dunsfort: Dunsfort, C of I. Vol. 8

—— Dunsfort, St Mary's, RC. Vol. 8

Garvaghy: Fedany (Garvaghy?), C of I. Vol. 19

—— Kilkinamurry, Pres. Vol. 19

—— Ballooly, Vol. 19

Greyabbey: Rosemount, Grey Abbey grounds and graveyard. Vol. 12

Hillsborough: Hillsborough, Main Street, C of I. Vol. 18

—— Ballykeel Edenagonnell (Annahilt), Pres. Vol. 18

—— Corcreeny, Moravian. Vol. 18

—— Corcreeny, C of I. Vol. 19

—— Hillsborough, Park Street, Quaker. Vol. 18

—— Reillys Trench, RC. Vol. 18

—— Corcreeny, C of I. Vol. 18

Holywood: Holywood, Old Church Lane, Priory?. Vol. 4

Inch: Inch, C of I. Vol. 7

Inishargy: Balliggan, C of I. Vol. 14

—— Kircubbin, Pres. Vol. 12

—— Inishargy, Old. Vol. 14

Kilclief: Kilclief, C of I. Vol. 8

—— Kilclief, St Malachy's, RC. Vol. 8

Kilkeel: Kilkeel, Bridge Street, Vol. 10

—— Mourne Abbey, 1 inscription only. Vol. 10

—— Glasdrumman, RC. Vol. 10

—— Moneydorragh More, C of I (Kilhorne). Vol. 10

—— Kilkeel, Newry Street, C of I. Vol. 10

Kilkeel, Greencastle Street, Pres. (Mourne). Vol. 10

—— Ballymartin, RC. Vol. 10

—— Ballymageogh, RC. Vol. 10

—— Kilkeel, Newcastle Street, Moravian. Vol. 10

Killaney: Carrickmaddyroe, Pres. (Boardmills). Vol. 2

—— Killaney, C of I. Vol. 2
Killinchy: Ballygowan (Killinchy?), Pres. Vol. 5
—— Killinakin, 2 inscriptions only. Vol. 6
—— Ballymacashen, Pres. (reformed). Vol. 6
—— Ravara, Unitarian. Vol. 5
—— Killinchy, C of I. Vol. 5
—— Balloo, Pres. Vol. 6
—— Drumreagh (Kilcarn?), RC. Vol. 5
Killyleagh: Killyleagh, Church Hill Street, C of I. Vol. 6
—— Killyleagh, The Plantation, Pres. Vol. 7
—— Toy and Kirkland, Killaresy graveyard. Vol. 6
—— Killyleagh Old, Vol. 6
—— Tullymacnous, 1 inscription. Vol. 6
Kilmegan: Moneylane (Kilmegan?), C of I. Vol. 9
—— Aghalasnafin, RC. Vol. 9
Kilmood: Kilmood and Ballybunden, C of I. Vol. 5
—— Ballyministragh, Pres. Vol. 5
Kilmore: Barmaghery, 1 inscription only. Vol. 1
—— Carnacully (Kilmore?), C of I. Vol. 3
—— Drumaghlis, Pres. (Kilmore). Vol. 3
—— Rademan, Pres. N.S. (Unitarian). Vol. 3
Lambeg: Lisnatrunk, Pres. (Hillhall). Vol. 1
Loughinisland: Tievenadarragh, Mixed. Vol. 9
—— Seaforde town, C of I. Vol. 9
—— Clough town, Pres. Vol. 9
—— Clough town, Unitarian. Vol. 9
—— Drumaroad, RC. Vol. 9
Magheradrool: Ballynahinch, C of I. Vol. 9
—— Ballynahinch, Windmill Street, Pres. Vol. 9
—— Ballynahinch, Dromore Street, Pres. Vol. 9
Magheralin: Ballymakeonan (Magheralin?), Vol. 19
Magherally: Magherally, C of I. Vol. 20
—— Magherally, Pres. Vol. 20
Moira: Moira (Clare). Vol. 18
—— Moira, Pres. (N.S.). Vol. 18
—— Lurganville, RC. Vol. 18
—— Moira, Pres. Vol. 18
Newtownards: Ballyblack, Pres. Vol. 12
—— Milecross, RC (Killysuggan). Vol. 5
—— Movilla, Vol. 11
—— Newtownards Chuch interior, C of I. Vol. 11
—— Newtownards Priory, Vol. 11
Rathmullan: Rathmulland Upper, C of I. Vol. 9
—— Rossglass, RC. Vol. 8

—— Killough, Palatine Square, C of I. Vol. 8
Saintfield: Saintfield town, Pres. Vol. 3
—— Saintfield town, C of I. Vol. 3
—— Saintfield, Cow Market, Pres. Vol. 3
Saul: Saul, C of I. Vol. 7
—— Ballysugagh (Saul?), RC. Vol. 8
Seapatrick: Banbridge, Scarva Street, Vol. 20
—— Kilpike (Seapatrick?), Vol. 20
Slanes: Slanes, Vol. 14
St Andrews alias Ballyhalbert:
Ballyesborough, C of I. Vol. 15
—— Ballyhemlin, Pres. (N.S.)/Unitarian. Vol. 14
—— Ballyhalbert, Vol. 15
—— Glastry, Pres. Vol. 15
Tullylish: Tullylish, C of I. Vol. 20
—— Moyallon, Quaker. Vol. 20
—— Laurencetown, Vol. 20
—— Clare, Vol. 19
Tullynakill: Tullynakill, C of I. Vol. 1

Estate Records
Anglesea: Tenants on the Anglesea estate, 1856, JCLAHS, 12 (2), 1950, 151–3, Covering areas in the civil parish of Newry.
Annesley, Earls: Rentals, 1650–1950 PRONI D/1503. Covering townlands in the civil parishes of: Clonduff; Drumballyroney; Drumgooland; Kilcoo; Kilmegan. May cover further parishes.
Chichester Fortescue: Rental, 1817–1817, NAI, M3610. Covering areas in the civil parishes of: Donaghcloney; Magherally; Seapatrick; Donaghadee.
Kilmorey: Rental, 1816 PRONI D/2638. Covering townlands in the civil parishes of: Kilkeel; Magheralin; Newry. May cover further parishes.
Londonderry, Marquis of: PRONI D/654. Rentals, 1750–1940. Covering townlands in the civil parishes of: Ballee; Ballywalter; Comber; Greyabbey; Newtownards. May cover further parishes.

DUBLIN

Census returns and substitutes
1568   Herald's Visitation of Dublin. GO 46. Also NLI Pos. 957
1607–1610 Herald's Visitation of Dublin city & county. GO 48. NLI Pos. 957
1621   St John's parish Cess lists. Also for years 1640, 1687. JPRS, Appendix to Vol. 1, 1906. LDS Film 82407
1634   Book of Survey and Distribution. NLI Ms. 964
1652   Inhabitants of the baronies of Newcastle & Uppercross NAI M.2467
1654–1656 Civil Survey. *Civil Survey*, Vol. VII

1659   Pender's 'Census'. Repr. GPC, 1997, IMC, 2002. LDS Film 924648

1663–1668 Subsidy roll for Co. Dublin NAI M.2468

1664   Persons with six hearths or upwards, Dublin city, RDKPRI, No. 57 p. 560

1667–1810 Assessments for the parish of St Bride's. TCD M.2063.

1680–1686 Index only to an applotment book for Dublin City. NAI M.4979

1680   Pipe water accounts. IG, 1987. Also 1703–4, IG 1994

1684   List of those eligible for jury service IG 8, No. 1 1990 49–57

1711–1835 Annual Cess Applotment books of St Michan's parish. RCBL

1730–1740 Index to marriages and deaths in 'Pue's Occurrences' and 'The Dublin Gazette'. NLI Ms. 3197

1756   Inhabitants of St Michael's parish. *The Irish Builder*, Vol. 33, pp170/1

1761   Dublin city voting freemen and freeholders NLI I 6511 Dubl.

1766   Crumlin. RCBL. Also in GO 537; Castleknock RCBL Ms. 37; Taney NAI M.2478, LDS Film 258517

1767   Freeholders. NAI M.4910–2

1778–1782 Catholic Merchants, Traders & Manufacturers of Dublin. *Reportorium Novum*, 2(2), 1960, p. 298 323

1791–1831 Register of children at Baggot St school. (Incorporated Soc. for Promoting Protestant Schools). NLI Pos. 2884

1791–1957 Register of Admissions to Pleasant's Female Orphan Asylum, including places of birth and families. NLI Ms. 1555. See also Mss. 1556 & 1558

1793–1810 Census of Protestants in Castleknock. GO 495. LDS Film 100225

1798   Persons who suffered losses in the 1798 rebellion. Propertied classes only. c.100 names. NLI I 94107.

1798–1831 Register of children at Santry school. (Incorporated Soc. for Promoting Protestant Schools). NLI Pos. 2884

1800–1816 Card index to biographical notices in Faulkner's *Dublin Journal.* NLI

1805–1839 Register of children at Kevin St school. (Incorporated Soc. for Promoting Protestant Schools). NLI Pos. 2884

1806   Voters' Lists, by occupation. NLI Ir. 94133 d 13

1807   Board of Works tradesmen's names and occupations, Dublin city, DLGSJ 4 (2) 1995

1820   Freemen voters. NLI P 734

1821   Some extracts. NAI Thrift Abstracts

1823–1838 Tithe Books

1826   Labourers' accounts May–June 1826. c.300 names. NAI OP 727 1–199. Relief tickets June–Sept. 1826. NAI OP 726. Almost all weavers from the Liberties. See Magee *Weavers* (1993)

1830   Freeholders. NLI Ms. 11,847

1831   Householders in St Bride's parish. NLI P. 1994

1834–1835 Returns of those liable for paving tax. Inquiry into the impeachment of Alderman Richard Smith (formerly in State Paper Office). NAI

1835   Alphabetical list of voters with addresses and occupations. NLI Ir. 94133 d 12

1835–1837   Dublin county freeholders & leaseholders. NLI Ms. 9363
1837   Memorial from Balbriggan for General Sessions (c.300 names) NAI OP
            1837/413 c
1840–1938   Admissions and Discharge registers for Dublin city workhouses
            (North and South Unions). NAI
1841   Some extracts. NAI Thrift Abstracts
1843   Voters. NAI 1843/52
1844–1850   Householders, St Peter's parish. RCBL P45/15/1, 2
1848–1851   Griffith's Valuation. Indexed online: Hayes
1848–1849   Smith O'Brien Petition ENE #CD2. More than 40,000 names for
            Dublin
1851   Index only to heads of households, by street and parish. NAI Cen
            1851/18/1; ENE #CD3, Online: Origins
1864   City of Dublin Voters List, by district and street. NLI Ir. 94133 d 16
1865–1866   Voters. NLI Ir. 94133 d 15
1878   Voters, South Dock Ward only. NLI ILB 324 d
1901   Census. See Keogh *Indexes* for Dublin suburbs
1911   Census

Online

Hayes, John	*www.failteromhat.com*	
Finlay, Ken	*www.chapters.eiretek.org*	Many Dublin histories
Loughman, Trish	*www.loughman.dna.ie*	
Origins	*www.originsnetwork.com*	
Uphill, Christine	*freepages.genealogy.rootsweb.* *com/~chrisu*	Howth

Publications

Local histories, etc.

St Peter's *Parochial Male & Female Boarding Schools, Sunday, Daily & Infant*
   Schools: Reports 1850–60, NLI, p. 439

Aalen, F.H., *Dublin city and county: From prehistory to present*, Dublin: Geography
   Publications, 1992, NLI Ir. 94133 d 48. Co-editor, Kevin Whelan 450 p.

Adams, B.N., *History and Description of Santry and Cloghran Parishes*, London:
   Mitchell and Hughes, 1883 NLI Ir. 94133 a 1. 144 p.

Appleyard, D.S., *Green Fields Gone Forever*, Coolock: Coolock Select Vestry, 1985.
   NLI Ir. 94133 a 5, 214 p. Coolock & Artane area

Ball, F.E., *A history of the county of Dublin, Vol 1–6*, Dublin: 1902–20. NLI Ir. 94133
   b 1. Online: Finlay
      1. Monkstown, Kill-o'-the Grange, Dalkey, Killiney, Tully, Stillorgan,
          Kilmacud.
      2. Donnybrook, Booterstown, St Bartholemew, St Mark, Taney, St Peter,
          Rathfarnham.

3. Tallaght, Cruagh, Whitechurch, Kilgobbin, Kiltiernan, Rathmichael, Old Connaught, Saggart, Rathcoole, Newcastle.
4. Clonsilla, Leixlip, Lucan, Aderrig, Kilmactalway, Kilbride, KIlmahuddrick, Esker, Palmerstown, Ballyfermot, Clondalkin, Drimnagh, Crumlin, St Catherine, St Nicholas Without, St James, St Jude, Chapelizod.
5. Howth.
6. Castleknock, Mulhuddert, Cloghran, Ward, St Margaret's, Finglas, Glasnevin, Grangegorman, St George, Clonturk.

Ball, F.E., *The Parish of Taney,* Dublin: 1895, NLI Ir. 94133 b 2. 256 p.

Black, A. & C., *Guide to Dublin & Co. Wicklow,* 1888

Blacker, Rev. Beaver H., *Sketches of the Parishes of Booterstown and Donnybrook,* Dublin: 1860–74 NLI Ir. 94133 b 6. 488 p.

Byrne, Joseph, *War and peace the survival of the Talbots of Malahide 1641–1671,* Dublin: Irish Academic Press, 1997, NLI Ir. 94133 b 17, 76 p.

Cantwell, Brian, *Memorials of the Dead, North-East Wicklow (1),* Dublin: Typescript, 1974, NLI Ir. 9295 c 2, Master Index Vol. 10

Cantwell, Brian, *Memorials of the Dead: South Dublin,* Dublin: 1990, DCLA

Carroll, Frieda, *Booterstown, Co. Dublin, Ireland school registers 1861–1872 & 1891–1939,* Dun Laoghaire: Dun Laoghaire Genealogical Society, 1998, NLI Ir. 9291 g 7

Clare, Liam, *Enclosing the commons: Dalkey, the Sugar Loaves and Bray, 1820–1870,* Dublin: Four Courts, 2004, NLI, 64 p.

Clark, Mary, 'Sources for Genealogical Research in Dublin Corporation Archives', IG, 1987

Clarke, H.B., *Irish Historic Towns Atlas 11: Dublin, part 1 to 1610,* Dublin: Royal Irish Academy, 2002, NLI

Collins, Sinead, *Balrothery Poor Law Union, County Dublin, 1839–51,* Dublin: Four Courts, 2005, NLI, 64 p.

Connell, Carmel, *Glasnevin Cemetery, Dublin, 1832–1900,* Dublin: Four Courts, 2004, NLI, 72 p.

Costello, Peter, *Dublin Churches,* Dublin: 1989, NLI Ir. 720 c 23

Craig, Maurice, *Dublin 1660–1800,* Dublin: 1952

Crawford, John, *St Catherine's Parish Dublin 1840–1900 portrait of a Church of Ireland community,* Blackrock, Co. Dublin: Irish Academic Press, 1996, NLI Ir. 27413 c 11, 57 p.

Cronin, Elizabeth, *Fr Michael Dungan's Blanchardstown, 1836–68,* Dublin: Four Courts, 2002, NLI, 64 p.

Cullen, L.N., *Princes and Pirates: the Dublin Chamber of Commerce 1783– 1983,* NLI Ir. 94133 c 17

Donnelly, N., *State of RC Chapels in Dublin 1749,* NLI, I 2820941 p 10

Donnelly, N., *Series of short histories of Dublin parishes,* NLI Ir. 27413 d 1

Doolin, W., *Dublin's surgeon-anatomists and other essays: a centenary tribute,* Dublin: Dept. of History of Medicine, RCSI, 1987, NLI Ir. 610 d 8, 232 p.

Dublin Public Libraries, *Dublin in Books: A reading list from the stock of Dublin Public Libraries,* Dublin: 1982, 22 p. NLI Ir. 941 p 127(1)

Egan, Michael E., *Memorials of the Dead: Dublin City and County Vols. 1–10*, Dublin: (Typescript), 1992–2004, NLI/NAI/DCLA

Fingal Heritage Group, 'Rest in Peace', St Colmcille's, Swords, Dublin: 1989, NLI Ir. 9295 p 1(3)

Fingal Heritage Group, 'In Fond Remembrance': Headstone Inscriptions No. 2, St. Columba's Graveyard, Dublin: 1990, NLI Ir. 9295 p 1(2), 24 p.

Gilbert Library, *Dublin and Irish Collections*, Dublin, NLI Ir. 02 p 50

Gilbert, Sir John T., *A History of the City of Dublin*, Dublin, 1885–9. 3 vols. NLI Ir. 94133 g 3

Goodbody, Rob, *Sir Charles Domvile and the management of his Shankill estate, Co. Dublin, 1857–68*, Dublin: Four Courts, 2003, NLI, 64 p.

Guilfoyle, Eithne, *Harold (Boys) School, Glasthule, county Dublin: registers, 1904–1948*, Dun Laoghaire: Dun Laoghaire Genealogical Society, 1998, NLI Ir. 9291 g 7, 145 p.

Harris, Walter, *The History and Antiquities of the city of Dublin:* Dublin: 1776 Online: Finlay

Harrison, W., *Dublin Houses/ or Memorable Dublin Houses*, Dublin: 1890, NLI Ir. 94133 h 5

Hughes, Anne, *Ardgillan Castle and the Taylor family*, Balbriggan: Ardgillan Castle, 1995, NLI Ir. 94133 a 8, 65 p. Edited by Rory Keane, Anne Hughes, Ronan Swan

Kelly, James, *The Liberty and Ormond Boys: factional riots in eighteenth-century Dublin*, Dublin: Four Courts, 2005, NLI, 64 p.

Keogh, Marie, *Dublin City 1901 census indexes*, Dun Laoghaire: Genealogical Society of Ireland, 1998–2002, NLI Ir. 9291 g 7. Irish genealogical sources series No. 5 (North Strand, Summerhill and Clonliffe); No. 22 (Blackrock Urban District); No. 28 (Howth, Sutton, Kilbarrack and Baldoyle)

Kingston, Rev. John, *The Parish of Fairview*, Dundalk: Dundalgan Press, 1953, 'Including the present parishes of Corpus Christi, Glasnevin, Larkhill, Marino, and Donnycarney'. NLI Ir. 94133 k 2, 121 p.

Le Fanu, T.P., *The Huguenot Churches of Dublin and their Ministries*, 1905, NLI, p. 2274

Leeper, A., *Historical handbook to the monuments, inscriptions, &c., of the collegiate, national & cathedral church of St. Patrick, Dublin*, Dublin: Hodges, Foster, & Figgis 1878. NLI Ir. 7266 L 11, 74 p.

MacGiolla Phadraig, Brian, *History of Terenure*, Dublin: 1954

MacSorley, Catherine M., *The Story of Our Parish: St Peter's Dublin*, Dublin: 1917 NLI P 1173(10)

Magee, Sean, *Weavers of Prosperous, County Kildare, Balbriggan, County Dublin & Tullamore, County Offaly in memorials of 1826*, Dublin: Dun Laoghaire Genealogical Society, 1998, NLI Ir. 9291 g 7

Magee, Seán, *Dublin street index 1798 extracted from Whitelaw's census*, Dun Laoghaire: Dun Laoghaire Genealogical Society, 1998, NLI Ir. 9291 g 7, 47 p.

Magee, Seán, *Weavers and related trades in Dublin 1826*, Dublin: Dun Laoghaire Genealogical Society, 1993, NLI Ir. 9292, Includes 'Labourers on Account' (1522 names) and 'List of Food Recipients on Account'

Maxwell, Constantia, *Dublin under the Georges, 1714–1830*, London: 1956, NLI Ir. 94133 h 5

McCready, C.T., *Dublin street names, dated and explained*, Dublin: 1892, NLI Ir. 92941 m 1 (& L.O.), including bibliography

McDonnell, Annette, *Petitioners against closure of Kill O' The Grange cemetery, County Dublin 1864*, Dun Laoghaire: Dun Laoghaire Genealogical Society, 1998, NLI Ir. 9291 g 7, 134 p.

Monks, W., *Lusk, a Short History*, Lusk: Old Fingal Society, 1978 8 p. NLI Ir. 9141 p 85

Mulhall, Mary, *A History of Lucan*, Lucan: 1991

Murphy, Sean, *Memorial Inscriptions from St. Catherine's Church and Graveyard*, Dublin: Divellina, 1987, NLI

Murphy, Sean, *Bully's Acre and Royal Hospital Kilmainham graveyards: history and inscriptions*, Dublin: Divellina, 1989, NLI Ir. 9295 p 2(2), 48 p.

Ó Maitiú, Séamas, *The humours of Donnybrook Dublin's famous fair and its suppression*, Blackrock, Co. Dublin: Irish Academic Press, 1995, NLI Ir. 94133 o 19, 56 p.

O'Connor, Barry, *Memorial inscriptions of Dun Laoghaire-Rathdown, Co. Dublin, Ireland Vol. 1*, Dun Laoghaire: Genealogical Society of Ireland, 2000, NLI Ir. 9295 m 7. Co-compiler, Brian Smith

O'Driscoll, J., *Cnucha: a history of Castleknock & district*, NLI Ir. 94133 o 9

O'Sullivan, Peter, *Newcastle Lyons, A Parish of the Pale*, Dublin: Geography Publications, 1986, NLI Ir. 941233 o 13, 139 p.

Parkinson, Danny, *Huguenot Cemetery 1693*, Dublin: Dublin Family History Society, 1988, NLI Ir. 941 p 105 (4), 49 p.

Refaussé, Raymond, *Directory of historic Dublin guilds*, Dublin: Dublin Public Libraries, 1993, NLI Ir. 94133 d 40, 65 p. Co-author, Mary Clark

Rosenblatt, Stuart, *Irish Jewish museum Dublin 1992: 12,300 listings*, Dublin: the author, 2004, NLI, 341 p.

Shepherd, W.E., *Behind the Scenes: the story of Whitechurch district*, Dublin: Whitechurch Publications, 1983. 80 p. NLI Ir. 94133 s 8

Smith, Charles V., *Dalkey society and economy in a small medieval Irish town*, Blackrock, Co. Dublin: Irish Academic Press, 1996, NLI Ir. 94133 s 15, 63 p.

Stephen's Green Club, *List of members, 1882*, 1882, NLI Ir. 367 s 12

TCD, *Alphabetical list of the constituency of the University of Dublin*, Dublin: 1865, NLI Ir. 37841 t 2 & 1832: JP 1375. Also LO

Twomey, Brendan, *Smithfield and the parish of St Paul, Dublin, 1698–1750*, Dublin: Four Courts, 2005, NLI, 64 p.

Tyrrell, J.H., *Genealogical History of the Tyrrells of Castleknock in Co. Dublin, Fertullagh in Co. Westmeath and now of Grange Castle, Co. Meath*, 1904, NLI Ir. 9292 t 6, 202 p.

Warburton, John, *History of the City of Dublin*, London: 1818. Co-authors, James Whitlow, Robert Walsh. 2 vols. NLI Ir. 94133 w 2

Local Journals
Dublin Historical Record (Journal of the Old Dublin Society), NLI Ir. 94133 d 23
Genealogical Society of Ireland Journal, NLI Ir. 9292 d 20
Reportorium Novum: Dublin diocesan historical record, NLI Ir. 27413 r 3
Dublin Historical Record (Journal of the Old Dublin Society), NLI Ir. 94133 d 23

Directories

1738	Dublin Corporation Public Libraries, *A directory of Dublin for the year 1738: compiled from the most authentic sources* (Dublin, 2000) NLI Ir. 94133 d 63
1751	Peter Wilson, *An Alphabetical List of Names and Places of Abode of the Merchants and Traders of the City of Dublin* (annual to 1837) NLI LO.85, DCLA
1820	J. Pigot, *Commercial Directory of Ireland* PRONI, NLI Ir. 9141 p 107, LDS Film 962702 Item 1
1824	J. Pigot and Co., *City of Dublin and Hibernian Provincial Directory*, NLI, LDS Film 451787
1834	Pettigrew and Oulton, *Dublin Almanack and General Register of Ireland*, NLI 1824. Online: Hayes
1844	Alexander Thom, *Irish Almanack and Official Directory*, NLI LDS (various years), DCLA (complete)
1846	Slater's *National Commercial Directory of Ireland*. PRONI, NLI LO, LDS Film 1696703 Item 3
1850	Henry Shaw, *New City Pictorial Directory of Dublin city*, NLI Ir. 914133 n 1. Online: Loughman
1856	Slater, *Royal National Commercial Directory of Ireland*, NLI, LDS Film 1472360 Item 1
1870	Slater, *Directory of Ireland*, NLI
1881	Slater, *Royal National Commercial Directory of Ireland*, NLI
1894	Slater, *Royal Commercial Directory of Ireland*, NLI

Gravestone Inscriptions
MDDCC = *Memorials of the Dead: Dublin City and County, Volumes 1–10* (Dublin 1988–2004), compiled and edited by Dr Michael T.S. Egan. NAI open shelves, NLI, DCLA
MDSD = *Memorials of the Dead: South Dublin* (Dublin, 1990) compiled and edited by Brian Cantwell. NAI open shelves, NLI, DCLA

Dublin County
Aderrig: MDSD, MDDCC Vol. 9
Baldongan: MDDCC Vol. 9
Baldoyle: Grange, MDDCC Vol. 4. Also IGRS Collection (3 entries), GO,
Ballyboghil: MDDCC Vol. 6
Ballymadun: MDDCC Vol. 5

Balrothery: Balbriggan, George's Street, C of I, MDDCC Vol. 6
—— Balrothery town, C of I, MDDCC Vol. 6
—— Bremore, MDDCC Vol. 6
—— Balrothery Union, MDDCC Vol. 6
Balscaddan: Tobertown (Balscaddan Old), MDDCC Vol. 6
—— Balscaddan New, MDDCC Vol. 6
Booterstown: Church interior, RC, MDSD
Castleknock: Abbotstown, MDDCC Vol. 3. Also IGRS Collection (29 entries), and GO
    622, p.82
Chapelizod: C of I, IG, Vol. 5, No. 4, 1977
Cloghran: C of I. *Santry and Cloghran,* Adams
—— Cloghran-hidart, MDDCC Vol. 4
—— Cloghran, MDDCC Vol. 4
Clondalkin: Mount St Joseph, MDDCC Vol. 2
Clonmethan: Glebe (Clonmethan), C of I, MDDCC Vol. 5
Clonsilla: MDDCC Vol. 8
Cruagh: MDDCC Vol. 4
Crumlin: C of I, IG, Vol. 7, No. 2, 1988
—— Mount Argus interior, RC, MDSD
Dalkey: Dalkey, MDSD, also IG, Vol. 5, No. 2, 1975
Deansgrange. *Memorial Inscriptions of Deansgrange Cemetery, Blackrock, Co.*
    Dublin, Dun Laoghaire Genealogical Society, 1993. NLI Ir. 9295 d
Donabate: Kilcrea, MDSD, MDDCC Vol. 8
—— Donabate: MDDCC Vol. 8
Donnybrook: Irishtown (St Mathew's), C of I, MDDCC Vol. 2
—— Merrion, MDDCC Vol. 2
—— St Bartholomew's interior, C of I, MDSD
—— Church of the Sacred Heart interior, RC, MDSD
—— Sandymount: Star of the Sea, RC interior, MDSD
Drimnagh: Bluebell, MDDCC Vol. 3
Garristown: Garristown, C of I, MDDCC Vol. 5
Grallagh: Grallagh, MDDCC Vol. 5
Hollywood: Hollywood Great, MDDCC Vol. 5
—— Damastown, MDDCC Vol. 5
Holmpatrick: Skerries, South Strand Street: MDDCC Vol. 7
Kilbride: Kilbride, IG, Vol. 6, No. 3, 1982
—— Kilbride, MDDCC Vol. 2
Kilgobbin: Kilgobbin, MDDCC Vol. 2
—— Kilgobbin New, MDDCC Vol. 3
Kill: Kill of the Grange, IG, Vol. 4, No. 5, 1972
Killeek: Killeek, MDDCC Vol. 5
Killiney: Killiney, IG, Vol. 4, No. 6, 1973
—— Killiney, MDSD
—— Ballybrack, RC interior, MDSD

Killossery: MDDCC Vol. 5

Kilmactalway: MDDCC Vol. 2

—— IG, Vol. 6, No. 3, 1982

—— Loughtown Lower, MDDCC Vol. 2

Kilmahuddrick: Kilmahuddrick, MDDCC Vol. 2

Kilsallaghan: Castlefarm (Kilsallaghan), C of I, MDDCC Vol. 4

—— Corrstown (Chapelmidway), MDDCC Vol. 5

Kiltiernan: Kiltiernan, MDDCC Vol. 2, also MDSD, & O'Connor *Memorial Inscriptions*

—— Glencullen, RC, MDSD

Lucan: Lucan and Pettycannon (St Mary's), RC, MDDCC Vol. 2. Also *IG*, Vol. 5, No. 6, 1976

Lusk: Whitestown: MDDCC Vol. 8

—— Lusk town (RC): MDDCC Vol. 8

—— Lusk town (C of I): MDDCC Vol. 8

Monkstown: York Road interior, Presbyterian, MDSD

—— St Paul's Glenageary, C of I interior, MDSD

—— Northumberland Avenue interior, Methodist, MDSD

—— Mariner's Church interior, C of I, MDSD

—— Christ Church Kingstown interior, C of I, MDSD

—— Monkstown, *IG*, Vol. 4, Nos 3, 4, 1970/1

—— Monkstown interior, C of I, MDSD

Mulhuddart: Buzzardstown (Mulhuddart), MDDCC Vol. 4, Also GO Ms. 622 p. 96

Naul: C of I, MDDCC Vol. 5

Newcastle: Colmanstown, MDDCC Vol. 3

—— Glebe, C of I, MDDCC Vol. 2

—— Esker, Old, MDDCC Vol. 2

—— Newcastle, RC, MDDCC Vol. 2

Oldconnaught: St James' interior, C of I, MDSD

—— Little Bray, RC, IGRS Collection (54 inscriptions), GO

—— Little Bray, RC, *Memorials of the Dead, North-East Wicklow* (1)

—— Oldconnaught, MDSD, & O'Connor *Memorial Inscriptions*

Palmerstown: Palmerstown (Oldtown), *IG*, Vol. 5, No. 8, 1978

—— Palmerstown (Oldtown), MDDCC Vol. 4

Portmarnock: Burrow: MDDCC Vol. 10

—— Portmarnock (C of I): MDDCC Vol. 7

Rathcoole: Rathcoole, C of I, MDDCC Vol. 2

—— Rathcoole, C of I, *IG*, Vol. 6, No. 4, 1983

Rathfarnham: Rathfarnham, *IG*, 1987

—— Rathfarnham interior, RC, MDSD

Rathmichael: Rathmichael interior, C of I, MDSD

—— Rathmichael: O'Connor *Memorial Inscriptions*

Saggart: Newtown Upper, MDDCC Vol. 3

—— Saggart New, MDDCC Vol. 3

Santry: Adams *[…] Santry and Cloghran*
St Peter's: Adelaide Road, Presbyterian, MDSD
—— Rathmines interior, RC, MDSD
Stillorgan: Stillorgan South, C of I, MDSD
Swords: Swords Glebe. C of I. Fingal Heritage "*In Fond Remembrance*"
Swords: Swords, St Colmcille's RC. Fingal Heritage "*Rest in Peace*"
Tallaght: Templeogue, MDDCC Vol. 2
—— Tallaght, C of I, *IG*, Vol. 4, No. 1, 1968
Taney: Dundrum, Churchtown Road. Ball *Taney*
—— Dundrum interior, RC, MDSD
Tully: Laughanstown, O'Connor *Memorial Inscriptions*
—— Laughanstown, MDSD
Ward: Ward Lower, MDDCC Vol. 4
Westpalstown: Westpalstown, MDDCC Vol. 5
Whitechurch: Whitechurch New, MDDCC Vol. 4
—— Whitechurch, MDDCC Vol. 3, also *IG*, 1990

Dublin City
St Andrew's: St Andrew's Street, C of I, MDSD
—— St Andrew's (Coffin plates), *IG*, Vol. 5, No. 1, 1974
St Anne's: Dawson Street, C of I, MDSD
St Bride's: Peter Street, French Protestant, MDSD
St Catherine's: Thomas Street, C of I. Murphy *Memorial Inscriptions*
St James': Military Road, Murphy *Bully's Acre*
—— Goldenbridge North, MDDCC Vol. 1
—— Royal Hospital, Murphy *Bully's Acre*
—— James' Street, C of I, Open shelves, NAI
St John's: SS Michael's & John's RC (coffin plates), *IG*, Vol. 5, No. 3, 1976
St Michael's: Merchant's Quay interior, RC, MDSD
St Nicholas Without: St Nicholas interior, RC, MDSD
—— St Patrick's Cathedral, Leeper, *Historical Handbook*
St Paul's: St Paul's, C of I, *JRSAI*, Vol. 104, 1974. Also IGRS Collection (6 inscriptions), GO
St Peter's: Harrington Street interior, RC, MDSD
—— Kevin Street Lower, C of I, MDSD
—— Merrion Row, French Protestant, MDDCC Vol. 2, & Parkinson *Huguenot Cemetery 1693*

FERMANAGH

Census returns and substitutes

1612–1613   'Survey of Undertakers Planted in Co. Fermanagh', *Historical Manuscripts Commission Report*, No. 4, (Hastings Mss), 1947 pp 159–82
1630   Muster Roll of Ulster; Armagh Co. Library and PRONI D.1759/3C/1; T/934; NLI Pos. 206

1630–1800	C of I Marriage Licence Bonds, Diocese of Clogher Online: Ulsterancestry
1631	Muster Roll. Trimble, *History of Enniskillen*, Online: Ulsterancestry
1659	Pender's 'Census'. Repr. GPC, 1997, IMC, 2002. LDS Film 924648
1660	Poll Tax Returns PRONI MIC/15A/80
1661	Books of Survey and Distribution. PRONI T.370/B & D.1854/1/20
1662	Subsidy roll, Enniskillen town NLI Ms. 9583. Also PRONI T.808/15068
1665–1666	Hearth Money Roll. NLI Ms. 9583 and PRONI T.808/15066 Lurg barony, *Clogher Record*, 1957
1747	Poll Book (votes cast). PRONI T.808/15063. Online: Freeholders
1766	Boho, Derryvullen, Devenish, Kinawley, Rossory. NAI 2476d
1770	Freeholders. NLI Ms. 787 8. Also GO 443
1785	Male Protestants aged over 17—Magheracloone, Errigal Trough & Trory, LDS Film 258517
1788	Poll Book (votes cast). PRONI T.808/15075, T.543, T.1385; LDS Films 100181, 1279356. Online: Freeholders
1794–1799	Militia Pay Lists and Muster Rolls. PRONI T.1115/5A–C
1796	Spinning-Wheel Premium List. 2,500 names for Co. Fermanagh. Online: Hayes
1796–1802	Freeholders. PRONI D.1096/90. Online: Freeholders
1797	Yeomanry Muster Rolls. PRONI T.1021/3
1821	Parishes of Derryvullan and Aghalurcher (part only); NAI & PRONI. Online: Fermanagh Genweb
1823–1838	Tithe Books
1832	Enniskillen registered voters. *Parliamentary Papers 1837, Reports from Committees*, Vol. 13 (2) pp 554 7
1836	Memorials from the inhabitants of the towns of Ballyshannon, Pettigo & Bundoran (c.70 names), NAI OP 1851/79 1836
1837	Freeholders. *Parliamentary Papers 1837, Reports from Committees*, Vol. 11 (1) pp (39) 7 21
1841	Certified copies of census returns for use in claims for old age pensions. NAI & PRONI; LDS Film 258357
1842	Voters NAI OP 1842/114
1845	Workhouse records, Irvinestown (1845–1918) and Enniskillen (1845–1913). PRONI. Also LDS Films 259187–90 and 25914–53, respectively
1846	Voters NAI OP 1846/145
1851	Clonee townland only. NAI CEN 1851/13/1
1851–1852	Galloon parish. PRONI D.2098
1861	Boho parish. Protestants only c.1861. NAI T.3723
1862	Griffith's Valuation. Indexed online: Hayes
1874	Census of Devenish C of I parish. Local custody
1901	Census. Meehan, index
1911	Census
1912	The Ulster Covenant. Almost half-a-million original signatures and

addresses of those who signed. c.15,000 names for Fermanagh.
Online: Covenant

Online

Covenant	*www.proni.gov.uk/ulstercovenant*	
Fermanagh Gold	*www.fermanagh.org.uk*	Cemeteries, rentals, family histories
Fermanagh Genweb	*www.rootsweb.com/~nirfer*	
Freeholders	*www.proni.gov.uk/freeholders*	5 freeholders/voters' lists, 1747–1802
Hayes, John	*www.failteromhat.com*	
Headstones	*www.historyfromheadstones.com*	Comprehensive collection of inscriptions
Ulsterancestry	*www.ulsterancestry.com*	Assorted records

Publications

Local histories, etc.

Belmore, Earl of, *Parliamentary Memoirs of Fermanagh and Tyrone 1613 1885*, Dublin: Alex. Thom & Co., 1887, NLI Ir. 94118 b 1 368 p.

Bradshaw, W.H., *Enniskillen Long Ago; an Historic Sketch of the Parish ...*, Dublin: G. Herbert, 1878, NLI Ir. 274118 b 1, 159 p.

Day, Angelique & McWilliams, Patrick (eds.), *Ordnance Survey Memoirs of Ireland series*, Belfast: Inst. of Irish Studies/RIA, 1990–7.

> *Vol. 4: Co. Fermanagh I* (1990), Aghalurcher, Aghavea, Clones, Derrybrusk, Drummully, Enniskillen, Galloon, Kinawley, Tomregan. NLI Ir. 914111 o 13

> *Vol. 14: Co. Fermanagh II* (1992), Belleek, Boho, Cleenish, Derryvullan, Devenish, Drumkeeran, Inishmacsaint, Killesher, Magheracross, Magheraculmoney, Rossorry, Templecarn, Trory, NLI Ir. 9141 o 13

Duffy, Joseph, *A Clogher Record Album; a diocesan history*, Enniskillen: Cumann Seanchais Chlochair, 1975, NLI Ir. 94114 c 3, 340 p.

Dundas, W.H., *Enniskillen parish and town*, Dundalk: 1913, NLI Ir. 94118 d 2 197 p.

Elliott, E.G., *The parish of Devenish and Boho*, Enniskillen: Elliott, 1990, NLI Ir. 27411 e 2, 198 p.

Graham, Rev. John, *Derriana, a History of the Siege of Derry and the Defence of Enniskillen in 1688 and 1689, with Biographical Notes*, Londonderry: pr. for the author by William M'Corkell, 1823, NLI, J94112, 64 p.

King, Sir Charles (ed.), *Henry's 'Upper Lough Erne in 1739'*, Dublin: 1892, NLI Ir. 914118 h 6 95 p.

Livingstone, Peadar, *The Fermanagh story; a documented history of the County Fermanagh from the earliest times to the present day*, Enniskillen: Clogher Historical Society, 1969, NLI Ir. 94118 L 1, 570 p.

MacDonald, Brian, *Time of Desolation, Clones Poor Law Union 1845–50*, Monaghan: Clogher Historical Society, 2002, Monaghan County Library, 941.67

Maguire, Thomas, *Fermanagh: its Native Chiefs and Clans*, Omagh: S.D. Montgomery, 1954, NLI Ir. 914118 m 9

Martin, Samuel, *Historical gleanings from Co. Derry, and some from Co. Fermanagh*, Dublin: 1955, NLI Ir. 94112 m 2

McCusker, Breege, *Lowtherstown workhouse*, Irvinestown: Necarne Press, 1997, NLI, 37 p.

McKenna, J.E., *Devenish, its history, antiquities and traditions*, Dublin: Gill, 1897, NLI Ir. 914118 m 2, 134 p.

Meehan, C.P., *Fermanagh: 1901 census index*, Alberta Largy Books: 1993. NLI

Moran, T. Whitley, *The Whitleys of Enniskillen*, Hoylake: T.W. Moran, 1962, NLI, GO 343, 39 leaves

O'Connell, Philip, *The Diocese of Kilmore: its History and Antiquities*, Dublin: Browne and Nolan, 1937, NLI Ir. 274119 o 3, 579 p.

Parke, W.K., *The parish of Inishmacsaint*, Fermanagh: Select Vestry, 1982, NLI Ir. 27411 p 6, 73 p.

Roslea Community Historical Society, *Roslea remembers*, Fermanagh: 2001?, NLI, 152 p.

Steele, W.B., *The parish of Devenish*, Enniskillen: *Fermanagh Times* Office, 1937, NLI Ir. 914118 s 12, 172 p.

Swanzy, Rev. H.B., *The later history of the Family of Rosborough of Mullinagoan, Co. Fermanagh*, 1898, Linen Hall Library, 929.2/ROSB, Mullynagowan, Galloon parish

Trimble, W.C., *The history of Enniskillen with reference to some manors in co. Fermanagh, and other local subjects*, Enniskillen: W. Trimble, 1919–21, NLI Ir. 94118 t 1, Vols I–III. McGuire family

Witherow, Thomas, *Derry and Enniskillen, in the year 1689*, 1873, 1885, Belfast: W. Mullen & Son, 1895, NLI Ir. 94112 w 8, 419 p.

Local Journals

Clogher Record, NLI Ir. 94114 c 2

North Irish Roots (*Journal of the North of Ireland Family History Society*), NLI Ir. 92905 n 4

Irish Family Links, NLI Ir. 9292 f 19

Ulster Journal of Archaeology, NLI Ir. 794105 u 1

Directories

1824   J. Pigot and Co., *City of Dublin and Hibernian Provincial Directory*, NLI, LDS Film 451787

1839   *Directory of the Towns of Sligo, Enniskillen, Ballyshannon, Donegal [...]*

1846   Slater's *National Commercial Directory of Ireland*. PRONI, NLI LO, LDS Film 1696703 Item 3

1852	James A. Henderson, *Belfast and Province of Ulster Directory.* Issued also in 1854, 1856, 1858, 1861, 1863, 1865, 1868, 1870, 1877, 1880, 1884, 1887, 1890, 1894, 1900, PRONI. LDS (various years)
1856	Slater, *Royal National Commercial Directory of Ireland,* NLI, LDS Film 1472360 Item 1
1870	Slater, *Directory of Ireland,* NLI
1881	Slater, *Royal National Commercial Directory of Ireland,* NLI
1887	*Derry Almanac and Directory* (Enniskillen) NLI Ir. 914112 d 1
1894	Slater, *Royal Commercial Directory of Ireland,* NLI

Gravestone Inscriptions

Heritage World has transcripts for forty-six graveyards in Fermanagh. These are searchable online, for a fee, at *www.historyfromheadstones.com.* Published or publicly available transcripts are given below, ordered by civil parish.

Aghavea: Aghavea, C of I, *Clogher Record,* Vol. 4, Nos 1, 2, 1960/1
Cleenish: Templenaffrin, *Clogher Record,* Vol. 2, No. 1, 1957
Clones: Rosslea, St Tierney's, RC, *Clogher Record,* 1982–84
Derryvullan: Monea, C of I, Steele, *The parish of Devenish*
Devenish: St Molaise's and Devenish Abbey, MacKenna, *Devenish, its history*
Drummully: *Clogher Record,* Vol. 1, No. 2, 1954
Enniskillen: St Macartin's, C of I, Dundas, *Enniskillen*
Galloon: Galloon, *Clogher Record,* Vol. 10, No. 2, 1980
Galloon: Donagh, *Clogher Record,* Vol. 1, No. 3, 1955

Estate Records

Archdale: Rental 1753. Online: Ulsterancestry. Devinish parish.

Balfour family: Tenants' list, 1735, NLI Mss. 10259, 10305 major tenants only. Rentals, 1735–1789, NLI Ms. 10259 major tenants only. Rentals, 1818–1822, NLI Ms. 10260 all tenants. Covering areas in the civil parishes of: Aghalurcher; and Kinawley.

Commissioners of Education: Rentals, 1832–1851, NLI Ms. 17956. All tenants. Covering areas in the civil parishes of: Cleenish; and Killesher.

Enniskillen, Viscounts: Rentals, 1810–1876 PRONI D/1702. Covering areas in the civil parishes of: Aghalurcher; Aghavea; Cleenish; Derryvullan; Drumkeeran; Enniskillen; Killesher; Kinawley; Rossorry; Trory.

Hassard family: Rentals, 1810–1820, NAI M.3136. Major tenants only. Covering areas in the civil parish of Enniskillen.

Hume, Nicholas (Ely estate): Online: Fermanagh Genweb.

Broomfield, J.C.: Rentals, 1810–1820, NAI M.3563. All tenants. Covering areas in the civil parish of Belleek.

GALWAY

Census returns and substitutes

1640	Irish Papist Proprietors, Galway Town. *History,* Hardiman
1641–1703	Book of Survey and Distribution. NLI Ms. 969
1657	English Protestant Proprietors, Galway town. *History of the town and county of Galway to 1820,* Galway: 1958
1727	A Galway election list. *JGAHS,* 1976
1749	Ahascra, Athleague, Ballynakill, Drimatemple, Dunamon, Kilbegnet, Killian, Killosolan. NAI MFS 6. LDS Film 101781. See Manning, *Elphin Index,* Ballynakill, Dunamon, Kilbegnet. Online: Creggs
1791	Survey of Loughrea town (occupiers). *JGAHS,* Vol. 24, No. 3
1794	Catholic Freemen of Galway town. *JGAHS,* Vol. 9, No. 1
1798	Convicted Rebels from Galway *JGAHS,* Vol. 23, No. 1
1798	Persons who suffered losses in the 1798 rebellion. Propertied classes only. c.100 names. NLI I 94107
1806–1810	Catholic householders, Killalaghten; In the Catholic parish registers of Cappataggle NLI. Pos. 2431
1810–1819	Names in account books of C. St George, Oranmore town, *IG,* Vol. 7 (1) 1986 pps 101–112
1821	Parishes of Aran, Athenry, Kilcomeen, Kiltallagh, Killimore, Kilconickny, Kilreekill. NAI CEN 1821/18–25; LDS Film 597734. Also Loughrea (fragments) GO Ms. 622, pp 53 & ff
1823–1838	Tithe Books
1827	Protestants in Aughrim parish. NAI M.5359
1830	Memorials:
	1. Killyan barony, (Athleague, Kilroran, Killyan and Tisrara), 1830, c.130 names, NAI OP 974/148.
	2. Galway city, 1830, c.100 signatures, NAI OP 974/145
	3. Fishermen of Claddagh, 1831, 59 names, NAI OP 974/101
	4. 'Urrismore' [Errismore], 1831, 85 names, NAI OP 974/121
1834	List of parishioners, Kinvara and Killina; NLI Pos. 2442. Also GFHSW. Online: Celtic Cousins
1837	Valuation of towns returning M.P.s (occupants and property values): Galway. *Parliamentary Papers 1837, Reports from Committees,* Vol. II (i), Appendix G
1838–1848	Reproductive Loan Fund records. Records of loan associations at Ahascragh, Ballygar, Castlehacket, Clifden, Corrandulla, Furbo, Loughrea, Galway city, Mountshannon (now in Clare), Mountbellew, covering more than fifty parishes and 8,000 individuals. NA (Kew). T 91. Partly online: Moving Here
1839–1846	List of subscribers to the RC Chapel at Dunmore, with name, townland and donation 1839–46. NLI Pos. 4211
1841	Fragments, for Loughrea town. NAI M 150(2). Also GO 622 pp 53 & ff

1848–1852	Ahascra assisted passages. AH, Vol. 22, 1960. Also Ellis *Emigrants*
1850–1859	Emigrants to Australia and the US from the parish of Kilchreest, with some from the parishes of Killogilleen, Killinane, Killora, Kilthomas and Isertkelly. GO Ms. 622
1851	Fragments, for Loughrea town. NAI M 150
1855	Griffith's Valuation. Online: Index, Hayes; 24 North Galway parishes: Lally
1901	Census. Headford & Killursa. Online: Lally
1911	Census

Online

Bishop	*pw2.netcom.com/~lgb1/ tuamcumm.html*	
Celtic Cousins	*www.celticcousins.net/ireland*	Assorted records, Beagh and Gort areas
Creggs	*www.strandnet.com/creggs*	Northeast Galway
Egan	*homepages.rootsweb.com/~egan*	
Hayes, John	*www.failteromhat.com*	
Lally, Joseph	*www.lalley.com*	
Leitrim-Roscommon	*www.leitrim-roscommon.com*	1901, Griffith's, Townlands. Elphin 1749
Moving Here	*www.movinghere.org.uk/search/*	

Publications

Local histories, etc.

'The Ethnography of the Carna and Mweenish in the Parish of Moyruss', *Proceedings of the Royal Irish Academy*, 3rd Ser. Vol. 6, 1900–2, 503–34

'The Ethnography of the Aran Islands', *Proceedings of the Royal Irish Academy*, 3rd Ser. Vol. 2, 1891–3, 827–9

Dillon papers (Clonbrock, Co. Galway), AH, XX, 17–55

Dunsandle papers, AH, XV, 392, 405

Barna/Furbo Irish Countrywomen's Assoc., *Barna and Furbo: A Local history*, Barna: Barna/Furbo Irish Countrywomen's Assoc., 1982

Beirne, Francis, *A history of the parish of Tisrara*, Tisrara: Tisrara Heritage Society, 1997, NLI Ir. 94125 h 5, 219 p.

Berry, J.F., *The Story of St Nicholas' Church, Galway*, 1912, NLI Ir. 7265 b 5

Breathnach, Pádraic, *Maigh Cuilinn: a táisc agus a tuairisc*, Indreabhán: Co. na Gaillimhe, Cló Chonamara, 1986, NLI Ir. 94124 m 6, 298 p.

Breatnach, Caoilte, *Memories in Time Folklore of Beithe: 1800–2000*, Tubber, Co. Galway: Beagh Integrated Rural Development Association, 2003, NLI, 224 p.

Candon, Geraldine, *Headford, County Galway, 1775–1901*, Dublin: Four Courts, 2003, NLI, 64 p.

Cantwell, Ian, *Memorials of the Dead, Counties Galway & Mayo (Western Seaboard)*, CD-ROM #4, Dublin, Eneclann, 2002. Galway County Library, DCLA

Carroll, Michael H., *Of beauty rarest: a history of Clydagh National School, Headford, Co. Galway*, Headford, Co. Galway: Michael H. Carroll, 2000, NLI, 206 p.

Carroll, Michael H., *Valley of the Milk: a history of the Carroll Family of Luggawannia, Headford, Co. Galway*, Luggawannia, Headford, Co. Galway, Ireland: M.H. Carroll, 2000, NLI Ir. 9292 c 65, 221 p.

Claffey, John A., *History of Moylough-Mountbellew. Part I, from the earliest times to 1601*, Tuam: Claffey, 1983, NLI Ir. 94124 c 13, 168 p.

Claregalway Historical & Cultural Society, *Claregalway parish history 750 years = Stair pharóiste Bhaile Chláir na Gaillimhe*, Claregalway: Claregalway Historical and Cultural Society, 1999, NLI Ir. 94124 c 14, 277 p.

Clarke, Joe, *Christopher Dillon Bellew and his Galway estates, 1763–1826*, Dublin: Four Courts, 2003, NLI, 64 p.

Connemara Orphans' Nursery, *The story of the Connemara Orphans' Nursery from its commencement to the year 1876*, Glasgow: Campbell & Tudhope, 1877, NLI Ir. 361.s[sic], 213 p. Records of the Connemara Orphans' Nursery

Conwell, John Joe, *Lickmolassy by the Shannon: a history of Gortanumera & surrounding parishes*, Galway: Conwell, 1998, NLI, 343 p.

Conwell, John Joe, *A Galway landlord and the Famine: Ulick John de Burgh*, Dublin: Four Courts, 2003, NLI, 64 p.

Cronin, Denis, *A Galway gentleman in the age of improvement: Robert French of Monivea, 1716–76*, Blackrock, Co. Dublin: Irish Academic Press, 1995, NLI Ir. 94124 c 12

D'Alton, E., *History of the Archdiocese of Tuam*, Dublin: Phoenix, 1928, NLI Ir. 27412 d 1, 2 vols.

Donnelly, Fr James, *Family history of the Donnellys and the Crushells of Belmont Co, Galway*, Kathmandu: the author, 1990, NLI Ir. 921 d Including references to: Maloney (Lissananny, Galway); Dowd (Kilconly, Galway); Devaney (Kilconly, Galway); Donnelly (Ballyglass, Mayo)

Dwyer, Philip, *The Diocese of Killaloe, from the Reformation to the Close of the Eighteenth Century*, Dublin: Hodges, Foster, and Figgis, 1878, NLI Ir. 94143 d 11, 602 p. Repr.: Newmarket-on-Fergus: O'Brien Book Publications, 1997

Egan, Patrick K., *The parish of Ballinasloe, its history from the earliest times to the present day*, Galway: Kennys Bookshops, 1994, NLI Ir. 94124 e 2, 355 p.

Ellis, Éilis, *Emigrants from Ireland 1847–52*, Baltimore: Genealogical Publishing Co., 1977, NLI Ir. 325 e 5

Faherty, Padhraic, *Barna—A History*, Barna: Faherty, 2000

Fahey, Jerome, *The History and Antiquities of the Diocese of Kilmacduagh*, repr. *Galway*: KG, 1986. NLI Ir. 274124 f 2. 480 p.

Fahy, Mary de Laordes, *Kiltartan: many leaves one root: a history of the parish of Kiltartan*, Gort, Co. Galway: The Kiltartan Gregory Cultural Society, 2004, NLI, 349 p.

Farrell, Noel, *County Galway, Tuam family roots: exploring family origins in Tuam,* Longford: Noel Farrell, 2004, NLI 48 p.

Farrell, Noel, *Exploring family origins in Ballinasloe town,* Longford: Noel Farrell, 1998, NLI, 48 p.

FÁS Galway Family History Project, *Forthill graveyard,* Galway: Galway Family History Society West, 1992, NLI Ir. 941 p 118 (4)

Finnegan, Eileen, *A History of the parish of Templetogher: and the town of Williamstown: from earliest times to 1990,* Williamstown: Finnegan, 1990, NLI Ir. 94124 p 5(3), 56 p.

Flynn, John S., *Ballymacward the story of an east Galway parish,* Mullingar: John S. Flynn, 1991, NLI Ir. 94124.f.3, 238 p.

Forde, Joseph, *The District of Loughrea Vol 1: History 1791–1918,* Loughrea, Co. Galway: Loughrea History Project, 2003, NLI. Co-editors, Christina Cassidy, Paul Manzor and David Ryan

Forde, Joseph, *The District of Loughrea Vol II: Folklore 1860–1960,* Loughrea, Co. Galway: Loughrea History Project, 2003, NLI 326 p.

Furey, Brenda, *Oranmore Maree a history of a cultural and social heritage,* Galway: the author, 1991, NLI Ir. 94124 f 4, 116 p.

Glynn, Sean M., *Williamstown County Galway Historical Sketch and Records,* Galway, Galway Printing Company: 1966, Galway County Library

Goaley, Rev. M., *History of Annaghdown,* Westport: Berry's Printing Works, 197?, NLI Ir. 274 p 31

Hardiman, James, *History of the town and county of Galway ... to 1820,* Repr. Galway: Kennys Bookshops and Art Galleries, 1975. 320 p. NLI Ir. 94124 h 1 (Repub. Archive CD Books Ireland, CD ROM #IET0043, 2005)

Hayes McCoy, G.A., *Index to 'The Compossicion Booke of Connoght, 1585',* Dublin: Irish Manuscripts Commission, 1945, NLI Ir. 9412 c 1, 179 p.

Higgins, Jim, *St. Mary's Cathedral (Church of Ireland) Tuam: an architectural, archaeological and historical guide,* Tuam: Friends of St Mary's Cathedral, c.1995, NLI Ir. 27412 s 1, 182 p. Co-author, Aisling Parsons

IGRS, *Tombstone inscriptions Vol. 1,* Dublin, IGRS Tombstone Committee, 2001, NLI, 850 p.

Irish Countrywomen's Association, *Portrait of a Parish: Ballynakill, Connemara,* Irish Countrywomen's Association

Jordan, Kieran, *Kiltullagh/Killimordaly as the centuries passed: a history from 1500–1900,* Kiltullagh: Kiltullagh/Killimordaly Historical Society, 2000, NLI, 378 p.

Kavanagh, Michael V., *A Bibliography of the Co. Galway,* Galway: Galway County Libraries, 1965, NLI Ir. 801 K 6, 187 p.

Kenney, James C., *Pedigree of the Kenney family of Kilclogher, Co. Galway,* Dublin: 1968, Killaclogher, Monivea

Knox, H.T., *Notes on the Early History of the Dioceses of Tuam, Killala and Achonry,* Dublin: Hodges Figgis, 1904, NLI Ir. 27412 k 1, 410 p.

Knox, H.T., *Portumna and the Burkes,* JGAHS, VI, 1909, 107–9

Lackagh Parish History Committee, *The parish of Lackagh Turloughmore*, Turloughmore: Lackagh Parish History Committee, 1990, NLI Ir. 94124 f 2, 292 p. Inc. 1901 census

MacLochlainn, Tadgh, *A Historical summary on the Parish of Ahascra, Caltra & Castleblakeney*, Ballinasloe: MacLochlainn, 1979, NLI Ir. 9141 p 79, 92 p.

MacLochlainn, Tadgh, *The Parish of Aughrim & Kilconnell, South Harrow*, MacLochlainn, 1980, NLI Ir. 94124 m 4, 79 p.

MacLochlainn, Tadgh, *The Parish of Laurencetown & Kiltormer*, Ballinasloe: MacLochlainn, 1981, NLI Ir. 94124 m 5, 73 p.

MacLochlainn, Tadgh, *Ballinasloe, inniu agus iné: a story of a community over the past 200 years*, Galway: Galway Print. Co, 1971?, NLI Ir. 94124 m 1, 223 p.

MacLochlainn, Tadgh, *A Short history of the Parish of Killure, Fohenagh and Kilgerrill*, Galway: MacLochlainn, 1975, NLI Ir. 9141 p 74, 54 p.

Madden, Gerard, *For God or King: the history of Mountshannon, Co. Clare 1742–1992*, Tuamgraney, Co. Clare: East Clare Heritage, 1993, NLI Ir. 94143 f 8, 204 p.

Manning, Peter, *Elphin Diocesan census 1749: surname index.*, Rainham, Kent: Manning, 1987. NLI Ir. 27412 m 20

McNamara, Marie, *Beagh a history & heritage*, Beagh: Beagh Integrated Rural Development Association, 1995?, NLI Ir. 94124 b 4, 276 p. Co-author, Maura Madden

Mulvey, Con, *The memorial inscriptions and related history of Kiltullagh, Killimordaly and Esker graveyards*, Kiltullagh, Co. Galway: Kiltullagh Community Council, 1998, NLI Ir. 9295 m 5/1, 146 p.

Naughton, M., *The History of St Francis' Parish, Galway*, Galway: Corrib Printers, 1984, NLI Ir. 27412 n 1, 60 p.

Ni Dhomhnaill, Cáit, *An Cheathrú Rua*, Baile Átha Cliath: An tOireachtas, 1984, NLI, 33 p.

Ó Concheanainn, Peadar, *Innismeadhoin, seanchas agus sgéalta*, Baile Átha Cliath: Oifig Díolta Foillseacháin Rialtais, 1931, NLI Ir. 89162 Oc 25, 76 p.

Ó Laoi, Padraic, *History of Castlegar Parish*, Galway, Ó Laoi, 1998?, NLI Ir. 94124 o 14, 216 p.

O'Donnell, Paul, *A Mullagh Miscellany, Vol. 1*, Galway Rural Development: 2002, Galway County Library, 49 p.

O'Donovan, John, *The Tribes and customs of Hy-Many, commonly called O'Kelly's country*, Dublin: for the Irish Archaeological Society, 1843. NLI Ir. 9412 o 1/1

O'Flaherty, Roderic, *A chorographical description of West or H-Iar Connaught: written A.D. 1684*, Dublin: for the Irish Archaeological Society, 1846, NLI Ir. 94124 o 2. Repr. 1978 Galway: Kennys Bookshops and Art Galleries

O'Gorman, Michael, *A pride of paper tigers: a history of the Great Hunger in the Scariff Workhouse Union from 1839 to 1853*, Tuamgraney, Co. Clare: East Clare Heritage, 1994, NLI Ir. 94143 o 8, 82 p.

O'Gorman, Tony, *History of Fohenagh*, Galway: Fohenagh Community Council, 2000?, NLI, 167 p.

O'Neill, T.P., *The tribes and other Galway families. Galway quincentennial, 1484–1984,* Galway: *Connaught Tribune,* 1984, NLI Ir. 927, p 5, 32 p.

O'Regan, Carol, *Moylough a people's heritage,* Moylough: Moylough Community Council, 1993, NLI Ir. 94124 p 5(4), 138 p. Co-editor, John Jones

O'Regan, Finbarr, *The Lamberts of Athenry: a book on the Lambert families of Castle Lambert and Castle Ellen, Co. Galway,* Athenry, Co. Galway: Finbarr O'Regan for the Lambert Project Society, 1999, NLI Ir. 9292 L 24, 254 p.

O'Sullivan, M.D., *Old Galway: the history of a Norman colony in Ireland,* Cambridge: W. Heffer and Sons, 1942, NLI Ir. 94124 04, 488 p.

Qualter, Aggie, *Athenry history from 1780, folklore, recollections,* Galway: Qualter, 1989, NLI Ir. 94124 p 3(2), 66 p.

Regan, Carol, *Moylough, a people's heritage,* Moylough: Moylough Community Council, 1993, NLI Ir. 94124 p 5(4), 138 p.

Regan, D., *Abbeyknockmoy, a time to remember,* Co. Galway: Abbeyknockmoy Community Council, 1996, NLI Ir. 94124 a 4

Robinson, Tim, *Connemara after the Famine: journal of a survey of the Martin Estate by Thomas Colville Scott, 1853,* Dublin: Lilliput Press, 1995, NLI Ir. 94124 s 10, 102 p.

Rynne, Etienne, *Athenry: a medieval Irish town,* Athenry: Athenry Historical Society, 1992, NLI Ir. 941 p 132(1)

Shiel, Michael, *A Forgotten Campaign and aspects of the heritage of south-east Galway,* Galway: East Galway Centenary Committee, NLI Ir. 94124 f. Co-author, Desmond Roche. Land wars and evictions, c.1886

Simington, Robert C., *The transplantation to Connacht, 1654–58,* Shannon: Irish University Press for the Irish Manuscripts Commission, 1970, NLI Ir. 94106 s 9, 306 p.

Smythe, Colin, *A guide to Coole Park, Co. Galway home of Lady Gregory,* Gerrards Cross: Colin Smythe Ltd, 1995, NLI Ir. 94124 s 9, with a foreword by Anne Gregory. 3rd ed. (rev.)

Tourelle, John F., *Forde, Forde, Forde: from Annagh West, Co. Galway, Ireland to Southland, New Zealand,* Alexandra, NZ: J.F. Tourelle, 1998, NLNZ, 180 p.

Villiers-Tuthill, Kathleen, *History of Clifden, 1810–1860,* Dublin: the author, c.1981, NLI Ir. 94124 V 1, 88 p. Dorsey family

Villiers-Tuthill, Kathleen, *Patient endurance: the great famine in Connemara,* Dublin: Connemara Girl Publications, 1997, NLI Ir. 94123 v 1, 189 p.

Villiers-Tuthill, Kathleen, *Beyond the Twelve Bens, a history of Clifden and district 1860–1923,* Dublin: the author, 1990, NLI Ir. 94124.v.3, 252 p.

White, Rev. P., *History of Clare and the Dalcassian Clans of Tipperary, Limerick and Galway,* Dublin: 1893, NLI Ir. 94143 w 4, 398 p. Repr. Newmarket-on-Fergus: O'Brien Book Publications, 1997

Local Journals
Galway Roots: Journal of the Galway Family History Society West, NLI
Journal of the Galway Archaeological and Historical Society, NLI Ir. 794105 g 1

Directories

1820   J. Pigot, *Commercial Directory of Ireland* PRONI, NLI Ir. 9141 p 107, LDS
           Film 962702 Item 1
1824   J. Pigot and Co., *City of Dublin and Hibernian Provincial Directory*, NLI,
           LDS Film 451787
1846   Slater's *National Commercial Directory of Ireland.* PRONI, NLI LO, LDS
           Film 1696703 Item 3
1856   Slater, *Royal National Commercial Directory of Ireland*, NLI, LDS Film
           1472360 Item 1
1870   Slater, *Directory of Ireland*, NLI
1881   Slater, *Royal National Commercial Directory of Ireland*, NLI
1894   Slater, *Royal Commercial Directory of Ireland*, NLI

Gravestone Inscriptions

Galway Family History Society West Ltd. has transcripts for sixty-one graveyards,
mainly in the west of the county. Contact details will be found in Chapter 15.
Published or publicly available transcripts are given below.

Addergoole: Carrowntomush: IGRS Collection: GO
Ballynakill (Ballynahinch): Ballynakill, Cantwell, *Memorials*
Claregalway: Claregalway (Abbey?): IGRS Collection (172 inscriptions): GO
Drumacoo: Drumacoo: *IGRS, Vol. 1*
Kilcummin: Canrawer West (Carraroe?), Cantwell, *Memorials*
    Oughterard, Main Street, C of I, Cantwell, *Memorials*
Killannin: Cloghmore, Cantwell, *Memorials*
Killimordaly: Killimor, RC, Mulvey, *Memorial inscriptions*
Kilmacduagh: Lisnagyreeny: *IA*, NLI Ir. 9205 i 3, Vol. Vii, No. 1, 1975
Kiltullagh: Kiltullagh North (Esker?), Mulvey, *Memorial inscriptions*
Kiltullagh: Mulvey, *Memorial inscriptions*
Moycullen: Moycullen, Cantwell, *Memorials*
—Spiddle town, Cantwell, *Memorials*
Moyrus: Ardbear, Cantwell, *Memorials*
—Roundstone town, C of I, Cantwell, *Memorials*
Omey: Clifden, Chapel Lane, RC, Cantwell, *Memorials*
—Clifden, Church Street, C of I, Cantwell, *Memorials*
Rahoon: Rahoon (Barna RC?), Cantwell, *Memorials*
St Nicholas: Galway, Forthill Road: RC: *Forthill graveyard*
—St Nicholas' Church: C of I: Higgins, *Monuments of St Nicholas*
Tuam: Tuam, Church Lane (St Mary's?), Higgins, *St Mary's Cathedral*

Estate Records

Bellew: estate wages book, 1679–1775. NLI Ms. 9200.
Blake Knox, Francis: Rental, 1845–66, NLI Ms. 3077. Covering townlands in the
    civil parishes of: Annaghdown; Kilmacduagh; Kilmoylan.

Browne, Col. John: NLI Pos. 940. Account of the sales of the estates of Col. John Browne in Counties Galway and Mayo, compiled in 1778, giving names of major tenants and purchasers 1698–1704, and those occupying the estates in 1778. Covering townlands in the civil parishes of: Ballynakill; Cong; Kilcummin; Killannin; Omey; Ross.

Clanmorris, Lord: Estate rental, 1833, NLI Ms. 3279. All tenants. Covering townlands in the civil parish of Claregalway.

Dillon, Barons Clonbrock: NLI Ms. 19501; tenants' ledger 1801–06, indexed. NLI Mss. 19585–19608 (24 vols); rentals and accounts, 1827–1840. All tenants. NLI Mss. 22008, 22009; maps of the Co. Galway estates, with full valuation of all tenants' holdings. NLI Mss. 19609–19616; Rentals and accounts, 1840–44. All tenants. Covering townlands in the civil parishes of: Ahascragh; Aughrim; Fohanagh; Kilcoona; Killaan; Killallaghtan; Killosolan; Kilteskil.

French family: NLI Ms. 4920; rent ledger, Monivea estate, 1767–77. Major tenants only. NLI Ms. 4929; estate accounts and wages book, 1811/12. All tenants, with index. NLI Ms. 4930; accounts and wages book, 1830–33. Covering townlands in the civil parishes of: Abbeyknockmoy; Athenry; Cargin; Claregalway; Monivea; Moylough; Oranmore.

Hodson, Lieut. Edward: NLI Ms. 2356. Rent rolls and tenants' accounts, 1797–1824, indexes. Covering townlands in the civil parish of Kiltormer.

St George, Richard St George Mansergh: NLI Pos. 5483. (a) Rental of Headford town (all tenants), (b) estate rentals (major tenants only), both 1775. Covering townlands in the civil parishes of: Cargin; Donaghpatrick; Kilcoona; Kilkilvery; Killursa.

Shee, George: NAI M.3105–3120. Yearly rentals of the estate in and around Dunmore, 1837–1859. All tenants. Covering townlands in the civil parishes of: Addergoole; Boyounagh; Clonbern; Dunmore.

Trench: NLI Ms. 2577. Estate rental, 1840–50. Covering townlands in the civil parishes of: Ballymacaward; Kilbeacanty; Killaan; Killimordaly.

Wolfe, Theobold: NLI Ms. 3876. Estate maps with names of major tenants, 1760, indexed. Covering townlands in the civil parishes of: Kilmallinoge; and Tiranascragh.

[No Landlord Given]: NLI 21 g 76 (14) and 21 g 76 (26). Maps of Cloonfane and Carogher townlands in Dunmore parish, with tenants' names. Mid-nineteenth century.

[No Landlord Given]: NLI Ms. 4633. Survey of occupiers, townlands of Ballinasoora, Streamsfort, Fortlands, Woodlands, parish of Killimordaly. 1851.

[No Landlord Given]: NLI Mss. 2277–2280. Rentals, 1854–85, townlands of Ballyargadaun, Leitrim More, Kylebrack, Knockash in the civil parishes of Leitrim and Kilteskil.

KERRY

Census returns and substitutes

1586	Survey of the estates of the Earl of Desmond recording leaseholders. NAI M.5037
1641	Book of Survey and Distribution. NLI Ms. 970
1654	Civil Survey, Vol. IV. Dysert, Killury, Rathroe. *Civil Survey*, Vol. IV. (NLI I 6551 Dublin)
1659	Pender's 'Census'. Repr. GPC, 1997, IMC, 2002. LDS Film 924648. Online: Genweb, Kerry
1799	Petition of 300 prominent Catholics of Co. Kerry. *The Dublin Evening Post*, June 9, 1799
1809	List of pupils at Tarbert school. NLI Ms. 17935
1821	Some extracts for Tralee and Annagh. NAI Thrift Abstracts
1821	Parish of Kilcummin. RIA, McSwiney papers, parcel f, No. 3. LDS Film 596419
1823–38	Tithe Books. NAI
1834–1835	Householders, parishes of Dunquin, Dunurlin, Ferriter, Killemlagh, Kilmalkedar, Kilquane, Marhin, Prior. *JKAHS*, 1974–5. Part online: Ballyferriter
1835	Tralee Voters. *JKAHS*, No. 19, 1986
1847–1851	Assisted passages Castlemaine estate, Kiltallagh parish. *AH*, Vol. 22, 1960
1852	Griffith's Valuation. Indexed online: Hayes
1901	Census. King's, *County Kerry, Past and Present* (1931) appears to have an index to the entire county
1911	Census

Online

Ballyferriter	*www.geocities.com/Athens/ Ithaca/7974/Ballyferriter*	
Genweb, Kerry	*www.rootsweb.com/~irlker*	Assorted records
Grogan, Margaret	*www.sci.net.au/userpages/mgrogan*	
Hayes, John	*www.failteromhat.com*	Dingle, 1901 & many others

Publications

Local histories, etc.

Allman, J., *Causeway, location, lore and legend*, Naas: *Leinster Leader*, 1983, NLI Ir. 94146 a 2, 117 p.

Barrington, T.J., *Discovering Kerry*, Dublin: 1976 NLI Ir. 94146 b 5 363 p.

Bary, V.A., *Houses of Co. Kerry*, Clare: Ballinakella Press, 1994, NLI Ir. 720 b 32, 247 p.

Brady, W. Maziere, *The McGellycuddy Papers*, London: 1867 NLI Ir. 9292 m 3, 209 p.

Brosnan, Donald Patrick, *The Brosnans of Glounlea, Co. Kerry*, Tucson, Arizona:

D.P. Brosnan, 1990, LOC

Browne, Bernard, *In the shadow of Sliabh Mish: Blennerville, Tonevane, Annagh, Curraheen, Derryquay, Derrymore,* Derryquay: Derryquay I.C.A., 2001, NLI, 176 p.

Casey, Albert, *O'Kief, Cosh Mang, Slieve Lougher, and Upper Blackwater in Ireland.* Privately printed, 1962–74, NLI Ir. 94145 c 12. Massive, multi-volume compendium of information on the Slieve Luachra/Blackwater Valley area on the Cork/Kerry border

Costello, Michael, *The famine in Kerry,* Tralee: Kerry Archaeological and Historical Society, 1997, NLI Ir. 94146 f 6, 108 p.

Cusack, Mary F., *History of the kingdom of Kerry,* Boston: Donohoe, 1871, NLI Ir. 94146 c 1, 453 p.

Denny, H.A., *A Handbook of Co. Kerry Family History etc,* 1923, NLI Ir. 9291 d 1

Donovan, T.M., *A Popular History of East Kerry,* Dublin: Talbot Press, 1931, NLI Ir. 94146 d 2, 230 p.

Farrell, Noel, *Killarney family roots book: exploring family origins in Killarney,* Longford: Noel Farrell, 2000, NLI, 48 p.

Finuge Heritage Society, *A span across time: Finuge, a folk history,* Finuge Heritage Society

Guerin, Michael, *Listowel Workhouse Union,* Clieveragh, Listowel: Michael Guerin, 1996, NLI Ir. 94146 g 27, 86 leaves

Hickson, Mary, *Selections from Old Kerry Records, Historical and Genealogical,* London: Watson & Hazell, 1872–4, NLI Ir. 94146 h 1, 337 p.

IGRS, *Tombstone inscriptions Vol. 1,* Dublin: IGRS Tombstone Committee, 2001, NLI, 850 p.

Keane, L., *Knocknagoshel: then and now,* Kerry County Library: 1985

Kelly, Liam, *Blennerville gateway to Tralee's past,* Tralee: Community Response Programme, 1989, NLI Ir. 94146 k 8, 463 p. Co-authors, Geraldine Lucid and Maria O'Sullivan

Kilcummin Rural Development Group, *Kilcummin: Glimpses of the Past,* Kilcummin: Kilcummin Rural Development Group, 1998

King, Jeremiah, *County Kerry, Past and Present,* Dublin: Hodges, Figgis & co, 1931, NLI Ir. 94146 k 3, 338 p.

King, Jeremiah, *King's history of Kerry, or, history of the parishes in the county. Part IV,* Tralee, pr. by Ryle and Quirke, 191–, NLI, Dix Tralee, 353 p.

Lansdowne, Marquis of, *Glanerought and the Petty-Fitzmaurices,* London: New York: Oxford University Press, 1937, NLI Ir. 94146 L 1, 226 p.

Lucey, Donnacha Seán, *The Irish National League in the Dingle Poor Law Union, 1885–91,* Dublin: Four Courts, 2003, NLI, 64 p.

Lyne, G.J., *The Lansdowne Estate in Kerry under the agency of William Steuart Trench 1849–72,* Dublin: Geography Publications, 2001, NLI Ir. 94146 L 3, 764 p.

MacLysaght, Edward, *The Kenmare Manuscripts,* Dublin: Irish Manuscripts Commission, 1947

MacMahon, Bryan, *The story of Ballyheigue,* Baile Uí Thaidhg: Oidhreacht, 1994, NLI Ir. 94146 m 9, 264 p.

MacSwiney [Unpublished manuscripts]; Royal Irish Academy. Historical notes and will abstracts, mainly from Counties Cork and Kerry

McMoran, R., *Tralee, a short history and guide to Tralee and environs*, 1980

Mitchell, Frank, *Man and Environment in Valencia Island*, Dublin: Royal Irish Academy, 1989, NLI Ir. 914146 p 19(4), 130 p.

Moreton, Cole, *Hungry for home: leaving the Blaskets ; a journey from the edge of Ireland*, London: Viking, 2000, NLI Ir. 94146 m 13, 287 p. Springfield, Mass. esp.

Mould, D.C. Pochin, *Valentia: portrait of an island*, Dublin: Blackwater Press, 1978, NLI Ir. 914146 m 7, 143 p.

O'Connor, Michael, *A Guide to Tracing your Kerry Ancestors*, Dublin: Flyleaf Press, 1994, NLI Ir. 9291 o 6, 96 p.

O'Connor, T., *Ardfert in times past*, Ardfert: Foilseachain Breanainn, 1990, NLI Ir. 94146 oo 11, History of Ardfert parish

O'Shea, Kieran, *Knocknagoshel Parish*, 1991, NLI Ir. 270 p 21(1), 47 p.

O'Shea, Kieran, *Castleisland: church and people*, Castleisland: the author, 1981, NLI Ir. 94146 o 6, 88 p.

Palmer, A.H., *Genealogical and historical account of the Palmer family of Kenmare, Co. Kerry*, 1872

Quane, Michael, *Castleisland charter school*, Kerry: Kerry Archaeological and Historical Society, 1968, NLI, 15 p.

Reedy, Rev. Donal A., *The diocese of Kerry (formerly Ardfert)*, Killarney: Catholic Truth Society, 1937, NLI, 46 p.

Siepmann, Dennis, *I am of Ireland: a family social history of the descendants of Dennis Scanlon and Mary Mullen of Lisselton Cross, County Kerry, Ireland, 1798–2002*, Knoxville, Tenn.: Tennessee Valley Pub., c.2002, LOC, 647 p.

Smith, Charles, *The Ancient and Present State of the County of Kerry: being a natural, civil, ecclesiastical, historical and topographical description thereof*, Dublin: 1756, NLI Ir. 94145 s 5. Reprint: Dublin, Mercier Press, 1979

Stoakley, T.E., *Sneem, The Knot in the Ring*, Sneem: Sneem Tourism Association, 1986, NLI Ir. 94146 s 7, 140 p.

Windele, J. [Unpublished manuscripts], NLI Pos. 5479. Information on Cork and Kerry families, including Coppinger, Cotter, Crosbie, O'Donovan, O'Keeffe, McCarthy, Sarsfield and others. See also Casey, O'K, Vol. 7

Local Journals
Journal of the Kerry Archaeological & Historical Society, NLI Ir. 794105 k 1
Kenmare Literary and Historical Society Journal

Directories

1824	J. Pigot and Co., *City of Dublin and Hibernian Provincial Directory*, NLI, LDS Film 451787
1846	Slater's *National Commercial Directory of Ireland*, PRONI, NLI LO, LDS Film 1696703 Item 3
1856	Slater, *Royal National Commercial Directory of Ireland*, NLI, LDS Film 1472360 Item 1

1870	Slater, *Directory of Ireland*, NLI
1881	Slater, *Royal National Commercial Directory of Ireland*, NLI
1886	Francis Guy, *Postal Directory of Munster*, NLI Ir. 91414 g 8, LDS Film 1559399 Item 8
1893	Francis Guy, *Directory of Munster*, NLI Ir. 91414 g 8
1894	Slater, *Royal Commercial Directory of Ireland*, NLI

Gravestone Inscriptions

The situation with transcripts compiled by the Kerry Genealogical Society and Finuge Heritage Society is unclear. They may be available through Killarney Library, Rock Road, Killarney.

Aghadoe: Parkavonear (Fossa?), O'K, Vol. 6
Aghadoe: Knoppoge (Aghadoe?), C of I, O'K, Vol. 6
Aghavallen: Rusheen, C of I, Kerry Genealogical Society
Aglish: C of I, O'K, Vol. 6
Ardfert: Ardfert town, C of I, O'K, Vol. 8
Ballincuslane: Cordal East, O'K, Vol. 6
Ballincuslane: Kilmurry, O'K, Vol. 6
Ballymacelligott: C of I, O'K, Vol. 8
—— Ballymacelligot, O'K, Vol. 11
Ballynahaglish: Spa, O'K, Vol. 11
Brosna: O'K, Vol. 6
Caher: Cahersiveen (Killevanoge), IGRS Collection, GO
Caher: Caherciveen Marian Place, IGRS Collection, GO. Also Finuge Heritage Society
Castleisland: Church Lane, C of I, O'K, Vol. 6
—— Kilbannivane, O'K, Vol. 6
—— Meenbannivane (Dysert?), O'K, Vol. 6
Clogherbrien: Clogherbrien, O'K, Vol. 8
Currans: Ardcrone, O'K, Vol. 6
Dingle: Raheenyhooig, IGRS, Vol. 1
Duagh: Islandboy (Duagh?), O'K, Vol. 11
Dysert: Kilsarkan East, O'K, Vol. 6
Finuge: Finuge Heritage Society. Also Kerry Genealogical Society
Kilcummin: Glebe, O'K, Vol. 6
—— Gneevegullia, O'K, Vol. 6
Kilcummin: Kilquane, O'K, Vol. 6
Killarney: Muckross, O'K, Vol. 6
—— Killarney (new), O'K, Vol. 6
Killeentierna: C of I, O'K, Vol. 6
Killehenny: (Ballybunion?), O'K, Vol. 11
Killorglin: O'K, Vol. 11
—— Dromavally (Killorglin?), O'K, Vol. 8

Kilnanare: Kilnanare, o'к, Vol. 6
Listowel: Listowel, o'к, Vol. 11
Molahiffe: Castlefarm (Molahiff?), o'к, Vol. 6
Murher: Murher, Kerry Genealogical Society
Nohaval: Ballyregan, o'к, Vol. 8
—— Nohaval, o'к, Vol. 11
O'Brennan: o'к, Vol. 11
—— Crag, o'к, Vol. 8
Tralee: Tralee, Nelson Street, C of I, o'к, Vol. 8
—— Tralee, Brewery Road, o'к, Vol. 8
—— Tralee, Castle Street Lower, C of I, o'к, Vol. 8

Estate Records

Asgill: Account book, 1709. NAI M.1854. Major tenants only. Covering townlands in the civil parishes of: Currans; Kilbonane; Kilcredane; Killarney; Killeentierna; Kiltomy; Tuosist.

Browne, Earls of Kenmare: assorted rentals, maps and estate accounts for areas around Kenmare and in the barony of Dunkerron, from 1620 to 1864 in MacLysaght, E., *The Kenmare Manuscripts*, Dublin: 1942. See also *O'Kief Coshe Nang*, etc. Vols 6, 7 and 9.

Crosbie, John Viscount: Rent ledger, 1805–1812. NLI Ms. 5033. Most tenants. Indexed, with detailed abstracts of lives in leases. Covering townlands in the civil parishes of: Currans; Kilbonane; Kilcredane; Killarney; Killeentierna; Kiltomy; Tuosist.

Fitzmaurice, F.T.: 7 sets of rentals 1742–86, with comments on lives in leases. NLI Pos. 176–7 (Paris, Archives Nationales). Major tenants only. Covering townlands in the civil parishes of: Aghavallen; Ardfert; Ballyconry; Ballynahaglish; Duagh; Dysert (Listowel); Fenit; Finuge; Galey; Kilcaragh; Kilcolman; Kilconly; Kilcredane; Kilfeighny; Killahan; Killeentierna; Killehenny; Killury; Kilmoyly; Kilnanare; Kilshenane; Kiltomy; Knockanure; Lisselton; Listowel; O'Dorney; Rattoo.

Gun Mahoney: Map, 1832. NLI Ms. 26812 (6). All tenants. Covering townlands in the civil parishes of: Aghavallen; Ardfert; Galey; Kilcrohane.

Herbert, Richard Townsend: Account book, 1709. NAI M.1854. Major tenants only. Covering townlands in the civil parishes of: Currans; Kilbonane; Kilflyn; Killeentierna. Rent and account book, 1741–1752. NAI M.1854. Covering townlands in the civil parishes of: Aghadoe; Aglish; Ballymacelligott; Ballynacourty; Brosna; Caher; Duagh; Dysert (Listowel); Galey; Garfinny; Kilbonane; Kilcredane; Kilcrohane; Kilcummin; Kilgarrylander; Killaha; Killarney; Killeentierna; Killorglin; Kilnanare; Kilquane; Kiltomy; Knockane; Minard; Molahiffe; Nohavaldaly; O'Brennan.

Herbert: Rent rolls, 1760, 1761. NAI M.1864. Covering townlands in the civil parishes of: Aghadoe; Aglish; Ballincuslane; Brosna; Castleisland; Cloghane; Dingle; Dysert (Trughanacmy); Garfinny; Kilcredane; Kilcrohane; Kilcummin;

Killaha; Killarney; Killeentierna; Killorglin; Kilnanare; Knockane; Valencia; Ventry.

Kerry, Earl of: Rent roll, 1761–64. NAI M.3302. Major tenants only. Covering townlands in the civil parishes of: Aghavallen; Ardfert; Ballymacelligott; Ballynahaglish; Dingle; Duagh; Dysert (Listowel); Fenit; Finuge; Galey; Kilcaragh; Kilcummin; Kilfeighny; Killahan; Killehenny; Kilmoyly; Kilshenane; Kiltomy; Lisselton; Listowel; O'Dorney; Rattoo.

Lefroy, Thomas: Abstract of leases, 1781. NLI Ms. 10933 (Part 5). Major tenants only. Covering townlands in the civil parishes of: Ballymacelligott; Kilmoyly; Kiltallagh.

Listowel, Earl of: Tithes, 1838. NAI M.2356. Most tenants. Covering the civil parishes of: Ardfert; Galey; Kilcaragh; Killahan; Kilshenane; Kiltomy; O'Dorney.

Locke: Summary of leases, 1801, with many comments on lives in leases. NAI M.3284. Major tenants only. Covering townlands in the civil parishes of: Ardfert; Ballincuslane; Duagh; Dysert (Listowel); Fenit; Kilcaragh; Kilfeighny; Killehenny; Kilshenane; Kiltomy; Lisselton; Rattoo.

Monsell: Rental, 1842. NLI Ms. 7868. All tenants. Covering townlands in the civil parishes of: Ballycahane; Kilkeedy; Killeely; Kiltallagh; Mungret; Rathronan.

Naper, James Lenox: Rental, mainly Co. Meath, 1733–1814. NLI Ms. 3031. Major tenants only. Covering townlands in the civil parish of Knockane.

MacGillicuddy: NLI Ms. 3014, the MacGillicuddy papers. Rentals, 1707 (p. 186), 1777 (p. 176) n.d., early eighteenth century? (p. 172). Major tenants only. Covering townlands in the civil parishes of: Kilbonane; Kilcummin; Killarney; Killorglin; Knockane; Tuosist.

Orpen: 'Land Tenure in Tuosist and Kenmare', *JKAHS* (1976), (1978), (1979). Rentals. All tenants. Covering townlands in the civil parishes of: Kenmare; Tuosist.

Rice, Stephen Edward: Summary of rents of Coolkeragh, Co. Kerry, parish of Galey 1806–23. NLI Ms. 605 F. All tenants.

Sandes, Thomas: Rental of the estate 1792–1828. Covering parts of the parishes of: Aghavallin; Kilnaughtin; Murher. NLI Ms. 1792.

Talbot-Crosbie, William: Rental, 1845–1849. NLI Ms. 5035. All tenants, with some comments on tenancies. Covering townlands in the civil parishes of: Ardfert; Duagh; Kilbonane; Kilgobban; Killahan; Kilmoyly; Kiltomy; O'Dorney; Rattoo.

[No landlord given—Locke?]: Rental of the Feale River fishery, early nineteenth century. NAI M3296. Major tenants only. Covering townlands in the civil parishes of: Ballyconry; Duagh; Dysert (Listowel); Finuge; Killeentierna; Killehenny; Listowel; Rattoo.

KILDARE

Census returns and substitutes

1641	Book of Survey and Distribution. Also NLI Ms. 971. *JKAS,* Vol. X, 1922–8
1654	Civil Survey, Vol. VIII. *Civil Survey,* Vol. VIII
1659	Pender's 'Census'. Repr. GPC, 1997, IMC, 2002. LDS Film 924648
1766	Catholic householders in Kilrush, Comerford, *Collections relating to Kildare and Leighlin.* Ballycommon, parish of Clonaghlis, *JKAS* 7 (4), 1913, 274–6
1798	Persons who suffered losses in the 1798 rebellion. Propertied classes only. c.320 names. NLI I 94107
1804	Yeomanry Order Book for Millicent townland, giving names and addresses of officers and men *JKAS* 13 (4) 1953 211–219
1823–1838	Tithe Books
1831	Kilcullen. Protestant returns only. GO Ms. 622, pp 53 & ff; NAI M.150(2)
1837	Memorial from inhabitants of Ballymore Eustace. c.100 names, NAI OP 1837/397
1837	Voters, NLI Ms. 1398
1840	Castledermot & Moone. NLI Pos. 3511
1843	Voters, NAI OP 1843/53
1851	Griffith's Valuation. Indexed online: Hayes
1901	Census
1911	Census

Online

Hayes, John   *www.failteromhat.com*

Publications

Local histories, etc.

Index to Ballyna Roman Catholic registers, 1785–1899, KAS, 1988. NLI Ir. 9293 i 4

Lest we forget: Kildare and the great famine, Naas: Kildare County Council, 1996, NLI Ir. 94108 L 21, 106 p.

Andrews, J.H., *Irish Historic Towns Atlas 1: Kildare,* Dublin: Royal Irish Academy, 1989, NLI, ILB 941 i 3(1)

Archbold, W.D., *The Archbolds of Roseville: an anthology of the Archbold family of Eadestown, County Kildare, Ireland, in the colony of New South Wales,* Birrong, NSW: Bill Archbold Ministries, 1997, NLI, 177 p. Rathmore parish

Athy Union, *Athy Union List of destitute persons relieved out of the workhouse in the Stradbally district Athy Union,* Naas: Athy Union, 1845, NLI, Poster

Behan, Vera Mahon, *Athy and district,* NLI, 56 p.

Brennan, M., *Schools of Kildare and Leighlin, 1775–1835,* Dublin: M.H. Gill and Son, 1935, NLI Ir. 37094135 b 4, 616 p.

Bunbury, Turtle, *The Landed Gentry & Aristocracy of Co. Kildare,* Wexford: Irish

Family Names, 2004, Aylmer, Barton, de Burgh, Clements, Conolly, Guinness, Henry, Fennell, FitzGerald, Latten, La Touche, Mansfield, Maunsell, Medlicott, More O'Ferrall, Moore, de Robeck, and Wolfe

Carville, Geraldine, *Monasterevin, Valley of Roses*, Moore Abbey, 1989

Carcy, Michael, 'Journal of Michael Carey, Athy, Co. Kildare'. NLI Ms. 25299 (Letters, leases, social commentary 1840–1859)

Comerford, Rev. M., *Collections relating to Kildare and Leighlin*, Dublin: J. Duffy, 1883–1886, NLI Ir. 27413 c 4, 3 vols.

Costello, Con, *A most delightful station: the British Army on the Curragh of Kildare, Ireland, 1855–1922*, Cork: Collins Press, 1996, NLI Ir. 355 c 18, 431 p.

Costello, Con, *Kildare: Saints, Soldiers & Horses*, Naas: *Leinster Leader*, 1991, NLI Ir. 94135.c.8184 p., 184 p.

Costello, Con, *Looking Back, Aspects of History, Co. Killdare*, Naas: *Leinster Leader*, 1988, NLI Ir. 94135 c 7, 113 p.

Coyle, James, *The Antiquities of Leighlin*, Dublin: Browne and Nolan, n.d., NLI Ir. 94138 c 1

Cullen, Seamus, *Unity in division: a history of Christianity in Kilcock and Newton Parish 400–2000*, Kilcock: Kilcock Publication Millennium Committee, 1999, NLI, 197 p.

Doohan, Tony, *A History of Celbridge*, Dublin n.d., NLI Ir. 94135 d 2 88 p.

Dunlop, Robert, *Waters under the bridge: the saga of the La Touches of Harristown, John Ruskin and his Irish Rose*, Brannockstown: 1988, NLI Ir. 9292 p 29(3), 64 p.

Flynn, Michael, *Outline histories ... Kelly of Youngstown, Kilmead, Athy, Co. Kildare, Murphy of Togher, Roundwood, Co. Wicklow, Masterson family of Ardellis, Athy, Co. Kildare (with descendants)*, Mullingar: Michael P. Flynn, 1997, NLI Ir. 9292 f [sic]

Gibson, Comdt. W.H., *St. Peter's Church, Two-Mile-House, 1790–1990*, Naas, Co. Kildare: St Peter's Church Bi-centenary Committee, 1990, NLI Ir. 27413 s 6, 176 p.

Horner, Arnold, *Irish Historic Towns Atlas 7: Maynooth*, Dublin: Royal Irish Academy, 1995, NLI, ILB 941 p 13 (4)

IGRS, *Tombstone inscriptions Vol. 1*, Dublin: IGRS Tombstone Committee, 2001, NLI, 850 p.

Kavanagh, Michael V., *A contribution towards a bibliography of the history of County Kildare in printed books*, Newbridge: Kildare Co. Library, 1976, NLI Ir. 94135 k 1, 328 p.

Leadbeater, Mary, *The Annals of Ballitore*, London: 1862, NLI Ir. 92 l 8, Shackleton

Mac Suibhne, Peadar, *Rathangan*, Maynooth: An t-Athair Ó Fiach, 1975, NLI Ir. 94135 m 3, 323 p.

MacKenna, John, *Castledermot and Kilkea—a social history, with notes on Ballytore, Graney, Moone and Mullaghmast*, Athy: Winter Wood Books, 1982, NLI Ir. 94135 m 5, 60 p.

Magee, Sean, *Weavers of Prosporous, County Kildare, Balbriggan, County Dublin & Tullamore, County Offaly in memorials of 1826*, Dublin: Dun Laoghaire Genealogical Society, 1998, NLI Ir. 9291 g 7

McAuliffe, E.J., *An Irish genealogical source: the roll of the Quaker School at Ballitore, County Kildare: with an index and notes on certain families*, Blackrock, Co. Dublin: Irish Academic Press, 1984, NLI Ir. 92001 m 26, 49 p.

Naas Local History Group, *Nas na Riogh: ... an illustrated history of Naas*, Naas: Naas Local History Group, 1990, NLI Ir. 94135 n 2, 144 p.

Nelson, Gerald, *A History of Leixlip*, Naas: Kildare Co. Library, 1990, NLI Ir. 94135.n.1, 68 p.

O Conchubhair, Seamus, *A History of Kilcock and Newtown*, 1987

O Muineog, Micheal, *Kilcock GAA, A History*, 1989

O'Dowd, Desmond J., *Changing times religion and society in nineteenth-century Celbridge*, Dublin: Irish Academic Press, 1997, NLI Ir. 94135 o 6, 73 p.

Paterson, J. (ed.), *Diocese of Meath and Kildare: an historical guide*, 1981, NLI Ir. 941 p 75

Quane, Michael, *Ballitore school*, Kildare: Kildare Archaeological Society, 1966/67, NLI, P [?sic], pp. 174–209

Reid, J.N.S., *Church of St Michael & All Angels, Clane*, 1983

Ryan, Eileen, *Monasterevan parish, Co. Kildare some historical notes compiled*, Naas: printed by *Leinster Leader*, 1958, NLI Ir. 91413.r.1, 75 p.

Shackleton, Betsy, *Ballitore & its inhabitants seventy years ago*, Dublin: printed by Richard D. Webb and Son, 1862, NLI, Oke 398, 110 p.

Shackleton, Jonathan, *The Shackletons of Ballitore: (1580–1987)*, Dublin: the author, 1988, NLI, GO 268

Wolfe, Major R., *Wolfes of Forenaghts, Blackhall, Baronrath, Co. Kildare, Tipperary, Cape of Good Hope, &c: also the old Wolfes of Co. Kildare, and the Wolfes of Dublin*, Guilford: W. Matthews, 1885, NLI Ir. 9292 w 4, 17, 23, 107 p.

Local Journals
Journal of the Kildare Archaeological Society, NLI Ir. 794106 k 2
The Bridge: Kilcullen community magazine, NLI Ir. 94135 b 2
Reportorium Novum, NLI Ir. 27413 r 3

Directories
1788   Richard Lucas, *General Directory of the Kingdom of Ireland*, NLI Pos. 3729. Repr. in Veale, *Lucas*, IG 1965, 1966, 1967, 1968
1824   J. Pigot and Co., *City of Dublin and Hibernian Provincial Directory*, NLI, LDS Film 451787
1846   Slater's *National Commercial Directory of Ireland*. PRONI, NLI LO, LDS Film 1696703 Item 3
1856   Slater, *Royal National Commercial Directory of Ireland*, NLI, LDS Film 1472360 Item 1
1870   Slater, *Directory of Ireland*, NLI
1881   Slater, *Royal National Commercial Directory of Ireland*, NLI
1894   Slater, *Royal Commercial Directory of Ireland*, NLI

Gravestone Inscriptions

Ardkill: Ballyshannon, GO. Ms. 622, p. 108, GO

Ballaghmoon: Ballaghmoon, KCL, *IGRS*, *Vol. 1*

Ballynafagh: Ballynafagh, C of I, KCL

Belan: Belan, KCL, *IGRS*, *Vol. 1*

Castledermot: Knockbane, IGRS Collection, GO

—— Castledermot town, C of I, KCL. Also *IGRS*, *Vol. 1*

—— Ballyhade, KCL, *IGRS*, *Vol. 1*

—— St James, KCL

—— Franciscan Friary, KCL

—— Prumplestown, KCL

Clane: Clane town, C of I, KCL

Donadea: Donadea South, C of I, KCL

Dunmanoge: KCL, *IGRS*, *Vol. 1*

Dunmanoge: Maganey Upper, RC, GO Ms. 622, p.108, GO

—— Castleroe Rath, KCL

—— Levistown, KCL

Dunmurraghill: Dunmurraghill, KCL

Fontstown: Fontstown Lower, GO Ms. 622, p.148/9, GO

Graney: Knockpatrick, KCL, *IGRS*, *Vol. 1*

Harristown: Harristown Lower, GO. Ms. 622, 126/7, GO

Kilcock: Kilcock, Church Lane, C of I, KCL

Kilcullen: Oldkilcullen, *Co. Carlow Tombstone Inscriptions*, Vol. 3 NLI Ir. 9295 c 3,

—— Kineagh, KCL, *IGRS*, *Vol. 1*

Kildare: Church and Friary Lane, C of I, *IGRS*, *Vol. 1*

Kilkea: Kilkea Lower, KCL

Killelan: Killelan, KCL, *IGRS*, *Vol. 1*

—— Killeen Cormac, KCL. Also *IGRS*, *Vol. 1*

Kilteel: JKAS, 1981/2 NLI Ir. 794106 k 2

Kyle: *IGRS*, *Vol. 1*

Moone: KCL, *IGRS*, *Vol. 1*

——Moone Abbey, KCL, *IGRS*, *Vol. 1*

Narraghmore: Moyleabbey, KCL, *IGRS*, *Vol. 1*

—— Mullamast, KCL

St Michaels: Athy, GO Ms. 622, 89, GO

Straffan: Barberstown, + JKAS, 1977/8

Taghadoe: C of I, KCL

Tankardstown: Levistown, KCL

Timahoe: Timahoe East, KCL

Timolin: C of I, *IGRS*, *Vol. 1*, KCL

—— Ballitore, Quaker, KCL

Estate records

Aylmer, Michael: Rent-roll, 1796. NLI Ms. 9056. Major tenants only. Covering townlands in the civil parishes of Kill; Lyons; Mylerstown.

Christ Church, Dublin, Dean and Chapter of: Maps and rentals, 1692–1838. NLI Mss. 2789–90. Major tenants only. Covering townlands in the civil parishes of: Ardkill; Kilcullen.

Cloncurry, Lord: Accounts and rentals, 1814–1853. NLI Ms. 8183. Major tenants only. Covering townlands in the civil parishes of: Castledermot; Cloncurry; Clonshanbo; Donadea; Lyons; Rathangan.

Colleys, Hon. Misses: Maps and rentals, with detailed comments, 1744. NLI Ms. 9212. Major tenants only. Covering townlands in the civil parishes of: Ardkill; Carbury; Carrick; Kilmore; Mylerstown.

De Burgh: Maps and rentals, 1787–1850. NLI Pos. 4576 (De Burgh Papers). Coverage unclear. Covering townlands in the civil parish of Naas.

Deane, J.W.: Rentals, 1845–1881. NLI Mss. 14281–2. All tenants. Covering townlands in the civil parishes of: Kilkea; Timolin.

Drogheda, Earl of: Rentals, 1746–1801. NLI Mss. 12720–12723. Principally major tenants. Covering townlands in the civil parishes of: Ballybrackan; Cadamstown; Fontstown; Harristown; Lackagh; Monasterevin; Narraghmore.

Drogheda, Earl of: Rentals, 1810–1815. NLI Mss. 12724–12733. All tenants. Covering townlands in the civil parishes of: Ballybrackan; Fontstown; Harristown; Kilrush; Monasterevin; Narraghmore.

Drogheda, Earl of: Rentals, 1838–1883. NLI Mss. 9737–9738. Most(?) tenants. Covering townlands in the civil parishes of: Ballybrackan; Fontstown; Harristown; Monasterevin; Narraghmore.

Edgeworth, Richard: Rental Book with details of leases, 1796. NAI M.1503. All tenants. Covering townlands in the civil parish of Kilkea.

Fitzgerald, Maurice: Accounts, 1768–1782, NLI Ms. 23458. Major tenants only. Covering townlands in the civil parishes of: Feighcullen; Rathangan.

Fitzwilliam, Earl: NLI Mss. 6069–6072, Rentals, 1796. NLI Mss. 6069–6072 Rentals, 1796–1808. NLI Mss. 6077–6081, Rentals, 1813–1825. Most tenants. Covering townlands in the civil parish of Naas.

Kildare, Earl of: NLI Pos. 1431 (BM: Harleian Ms. 7200), Rent roll, 1684. Principally major tenants. Covering townlands in the civil parishes of: Ballaghmoon; Ballybrackan; Balraheen; Castledermot; Churchtown; Clane; Cloncurry; Donaghmore; Duneany; Dunmanoge; Dunmurry; Feighcullen; Fontstown; Graney; Grangerosnolvan; Harristown; Kilberry; Kilcock; Kildare; Kilkea; Killelan; Kineagh; Lackagh; Laraghbryan; Leixlip; Moone; Morristownbiller; Naas; Narraghmore; Oughterard; Pollardstown; Rathangan; Rathernan; St Johns; St Michaels; Taghadoe; Tankardstown; Thomastown; Tipper; Walterstown.

Lattin, George: Mansfield Papers. Rent ledgers, 1742–1773. NLI Mss. 9635–9636. All tenants. Covering townlands in the civil parishes of: Forenaghts; Greatconnell; Killashee; Ladytown; Naas.

Leinster, Duke of: Lease books, 1780–1850. NLI Mss. 19908–19910. All tenants. Covering townlands in the civil parishes of: Ballybrackan; Ballysax; Cloncurry; Duneany; Dunmurry; Feighcullen; Grangeclare; Harristown; Haynestown; Kildare; Naas; Oughterard; Pollardstown; Rathangan;

Rathernan; Rathmore; Thomastown; Tipper; Tipperkevin; Walterstown. NLI Mss. 19911–19912, Lease books, 1780–1850. Covering townlands in the civil parishes of: Ballaghmoon; Castledermot; Dunmanoge; Graney; Grangerosnolvan; Kilkea; Killelan; Kineagh; Moone; Narraghmore; Tankardstown. NLI Mss. 19921–19922, tenants' registers. All tenants. Covering townlands in the civil parishes of: Ballybrackan; Ballysax; Castledermot; Duneany; Dunmurry; Feighcullen; Grangeclare; Kildare; Pollardstown; Thomastown; Walterstown.

Magan, William Henry: Maps, 1848. NLI Ms. 14.A.27. All tenants. Covering townlands in the civil parishes of: Ballyshannon; Cloncurry; Kilrush.

Mansfield, John: Map, 1813. NLI Ms. 16.H.34(5). All tenants. Covering townlands in the civil parish of Carragh.

Oxmantown, Lord: Accounts, 1798–9. NAI M.1279. Major tenants only. Covering townlands in the civil parish of Clane.

Rockingham, Marquess of: Rent-roll, 1735–1748. NLI Ms. 6054. Most tenants. Covering townlands in the civil parish of Naas. NLI Ms. 6053, accounts and rentals. Major tenants only. Covering townlands in the civil parishes of: Kilcullen; Naas; Tipperkevin. NLI Mss. 6062–6063, Rentals, 1778–1781. Most tenants. Covering townlands in the civil parishes of: Carragh; Naas; Tipperkevin.

Sabine, Joseph: Maps and rentals, 1777–1783. NLI Ms. 679. Principally major tenants. Covering townlands in the civil parishes of: Ballymore Eustace; Ladytown.

Sarsfield-Vesy: Rentals and accounts, NAI, see *RDKPRI* 56. Covering townlands in the civil parishes of: Carn; Clane; Feighcullen; Morristownbiller; Naas; Tully.

[No landlord]: Map & survey, 1840. NLI Ms. 21.F.103(6). All tenants. Covering townlands in the civil parishes of: Ballybought; Ballymore Eustace; Ballysax; Bodenstown; Carn; Carnalway; Churchtown; Fontstown; Gilltown; Jago; Kilberry; Kill; Killashee; Naas; Narraghmore; Rathmore; Sherlockstown.

[No landlord]: Maps, 1707–1838. NLI Ms. 21.F.34(1–38). Most tenants. Covering townlands in the civil parishes of: Aghavallen; Balraheen; Brideschurch; Carragh; Carrick; Downings; Dunfierth; Greatconnell; Kilcock; Kilcullen; Killelan; Kilrainy; Kineagh; Moone; Naas; Nurney; Rathernan.

Valentia, Viscount: Maps and rentals, 1773. NLI Ms. 19024. Major tenants only. Covering townlands in the civil parishes of: Ballysax; Cloncurry; Lullymore.

KILKENNY

Census returns and substitutes

1641	Book of Survey and Distribution. NLI Ms. 975
1650–1800	Dunnamaggan. *Old Kilkenny Review,* 1992, 958
1654	Kilkenny City. *Civil Survey,* Vol. Vl (NLI I 6551 Dublin)
1659	Pender's 'Census'. Repr. GPC, 1997, IMC, 2002. LDS Film 924648
1664	Hearth Money Rolls. Parishes of: Agherney, Aghavillar, Bellaghtobin, Belline, Burnchurch, Callan, Castleinch, Clone, Coolaghmore,

Coolcashin, Danganmore, Derrinahinch, Dunkitt, Earlstown, Eyverk, Fartagh, Inishnagg & Stonecarthy, Jerpoint, Kells, Kilbeacon & Killahy, Kilcolm, Kilferagh, Kilkredy, Killamery, Killaloe, Killree, Kilmoganny, Kiltackaholme, Knocktopher & Kilkerchill, Muckalee & Lismatigue, Outrath, Ratbach, Rathpatrick, Tullaghanbrogue, Tullaghmaine, Urlingford. *IG*, 1974–5.

1684–1769	Registers of Kilkenny College. NLI Pos. 4545
1702	Partial parishioners' lists, St Mary's and St Canice's parishes, Kilkenny City. NAI List 63 (Priim 8, 11, 15, 16)
1715	Protestant males between 16 and 60 in St John's parish, Kilkenny City. NAI
1750–1844	Inistiogue emigrants in Newfoundland. Whelan, *Kilkenny History and Society*
1766	Portnascully, Catholic householders. GO 683–4. Also LDS Film 100158
1775	Landowners. GO 443
1785	Freeholders (incomplete). GO 443, LDS Film 100158
1785–1879	Kilkenny city deeds. *Old Kilkenny Review,* Vol. 2, No. 4
1797	Chief Catholic inhabitants, Parishes of Graiguenamanagh and Knocktopher. *IA*, 1978
1785–1819	Freeholders: 1785 (incomplete), GO 443, LDS Film 100158; 1768–1809, (Iverk only), GO 684, LDS Film 100158 1809–1819, NLI Ms. 14181
1811–1858	Registers & Accounts of St Kieran's College. NLI Pos. 973
1819	Memorial of the inhabitants of Ballyraggett, c.50 names. NAI OP 1832/49
1821	Extracts only for Pollrone *IA* 1976, 1977; Extracts from the 1821 census, parishes of Aglish, Clonmore, Fiddown, Kilmacow, Polerone, Rathkyran, Whitechurch. GO 684 (Walsh-Kelly notebooks). Also *IG*, Vol. 5, 1978, Veale *Census*
1822–1830	*Co Kilkenny, Division of Kilkenny and Thomastown, applicants for the vote.* (Kilkenny 1,285 names; Thomastown 2,525 names) NLI ILB 324
1823–1838	Tithe Books. Part online: Connors
1831	Extracts from the 1831 census, parishes of Aglish, Clonmore, Kilmacow, Polerone, Rathkyran, Tybroghney. GO 684 (Walsh-Kelly notebooks)
1841	Extracts from the 1841 census, parishes of Aglish and Rathkyran. GO 684 (Walsh-Kelly notebooks). Townlands of Aglish and Portnahully only. *IA*, 1977
1842	Voters NAI OP 1842/79
1847–1853	Assisted emigration from Castlecomer Union, Lyng, *Castlecomer.* Online: Connors. c.650 names
1849–1850	Griffith's Valuation. Indexed online: Hayes, NLI
1851	Parish of Aglish. *IA,* 1977. Also GO 684 (Walsh-Kelly notebooks)
1901	Census. For Castlecomer, see Delaney, *Castlecomer: 1901 census*
1911	Census

Online

Celtic cousins	www.celticcousins.net	Walsh-Kelly parish extracts
Connors	www.connorsgenealogy.com	
Genweb, Kilkenny	www.rootsweb.com/~irlkik/	
Hayes, John	www.failteromhat.com	
Rosbercon	home.att.net/~mojo2/rosbercon	Assorted records

Publications

Local histories, etc.

Alsworth, W.J., *History of Thomastown and District*, 1953, NLI, JP. 1996

Birtwhistle, D., 'Inistioge', *Old Kilkenny Review*, 1969, 31

Bradley, John, *Irish Historic Towns Atlas 10: Kilkenny*, Dublin: Royal Irish Academy, 2000, NLI

Brennan, M., *Schools of Kildare and Leighlin, 1775–1835*, Dublin: M.H. Gill and Son, 1935, NLI Ir. 37094135 b 4, 616 p.

Brennan, T.A., *A History of the Brennans of Idaugh in Co. Kilkenny*, New York: 1979, NLI Ir. 9292 b 45

Burtchaell, G., *Genealogical memoirs of the members of Parliament for the county and city of Kilkenny ... 1295–1888*, Dublin: Sealy, Bryers & Walker, 1888, NLI Ir. 920041 b 3, 276 p.

Carrigan, Rev. William, *The History and Antiquities of the Diocese of Ossory*, Kilkenny: Roberts Books, 1980, NLI Ir. 27413 c 9, 4 vols. Repr. of 1905 edition

Carville, Geraldine, *A town remembers Duiske Abbey, Graignamanagh: an illustrated history and guide*, 1980, NLI, 48 p.

Carville, Geraldine, *Norman splendour: Duiske Abbey, Graignamanagh*, Belfast: Blackstaff Press, 1979, NLI Ir. 270 c 30, 119 p.

Coyle, James, *The Antiquities of Leighlin*, Dublin: Browne and Nolan, n.d., NLI Ir. 94138 c 1

Delaney, Tom, *Castlecomer Co. Kilkenny: 1901 census*, Dun Laoghaire: Genealogical Society of Ireland, 2000, NLI Ir. 94139 d 3, 286 p.

Gulliver, P.H., *Merchants and shopkeepers: a historical anthropology of an Irish market town 1200–1991*, Toronto: University of Toronto Press, 1995, NLI Ir. 94139 g 1, 440 p. Co-author, Marilyn Silverman

Healy, William, *History & antiquities of Kilkenny county & city*, Kilkenny: 1893, NLI Ir. 94139 h 1

Hogan, John, *Kilkenny, the Ancient City of Ossory*, Kilkenny: P.M. Egan, 1884. NLI Ir. 94139 h 2. 462 p.

Hogan, John, *Kilkenny; the ancient city of Ossory, the seat of its kings, the see of its bishops and the site of its cathedral*. Kilkenny: P. M. Egan, 1884, NLI Ir. 94139 h 2, 462 p.

Holahan, J., *Notes on the antiquities of the united parishes of Ballycallan, Kilmanagh & Killaloe; with notices of the late parish priests ...*, Kilkenny: *Journal* office, 1875, NLI Ir. 274144 h 1, 50 p.

Hore, H.F., *The Social State of the Southern and Eastern Counties of Ireland in the Sixteenth Century*, Dublin, 1870, NLI Ir. 794105 r 2, 'being the presentments of the gentlemen, commonalty, and citizens of Carlow, Cork, Kilkenny, Tipperary, Waterford, and Wexford, made in the reigns of Henry VIII. and Elizabeth. / Printed from the originals in the Public Record Office, London. Edited by the late Herbert J. [i.e. F.] Hore, ... and the Rev. James Graves'

IGRS, *Tombstone inscriptions Vol. 1*, Dublin: IGRS Tombstone Committee, 2001, NLI, 850 p.

Joyce, John, *Graiguenamanagh and the South Carlow– Kilkenny area in 1798*, Graignamanagh Historical Society, 1998, NLI, 20 p.

Joyce, John, *Graiguenamanagh a town and its people: an historical and social account of Graiguenamanagh & Tinnahinch*, Graiguenamanagh, [Co. Kilkenny], Graigue Publications, 1993, NLI Ir. 94139 j 2, 198 p.

Kenealy, M., *The Parish of Aharney and the Marum Family*, Old Kilkenny Review, 1976, NLI Ir. 94139 o 3

Kennedy, Edward, *The land movement in Tullaroan, County Kilkenny, 1879–1891*, Dublin: Four Courts, 2004, NLI, 68 p.

Kilkenny Archaeological Society, *St. Patrick's, Kilkenny gravestone inscriptions: with historical notes on the parish*, Kilkenny: Kilkenny Archaeological Society, 1990?, NLI Ir. 9295 k 1, 100 p.

Kirwan, John, *The Kirwan's of Lowergrange, Goresbridge, Co. Kilkenny and their associated familie*, 1995, NLI, 1 sheet

Laffan, Thomas, *Kilmacow ... A south Kilkenny parish*, Kilkenny: *Kilkenny People*, 1998

Lyng, Tom, *Castlecomer connections: exploring history, geography, and social evolution in North Kilkenny environs*, Castlecomer: Castlecomer History Society, 1984, NLI Ir. 94139 L 4, 429 p.

Neely, W.G., *Kilkenny, an urban history, 1391–1843*, Belfast: Institute of Irish Studies, 1989, NLI Ir. 94139 n 2, 306 p.

Nolan, W., *Fassidinin: Land, Settlement and Society in South East Ireland, 1600–1850*, Dublin: Geography Publications, 1979, NLI Ir. 94139 n 1, 259 p.

O'Dwyer, Michael, *Coolagh its history and heritage*, Coolagh: Coolagh Centenary Committee, 1996, NLI Ir. 94139 c 3, 213 p.

O'Shea, Mary, *Parish of Templeorum: a historical miscellany 1999–2000*, Raheen, Co. Kilkenny: the author, 2000, NLI, 72 p.

O'Sullivan, Michael, *Rathpatrick Graveyard, Co. Kilkenny memorial inscriptions*, Waterford: Michael O'Sullivan, 1998, NLI Ir. 9295 p, 21 p.

Phelan, M., *Callan Doctors*, Old Kilkenny Review, 1980, NLI Ir. 94139 o 3

Phelan, M.M., *Kilkenny Gravestone Inscriptions: 1 Knocktopher*, Kilkenny: Kilkenny Archaeological Society, 1988, NLI, 44 p.

Prim, J.G.A., *The History (...) of St. Canice, Kilkenny*, Dublin: Hodges, Smith, & Company, 1857, NLI Ir. 7266 g 5/1, 360 p. Co-author, James Graves

Prim, J.G.A., 'Documents connected with the city of Kilkenny militia in the 17th and 18th centuries', NLI, *Kilkenny & SE Ire Arch. Soc. Jnl*, 1854 5, 231–74

Raymond, B., *The Story of Kilkenny, Kildare, Offaly and Leix*, 1931, NLI I 9141 p 1

Shaw, William, *Survey of Tullaroan, or Grace's Parish, in the cantred of Grace's Country, and county of Kilkenny; taken from the statistical account, or parochial survey of Ireland*, Dublin: Faulkner Pr., 1819, NLI Ir. 94137 m 1, 160 p.

Silverman, M., *In the Vally of the Nore: Social History of Thomastown, Co. Kilkenny 1843–1983*, Dublin: Geography Publication, 1986. Co-editor, P. Gulliver

Sullivan, Joe, *To school by the banks: a history of the origins and development of the primary schools in Carrigeen, Co. Kilkenny*, Carrigeen: Carrigeen School Centenary Committee, 2000, NLI, 163 p.

Thomastown Vocational School, *Thomastown: through the mists of time*, Kilkenny: Transition Year, Thomastown Vocational School, n.d., NLI Ir. 94139 t 1, 138 p.

Veale, Tom, *Index of Surnames in 'The New Commercial Directory for the cities of Waterford and Kilkenny and the towns of Clonmel, Carrick-on-Suir, New Ross and Carlow'*, Dublin: Veale, 1996, NLI Ir. 9414 p.

Veale, Tom, *Richard Lucas 1788: directory extract for south east of Ireland*, Dublin: Veale, 1995, NLI Ir. 9414

Veale, Tom, *Census extract 1821 Mooncoin area of Co. Kilkenny, Ireland: surname index*, Dublin: Veale, 1997, NLI Ir. 94139 v 1 97 p.

Walsh, Christopher, *A place of memories*, Tullaroan, Christopher Walshe, 1991, NLI Ir. 94139 w 1

Walsh, Jim, *Sliabh Rua: a history of its people and places*, Slieverue: Slieverue Parish Pastoral Council, 2001, NLI, 612 p.

Whelan, Kevin, *Kilkenny History and Society*, Dublin: Geography Publications, 1990, NLI Ir. 94139 k 8, 715 p. Co-editor, W. Nolan

Local Journals
Deenside, NLI Ir. 914139 d 3
Journal of the Butler Society, NLI Ir. 9292 b 28
Kilkenny & South-East of Ireland Archaeological Society Journal, NLI J 7914 (to 1890); Ir. 794105 r 1 (after 1890)
Old Kilkenny Review, NLI Ir. 94139 o 3
Transactions of the Ossory Archaeological Society, NLI Ir. 794105 o 1

Directories

1788	Richard Lucas, *General Directory of the Kingdom of Ireland*, NLI Pos. 3729. Repr. in Veale, *Lucas*, IG 1965, 1966, 1967, 1968
1820	J. Pigot, *Commercial Directory of Ireland* PRONI, NLI Ir. 9141 p 107, LDS Film 962702 Item 1
1824	J. Pigot and Co., *City of Dublin and Hibernian Provincial Directory*, NLI, LDS Film 451787
1839	T. Shearman, *New Commercial Directory for the cities of Waterford and Kilkenny, Towns of Clonmel, Carrick-on-Suir, New Ross and Carlow* Indexed in Veale, *Index*

1846   Slater's *National Commercial Directory of Ireland*. PRONI, NLI LO, LDS
          Film 1696703 Item 3
1856   Slater, *Royal National Commercial Directory of Ireland*, NLI, LDS Film
          1472360 Item 1
1870   Slater, *Directory of Ireland*, NLI
1881   Slater, *Royal National Commercial Directory of Ireland*, NLI
1884   George Henry Bassett, *Kilkenny City and County Guide and Directory*
1885   George Henry Bassett, *Wexford County Guide and Directory*. Repr.
          Kilkenny, Grangesilvia Publications, 2001. NLI
1894   Slater, *Royal Commercial Directory of Ireland*, NLI

Gravestone Inscriptions

Ballygurrim: Jamestown, *IGRS*, *Vol. 1*
Ballytarsney: *IGRS*, *Vol. 1*
Blackrath: Maddockstown, IGRS Collection, GO
Castlecomer: Dysert, IGRS Collection, GO
Castleinch or Inchyolaghan: IGRS Collection, GO
Clara: Churchclara, IGRS Collection, GO
Clashacrow: Clashacrow, IGRS Collection, GO
Clonmore: *IGRS*, *Vol. 1*
Danesfort: GO Ms. 622, p.147, GO
—— Annamult, IGRS Collection, GO
Dunkitt: *IGRS*, *Vol. 1*
—— Killaspy, IGRS Collection, GO
Dunmore: Dunmore, C of I, IGRS Collection, GO
Fiddown: Fiddown, C of I, GO Ms. 622, p.150
Freshford: Freshford, Kilkenny Street, C of I, IGRS Collection, GO
Gaulskill: Ballynamorahan, C of I, *IGRS*, *Vol. 1*
Inistioge: Cappagh, IGRS Collection, GO
Jerpointchurch: Kilvinoge, *IGRS*, *Vol. 1*
Kells: Glebe, IGRS Collection, GO
—— St Kieran's, IGRS Collection, GO
Kilbeacon: Garrandarragh, RC, *IGRS*, *Vol. 1*
Kilbride: Kilbride, *IGRS*, *Vol. 1*
Kilcolumb: Rathinure *IGRS*, *Vol. 1*
Kilferagh, IGRS Collection, GO
—— Sheastown, IGRS Collection, GO
Killahy: Killahy, *IGRS*, *Vol. 1*
Kilmacow: Kilmacow, C of I, *IGRS*, *Vol. 1*
Kilmademoge: Kilmademoge, IGRS Collection, GO
Kilree: Kilree, IGRS Collection, GO
Knocktopher: Kilcurl (Anglesea), IGRS Collection, GO
—— Knocktopher town, *Kilkenny Gravestone Inscriptions: 1*
—— Sheepstown, *IGRS*, *Vol. 1*

Muckalee: Muckalee, *IGRS*, *Vol. 1*
Odagh: Threecastles, IGRS Collection, GO
Outrath: Outrath, IGRS Collection, GO
Portnascully: Portnascully, *IGRS*, *Vol. 1*
Rathcoole: Johnswell, IGRS Collection, GO
—— Carrigeen, IGRS Collection, GO
Rathpatrick: O'Sullivan, *Rathpatrick Graveyard*
Rosbercon: Rosbercon town, C of I, Cantwell, *West Wexford*
—— Rosbercon, RC, Cantwell, *West Wexford*
St Canice: St Canice's interior, RC, IGRS Collection, GO
—— St Canice's Cathedral, Prim, J.G.A., *St. Canice*
—— Kilkenny, the Colonnade, C of I, IGRS Collection, GO
St John's: Kilkenny, John Street Lower, C of I, IGRS Collection, GO
—— Radestown North, IGRS Collection, GO
—— Kilkenny, Dublin Road, RC, IGRS Collection, GO
St Martin's: Templemartin, IGRS Collection, GO
St Mary's: Kilkenny, St Mary's Lane, C of I, *Old Kilkenny Review*, 1979/1980/1981
St Maul's: Kilkenny, Green's Bridge Street, IGRS Collection, GO
St Patrick's: Kilkenny, Patrick Street Upper, IGRS Collection, GO
Stonecarthy: Stonecarthy East, IGRS Collection, GO
Tiscoffin: Freynestown, C of I, IGRS Collection, GO
Treadingstown: Ballyredding, IGRS Collection, GO
Tubbrid: Tubbrid, *IGRS*, *Vol. 1*
Tullaghanbrogue: Grove, IGRS Collection, GO
Tullamaine: Tullamaine (Ashbrook), IGRS Collection, GO
Ullid: Ullid, *IGRS*, *Vol. 1*

Estate records
Tuthill: Rental, 1812. NAI M.5825 (48). Principally major tenants. Covering townlands in the civil parish of Dunnamaggan.

LAOIS

Census returns and substitutes
1641	Book of Survey and Distribution. NLI Ms. 972
1659	Pender's 'Census'. Repr. GPC, 1997, IMC, 2002. LDS Film 924648. Online: Rootsweb, Laois
1664	Hearth Money Roll. NAI Thrift Abstracts 3737
1668–1669	Hearth Money Roll. Baronies of Maryborough and Clandonagh (Upper Ossory). NAI Thrift Abstracts 3737
1758–1775	Freeholders. *JKAS*, Vol. VIII, pp. 309 27. Online: Rootsweb, Laois
1766	Lea parish RCBL; Also LDS Film 258517
1821	Mountrath. NAI m6225(1)–(5)
1823–1838	Tithe Books

1832–1840   Owners and occupiers, Lea parish. NLI Ms. 4723/4
1844   Register of Arms, baronies of Clandonagh (Upper Ossory), Maryborough, Cullenagh. 433 names. NAI
1847   Voters. NLI ILB O4 P12
1851–1852   Griffith's Valuation. Indexed online: Hayes
1901   Census
1911   Census

Online

Connors	www.connorsgenealogy.com
Genweb, Laois	www.rootsweb.com/~irllex/
Hayes, John	www.failteromhat.com

Publications

Local histories, etc.
An Tostal, *The story of Abbeyleix: An tóstal souvenir 1953*, Abbeyleix: An Tostal, 1953, NLI Ir. 94137 s 1, 76 p.
Athy Union, *Athy Union List of destitute persons relieved out of the workhouse in the Stradbally district Athy Union*, Naas: Athy Union, 1845, NLI, Poster
Brennan, M., *Schools of Kildare and Leighlin, 1775–1835*, Dublin: M.H. Gill and Son, 1935, NLI Ir. 37094135 b 4, 616 p.
Campbell, Rosaleen, *Tombstone Inscriptions of Castlebrack*, Castlebrack: 1990, NLI Ir. 9295 p 2(3), 32 p.
Carrigan, Rev. William, *The History and Antiquities of the Diocese of Ossory*, Kilkenny: Roberts Books, 1980, NLI Ir. 27413 c 9, 4 vols. Repr. of 1905 edition
Coyle, James, *The Antiquities of Leighlin*, Dublin: Browne and Nolan, n.d., NLI Ir. 94138 c 1
Dwyer, Philip, *The Diocese of Killaloe, from the Reformation to the Close of the Eighteenth Century*, Dublin: Hodges, Foster, and Figgis, 1878, NLI Ir. 94143 d 11, 602 p. Reprint: Newmarket-on-Fergus: O'Brien Book Publications, 1997
Feehan, John, *The Landscape of Slieve Bloom: a study of the natural & human heritage*, Dublin: Blackwater Press, 1979, NLI Ir. 91413 f 4, 284 p.
Flynn, Michael, *An outline history of the Flynn family of Coolroe, Ballybrittas, Co. Leix [...] details of the Devoy family of Ballybrittas [..] the Lapham and Beasley families*, Mullingar: the author, 1995, NLI Ir. 9292 d 37
Flynn, Thomas S., *The Dominicans of Aghaboe (c.1382–c.1782)*, Dublin: Dominican Publications, 1975, NLI Ir. 270 p 10, 57 p.
Hovenden, Robert, *Lineage of the family of Hovenden (Irish branch) by a member of the family*, London: 1892, NLI Ir. 9292 h 6, 8 p.
Jolly, M.A., *A Portarlington settler and his descendants*, London: Spottiswoode, Ballantyne & Co., 1935, NLI, GO 415, 6 p.
Mac Suibhne, Peadar, *Parish of Killeshin, Graigcullen*, Carlow: St Patrick's College, 1975, NLI Ir. 94136 m 3, 192 p.

Meehan, Patrick, *Members of Parliament for Laois and Offaly 1801–1918*, Portlaoise: Leinster Express, 1983, NLI Ir. 328 m 6, 246 p.

Merrigan, Michael, *Croasdaile's History of Rosenallis, Co. Laois, Ireland*, Dun Laoghaire: Dun Laoghaire Genealogical Society, 1998, NLI Ir. 9291 g 7, 70 p.

O'Brien, Edward, *An historical and social diary of Durrow, County Laois, 1708–1992*, Durrow: Millfield Press, 1992, NLI Ir. 94137 o 8

O'Byrne, Daniel, *The history of the Queen's county: containing an historical and traditional account of is foundries, duns, (-) & an account of some noble families of English extraction*, Dublin: J. O'Daly, 1856, NLI Ir. 94137 o 2, 159 p.

O'Dea, Kieran, *Errill Cemetary*, Kilkenny: Errill Tidy Towns Committee, 1994, NLI, 46 p.

O'Hanlon, John, *History of the Queen's County*, Dublin: Sealy, Bryers & Walker, 1907–14, 2 vols. NLI Ir. 94137 o 3. Co-author, Edward O'Leary

O'Shea, Christopher, *Aspects of Local History*, Pallaskenry, Salesian Press, 1977, NLI Ir. 941 p 56, 39 p.

Paterson, J. (ed.), *Diocese of Meath and Kildare: an historical guide*, 1981, NLI Ir. 941 p 75

Powell, John S., *'Shot a buck....', the Emo estate, 1798–1852*, York: Frenchchurch, 1998, NLI, No. 3 from the Documents of Portarlington series

Redmond, Paul, *Gravestone Inscriptions from Killeshin, Sleaty, Graiguecullen, Mayo, Arles, Doonane, Castletown, Rathsapick, Shrule, Rathnure etc. with historical notes*, 1997, NLI Ir. 3991 r 16, 119 p.

Rudd, Norman N., *An Irish Rudd family 1760–1988 progeny of Gordon Arthur Rudd and Alicia Wellwood Rathsarn Parish, Queens County, Ireland: Rudd origins and other Irish Rudds*, California: Rudd Family Research Association, 1992, NLI Ir. 9292 r 22, 488 p.

Walker, Linus H., *Beneath Slievemargy's brow*, Portlaoise: Leinster Express, 2001, NLI, 302 p.

Walsh, Hilary D., *Borris-in-Ossory, Co. Laois; an Irish rural parish and its people*, Kilkenny: Kilkenny Journal, 1969, NLI Ir. 94137 w 1, 256 p.

Local Journals
Laois Heritage: bulletin of the Laois Heritage Society, NLI Ir. 9413705 l 1

Directories

1788	Richard Lucas, *General Directory of the Kingdom of Ireland*, NLI Pos. 3729. Repr. in Veale, *Lucas*, IG 1965, 1966, 1967, 1968
1824	J. Pigot and Co., *City of Dublin and Hibernian Provincial Directory*, NLI, LDS Film 451787
1846	Slater's *National Commercial Directory of Ireland*. PRONI, NLI LO, LDS Film 1696703 Item 3
1856	Slater, *Royal National Commercial Directory of Ireland*, NLI, LDS Film 1472360 Item 1
1870	Slater, *Directory of Ireland*, NLI

1881   Slater, *Royal National Commercial Directory of Ireland*, NLI
1894   Slater, *Royal Commercial Directory of Ireland*, NLI

Gravestone Inscriptions
Irish Midlands Ancestry has transcripts for a large number of graveyards in the
county. Contact details will be found in Chapter 15. Published or publicly available transcripts are given below.

Castlebrack: Campbell, *Castlebrack*
Killabban, Mayo: Redmond, *Gravestone Inscriptions*
Killabban, Castletown: Redmond, *Gravestone Inscriptions*
Killeshin, Graigue: Redmond, *Gravestone Inscriptions*
Killeshin, Killeshin Redmond, *Gravestone Inscriptions*
Rathaspick, Doonane: Redmond, *Gravestone Inscriptions*
Shrule: Redmond, *Gravestone Inscriptions*
Sleaty: Redmond, *Gravestone Inscriptions*
Rathsaran: Online: Genweb, Laois
Rathdowney: Errill, O'Dea, *Errill Cemetary*

Estate records
Fitzmaurice, James: Rent book, 1851–1871. NLI Ms. 19451. Most tenants. Covering
     townlands in the civil parish of Killeshin.

LEITRIM

Census returns and substitutes
1600–1868 Roll of all the gentlemen. NLI P 2179
1659   Pender's 'Census'. Repr. GPC, 1997, IMC, 2002. LDS Film 924648
1726–1727 Protestant Householders. Edgeworth papers. NAI M.1501 Annaduff,
           Kiltogher, Kiltubbrid, Fenagh, Mohill
1791   Freeholders. GO 665; Also LDS Film 100213
1792   Protestants in the barony of Mohill. *IA*, Vol. 16, No. 1
1796   Spinning-Wheel Premium List. 1,875 names for Co. Leitrim. Online:
           Hayes
1807   Freeholders, Mohill barony. NLI Ms. 9628
1820   Voting freeholders. NLI Ms. 3830
1821   Parish of Carrigallen. NLI Pos. 4646
1823–1838 Tithe Books
1839–1883 Workhouse records, Mohill (1839–83) Manorhamilton (1839–81) and
           Carrick-on-Shannon (1843–82) unions. LCL
1842   Voters NAI OP 1842/4
1852   Voters, Oughteragh, Cloonclare, Cloonlogher. *Breifne*, Vol. 5, No. 20
1856   Griffith's Valuation. Indexed online: Hayes
1861   Catholic Householders, Mohill parish. LHC

| 1901 | Census. Online: Leitrim-Roscommon |
| 1911 | Census |

Online

Grieves	*members.iinet.net.au/~sgrieves/*	Gravestones
Hayes, John	*www.failteromhat.com*	Large compendium of transcribed records
Leitrim-Roscommon	*www.leitrim-roscommon.com*	1901, Griffith's, Townlands

Publications

Local histories, etc.

Manorhamilton parish church 1783–1983: 'Glimpses of our History', Cavan: Blacks, 1983, NLI Ir. 200 p 48, 20 p.

Breen, Father Mark, *The Gray Family: Anskirt, Gortletteragh*, Leitrim County Library, 929.2.Gra

Clancy, Eileen, *Ballinaglera Parish, Co. Leitrim: aspects of its history and traditions*, Dublin: Authors, 1980, NLI Ir. 94121 c 2, 212 p. Co-author, P. Forde

Clancy, P.S., *Historical Notices of the Parish of Inishmagrath: Diocese of Kilmore, Co. Leitrim*, Carrick-on-Shannon: Maura Clancy, 1972

Day, Angelique, & McWilliams, Patrick (eds.), *Ordnance Survey Memoirs of Ireland: Volume 40 Counties of South Ulster, 1834–8, Cavan, Leitrim, Louth, Monaghan and Sligo*, Belfast: Institute of Irish Studies, 1997, NLI Ir. 9141 o 80, 216pp. Co. Leitrim: Manorhamilton Union

Farrell, Noel, *Exploring Family origins in Carrick-on-Shannon*, Longford: Longford Leader, 1994, NLI, 47 p.

Freeman, T.W., *The Town & District of Carrick on Shannon*, 1949, NLI P. 1916

Hackett, Raymond, *Carrigallen Parish—A History*, Carrigallen: [Design Inc.?]: 1996, Leitrim County Library, 941.71. Co-editor, Michael Reilly

Hayes McCoy, G.A., *Index to 'The Compossicion Booke of Connoght, 1585'*, Dublin: Irish Manuscripts Commission, 1945, NLI Ir. 9412 c 1, 179 p.

Kelly, Liam, *Kiltubbrid*, Carrick-on-Shannon, Kiltubrid GAA, 1984, NLI Ir. 397 k 4, 144 p.

Kelly, Liam, *Kiltubrid, County Leitrim: snapshots of a parish in the 1890s*, Dublin: Four Courts, 2005, NLI, 64 p.

Logan, Patrick, *Outeragh, My Native Parish*, Dublin, 1963, NLI Ir. 941 p 74, 24 p.

MacAtasney, Gerard, *Leitrim and the great hunger 1845–50 '...a temporary inconvenience...'?*, Leitrim: Carrick-on-Shannon & District Historical Society, 1997, NLI Ir. 94121 m 2, 177 p.

MacNamee, James J., *History of the Diocese of Ardagh*, Dublin: Browne and Nolan, 1954, NLI Ir. 274131 m 5, 858 p.

McNiffe, Liam, 'Short History of the Barony of Rosclogher, 1840–60', *Breifny*, 1983–4

Monahan, Rev. J., *Records Relating to the Diocese of Ardagh and Clonmacnoise*, Dublin: M.H. Gill and son, 1886, NLI Ir. 27413 m 3, 400 p.

Ó Duigneáin, Proinnsíos, *North Leitrim in famine times, 1840–50*, Nure, Manorhamilton, Co. Leitrim: P. Ó Duigneáin, 1987?, NLI, 48 p.

O'Connell, Philip, *The Diocese of Kilmore: its History and Antiquities*, Dublin: Browne and Nolan, 1937, NLI Ir. 274119 o 3, 579 p.

O'Flynn, T., *History of Leitrim*, Dublin: C.J. Fallon, 1937, NLI Ir. 94121 o 3, 109 p.

Simington, Robert C., *The transplantation to Connacht, 1654–58*, Shannon: Irish University Press for the Irish Manuscripts Commission, 1970, NLI Ir. 94106 s 9, 306 p.

Local Journals
Ardagh & Clonmacnoise Historical Society Journal, NLI Ir. 794105
Breifne, NLI Ir. 94119 b 2
Breifny, NLI Ir. 794106 b 1
The Drumlin: a Journal of Cavan, Leitrim and Monaghan, NLI Ir. 05 d 345

Directories

1824	J. Pigot and Co., *City of Dublin and Hibernian Provincial Directory*, NLI, LDS Film 451787
1846	Slater's *National Commercial Directory of Ireland*. PRONI, NLI LO, LDS Film 1696703 Item 3
1856	Slater, *Royal National Commercial Directory of Ireland*, NLI, LDS Film 1472360 Item 1
1870	Slater, *Directory of Ireland*, NLI
1881	Slater, *Royal National Commercial Directory of Ireland*, NLI
1894	Slater, *Royal Commercial Directory of Ireland*, NLI

Gravestone Inscriptions
Leitrim Heritage Centre/Leitrim County Library have transcripts for 105 graveyards in the county. Contact details will be found in Chapter 15. Published or publicly available transcripts are given below.

Cloonclare: Manorhamilton C of I. Online: Grieves
Killasnet: Lurganboy Presbyterian. Online: Grieves
Kiltubbrid: Church & Graveyard, C of I, RCBL

Estate Records
Bessborough, Earl of: Rental, 1805. NAI M.3374; Major tenants only. NAI M.3370; valuation of estate, 1813. All tenants. NAI M.3383; tenants with leases, 1813. NAI M.3384; rental, 1813. All tenants. Covering townlands in the civil parishes of: Fenagh; and Kiltubbrid.
Clements: Rentals of the Woodford estate, 1812–1828. NLI Mss. 3816–3827. All tenants. Covering townlands in the civil parish of: Carrigallen. NLI Mss. 12805–7, 3828; rental, 1812–1824 (with gaps) of Bohey townland in Cloone civil parish.

Crofton, Sir Humphrey: Rental, March 1833, with tenants' names in alphabetical order. NLI Ms. 4531. Covering townlands in the civil parishes of: Cloone; Kitoghert; Mohill; Oughteragh.

Johnson, William: Rental of the Drumkeeran estate, 1845–56. NLI Ms. 9465. All tenants. Covering townlands in the civil parish of Inishmagrath.

King, John: Rent and miscellaneous accounts, 1757–1786. NLI Ms. 3520, 3125. All tenants. Covering townlands in the civil parishes of: Fenagh; and Mohill.

King: Rent roll and estate accounts, 1801–1818. NLI Ms. 4170. Major tenants only. Covering townlands in the civil parishes of: Fenagh; and Kiltubbrid.

Leitrim, Earl of: Rental and accounts 1837–42. NLI Ms. 12787. All tenants. NLI Mss. 5728–33; rentals 1838–65. All tenants. NLI Mss. 5803–5; rentals 1842–55. All tenants. NLI Mss. 12810–12; rentals 1844–8. All tenants. NLI Mss. 179, 180; rentals 1844 & 1854. All tenants. Covering townlands in the civil parishes of: Carrigallen; Cloone; Clooneclare; Inishmagrath; Killasnet; Kiltoghert; Mohill.

Newcomen, Viscount: Rental, 1822, NAI M.2797. Mainly larger tenants. Covering townlands in the civil parish of Drumlease.

O'Beirne, Francis: Rental, 1850. NLI Ms. 8647 (14). Mainly large tenants. Covering townlands in the civil parishes of: Cloone; Drumlease; Kiltoghert.

St George, Charles Manners: Annual accounts and rentals. NLI Mss. 4001–22. Covering townlands in the civil parish of Kiltoghert.

Tottenham, Nicholas Loftus: 26 maps. NLI Ms. 9837. Major tenants only. Covering townlands in the civil parishes of: Clooneclare; Inishmagrath; Rossinver.

Tottenham, Ponsonby: Printed rental, 1802. NLI Ms. 10162. Mainly larger tenants. Covering townlands in the civil parishes of: Clooneclare; and Rossinver.

Wynne, Owen: Rentals and expense books, 1737–68. NLI Mss. 5780–5782. Major tenants only. NLI Mss. 5830–1; rent ledgers 1738–53, 1768–73. Major tenants only, indexed. NLI Mss. 3311–3; a rental and two rent ledgers, yearly from 1798 to 1825, with all tenants. Covering townlands in the civil parishes of: Clooneclare; Cloonlogher; Killanummery; Killasnet; Rossinver.

LIMERICK

Census returns and substitutes

1569	Freeholders. NLI Pos. 1700
1570	Freeholders & Gentlemen. *JNMAS*, 1964
1586	Survey of leaseholders on the Desmond estates. NAI M.5037
1641	Book of Survey and Distribution. NLI Ms. 973
1654–1656	Civil Survey, Vol. IV. *Civil Survey*, Vol. IV (NLI I 6551 Dublin)
1659	Pender's 'Census'. Repr. GPC, 1997, IMC, 2002. LDS Film 924648
1660	Rental of lands in Limerick City and County. NLI Ms. 9091
1664	Hearth Money Rolls, Askeaton *JNMAS*, 1965
1673	Valuation of part of Limerick city (estates of the earls of Roscommon and Orrery) with occupiers' names and valuation. NLI Pos. 792
1715–1794	Limerick City Freemen, LDS Film 477000 from NA (Kew)

1746–1836	Freemen, Limerick. NLI, Pos. 5526. *JNMAS*, 1944–5. Online: Celtic cousins
1761	Freeholders, Limerick city (16092) and county (16093). NLI Ms. 16092; Ms. 16093
1766	Abington, Cahircomey, Cahirelly, Carrigparson, Clonkeen, Kilkellane, Tuogh NAI Parl. Ret. 681/684. Protestants only Croagh, Kilscannel, Nantinan and Rathkeale. *IA*, 1977. Tuogh in Duggan, *Cappamore*. Online: Connors
1776	Freeholders entitled to vote. NAI M.1321–2. Voters. NAI M.4878
1783	Burgesses of Kilmallock, NLI Ms. 10941
1793–1821	Two Lists of People Resident in the Area of Newcastle in 1793 and 1821. *IA*, Vol. 16, No. 1 (1984)
1798	Rebel Prisoners in Limerick Jail. *JNMAS*, Vol. 10 (1), 1966
1813	Chief inhabitants of the parishes of St Mary's and St John's, Limerick. *IA*, Vol. 17, No. 2, 1985
1816–28	Freeholders. GO 623. Also LDS Film 100224
1821	Some extracts. NAI Thrift Absracts
1821	Fragments only, Kilfinane district. *JNMAS*, 1975
1823–1838	Tithe Books. Part online: Connors
1829	Freeholders. GO 623
1835	Householders, Parish of Templebredin. *JNMAS*, 1975
1835–1839	List of inhabitants of Limerick taking water (Waterworks accounts). NLI Pos. 3451
1838–1848	Reproductive Loan Fund records. Administered from Limerick city, for all areas of the city and county. More than 5,000 names. NA (Kew), T 91. Partly online: Moving Here
1840	Freeholders, Barony of Coshlea. NLI Ms.9452
1840	Rate Books: Kilfinnane NLI Ms. 2026, Kilmallock NLI Ms. 9449. With comments
1843	Voters. NAI OP 1843/66
1846	Survey of Households in connection with famine relief. Loughill, Foynes, Shanagolden areas. NLI Ms. 582
1848–1851?	Undated lists of paupers in the Loughill E. Division showing families and individual's names, ages and address. Lists of inmates of Glin Union workhouse. NLI Ms. 13413
1851–1852	Griffith's Valuation. Indexed online: Hayes. 24 parishes transcribed online: Leitrim-Roscommon
1851	Some extracts. NAI Thrift Absracts
1852	'Analysis of the late election showing the entire list of the poll' Limerick County Library
1870	Rate Book for Clanwilliam barony. NAI M.2434
1901	Census
1911	Census

Online

Celtic cousins	*www.celticcousins.net*
Connors	*www.connorsgenealogy.com*
Devries	*www.geocities.com/luanndevries*
Hayes, John	*www.failteromhat.com*
Leitrim-Roscommon	*www.leitrim-roscommon.com*
Moving Here	*www.movinghere.org.uk/search/*

Publications

Local histories, etc.

Famine Ireland: Limerick. Extracts from British Parliamentary Papers, 1846–49, relating to Limerick City and County, Limerick Corporation Public Library, [Photocopied and bound into two vols, 274 pp.]

O'Grady Papers (Kilballyowen, Co. Limerick), *AH*, XV, 35–62

Barry, J.G., 'Cromwellian Settlement of Co. Limerick', NLI, *Limerick Field Journal*, Vols 1–8, 1897–1908, IIr 794205 l 1, effectively an edition of the Books of Survey and Distribution

Begley, Canon John, *The Diocese of Limerick,* Dublin: Browne and Nolan, 1906–38, NLI, 3 vols. Vol. I Ancient and Medieval, 1906. Vol. II Sixteenth and Seventeenth Centuries, 1927. Vol. III 1691 to the Present, 1938. Reprinted, Limerick, 1993

Bennis, E.H., *Reminiscences of Old Limerick,* Limerick: George McKern & Sons, 1939, NLI, GO 674, 30 p.

Carroll, J., *Village by the Shannon,* Limerick, 1991, 144 p. Co-Author, R. Tuohy. A history of Castleconnell

Cochrane, Mary, *Clounleharde, Ireland to MT Ararat, Gippsland: a history of the Dore family, 1841–1982,* Victoria, Australia: Parkenham Gazette, 1982, NLI, GO 414, 50 p.

Connellan, Canon Brendan, *Light on the Past—Story of St. Mary's Parish,* Limerick: Connellan, 2001, Limerick City Library, 147 p.

Cronin, Patrick, *The auld town: a chronicle of Askeaton,* Limerick: Askeaton Civic Trust, 1995, NLI Ir. 94144 c, 111 p.

Cronin, Patrick J., *Eas Céad Tine, 'The Waterfall of the Hundred Fires',* Askeaton: 1999, 90 p. [A history of Askeaton.]

Curtin, Gerard, *Recollections of our native valley. A history of Loughill-Ballyhahill and the Owavaun Valley,* Ballyhahill: 1996, NLI Ir. 94144 c 13, 405 p.

Curtin, Gerard, *A pauper warren: West Limerick 1845–49,* Ballyhahill, Co. Limerick: Sliabh Luachra Books, 2000, NLI Ir. 94144 c 19

Dowd, Rev. James, *St Mary's Cathedral Limerick,* Limerick: 1936, NLI Ir. 7266 d 6, Rev. by T.F. Abbott, 'who has included notes on the cathedral organ with a succession of bishops and a list of deans'

Dowd, Rev. James, *Limerick and its Sieges*, Limerick: M'Kern & sons 1896 NLI Ir. 94144 d 2, 195 p.

Duggan, Eileen, *Cappamore a parish history*, Cappamore: Cappamore Historical Society, 1992, NLI Ir. 94145 c 22, 438 p.

Dunraven, Countess of, *Memorials of Adare Manor*, Oxford: 1865, NLI Ir. 94144 d 3, c.350 p.

Dwyer, Philip, *The Diocese of Killaloe, from the Reformation to the Close of the Eighteenth Century*, Dublin: Hodges, Foster, and Figgis, 1878, NLI Ir. 94143 d 11, 602 p. Reprint: Newmarket-on-Fergus: O'Brien Book Publications, 1997

Farrell, Noel, *Rathkeale/Newcastle family roots: exploring family origins in Rathkeale & Newcastle West*, Longford: Noel Farrell, 2001, NLI, 3B 500, 48 p.

Feheny, J.P.M., *Ballysteen, the people and the place*, Blarney: Iverus, 1998, NLI, 201 p.

Fennell, Paul D., *The Fennells of Manister, Co. Limerick, Eire*, Baltimore, MD: Gateway Press, 2000, NLI Ir. 9292 f 34, 309 p.

Ferrar, John, *The History of Limerick, Ecclesiastical, Civil and Military, from the earliest records to the year 1787*, Limerick, 1767, NLI, J.94144.FER/1787, 492p .2nd ed., much revised and enlarged, 1787

Fitzgerald, P., *The history, topography and antiquities of the city and county of Limerick*, Dublin: 1826–1827, NLI. Co-author, J.J. McGregor

Fitzgerald, Séamus, *Cappawhite and Doon*, Pallasgrean: S. Fitzgerald, 1983, NLI Ir. 9141 p 43, 124 p.

Fleming, John, *Reflections, historical and topographical on Ardpatrick, Co. Limerick*, Limerick: the author, 1979, NLI Ir. 94144 f 5, 165 p.

Gaughan, Rev. J.A., *The Knights of Glin: a Geraldine family*, Dublin: Humanities Press, 1978, NLI Ir. 9292 g 17, 222 p.

Hamilton, G.F., *Records of Ballingarry*, Limerick, 1930, NLI Ir. 94144 h 2

Hannan, Kevin, *Limerick historical reflections*, Limerick: 1996, 352 p.

Hayes, Richard, 'Some Notable Limerick Doctors', *JNMAS*, I, 3, 1938, 113–123

Hayes, Richard, *The German Colony in County Limerick*, NLI, *JNMAS*, 1937, Palatines

Herbert, Robert, *Worthies of Thomond: a compendium of short lives of the most famous men and women of Limerick and Clare*, Limerick: printed by the *Limerick Leader* Ltd., and published by the author, 1946, NLI, 3 parts

Hynes, G. Carew, *Dún Bleisce, a history*, Doon: Cumann Forbartha Dhún Bleisce, 1990, NLI Ir. 94144 d 10, 200 p.

IGRS, *Tombstone inscriptions Vol. 1*, Dublin: IGRS Tombstone Committee, 2001, NLI, 850 p.

Jackson, R.W., *Freemasonry in Sligo 1767 to 1867* Beverley: Wright & Hoggard, 1909, NLI, 16 p.

Jackson, R.W., *The History of St Michael's Church, Limerick, 1844–1944*, Limerick: 1944

Jones, Hank, *The Palatine Families of Ireland*, San Leandro, 1965, NLI Ir. 9292 p 6

Kerins, C., *Ballingarry, Granagh, and Clouncagh, archival records 1800–1900*, Dublin: Christy Kerins, 2000, NLI Ir. 94144 b 11, 184 p.

Lee, David, *Remembering Limerick*, Limerick: Limerick Civic Trust/FÁS, 1997, NLI Ir. 94144 r 1, 407 p. [Essays on the 800th anniversary of the charter]

Lee, Rev. Dr C., 'Statistics from Knockainy and Patrickswell parishes, 1819–1940', NLI, *JCHAS*, Vol. 47, No. 165

Lenihan, Maurice, *Limerick, its history and antiquities*, Dublin: 1866, NLI Ir. 94144 l 1, Facsimile reprint, Cork (Mercier Press), 1967, 780 p. Reprint, with new index, 1991

Lyddy, Margaret, *St Joseph's Parish, A history*, Limerick: 1990, 31 p. Lists Quaker gravestones in Ballinacurra

MacCaffrey, James, *The Black Book of Limerick*, Dublin: M.H. Gill & Son, 1907. NLI Ir. 27414 m 1

Meistrell, Rita J., *The James Sullivan family: Emigrants from Lisready Cripps, Loughill, County Limerick and their descendants*, Los Angeles: Rita J. Meistrell, 1999, NLI Ir. 9292 m 87, 258 p.

Meredyth, Francis, *Descriptive and Historic Guide, St Mary's Cathedral*, Limerick: 1887

Moloney, Rev. M., 'The Parish of St Patrick, Limerick', *JNMAS*, I, 1937, 102

Nash, Roisín, *A bibliography of Limerick*, Limerick: 1962

O'Connor, Patrick J., *People make places: the story of the Irish Palatines*, Newcastle West: Oireacht na Mumhan Books, 1989, NLI Ir. 941 o 71, 229 p.

O'Connor, Patrick J., *Hometown. A Portrait of Newcastle West, Co Limerick*, Oireacht na Mumhan Books, NLI

O'Donovan, John, *Letters and extracts relative to ancient territories in Thomond*, Dublin: Ordnance Survey, 1841, NLI Ir. 9141 o 19

O'Sullivan, Michael F., *A History of Hospital and its environs*, Cullen: Michael F. O'Sullivan, 1995, NLI Ir. 94144 o 7, 135 p.

Press, Kate, *West Limerick families abroad*, Melbourne: Press, Kate, 2001, NLA 217 p. Co-author, Valerie Thompson

Seoighe, Mainchin, *Sean Chill Mocheallóg = Old Kilmallock*, Cumann na Máighe, 1975, NLI Ir. 941 p 87, 26 p.

Seoighe, Mainchin, *Dromin Athlacca: the story of a rural parish in Co. Limerick*, Athlacca: Glór na nGael, 1978, NLI Ir. 94144 s 3, 214 p.

Seoighe, Mainchin, *From Bruree to Corcomhide: the district where world statesman Éamon de Valera grew up and where the illustrious Mac Eniry family ruled*, Bruree, Co. Limerick: Bruree/Rockhill Development Association, 2000, NLI Ir. 91414 s 15, 562 p.

Seoighe, Mainchin, *Bruree; the history of the Bruree district i.e., the history of the parish of Bruree and of the old parish of Tankardstown*, Bruree: Rockhill Development Assoc, 1973, NLI Ir. 94144 s 4, 184 p.

Seoighe, Mainchin, *Portrait of Limerick*, London: R. Hale, 1982, NLI Ir. 914144 s 6, Wide-ranging historical and geographical tour of City and County

Seymour, St John D., *The Diocese of Emly*, Dublin: C of I Print, 1913, NLI Ir. 27414 s 1, 297 p.

Sheehan, John, *A corner of Limerick history, recollections and photographs,*

Ballybrown, Co. Limerick: John Sheehan, 1989, NLI Ir. 94144 s 8, History of Ballybrown 311 p.

Spellisy, Seán, *Limerick, the Rich Land,* O'Brien's Bookshop, 1989, NLI Ir. 94144 s 7, 286 p.

Stewart, Dorothy, *A Short history of St John's Church, Limerick,* Ballysimon [Co. Limerick], 1952, NLI Ir. 2741 p 23, 12 p.

Tierney, Mark, *Murroe and Boher, history of an Irish country parish,* Dublin: Browne and Nolan, 1966, NLI Ir. 94144 t 1, 251 p.

Toomey, Thomas, *An antique and storied land a history of the parish of Donoughmore, Knockea, Roxborough and its environs in County Limerick by Thomas Toomey,* Limerick: 1991, NLI Ir. 94144.t.4. Co-author, Harry Greensmyth. 374 p.

Tuthill, P.B., *Pedigree of the family of Villiers of Kilpeacon, Co. Limerick,* London: 1907

Walter, J. & S., *A little of Limerick, an account of the Hickey, Scanlan, and Baggott families of Camperdown and Cobden,* Australia: 1999, 319 p.

Westropp, *Westropp Manuscripts, Royal Irish Academy,* Will abstracts mainly for Counties Clare and Limerick

Whelan, Frank, *Cappagh: a sense of history,* Ballingrane: Whelan, 2003, NLI, 147 p. 2nd ed.

White, John D., *The History of the Family of White of Limerick, Knockcentry, etc.,* 1887, NLI Ir. 9292 w 10

White, Rev. P., *History of Clare and the Dalcassian Clans of Tipperary, Limerick and Galway,* Dublin: 1893, NLI Ir. 94143 w 4, 398 p. Repr. Newmarket-on-Fergus: O'Brien Book Publications, 1997

Winkler, Rosemary McNerney, *McNerney, Mc Inerney genealogy: a family from Glin, Kilfergus Parish, County Limerick, Ireland,* Albuquerque, NM: R.M. Winkler, 2001, LOC

Local Journals

Journal of the North Munster Archaeological Society, NLI Ir. 794105 n 1

Journal of the Newcastle West Historical Society, NLI Ir. 94143 n 2

The Dawn (Journal of the Bruff Historical Society), NLI Ir. 94144 d

The Glencorbry Chronicle

Limerick Field Journal, NLI Ir. 794205 l 1

Lough Gur Historical Society Journal, LCL

Old Limerick Journal, NLI Ir. 94144 o 2

Directories

1769   John Ferrar, *Directory of Limerick.* Online: Celtic cousins

1788   Richard Lucas, *General Directory of the Kingdom of Ireland,* NLI Pos. 3729. Repr. in Veale, *Lucas, IG* 1965, 1966, 1967, 1968. Online: Celtic cousins

1809   Holden's *annual London and country directory of the United Kingdoms & Wales, in three volumes, for … 1811.* (3 vols. Facsimile repr. Norwich M. Winton, 1996) NLI G 942 h 23, LDS Film 258722 Item 2

1820   J. Pigot, *Commercial Directory of Ireland* PRONI, NLI Ir. 9141 p 107, LDS
            Film 962702 Item 1
1824   J. Pigot and Co., *City of Dublin and Hibernian Provincial Directory*, NLI,
            LDS Film 451787
1846   Slater's *National Commercial Directory of Ireland*. PRONI, NLI LO, LDS
            Film 1696703 Item 3
1856   Slater, *Royal National Commercial Directory of Ireland*, NLI, LDS Film
            1472360 Item 1
1866   George Henry Bassett, *Directory of the City and County of Limerick, and of
            the Principal Towns in the Cos. of Tipperary and Clare*, NLI Ir. 914144 b 5
1870   Slater, *Directory of Ireland*, NLI
1879   George Henry Bassett, *Limerick Directory*
1881   Slater, *Royal National Commercial Directory of Ireland*, NLI
1886   Francis Guy, *Postal Directory of Munster*, NLI Ir. 91414 g 8, LDS Film
            1559399 Item 8
1889   George Henry Bassett, *The Book of Tipperary* (Ballylooby)
1893   Francis Guy, *Directory of Munster*, NLI Ir. 91414 g 8
1894   Slater, *Royal Commercial Directory of Ireland*, NLI

Gravestone Inscriptions
Abbeyfeale: Main Street, RC, O'K, Vol. 11
Ardcanny: Melllon, *IA*, Vol. 9, No. 1, 1977
Ardpatrick: Fleming, John, *Reflections (...) on Ardpatrick*, 1979
Askeaton: C of I, *IGRS*, Vol. 1
Athlacca: Athlacca South, C of I, Seoighe, Mainchin, *Dromin, Athlacca*, 1978
Ballingarry: Hamilton, *Ballingarry*
Bruree: Howardstown North, Seoighe, *Brú Rí*
—— Ballynoe, C of I, Seoighe, *Brú Rí*
Dromin: Dromin South, Seoighe, *Dromin, Athlacca*
Grange: Grange Lower, *IA*, NLI Ir. 9205 i 3
Limerick, St Michael's: Ballinacurra (Bowman), Quaker, Lyddy, *St Joseph's Parish*
Kilbeheny: Churchquarter, C of I, *IG*
Killeedy: Mountcollins, Casey, Albert, O'K, Vol. 11
Knockainy: Loughgur, *Lough Gur Historical Society Journal*, 1 (1985) 51–61
—— Patrickswell, RC, *Lough Gur Historical Society Journal*, 2 (1986) 71–9
Nantinan: Nantinan, C of I, *IA*, NLI Ir. 9205 i 3
Rathkeale: Rathkeale, Church Street, C of I, *IA*, NLI Ir. 9205 i 3, Vol. 14, No. 2, 1982
Stradbally: Stradbally North, Shannon Lodge, C of I, *IGRS*, Vol. 1
Tankardstown: Tankardstown Sough, Seoighe, *Brú Rí*

Estate Records
Ashtown, Lord: Rent Ledger, 1839–1882 NLI Mss. 5823–5. All tenants. Covering
    townlands in the civil parishes of: Athneasy; Ballingarry (Coshlea); Crecora;
    Darragh; Emlygrennan; Galbally; Kilbreedy Major; Kilfinnane; Kilflyn;
    Knocklong; Particles.

Bourke, Major General Richard: Rent rolls, 1831. NLI Mss. 19787, 19790–19798. Principally major tenants. Covering townlands in the civil parishes of: Abington; Ballingarry (Connello); Ballybrood; Ballynaclogh; Doon; Uregare.

Castle Oliver estate: NLI Ms. 10933 (Part 1). Some tenants only, 1827–1832. Coverage unclear. Covering townlands in the civil parishes of: Ballingarry (Connello); Ballingarry (Coshlea); Darragh; Emlygrennan; Kilfinnane; Kilflyn; Knocklong; Particles; St Peter's and St Paul's.

Chetwood, Jonathan: Rent ledger, 1816–1822. NLI Ms. 14250. Most tenants. Covering townlands in the civil parishes of: Limerick; St Patrick's; Ludden.

Cloncurry, Lord: Rentals, 1825–1850. NLI Mss. 3417, 5661–6, 5693–5, 9053. Principally major tenants. Covering townlands in the civil parishes of: Abington; Loghill.

Collins: Tenants, 1859–1889, NLI Ms. 17718. All tenants. Covering townlands in the civil parishes of Abbeyfeale.

Creaghe, John Fitzstephen: Printed LEC Rental, 1820–1868. NAI M.3703 (183). Principally major tenants. Covering townlands in the civil parishes of: Kilfergus; St Peter's and St Paul's.

de Lacy Smith: Rental, 1740–1744. NLI Ms. 869. Major tenants only. Covering townlands in the civil parishes of: Ardcanny; Ballycahane; Kilcornan; Knockainy.

Fitzmaurice, James: Rent book, 1851–1871. NLI Ms. 19451. Most tenants. Covering townlands in the civil parishes of Templebredon.

Gascoigne, Richard Oliver: Leases, 1764–1772. NLI Ms. 10930 (2) (Part 2). Principally major tenants. Covering townlands in the civil parishes of: Abbeyfeale; Ballingarry (Connello); Croom; Grean; Kilcornan.

Gascoigne, Richard Oliver: Rent books, tenants' lists, etc. 1816–1840. NLI Ms. 10930, 10936. Most tenants. Covering townlands in the civil parishes of: Ballingarry (Connello); Darragh; Emlygrennan; Kilbreedy Major; Kilfinnane; Kilflyn; Knocklong; Particles; Uregare.

Greene, Henry: Tenants' list, 1775–1790. NAI M.5555(1). Major tenants only. Covering townlands in the civil parishes of: Ballynaclogh; Cahernarry; Ludden.

Kingston, Earl of: Rental, 1840. NLI Ms. 3276. All tenants. Covering townlands in the civil parishes of: Ballingarry (Coshlea); Ballylanders; Brigown; Effin; Glenkeen; Kilbeheny; Knockainy; Macroney; Templetenny.

Lefroy, Seycant: Rental, 1812. NLI Ms. 10930 (3) (Part 2). Major tenants only. Covering townlands in the civil parishes of: Kilbreedy Major; Kilmeedy; St Peter's and St Paul's.

Kingston, Earl of: Rental, 1840. NLI Ms. 3276. All tenants. Covering townlands in the civil parishes of: Ballingarry (Coshlea); Ballylanders; Brigown; Effin; Glenkeen; Kilbeheny; Knockainy; Macroney; Templetenny.

Lefroy, Seycant: Rental, 1812. NLI Ms. 10932 (Part 1). Major tenants only. Covering townlands in the civil parishes of: Kilbreedy Major; Kilmeedy; St Peter's and St Paul's.

Lefroy, Thomas: Rental, Leases, 1807–1812. NLI Ms. 10933 (Part 6). Major tenants only. Covering townlands in the civil parishes of: Kilbreedy Major; Kilmeedy.

Lloyd, Dr Thomas: Rent roll, 1843. NLI Ms. 11429 (2). Most tenants. Covering townlands in the civil parishes of: Caherconlish; Doon; Fedamore; Knocknagaul; Oola; Particles.

Monsell: Rentals, 1840–1848. NLI Ms. 7868, 7869. All tenants. Covering townlands in the civil parishes of: Ballycahane; Kilkeedy; Killeely; Kiltallagh; Mungret; Rathronan.

Monsell, William: Rental, 1852–1855. NLI Ms. 7870. Major tenants only. Covering townlands in the civil parishes of Athlacca, Donaghmore, Kilkeedy, Killeely, Killeenagarriff, Mungret, Rathronan, Stradbally.

Monteagle papers: Rent book, 1800–1807, NLI Ms. 605A. Major tenants only. Covering townlands in the civil parishes of: Cappagh; Kilmoylan; Loghill; Robertstown; Shanagolden; St Peter's and St Paul's.

Oliver estate: Rentals, 1775–1831 (intermittent). NLI Mss. 10930–4, 9091. Principally major tenants. Covering townlands in the civil parishes of: Athneasy; Ballingaddy; Ballingarry (Connello); Ballingarry (Coshlea); Darragh; Emlygrennan; Kilfinnane; Kilflyn; Knocklong; Particles; St Peter's and St Paul's; Uregare.

Sexton, Edmond: Tenants, 1725. NLI Ms. 16085. Major tenants only. Covering townlands in the civil parishes of: Adare; Croom; Killeedy.

Tuthill: Rentals, 1745–1841. NAI M.5825. Principally major tenants. Covering townlands in the civil parishes of: Adare; Ballycahane; Bruree; Caherconlish; Caherelly; Crecora; Croagh; Croom; Doon; Fedamore; Grean; Kilfrush; Kilpeacon; Knocknagaul.

Wandesforde, Prior: Rent book, 1804–1819. NLI Ms. 14171. Principally major tenants. Covering townlands in the civil parishes of Clonagh; Cloncagh; Corcomohide; Darragh; Dromcolliher; Kilmeedy; Kilmoylan; Kilscannell; Rathkeale.

Webb, James: Rental, 1765–1772. NLI Ms. 7867. Major tenants only. Covering townlands in the civil parishes of: Adare; Ballycahane; Monasteranenagh.

[No landlord given]: Rental. Townlands of Leheys and Ballinree, 1815–1818. NLI Ms. 13413 (7). Major tenants only. Civil parishes of: Robertstown; Shanagolden.

[No landlord given]: NAI M.3668 (12). Map, 1840. All tenants. Covering townlands in the civil parish of Newcastle.

LONGFORD

Census returns and substitutes

1641   Book of Survey and Distribution. NLI Ms. 965

1659   Pender's 'Census'. Repr. GPC, 1997, IMC, 2002. LDS Film 924648. Online: Genweb Longford

1726–1727 Protestant householders, Abbeylara, Abbeyshrule, Ardagh, Clonbroney, Clongesh, Kilcommock, Killashee, Rathreagh, Shrule, Taghshiny (Longford); Rathsapick, Russagh (Westmeath). List compiled for the distribution of religious books. NAI M.1502

1729   Presbyterian exodus from Co. Longford. *Breifny*, 1977–1978
1740   Protestants, Shrule & Rathreagh (Longford); Rathaspick (Westmeath)
            RCBL GS 2/7/3/25
1747–1806 Freeholders. Registration book. NAI M.2745
1790   Freeholders c.1790 NAI M.2486 8. NLI Pos. 1897. LDS Film 100888
1795–1862 Charleton Marriage Certificates. NAI M.2800. Indexed in Accessions,
            Vol. 37.
1796   Spinning-Wheel Premium List. 2,550 names for Co. Longford. Online:
            Hayes
1800–1835 Freeholders. GO 444. Also LDS 100181
1823–1838 Tithe Books. Fully transcribed and indexed in Rymsza, *Co. Longford
            Residents*
1834   Granard RC parish; heads of household—with Catholic registers. NLI
1828–1836 Freeholders' certificates. NAI M.2781
1838   Mullinanalaghta RC parish—contributors to new church *Teathbha*, 1
            (3), 1978, 244–51
1843   Voters NAI OP 1843/62
1854   Griffith's Valuation. Indexed online: Hayes. Indexed in Leahy, *Co.
            Longford Survivors*
1901   Census. Full index in Leahy *Co. Longford and its People*. Part online:
            Genweb Longford
1911   Census

Online

Genweb Longford	*www.rootsweb.com/~irllog*	Many records transcribed
Hayes, John	*www.failteromhat.com*	

Publications
Local histories, etc.

Brady, G., *In Search of Longford Roots,* Offaly Historical Society, 1987, NLI Ir. 94136
    t 1
Brady, J., *A short history of the parishes of the diocese of Meath, 1867–1944,* NLI Ir.
    94132 b 2
Butler, H.T. & H.E., *The Black Book of Edgeworthstown 1585 1817,* 1927
Cobbe, D., *75 Years of the Longford Leader,* 1972, NLI, ILB 07
Devaney, O., *Killoe: History of a Co. Longford Parish,* 1981, NLI Ir. 9413 d 1
Farrell, James P., *History of the county of Longford,* Dublin, 1891, NLI Ir. 94131 f 2
Farrell, Noel, *Exploring Family origins in Longford,* Longford, Longford Leader,
    1991
Gillespie, Raymond, *Longford: Essays in County History,* Dublin: Lilliput Press,
    1991, Dublin City Library (1), 941.812. Co-editor, Gerard Moran
Healy, John, *History of the Diocese of Meath,* Dublin, 1908, 2 vols
Kelly, Francis, *Window on a Catholic parish St Mary's, Granard, Co. Longford,*
    Blackrock, Co. Dublin: Irish Academic Press, 1996, NLI Ir. 27413 k 5, 63 p.

Leahy, David, *Co. Longford Survivors of the Great Famine: index to Griffith's for Co. Longford*, Raheen: Derryvrin Press, 1996, NLI Ir. 94131 L 3, 236 p.

Leahy, David, *Co. Longford and its People*, Dublin: Flyleaf Press, 1990, NLI GS/ Ir. 9413.L.1, 214 p. 1901 census index

Lefroy, Sir J.H., *Notes and Documents relating to the Lefroy family (...) of Carrickglas, Co. Longford*, Woolwich: The Royal Artillery institution, 1868, NLI Ir. 9292 l 18, 233 p.

MacNamee, James J., *History of the Diocese of Ardagh*, Dublin: Browne and Nolan, 1954, NLI Ir. 274131 m 5, 858 p.

McGivney, J., *Placenames of the Co. Longford*, Longford: 1908

Mimnagh, John, *'To the four winds': famine times in north Longford*: Mullingar: the author, 1997, NLI Ir. 9413 m 3, 112 p.

Monahan, Rev. J., *Records Relating to the Diocese of Ardagh and Clonmacnoise*, Dublin: M.H. Gill and son, 1886, NLI Ir. 27413 m 3, 400 p.

Murray, Mary Celine, *Bibliography of the Co. Longford*, Longford: 1961, LDS Film 1279275

Murtagh, H., *Irish Midland Studies*, Athlone: Old Athlone Society, 1980, NLI Ir. 941 m 58, 255 p.

Rymsza, Guy, *County Longford Residents Prior to the Famine*, South Bend, Indiana: Dome Shadow Press, 2004, Longford County Library, 439 p.; A Transcription and Complete Index of the Tithe Applotment Books of County Longford, Ireland (1823–1835), DCLA

Stafford, R.W., *St Patrick's Church of Ireland Granard: Notes of Genealogical & Historical Interest*, 1983, NLI Ir. 914131 s 3

Local Journals
Ardagh & Clonmacnoise Historical Society Journal, NLI Ir. 794105
Teathbha, NLI Ir. 94131 t 1

Directories

1824 J. Pigot and Co., *City of Dublin and Hibernian Provincial Directory*, NLI, LDS Film 451787

1846 Slater's *National Commercial Directory of Ireland*. PRONI, NLI LO, LDS Film 1696703 Item 3

1856 Slater, *Royal National Commercial Directory of Ireland*, NLI, LDS Film 1472360 Item 1

1870 Slater, *Directory of Ireland*, NLI

1881 Slater, *Royal National Commercial Directory of Ireland*, NLI

1894 Slater, *Royal Commercial Directory of Ireland*, NLI

Gravestone Inscriptions
Ballymacormick: RC, Farrell, *Exploring Family origins*
—— Ballinamore, Farrell, *Exploring Family origins*
Granard: Granard, The Hill, C of I, Stafford, *St Patrick's*

Templemichael: Longford town, Pres, Farrell, *Exploring Family origins*
Templemichael: Longford, Church Street, C of I, Farrell

Estate Records

Adair, John: Rentals, 1738–1767. NLI Ms. 3859. Coverage unclear. Covering townlands in the civil parish of Clonbroney.

Aldborough estate: rentals, 1846. NAI M.2971.

Barbon, James: Map, 1815. NAI M.771. All tenants. Covering townlands in the civil parish of Cashel.

Buckingham, Duke of: Estate sale, 1848. NLI 14.A.20. All tenants. Covering townlands in the civil parish of Granard.

Coates, Thomas: Rental, 1822. NAI M.1883(iv). Major tenants only. Covering townlands in the civil parish of Abbeyshrule.

Crofton, Sir Humphrey: Rental and Account, 1832–1833. NLI Ms. 4531. All tenants. Covering townlands in the civil parish of Killashee.

Dopping: Rentals, 1833–1882. NLI Ms. 9,993. All tenants. Covering townlands in the civil parish of Columbkille.

Edgeworth: Map, 1727. NLI 16. H.28(10). All tenants. Covering townlands in the civil parish of Clonbroney.

Edgeworth, Rev. Essez: Account Book of Tithes, 1719–1727. NAI M.1502. Most tenants. Covering townlands in the civil parishes of: Ballymacormick; Clongesh; Granard; Kilcommock; Killoe; Mostrim; Templemichael.

Edgeworth, Richard: Rental, accounts, valuations, 1760–1849. NAI M.1497, M.1503, M.1505. All tenants. Covering townlands in the civil parishes of: Ardagh; Clonbroney; Granard; Mostrim; Templemichael.

Enery, John: Rental, 1750 NAI M.1883(ii). All tenants. Covering townlands in the civil parishes of: Agharra; Kilglass; Killoe.

Fetherstonh, Sir Thomas: Rental, 1820. NAI M.1314. All tenants. Covering townlands in the civil parish of Killoe.

Fox, James: Rental, 1819. NLI Pos. 4065. All tenants. Covering townlands in the civil parishes of: Cashel; Mostrim; Rathcline.

Harman/King Harman: Rentals, accounts and maps, 1757–1846. NAI M.1259, 1273, 1311, 1865, 1866, 1869, 1883, 1918, 1921, 1922, 1924. All tenants. Covering townlands in the civil parishes of: Abbeyshrule; Agharra; Cashel; Columbkille; Forgney; Kilcommock; Kilglass; Killashee; Killoe; Mostrim; Noughaval; Rathcline; Shrule; Taghshinny; Templemichael.

King, John: Rent and Miscellaneous accounts, 1757–1786. NLI Mss. 3520,3125. All tenants. Covering townlands in the civil parish of Rathcline.

Jessop, John H.: Survey, 1801. NLI Ms. 10,209. All tenants. Covering townlands in the civil parishes of: Ardagh; Ballymacormick; Clongesh; Forgney; Moydow; Taghsheenod; Taghshinny.

Lorton, Lord: Tenants list, 1847–1847. NLI Ms. 18,244. All tenants. Covering townlands in the civil parishes of: Cashel; Clongesh; Granard; Mostrim; Shrule; Taghshinny.

Montfort, H.: Rental, 1845–1848. NLI Ms. 16,843. Most tenants. Covering townlands in the civil parish of Killashee.

Newcommen, Viscount: Maps, 1826–1827. NLI Ms. 2766. All tenants. Covering townlands in the civil parishes of: Abbeylara; Ardagh Cashel; Clonbroney; Clongesh; Granard; Kilcommock; Killashee; Killoe; Templemichael.

Oxmantown, Lord: Accounts, 1798–9. NAI M.1279. Major tenants only. Covering townlands in the civil parishes of: Abbeyshrule; Agharra; Ballymacormick; Cashel; Columbkille; Forgney; Kilcommock; Kilglass; Killashee; Mostrim; Noughaval; Rathcline; Shrule; Taghsheenod; Taghshinny.

Rochfort: Poor Rent, 1851–1854. NAI M.1262. Most tenants. Covering townlands in the civil parishes of: Columbkille; Killoe.

Rosse, Countess Dowager of: Surveys, rentals, tithes, maps and valuations, 1810–1837. NAI M.1883(v), 1914–6, 1284, 1286, 1290, 1294–5, 1301. All tenants. Covering townlands in the civil parishes of: Abbeyshrule; Agharra; Columbkille; Ballymacormick; Cashel; Clonbroney; Forgney; Kilcommock; Kilglass; Killashee; Killoe; Mostrim; Noughaval; Rathcline; Taghsheenod; Taghshinny; Templemichael; Shrule.

[No landlord given]: Survey and Valuation, 1810–1871. NAI M.1309. All tenants. Covering townlands in the civil parishes of: Columbkille; Killoe.

LOUTH

Census returns and substitutes

1538–1940	A Genealogical Survey of the Townland of Dowdallshill, Dundalk, Co. Louth. Online: Hall
1600	Gentlemen of Co. Louth. *JCLAHS*, Vol. 4, No. 4 1919/20
1625–1627	Leet Court Rolls. Jurors and litigants in Armagh Manor; Arboe, Ardtrea, Donaghmore (Tyrone); Termonfeckin (Louth) SA, Vol. 11, No. 9, 1957 pp. 295–322
1641	Book of Survey and Distribution. NLI Ms. 974
1659	Pender's 'Census'. Repr. GPC, 1997, IMC, 2002. LDS Film 924648
1663	Hearth Money Roll. *JCLAHS*, Vol. 6, Nos 2 & 4, Vol. 7, No. 3
1666	Hearth Money Roll, Dunleer parish *IG*, 1969
1670/1	Armagh diocese gentry, clergy and parishioners supporting the Franciscans. SA Vol. 15, No. 1, 1992, 186–216
1683	Louth brewers and retailers. *JCLAHS*, Vol. 3, No. 3
1683	Drogheda merchants. *JCLAHS*, Vol. 3, No. 3
1715	Dunleer Freemen *IG* 4(2), 1969, 142–4
1739–1741	Corn census of Co. Louth. *JCLAHS*, Vol. 11, No. 4, pp. 254 86
1756	Commissions of Array, giving lists of Protestants who took the oath. NLI Pos. 4011 Online: Hall
1760	Ardee parish, *IG*, 1961. PRONI
1766	Ardee, Ballymakenny, Beaulieu, Carlingford, Charlestown, Clonkeehan, Darver, Drumiskan, Kildermock, Kileshiel, Louth,

Mapastown, Philipstown, Shanlis, Smarmore, Stickallen, Tallonstown, Termonfeckin. NAI M.2476 (b); Creggan NAI Parl. Ret. 657 and Nelson, *History of the Parish of Creggan* ....

1775	Collon Cess Payers RCBL MIC 1/163. Online: Hall
1782–1792	Cess payers. Parishes of Cappoge, Drumcar, Dysart Monasterboice, Mullary *JCLAHS*, Vol. 9, No. 1
1791	Landholders Dromiskin parish: Leslie, *History of Kilsaran* ...
1793–1798	County Louth Assizes 1793–99 from 'The Freeman's Journal'. Online: Hall
1796	Spinning-Wheel Premium List. 3,150 names for Co. Louth. Online: Hayes
1798	Drogheda voters' list. *JCLAHS*, Vol. XX, 1984
1801	Tithe applotment Stabannon & Roodstown. *Leslie, History of Kilsaran* ...
1802	Drogheda Voters. *JCLAHS*, Vol. XX, 1984
1802	Carlingford. Protestants only. *JCLAHS*, Vol. 16, No. 3
1804	Drogheda Militia. Online: Hall
1806	Louth Militia Enlisted Recruits. Online: Hall
1816	Grand Jurors. NLI Ir. 6551 Dundalk
1821–1827	Freeholders 1821: NLI Ir. 94132 L 3; 1822 Online: Hall; 1824–7: Online: Hall; Dundalk Voters' List: Online: Hall
1823–1838	Tithe Books
1833	Memorial of the inhabitants of Drogheda about cholera. c.250 signatures NAI OP 1833/51
1834	Tallanstown parish census. *JCLAHS*, Vol. 14
1836	Memorial from inhabitants of Dundalk. c.100 names. NAI OP 1838/26
1837	Valuation of towns returning M.P.s (occupants and property values): Drogheda, Dundalk. *Parliamentary Papers 1837, Reports from Committees*, Vol. II (i), Appendix G
1837	Marksmen (illiterate voters) in parliamentary boroughs: Drogheda, Dundalk. *Parliamentary Papers 1837, Reports from Committees*, Vol. II (i), Appendix A
1837–1838	Memorials from inhabitants of Ardee. 1837 (c.90 names), 1838 (c.100 names) NAI OP 1838/26
1839	Tenants of Lord Roden—Dundalk area. Online: Hall
1842	Voters. NAI 1842/70. Online: Hall
1852	Mosstown and Phillipstown. *JCLAHS*, 1975
1852	Voting electors. NLI Ms. 1660
1854	Griffith's Valuation. Indexed online: Hayes
1854	Louth Patriotic Fund for the dependants of Crimean War soldiers. Online: Hall
1855–1856	Ardee Convent Building Fund. Online: Hall
1865	Parliamentary voters. NLI P. 2491. Online: Hall
1901	Census
1911	Census

Online

Hall, Brendan   *www.jbhall.freeservers.com*   Large compendium of
Louth records

Hayes, John   *www.failteromhat.com*

Publications

Local histories, etc.

A copy of the book of the corporation of Atherdee [Ardee] (manuscript), NLI Ms. 31778

'Families at Mosstown & Phillipstown in 1852', NLI, *JCLAHS*, Vol. XVIII, 3, 1975

'Old Title Deeds of Co. Louth; Dundalk 1718 1856', *JCLAHS*, Vol. XX, 1 1981

'Cromwellian & Restoration settlements in the parish of Dundalk', *JCLAHS*, Vol. XIX, 1 1977

'Notes on the Volunteers, Militia & Yeomanry, and Orangemen of Co. Louth', *JCLAHS*, Vol. XVIII, 4, 1976

Bernard, Nicholas, *The Whole Proceedings of the Siege of Drogheda [&] Londonderry*, Dublin, 1736. NLI Ir. 94106.b2

Boyle, Sean, *Looking Forward, Looking Back: Stories, Memories and Musings of Castlebellingham/ Kilsaran/ Stabannon*, Dundalk: 2004

Conlon, Larry, *The Heritage of Collon, 1764–1984*, Ardee: Conlon, 1984, NLI Ir. 94132 c 5, 87 p.

D'Alton, John, *The history of Drogheda*, Dublin: McGlashan and Gill, 1844, NLI Ir. 94132 d 1, 2 vols.

Day, Angelique, & McWilliams, Patrick (eds.), *Ordnance Survey Memoirs of Ireland: Volume 40 Counties of South Ulster, 1834–8, Cavan, Leitrim, Louth, Monaghan and Sligo*, Belfast: Institute of Irish Studies, 1997, NLI Ir. 9141 o 80, 216p. Co. Louth: Ballymascanlan, Carlingford, Castletown

Duffner, P., *Drogheda: the Low Lane Church 1300–1979*, NLI Ir. 94132 d 7

Duffy, Joseph, *A Clogher Record Album; a diocesan history*, Enniskillen: Cumann Seanchais Chlochair, 1975, NLI Ir. 94114 c 3, 340 p.

Garry, James, *Clogherhead through the years*, Drogheda: Old Drogheda Society, 1999, NLI Ir. 94132 g 24, 226 p.

Garry, James, *The Streets and Lanes of Drogheda*, Drogheda, 1996, NLI Ir. 91413 g 4/1, 120 p.

Gavin, Joseph, *Military barracks Dundalk: a brief history*, Dublin: Defence Forces Printing Press, 1999, NLI Ir. 355 g 9, 102 p. Co-author, Stephen O'Donnell.

Gerrard, Richard, *The story of Newtownstalaban*, Drogheda: Old Drogheda Society, 2003, NLI, 240 p.

Hall, Brendan, *Officers and recruits of the Louth Rifles, 1854–1876*, Dun Laoghaire: Genealogical Society of Ireland, 2001, NLI Ir. 94132 h 3, 188 p. (2nd ed.)

Irish Countrywomen's Association, *A Local History Guide to Summerhill and Surrounding Areas*, NLI Ir. 94132 i 1

King, Philip, *Monasterboice heritage: a centenary celebration [...]*, Monasterboice, Philip King, 1994, NLI Ir. 94132 k 1, 352 p.

Leslie, Canon J.B., *History of Kilsaran Union of Parishes*, Dundalk: Tempest, 1908, NLI Ir. 94132 l 1, 350 p.

L'Estrange, G., *Notes and Jottings concerning the parish of Charlestown Union*, Charlestown: Rectory Press, 1912, NLI Ir. 94132 l 2, 94 p.

Mac Iomhair, D., *Tombstone Inscriptions from Fochart*, Dundalk: Dundalgan press, 1968, NLI Ir. 94132 p 1, 20 p.

MacAllister, Robert Alexander Stewart, *Monasterboice, Co. Louth*, Dundalk: Tempest, 1946, NLI Ir. 7941 m 11, 79 p.

McHugh, Ned, *Drogheda before the Famine: urban poverty in the shadow of privilege 1826–45*, Maynooth: Irish Academic Press, 1998

McNeill, Charles, *Dowdall deeds*, Dublin: The Stationery Office for the Irish Manuscripts Commission, 1960, NLI Ir. 091 m 9, 416 p. Co. editor, A.J. Otway-Ruthven

McNeill, Charles, 'Some early documents relating to English Uriel, and Drogheda and Dundalk, 1: The Draycott family', *JCLAHS*, V, 1924, 270–5

McQuillan, Jack, *The railway town the story of the Great Northern Railway Works and Dundalk*, Dundalk: Dundalgan Press, 1993, NLI Ir. 625 m 17, 212 p.

Murphy, Peter, *Together in Exile*, Nova Scotia, 1991, Carlingford Library, Carlingford emigrants to St John's, New Brunswick

Murray, Rev. Lawrence P., *History of the Parish of Creggan in the Seventeenth and Eighteenth Centuries*, Dundalk: 1940

Nelson, Simon, *History of the Parish of Creggan in Cos Armagh and Louth from 1611 to 1840*, Belfast: PRONI, 1974, NLI Ir. 941 p 43, 37 p.

O'Neill, C.P., *History of Dromiskin, Darver Parish*, Dundalk: Annaverna Press, 1984, NLI Ir. 94132 o 4, 101 p.

Redmond, Brigid, *The Story of Louth*, Dublin, 1931, NLI Ir. 9141 p 1

Reynolds, F., *The Medieval Parishes of Clogherhead and Walshestown (1300– 1857)*, Drogheda: Reynolds, 2003, NLI, 25 p.

Ross, Noel, *Tombstone Inscriptions in Castletown Graveyard, Dundalk*, Dundalk: Old Dundalk Society, 1992, NLI Ir. 9295 p1 (1). Co-author, Maureen Wilson

Sharkey, Noel, *The Parish of Haggardstown and Blackrock: A History*, Dundalk: Sharkey, 2003, Louth County Library

Tempest, H.S., *Descriptive and Historical Guide to Dundalk and District*, 1916, NLI Ir. 94132 t 1

Ua Dubhthaigh, Padraic, *The book of Dundalk*, Sligo: Champion Publications, 1946, NLI Ir. 914132 u 2, 148 p.

Local Journals

Journal of the County Louth Archaeological and Historical Society, NLI Ir. 794105 L 2

Journal of the Old Drogheda Society, NLI Ir. 94132 o 3

Journal of the Termonfeckin Historical Society

Seanchas Ardmhacha, NLI Ir. 27411 s 4

Directories

1820	J. Pigot, *Commercial Directory of Ireland* PRONI, NLI Ir. 9141 p 107, LDS Film 962702 Item 1
1824	J. Pigot and Co., *City of Dublin and Hibernian Provincial Directory*, NLI, LDS Film 451787
1830	McCabe, *Drogheda Directory*, NLI Pos. 3986
1846	Slater's *National Commercial Directory of Ireland*. PRONI, NLI LO, LDS Film 1696703 Item 3
1856	Slater, *Royal National Commercial Directory of Ireland*, NLI, LDS Film 1472360 Item 1
1861	Henderson, *Post Office Directory of Meath & Louth*
1870	Slater, *Directory of Ireland*, NLI
1881	Slater, *Royal National Commercial Directory of Ireland*, NLI
1886	George Henry Basset, *Louth County Guide and Directory* NLI Ir. 914132 b 2/1
1894	Slater, *Royal Commercial Directory of Ireland*, NLI

Gravestone Inscriptions

Ardee: Ardee, Market Street, C of I, *IG*, 3 (1) 1956

Ballymakenny: C of I, *SA*, 1983/4

Ballymascanlan: C of I, *JCLAS*, Vol. 17, No. 4, 1972

—— Faughart Upper, HW

Beaulieu: C of I, *JCLAS*, Vol. 20, No. 1

Carlingford: Church Lane, C of I, *JCLAS*, Vol. 19, No. 2, 1978

Castletown: Ross, Noel, *Tombstone Inscriptions*

Charlestown: C of I, L'Estrange, G., *Notes and Jottings*

Clonkeen: Churchtown, C of I, L'Estrange, G., *Notes and Jottings*

Clonmore: C of I, *JCLAS*, Vol. 20, No. 2

Collon: Church Street, LDS Family history library, 941.825/k29c

Darver: C of I, CHGC. Also *Breifne*, 1922

Dromin: LDS Family history library, 941.825/k29c

Drumshallon: *JCLAS*, Vol. 19, No. 3, 1979

Dunany: *JCLAS*, Vol. 20, No. 3, 1983

Dundalk: Seatown, *Tempest's Annual*, 1967, 1971/2

Dunleer: Main Street, C of I, *JCLAS*, Vol. 22, No. 4, 1992

Dysart: *JCLAS*, Vol. 19, No. 3, 1979

Faughart: Dungooly, Mac Iomhair *Tombstone Inscriptions*

Gernonstown: Castlebellingham, Leslie, *History of Kilsaran*

Kildemock: Drakestown, *JCLAS*, Vol. 13, No. 1

—— Millockstown, Leslie, *History of Kilsaran*

—— Kilsaran, Leslie, *History of Kilsaran*

Louth: Priorstate, *JCLAS*, Vol. 19, No. 4, 1980

—— Grange, *JCLAS*, Vol. 19, No. 3, 1979

Mansfieldstown: Mansfieldstown, Leslie, *History of Kilsaran*

Mayne: Glebe East, *JCLAS,* Vol. 20, No. 4, 1984

Monasterboice: King, *Monasterboice*

Mosstown: Mosstown North, LDS Family history library, 941.825/k29c

Port: *JCLAS,* 21 (2), 1986, 208–18

Rathdrumin: Glebe, C of I, *JCLAS,* Vol. 19, No. 1, 1970

Salterstown: *JCLAS,* Vol. 20, No. 3, 1983

Shanlis: *JCLAS,* Vol. 22, No. 1, 1989

Smarmore: *JCLAS,* Vol. 22, No. 1, 1989

Stabannan: C of I, Leslie, *History of Kilsaran*

Stickillin: *JCLAS,* Vol. 22, No. 1, 1989

Tullyallen: RC, *SA,* Vol. 7, No. 2, 1977

Tullyallen: Newtownstalaban, *JCLAS,* Vol. 17, No. 2, 1970

Estate Records

Anglesea: Tenants' list for Anglesea estate, Carlingford parish, 1810, *JCLAS,* 12 (2) (1950), 136–43. Covering areas in the civil parish of Carlingford.

Anglesea: Tenants on the Anglesea estate, 1856, *JCLAS,* 12 (2) (1950), 143–51. Covering areas in the civil parish of Carlingford.

Details of the Anglesea estate papers in PRONI: *JCLAS* Vol. 17, 1 (1973) (See also *JCLAS* 12, 2)

Balfour: Tenants, Ardee parish 1838, *JCLAS,* 12 (3) (1951), 188–90. Covering areas in the civil parish of Ardee.

Drumgooter: 'A Tenant Farm in the 18th & 19th Centuries (from a rent roll of the estate of Sir John Bellew)', *JCLAS,* Vol. 20, 4 (1984). Rathdrumin civil parish.

Caraher: Cardistown, tenants on potato land, 1810–1817, *JCLAS,* 165 (3) (1967), 177–83. Covering areas in the civil parish of Clonkeen.

Clanbrassil: Tenants on two Clanbrassil estate maps of Dundalk, 1782–1788, *JCLAS,* 15 (1) (1961), 39–87. Covering areas in the civil parish of Dundalk.

John Foster: Rental and Accounts of Collon Estate, 1779–1781, *JCLAS,* 10 (3) (1943), 222–9. Covering areas in the civil parish of Collon.

McClintock: Tenants on the McClintock estate, Drumcar & Kilsaran, 1852, *JCLAS,* 16 (4) (1968), 230–2. Covering areas in the civil parishes of: Drumcar; and Kilsaran.

Papers from the Roden estate: Clanbrassel estate map, 1785, *JCLAS,* Vol. 20, 1 (1981).

Trench estate rentals: Drogheda. NLI Ms. 2576.

[No Landlord given]: Families (all) in the townlands of Mosstown and Philipstown, 1852, *JCLAS,* 18 (3) (1975), 232–7. Covering areas in the civil parish of Mosstown.

[No Landlord given]: 'Tenants in Culver House Park Drogheda.' 30 Tenants, with maps, 1809, *JCLAS,* 11 (3) (1947), 206–8. Covering areas in the civil parish of St Peter's.

[No Landlord given]: 'Tenants of Omeath', 1865: *JCLAS,* Vol. XVII, 1 (1973).

MAYO

Census returns and substitutes

1600–1700	Mayo landowners in the 17th century. *JRSAI*, 1965, 153–62
1693	List of those outlawed after the Williamite wars; In some cases, addresses and family relationships are specified. AH, 22, 1–240.
1716	Ballinrobe Protestant freeholders requesting the building of walls. 70 names. *JGAHS*, 7, 1911/2, 168–170
1783	Ballinrobe householders. AH, Vol. 14
1786	Petition for a postal service between Westport and Castlebar. 70 inhabitants of Westport listed. *Cathair Na Mart*, 16, 1996.
1796	Catholics Emigrating from Ulster to Mayo. SA, 1958, pp. 17–50. See also 'Petition of Armagh migrants in the Westport area', *Cathair na Mart*, Vol. 2, No. 1 (Appendix). Online: Dees
1796	Spinning-Wheel Premium List. 1,900 names for Co. Mayo, Online: Hayes
1798	Persons who suffered losses in the 1798 rebellion. Propertied classes only. *c.*650 names. NLI I 94107
1818	Tithe Collectors' account book, parishes of Kilfian and Moygawnagh. NAI M.6085
1820	Protestants in Killala. NAI MFCI 32
1823–1838	Tithe Books. Part online: Connors
1823	Defendants at Westport Petty sessions. NLI Ms. 14902
1825	Petition to have the River Moy dredged (100 names, Ballina). NAI OP 974/131
1831	750 names in a petition for poor relief in Coolcarney (Kilgarvan and Attymass). NAI OP 9974/116
1832–1839	Freeholders. Alphabetical listing showing residence and valuation. NAI OP 1839/138
1832	Protestants in Foxford. NLI Ms. 8295
1833	Defendants at Mayo Lent Assizes. Mahon, *Claremorris*
1836	Defendants at Mayo Summer Assizes. Mahon, *Claremorris*
1838	Memorial from Achill opposing Edward Nangle's request for the establishment of petty sessions. c.250 names (signatures and marks) OP 1838/214
1838–1848	Reproductive Loan Fund records. Records of loan associations at Ballina (Carramore), Ballindangan, Ballinrobe, Castlebar, Claremorris, Newport, Swineford, Westport, covering more than 4,000 individuals. NAI (Kew). T 91. Partly online: Moving Here
1839	Crossmolina parishioners. 170 names of nominators of Tithe apploters. NAI OP/1839/77
1841	Some extracts only, for Newport. NAI Thrift Abstracts
1842	Freeholders (Excludes the baronies of Erris and Tirawley). NAI OP/1842/71

1845   Defendants at Mayo Summer Assizes (Notebook of Justice Jackson).
            NAI M.55249
1845   Clare Island tenants. *South Mayo Family History Research Journal*, 7,
            1994, 46–7
1845   Defendants at Mayo Summer Assizes, Notebook of Justice Jackson
            NAI M.55249
1850   Voters' lists. *South Mayo Family History Research Journal*, 1996, 27–41
1856–1857   Voters' registers. Costello barony (NAI M.3447), Clanmorris barony
            (NAI M.3448), Tirawley barony (NAI M.2782), Kilmaine barony (NAI
            M.2783); Gallen barony (NAI M.2784).
1856–1857   Griffith's Valuation. Indexed online: Hayes
1901   Census (Masterson *1901 Achill* and *1901 Burrishoole*) Part online:
            Leitrim-Roscommon & Celtic cousins
1911   Census. (Burrishoole, Masterson *1911 census Burrishoole*)

Online

Celtic cousins	*www.celticcousins.net*	
Connors	*www.connorsgenealogy.com*	
Dees	*freepages.genealogy.rootsweb.com/~deesegenes*	
Glanduff	*www.geocities.com/lorettagb*	
Hayes, John	*www.failteromhat.com*	
Leitrim-Roscommon	*www.leitrim-roscommon.com*	1901, Griffith's, Townlands. Elphin 1749
Moving Here	*www.movinghere.org.uk/search/*	

Publications

Local histories, etc.
St Muiredach's College, Ballina. Roll *1906–1979*, NLI Ir. 259 m 2/ Ir. 37941 s 18
'The Ethnography of Inishbofin and Inishark', *Proceedings of the Royal Irish Academy*, 3rd Ser. Vol. 3, 1893–6, 360–80
Achill Orphan Refuges, Achill, *15th report of the mission report of Achill Orphan Refuges*, 1849, NLI Ir. 266 a 8
Butler, Patrick, *Turlough Park and the FitzGeralds*, Butler, 2002, NLI, 48 p.
Cantwell, Ian, *Memorials of the Dead, Counties Galway & Mayo (Western Seaboard)*, CD-ROM#4, Dublin, Eneclann, 2002. DCLA
Comer, Michael, *Béacán/Bekan: portrait of an East Mayo parish*, Ballinrobe: Comer, 1986, NLI Ir. 94123 b 1, 208 p. Co-editor, Nollaig Ó Muraíle
Crossmolina Historical & Archaeological Society, *The Deel basin: a historical survey* Mayo, 1985–1990. NLI Ir. 94123 c 5
Donohoe, Tony, *History of Crossmolina*, Dublin: De Burca, 2003, NLI, 627 p.
Farrell, Noel, *Exploring Family Origins in Ballina Town*, Longford: Noel Farrell, 2001?, 48 p.

Fitzgerald, Patricia, *An gorta mór i gCill Alaidhe [the great famine in Killala]*, Killala: the authors, 1996, NLI, 66 p. Co-author, Olive Kennedy

Garvey, Rosemary, *Kilkenny to Murrisk: a Garvey family history*, Killadoon, Co. Mayo: the author, 1992, NLI Ir. 9292 g 30

Hayes McCoy, G.A., *Index to 'The Compossicion Booke of Connoght, 1585'*, Dublin: Irish Manuscripts Commission, 1945, NLI Ir. 9412 c 1, 179 p.

Higgins, Tom, *Through Fagan's Gates: the parish and people of Castlebar down the ages*, Castlebar: Higgins, 2001, NLI, 224 p.

Jennings, Martin, *Swinford re-echo: parish inscapes*, Swinford: Swinford Community Council, 1981, NLI Ir. 94123 s 2, 92 p.

Kennedy, Gerald Conan, *North Mayo (Tirawley) history & folklore, landscape, environment, places of historic interest*, Killala: Morrigan Books, 1992, NLI Ir. 941 p 122(3), 3 folded sheets

Kingston, Rev. John, *Achill Island, the deserted village at Slievemore: a study ...*, Achill Island: Bob Kingston, 1990, NLI Ir. 720 k 6

Knight, P., *Erris in the Irish highlands and the Atlantic railway*, Dublin: M.Keene, 1836, NLI Ir. 914123 k 2, 178 p.

Knox, H.T., *The history of Mayo to the close of the 16th century*, Dublin: Hodges, Figgis, 1908, NLI Ir. 94123 k 2 (& L.O.), 451 p., Repr. De Burca Rare Books, 1982.

Knox, H.T., *Notes on the Early History of the Dioceses of Tuam, Killala and Achonry*, Dublin: Hodges Figgis, 1904, NLI Ir. 27412 k 1, 410 p.

Mac Néill, Eoin, *Clare Island survey. Place-names and family names*, Dublin: Royal Irish Academy. Proceedings. v.31, sect.1, pt.3, 1911–1915, NLI Ir. 92942 m 6, 42 p.

MacHale, Edward, *The Parishes in the Diocese of Killala: [1]: South Tirawley, (2) North Tirawley, 3 (Erris), (4) Tireragh*, Killala, [s.n], 1985, NLI Ir. 27414 m 6, 166/ 104/ 88/ 79 p.

Mahon, Marie, *Claremorris in History*, Mayo: Mayo Fam. Hist. Soc., 1987, NLI, 92 p.

Masterson, William G., *County Mayo, families of Ballycroy parish 1856–1880*, Indianapolis: the author, 1995, NLI Ir. 9292 m 74

Masterson, William G., *County Mayo, Ireland, Newport area families, 1864–1880*, Indianapolis, Ind.: W.G. Masterson, 2000, NLI Ir. 9291 m31, 157 p.

Masterson, William G., *Achill parish: Census Index*, Indianapolis, 1994, NLI Ir. 94123 m 21

Masterson, William G., *1911 census, Burrishoole Parish, County Mayo, Ireland: a transcription and index*, Indianapolis, Ind.: Masterson, 2002, NLI, 144 p.

Masterson, William G., *1901 census, Burrishoole Parish, County Mayo, Ireland*, Indianapolis, Ind.: Masterson, 1990, NLI, 45 p.

McDonald, Theresa, *Achill 5000 B.C. to 1900 A.D.: archaelogy, history. folklore*, I.A.S. Publications, 1992, NLI Ir. 94123 m 12

McDonnell, Thomas, *The diocese of Killala: from its institution to the end of the penal times*, Ballina: R. & S. Monaghan, 1975, NLI Ir. 27412 m 1, 143 p.

McGrath, Fiona, *Emigration and landscape: the case of Achill Island*, Dublin: TCD Dept of Geography, 1991, NLI Ir. 900 p 10 (3)

Moffitt, Miriam, *The Church of Ireland community of Killala & Achonry, 1870–1940*, Dublin: Irish Academic Press, 1999, NLI Ir. 283 m 4, 64 p.

Moran, Gerard, *The Mayo evictions of 1860: Patrick Lavelle and the "War" in Partry*, Contae Mhaigh Eo: Foilseacháin Náisiúnta Teoranta, 1986, NLI Ir. 94123 m 9, 143 p.

Mulloy, Bridie, *Itchy feet & thirsty work: a guide to the history and folklore of Ballinrobe*, Ballinrobe: Lough Mask and Lough Carra Tourist Development Association, 1991, NLI Ir. 94123.m.11, 268 p.

Ní Ghiobúin, Mealla C., *Dugort, Achill Island, 1831–1861: a study of the rise and fall of a missionary community*, Dublin: Irish Academic Press, 2001, NLI, 78 p.

Noone, Sean, *Where the sun sets: Ballycroy, Belmullet, Kilcommon & Kiltane County Mayo*, Ballina: Erris Publications, 1991, NLI Ir. 94123 n 5, 351 p.

O'Donovan, John, *Tribes and customs of Hy Fiachra*, Kansas City: Kansas City Irish Genaelogical Foundation, 1993, NLI Ir. 941 t 21

O'Flaherty, Roderic, *A chorographical description of West or H-Iar Connaught: written A.D. 1684*, Dublin: for the Irish Archaeological Society, 1846, NLI Ir. 94124 o 2. Repr. 1978 Galway: Kennys Bookshops and Art Galleries

O'Hara, B., *Killasser: a history*, Galway: O'Hara, 1981, NLI Ir. 94123 o 6, 104 p.

O'Sullivan, William, *The Strafford inquisition of County Mayo (R.I.A. ms. 24 E 15)*, Dublin: IMC, 1958, NLI Ir. 94123 o 4, 245 p.

People of Bohola, *Bohola: its history and its people*, Bohola: Sheridan Memorial Community Centre Committee, 1992, NLI, 312 p.

Simington, Robert C., *The transplantation to Connacht, 1654–58*, Shannon: Irish University Press for the Irish Manuscripts Commission, 1970, NLI Ir. 94106 s 9, 306 p.

Smith, Brian, *Tracing your Mayo Ancestors*, Dublin: Flyleaf Press, 1997, NLI, GS, 96 p.

Sobolewski, Peter, *Kiltimagh our life & times*, Kiltimagh: Kiltimagh Historical Society, 1996, NLI, 94123 k[sic], 318 p. Co-editor, Betty Solan

Suttle, Sam, *Roots and branches: a history of the Hughes family of Islandeady*, Dublin, 1999, NLI, 88 p.

Swinford Historical Society, *An Gorta Mór: famine in the Swinford Union*, Swinford: Swinford Historical Society, 1996, NLI Ir. 94123 f 3, 80 p.

Walsh, Marie, *An Irish country childhood: memories of a bygone age*, London: Smith Gryphon, 1995, NLI Ir. 92 w 242, Attymass

Local Journals

Cathair na Mart (Journal of the Westport Historical Society), NLI Ir. 94123 c 4

North Mayo Historical & Archaeological Journal, NLI Ir. 94123 n 4

South Mayo Family History Research Journal, Mayo Co. Library

Directories

1824   J. Pigot and Co., *City of Dublin and Hibernian Provincial Directory*, NLI, LDS Film 451787

1846	Slater's *National Commercial Directory of Ireland*. PRONI, NLI LO, LDS Film 1696703 Item 3
1856	Slater, *Royal National Commercial Directory of Ireland*, NLI, LDS Film 1472360 Item 1
1870	Slater, *Directory of Ireland*, NLI
1881	Slater, *Royal National Commercial Directory of Ireland*, NLI
1894	Slater, *Royal Commercial Directory of Ireland*, NLI

Gravestone Inscriptions

Mayo South Family Research Centre has transcripts for 142 graveyards, mainly in the south of the county. Mayo North Family History Research also has a large number of transcripts. Galway Family History Society has transcripts for Inishbofin, and Sligo Heritage and Genealogy Centre has transcripts for the parish of Kilmoremoy. Contact details will be found in Chapter 15.

Achill: Doogort East, Cantwell, *Memorials*
Aghagower: Aghagower, RC, Cantwell, *Memorials*
Aglish: Knockacroghery (Castlebar?), Cantwell, *Memorials*
Ballintober: Ballintober (Abbey), Cantwell, *Memorials*
Ballyovey: Gorteenmore (Tourmakeedy?), RC, Cantwell, *Memorials*
Burrishoole: Tierna (Carrowkeel ?), Cantwell, *Memorials*
Newport: Church Lane, C of I, Cantwell, *Memorials*
Islandeady: Islandeady, Cantwell, *Memorials*
Kilcommon (Erris): Fahy, Cantwell, *Memorials*
Kilcommon or Pollatomish: Cantwell, *Memorials*
Kilteany: Cantwell, *Memorials*
Bunnahowen: RC, Cantwell, *Memorials*
Kilgeever: Louisburgh, Bridge Street, C of I, Cantwell, *Memorials*
Lecarrow: (Killeen?), RC, Cantwell, *Memorials*
Kilgeever: Cantwell, *Memorials*
Kilmaclasser: Rushbrook (Fahy? Clogher Lough?), Cantwell, *Memorials*
Kilmeena: Kilmeena, Cantwell, *Memorials*
Kilmore: Binghamstown, C of I, Cantwell, *Memorials*
Cross (Boyd): Cantwell, *Memorials*
Termoncarragh: Cantwell, *Memorials*
Oughaval: Drumin East, Cantwell, *Memorials*

Estate Records

Altamont, Lord: NAI M.5788(2), Rental of the Westport estate, 1787. Principally major tenants. The section on Westport town is published in *Cathair na Mart*, Vol. 2, No. 1, along with a rent roll for the town from 1815. Covering townlands in the civil parishes of: Aghagower; Burriscarra; Burrishoole; Kilbelfad; Kilbride; Kilconduff; Kildacomoge; Kilfian; Killdeer; Kilmaclasser; Kilmeena; Moygownagh; Oughaval.

Arran, Earl of: NLI Ms. 14087; leases on the Mayo estate, 1720–1869, mentioning lives in the leases. NLI Ms. 14086; valuation survey of the Mayo estates, 1850–52. All tenants. Covering townlands in the civil parishes of: Addergoole; Ardagh; Ballysakeery; Crossmolina; Kilbelfad; Kilcummin; Kilfian; Killala; Kilmoremoy.

Browne, Col. John: NLI Pos. 940. Account of the sales of the estates of Col. John Browne in Counties Galway and Mayo, compiled in 1778, giving names of major tenants and purchasers 1698–1704, and those occupying the estates in 1778. Covering townlands in the civil parishes of: Addergoole; Aghagower; Aglish; Ballintober; Ballyhean; Ballyovey; Ballysakeery; Breaghwy; Burrishoole; Cong; Crossmolina; Drum; Islandeady; Kilcommon; Kilgeever; Killeadan; Kilmaclasser; Kilmainemore; Kilmeena; Manulla; Moygownagh; Oughaval; Robeen; Tonaghty; Turlough.

Clanmorris, Lord: NLI Ms. 3279. Rental, 1833. All tenants. Covering townlands in the civil parishes of: Kilcommon; Kilmainemore; Mayo; Robeen; Rosslee; Tonaghty; Toomour.

Domville: NLI Ms. 11816. Rentals, 1833–36, 1843, 1847, 1851. All tenants. Covering townlands in the civil parishes of: Killasser; Manulla; Robeen.

Knox, Henry: NAI M.5630 (1). Rental, early nineteenth century. All tenants. Covering townlands in the civil parishes of: Crossmolina; Doonfeeny; Kilfian; Kilmoremoy.

Medlicott, Thomas: NLI Ms. 5736 (3), Tithe Applotment Book, Achill. NLI Mss. 5736 (2), 5821. Rent rolls, showing lives in leases, 1774, 1776. Major tenants only. Covering townlands in the civil parishes of: Achill; Aghagower; Burrishoole; Kilcommon; Kilmeena; Kilmore.

O'Donel, Sir Neal: NLI Ms. 5738 & 5744; leaseholders on the estates, 1775–1859, 1828, giving lives mentioned in leases. Mainly major tenants. NLI Ms. 5736; Rental, 1788. Major tenants only. NLI Ms. 5281; Rental, 1805. Major tenants only. NLI Ms. 5743; Rental, 1810. Major tenants only. NLI Ms. 5281; Rental, 1828. Major tenants only. Covering townlands in the civil parishes of: Achill; Aghagower; Burrishoole; Cong; Kilcommon; Kilgeever; Kilmore; Kilmaclasser.

O'Malley, Sir Samuel: NAI M.1457 (published in *Cathair na Mart*, Vol. 6, No. 1). Valuation of the Mayo estates, 1845. All tenants. Covering townlands in the civil parishes of: Aglish; Kilgeever; Kilmeena.

MEATH

Census returns and substitutes

1641	Book of Survey and Distribution. NLI Ms. 974
1654–1656	Civil Survey, Vol. lll. *Civil Survey,* Vol. lll (NLI I 6551 Dublin)
1659	Pender's 'Census'. Repr. GPC, 1997, IMC, 2002. LDS Film 924648
1663	Hearth Money Roll. *JCLAHS,* Vol. 6, Nos 2 & 4, Vol. 7, No. 3
1670/1	Armagh diocese gentry, clergy and parishioners supporting the Franciscans. SA, Vol. 15, No. 1, 1992, 186–216
1710	Voters in Kells. PRONI T 3163, NLI Headford papers

1766	Ardbraccan. Protestants only. GO 537. Also RCBL.
1770	Freeholders. NLI Ms. 787–8 Also LDS Film 100181
1781	Voters. NAI M.4910–12
1792	Hearth tax collectors account and collection books, parishes of Colp, Donore, Duleek, Kilshalvan, NLI Ms. 26735; Ardcath, Ardmulchan, Ballymagarvy, Brownstown, Clonalvy, Danestown, Fennor, Kentstown, Knockcommon, Rathfeigh, NLI Ms. 26736; Athlumney, Danestown, Dowdstown, Dunsany, Kilcarn, Killeen, Macetown, Mounttown, Tara, Trevet, NLI Ms. 26737; St Mary's Drogheda, NLI Ms. 26739. NLI Ms. 26735
1793	Hearth tax collectors account and collection books; parishes of Ardagh, Dowth, Gernonstown, Killary, Mitchelstown, Siddan, Slane, Stackallan, NL Ms. 26738. NLI Ms. 26738
1795–1862	Charleton Marriage Certificates NAI. M.2800. Indexed in Accessions, Vol. 37.
1796	Spinning-Wheel Premium List. 1,450 names for Co. Meath. Online: Hayes
1797–1801	Tithe Valuations Athboy. NAI MFCI 53, 54
1798	Drogheda voters' list. *JCLAHS*, Vol. XX, 1984
1802–1806	Protestants in the parishes of Agher, Ardagh, Clonard, Clongill, Drumconrath, Duleek, Emlagh, Julianstown, Kentstown, Kilbeg, Kilmainhamwood, Kilskyre, Laracor, Moynalty, Navan, Robertstown, Raddenstown, Rathcore, Rathkenny, Rathmolyon, Ratoath, Skryne, Straffordstown, Stamullin, Tara, Trevet, Templekeeran. *IA*, 1973. Indexed online: From Ireland
1802	Drogheda Voters. *JCLAHS*, Vol. XX, 1984
1804	Drogheda Militia. Online: Hall
1813	Protestant children at Ardbraccan school. *IA*, 1973
1815	Voters. PRONI T3163. Also NLI Headford papers
1816	Grand Jurors. NLI Ir. 6551 Dundalk
1821	Parishes of Ardbraccan, Ardsallagh, Balrathboyne, Bective, Churchtown, Clonmacduff, Donaghmore, Donaghpatrick, Kilcooly, Liscartan, Martry, Moymet, Navan, Newtownclonbun, Rathkenny, Rataine, Trim, Trimblestown, Tullaghanoge. NAI
1823–1838	Tithe Books
1830	Census of landowners in Julianstown, Moorchurch, Stamullen, and Clonalvey, *Riocht na Midhe* 3 (4), 1966, 354–8
1833	Protestant Cess payers, parishes of Colpe and Kilshalvan. *Riocht na Midhe*, 4 (3), 1969, 61–2
1833	Memorial of the inhabitants of Drogheda about cholera. c.250 signatures NAI OP 1833/51
1837	Valuation of towns returning M.P.s (occupants and property values): Drogheda, Dundalk. *Parliamentary Papers 1837, Reports from Committees,* Vol. II (i), Appendix G

1837   Marksmen (illiterate voters) in parliamentary boroughs: Drogheda,
              Dundalk. *Parliamentary Papers 1837, Reports from Committees*, Vol. II
              (i), Appendix A
1843   Voters NLI Ms. 1660
1848–1849   Smith O'Brien Petition, ENE # CD2. Almost 1,000 names for Kells
1850   Register of land occupiers, with particulars of land and families, in
              the Unions of Kells and Oldcastle. NLI Ms. 5774
1852   Voting electors. NLI Ms. 1660
1855   Griffith's Valuation. Indexed online: Hayes
1865   Parliamentary voters. NLI P. 2491
1866–1873   Emigrants from Stamullen Catholic parish, Co. Meath *IG* 8, No. 2,
              1991 290–92. Original with RC registers
1871   Drumcondra and Loughbrackan NLI Pos. 4184
1901   Census. Part online: Ashbourne
1911   Census

Online

Ashbourne	*www.angelfire.com/ak2/ashbourne*
From Ireland	*www.from-ireland.net*
Hall, Brendan	*www.jbhall.freeservers.com*
Hayes, John	*www.failteromhat.com*

Publications

Local histories, etc.
Parish Guide to Meath, Dublin: Irish Church Publications, 1968, NLI Ir. 270 p 2, 48
    p.
Bernard, Nicholas, *The Whole Proceedings of the Siege of Drogheda [&]*
    Londonderry, Dublin, 1736. NLI Ir. 94106.b2
Bolton, Michael D.C., *Headfort House,* Kells, Co. Meath: Fieldgate Press, 1999, NLI,
    57 p.
Brady, J., *A short history of the parishes of the diocese of Meath, 1867–1944,* NLI Ir.
    94132 b 2
Carty, Mary Rose, *History of Killeen Castle,* Dunsany: Carty/Lynch, 1991, NLI Ir.
    94132 c 8, 87 p.
Cogan, A., *The diocese of Meath: ancient and modern,* Dublin: J. F. Fowler, 1874, NLI
    Ir. 27413 c 3, 3 vols.
Cogan, J., *Ratoath,* Drogheda: *Drogheda Independent,* 19?, NLI Ir. 9141 p 84, 56 p.
Coldrick, Bryn, *Rossin, Co. Meath: an unofficial place,* Dublin: Four Courts, 2002,
    NLI, 3B 726, 63 p.
Conlon, Larry, *The Heritage of Collon, 1764–1984,* Ardee: Conlon, 1984, NLI Ir.
    94132 c 5, 87 p.
Connell, P., *Changing Forces Shaping a Nineteenth Century town: A Case Study of*
    Navan, Maynooth: Geography Dept., St Patrick's College, 1978, NLI Ir. 94132 c 1

Coogan, Oliver, *A History of Dunshaughlin, Culmullen & Knockmark*, Dunshaughlin: Coogan, 1988, NLI, 132 p.

Coogan, Oliver, *A short history of south-east Meath*, 1979

Coogan, Tony, *Charlesfort: the story of a Meath estate and its people 1668–1968*, Kells: the author, 1991, NLI Ir. 94132 9 2(2), 72 p.

Cusack, Danny, *Kilmainham of the woody hollow: a history of Kilmainhamwood for the centenary of the Church of the Sacred Heart Kilmainhamwood (1898–1998)*, Kells: Kilmainhamwood Parish Council, 1998, NLI Ir. 94132 c 11, 166 p.

D'Alton, John, *The history of Drogheda*, Dublin: McGlashan and Gill, 1844, NLI Ir. 94132 d 1, 2 vols.

D'Alton, John, *Antiquities of the County of Meath*, Dublin: 1833

Duffner, P., *Drogheda: the Low Lane Church 1300–1979*, NLI Ir. 94132 d 7

Duleek Heritage, *The parish of Duleek and 'over the ditches': a ramble calling at Bellewstown, Kilsharvan, Mount Hanover, Donore, Duleek, Athcarne, Riverstown, Cushenstown and Boolies*, Duleek: Duleek Heritage, 2001, NLI, 266 p.

Falsey, Olive, *Kildalkey: a parish history*, Meath: Falsey, 2001, NLI, 155 p.

Farrell, Nocl, *Exploring family origins in Navan Town*, Longford: Noel Farrell, 1998, NLI, 1B 2149, 48 p. Includes transcripts of 1901, 1911 censuses, 1838 Thoms, 1941 Electors, Griffith's, etc.

Farrell, Valentine, *Not so much to one side*, Upholland: Farrell, 1984, NLI Ir. 94132 f 6, 214 p.

Fitzsimons, J., *The Parish of Kilbeg*, Kells: Kells Art Studios, 1974, NLI Ir. 914132 f 3, 287 p.

French, Noel, *Bellinter House*, Trim, Co. Meath: Trymme Press, 1993, NLI Ir. 941 p 124(3)

French, Noel, *Nobber, a step back in time*, Trim, Co. Meath: Meath Heritage Centre, 1991, NLI Ir. 941 p 103 (3), 56 p.

French, Noel, *Trim Traces and Places*, Trim, 1987, NLI, 54 p.

French, Noel, *A short history of Rathmore and Athboy*, 1995, NLI Ir. 94132 f 3, 79 p.

French, Noel, *Navan by the Boyne*, Athboy: French, 1986, NLI, 116 p.

French, Nocl, *Monumental Inscriptions from Some Graveyards in Co. Meath*, Typescript, 1990, NAI Open shelves, Also NLI Ir. 9295 f 2

French, Noel, *Meath ancestors, a guide to sources for tracing your ancestors in Co. Meath*, Trim: Trymme Press, 1993, NLI Ir. 921 p 12(4), 68 p.

Garry, James, *The Streets and Lanes of Drogheda*, Drogheda, 1996, NLI Ir. 91413 g 4/1, 120 p.

Gerrard, Richard, *The annals of St. Mary's Boys School, Drogheda, 1865–2000*, Drogheda: St Mary's School, 2000, NLI Ir. 370 g 26, 3 vols.

Gilligan, Jim, *Graziers and Grasslands: portrait of a rural Meath Community 1854–1914*, Maynooth: Irish Academic Press, 1998, NLI

Healy, John, *History of the Diocese of Meath*, Dublin, 1908, 2 vols

Hennessy, Mark, *Irish Historic Towns Atlas 14: Trim*, Dublin: Royal Irish Academy, 2004, NLI

IGRS, *Tombstone inscriptions Vol. 2*, Dublin: IGRS Tombstone Committee, 2001, NLI, c. 900 p.

Irish Countrywomen's Association, *Kentstown in bygone days*, 1997, NLI Ir. 94132 k 3, 132 p.

Kieran, Joan S., *An Outline History of the Parish of St Mary's Abbey, Ardee*, 1980, NLI Ir. 91413 p 12, 5 p.

MacLochlainn, Tadgh, *The Parish of Laurencetown & Kiltormer*, Ballinasloe: MacLochlainn, 1981, NLI Ir. 94124 m 5, 73 p.

Matthews, Bredan, *A history of Stamullen*, Stamullen: Matthews, 2003, NLI, 138 p.

McCullen, John, *The Call of St Mary's: a hundred years of a parish*, Drogheda: McCullen, 1984, NLI Ir. 27413 m 8, 92 p.

McHugh, Ned, *Drogheda before the Famine: urban poverty in the shadow of privilege 1826–45*, Maynooth: Irish Academic Press, 1998

McNeill, Charles, *Dowdall deeds*, Dublin: The Stationery Office for the Irish Manuscripts Commission, 1960, NLI Ir. 091 m 9, 416 p. Co. editor, A.J. Otway-Ruthven

McNiffe, Liam, *A history of Williamstown, Kells*, Williamstown: McNiffe, 2003, NLI, 68 p.

Murchan, Maureen, *Moynalty Parish: the millennium record: 'a moment in time'*, Moynalty: The Millennium Record Book Committee, 2000, NLI Ir. 94132 m 10, 468 p. Co-editor, Joe McKenna

O'Boyle, Edna, *A history of Duleek*, Duleek: Duleek Historical Society, 1989, NLI Ir. 94132 o 8, 129 p.

Paterson, J. (ed.), *Diocese of Meath and Kildare: an historical guide*, 1981, NLI Ir. 941 p 75

Quane, Michael, *Gilson Endowed School, Oldcastle*, Meath: Meath Archaeological and Historical Society, 1968, NLI, 23 p.

Rathkenny Local History Group, *Rathkenny Parish: a local history*, Rathkenny: 1983, NLI, 176 p.

Simms, Angret, *Irish Historic Towns Atlas 4: Kells*, Dublin: Royal Irish Academy, 1990, NLI, ILB 941 p 13 (2)

Local Journals
Annala Dhamhliag: The annals of Duleek, NLI I 94132 a 1
Riocht na Midhe, NLI Ir. 94132 r 1
Journal of the Old Drogheda Society, NLI Ir. 94132 o 3

Directories
1824   J. Pigot and Co., *City of Dublin and Hibernian Provincial Directory*, NLI, LDS Film 451787

1846   Slater's *National Commercial Directory of Ireland*. PRONI, NLI LO, LDS Film 1696703 Item 3

1856   Slater, *Royal National Commercial Directory of Ireland*, NLI, LDS Film 1472360 Item 1

1861   Henderson, *Post Office Directory of Meath & Louth*
1870   Slater, *Directory of Ireland*, NLI
1881   Slater, *Royal National Commercial Directory of Ireland*, NLI
1894   Slater, *Royal Commercial Directory of Ireland*, NLI

Gravestone Inscriptions

Agher: C of I, *IA*, Vol. 10, No. 2, 1978
Agher: C of I, GO, *IGRS*, Vol. 1
Ardmulchan: French, *Monumental Inscriptions*
Ardsallagh: French, *Monumental Inscriptions*
Assey, *IGRS*, Vol. 2
Athboy: Church Lane, C of I, *IA*, Vol. 12, Nos 1 and 2, 1981, *IGRS*, Vol. 2
Athlumney: IGRS Collection, GO
Balfeaghan: *IGRS*, Vol. 1
Ballygarth: *IGRS*, Collection, GO
Balrathboyne: Cortown, GO, *IGRS*, Vol. 2
Balsoon: *IA*, Vol. 7, No. 2, 1976, *IGRS*, Vol. 2
Bective: Clady, GO
Castlejordan: C of I, *IGRS*, Vol. 2
Churchtown: *IGRS*, Vol. 2
Clonard: Tircroghan, *IGRS*, Vol. 2
Colp: Mornington town, RC, *Journal of the Old Drogheda Society*, 1989
—— Stagreenan, *Journal of the Old Drogheda Society*, 1977
—— Colp West, C of I, LDS Family history library
Danestown: Danestown, *Riocht na Midhe*, Vol. 5, No. 4, 1974, *IGRS*, Vol. 2
Diamor: Clonabreaney, *Riocht na Midhe*, Vol. 6, No. 2, 1976
Donaghmore: Donaghmore, RC, French, *Monumental Inscriptions*
Dowdstown: French, *Monumental Inscriptions*
Drumlargan: *IA*, Vol. 12, Nos 1 & 2, 1980
Duleek: Church Lane, C of I, *IG*, Vol. 3, No. 12, 1967, *IGRS*, Vol. 2
Dunboyne: Dunboyne, *IGRS*, Vol. 2. Also *IA*, Vol. 11, Nos 1 & 2, 1979
Dunmoe: French, *Monumental Inscriptions*
Gallow: Gallow, *IGRS*, Vol. 2
Gernonstown: French, *Monumental Inscriptions*
Girley: Girley, French, *Monumental Inscriptions*
Kells: Headford Place, *IG*, Vol. 3, No. 11, 1966
Kilbride: Baytown, *Riocht na Midhe*, Vol. 6, No. 3, 1977, *IGRS*, Vol. 2
Kilcarn: French, *Monumental Inscriptions*
Kilcooly: Kiltoome (Kilcooly?), *IGRS*, Vol. 2
Kildalkey: *IGRS*, Vol. 2
Killaconnigan: Killaconnigan, *IGRS*, Vol. 2
Killeen: Killeen, *Riocht na Midhe*, Vol. 4, No. 3, 1970
Kilmore: Arodstown, *Riocht na Midhe*, Vol. 6, No. 1, 1975, *IGRS*, Vol. 2
—— Kilmore, C of I, *Riocht na Midhe*, Vol. 6, No. 1, 1975

Laracor: Moy, *IA*, Vol. 6, No. 2, 1974
—— Summerhill Demesne, LDS Family history library
Loughan or Castlekeeran: *IGRS*, Vol. 2
Loughcrew: C of I, *IA*, Vol. 9, No. 2, 1977
Macetown: IGRS Collection (7), GO
Martry: Allenstown Demesne, French, *Monumental Inscriptions*
Moymet: *IGRS*, Vol. 2
Moynalty: Hermitage, French, *Monumental Inscriptions*
Navan: Church Hill, C of I, MF CI 45, NAI
Oldcastle: *Riocht na Midhe*, Vol. 4, No. 2, 1968
Rataine: *IGRS*, Vol. 2
Rathfeigh: *IGRS*, Vol. 2
Rathkenny: C of I, French, *Monumental Inscriptions*
Rathmore: RC, *IA*, Vol. 7, No. 2, 1975, *IGRS*, Vol. 2
Rathmore: Moyagher Lower, *IA*, Vol. 8, No. 1, 1976, *IGRS*, Vol. 2
Ratoath: Main Street, C of I, French, *Monumental Inscriptions*
Scurlockstown: *IGRS*, Vol. 2
Skreen: French, *Monumental Inscriptions*
St Mary's: Drogheda, New Road, C of I, *Journal of the Old Drogheda Society*, 1986
Stackallan: French, *Monumental Inscriptions*
Tara: Castleboy, C of I, Meath Heritage Centre
Trim: Tremblestown, RC, French, *Monumental Inscriptions*
Trim: Maudlin, IGRS Collection (3), GO
Tullaghanoge: French, *Monumental Inscriptions*

Estate Records
Balfour: Balfour tenants in the townlands of Belustran, Cloughmacow, Doe and Hurtle, 1838, *JCLAHS*, 12 (3) (1951), 190, Nobber civil parish.
Edgeworth, Richard: Rental, NAI M.1503. 1760–1768. All tenants. Covering townlands in the civil parish of Scurlockstown.
Newcomen estates: maps of estates to be sold, July 20, 1827. NLI Ms. 2766. All tenants. Covering townlands in the civil parishes of: Clonmacduff; and Moymet.
Reynell family: rent books 1834–48. NLI Ms. 5990.
Smythe, William Barlow: Collinstown. Farm a/c book. NLI Ms. 7909.
Trench estate rentals: Drogheda. NLI Ms. 2576.
Wellesley: Tenants of the Wellesley estate at Dangan, Ballymaglossan, Moyare, Mornington and Trim, 1816, *Riocht na Midhe*, 4 (4) (1967), 10–25, Ballymaglassan, Colp, Laracor, Rathmore and Trim civil parishes.

MONAGHAN

Census returns and substitutes

	Medieval Clones families. *Clogher Record,* 1959
1630	Muster Roll of Ulster; Armagh Co. Library, PRONI D.1759/3C/1; T. 808/15164, NLI Pos. 206
1630–1800	Church of Ireland Marriage Licence Bonds, Diocese of Clogher. Online: Ulsterancestry
1641	Index to the rebels of 1641 in the Co. Monaghan depositions, *Clogher Record,* 15 (2), 1995, 89–89
1659	Pender's 'Census'. Repr. GPC, 1997, IMC, 2002. LDS Film 924648
1663–1665	Hearth Money Roll. *History of Monaghan for two hundred years 1660–1860,* Dundalk, 1921
1738	Some Clones Inhabitants. *Clogher Record,* Vol. 2, No. 3, 1959
1777	Some Protestant Inhabitants of Carrickmacross. *Clogher Record,* Vol. 6, No. 1, 1966
1785	Male Protestants aged over 17—Magheracloone & Errigal Trough LDS Film 258517
1796	Spinning-Wheel Premium List. 4,400 names for Co. Monaghan. Online: Hayes
1821	Some abstracts only; See *Clogher Record,* 1991. NAI Thrift Abstracts
1823	Some C of I members in the Aghadrumsee area, *Clogher Record,* 15 (1), 1994
1823–1838	Tithe Books
1824	Protestant householders, Aghabog parish. RCBL D1/1/1
1832	Donagh parish Co. Monaghan (with C of I records) PRONI MIC.1/127
1835–1849	Shirley Estate Loan Book. Carrickmacross Library
1841	Some abstracts only. NAI Thrift Abstracts
1842–1849	Workhouse records, Castleblayney Union. MAR
1843	Magistrates, landed proprietors, 'etc.', NLI Ms. 12,767
1847	Poor Law Rate Book, Castleblayney. *Clogher Record,* Vol. 5, No. 1, 1963
1851	Some abstracts only. NAI Thrift Abstracts
1858–1860	Griffith's Valuation. Indexed online: Hayes
1901	Census
1911	Census
1912	The Ulster Covenant. Almost half-a-million original signatures and addresses of those who signed. Almost 11,000 names for Monaghan. Online: Covenant

Online

Clogher	www.clogherhistoricalsoc.com	Clogher Historical Society
Covenant	www.proni.gov.uk/ulstercovenant	
Hayes, John	www.failteromhat.com	
McGeough	ahd.exis.net/monaghan	Good maps
Ulsterancestry	www.ulsterancestry.co.uk	

Publications

Local histories, etc.

A Clones miscellany / [Compiled by Clones Community Forum], Clones Community Forum, 2004, NLI, 170 p.

Monaghan Election Petition 1826; minutes of evidence, NLI Ir. 32341 m 52

Duffy, Joseph, *A Clogher Record Album; a diocesan history,* Enniskillen: Cumann Seanchais Chlochair, 1975, NLI Ir. 94114 c 3, 340 p.

[Unknown], *St. Macartan's College 1840–1990,* Monaghan: St Macartan's College, 1990, Monaghan County Library, 371.20094167

Brown, Dr. L.T., *Shepherding the Monaghan Flock, The Story of First Monaghan Presbyterian Church 1697–1997,* Monaghan: Monaghan County Library, 1997, 262.3

Carville, Gary, *Parish of Clontibret,* Castleblayney, 1984, NLI Ir. 941 p 74, 59 p.

Copeland, Henry deSaussure, *Lynch family, 2nd–8th generations: line of Conlaw Peter Lynch descendants of Conlaw Peter Lynch and Eleanor (MacMahon) Neison of Clones, Monaghan, ...and Cheraw, South Carolina,* South Carolina, the compiler, 1993, NLI, GO 617, 5 p.

Cotter, Canon J.B.D., *A Short History of Donagh Parish,* Enniskillen: 1966

Day, Angelique, & McWilliams, Patrick (eds.), *Ordnance Survey Memoirs of Ireland: Volume 40 Counties of South Ulster, 1834–8, Cavan, Leitrim, Louth, Monaghan and Sligo,* Belfast: Institute of Irish Studies, 1997, NLI Ir. 9141 o 80, 216p. Co. Monaghan: Aghabog, Aughnamullen, Ballybay, Clontibret, Currin, Donagh, Donaghmoyne, Ematris, Errigal Truagh, Inniskeen, Killanny, Kilmore, Magheracloone, Magheross, Monaghan, Muckno, Tydavnet, Tyholland

Doyle, Anthony, *Charles Powell Leslie (II)'s estates at Glaslough, County Monaghan, 1800–4: portrait of a landed estate business and its community in changing times,* Dublin: Irish Academic Press, 2001, NLI, 68 p.

Farrell, Noel, *Exploring family origins in Monaghan town,* Longford: Noel Farrell, 1998, NLI, 48 p.

Gilsenan, M., *Hills of Magheracloone 1884 1984,* Magheracloone: Magheracloone Mitchells GAA, 1985, NLI Ir. 94117 g 1, 480 p.

Guest, Bill L., *American descendants of John Moorhead of Drumsnat, Monaghan County, Ireland,* Spring, Tex.?: B.L. Guest, 1992?, LOC 50 p.

Haslett, A., *Historical sketch of Ballyalbany Presbyterian Church. Formerly Second Monaghan. Formerly Belanalbany. Formerly New Monaghan Secession Presbyterian Church. [1750–1940],* Belfast: 1940, NLI Ir. 285 o 4, 231 p. Co-author, Rev. S.L. Orr

Killeevan Heritage Group, *From Carn to Clonfad, Killeevan Heritage Group takes a Journey through some pages out of the history of Currin, Killeevan and Aghabog,* Killeevan: Killeevan Heritage Group, n.d., Monaghan County Library, 941.67

Leslie, Seymour, *Of Glaslough in Oriel,* Glaslough: The Glaslough Press, 1912, NLI Ir. 9292 l 6, 114 p.

Livingstone, Peadar, *The Monaghan story: a documented history of the County Monaghan from the earliest times to 1976*, Enniskillen: Clogher Historical Society, 1980, NLI Ir. 94117 L 2, 693 p.

Lockington, John W., *Full circle—a story of Ballybay Presbyterians*, Monaghan, Cahans, NLI

M., G.S., *A Family History of Montgomery of Ballyleck, County Monaghan, now of Beaulie*, Belfast, 1850, Linen Hall Library, 929.2/MONT

Mac Annaidh, S., 'Cholera in Tonytallagh townland in Currin 1834', *Clogher Record*, Vo. 16, No. 1, 1997, 180–1

MacDonald, Brian, *Time of Desolation, Clones Poor Law Union 1845–50*, Monaghan: Clogher Historical Society, 2002, Monaghan County Library, 941.67

Madden, Lucy, 'The Town of Clones', Ir., No. 2, 1993, 18–19

Maisel, Rosemary Virginia, *The Patrick Kirwan family of Carrickmacross, County Monahan, Ireland*, Catonsville, Md: R.V. Maisel, c.1991, LOC, 76 leaves

Marshall, J.J., *History of the Town & District of Clogher, Co. Tyrone, parish of Errigal Keerogue, Tyrone, & Errigal Truagh in the Co. of Monaghan*, Dungannon: Tyrone Printing Co., 1930, NLI Ir. 94114 m 2, 97 p.

McCluskey, Seamus, *Emyvale McKenna country*, Emyvale: 1996, NLI Ir. 94117 m 15, 226 p.

McCluskey, Seamus, *Emyvale Sweet Emyvale*, Monaghan: R. & S. Printers, 1985, NLI Ir. 94117 m 13, 70 p.

McDonald, Brian, 'Church of Ireland members in the Aghadrumsee area in 1823', *Clogher Record*, Vol. 15, No. 1, 1994, 107–121

McGeough, Paula, *Beyond the Big Bridge: A History of Oram and Surrounding Townlands*, Monaghan: R. & S. Printers, 2002, Monaghan County Library, 941.67

McIvor, John, *Extracts from a Ballybay Scrapbook*, Monaghan: 1974, NLI Ir. 9141 p 61, 51 p.

McKenna, J.E., *Parochial Records*, Enniskillen: 1920, 2 vols

McMahon, Theo, *Old Monaghan 1775–1995*, Monaghan: Clogher Historical Society, 1995, NLI Ir. 94117 m 12, 224 p.

Mulligan, Eamonn, *The Replay: A Parish History: Kilmore & Drumsnat*, Monaghan: Sean McDermotts GFC, 1984, NLI Ir. 94117 m 10, 376 p. Co-author, Fr Brian McCluskey

Murnane, Peadar, *At the ford of the birches: the history of Ballybay, it's people and vicinity*, Ballybay: Murnane brothers, 1999, NLI Ir. 94117 m 19, 670 p. Co-author, James H. Murnane

Na Braithre Criostai Mhuineachain, *Monaghan Memories Na Bráithre Criostai Muineachán 1867–1984*, Monaghan: Christian Brothers, 1984, Monaghan County Library

Ó Dufaigh, Brendan, *The book of Clontibret*, Monaghan, Ó Dufaigh, 1997, NLI, 390 p.

Ó Mórdha, P., *The Story of the G.A.A. in Currin and an outline of Parish History*, Currin: Currin GAA Club, 1986, NLI Ir. 396.0.48, 208 p.

Ó Mórdha, P., 'Early schools and schoolteachers in Clones', *Clogher Record*, Vol. 15, No. 1, 1994, 48–50

Ó Mórdha, P., 'Some notes on Clones workhouse', *Clogher Record*, Vol. 15, No. 1, 1994, 74–5

Ó Mórdha, P., 'Summary of inquests held on Currin, Co. Monaghan victims, 1846–1855', *Clogher Record*, Vol. 15, No. 2, 1995, 90–100

O'Donnell, Vincent, *Ardaghey Church and people*, Ardaghey: St Naul's Church, 1995, NLI Ir. 94113 a 5, 146 p.

Quinn, Daig, *St. Anne's Church Drumcatton & Blackstaff 1796 to 1996*, Carrickmacross: Drumcatton 200 Committee, 1996, Monaghan County Library, 941.697, Donaghmoyne

Rushe, Denis Carolan, *Monaghan in the 18th century*, Dublin & Dundalk: M.H. Gill, 1916, NLI Ir. 94117 r 2, 139 p.

Rushe, Denis Carolan, *Historical Sketches of Monaghan*, Dublin: J. Duffy, 1895, NLI Ir. 94117 r 1, 120 p.

Schlegel, Donald M., 'An index to the rebels of 1641 in the County of Monaghan deposition', *Clogher Record*, Vol. 15, No. 2, 1995, 69–89

Shirley, E.P., *The history of the county of Monaghan*, London: Pickering, 1879, NLI Ir. 94117 s 2, 618 p. Repr. Bangor: Fox, 1988

Swanzy, D., 'The Swanzys of Clontibret', *Clogher Record*, Vol. 16, No. 1, 1997, 166–176

Local Journals

Clann MacKenna Journal, NLI Ir. 9292 c 54
Clogher Record, NLI Ir. 94114 c 2
Macalla, NLI Ir. 94116 m 8
The Drumlin: a Journal of Cavan, Leitrim and Monaghan, NLI Ir. 05 d 345

Directories

1824   J. Pigot and Co., *City of Dublin and Hibernian Provincial Directory*, NLI, LDS Film 451787

1846   Slater's *National Commercial Directory of Ireland*. PRONI, NLI LO, LDS Film 1696703 Item 3

1854–   *Belfast and Province of Ulster Directory*. Also 1856, 1858, 1861, 1863, 1865, 1868, 1870, 1877, 1880, 1884, 1887, 1890, 1894, 1900. PRONI. LDS (various years)

1856   Slater, *Royal National Commercial Directory of Ireland*, NLI, LDS Film 1472360 Item 1

1865   R. Wynne, *Business Directory of Belfast*, NLI Ir. 91411 b 2

1870   Slater, *Directory of Ireland*, NLI

1881   Slater, *Royal National Commercial Directory of Ireland*, NLI

1894   Slater, *Royal Commercial Directory of Ireland*, NLI

1897   Gillespie's *Co. Monaghan Alamanack and Directory*

Gravestone Inscriptions

Aghabog: Crover (Aghabog?), C of I. *Clogher Record*, 1982

Clones: Abbey Lane. *Clogher Record*, 1982–84

Clontibret: Annayalla, RC. *Clogher Record*, Vol. 7, No. 2, 1974

Gallagh, C of I, MAR

Clontibret, Pres, MAR

The Diamond, C of I. *Clogher Record*, Vol. 13, No. 1, 1988

Donagh: Glaslough town, C of I. *Clogher Record*, Vol. 9, No. 3, 1978

Donagh. *Clogher Record*, Vol. 2, No. 1, 1957

Drumsnat: Mullanacross, C of I. *Clogher Record*, Vol. 6, No. 1, 1966

Ematris: Rockcorry town, C of I. *Clogher Record*, Vol. 6, No. 1, 1966

Edergoole, MAR

Errigal Trough: Attiduff, St Jospeh's, RC, HW

Killanny: Aghafad, C of I. *Clogher Record*, Vol. 6, No. 1, 1966

Killeevan: Drumswords. *Clogher Record*, 1985

Killeevan Glebe. *Clogher Record*, 1982

Killyfuddy, RC, HW

Kilmore: Kilnahaltar (Kilmore?), C of I. *Clogher Record*, 1983, 1985

Monaghan: Aghananimy, RC, MAR

Rackwallace. *Clogher Record*, Vol. 4, No. 3, 1962

Tedavnet: Drumdesco (Urbeshanny?), RC, MAR

Tehallan: Templetate, C of I, GO

Tullycorbet: Creevagh, Murnane, *At the ford of the birches*

Corvoy (RC): Murnane, *At the ford of the birches*

Estate Records

Anketell estate rentals: 1784–89; *Clogher Record*, Vol. XI, No. 3.

Balfour rentals: of 1632 & 1636. *Clogher Record*, 1985.

Bath, Earl of: NLI Pos. 5894, Rentals, 1784–1809. Major tenants only. Covering townlands in the civil parishes of: Donaghmoyne; Iniskeen; Magheracloone; and Magheross.

Crofton: NLI Ms. 4530, Rental, 1792. All tenants. NLI Ms. 8150, Rentals 1769–1851, some full, some major tenants only. NLI Ms. 20783, Rentals 1853, 1854, 1859. All tenants. Covering townlands in the civil parish of: Aghnamullen; Errigal Trough; and Tednavnet.

Dartry, Earl of (later Viscount Cremorne): NLI Ms. 3181, Maps with tenants' names, 1779. NLI Ms. 3282, Rental, 1780. Major tenants only. NLI Ms. 3184 Rental 1790. Major tenants only. NLI Ms. 1696, Leaseholders. NLI Ms. 3674, Rental, 1796–7. Major tentants only. NLI Mss. 3186–7, Rental, 1800–1. Major tenants only. NLI 3189, Rental, 1838. All tenants. NLI Ms. 1648, Rental 1846. All tenants. NLI Ms. 1698, Valuation, 1841–2. All tenants. Covering townlands in the civil parishes of: Aghabog; Aghnamullen; Donagh; Ematris; Errigal Trough; Killeevan; Kilmore; Monaghan; Tyholland.

Forster, James: Five Rent Rolls, 1803–08, 1812–24. Covering areas in the parishes of: Aghabog; Killeevan; Tydavnet; Tyholland. MA.

Kane: Rentals and Reports for the Kane estates, Errigal Truagh, 1764. Also 1801, 1819–21, *Clogher Record,* 13 (3) (1990), Errigal Trough civil parish.

Kane: Rentals 1840–1; Account Books, 1842–4; Arrears, 1848, 1849, 1852; Rent Receipts, 1851–2. Covering townlands in the parish of Tydavnet. MA.

Ker: Landholders, Newbliss, 1790–c.1830. Killeevan civil parish. *Clogher Record,* 1985.

Leslie: NLI 5783, Rentals 1751–66. Major tenants only & leases. Donagh civil parish NLI 5809 Rent rolls, 1751–1780, NLI Ms. 13710 (part 3); 5809. Coverage unclear. Glaslough and Emy estates, Donagh civil parish. NLI Ms. 5813, Rental, 1839–40. All tenants. Covering townlands in the civil parishes of: Aghabog; Drummully; Drumsnat; Errigal Trough; Kilmore.

Mayne, Edward: NAI M.7036 (18 & 19), Rental, 1848 and 1853. All tenants.

Murray-Ker: Full rentals, 1840–3 (NAI BR Mon 8/1), and 1853–4 (NAI BR Mon 9/1). Covering townlands in the civil parishes of: Aghabog; Aghnamullen; and Killeevan.

Rossmore estate: Maps with tenants' names, c.1820–1852. Monaghan town and surrounding areas. MA.

Smyth, Edward: NAI M.7069, Rental, n.d. All tenants. Covering townlands in the civil parishes of: Ballybay; and Clontibret.

Weymouth estate, Magheross: Survey. Major tenants only. MA.

Wingfield estate: Rentals and arrears, 1852. County and town of Monaghan. MA.

[No Landlord Given:]
Ballybay estate rentals: 1786; *Clogher Record,* Vol. XI, No. 1.
Castleblayney Rent Book: 1772; *Clogher Record,* Vol. X, No. 3.
'Clones rent roll, 1821': *Clogher Record,* 13 (1) (1988).
Emy and Glaslough estates: Rent Roll, 1752–60. Principally major tenants. Civil parishes of: Donagh; and Errigal Truagh. MA.
Rent book, 1772: Most tenants, Castleblayney rent book 1772, *Clogher Record,* 11 (1) (1982), Muckno civil parish.

OFFALY

Census returns and substitutes

1641	Book of Survey and Distribution. NLI Ms. 972
1659	Pender's 'Census'. Repr. GPC, 1997, IMC, 2002. LDS Film 924648
1766	Ballycommon. JKAS, Vol. VII, GO 537
1770	Voters. NLI Ms. 2050
1773–1907	Register of tenants who planted trees: Geashill 1793–1907, Eglish 1809–37, JKAS, 15 (3), 1973/4, 310–18
1802	Protestants in the parishes of Ballyboggan, Ballyboy, Castlejordan, Clonmacnoise, Drumcullin, Eglish, Gallen, Killoughey, Lynally, Rynagh, Tullamore. IA, 1973

1821	Parishes of Aghacon, Birr, Ettagh, Kilcolman, Kinnitty, Letterluna, Roscomroe, Roscrea, Seirkieran. NAI CEN 1821/26–34
1823–1838	Tithe Books. NAI
1824	Catholic householders, Lusmagh parish. In Roman Catholic parish registers. NLI
1830	Contributors to new Catholic church in Lusmagh. In Roman Catholic parish registers. NLI
1835	Tubber parish. NLI Pos. 1994
1840	Eglish and Drumcullin parishes. In Roman Catholic parish registers. NLI Pos. 4175
1842	Voters, NAI OP 1842/27
1852	Assisted passages from Kilconouse, Kinnitty parish. AH, Vol. 22, 1960
1854	Griffith's Valuation. Indexed online: Hayes
1901	Census. Database version in IMA
1911	Census

Online

Hayes, John	*www.failteromhat.com*	Large compendium of transcribed records

Publications

Local histories, etc.

Ferbane Parish & its Churches, NLI Ir. 91413 f 4

Memoir of the Warburton family of Garryhinch, King's Co., Dublin, 1842, 2nd ed. 1881

Boruwlaski, Joseph, *Joseph Boruwlaski, his visit to Portarlington, 1795*, York: Frenchchurch Press, 1997, NLI, 5 p.

Brady, J., *A short history of the parishes of the diocese of Meath, 1867–1944*, NLI Ir. 94132 b 2

Byrne, Michael, *Tullamore Catholic parish: a Historical Survey*, Tullamore: Tullamore Parish Committee, 1987, NLI Ir. 27414 b 7, 188 p.

Byrne, Michael, *Towards a History of Kilclonfert*, Tullamore: AnCo/Offaly Historical Society, 1984, NLI Ir. 94136 t 1, 141 p.

Byrne, Michael, *Durrow and its History: a celebration of what has gone before*, Tullamore: Esker Press, 1994, NLI Ir. 9141 p 71, 303 p.

Byrne, Michael, *Tullamore Catholic Parish: a historical survey*, Tullamore: Tullamore Parish Committee, 1987, NLI Ir. 27414 b 7, 188 p.

Byrne, Michael, *Sources for Offaly History*, Tullamore: Offaly Research Library, 1977, NLI Ir. 94136 b 1, 102 p.

Carville, Geraldine, *Birr, the monastic city St. Brendan of the water cress*, Bray: Kestrel Books Ltd., 1997, NLI Ir. 94101 c 4, 103 p.

Clonbullogue Book Committee, *The Life, the times, the people*, Clonbullogue: Clonbullogue Book Committee, 1993, NLI Ir. 94136 L 3, 416 p.

Cooke, William Antisell, *History of Birr*, Dublin: 1875

Darby, Stephen, *Ballybryan a step back in time*, Ballybryan: Ballybryan National School, 1994, NLI Ir. 94136 d 3, 216 p.

Dwyer, Philip, *The Diocese of Killaloe, from the Reformation to the Close of the Eighteenth Century*, Dublin: Hodges, Foster, and Figgis, 1878, NLI Ir. 94143 d 11, 602 p. Reprint: Newmarket-on-Fergus: O'Brien Book Publications, 1997

Farrell, Noel, *Exploring family origins in Birr*, Longford: Noel Farrell, 1998, NLI

Farrell, Noel, *Exploring family origins in old Tullamore Town*, Longford: Noel Farrell, 1998, NLI

Feehan, John, *The Landscape of Slieve Bloom: a study of the natural & human heritage*, Dublin: Blackwater Press, 1979, NLI Ir. 91413 f 4, 284 p.

Finney, Charles W., *Monasteroris Parish, 8th May 1778–8th May 1978*, Monasteroris: 1978, NLI Ir. 200 p 23, 14 p.

Gleeson, John, *History of the Ely O'Carroll Territory or Ancient Ormond*, Dublin: Gill, 1915, NLI Ir. 94142 g 1, Repr. Roberts' Books, c.1982, with an introduction and bibliography by George Cunningham.

Healy, John, *History of the Diocese of Meath*, Dublin: 1908, 2 vols

Irish Countrywomen's Association, *Approach the fountain, a history of Seir Kieran*, Seir Kieran: Seir Kieran ICA, 1992, NLI Ir. 94136 p 2(4), 163 p.

Kearney, John, *Daingean: pages from the past*, Daingean, 1988, NLI, 48 p.

Kelly, Denis, *Famine: Gortá í Lusmá*, 1996, NLI, 50 p.

Magee, Sean, *Weavers of Prosporous, County Kildare, Balbriggan, County Dublin & Tullamore, County Offaly in memorials of 1826*, Dublin: Dun Laoghaire Genealogical Society, 1998, NLI Ir. 9291 g 7

Meehan, Patrick, *Members of Parliament for Laois and Offaly 1801–1918*, Portlaoise: Leinster Express, 1983, NLI Ir. 328 m 6, 246 p.

Monahan, Rev. J., *Records Relating to the Diocese of Ardagh and Clonmacnoise*, Dublin, M.H. Gill and son, 1886, NLI Ir. 27413 m 3, 400 p.

O Riain, Seamus, *Dunkerrin: a parish in Ely O Carroll: a history of Dunkerrin Parish from 1200 A.D. to the present time*, Dunkerrin: Dunkerrin History Committee, 1988, NLI Ir. 94136 O 5, 256 p.

Offaly Historical Society, *Offaly Tombstone Inscriptions Vols 1–4*, Tullamore: Offaly Historical Society, 1981(?), NLI

O'Reilly, Joe, *From Clonsast to Ballyburley*, Edenderry: O'Reilly, 1994, NLI Ir. 94136 f 2, 176 p.

Paterson, J. (ed.), *Diocese of Meath and Kildare: an historical guide*, 1981, NLI Ir. 941 p. 75

Pey, Brian, *Eglish and Drumcullen: a parish in Firceall*, Offaly: Firceall Heritage Group, 2003, NLI, 435 p.

Ryan, Brendan, *A land by the river of God: a history of Ferbane Parish from earliest times to c.1900*, Ferbane: St Mel's Diocesan Trust, 1994, NLI Ir. 94136 r 1, 348 p.

Sheil, Helen, *Falling into wretchedness: Ferbane in the late 1830s*, Dublin: Irish Academic Press, 1998, NLI Ir. 94136 s 3, 64 p.

Simons, P. Frazer, *Tenants no more: Voices from an Irish Townland 1811–1901 and the Great Migration to Australia and America*, Richmond, Australia: Prowling

Tiger Press, 1996, NLI Ir. 994 s 32, 288 p. Clay family from Gurteen, Offaly (King's), Methodist migrants to the US and Australia

Trodd, Valentine, *Clonmacnois and West Offaly,* Banagher: Banagher, 1998, NLI Ir. 94136 t 5, 224 p.

Trodd, Valentine, *Midlanders: chronicle of a Midland parish,* Banagher: Scéal Publications, 1994, NLI Ir. 94136 t 3, 226 p. Banagher

Local Journals
Offaly heritage: Journal of the Offaly Historical and Archaeological Society. (2003–), NLI
Ardagh & Clonmacnoise Historical Society Journal, NLI Ir. 794105

Directories

1824	J. Pigot and Co., *City of Dublin and Hibernian Provincial Directory,* NLI, LDS Film 451787
1846	Slater's *National Commercial Directory of Ireland.* PRONI, NLI LO, LDS Film 1696703 Item 3
1856	Slater, *Royal National Commercial Directory of Ireland,* NLI, LDS Film 1472360 Item 1
1870	Slater, *Directory of Ireland,* NLI
1881	Slater, *Royal National Commercial Directory of Ireland,* NLI
1894	Slater, *Royal Commercial Directory of Ireland,* NLI

Gravestone Inscriptions
Irish Midlands Ancestry has transcripts for a large number of graveyards in the county. Contact details are given in Chapter 15.

Ballykean: Stranure (Cloneygowan?), C of I, GO Ms. 622, p. 182
Kilclonfert: Kilclonfert, Byrne, *Kilclonfert*
Killaderry: Phillipstown, Main Street, *Offaly Tombstone Inscriptions, Vol. 4*
Lusmagh: *Offaly Tombstone Inscriptions, Vol. 3*
Monasteroris: *Offaly Tombstone Inscriptions, Vol. 2*
Rahan: Rahan Demesne, C of I, *Offaly Tombstone Inscriptions, Vol. 1*

Estate Records
Charleville, Earl of: Tullamore tenants, 1763–1763, LDS Family history library, 941.5 A1, Kilbride civil parish.
Magan, William Henry: NLI Ms. 14.A.27, Maps, 1848. All tenants. Covering townlands in the civil parish of Killaderry.
[No Landlord given]: Rental & maps, 1855–1855, NAI, M.601, Killoughy parish, Ballyfarrell & Derrymore townlands
[No Landlord given]: Rentals, 1840–1850, NLI Ms. 4337 Clonsast parish; seven townlands, 154 tenants

ROSCOMMON

Census returns and substitutes

1659   Pender's 'Census'. Repr. GPC, 1997, IMC, 2002. LDS Film 924648

1749   Aughrim, Ardcarn, Ballintober, Ballynakill, Baslick, Boyle, Bumlin, Cam, Clontuskert, Cloocraff, Cloonfinlough, Cloonygormican, Creeve, Drimatemple, Dunamon, Dysart, Estersnow, Elphin, Fuerty, Kilbride, Kilbryan, Kilcolagh, Kilcooley, Kilcorkey, Kilgefin, Kilglass, Kilkeevin, Killinvoy, Killuken, Kilumnod, Kilmacallen, Kilmacumsy, Kilmore, Kilronan, Kiltoom, Kiltrustan, Kilnamagh, Lisonuffy, Ogulla, Oran, Rahara, Roscommon, St John's, St Peter's Athlone, Shankill, Taghboy, Termonbarry, Tibohine, Tisrara, Tumna. NAI MFS 6. See also Manning, *Elphin Index*. Part online: Leitrim-Roscommon

1780   Freeholders. GO 442. Also LDS Film 100181

1790–1799 Freeholders c.30 lists. NLI Ms. 10130

1796   Spinning-Wheel Premium List. 1,650 names for Co. Roscommon. Online: Hayes

1813   Freeholders. NLI ILB 324

1821   Some extracts. NAI Thrift Abstracts

1823–1838 Tithe Books

1830–1847 Ballykilcline, Kilglass parish. Scally, *Hidden Ireland*. Online: Ballykilcline

1837   Memorial for Quarter Sessions at Castlerea. Parishes of Kiltullagh and Loughglyn esp. Also mentioned Baslick, Kilkeevin Ballintubber, Aughamore. c.260 names. NAI OP 1837/3

1838   Memorial from inhabitants of Frenchpark for Quarter Sessions. c.250 names NAI OP 1850/114

1837   Marksmen (i.e. illiterate voters), Athlone Borough. *Parliamentary Papers 1837, Reports from Committees*, Vol. II (1), Appendix A

1838–1848 Reproductive Loan Fund records. Covering parishes of Ardcarn, Aughrim, Ballintober, Baslick, Boyle, Bumlin, Clooncraff, Cloonfinlough, Creeve, Elphin, Estersnow, Kilglass, Kilkeevin, Killukin (Boyle), Kilmore, Kilteevan, Kiltoom, Kiltullagh, Ogulla, Oran, Termonbarry, Tibohine. More than 9,000 names NAI (Kew). T 91. Partly online: Moving Here

1841   Some extracts. NAI Thrift Abstracts

1843   Petition for Quarter Sessions at Frenchpark 'inhabitants of the western districts of Castlerea and Frenchpark'. More than 350 names and signatures NAI OP 1850/114

1843   Voters NAI OP 1843/59

1843   Workhouse records Carrick-on-Shannon union 1843–82. LCL

1848   Male Catholic inhabitants of the parish of Boyle. NLI Pos. 4692

1851   Some extracts. NAI Thrift Abstracts

1857–1858 Griffith's Valuation. Indexed online: Hayes. Part transcription online:

Leitrim-Roscommon
1861   Athlone voters. WCL. Also LDS Film 1279285
1901   Census. Online: Leitrim-Roscommon
1911   Census

Online

Ballykilcline	www.ballykilcline.com	
Hayes, John	www.failteromhat.com	
Leitrim-Roscommon	www.leitrim-roscommon.com	1901, Griffith's, Townlands. Elphin 1749
Moving Here	www.movinghere.org.uk/search/	
Williams, Brenda	www.puregolduk.com/bren/ kilglass_co_sligo1.htm	

Publications

Local histories, etc.

Notes on the O'Kellys and other families of Kilkeerin parish Co. Roscommon (type-script), NLI Ir. 9292 k 5, Kilkeevin?

Taughmaconnell: a history / compiled by the Taughmaconnell Historical and Heritage Group, Taughmaconnell: Taughmaconnell Historical and Heritage Group, 2000, NLI, 256 p.

Kingsland co. Roscommon: its people past and present, Kingsland Reunion Committee, 1994, Roscommon County Library

Athlone: Materials from printed sources relating to the history of Athlone and surrounding areas, 1699–1899, NLI Mss. 1543–7, including an index volume

Beckett, Rev. M., *Facts and Fictions of Local History,* 1929, Kiltullagh district

Beirne, Francis, *A history of the parish of Tisrara,* Tisrara: Tisrara Heritage Society, 1997, NLI Ir. 94125 h 5, 219 p.

Burke, Francis, *Lough Ce and its annals: North Roscommon and the diocese of Elphin in times of old,* Dublin, 1895, NLI Ir. 27412 b 1

Clarke, Desmond, 'Athlone, a bibliographical study', *An Leabhar,* No. 10, 1952, 138–9

Clonown Community Centre, *Clonown the history, traditions and culture of a South Roscommon community,* Clonown: Clonown Community Centre, 1989, NLI Ir. 94125.c.6, 180 p.

Coleman, Anne, *Riotous Roscommon: social unrest in the 1840s,* Dublin; Portland, OR: Irish Academic Press, 1999, NLI Ir. 94125 c 12, 64 p.

Coyle, Liam, *A parish history of Kilglass, Slatta, Ruskey,* Kilglass: Kilglass Gaels GAA Club, 1994, NLI Ir. 94125 C 9, 559 p.

Drum Heritage Group, *Drum and its hinterland,* Drum: Drum Heritage Group, 1994, NLI Ir. 94125 d 3, 368 p.

Egan, Patrick K., *The parish of Ballinasloe, its history from the earliest times to the present day,* Galway: Kennys Bookshops, 1994, NLI Ir. 94124 e 2, 355 p.

Farrell, Noel, *Exploring family origins in old Roscommon town*, Longford: Noel Farrell, 1998, NLI, 48 p.

Gacquin, William, *Roscommon before the Famine—the parishes of Kiltoom and Cam*, Dublin: Irish Academic Press, 1996, NLI Ir. 94125 g 9, 64 p.

Gacquin, William, *Tombstone inscriptions Cam Old Cemetery*, Cam: Cam Cemetery Committee, 1992, NLI Ir. 941 p 120(1), 49 p.

Gibbon, Skeffington, *The recollections of Skeffington Gibbon, from 1796 to the present year, 1829*, Dublin: printed by Joseph Blundell, 1829, NLI Ir. 92 g 94, 170 p.

Gormley, Mary, *Tulsk Parish in historic Magh Ai, aspects of its history and folklore compiled*, Roscommon: County Roscommon Historical & Archaeological Society, 1989, NLI Ir. 94125 g 8, 160 p. Baslick, Killukin (Roscommon), Ogulla

Grenham, John Joe, *Moore: the customs and traditions of a rural community*, Moore Community Council, 1983, Roscommon County Library, 941.75

Hayes McCoy, G.A., *Index to 'The Compossicion Booke of Connoght, 1585'*, Dublin: Irish Manuscripts Commission, 1945, NLI Ir. 9412 c 1, 179 p.

Higgins, Jim, *The Tisrara medieval church Carrowntemple [...]*, Four Roads, Tisrara Heritage [...] Committee, 1995, NLI Ir. 7941 h 25

Hurley, Rev. Timothy, *St Patrick and the Parish of Kilkeevan Vol. 1*, Dublin: Dollard, 1944, NLI Ir. 27412 h 2, 618 p.

IGRS, *Tombstone inscriptions Vol. 2*, Dublin: IGRS Tombstone Committee, 2001, NLI, c. 900 p.

Keaney, Marion, *Athlone bridging the centuries*, Mullingar: Westmeath county council, 1991, NLI Ir. 94131 a 2. Co-editor, Gearóid Ó Briain

Knox, H.T., *Notes on the Early History of the Dioceses of Tuam, Killala and Achonry*, Dublin: Hodges Figgis, 1904, NLI Ir. 27412 k 1, 410 p.

Lenehan, Jim, *Politics and Society in Athlone, 1830–1885: A Rotten Borough*, Irish Academic Press, 1999, NLI

MacNamee, James J., *History of the Diocese of Ardagh*, Dublin: Browne and Nolan, 1954, NLI Ir. 274131 m 5, 858 p.

Manning, Peter, *Elphin Diocesan census 1749: surname index*, Rainham, Kent: Manning, 1987, NLI Ir. 27412 m 20

Mattimoe, Cyril, *North Roscommon its people and past*, Kildare: Cyril Mattimoe, 1992, NLI Ir. 94125 m 8, 214 p.

Monahan, Rev. J., *Records Relating to the Diocese of Ardagh and Clonmacnoise*, Dublin: M.H. Gill and son, 1886, NLI Ir. 27413 m 3, 400 p.

Moran, James M., *Stepping on stones: Roscommon Mid West, the Suck lowlands, the Ballinturly-Correal valley*, Cartur, Co. Roscommon: James Moran, 1993, NLI Ir. 94125 m 10

Moran, James M., *Vignettes*, Athleague: Moran/Cartur Publications, 1996, NLI Ir. 94125 m 12, 296 p.

Murtagh, H., *Athlone: history and settlement to 1800*, Athlone: Old Athlone Society, 2000, NLI Ir. 94131 m 6, 256 p.

Murtagh, H., *Irish Historic Towns Atlas 6: Athlone*, Dublin: Royal Irish Academy, 1994, NLI, ILB 941 p (13) 3

Murtagh, H., *Athlone besieged*, Athlone: Temple Printing Co., 1991, NLI Ir. 94107 p 21(1), Eyewitness and other contemporary accounts of the siege of Athlone 1690, 1691

O'Brien, Brendan, *Athlone Workhouse and the Famine*, Athlone: Old Athlone Society, 1995, NLI Ir. 300 p 207(8). Edited by Gearóid O'Brien

Scally, Robert, *The End of Hidden Ireland*, Oxford: Oxford University Press, 1997, NLI Ir. 94125 s 7, 266 p. Ballykilcline townland

Schmidt, Joanne C. Fisher, *Tombstones of Ireland: counties Down & Roscommon*, Bowie, MD: Heritage Books, c.2000, LOC, 110 p.

Simington, Robert C., *The transplantation to Connacht, 1654–58*, Shannon: Irish University Press for the Irish Manuscripts Commission, 1970, NLI Ir. 94106 s 9, 306 p.

Stokes, George T., *Athlone, the Shannon & Lough Ree*, Dublin & Athlone, 1897, NLI Ir. 91413 s 1

Tonra, Henry, *The Parish of Ardcarne*, 2001, NLI, 244 p.

Local Journals
Journal of the Old Athlone Society, NLI Ir. 94131 o 1
Journal of the Roscommon Historical and Archaeological Society, NLI Ir. 94125 r 5
The Moylfinne: Journal Of The Old Taughmaconnell Society, Roscommon Co. Library

Directories

1824	J. Pigot and Co., *City of Dublin and Hibernian Provincial Directory*, NLI, LDS Film 451787
1846	Slater's *National Commercial Directory of Ireland*. PRONI, NLI LO, LDS Film 1696703 Item 3
1856	Slater, *Royal National Commercial Directory of Ireland*, NLI, LDS Film 1472360 Item 1
1870	Slater, *Directory of Ireland*, NLI
1881	Slater, *Royal National Commercial Directory of Ireland*, NLI
1894	Slater, *Royal Commercial Directory of Ireland*, NLI

Gravestone Inscriptions
Ardcarn (C of I): Schmidt, *Tombstones*
Aughrim: RHGC
Bumlin: Killinordin RHGC
Cam: *IGRS*, Vol. 2. Also Gacquin, *Tombstone inscriptions*
Cloonfinlough: Ballintemple, RHGC
Cloontuskert: IGRS Collection, GO
Dysart: RHGC. Also IGRS Collection (103 inscriptions), GO
Elphin: Elphin Cathedral, C of I, GO Ms. 622 p. 151, GO
Estersnow (C of I): Schmidt, *Tombstones*
Fuerty: RHGC

Kilmore: (C of I): Schmidt, *Tombstones*

Kiltrustan: RHGC

Lissonuffy: RHGC

Roscommon: Hill Street C of I, GO. Ms. 622, p. 170, GO. Also RHGC

St Peter's: Athlone, King Street, C of I, Pos. 5309 (with parish registers), NLI

Taghboy: Jamestown?, GO Ms. 622, p. 170, GO

Taghmaconnell: *IGRS*, Vol. 2

Tisrara: Mount Talbot (Tisrara?), C of I, *IGRS, Vol. 2*

Tisrara: Carrowntemple, Higgins, *The Tisrara medieval church*

Estate Records

Blake Knox, Francis: NLI Ms. 3077. Rentals, 1845–66. Covering townlands in the civil parishes of: Cloonfinlough; Rahara.

Boswell, Frances: NLI Pos. 4937. Rent ledger, c.1760–86. Major tenants only. Covering townlands in the civil parish of Kilronan.

Browne, John: NLI 16 1 14(8). Map of Carronaskeagh, Cloonfinlough parish, May 1811, with tenants' names.

Clonbrock, Baron: NLI Ms. 19501. Tenants' ledger, 1801–06, indexed. Covering townlands in the civil parish of Taughmaconnell.

Crofton, Edward: NLI Ms. 19672. Rent roll, May 1778. Major tenants only. Covering townlands in the civil parishes of: Baslick; Estersnow; Kilbryan; Kilgefin; Killinvoy; Killumod; Kilmeane; Kiltrustan; Ogulla.

Crofton, Sir Humphrey: NLI Ms. 4531. Rental, March 1833, tenants' names alphabetically. Covering townlands in the civil parish of Tumna.

Dundas, Sir Thomas: NLI Mss. 2787, 2788. Rentals, 1792, 1804. Major tenants only. Covering townlands in the civil parishes of: Boyle; Estersnow; Kilnamanagh; Tumna.

Evans, Walker: NLI Ms. 10152. Leases, c.1790. Covering townlands in the civil parish of Creeve.

Fox, James: NLI Pos. 4065, Rental, 1819. All tenants. Covering townlands in the civil parish of Ogulla.

Gunning, Gen'l (?): NLI Ms. 10152. Rental, 1792. Major tenants only. Covering townlands in the civil parishes of: Athleague; Fuerty; Kilcooley.

King: NLI Ms. 4170. Rent rolls and accounts, 1801–1818. Major tenants only. Covering townlands in the civil parishes of: Creeve; Elphin; Kilmore.

King, John: NLI Mss. 3520,3125, Rent and Miscellaneous accounts, 1757–1786. All tenants. Covering townlands in the civil parishes of: Creeve; Elphin; Kilmacumsy; Kilmore; Roscommon; Taghboy; Tisrara.

Lorton, Lord: NLI Mss. 3104/5. Lease Books, 1740–1900, including many leases to small tenants, with lives mentioned in the leases. Covering townlands in the civil parishes of: Ardcarn; Aughrim; Boyle; Creeve; Elphin; Estersnow; Kilbryan; Kilnamanagh.

Ormsby, Rev. Rodney: NLI Ms. 10152. Leases c.1803, Grange townland.

Pakenham-Mahon: NLI Ms. 10152; Rent roll, 1725. Major tenants only. NLI Ms. 10152; rent roll, 1765–68. Major tenants only. NLI Ms. 2597; rent ledger, 1795–1804, indexed. NLI Mss. 5501–3; rent ledgers, 1803–1818, 1824–36, part indexed. NLI Ms. 9473; tenants of Maurice Mahon, c.1817. NLI Ms. 9471; rentals and accounts, 1846–54. Covering townlands in the civil parishes of: Bumlin; Cloonfinlough; Elphin; Kilgefin; Kilglass; Kilnamanagh; Kiltrustan; Lisonuffy; Shankill. Also NLI Ms. 9472; rent ledger 1840–48, Kilmacumsy parish.

St George, Charles Manners: NLI Mss. 4001–22. Accounts and rentals (annual), 1842–46, 50–55, 61–71. Covering townlands in the civil parishes of: Ardcarn; Killukin; Killumod.

Sandford: NLI 10,152; Rental (major tenants only), 1718. NLI Ms. 10,152; Leases, c.1750. NLI Ms. 10,152; Lands to be settled on the marriage of Henry Sandford, with tenants' names, 1750. NLI Mss. 4281–9; Annual Rentals, 1835–45. Covering townlands in the civil parishes of: Ballintober; Baslick; Kilkeevin; Boyle; Kiltullagh; Tibohine.

Tenison, Thomas: NLI Ms. 5101. Rental & Accounts, 1836–40. Covering townlands in the civil parishes of: Ardcarn; Kilronan.

[No Landlord Given]: NLI Ms. 24880. List of tenants, Moore parish, 1834.

SLIGO

Census returns and substitutes

1659	Pender's 'Census'. Repr. GPC, 1997, IMC, 2002. LDS Film 924648
1664	MacLysaght, *Hearth money rolls*
1749	Parishes of Aghanagh, Ahamlish, Ballynakill, Ballysumaghan, Drumcliff, Drumcolumb, Killadoon, Kilmacallan, Kilmactranny, Kilross, Shancough, Sligo, Tawnagh. NAI MFS 6. See also Manning, *Elphin Index*. Part online: Genweb, Sligo
1790	Voters. NLI Ms. 2169
1795–1796	Freeholders. NLI Ms. 3136
1798	Persons who suffered losses in the 1798 rebellion. Propertied classes only. c.250 names. NLI I 94107
1822–1848	Reproductive Loan Fund records, Templehouse loan association. Mainly parishes of Emlaghfad and Kilvarnet NAI (Kew) T/91
1823–1838	Tithe Books. Part online: Genweb, Sligo
1832–1837	Voters registered in Sligo borough. *Parliamentary Papers 1837, Reports from Committees*, Vol. II (2), 193–6
1842–1843	Voters OP 1843/61
1852	Sligo electors. NLI Ms. 3064
1858	Griffith's Valuation. Indexed online: Hayes
1901	Census. Part online: Genweb, Sligo, Leitrim-Roscommon
1911	Census

Online

Genweb, Sligo	*www.rootsweb.com/~irlsli*	
Hayes, John	*www.failteromhat.com*	
Leitrim-Roscommon	*www.leitrim-roscommon.com*	1901, Griffith's, Townlands. Elphin 1749
Williams, Brenda	*www.puregolduk.com/bren/kilglass_co_sligo1.htm*	

Publications

Local histories, etc.

Petition by Sligo Protestants, 1813, 1813, NLI, p. 504

Carroll, P.J., *Cillglas—Kilglas the church by the stream: a history of the confiscation settlement and vesting of its lands*, Carroll, 1995, NLI, 32 p.

Day, Angelique, & McWilliams, Patrick (eds.), *Ordnance Survey Memoirs of Ireland: Volume 40 Counties of South Ulster, 1834–8, Cavan, Leitrim, Louth, Monaghan and Sligo*, Belfast: Institute of Irish Studies, 1997, NLI Ir. 9141 0 80, 216p. Co. Sligo: Emlaghfad, Killoran and Kilcarnet: Kilmactigue

Farry, M., *Killoran and Coolaney: a local history*, 1985, NLI Ir. 94122 f 1

Finn, J., *Gurteen, Co. Sligo, its history, antiquities and traditions*, Boyle, Ireland: Roscommon Herald, 1981, NLI Ir. 94122 p 1, 64 p.

Greer, James, *The windings of the Moy with Skreen and Tirerogh*, Dublin: Thom, 1923, NLI Ir. 91412 g 3, 232 p. Repr. Western People, Ballina, 1986

Halloran, Canon Martin, *Templeboy 2000*, Templeboy: Halloran, 2000

Hayes McCoy, G.A., *Index to 'The Compossicion Booke of Connoght, 1585'*, Dublin: Irish Manuscripts Commission, 1945, NLI Ir. 9412 c 1, 179 p.

Heneghan, Susan, *Laethanta scoile: Castlerock townland, Castlerock school, & its surrounds*, 2003, Sligo, 2003, NLI, 131 p.

Henry, Patrick J., *Sligo: medical care in the past 1800–1965*, 1995, NLI Ir. 362 h 11, 144 p.

Higgins, John, *Keash and Culfadda: a local history*, Keash: The Keash–Culfadda Local History Committee, 2001, NLI, 245 p. Co-editors, Mary B. Timoney, Br. Thomas Connolly and John Kielty.

IGRS, *Tombstone inscriptions Vol. 2*, Dublin: IGRS Tombstone Committee, 2001, NLI, c.900 p.

Knox, H.T., *Notes on the Early History of the Dioceses of Tuam, Killala and Achonry*, Dublin: Hodges Figgis, 1904, NLI Ir. 27412 k 1, 410 p.

MacHale, Edward, *The Parishes in the Diocese of Killala: [1]: South Tirawley, (2) North Tirawley, 3 (Erris), (4) Tireragh*, Killala, [s.n], 1985, NLI Ir. 27414 m 6, 166/ 104/ 88/ 79 p.

MacLysaght, Edward, *Seventeenth century hearth money rolls, with full transcript for County Sligo*, Dublin: IMC, 1967. NLI Ir. 94122 m 5. From NLI Ms. 2165

MacNamee, James J., *History of the Diocese of Ardagh*, Dublin: Browne and Nolan, 1954, NLI Ir. 274131 m 5, 858 p.

Manning, Peter, *Elphin Diocesan census 1749: surname index*, Rainham, Kent: Manning, 1987. NLI Ir. 27412 m 20

McDonagh, J.C., *History of Ballymote and the Parish of Emlaghfad*, 1936, NLI Ir. 94122 m 1, 205 p.

McDonnell, Thomas, *The diocese of Killala: from its institution to the end of the penal times*, Ballina: R. & S. Monaghan, 1975, NLI Ir. 27412 m 1, 143 p.

McGloin, Atlanta, *In the shadow of Carran Hill historical perspectives of Gleann and its surroundings*, 1997, NLI Ir. 94122 i 1, 195 p.

McGowan, Joe, *Inishmurray gale, stone and fire: portrait of a fabled island*, Mullaghmore: Aeolus, 1998, NLI Ir. 94122 m 23, 64 p.

McGowan, Joe, *In the shadow of Benbulben*, Mullaghmore: Aeolus, 1993, NLI Ir. 94122 m 14, 336 p.

McGuinn, J., *Curry*, the author, 1984, NLI Ir. 94122 m 8, 102 p.

McTernan, John C., *At the foot of Knocknarea a chronicle of Coolera in bygone days*, Coolera, Coolera/Strandhill GAA; 1990, NLI Ir. 94122.m.10, 188 p. Killaspugbrone

McTernan, John C., *Memory harbour the Port of Sligo: an outline of its growth and decline and its role as an emigration port*, Sligo: Avena Publications, 1992, NLI Ir. 387 m 16, 96 p.

McTernan, John C., *Historic Sligo*, Sligo: Yeats Country Publications, 1965, NLI Ir. 94122 m 4, 156 p. A bibliographical introduction to the antiquities, history, maps and surveys, mss, newspapers, historic families, and notable individuals of Co. Sligo

Moffitt, Miriam, *The Church of Ireland community of Killala & Achonry, 1870–1940*, Dublin: Irish Academic Press, 1999, NLI Ir. 283 m 4, 64 p.

O'Connell, Philip, *The Diocese of Kilmore: its History and Antiquities*, Dublin: Browne and Nolan, 1937, NLI Ir. 274119 o 3, 579 p.

O'Connor, Watson B., *The O'Connor family: families of Daniel and Mathias O'Connor of Carsallagh House, Achonry, Co. Sligo ...1750*, Brooklyn, 1914

O'Rorke, T., *History and Antiquities of the Parishes of Ballysadare and Kilvarnet*, 1878, NLI, I 9412201. Including histories of the O'Haras, Coopers, Percevals, and other families

Ridge, John T., *Sligo in New York: the Irish from County Sligo, 1849–1991*, New York: County Sligo Social & Benevolent Association, c.1991, NLI Ir. 947 r 21, 157 p.

Simington, Robert C., *The transplantation to Connacht, 1654–58*, Shannon: Irish University Press for the Irish Manuscripts Commission, 1970, NLI Ir. 94106 s 9, 306 p.

Sligo Family Research, *Doo Chapel Kilmorgan*, Sligo: Sligo Family Research, 1980?, NLI, 7 p.

Wood Martin, W.G., *Sligo and the Enniskilleners, from 1688–91*, Dublin: 1882

Wood Martin, W.G., *History of Sligo, county and town, from the close of the Revolution of 1688 to the present time*, Dublin: Hodges, Figgis, & Co, 1892, NLI Ir. 94122 w 1, 3 vols, 510 p.

Directories

1820   J. Pigot, *Commercial Directory of Ireland* PRONI, NLI Ir. 9141 p 107, LDS
              Film 962702 Item 1
1824   J. Pigot and Co., *City of Dublin and Hibernian Provincial Directory*, NLI,
              LDS Film 451787
1839   *Directory of the Towns of Sligo, Enniskillen, Ballyshannon, Donegal [...]*
1846   Slater's *National Commercial Directory of Ireland*. PRONI, NLI LO, LDS
              Film 1696703 Item 3
1856   Slater, *Royal National Commercial Directory of Ireland*, NLI, LDS Film
              1472360 Item 1
1870   Slater, *Directory of Ireland*, NLI
1881   Slater, *Royal National Commercial Directory of Ireland*, NLI
1889   *Sligo Independent County Directory*
1894   Slater, *Royal Commercial Directory of Ireland*, NLI

Gravestone Inscriptions

Sligo Heritage and Genealogy Centre has transcripts for 146 graveyards in the
county. Contact details will be found in Chapter 15. Published or publicly available transcripts are given below.

Calry C of I, *IGRS*, Vol. 2
St John's, Sligo Abbey, *IGRS*, Vol. 2

Estate Records

Boswell, Francis: NLI Pos. 4937. Rental, c.1760–1786. Major tenants only. Covering
   townlands in the civil parishes of: Ahamlish; Drumrat.
Cooper family: NLI Mss. 3050–3060; eleven volumes of rentals and rent ledgers,
   1775–1872. Major tenants only. NLI Ms. 3076; rental 1809/10. Major tenants only.
   NLI Ms. 9753–57; rentals and accounts. Major tenants only. Covering townlands
   in the civil parishes of: Achonry; Ahamlish; Ballysadare; Ballysumaghan;
   Drumcolumb; Drumcliff; Killery; Killaspugbrone; Kilmacallan; Kilmorgan;
   Kilross; Tawnagh; Templeboy.
Crofton, Sir Malby: NAI M.938X; rental, 1853, with all tenants. NAI M.940X; leases on
   the estate, including many small tenants, and mentioning lives in the leases.
   Covering townlands in the civil parishes of: Dromard; Templeboy.
Dundas, Sir Thomas: NLI Mss. 2787, 2788; rentals, 1792, 1804. Major tenants only.
   Covering townlands in the civil parishes of: Aghanagh; Drumrat; Emlaghfad;
   Kilcolman; Kilfree; Kilglass; Kilmacallan; Kilmacteigue; Kilmactranny;
   Kilmoremoy; Kilshalvey; Skreen.
Lorton, Lord: NLI Mss. 3104, 3105; lease books, 1740–1900, including many leases
   to small tenants, with lives mentioned in leases. Covering townlands in the
   civil parishes of: Aghanagh; Drumcolumb; Kilfree; Killaraght; Kilmacallan;
   Kilshalvey; Toomour.
O'Hara the younger, Charles: NLI Pos. 1923. Rent roll. c.1775. All tenants, giving

lives named in leases. Covering townlands in the civil parishes of: Achonry; Ballysadare; Killoran; Kilvarnet.

Strafford, The Earl of (and others): NLI Ms. 10223. Estate rentals, 1682 and 1684. Major tenants only. Includes a large part of Sligo town. Covering townlands in the civil parishes of: Ahamlish; Ballysadare; Ballysumaghan; Calry; Cloonoghill; Dromard; Drumcliff; Kilfree; Killoran; Killaspugbrone; Kilmacallan; Kilmacowen; Kilmacteigue; Kilross; St John's; Skreen; Templeboy; Toomour.

Wynne, Owen: NLI Mss. 5780–5782; rentals and expense books, 1737–68. Major tenants only. NLI Mss. 5830–1; rent ledgers 1738–53, 1768–73. Major tenants only, indexed. NLI Mss. 3311–3; a rental and two rent ledgers, yearly from 1798 to 1825, with all tenants. Covering townlands in the civil parishes of: Ahamlish; Ballysadare; Calry; Drumcliff; Killoran; St John's; Tawnagh; Templeboy.

TIPPERARY

Census returns and substitutes

1595	Freeholders. NLI Pos. 1700
1641	Book of Survey and Distribution. NLI Ms. 977
1641–1663	Proprietors of Fethard. *IG*, Vol. 6, No. 1, 1980
1653	Names of soldiers & adventurers who received land in the county under the Cromwellian settlement. Prendergast, *The Cromwellian Settlement …*,
1654	Civil Survey, Vol. l & ll. *Civil Survey*, Vol. l & ll. (NLI I 6551 Dublin). Part online: Pitskar
1659	Pender's 'Census'. Repr. GPC, 1997, IMC, 2002. LDS Film 924648. Online: Genweb Tipperary
1666–1668	Three Hearth Money Rolls. Laffan, *Tipperary's Families*, Part online: Rootsweb Tipperary
1703	Minister's money account, Clonmel. *AH*, 34
1750	Catholics in the parishes of Barnane, Bourney, Corbally, Killavanoge, Killea, Rathnaveoge, Roscrea, Templeree, Templetouhy. *IG*, 1973. Online: Rootsweb Tipperary
1766	Ballingarry, Uskeane GO 536; Athassel, Ballintemple, Ballycahill, Ballygriffin, Boytonreth, Brickendown, Bruis, Clerihan, Clonbeg, Cloneen, Clonoulty, Clonbolloge, Clonpet, Colman, Cordangan, Corrogue, Cullen, Dangandargan, Drum, Dustrileague, Erry, Fethard, Gaile, Grean, Horeabbey, NAI. Parl. Ret. 682–701. Online: Genweb Tipperary, Pitskar
1776	Voters. NAI M.4910 12
1776	Freeholders. NAI M.1321–2. Also GO 442. Online: Rootsweb Tipperary
1790–1801	Tithe Book, Ardmayle & Ballysheehan parishes. NLI Pos. 5553
1799	Census of Carrick-on-Suir. BL Add. Ms. 11722, NLI Pos. 28, Carrick-on-Suir heritage centre

1813   Valuation of Roscrea. NAI MFCI 3
1821   Clonmel NAI M. 242(2); Modreeny (extracts only) GO 572
1823–1838 Tithe Books. Part online: Connors, Genweb Tipperary, Rootsweb
           Tipperary
1828   Clonmel, houses & occupiers. *Parliamentary Papers 1837, Reports from
           Committees*, Vol. 11 (2)
1832–1837 Registered voters, Clonmel and Cashel boroughs. *Parliamentary Papers
           1837, Reports from Committees*, Vol. II (2)
1835   Census of Newport and Birdhill. NLI Pos. 1561 Templebredin *JNMAS*, 1975
1837   Protestant parishioners, Clogheen union, 1837, 1877, 1880. *IA*, Vol. 17,
           No. 1, 1985
1838–1848 Reproductive Loan Fund records. Tipperary town Loan Association.
           Covering parishes of Bruis, Clonpet, Cordangan, Corroge,
           Solloghodbeg, Solloghodmore, Templenoe, Tipperary. c.450 individu-
           als. NAI (Kew). T 91. Partly online: Moving Here
1851   Griffith's Valuation. Indexed online: Hayes
1864–1870 Protestants in the parishes of Shanrahan and Tullagherton, *IA*, 16 (2),
           1984, 61–7
1901   Census
1911   Census

Online

Connors	*www.connorsgenealogy.com*
Devries	*www.geocities.com/luanndevries*
Genweb Tipperary	*www.rootsweb.com/~irltip/records.htm*
Grieves	*members.iinet.net.au/~sgrieves/*
Hayes, John	*www.failteromhat.com*
Moving Here	*www.movinghere.org.uk/search/*
Pitskar	*freepages.genealogy.rootsweb.com/~irish*
Rootsweb Tipperary	*www.rootsweb.com/~irltip2/*

Publications

Local histories, etc.
'Emigration from the Workhouse of Nenagh Union, Co. Tipperary', 1849–1860,
    IA, 17 (1), 1985
Bateman, Paul, *Heffernans from Clonbonane, Co. Tipperary*, Canberra?, The
    author, 1991, NAI, Ir. 9292 H 18, 133 p.
Bell, Eileen, *Around New Inn & Knockgraffon*, Cashell, Lion Print, 2003, NLI, 120 p.
Burke, William P., *History of Clonmel*, Waterford, 1907, NLI Ir. 94142 b 1. Incl.
    Grubb, *Commercial Directory of Clonmel*. Online: Rootsweb Tipperary
Carville, Geraldine, *The heritage of Holy Cross*, Belfast: Blackstaff Press, 1973, NLI
    Ir. 271 c 27, 175 p.

Coffey, G., *Evicted Tipperary*, NLI Ir. 330 p 22

Collins, Michael, *The Famine in Newport*, Newport: Newport Historical and Archaelogical Society, 1996?, NLI, 56 p.

Dunne, Katie, *Grangemockler Church and People 1897–1997*, Grangemockler: Grangemockler Centenary Committee, 1997, NLI

Farrell, Noel, *Carrick-on-Suir family roots: exploring family origins in Carrick-on-Suir, County Tipperary*, Longford: Noel Farrell, 2001, NLI, 48 p.

Fitzgerald, Séamus, *Cappawhite and Doon*, Pallasgrean: S. Fitzgerald, 1983, NLI Ir. 9141 p 43, 124 p.

Flood, John, *Kilcash: a history, 1190–1801*, Dublin: Geography Publications, 1999, NLI Ir. 94142 F 6, 135 p. Co-author, Phil Flood.

Flynn, Paul, *The book of the Galtees and the golden vale: a border history of Tipperary, Limerick and Cork*, Dublin: Hodges, Figgis & co, 1926, NLI Ir. 94142 f 2, 417 p.

Gleeson, John, *Cashel of the kings: a history of the ancient capital of Munster from the date of its foundation until the present day*, Dublin: J. Duffy & co, 1927, NLI Ir. 94142 g 2, 312 p. Repr. Dublin: Edmund Burke, 2001.

Gleeson, John, *History of the Ely O'Carroll Territory or Ancient Ormond*, Dublin: Gill, 1915, NLI Ir. 94142 g 1. Repr. Roberts' Books, c.1982, with an introduction and bibliography by George Cunningham

Gorman, Edward, *Records of Moycarkey and Two Mile Borris with some fireside stories*, Galway: Printinghouse, 1955, NLI Ir. 94142 g 4, 58 p.

Grace, Daniel, *Cloughjordan heritage*, Cloughjordan, NLI Ir. 914142 c 37. Co-editor, Edward J. Whyte, P.P.

Grace, Daniel, *Portrait of a parish Monsea & Killodiernan, Co. Tipperary*, Tyone: Nenagh Relay Publications, 1996, NLI Ir. 94142 g 5, 346 p.

Grace, Daniel, *The great famine in Nenagh poor law union Co. Tipperary*, Nenagh: Relay Books, 2000, NLI Ir. 94142 g 8, 230 p.

Griffin, Kevin M., *Ballina/Boher parish: our history and traditions*, Killaloe: Ballina Killaloe Print, 2000, NLI Ir. 94142 g 9, 389 p. Co-author, Kevin A. Griffin

Gwynn, A., *A history of the diocese of Killaloe*, Dublin: M.H. Gill and Son, 1962, NLI Ir. 27414.g.3, 566 p.

Hayes, W.J., *Newport, Co. Tipperary the town, its courts and gaols*, Roscrea: Lisheen Publications, 1999, NLI, 72 p.

Hayes, W.J., *Thurles a guide to the cathedral town*, Roscrea: Lisheen Publications, 1999, NLI, 54 p.

Hayes, W.J., *The Keeffes of the Jockey*, Roscrea: Lisheen Publications, 2001, NLI, A 80 p.

Hayes, W.J., *Moyne-Templetuohy a life of its own: the story of a Tipperary parish*, Tipperary: Moyne-Templetuohy History Group, 2001, NLI, 3 vols.

Hayes, W.J., *Tipperary Remembers*, 1976, NLI Ir. 914142 H 9

Hore, H.F., *The Social State of the Southern and Eastern Counties of Ireland in the Sixteenth Century*, Dublin: 1870, NLI Ir. 794105 r 2, 'being the presentments of the gentlemen, commonalty, and citizens of Carlow, Cork, Kilkenny,

Tipperary, Waterford, and Wexford, made in the reigns of Henry VIII and Elizabeth. Printed from the originals in the Public Record Office, London. Edited by the late Herbert J. [i.e. F.] Hore, ... and the Rev. James Graves'

IGRS, *Tombstone inscriptions Vol. 2*, Dublin: IGRS Tombstone Committee, 2001, NLI, c.900 p.

Kenny, Michael, *Glankeen of Borrisoleigh: a Tipperary Parish*, Dublin: J. Duffy & Company, 1944, NLI Ir. 94142 k 2, 6 p.

Laffan, Thomas, *Tipperary's families: being the hearth money records for 1665–67* ..., Dublin: James Duffy & Co, 1911. NLI Ir. 9292 l 11 205 p.

Mac Cárthaigh, Micheál, *A Tipperary parish: a history of Knockavilla-Donaskeigh*, Leemount, Carrigrohane, Co. Cork: S. Moran, 1986, NLI Ir. 94142 m 5, 302 p.

McIlroy, M., *Gleanings from Garrymore*, n.d.

Meskell, Peter, *History of Boherlahan- Dualla*, Midleton: Litho Press Co., 1987

Moloney, Bernie, *Times to cherish: Cashel and Rosegreen parish history 1795–1995*, Cashel: Cashel and Rosegreen parish, 1994, NLI Ir. 27414 T 2, 224 p.

Murphy, Ignatius, *The Diocese of Killaloe 1850–1904*, Dublin: Four Courts Press, 1995, NLI Ir. 27414 m 9, 527 p.

Murphy, Ignatius, *The Diocese of Killaloe 1800–1850*, Dublin: Four Courts Press, 1992, NLI Ir. 27414 m 7, 488 p.

Murphy, Ignatius, *The diocese of Killaloe in the eighteenth century*, Dublin: Four Courts Press, 1991, NLI Ir. 27414 m 8, 373 p.

Murphy, Nancy, *More of Nenagh's yesterdays*, Nenagh: Relay Publications, 1997, NLI Ir. 9141 m 102, 128 p.

Murphy, Nancy, *Tracing Northwest Tipperary Roots*, Nenagh, 1982

Neely, W.G., *Kilcooley: land and parish in Tipperary*, W.G. Neely, 1983, NLI Ir. 94142 n 1, 168 p.

Nolan, W., *Tipperary: History and Society*, Dublin: Geography Publications, 1985, NLI Ir. 94142 t 6, 493 p. Co-editor, Thomas G. McGrath.

O Riain, Seamus, *Dunkerrin: a parish in Ely O Carroll: a history of Dunkerrin Parish from 1200 A.D. to the present time*, Dunkerrin: Dunkerrin History Committee, 1988, NLI Ir. 94136 o 5, 256 p.

O'Brien, Bridie, *How we were—in the parish of Kilbarron—Terryglass Co. Tipperary*, Nenagh: Relay Books, 1999, NLI Ir. 94142 o 7, 396 p.

O'Donnell, Seán, *Clonmel 1840–1900: anatomy of an Irish town*, Dublin: Geography Publications, 2000, NLI, 337 p.

O'Keeffe, Tadhg, *Irish Historic Towns Atlas 13: Fethard*, Dublin: Royal Irish Academy, 2003, NLI

O'Riordan, Edmund, *Famine in the Valley*, Cahir: Galty Vee Valley Tourism, 1995, NLI Ir. 94142 o 4, 85 p.

O'Riordan, Edmund, *Historical guide to Clogheen*, O'Riordan, 1996, Tipperary County Library, 941.92, 76p

Poulacapple National School, *Centenary of a rural school Poulacapple 1891–1991*, Poulacapple, 1991, NLI Ir. 94142 p 5(2), 144 p.

Power, Martin, *Dear land—native place Monsea and Dromineer a history*, Nenagh:

Nenagh Guardian, 1998, NLI Ir. 94142 p 7, 390 p.

Power, V. Rev. P., *Waterford and Lismore: A Compendious History of the Dioceses,* Dublin: Cork University Press, 1937, NLI Ir. 274141 p 1, 402 p.

Prendergast, John, *The Cromwellian Settlement of Ireland,* Dublin, 1865. Repr. London: Constable, 1996, NLI Ir. 94106 p 14 304 p.

Pyke, D., *Parish Priests and Churches of St Mary's, Clonmel,* 1984, NLI Ir. 274 p 40, 54 p.

Resch, M.L., *The descendants of Patrick Halloran of Boytonrath, Co. Tipperary,* Baltimore: Gateway Press, 1987, NLI Ir. 9292 r 12, 627 p.

Ryan, C.A., *Tipperary Artillery, 1793–1889,* 1890, NLI Ir. 355942 t 1

Ryan, Senator Willic, *Golden-Kilfeacle the parish and its people,* Tipperary: Kilfeacle, 1997, NLI Ir. 94142 r 2, 371 p.

Seymour, St John D., *The Diocese of Emly,* Dublin: C of I Print, 1913, NLI Ir. 27414 s 1, 297 p.

Sheehan, E.H., *Nenagh and its Neighbourhood,* Nenagh: Nancy Murphy, 1976, NLI Ir. 914142 s 4, 98 p. Including many family records

Tierney, Mark, *Murroe and Boher, history of an Irish country parish,* Dublin: Browne and Nolan, 1966, NLI Ir. 94144 t 1, 251 p.

Treacy, Brendan, *Nenagh yesterday,* Nenagh: Nenagh Relay Publications, 1993, NLI Ir. 94142 t 4, 144 p.

Veale, T., *Richard Lucas 1788: directory extract for south east of Ireland,* Dublin: Veale, 1995 NLI Ir. 9414 v

Veale, T., *Index of Surnames in 'The New Commercial Directory for the cities of Waterford and Kilkenny and the towns of Clonmel, Carrick-on-Suir, New Ross and Carlow',* Dublin: Veale, 1996 NLI Ir. 9414 p.

Walsh, Paul P., *A history of Templemore and its environs,* Templemore, Paul P. Walsh, 1991, NLI Ir. 94142 w 2, 141 p.

Watson, Col. S.J., *A Dinner of Herbs: a history of Old St Mary's church, Clonmel,* Clonmel: Watson Books, 1988, Tipperary County Library, 284.094193, 259p.

White, James (ed.), *My Clonmel Scrap Book,* Clonmel: Tentmaker Publications, 1995, NLI Ir. 94142 w 3, 376 p. Repr. of 1907 edition

White, John D., *The History of the Family of White of Limerick, Knockcentry, etc.,* 1887, NLI Ir. 9292 w 10

White, Rev. P., *History of Clare and the Dalcassian Clans of Tipperary, Limerick and Galway,* Dublin, 1893, NLI Ir. 94143 w 4, 398 p. Repr. Newmarket on-Fergus: O'Brien Book Publications, 1997

Local Journals

Clonmel Historical and Archaeological Society Journal, NLI Ir. 94142 c 2

Cois Deirge, NLI Ir. 94142 c 4

Boherlahan/Dualla historical journal (1998–), NLI

Tipperary historical journal = Irisleabhar staire Thiobraid Arann., NLI Ir. 94142 t 2

Eile (Journal of the Roscrea Heritage Society), NLI Ir. 94142 e 1

Journal of the North Munster Archaeological Society, NLI Ir. 794105 n 1

Directories

1788	Richard Lucas, *General Directory of the Kingdom of Ireland,* NLI Pos. 3729. Repr. in Veale, *Lucas,* IG 1965, 1966, 1967, 1968
1820	J. Pigot, *Commercial Directory of Ireland* PRONI, NLI Ir. 9141 p 107, LDS Film 962702 Item 1
1824	J. Pigot and Co., *City of Dublin and Hibernian Provincial Directory,* NLI, LDS Film 451787. Part online: Rootsweb Tipperary
1839	T. Shearman, *New Commercial Directory for the cities of Waterford and Kilkenny, Towns of Clonmel, Carrick-on-Suir, New Ross and Carlow*
1846	Slater's *National Commercial Directory of Ireland.* PRONI, NLI LO, LDS Film 1696703 Item 3
1856	Slater, *Royal National Commercial Directory of Ireland,* NLI, LDS Film 1472360 Item 1. Part online: Rootsweb Tipperary
1866	George Henry Bassett, *Directory of the City and County of Limerick, and of the Principal Towns in the Cos. of Tipperary and Clare,* NLI Ir. 914144 b 5
1870	Slater, *Directory of Ireland,* NLI
1881	Slater, *Royal National Commercial Directory of Ireland,* NLI
1886	Francis Guy, *Postal Directory of Munster,* NLI Ir. 91414 g 8, LDS Film 1559399 Item 8
1889	George Henry Bassett, *The Book of Tipperary* NLI Ir. 914142 b 25. Online: Pitskar
1889	Francis Guy, *City and County Cork Almanack and Directory*
1894	Slater, *Royal Commercial Directory of Ireland,* NLI

Gravestone Inscriptions

Ardfinnan: Rochestown: Online: Devries
Ballyclerahan: *IGRS,* Vol. 2
Bansha: Online: Devries
Barnane-Ely: Barnane: Online, Grieves
Cahir—Kilcommon (Quaker): Online: Devries
Kilcommon (C of I): Online: Devries
Loughloher. Online: Devries
Old Church: Online: Devries
Derrygrath: Online: Devries
Drom: Online: Grieves
Glenkeen: Kylanna: Online: Grieves
Holycross: C of I, GO Ms. 622 P. 176/7
Inch: Dovea C of I. Online: Grieves
Inch Old Online: Grieves
Inishlounaght: Marlfield: Online: Devries
Kilfithmone: C of I. Online, Grieves
Kilgrant: Powerstown RC. Online: Grieves
—Old Powerstown. Online: Grieves

Kilmore: *IG*, Vol. 2, No. 10, 1953
Kiltinan: GO Ms. 622, P. 144
Knigh: Open shelves, NAI, *IGRS*, Vol. 2
Loughmoe West: Online: Grieves
Mortlestown: Online: Devries
Newchapel: *IGRS*, Vol. 2
Outeragh: Online: Devries
Shanrahan: Online: Devries
St Patricksrock, Cashel, The Rock: *IGRS*, Vol. 2
Tullaghorton: Castlegrace. Online: Devries
Doughill. Online: Devries
Twomileborris: Littleton, GO Ms. 622, p. 171
Uskane: *IG*, Vol. 3, No. 2, 1957
Whitechurch: Online: Devries

Estate Records

Burton, Edward William: Rental, 1828. All tenants, NLI Ms. 8683. Covering areas in the civil parish of Kilmurry.

Kingston, Earl of: NLI Ms. 3276, Rental, 1840. All tenants. Covering townlands in the civil parishes of: Glenkeen; Templetenny.

Newcommen, Viscount: NLI Ms. 2766, Maps, 1826–1827. All tenants. Covering townlands in the civil parishes of: Bourney; Dolla; Dolla; Kilnaneave; Peppardstown; Templederry.

TYRONE

Census returns and substitutes

1612–1613	Survey of Undertakers Planted in Co. Tyrone. *Historical Manuscripts Commission Report*, No. 4 (Hastings Mss.), 1947. p. 159 82
1625–1627	Leet Court Rolls. Jurors and litigants in Armagh Manor; Arboe, Ardtrea, Donaghmore (Tyrone); Termonfeckin (Louth) SA, Vol. 11, No. 9, 1957 pp. –322
1630	Muster Roll of Ulster; Armagh Co. Library and PRONI D.1759/3C/1; T. 808/15164; NLI Pos. 206. Online: Genweb Tyrone
1631	Muster Roll, Co. Tyrone PRONI T.934
1654–1656	Civil Survey. *Civil Survey*, Vol. lll (NLI I 6551 Dublin)
1661	Books of Survey and Distribution. PRONI T.370/C & D.1854/1/23
1664	Hearth Money Roll: NL Mss. 9583/4. Also PRONI T283/D/2. Clogher diocese in *Clogher Record*, (1965); Dungannon barony in SA, (1971)
1665	Subsidy roll. PRONI T.283/D/1. Also NLI Pos. 206
1666	Hearth Money Roll. PRONI T.307 Donagheady online: Genweb Tyrone
1699	Protestants in the parishes of Drumragh, Bodoney and Cappagh. GO Sources Box 6.
1740	Protestants, Derryloran and Kildress. PRONI T.808/15258. RCBL. LDS

Film 1279327

| 1766 | Aghaloo, Artrea, Carnteel, Clonfeacle, Derryloran, Donaghendry, Drumglass, Dungannon, Kildress, Tullyniskan, Errigal Keerogue, Kildress. PRONI T.808/15264 7. Also NAI Parliamentary returns 648–66, LDS Film 258517 |

1775   Arboe. With Arboe C of I registers. PRONI T.679/111, 115–119; D.1278

1780   Householders, Ternonmaguirk RCBL GS 2/7/3/25

1795–1798 Voters List, Dungannon barony. PRONI TYR5/3/1. Online: Freeholders

1796   Spinning-Wheel Premium List. 7,150 names for Co. Tyrone. Online: Hayes

1821   Some extracts, Aghaloo. NAI Thrift Abstracts

1823–1838 Tithe Books

1830   Census of the C of I parish of Donaghenry Co. Tyrone c.1830. PRONI C.R.1/38

1832   Memorial of the […] inhabitants of Strabane protesting at vexatious prosecutions. c.70 names NAI OP 964/16

1832   Census of rural deanery of Derryloran, 1832, PRONI T.2574

1834   Valuation of Dungannon. *Parliamentary Papers 1837, Reports from Committees,* Vol. II (i), Appendix G

1834   Clonoe (Coalisland); NLI Pos. 5579.

1838   Memorial from inhabitants of Dungannon to reinstate Richard Murray J.P., c.150 signatures NAI OP 1838/171

1840   Ratepayers for the Union of Armagh PRONI D/1670/13/6

1842   Voters. NAI OP 1842/77

1842   Workhouse records Clogher (1842–9), Irvinestown (1845–1918) Enniskillen (1845–1913) and Strabane (1861–83) unions. PRONI. Also LDS Films 259162–3, 259187–90, 25914–53 and 259164–5, respectively

1851   Griffith's Valuation. Indexed online: Hayes

1851–1852 Clogherny C of I parishioners. PRONI DIO 4.32C/9/4/2

1866   Parishioners' list. C of I parish of Termonmaguirk. Local custody

1901   Census. See Meehan, *Tyrone: 1901 census index*

1911   Census

1912   The Ulster Covenant. Almost half-a-million original signatures and addresses of those who signed. c.29,000 names for Tyrone. Online: Covenant

Online

Freeholders	*www.proni.gov.uk/freeholders*
Genweb Tyrone	*freepages.genealogy.rootsweb.com/~tyrone*
Hayes, John	*www.failteromhat.com*
Headstones	*www.historyfromheadstones.com*

Publications

Local histories, etc.

Drumquin ... A Collection of Writings and Photographs of the Past, NLI Ir. 91411 p 10

Provisional list of pre-1900 School Registers in the Public Record Office of Northern Ireland, *UHGGN*, 9, 1986, 60–71

[Unknown], *Donoughmore Presbyterian Church: 1658–1958*, Omagh, Co. Tyrone, Stule Press, 1958, NLI, 24 p.

[Unknown], *Ballymagrane Presbyterian Church: a short history of the congregation*, Ballymagrane, the Church, 1959, NLI, 24 p.

Bailie, W.D., *Benburb Presbyterian Church 1670–1970*, Benburb: Benburb Presbyterian Church, 1970, NLI, 11 p.

Belmore, Earl of, *Parliamentary Memoirs of Fermanagh and Tyrone 1613–1885*, Dublin: Alex. Thom & Co., 1887, NLI Ir. 94118 b 1 368 p.

Bradley, Rev. John, *The life and times of Father Bernard Murphy, Termon, Carrickmore 1832–1897*, Belfast: Eddie Murphy, 1994, NLI Ir. 92 m 511, 96 p., updated 1994.

Bradley, William John, *Gallon: the history of three townlands in County Tyrone from the earliest times to the present day*, Derry: Guildhall Press, c.2000, NLI, 216 p.

Day, Angelique & McWilliams, Patrick (eds.), *Ordnance Survey Memoirs of Ireland series*, Belfast: Inst. of Irish Studies/RIA, 1990–7.

    Vol. 5: Co. Tyrone I (1990) Aghaloo, Artrea, Ballinderry, Ballyclog, Bodoney, Carnteel, Clogherny, Clonoe, Desertcreat, Donaghenry, Drumglass, Errigal Keerogue, Kildress, Killyman, Lissan, Pomeroy, Tamlaght, Tullyniskan, NLI Ir. 914111 o 14

    Vol. 20: Co. Tyrone II (1993) Aghaloo, Artrea, Ballinderry, Ballyclog, Bodoney, Carnteel, Clogherny, Clonoe, Desertcreat, Donaghenry, Drumglass, Errigal Keerogue, Kildress, Killyman, Lissan, Pomeroy, Tamlaght, Tullyniskan, NLI Ir. 9141 o 28.

Donnelly, T.P., *A History of the Parish of Ardstraw West and Castlederg*, 1978, NLI Ir. 94114 d 6

Duffy, Joseph, *A Clogher Record Album; a diocesan history*, Enniskillen: Cumann Seanchais Chlochair, 1975, NLI Ir. 94114 c 3, 340 p.

Gartland, Joseph, *The Gartlands of Augher, Tyrone*, Dedham, Mass.: Joseph A. Gartland Jr., 1983, NLI, GO 218, 213 leaves. Gartland, Healy, Kerr, Grady, Magee families

Gebbie, John H., *Ardstraw (Newtownstewart); historical survey of a parish, 1600–1900*, Omagh: Strule Press, 1968, NLI Ir. 94114 g 2, 143 p.

Glasgow, John, *History of the Third Presbyterian Church, Cookstown: 1835–1935 a century in progress*, Cookstown, Mid-Ulster Printing Company, 1935, NLI, 44 p.

Gortin & District Historical Society, *Meetings and memories in Lower Badoney*, Gortin & District Historical Society, 1995–2000, NLI, 2 vols

Historical Committee of the Grouped Parishes, *The changing years: in the grouped parishes of Ardstraw, Baronscourt and Badoney Union*, Omagh: Grahams

Printers, 2000, NLI, 157 p.

Hutchison, W.R., *Tyrone precinct: a history of the plantation settlement of Dungannon and Mountjoy to modern times*, Belfast: W.E. Mayne, 1951, NLI Ir. 94114 h 2, 236 p.

Johnson, Norman, *Methodism in Omagh: an historical account of Methodism, over two centuries, in the Omagh and Fintona Circuit*, Omagh: Omagh Methodist Church, 1982, NLI Ir. 27411 p 5, 36 p. Co-author, Preston

Johnstone, John, *Clogher Cathedral Graveyard*, Omagh: Graham, 1972, NLI Ir. 9292 p 9, 54 p.

Kerr, Peter, Families and holdings in the Townland of Innishatieve, Carrickmore: SA, 15, No. 2, 1993, 151–235

Keys, John, *Fivemiletown Methodist Church jubilee 1897–1947: a short account of the Fivemiletown circuit*, Cookstown, Mid-Ulster Printing Company, 1947, NLI, 1A 2063, 16 p.

Mac an Ultaigh, Críostóir, *Urney a portrait of an Irish parish*, Urney: Urney GAA Club, 1994, NLI Ir. 396 m 73, 145 p.

Marsh, Robert G., *Brackaville: a parish of the Church of Ireland*, Dungannon: Tyrone Printing Co., 1981, NLI, 79 p.

Marshall, J.J., *Annals of Aughnacloy and of the parish of Carnteel, County Tyrone*, Dungannon: Tyrone Printing Co., 1925, NLI, P 1167(3), 76 p.

Marshall, J.J., *Vestry book of the Parish of Aghalow, Caledon, Co. Tyrone: with an account of the family of Hamilton of Caledon, 1691–1807*, Dungannon: Tyrone Printing Co., 1935, NLI Ir. 27411 a 2, 66 p.

Marshall, J.J., *History of the Town & District of Clogher, Co. Tyrone, parish of Errigal Keerogue, Tyrone, & Errigal Truagh in the Co. of Monaghan*, Dungannon: Tyrone Printing Co., 1930, NLI Ir. 94114 m 2, 97 p.

Marshall, J.J., *History of Dungannon*, Dungannon: Tyrone Printing Co., 1929, NLI Ir. 94114 m 3, 137 p.

McEvoy, J., *County of Tyrone 1802 a statistical survey by John McEvoy; with introduction by W.H. Crawford*, Belfast: Friar's Bush Press, 1991, NLI Ir. 3141 m 13

McGrew, William J., *Tombstones of the Omey: [15 graveyards transcribed within Omagh District, Co. Tyrone (1688–1900)]*, Omagh: Omagh Branch of the NIFHS, 1998, NLI Ir. 9295 m 6, 184 p.

McKee, Rev W.J.H., *Aspects of Presbyterianism in Cookstown*, Belfast, Presbyterian Historical Society of Ireland, 1995 [Examination of the beginnings of Presbyterianism in Cookstown, County Tyrone]

Meehan, C.P., *Tyrone: 1901 census index*, Alberta: Largy Books, 1995. NLI

Mongan, Norman, *Notes on an Erenagh family: the sacred clan of O Mongan of Ballymongan and Termonomongan*, Norman Charles Mongan, 1987, NLI, GO 686, 37 p.

Montgomery, S.D., *Ministries in miniature: Aughnacloy Presbyterian Church 1697–1938*, Omagh: the church, 1938, NLI, 36 p.

Murphy, H.B., *Three hundred years of Presbyterianism in Clogher*, Belfast: *Belfast NewsLetter*, 1958, NLI Ir. 285 m 42, 159 p.

O'Daly, B., 'Material for a history of the parish of Kilskeery', NLI, *Clogher Record*, 1953/4/5

Rutherford, J., *Donagheady: Presbyterian Churches & Parish*, Belfast: McGraw, Stevenson and Orr, 1953, NLI Ir. 285 r 7, 117 p.

Stewart, Austin, *Coalisland, county Tyrone, in the Industrial Revolution, 1800–1901*, Dublin: Four Courts, 2002, 64 p.

Todd, Sheelagh, *Register of gravestones in Leckpatrick Old Burial Ground*, the author, 1991, NLI Ir. 9295 p 1(4), 105 p.

Local Journals

Clogher Record, NLI Ir. 94114 c 2

Derriana, NLI Ir. 27411 d 4

Dúchas Néill: Journal of the O'Neill Country Society

North Irish Roots (Journal of the North of Ireland Family History Society), NLI Ir. 92905 n 4

Irish Family Links, NLI Ir. 9292 f 19

Seanchas Ardmhacha, NLI Ir. 27411 s 4

Ulster Journal of Archaeology, NLI Ir. 794105 u 1

Directories

1819   Thomas Bradshaw's *general directory of Newry, Armagh, and the towns of Dungannon, Portadown, Tandragee, Lurgan, Waringstown, Banbridge, Warrenpoint, Rosstrevor, Kilkeel, Rathfriland, 1820*. PRONI, NLI Ir. 91411 b 18, LDS Film 258723

1820   J. Pigot, *Commercial Directory of Ireland* PRONI, NLI Ir. 9141 p 107, LDS Film 962702 Item 1

1824   J. Pigot and Co., *City of Dublin and Hibernian Provincial Directory*, NLI, LDS Film 451787

1839   Martin *Belfast Directory*. Also 1841, 1842 PRONI, NLI Ir. 9141111 m 4

1846   Slater's *National Commercial Directory of Ireland*. PRONI, NLI LO, LDS Film 1696703 Item 3

1854   *Belfast and Province of Ulster Directory*. Also 1856, 1858, 1861, 1863, 1865, 1868, 1870, 1877, 1880, 1884, 1887, 1890, 1894, 1900. PRONI. LDS (various years)

1856   Slater, *Royal National Commercial Directory of Ireland*, NLI, LDS Film 1472360 Item 1

1865   R. Wynne, *Business Directory of Belfast*, NLI Ir. 91411 b 2

1870   Slater, *Directory of Ireland*, NLI

1881   Slater, *Royal National Commercial Directory of Ireland*, NLI

1872   *Tyrone Almanac & Directory*

1882   *Omagh Almanac* NLI Ir. 914114 o 1

1887   *Derry Almanac and Directory*, annually from this year. NLI Ir. 914112 d 1

1888   George Henry Bassett, *The Book of Armagh* (Moy) NLI Ir. 94116 b 3

1891   *Omagh Almanac* NLI Ir. 914114 o 1

1894   Slater, *Royal Commercial Directory of Ireland*, NLI

Gravestone Inscriptions

Heritage World has transcripts of 112 graveyards in Tyrone. The UHF has transcripts for fifty-three graveyards. See *www.historyfromheadstones.com*. Published or publicly available transcripts are given below.

Cappagh: Dunmullin: McGrew, *Tombstones of the Omey*
Killclogher (RC): McGrew, *Tombstones of the Omey*
Knockmoyle (RC): McGrew, *Tombstones of the Omey*
Mountjoy Forest East Division (C of I): McGrew, *Tombstones of the Omey*
Edenderry (Omagh) (Pres.) McGrew, *Tombstones of the Omey*
Lislimnaghan, Omagh (C of I): McGrew, *Tombstones of the Omey*
Carnteel: Pres, Johnstone, *Clogher Cathedral Graveyard*
Clogherny Donaghane (Donaghanie?): McGrew, *Tombstones of the Omey*
Donacavey: *Clogher Record*, Vol. 7, No. 2, 1970
Drumglass: Dungannon, Old Drumglass, RC, SA, Vol. 7, No. 2, 1974
Drumragh: Clanabogan (C of I): McGrew, *Tombstones of the Omey*
Drumragh (Old) (RC): McGrew, *Tombstones of the Omey*
Kilskeery: C of I, *Clogher Record*, Vol. 8, No. 1, 1973
Leckpatrick: Todd, *Register of gravestones*
Termonmaguirk: Drumnakilly (C of I): McGrew, *Tombstones of the Omey*

Estate Records

Abercorn, Earls of: Rentals, 1777–1832. PRONI D/623. Most tenants. Covering areas in the civil parishes of: Ardstraw; Camus; Donacavey; Donaghedy; Leckpatrick; Urney. May cover further parishes.

Charlemont: Rentals, 1798–1802, NLI Ms. 2702. Major tenants only. Covering areas in the civil parishes of: Clonfeacle; and Donaghmore.

Leslie: Rental, 1846, NLI Ms. 5813. All tenants. Valuation, with names and observations, 1833, NLI Ms. 5813. All tenants. Covering areas in the civil parishes of: Carnteel; and Errigal Keerogue.

Lindsay: Rentals, 1745–1761, NLI Ms. 5204. All tenants. Rentals, 1778–1817, NLI Ms. 5205. All tenants. Survey, 1800 NLI Ms. 2584. Major tenants only. Rentals, 1808–1817, NLI Ms. 5206. All tenants. Rentals, 1836–1848, NLI Ms. 5208. All tenants. Covering areas in the civil parishes of: Artrea; Derryloran; Desertcreat; and Donaghenry.

MacKenzie, Alexander: Rentals, 1825, NLI Ms. 18980. All tenants. Covering areas in the civil parish of Drumglass.

Maxwell: Valuation, with names, 1807, NLI Ms. 5379. All tenants. Survey and valuation, 1830, NLI Ms. 5380. All tenants. Covering areas in the civil parish of Urney.

Powerscourt: Rentals, 1809, NLI Ms. 19191. All tenants. Rentals, 1835, 1838, NLI Ms. 19192. All tenants. Covering areas in the civil parish of Clonfeacle.

Stewart: Survey, with tenants' names, 1730, NLI Ms. 8734 (1). Major tenants only. Covering areas in the civil parishes of Carnteel; Clonfeacle; and Killeeshil.

Stewart: Survey with tenants' names, 1767, NLI Ms. 9627. Major tenants only. Covering areas in the civil parish of Derryloran.

Stewart: Rentals, 1786–1788, NLI Ms. 766. All tenants. Covering areas in the civil parishes of: Artrea; Carnteel; Clonfeacle; Derryloran; Desertcreat; Donaghenry; Donaghmore; Kildress; Killeeshil; and Pomeroy.

Verner/Wingfield: Rental, PRONI D/2538, 1830. Covering areas in the civil parishes of: Cappagh; Clogherny; Donaghmore; Errigal Keerogue; Killeeshil; Termonmaguirk. May cover further parishes.

WATERFORD

Census returns and substitutes

1542–1650	Freemen of Waterford. *IG*, Vol. 5, No.5, 1978
1641	Houses and tenants, Waterford city, *JCHAS*, Vol. 51, 1946. Also NAI, Quit Rent Office Papers
1641	Book of Survey and Distribution. NLI Ms. 970
1659	Pender's 'Census'. Repr. GPC, 1997, IMC, 2002. LDS Film 924648
1662	Subsidy Roll of Co. Waterford. *AH*, 30, 1982, 47–96
1663	Inhabitants of Waterford City, including occupations. *JCHAS*, Vol. 51
1664–1666	Civil Survey. *Civil Survey*, Vol. VI
1700	Members of some Waterford Guilds, *WSIHSJ* 7, 1901, 61–5
1766	Killoteran householders. NAI Parl. Ret 1413; GO 684; LDS Film 100158
1772	Hearth Money Rolls. For parts of Co. Waterford only. *WSIHSJ*, Vol. XV, 1912
1775	Gentry of Co. Waterford. *WSIHSJ*, Vol. XVI, No. 1, 1913
1778	Inhabitants of Waterford city. *Freeman's Journal*, 29 Oct 1778, 5 Nov. 1778
1792	Leading Catholics of Waterford. *IA*, Vol. 8, No. 11
1792	Rent & arrears due to Waterford corporation, 1. NLI P 3000
1807	Waterford city voters. *IA*, Vol. 8, No. 11
1821	Townland of Callaghane, parish of Ballygunner, *Decies* 16. Extracts from Waterford city, *IG* 1968/9. Index to Waterford City, Veale *Extract*. Online: Rootsweb Waterford
1823–1838	Tithe Books
1839	Waterford City Polling List *IG* 8 (2), 1991, 275–89
1841	Memorial of inhabitants of Waterford City. More than 1,500 names and signatures, unindexed. NAI OP 1841/43
1843	Voters, NAI OP 1843/65
1847	Principal fishermen, Ring. Alcock, *Facts* …,
1848–1849	Smith O'Brien Petition ENE #CD2. More than 3,000 names for Waterford City.
1848–1851	Griffith's Valuation. Indexed online: Hayes. Complete online: Waterford Library
1864–1901	Civil death registers. Online: Waterford Library

1901   Census
1911   Census

Online

Celtic cousins	www.celticcousins.net	Walsh-Kelly parish extracts
Hayes, John	www.failteromhat.com	Large compendium of transcribed records
Rootsweb Waterford	www.rootsweb.com/~irlwat2	
Waterford Library	www.waterfordcountylibrary.ie	

Publications

Local histories, etc.

Waterford Historical Society Proceedings, NLI, ILB 94141, Newspapers cuttings relating to Waterford in 9 vols.

Ussher Papers (Cappagh, Co. Waterford), *AH*, XV, 63–78

Power-O'Shee papers (Gardenmorris, Co. Waterford), *AH*, XX, 216–58

Alcock, J., *Facts from the Fisheries, 1848*, Waterford, 1848. NLI I 6551

Brennan, T.A., *The Gearons of Janeville, Tallow, county Waterford*, New York, 1966, NLI, GO 466, 12 leaves

Butler, M., *A history of the barony of Gaultier. By M. Butler ... with a map of Gaultier*, Waterford, Downey & co., 1913, NLI Ir. 94141 b 1, 217 p.

Cuffe, Major O.T., *Records of the Waterford Militia 1584–1885*, London: 1885, NLI Ir. 355942 c 3, 112 p.

Downey, Edmund, *The story of Waterford to the middle of the 18th century*, Kilkenny, 1891, NLI Ir. 94191

Farrell, Noel, *County Waterford, Dungarvan family roots: exploring family origins in Dungarvan*, Longford: Noel Farrell, 2001, NLI, 48 p.

Fitzpatrick, Thomas, *Waterford during the Civil War, 1641–53*, Waterford, Downey, 1912, NLI Ir. 94106 f 5, 144 p.

Fraher, William, *Desperate haven: the Poor Law, famine, & aftermath in Dungarvan Union*, Dungarvan: Dungarvan Museum Society, 1996, NLI Ir. 94141 d 6, 415 p.

Fraher, William, *A guide to historic Dungarvan incorporating a town trail*, Dungarvan: Dungarvan Museum Society, 1991, NLI Ir. 941 p 103 (2), 48 p.

Hore, H.F., *The Social State of the Southern and Eastern Counties of Ireland in the Sixteenth Century*, Dublin: 1870, NLI Ir. 794105 r 2 [See Carlow]

IGRS, *Tombstone inscriptions Vol. 2*, Dublin: IGRS Tombstone Committee, 2001, NLI, 3B 29, c.900 p.

Keohan, Edmond, *Illustrated history of Dungarvan*, Waterford: *Waterford News*, 1924, NLI Ir. 94141 k 1, 156 p.

Kerr, Elizabeth M.F., 'Methodist New Chapell, Waterford', *IG*, 10, 4, 2001, 396–400

Nolan, W., *Waterford History and Society*, Dublin: Geography Publications, 1986, NLI Ir. 94141 w 6, 754 p.

O Cadhla, Stiofan, *The holy well tradition: the pattern of St Declan at Ardmore, county Waterford, 1800–2000*, Dublin: Four Courts, 2002, NLI, 64 p.

Ochille, F., *The Holy City of Ardmore, Co. Waterford*, Youghal: J.W. Lindsay, 1852, NLI, Dix Youghal [1852], 73 p.

O'Donnell, Seán, *Clonmel 1840–1900: anatomy of an Irish town*, Dublin: Geography Publications, 2000, NLI, 337 p.

O'Sullivan, Michael, *Kilbarry Graveyard, Waterford, Ireland: memorial inscriptions*, Waterford: Michael O'Sullivan, 1995, NLI Ir. 9295 p[sic], 12 p.

O'Sullivan, Michael, *Memorial inscriptions and obituaries: Abbey Church, Kilculliheen, Waterford*, Waterford: Michael O'Sullivan, 1995, NLI, 235 p.

O'Sullivan, Michael, *Killotteran, Co. Waterford: memorial inscriptions*, Waterford: Michael O'Sullivan, 1995, NLI Ir. 9295 p, 12 p.

O'Sullivan, Michael, *Lisnakill Graveyard, Co. Waterford memorial inscriptions*, Waterford: Michael O'Sullivan, 1999, NLI Ir. 9295 p, 10 p.

O'Sullivan, Michael, *Memorial Inscriptions Quaker Cemetery: Newtown, Waterford City, Ireland*, Waterford: Michael O'Sullivan, 1996, NLI, 69 p.

O'Sullivan, Michael, *Holy Trinity Church, Ballybricken, Waterford city memorial inscriptions*, Waterford: Michael O'Sullivan, 1998, NLI Ir. 9295 h 1, 119 p.

Power, V. Rev. P., *A short history of County Waterford*, Waterford: The Waterford News, 1933, NLI Ir. 94141 p 2, 98 p.

Power, V. Rev. P., *Waterford and Lismore: A Compendious History of the Dioceses*, Dublin: Cork University Press, 1937, NLI Ir. 274141 p 1, 402 p.

Pyke, D., *Parish Priests and Churches of St Mary's, Clonmel*, 1984, NLI Ir. 274 p 40, 54 p.

Reference committee, *Abbeyside reference archive*, Abbeyside: Abbeyside reference committee, 1995, NLI, 12 p.

Reilly, Jospeh F., *Reilly of Ballintlea, Kilrossanty, Co. Waterford ... with Amercian descendants*, Hartland VT: the author, 1981, NLI Ir. 9292 r 21, 42 p.

Ryland, R.H., *The history, topography and antiquities of the county and city of Waterford*, London: J. Murray, 1824, NLI Ir. 9141 r 1, 419 p. Repr. Kilkenny: Wellbrook, 1982

Smith, Charles, *The ancient and present state of the county and city of Waterford: being a natural, civil, ecclesiastical, historical and topographical description thereof*, Dublin: A. Reilly, 1774, NLI Ir. 94141 s 1. Reprint Cork: Mercier Press, 1969

Veale, T., *Index of Surnames in 'The New Commercial Directory for the cities of Waterford and Kilkenny and the towns of Clonmel, Carrick-on-Suir, New Ross and Carlow'*, Dublin: Veale, 1996 NLI Ir. 9414 p.

Veale, T., *Extract from 1821 census Waterford City: surname index*, Dublin: Tom Veale 1993, 40 p. NLI Ir. 94141 p.

Veale, T., *Richard Lucas 1788: directory extract for south east of Ireland*, Dublin: Veale, 1995, NLI Ir. 9414 v

Watson, Col. S.J., *A Dinner of Herbs: a history of Old St Mary's church, Clonmel*, Clonmel: Watson Books, 1988, Tipperary County Library, 284.094193, 259p.

White, James (ed.), *My Clonmel Scrap Book*, Clonmel: Tentmaker Publications, 1995, NLI Ir. 94142 w 3, 376 p. Repr. of 1907 edition

Young, John M., *A maritime and general history of Dungarvan 1690–1978*, Dungarvan: the author, 1978, NLI Ir. 94141 y 1, 87 p.

Local Journals

Decies, NLI Ir. 9414 d 5

Journal of the Waterford & South-East of Ireland Archaeological Society. Online: Waterford Library, NLI Ir. 794105 w 1

Directories

1788	Richard Lucas, *General Directory of the Kingdom of Ireland*, NLI Pos. 3729. Repr. in Veale, *Lucas*, IG 1965, 1966, 1967, 1968
1809	Holden, *Triennal Directory*
1820	J. Pigot, *Commercial Directory of Ireland* PRONI, NLI Ir. 9141 p 107, LDS Film 962702 Item 1
1824	J. Pigot, and Co., *City of Dublin and Hibernian Provincial Directory*, NLI, LDS Film 451787. Online: Waterford Library
1839	T. Shearman, *New Commercial Directory for the cities of Waterford and Kilkenny, Towns of Clonmel, Carrick-on-Suir, New Ross and Carlow.* Indexed in Veale, *Index*. Online: Waterford Library
1839	T.S. Harvey, *Waterford Directory*
1846	Slater's *National Commercial Directory of Ireland*. PRONI, NLI LO, LDS Film 1696703 Item 3. Online: Waterford Library
1856	Slater, *Royal National Commercial Directory of Ireland*, NLI, LDS Film 1472360 Item 1. Online: Waterford Library
1866	T.S. Harvey, *Waterford Almanac and Directory* (Repub. Archive CD Books Ireland, CD ROM #IET0017, 2005)
1869	Newenham Harvey, *Waterford Directory*, WDCL
1870	Slater, *Directory of Ireland*, NLI
1877	Harvey's *Waterford Almanack and Street Directory for 1877*. Online: Waterford Library
1881	Slater, *Royal National Commercial Directory of Ireland*, NLI. Online: Waterford Library
1884	George Henry Bassett, *Kilkenny City and County Guide and Directory*
1886	Francis Guy, *Postal Directory of Munster*, NLI Ir. 91414 g 8, LDS Film 1559399 Item 8
1894	Slater, *Royal Commercial Directory of Ireland*, NLI

Gravestone Inscriptions

Affane: Affane Hunter, C of I, *IG*, Vol. 2, No. 9, 1952

Ballygunner: Ballygunnertemple, *IGRS*, Vol. 2

Ballynakill: C of I, *IGRS*, Vol. 2

Ballynakill: Ballynakill House, *IGRS*, Vol. 2

Clashmore: Clashmore town, C of I, *IG*, Vol. 2, No. 8, 1950

Clonagam: Portlaw, C of I, IGRS Collection (7), GO

Corbally: Corbally Beg, RC, *IGRS*, Vol. 2

Crooke: IGRS Collection (138), GO

Crooke: RC, *IGRS*, Vol. 2

Drumcannon: *IGRS*, Vol. 2

Dunhill: *IGRS*, Vol. 2

Dysert: Churchtown, C of I, *Decies*, No. 25, 1984

Faithlegg: Coolbunnia (Faithlegg?), RC, *IGRS*, Vol. 2

Fenoagh, Curraghnagarragha: *IGRS*, Vol. 2

Guilcagh: C of I, IGRS Collection (11), GO

Islandikane: Islandikane South, *IGRS*, Vol. 2

Kilbarry: *IGRS*, Vol. 2, also O'Sullivan, *Kilbarry Graveyard*

Kilburne: Knockeen, *IGRS*, Vol. 2

Kilculliheen: Abbeylands (C of I): O'Sullivan. *Memorial inscriptions*

Kill St Lawrence: *IGRS*, Vol. 2

Kill St Nicholas: Passage, 1 inscription, IGRS Collection, GO

Killea: Commons (Killea Old?), RC, *IGRS*, Vol. 2

Killea: Dunmore East, C of I, IGRS Collection (123), GO

Killoteran: C of I, *IGRS*, Vol. 2, also O'Sullivan, *Killotteran, Co. Waterford*

Kilmeadan: Coolfin (Kilmeadan?), *IGRS*, Vol. 2

Lisnakill: *IGRS*, Vol. 2, also O'Sullivan, *Lisnakill Graveyard*

Mothel: C of I, *Decies*, Nos 38, 39, 40, 41, 42

Newcastle: Ardeenloun East (Newcastle?), *IGRS*, Vol. 2

Rathgormuck: *Decies*, No. 37

Reisk: *IGRS*, Vol. 2

St John's Without, Lower Newton Road (Quaker), O'Sullivan, *Quaker Cemetey*

John's Lane (Quaker), O'Sullivan, *Quaker Cemetey*

Stradbally: Faha Chapel of Ease, *Decies*, No. 17, 1981

Stradbally: *Decies*, No. 16, 1981

Trinity Without: Waterford, Chapel Lane, RC (Ballybricken), Power, *Catholic Records* also O'Sullivan, *Holy Trinity Church, Ballybricken*

Whitechurch: Ballykennedy (Whitechurch?), C of I, *IA*, NLI Ir. 9205 i 3, Vol. 5, No. 1, 1973

Estate Records

Bellew: Tenants list, 1760, *IWSLAHSJ*, Vol. XIX, No. 4 (1911). All tenants. Covering areas in the civil parish of Dungarvan.

Chearnley family: Rental, 1752, NLI Ms. 8811. Major tenants only. Covering areas in the civil parishes of: Lismore; and Mocollop.

Crown Lands: Rental, 1784, NAI M.3199. All tenants. Covering areas in the civil parishes of: Crooke; Faithlegg; and Kill St Nicholas.

Cunningham, Patrick: LEC Rental, 1869, NAI M.1834. Coverage unclear. Covering areas in the civil parish of Fenoagh.

Dawson, Richard: rental, 1781–1901, NLI Ms. 3148. Major tenants only. Covering areas in the civil parishes of: Colligan; Dungarvan; Fews; Kilgobnet; Kilrossanty; Lismore and Mocollop; Modelligo, Templemichael.

Fox, James: Rental, 1745–1773, NLI Pos. 4065. Major tenants only. Covering areas in the civil parishes of: Drumcannon; Kilbarry.

Lane Fox, George: Tenants list, 1857, *Decies*, No. 26 (1984). All tenants. Covering areas in the civil parish of Kilbarry.

Mansfield, John: rent ledger, 1783–1794, NLI Ms. 9633. Major tenants only. Covering areas in the civil parishes of: Clashmore; Clonea; Dungarvan; Kilmolash; Lisgenan or Grange; Modelligo, Rathgormuck.

Middleton, Lord: Estate survey, 1784, NLI Ms. 9977. Coverage unclear. Covering areas in the civil parish of Kilronan.

Newport-Bolton family: Rental, 1840–1876, NLI Ms. 8488. All tenants. Covering areas in the civil parishes of: Drumcannon; and Kilmacomb.

Osborne Family: Rentals, 1850, NAI D.6057. All tenants. Rentals, 1863–1877, NAI M.3052. All tenants. Covering areas in the civil parishes of: Clashmore; Colligan; Dungarvan; Kilbarrymeaden; Kilgobnet; Killaloan; Kilronan; Kilrossanty; Monksland; Rathgormuck; Ringagonagh; St Mary's; Clonmel; Stradbally; Whitechurch.

Power, Anne: Rental, 1853, NAI M.1830. All tenants. Covering areas in the civil parish of Dysert.

St George, Charles Manners: Rentals and accounts, 1842–1871, NLI Mss. 4001–22. All tenants. Covering areas in the civil parishes of: Affane; Fews; Whitechurch.

Sargeant, Francis: Rentals, 1798, NLI Ms. 10,072. All tenants. Covering areas in the civil parish of Clashmore.

[No Landlord given]: Rentals, 1849, *Decies*, No. 27 (1984). All tenants. Covering areas in the civil parishes of Lismore and Mocollop.

WESTMEATH

Census returns and substitutes

1640   Irish Proprietors in Moate and District, in Cox *Moate*
1641   Book of Survey and Distribution. NLI Ms. 965
1659   Pender's 'Census'. Repr. GPC, 1997, IMC, 2002. LDS Film 924648
1666   Hearth Money Roll of Mullingar. *Franciscan College Journal,* 1950
1726–1727 Protestant householders, Abbeylara, Abbeyshrule, Ardagh, Clonbroney, Clongesh, Kilcommock, Killashee, Rathreagh, Shrule, Taghshiny (Longford); Rathsapick, Russagh (Westmeath). List compiled for the distribution of religious books. NAI M.1502. Indexed online: From Ireland
1731   Protestants, Shrule & Rathreagh (Longford); Rathaspick (Westmeath) RCBL GS 2/7/3/25
1749   St Peter's Athlone. NAI MFS 6
1761–1788 Freeholders. NLI Mss. 787/8

1763	Poll Book. GO 443

1763   Poll Book. GO 443

1766   Russagh. LDS Film 258517

1796   Spinning-Wheel Premium List. 1,250 names for Co. Westmeath. Online: Hayes

1802–1803 Protestants in the parishes of Ballyloughloe, Castletown Delvin, Clonarney, Drumraney, Enniscoffey, Kilbridepass, Killalon, Kilcleagh, Killough, Killua, Killucan, Leney, Moyliscar, Rathconnell. *IA*, 1973

1823–1838 Tithe Books

1832   Voters. *IG*, Vol. 5, Nos 2 & 6, Vol. 6, No 1 (1975, 1979, 1980)

1835   Tubber parish. NLI Pos. 1994

1837   Marksmen (i.e. illiterate voters), Athlone Borough. *Parliamentary Papers 1837, Reports from Committees*, Vol. II (1), Appendix A

1854   Griffith's Valuation. Indexed online: Hayes

1855   Partial census of Streete parish c.1855. NLI Pos. 4236

1861   Athlone Voters. WCL. Also LDS Film 1279285

1863–1871 Census for the parish of Rathaspick and Russagh. PRONI T.2786

1901   Census

1911   Census

Online

From Ireland	*www.from-ireland.net*	
Hayes, John	*www.failteromhat.com*	
Leitrim-Roscommon	*www.leitrim-roscommon.com*	1901 for Athlone
Rootsweb Westmeath	*www.rootsweb.com/~irlwem2*	

Publications

Local histories, etc.

Athlone: Materials from printed sources relating to the history of Athlone and surrounding areas, 1699 1899, NLI Mss. 1543–7, including an index volume

Genealogies of the grand jurors of Co. Westmeath, 1727–1853, NLI Ir. 94131 g 1

Andrews, J.H., *Irish Historic Towns Atlas 5: Mullingar*, Dublin: Royal Irish Academy, 1992, NLI

Brady, J., *A short history of the parishes of the diocese of Meath, 1867–1944*, NLI Ir. 94132 b 2

Brady, Rev. John, *The parish of Mullingar*, Mullingar: the Parish, 1962, NLI Ir. 274108 p 12, 31 p.

Clarke, Desmond, 'Athlone, a bibliographical study', *An Leabhar*, No. 10, 1952, 138–9

Clarke, Joe, *Coosan school 1836–1988: school memories and local history*, 1988, NLI, 48 p.

Clarke, M.V., *Register of the priory of the Blessed Virgin Mary at Tristernagh*, IMC, NLI Ir. 271 c 22

Cox, Liam, *Moate, Co. Westmeath: a history of the town and district*, Athlone: 1981, NLI Ir. 994131 c 2, Also LDS Film 1279227

Egan, Oliver, *Tyrellspass, Past and Present*, Ireland: Tyrrellspass Town Development Committee, 1986, NLI Ir. 271 c 22, 212 p.

Farrell, Mary, *Mullingar: essays on the history of a Midlands town in the 19th century*, Mullingar: Westmeath County Library, 2002, NLI, 207 p.

Farrell, Noel, *Exploring Family Origins in Mullingar Town*, Longford: Noel Farrell, 2005, 48 p.

Grouden, Breda, *The contribution of the Clibborn family to Moate town and district*, Moate: Moate Historical Society, 1990, NLI Ir. 941 P 108(4), 40 p.

Healy, John, *History of the Diocese of Meath*, Dublin: 1908, 2 vols

IGRS, *Tombstone inscriptions Vol. 2*, Dublin: IGRS Tombstone Committee, 2001, NLI, c. 900 p.

Keaney, Marian, *Westmeath Local Studies; a guide to sources*, Mullingar: Longford-Westmeath Joint Library Committee, 1982, NLI Ir. 94131 k 1, 50 p.

Keaney, Marion, *Athlone bridging the centuries*, Mullingar: Westmeath county council, 1991, NLI Ir. 94131 a 2. Co-editor, Gearóid Ó Briain

Kieran, K., *Bibliography of the History of the Co. Westmeath*, Mullingar: 1959

Lenehan, Jim, *Politics and Society in Athlone, 1830–1885: A Rotten Borough*, Irish Academic Press, 1999, NLI

MacNamee, James J., *History of the Diocese of Ardagh*, Dublin: Browne and Nolan, 1954, NLI Ir. 274131 m 5, 858 p.

Monahan, Rev. J., *Records Relating to the Diocese of Ardagh and Clonmacnoise*, Dublin: M.H. Gill and son, 1886, NLI Ir. 27413 m 3, 400 p.

Moyvoughley Historical Committee, *Moyvoughley and its hinterland*, Moyvoughley, 2000, NLI Ir. 94131 m 5, 400 p.

Murtagh, Harman, *Irish Midland Studies*, Athlone: Old Athlone Society, 1980, NLI Ir. 941 m 58 255 p.

Murtagh, H., *Irish Historic Towns Atlas 6: Athlone*, Dublin: Royal Irish Academy, 1994, NLI, ILB 941 p (13) 3

Murtagh, H., *Athlone besieged*, Athlone: Temple Printing Co., 1991, NLI Ir. 94107 p 21(1), Eyewitness and other contemporary accounts of the siege of Athlone 1690, 1691

Murtagh, H., *Athlone: history and settlement to 1800*, Athlone: Old Athlone Society, 2000, NLI Ir. 94131 m 6, 256 p.

O'Brien, Brendan, *Athlone Workhouse and the Famine*, Athlone: Old Athlone Society, 1995, NLI Ir. 300 p 207(8). Edited by Gearóid O'Brien

O'Brien, Gearóid, *St. Mary's Parish Atlone, a history*, Longford: St Mel's Trust, 1989, NLI Ir. 27412 o 3, 213 p.

O'Brien, Gearóid, *Clonbonny a centre of learning*, Athlone, 1995, NLI Ir. 300 p 207(9), 64 p.

O'Brien, Seamus, *Famine and community in Mullingar poor law union, 1845–1849: mud cabins and fat bullocks*, Dublin ; Portland, OR: Irish Academic Press, 1999, NLI Ir. 94132 o 13, 64 p.

Paterson, J. (ed.), *Diocese of Meath and Kildare: an historical guide*, 1981, NLI Ir. 941 p 75

Ryan, Hazel A., *Athlone Abbey Graveyard Inscriptions*, Mullingar: Longford Westmeath Joint Library Committee, 1987, NLI Ir. 9295 p (2(1)

Sheehan, Jeremiah, *Westmeath, as others saw it: excerpts from the writings of 35 authors, who recorded ... observations on various aspects of Westmeath and its people, from 900 AD to the present*, Avila, Moate, Co. Westmeath: J. Sheehan, 1982, NLI Ir. 94131 s 5, 224 p.

Sheehan, Jeremiah, *Worthies of Westmeath: a biographical dictionary of brief lives of famous Westmeath people*, Westmeath: Wellbrook Press, 1987, Westmeath County Library, 920.041815, 130 p.

SS. Peter's & Paul's Foróige, *Our local history Streamstown, Horseleap & Boher*, Kilbeggan: Foróige, 1990, NLI Ir. 94131.0.4, 246 p.

Stokes, George T., *Athlone, the Shannon & Lough Ree*, Dublin & Athlone: 1897, NLI Ir. 91413 s 1

Tormey, John, *Rathaspic & Russagh: a history of the parish*, Mullingar: Tormey & Wallace, 1983, NLI Ir. 94131 t 2, 176 p. Co-author, Peter Wallace

Upton, *Upton Papers, Royal Irish Academy*, NLI Pos. 1997, Wills and Deeds mainly relating to Co. Westmeath. Originals in Royal Irish Academy; Microfilm in the NLI

Woods, James, *Annals of Westmeath*, Dublin: Sealy, Bryers & Walker, 1907, NLI Ir. 94131 w 1, 345 p.

Local Journals
Ardagh & Clonmacnoise Historical Society Journal, NLI Ir. 794105
Journal of the Old Athlone Society, NLI Ir. 94131 o 1
Ríocht na Midhe, NLI Ir. 94132 r 1

Directories

1820	J. Pigot, *Commercial Directory of Ireland* PRONI, NLI Ir. 9141 p 107, LDS Film 962702 Item 1
1824	J. Pigot and Co., *City of Dublin and Hibernian Provincial Directory*, NLI, LDS Film 451787
1846	Slater's *National Commercial Directory of Ireland*, PRONI, NLI LO, LDS Film 1696703 Item 3
1856	Slater, *Royal National Commercial Directory of Ireland*, NLI, LDS Film 1472360 Item 1
1870	Slater, *Directory of Ireland*, NLI
1881	Slater, *Royal National Commercial Directory of Ireland*, NLI
1894	Slater, *Royal Commercial Directory of Ireland*, NLI

Gravestone Inscriptions
Ardnurcher or Horseleap: Ardnurcher. Online: Rootsweb Westmeath
Ballyloughloe, Labaun (Mount Temple?), C of I, *IA*, Vol. 4, No. 2, 1972
Carrick, GO Ms. 622 p. 171
Foyran, Castletown (Finnea), GO Ms. 622 p. 107

Kilcleagh, Killomenaghan, Cox, *Moate*
Kilcleagh, Moate, Main Street, C of I, Cox, *Moate*
—— Moate, Main Street, Quaker, Cox, *Moate*
Killua, French, French, *Monumental Inscriptions*—see 'Meath'
Mullingar, Church Street, C of I, DSHC
St Feighin's, Fore, RC: *IGRS*, Vol. 2
St Mary's, Athlone, Church Street, C of I, Pos. 5309 (with parish registers), NLI
——Athlone, Abbey ruins, Ryan, *Athlone Abbey, IGRS*, Vol. 2
Stonehall, C of I, GO Ms. 622 p. 183
Street, Barradrum (Street?), C of I, *Ríocht na Midhe*, Vol. 4, No. 3, 1969

Estate records

Adams, Randal: Maps, 1697. *AH*, No. 10 (1941). Principally major tenants. Covering areas in the civil parishes of: Ardnurcher or Horseleap; Castletownkindalen; Churchtown; Mullingar; Rathconrath.

Boyd, G.A.: Rentals, 1842–1854. NLI Ms. 3108. All tenants. Covering areas in the civil parishes of: Ardnurcher or Horseleap; Ballymore; Castlelost; Castletownkindalen; Clonfad; Drumraney; Dysart; Kilbride; Kilcumreragh; Lynn; Moylisker; Mullingar; Newtown; Pass of Kilbride; Rahugh; Rathconnell; Rathconrath.

Buckingham, Duke of: Estate sale & map, 1848. All tenants, NLI Ms. 14.A.20. Covering areas in the civil parishes of: Foyran; Kilcleagh; Lickbla; Rathgarve.

Caulfield, Col. W: Maps, 1811–1837. NLI 21.F.125. Principally major tenants. Covering areas in the civil parishes of: Piercetown; Rathconrath.

Clonbrock: Rental 1624–1695. NLI Ms. 35,722. Major tenants only. Covering areas in the civil parishes of: Ballymore; Drumraney; Killare.

Dobbyn, George: Rental, 1849. NLI D.26410. Most tenants. Covering areas in the civil parishes of: Mullingar; Rathconnell.

Eustace, Charles Stannard: Map, 1847. NLI 21.F.80 (27). Most tenants. Covering areas in the civil parishes of: Ballymore; Kilcleagh; Templepatrick.

Gibbons, James: Valuation, 1818–1821. NAI M.6994. Coverage unclear. Covering areas in the civil parishes of: Castlelost; Kilbride.

Harman: Tenants' names, 1846. NAI M.1865. All tenants. Covering areas in the civil parish of St Mary's, Athlone.

Harman, Mrs Frances: Rent Roll, 1757–1758. NAI M.1311. All tenants. Covering areas in the civil parish of Noughaval.

Hinds, George: Map, 1843. NLI 16.J.10 (8). Principally major tenants. Covering areas in the civil parish of Castletowndelvin.

Hodson, Sir George: Rent ledger, 1840–1849. NLI Ms. 16409. Principally major tenants. Covering areas in the civil parish of Mullingar.

Hopkins, Sir Francis: Rent Rolls, 1795–1839. NLI Ms. 3195. Major tenants only. Covering areas in the civil parish of Killua.

Ireland, Sophia Mary: Rental, 1851. NAI M.5595. Most tenants. Covering areas in the civil parish of Noughaval.

Jones, Walter: Map of the lands of Anaugh, 1752. NLI 21.F.80 (1). Coverage unclear. Covering areas in the civil parish of St Mary's, Athlone.

Lyons: Rent roll and timber accounts, 1786–1792. NLI Ms. 4249. All tenants. Covering areas in the civil parishes of: Killulagh; Mullingar.

Lyons, John Charles: Map, 1834. NLI 21.F.80 (15). All tenants. Covering areas in the civil parishes of: Lynn; Mullingar.

Magan, William Henry: Maps, 1848. NLI Ms. 14.A.27. All tenants. Covering townlands in the civil parishes of: Ardnurcher or Horseleap; Castletowndelvin; Castletownkindalen; Churchtown; Conry; Kilcleagh; Kilcumreragh; Killare; Kilmacnevan; Lynn; Rathconrath.

Maunsell, George Meares: Map of part of the lands of Ballymore, 1827. NLI 16.J.10(6). Most tenants.

Meares: Papers, 1650–1750. NLI Ms. 33,003. Coverage unclear. Covering areas in the civil parishes of: Ballymorin; Killare; Piercetown; Rathconrath; Templepatrick.

Moland, Thomas: Maps, 1782. NLI Ms. 32,505. Major tenants only. Covering areas in the civil parishes of: Lynn; Mullingar.

Nugent: Rent accounts, 1736–1762. NLI Ms. 5991. Major tenants only. Covering areas in the civil parish of Rathconnell.

Oxmantown, Lord: Accounts, 1798–9. NAI M.1279. Major tenants only. Covering townlands in the civil parish of: Drumraney; Noughaval; St Mary's, Athlone.

Pratt, John: Accounts of rents, 1710–1739. NLI Mss. 2587, 5247. Coverage unclear. Covering areas in the civil parishes of: Killucan; Mullingar; Rathconnell.

Reynell: Rentals, 1834–1848. NLI Ms. 5990. All tenants. Covering areas in the civil parishes of: Killua; Killulagh; Mullingar; Rathconnell.

Rochfort: Poor Rent, 1851–1854. NAI M.1262. Most tenants. Covering areas in the civil parishes of: Columbkille; Kilcumreragh; Killoe; Kilmanaghan.

Rosse, Countess Dowager of: Rents and Arrears, 1836–1837. NAI M.1291, 1301. All tenants. Covering areas in the civil parishes of: Drumraney; Noughaval; St Mary's, Athlone.

Smyth, Ralph: Maps and surveys, 1783–1813. NLI Ms. 2799. Principally major tenants. Covering areas in the civil parishes of: Durrow; Dysart; Mullingar; Portloman; Rahugh; Templeoran.

Smythe, Ralph: Rent ledger, 1775–1779. NLI Ms. 9986. All tenants. Covering areas in the civil parishes of: Faughalstown; St Feighin's.

Smythe, William: Map and survey, 1831–1840. NLI 21.F.80 (3). Coverage unclear. Covering areas in the civil parishes of: Faughalstown; St Feighin's.

Smythe, William: Rent ledger, 1802–1809. NLI Ms. 9985. All tenants. Covering areas in the civil parishes of St Feighin's.

Smythe, William: Rent ledger, receipts, 1723–1737. NLI Ms. 9990. Most tenants. Covering areas in the civil parishes of St Feighin's.

Smythe, William Barlow: Rent book, 1835–1847. NLI Ms. 9982. All tenants. Covering areas in the civil parishes of: Faughalstown; St Feighin's.

Smythe, William Barlowe: Map, 1831–1836 NLI Ms. 83. Most tenants. Covering areas in the civil parishes of: Faughalstown; Kilcumny; St Feighin's.

Talbot, Sir John: Rental, 1841. NAI M.2246. Major tenants only. Covering areas in the civil parishes of: Dysart; Lackan; Leny; Lickbla; Mullingar; Multyfarnham; Portloman; Templeoran; Tyfarnham.

Temple, Gustavus Handcock: Maps, 1786. NLI 14.A.29. Principally major tenants. Covering areas in the civil parishes of: Ballyloughloe; Bunown; Churchtown; Drumraney; Dysart; Kilkenny West; Mullingar; Noughaval; St Mary's, Athlone.

Towers, Thomas: Rental, 1801–1804 NLI Ms. 4847. Major tenants only. Covering areas in the civil parish of Mayne.

Wilson's Hospital: Rentals, 1822–1860. NLI Mss. 1000, 3098. All tenants. Covering areas in the civil parishes of: Bodenstown; Castlelost; Churchtown; Foyran; Piercetown; Portloman; Portnashangan; St Mary's; Stonehall; Taghmon.

[No landlord given]: Rental, 1831–1833. NAI M.5872. Most tenants. Covering areas in the civil parish of Foyran.

[No landlord given]: Rent accounts, 1766–1782. NLI Ms. 3157. Major tenants only. Covering areas in the civil parish of Kilcleagh.

WEXFORD

Census returns and substitutes

1618	Herald's Visitation of Co. Wexford. GO 48. Also NLI Pos. 957
1641	Book of Survey and Distribution. NLI Ms. 975
1654–1656	*Civil Survey,* Vol. IX (NLI I 6551 Dublin)
1659	Pender's 'Census'. Repr. GPC, 1997, IMC, 2002. LDS Film 924648
1665–1839	Free Burgesses of New Ross. *Proceedings of the Royal Society of Antiquaries of Ireland,* Ser. 5, Vol. pt 1, (1890) p. 298 309
1766	Edermine, Protestants only, GO 537, LDS Film 258517; Ballynaslaney NAI. M.2476
1776	Freemen of Wexford, *IG,* 5, Nos 1, 3, 4, 1973
1789	Protestant householders in the parish of Ferns. *IA,* Vol. 13, No. 2, 1981
1792	Some Protestant householders in the parishes of Ballycanew and Killisk. *IA,* Vol. 13, No. 2, 1981
1798	Protestants murdered in the 1798 rebellion, Cantwell *Memorials of the Dead … supplementary volume,* Dublin, 1986, Vol. 10, p.432
1798	Persons who suffered losses in the 1798 rebellion. Propertied classes only. c.2,000 names NLI I 94107
1817	Emigrants from Counties Carlow and Wexford to Canada. Whelan, *Wexford: History and Society.* Online: Emigrants
1823–1838	Tithe Books
1840	Wexford electors. NAI OP 1840/103
1842	Voters. NAI OP 1842/82
1846	Memorial of the poor fishermen and labourers of Fethard, c.82 names, with occupations, & numbers in family. NAI OP 1846/152
1853	Griffith's Valuation. Indexed online: Hayes

1861   Catholics in Enniscorthy parish. With Catholic records. NLI
1867   Marshallstown. *IG*, 1985
1901   Census. 40% online: Leitrim-Roscommon
1911   Census

Online

Emigrants	*www.rootsweb.com/~irish/igsi_published/wextocan.htm*	
Hayes, John	*www.failteromhat.com*	Large compendium of transcribed records
Leitrim-Roscommon	*www.leitrim-roscommon.com*	1901 25% complete

Publications

Local histories, etc.

Browne, Bernard, *Old Ross the town that never was, a community biography*, [Wexford?], Sean Ros Press, 1993, NLI Ir. 94138 b 7, 133 p.

Butler, Thomas C., *A parish and its people: history of Carrig-on-Bannow Parish*, Wellingtonbridge: 1985, NLI Ir. 94138 b 4, 254 p.

Cantwell, Brian, *Memorials of the Dead, Wexford Vols. 5–9*, Dublin: Typescript, 1984, NLI Ir. 9295 c 2, Master Index Vol. 10

Coyle, James, *The Antiquities of Leighlin*, Dublin: Browne and Nolan, n.d., NLI Ir. 94138 c 1

Culleton, Edward, *By bishop's rath and Norman fort: the story of Piercestown-Murrintown*, Wexford: Drinagh Enterprises, 1994, Wexford County Library, 285 p.

de Vál, Séamas S., *Templeudigan—yesterday and today*, Templeudigan: Templeudigan Historical Society, 2001, Wexford County Library, 184 p.

de Vál, Séamas S., *Bun Cloidi a history of the district down to the beginning of the twentieth century compiled*, Bun Cloidi: An t-Udar, 1989, NLI Ir. 94138 b 5, 319 p.

Doyle, Martin, *Notes and Gleanings Relating to the County of Wexford*, Dublin: 1868

Farrell, Noel, *Exploring family origins in New Ross*, Longford: Noel Farrell, 1998, NLI, 1B 1174

Farrell, Noel, *Exploring family origins in Enniscorthy*, Longford: Noel Farrell, 1998, NLI, 1B 2233

Flood, W.H. Grattan, *History of Hooke (Templetown) parish, County Wexford*, Wexford: the author, 1968, Wexford County Library, 28 p.

Flood, W.H. Grattan, *History of Enniscorthy, County Wexford*, Enniscorthy: Flood, 1898, NLI Ir. 941382 f 1, 233 p.

Flood, W.H. Grattan, *History of the Diocese of Ferns*, Waterford: Downey, 1916, NLI Ir. 27413 f 1, 246 p.

Griffiths, George, *The chronicles of the county of Wexford*, NLI Ir. 94138 g 1

Hay, Edward, *History of the Insurrection of County Wexford in 1798*, Dublin: J. Duffy, 1847, NLI, J 94107

Hennessy, Patrick, *Davidstown, Coutrnacuddy—A Wexford Parish*, Enniscorthy: Hennessy, 1986, NLI Ir. 94138 h 3, 138 p.

Hore, H.F., *The Social State of the Southern and Eastern Counties of Ireland in the Sixteenth Century*, Dublin: 1870, NLI Ir. 794105 r 2 [See Carlow]

Hore, P.H., *History of the town and county of Wexford*, London: 1900–11, NLI Ir. 94138 h 2, 6 vols

Jeffrey, William H., *The Castles of Co. Wexford*, Wexford: Old Wexford Society, 1979, Wexford County Library

Kinsella, A., *The Waveswept Shore—A history of the Courtown district*, Wexford: Kinsella, 1982, Wexford County Library, 162 p.

Kirk, Francis J., *Some Notable Conversions in the Co. of Wexford*, London: Burns & Oates, 1901, NLI Ir. 2828 k 1, 114 p.

Lambert, Richard, *Rathangan, a County Wexford parish: its emerging story*, Rathangan: Lambert, 1995, NLI Ir. 94138 L 3, 282 p.

Mac Suibhne, Peadar, *Clonegal Parish*, Carlow: Newark Printers, 1975, NLI Ir. 2741 m 14, 190 p.

McDonald, Danny, *Tomhaggard: a sacred place*, Tomhaggard: Tomhaggard Heritage Group, 2002, NLI, 120 p.

Monageer Comóradh '98, *Monageer Parish: a rural district in 1798: a short history*, Monageer: Monageer Comóradh '98, 1998, NLI, 59 p.

Murphy, Hilary, *The parish of Mulrankin ancient and modern*, Wexford: Mulrankin-Tomhaggard Parish Council, 2004, NLI, 196 p.

Murphy, Rory, *Memorials to the dead: Templeshanbo*, Bunclody: Glór na nGael, 1990, NLI Ir. 94138.m.4, 59 p.

Murray, Patsy, *A history of Coolgreany*, Coolgreany: Coolgreany Historical Society, 1992, NLI Ir. 94138 m 5, 88 p.

Rees, J., *A farewell to famine*, Arklow: Arklow Enterprise Centre, 1994, NLI Ir. 94138 r 6, 174 p.

Rossiter, Nicholas, *Wexford Port—a history*, Wexford: Wexford Council of Trade Unions, 1989, NLI Ir. 94138 r 4, 95 p.

Urwin, Margaret, *County Wexford family in the land war: by the O'Hanlon Walshs of Knocktartan*, Dublin: Four Courts, 2002, NLI, 64 p.

Vandeleur, Rev. W.E., *Notes on the history of Kiltennel*, Dundalk: W. Tempest, 1927, Wexford County Library, 16p

Veale, T., *Richard Lucas 1788: directory extract for south east of Ireland*, Dublin: Veale, 1995 NLI Ir. 9414 v

Veale, T., *Index of Surnames in 'The New Commercial Directory for the cities of Waterford and Kilkenny and the towns of Clonmel, Carrick-on-Suir, New Ross and Carlow'*, Dublin: Veale, 1996 NLI Ir. 9414 p.

Whelan, Kevin, *Tintern Abbey, Co. Wexford: Cistecians and Colcloughs—8 centuries of occupation*, Saltmills, Co. Wexford: Friends of Tintern, 1990, NLI Ir. 700 p 77 (5)

Whelan, Kevin, *A History of Newbawn*, Newbawn: Macra na Feirme, 1989, Wexford County Library, 118 p.

Whelan, Kevin, *Wexford History and Society*, Dublin: Geography Publications, 1987, NLI, LO, 564 p. Associate editor, William Nolan

White, W.D., *Heirs to a heritage: a story of the people and places of the Clonegal area of Clonegal Parish*, Clonegal, Co. Carlow, 1992, NLI Ir. 941 p 132(2), 72 p.

Local Journals
Journal of the Wexford Historical Society, NLI Ir. 94138 o 5
The journal of the Taghmon Historical Society, NLI
Journal of the Old Wexford Society, NLI Ir. 94138 o 5
The Past (Journal of the Ui Cinsealaigh Historical Society), NLI Ir. 941382 p 1

Directories

1788	Richard Lucas, *General Directory of the Kingdom of Ireland*, NLI Pos. 3729. Repr. in Veale, *Lucas, IG* 1965, 1966, 1967, 1968
1820	J. Pigot, *Commercial Directory of Ireland*, PRONI, NLI Ir. 9141 p 107, LDS Film 962702 Item 1
1824	J. Pigot and Co., *City of Dublin and Hibernian Provincial Directory*, NLI, LDS Film 451787
1839	T. Shearman, *New Commercial Directory for the cities of Waterford and Kilkenny, Towns of Clonmel, Carrick-on-Suir, New Ross and Carlow.* Indexed in Veale, *Index*
1846	Slater's *National Commercial Directory of Ireland*. PRONI, NLI LO, LDS Film 1696703 Item 3
1856	Slater, *Royal National Commercial Directory of Ireland*, NLI, LDS Film 1472360 Item 1
1867	Coghlan, P.J., *A directory for the co. of Wexford ... townlands, gentlemen's seats & noted places*, Galway, NLI Ir. 914138 c 4, 59 p.
1870	Slater, *Directory of Ireland*, NLI
1872	George Griffith, *County Wexford Almanac* NLI Ir. 914138 g 2
1881	Slater, *Royal National Commercial Directory of Ireland*, NLI
1885	George Henry Bassett, *Wexford County Guide and Directory* NLI Ir. 914138 b 8
1894	Slater, *Royal Commercial Directory of Ireland*, NLI

Gravestone Inscriptions
Memorials of the Dead, Brian J. Cantwell.
Co. Wexford (complete): Vols V–IX.
Master Index: Vol. X.
Ir 9295 c 2 & NAI Search Room, DCLA.

Estate Records
Alcock estate tenants: Clonmore, 1820. NL Ms. 10169.
Baron Farnham estate rent books for Bunclody: 1775–1820. NLI Mss. 787–8.

Farnham: Tenants and Tradesmen from Baron Farnham's Estate of Newtownbarry, 1774, *Irish Family History Society Newsletter*, 10 (1993), 5–7.

Co. Wexford rent lists, eighteenth century. NL Ms. 1782.

WICKLOW

Census returns and substitutes

1641	Book of Survey and Distribution. NLI Ms. 969
1669	Hearth Money Roll. NAI M.4909 Also GO 667
1745	Poll Book. PRONI 2659
1766	Parishes of Drumkay, Dunganstown, Kilpoole, Rathdrum, Rathnew. GO 537. Also WHC and LDS Film 258517
1798	Persons who suffered losses in the 1798 rebellion. Propertied classes only. c.950 names. NLI I 94107
1823–1838	Tithe Books
1837	Memorial from inhabitants of Ballinacor Sth and Shillelagh for Quarter Law sessions at Tinahely. More than 1,500 names. Most (?) from Tinahely district NAI OP 1837/133. See Magee, *Shillelagh & Ballinacor South*
1842–1848	Emigrants list. Shilelagh; NLI Ms. 18,429, 18,524. See also *West Wicklow Historical Journal*, No. 1 *et seq.*
1852–1853	Griffith's Valuation. Indexed online: Hayes
1901	Census. Arklow online: CMC, Wicklow; Avoca; Rootsweb Wicklow
1911	Census. Arklow online: CMC, Wicklow

Online

CMC, Wicklow	*www.cmcrp.net/Wicklow*
Hayes, John	*www.failteromhat.com*
Rootsweb Wicklow	*www.rootsweb.com/~irlwic2*

Publications

Local histories, etc.

Bland, F.E., *The Story of Crinken 1840–1940*, Bray: 1940, NLI Ir. 941 p 26, 26 p.

Brien, C., *In the Land of Brien: a short history of the Catholic Church and other institutions in Bray and district from earliest times*, Bray: 1984

Cantwell, Brian, *Memorials of the Dead, Wicklow Vols. 1–4*, Dublin: Typescript, 1978, NLI Ir. 9295 c 2, Master Index Vol. 10

Carville, Geraldine, *Baltinglass: abbey of the three rivers*, Moone, Co. Kildare: West Wicklow Historical Societ, 1984, NLI Ir. 94134 c 5, 87 p.

Chavasse, C., *The story of Baltinglass: a history of the parishes of Baltinglass, Ballynure and Rathbran in County Wicklow*, Kilkenny: Kilkenny Journal, 1970, NLI Ir. 9141 p 40, 75 p.

Clare, Liam, *Victorian Bray: a town adapts to changing times*, Dublin: Irish

Academic Press, 1998, NLI Ir. 94134 c 14, 82 p.

Clare, Liam, *Enclosing the commons: Dalkey, the Sugar Loaves and Bray, 1820–1870*, Dublin: Four Courts, 2004, NLI, 64 p.

Clarke, Sheila, *Ashford: a journey through time*, Blackrock, Dublin: Ashford Books, 2003, NLI, 215 p.

Cleary, Jimmy, *Wicklow harbour: a history*, Wicklow: Wicklow Harbour Commissioners, 2001, NLI, 78 p. Co-author, Andrew O'Brien

Corbett, R. John H., *A short history of Glenealy and its Church of Ireland parish bicentenary 1792–1992*, Glenealy: the parish, 1992, NLI Ir. 200 p 91(6), 21 p.

Coyle, James, *The Antiquities of Leighlin*, Dublin: Browne and Nolan, n.d., NLI Ir. 94138 c 1

Davies, K.M., *Irish Historic Towns Atlas 9: Bray*, Dublin: Royal Irish Academy, 1998, NLI

de Lion, C., *The vale of Avoca*, Dublin: Kamac Publications, 1967/91, NLI Ir. 914134 p 4, 48 p.

Doran, A.L., *Bray and environs*, Bray: 1903. Repr. 1985

Earl, L., *The battle of Baltinglass*, London: Alfred Knopf, 1952, NLI Ir. 94134 e 1, 241 p.

Eustace, E.A.R., *Short history of Ardoyne Parish*, Carlow: 1967

Farrell, Noel, *Exploring family origins in Arklow town*, Longford: Noel Farrell, 1998, NLI 48 p.

Flannery, Judith, *Christ Church Delgany 1789–1990 between the mountains and the sea: a parish history*, Delgany: Select Vestry of Delgany Parish, 1990, NLI Ir. 27413 f 3, 162 p.

Flynn, A., *History of Bray*, Cork: Mercier Press, 1986, NLI Ir. 94134 f 1

Flynn, A., *Famous Links with Bray*, Bray: Falcon Print & Finish, 1985, NLI Ir. 941 p 85, 51 p.

Flynn, Michael, *Outline histories ... Kelly of Youngstown, Kilmead, Athy, Co. Kildare, Murphy of Togher, Roundwood, Co. Wicklow, Masterson family of Ardellis, Athy, Co. Kildare (with descendants)*, Mullingar: Michael P. Flynn, 1997, NLI Ir. 9292 f [sic]

Forde, F., *Maritime Arklow*, Arklow: 1988

Garner, W., *Bray: architectural heritage*, Dublin: 1980

Hannigan, Ken, *Wicklow History and Society*, Dublin: Geography Publications, 1994, Dublin City Library (1), 941.84, 1005 p. Co-edited by William Nolan

Heavener, Robert, *Credo Dunganstown: an age-old Irish parish with a living message for everyman today*, Jordanstown, Co. Antrim: Cromlech Books, 1993, NLI Ir. 27413 h 7, 145 p.

Hood, Susan, 'Marriage in Ireland before the famine: case study of Rathvilly parish', *Journal of the West Wicklow Historical Society*, 3, 1989, 33–40

Irish Countrywomen's Association, *Avoca Local History Guide presented by Avoca Guild* ICA, Avoca, ICA, 1987, NLI Ir. 94134 p 3(3), 52 p.

Jennings, Robert, *Kilcoole, County Wicklow History and folklore, historical walks & drives*, Kilcoole: Kilcoole Millennium and Residents' Association, 1998, NLI Ir. 94134 j 1, 130 p.

Jennings, Robert, *Glimpses of an ancient parish, Newcastle, Co. Wicklow 1189–1989*, 1989, NLI Ir. 94134 p 3(2), 42 p.

Mac Suibhne, Peadar, *Clonegal Parish*, Carlow: Newark Printers, 1975, NLI Ir. 2741 m 14, 190 p.

MacEiteagain, E., *Ballynagran: an historical perspective, Wicklow*, Ashford Historical Society, 1994, NLI, 21 p.

Magee, Seán, *Shillelagh & Ballinacor South, Co. Wicklow 1837—A Memorial*, Dun Laoghaire: Dun Laoghaire Genealogical Society, 1997. NLI Ir. 9291 g 7 64 p.

Mansfield, C., *The Aravon Story*, Dublin: 1975, NLI Ir. 372 p 237, 26 p. History of Aravon School

Martin, C., *The Woodcarvers of Bray 1887–1914*, Bray: 1985

Martin, C., *A drink from Broderick's well*, Dublin: 1980, NLI Ir. 94134 m 4, 167 p.

Morris, J., *The story of the Arklow lifeboats*, Coventry: 1987

Murphy, Hilary, *The Kynoch era in Arklow 1895–1918*, Wexford: Murphy, 1976, NLI Ir. 600 p 29, 76 p.

O'Reilly, George H., *Newcastle, County Wicklow school registers 1864–1947*, Dun Laoghaire: Dun Laoghaire Genealogical Society, 1997, NLI Ir. 9291 g 7, 159 p.

O'Reilly, George H., *Corn growers, carriers & traders county Wicklow 1788, 1789 & 1790*, Dun Laoghaire: Dun Laoghaire Genealogical Society, 1997, NLI Ir. 9291 g 7, 27 p. Co-author, James O. Coyle

Power, P.J., *The Arklow calendar, a chronicle of events from earliest times to 1900 AD*, Arklow: Elizabeth Press, 1981, NLI Ir. 94134 p 1, 129 p.

Power, Pat, *People of the rebellion: Wicklow 1798*, Dun Laoghaire: Dun Laoghaire Genealogical Society, 1999, NLI Ir. 9291 g 7, 116 p.

Rees, J., *Fitzwilliam tenants listed in the Coolattin Estate emigration 1847–56*, Wicklow: Dee-Jay Publications, 1998, NLI Ir. 94108 r 23, 84 leaves

Rees, J., *Arklow—last stronghold of sail: Arklow ships 1850–1985*, Arklow: Arklow Historical Society, 1985, NLI Ir. 386 r 7, 178 p. Co-author, L. Charlton

Scott, G.D., *The stones of Bray*, Dublin: Hodges, Figgis, 1913, NLI Ir. 914133 b 2, The barony of Rathdown

Stokes, A.E., *The parish of Powerscourt*, Bray: Old Bray Society, 1986, NLI, 16 p.

Taylor, R.M., *St. Mary's Church Blessington, 1683–1970*, Greystones: 1970

Veale, T., *Richard Lucas 1788: directory extract for south east of Ireland*, Dublin: Veale, 1995 NLI Ir. 9414 v

White, W.D., *Heirs to a heritage: a story of the people and places of the Clonegal area of Clonegal Parish*, Clonegal, Co. Carlow, 1992, NLI Ir. 941 p 132(2), 72 p.

Local Journals
Ashford and District Historical Journal, NLI Ir. 94134.a.
Bray Historical Record, NLI Ir. 94134 o 3
Glendalough: (...) Journal of the Glendalough Historical and Folklore Society
Imaal: Journal of the St. Kevin's Local Studies Group
Journal of the Arklow Historical Society, NLI Ir. 94134 a

Journal of the Cualann Historical Society, NLI Ir. 94134 b
Journal of the Greystones Historical & Archeological Society, NLI Ir. 94134 g V.1
Journal of the West Wicklow Historical Society, NLI Ir. 94134 w 5
Report of the Old Bray Society, NLI Ir. 94134 o 3
Reportorium Novum, NLI Ir. 27413 r 3
Roundwood and District History and Folklore Journal, NLI Ir. 94134 r 1
Wicklow Historical Society Journal
Wicklow Journal

Directories

1788	Richard Lucas, *General Directory of the Kingdom of Ireland,* NLI Pos. 3729. Repr. in Veale, *Lucas,* IG 1965, 1966, 1967, 1968
1824	J. Pigot and Co., *City of Dublin and Hibernian Provincial Directory,* NLI, LDS Film 451787
1846	Slater's *National Commercial Directory of Ireland.* PRONI, NLI LO, LDS Film 1696703 Item 3
1856	Slater, *Royal National Commercial Directory of Ireland,* NLI, LDS Film 1472360 Item 1
1870	Slater, *Directory of Ireland,* NLI
1881	Slater, *Royal National Commercial Directory of Ireland,* NLI
1894	Slater, *Royal Commercial Directory of Ireland,* NLI

Gravestone Inscriptions

Memorials of the Dead, Brian J. Cantwell.
Co. Wicklow (complete): Vols I–IV.
Master Index: Vol. X.
Ir. 9295 c 2, NAI Search Room, DCLA.

Estate records

Adair: Rent ledger, n.d. NLI Ms. 16410. Principally major tenants. Covering areas in the civil parish of Kilmacanoge.

Cobbe: Rental & maps, 1771, 1830–1882. NLI Pos. 4033. All tenants. Covering areas in the civil parish of Boystown.

Education, Commissioners of: Valuation, 1816. NLI Ms. 16925. Most tenants. Covering areas in the civil parish of Ballykine.

Fitzwilliam, Earl: NLI Ms. 6068, Lease book, 1795–1808; Ms. 6074 Rental, 1811–12; Ms. 6076 Rental 1809–1811; Ms. 6082, occupiers 1827–1868; Mss. 6001–6051, rentals 1782–1855; Mss. 6083–6087, rentals, 1828–33; Mss. 6088–6118, rentals, 1834–1866. Most tenants. Covering areas in the civil parishes of: Aghowle; Ardoyne; Carnew; Crecrin; Crosspatrick; Derrylossary; Dunganstown; Glenealy; Hacketstown; Kilcommon (Arklow); Kilcommon (Ballinacor); Killiskey; Kilpipe; Kilpoole; Kiltegan; Liscolman; Moyacomb; Moyne; Mullinacuff; Newcastle Lower; Preban; Rathdrum; Rathnew.

Hatch: NLI Mss. 11996–11997, Rent survey, 1817 (most tenants); Ms. 11341, Rental, 1750, Ms. 11995, Rental, 1785 (major tenants). Covering areas in the civil parishes of: Aghowle; Calary; Derrylossary; Newcastle Lower; Rathnew.

Hepenstal, Rev. L.W.: Map, 1818. NLI Ms. 16.J.22 (1). Most tenants. Covering areas in the civil parishes of: Ballinacor; Ballykine; Ballynure; Donaghmore; Knockrath.

Hodson: NLI Mss. 16390–96, Rent ledger, 1799–1887. Principally major tenants. Covering areas in the civil parishes of: Bray; Calary; Kilmacanoge; Powerscourt.

Hodson, Sir George: NLI Ms. 16418, Rent ledger, 1841–1850. Principally major tenants. Covering areas in the civil parishes of: Bray; Calary; Kilmacanoge.

Kemmis: NLI Ms. 15161, 1803–1923. Principally major tenants. Covering areas in the civil parishes of: Ballinacor; Ballykine; Kilpipe; Knockrath.

Miley, Rev. Edward: NAI M.5679, Rental, [n.d.]. Most tenants. Covering areas in the civil parishes of Kilbride (Talbotstown).

Ormonde, Duke of: NLI Ms. 23789, 1706, rental. Principally major tenants. Covering areas in the civil parishes of: Arklow; Kilcommon (Arklow).

Paul, Sir R.J.: Map. 1843, NLI Ms. 21.F.136. Most tenants. Covering areas in the civil parish of Ballynure.

Pembroke estate: NLI M.2011, Rent rolls, 1754–1806. Most tenants. Covering areas in the civil parish of Bray.

Percy, Anthony: NLI Ms. 10265, n.d. Major tenants only. Covering areas in the civil parishes of: Donaghmore; Rathnew.

Powerscourt: NLI Ms. 16386, register of leases, 1775–1862 (many with comments); Ms. 4882 rental, 1836–1841; Ms. 19298, rentals 1840–1850; Mss. 19189–19190, rentals 1803–1813; Mss. 19197–199, rentals 1841–44; Mss. 19202–09, rentals, 1846–1857. Most tenants. Covering areas in the civil parishes of: Bray; Calary; Castlemacadam; Derrylossary; Kilmacanoge; Newcastle Lower; Powerscourt; Rathnew.

Proby: NLI Ms. 3149, Rental, 1826. All tenants. Covering areas in the civil parishes of: Arklow; Ballintemple; Inch; Kilbride (Arklow); Killahurler.

Putland, George: NLI Mss. 12768–12778, Rentals, 1814–1827. Principally major tenants. Covering areas in the civil parishes of: Castlemacadam; Garrycloyne; Matehy; Templeusque.

Ram: NLI Ms. 8238, Rental, 1810–1820. Principally major tenants. Covering areas in the civil parishes of: Ballinacor; Donaghmore; Kilcommon (Ballinacor).

Rockingham, Marquess of: NLI Mss. 6055, 6056, Rentals, 1748, 1754. Most tenants; Mss. 6058, 6059 Rentals, 1763, 1770. Most tenants. Most tenants. Covering areas in the civil parishes of: Aghowle; Ardoyne; Carnew; Crecrin; Crosspatrick; Hacketstown; Kilcommon (Ballinacor); Kilpipe; Kiltegan; Liscolman; Moyacomb; Moyne; Mullinacuff; Preban.

Stone, Richard: NLI Ms. 16584, Rent ledger, 1712–1718. Major tenants only. Covering areas in the civil parishes of: Delgany; Drumkay; Dunganstown; Glenealy; Kilbride (Arklow); Kilcoole; Killiskey; Knockrath; Preban; Rathnew.

Westby, William Jones: NLI Mss. 14291–2, Rentals, 1836–1841. Most tenants. Covering areas in the civil parishes of: Hacketstown; Kiltegan.

Wicklow papers: NLI Ms. 9580, Rental, 1704–1705. Principally major tenants. Covering areas in the civil parishes of: Arklow; Calary; Kilcoole; Killiskey; Kiltegan; Newcastle Lower; Newcastle Upper.

Chapter 14 ～

ROMAN CATHOLIC PARISH REGISTERS

What follows is a listing of all copies of Roman Catholic parish registers, microfilm and database transcript, to be found at present (2005) in the NLI, PRONI, the LDS Family History Library and local heritage centres, as well as any that have been published or transcribed online. The aim here is to assist research by providing an overview of the dates and locations of records available, in any sense, to the public. For this reason, and because such an undertaking is beyond the scope of the present work, no attempt has been made to list the dates of the originals held in local custody, except where no other copy is known. Online references are detailed in that section of the county source-lists, except for LDS records: 'Familysearch' refers to the main LDS site, *www.family-search.org*, where any Irish parish records are included as part of the International Genealogical Index (IGI). The transcripts in the IGI are not complete, covering only dates and personal names. The same is true of the transcripts in the LDS CD-ROM set British Isles Vital Records Index (2nd ed., 2001), which includes some thirteen parishes, mainly in Roscommon, and overlaps to some extent with the IGI. It should be added that it is very difficult to pin down what exactly the IGI includes; it is perfectlly possible that I have missed something.

The parish names used in the tables are those found on the accompanying maps. For the most part these are the historic names used in the nineteenth-century records. A listing of variant and modern names will be found at the end of this chapter. This can sometimes clarify the evolution of a parish. Once again, some caution is needed in using the maps. Based largely on Lewis' *Topographical Dictionary of Ireland* (1837), they attempt to show all parishes with baptism, marriage or burial records before 1880. The problems are obvious. To put it at its kindest, the maps can only be taken as indicative, to be used primarily in identifying which parishes adjoin one other. In the case of Dublin City and County, the rapid creation and subdivision of parishes from the 1850s on makes it impossible to include them all on the maps, though any available records are listed.

Antrim

An index to all UHF records is searchable online, at *www.ancestryireland.co.uk.*

Parish (Diocese)	Baptisms	Marriages	Burials	Location	Reference
Aghagallon	Apr 1 1828–Dec 20 1880	May 25 1828–Nov 8 1880	Mar 29 1828–July 5 1848	NLI	Pos. 5467
(Down and Connor)			May 25 1872–Dec 22 1880		
	1828–1889	1828–1889	1828–1848; 1873–1881	PRONI	MIC.1D/6.63
	1828–1900	1828–1900	1828–1900	UHF	
Ahoghill	1833–1863	1833–1863	1833–1863	NLI	Pos. 5472
(Down and Connor)	Jan 10 1964–Dec 25 1880	Apr 3 1864–Dec 25 1880			
	1833–1881	1833–1881	1833–1847 (patchy)	PRONI	MIC.1D/68
	1864–1900	1866–1900		UHF	
Antrim	Jan 19 1874–Dec 3 1880			NLI	Pos. 5472
(Down and Connor)	1873–1881			PRONI	MIC.1D/68
	1873–1900	1873–1900		UHF	
Armoy	Apr 23 1848–Mar 10 1872	May 18 1848–Jan 7 1872		NLI	Pos. 5473
(Down and Connor)	Oct 12 1873–Dec 23 1880	Nov 29 1973–Oct 24 1880			
	1848–1880	1848–1882		PRONI	MIC.1D/69
	1872–1900	1872–1900		UHF	
Ballintoy	Apr 14 1872–Nov 6 1880	May 20 1872–Mar 27 1879		NLI	Pos. 5473
(Down and Connor)	1872–1882	1872–1882		PRONI	MIC.1D/69
	1872–1900	1872–1900		UHF	
Ballyclare	July 4 1869–Dec 25 1880	Feb 26 1870–Dec 29 1880		NLI	Pos. 5467
(Down and Connor)	(original and transcript)	(original and transcript)			
	1869–1881	1870–1872		PRONI	MIC.1D/63
	1869–1900	1870–1900		UHF	
Ballymoney	Mar 9 1853–Oct 15 1880	Apr 1853–June 30 1879		NLI	Pos. 5473
(Down and Connor)	1853–1882	1853–1879		PRONI	MIC.1D/69A
	1853–1900	1853–1900	1879–1887	UHF	

Parish (Diocese)	Baptisms	Marriages	Burials	Location	Reference
Blaris (Down and Connor)	See Down				
Braid (Down and Connor)	Sept 1878–Dec 22 1880	Nov 2 1878–Dec 25 1880		NLI	Pos. 5473
	1878–1881	1878–1881		PRONI	MIC.1D/69A
	1878–1881	1878–1881		UHF	
Carnlough (Down and Connor)	Aug 4 1869–Dec 18 1880	Aug 15 1869–Oct 21 1880		NLI	Pos. 5474
	1825–1880	1869–1882		PRONI	MIC.1D/70–71
	1857–1869	1869–1900		UHF	
Carrickfergus (Down and Connor)	Aug 15 1821–Nov 23 1828	Sept 21 1821–Nov 9 1828		NLI	Pos. 5472
	Dec 14 1828–Feb 9 1841	Dec 28 1828–Oct 1 1840			
	Mar 8 1852–May 12 1872	Apr 11 1852–June 3 1872			
	1852–1872	1852–1872		PRONI	MIC.1D/68, 90
	1820–1900	1821–1900		UHF	
Culfeightrin (Down and Connor)	July 3 1825–Apr 7 1834 (also a transcript)	Nov 1834–Dec 1838		NLI	Pos. 5472; with Cushendun and Ennispollan, Pos. 5473
	Dec 20 1834–Dec 26 1838	Jan 1 1839–June 9 1844			
	May 1839–Feb 5 1847	Aug 3 1845–Mar 6 1848			
	1845–Apr 17 1848	June 2 1848–Feb 27 1867			
	May 7 1848–May 15 1867	June 18 1867–Nov 14 1880			
	1825–1881	1834–1880		PRONI	MIC.1D/68, 69A
	1834–1900	1845–1900		UHF	
Cushendun (Down and Connor)	Apr 1848–Feb 24 1852	May 1 1848–Feb 24 1852		NLI	Pos. 5473
	June 8 1862–Nov 11 1880	June 15 1862–Sept 28 1880			
	1848–1852	1848–1852	1845–1852	PRONI	MIC.1D/59 A–B
	1862–1881	1862–1881			
	1834–1900	1845–1900		UHF	
Drumaul (Down and Connor)	Oct 5 1825–May 25 1832	Apr 21 1835–Oct 23 1842	Apr 21 1835–Oct 23 1842	NLI	Pos. 5474 to 1842; remainder on Pos. 5475
	May 27 1832–Aug 1835	Oct 30 1842–May 13 1854			
	Aug 30 1835–Aug 14 1842	May 16 1858–Nov 14 1867			
	Aug 23 1842–Sept 5 1854	(fragmented)			
	Aug 1855–Jan 1 1868	1871–July 4 1873			
	Sept 5 1871–May 18 1873	Oct 13 1872–Nov 11 1880			
	Jan 2 1866–Jan 1 1868				
	Feb 2 1872–Dec 26 1880				
	1825–1881	1825–1884	1837–1848	PRONI	MIC.1D/70–71
	1825–1900	1825–1900	1837–1848	UHF	
Dunean (Down and Connor)	May 16 1834–June 1844	May 16 1835–May 2 1844		NLI	Pos. 5474
	June 4 1844–Apr 13 1847	June 14 1844–Feb 20 1847			
	Sept 26 1847–Feb 3 1861	Oct 10 1847–Dec 29 1880			
	1834–1861	1835–1861		PRONI	MIC.1D/70
	1834–1900	1835–1900	UHF		
Dunloy (Down and Connor)	June 17 1860–Dec 26 1876	June 4 1877–Nov 23 1880	Apr 26 1877–Dec 24 1880	NLI	Pos. 5475
	Apr 25 1877–Nov 21 1880				
	1840–1881	1877–1881	1877–1881	PRONI MIC.	1D/71
	1860–1900	1877–1900	1877–1900	UHF	
Glenariffe (Down and Connor)	1872–1900			UHF	
Glenarm (Down and Connor)	Dec 18 1825–Mar 6 1859				
	June 7 1857–Dec 8 1862 (transcript)	Oct 6 1825–Mar 6 1859	Jan 24 1931–May 15 1838	NLI	Pos. 5475
		May 3 1859–Dec 30 1880			
	June 6 1865–Dec 26 1880 (transcript)				

Parish (Diocese)	Baptisms	Marriages	Burials	Location	Reference
Glenarm	1865–1880	1825–1880	1831–1838	PRONI	MIC.1D/71
(Down and Connor)	1859–1900		UHF		
Glenavy and Killead	May 30 1849–Dec 31 1880	Mar 25 1848–Dec 31 1880		NLI	Pos. 5467
(Down and Connor)	1849–1881	1848–1883		PRONI	MIC.1D/63
	1849–1900	1848–1900		UHF	
Glenravel	June 25 1825–1832	June 25 1825–1832	June 25 1825–1832	NLI	Pos. 5474
(Down and Connor)	July 3 1825–Sept 30 1856	(also a transcript)	July 8 1832–Sept 13 1841		
	July 8 1832–Sept 13 1841	July 8 1832–Sept 13 1841			
	Feb 15 1864–July 21 1878	Nov 19 1864–Jan 11 1869			
	Oct 10 1878–Dec 24 1880	Oct 20 1878–Nov 25 1880			
	1825–1856	1825–1841	1825–1841	PRONI	MIC.1D/70
	1864–1881	1864–1869	1864–1869		
		1878–1882			
	1825–1881	1825–1882	1825–1869	UHF	
Greencastle	Mar 21 1854–Dec 25 1880	Apr 3 1854–Oct 21 1880		NLI	Pos. 5475
(Down and Connor)	1854–1881	1854–1881		PRONI	MIC.1D/71
	1854–1900	1854–1900		UHF	
Hannastown, Rock	Oct 7 1877–Dec 30 1880	Oct 13 1877–Nov 7 1880		NLI	Pos. 5467
and Derriaghy	1877–1880	1877–1880		PRONI	MIC.1D/63
(Down and Connor)	1848–1900	1848–1900		UHF	
Kirkinriola	1848–Dec 25 1880	Jan 22 1847–Nov 27 1880		NLI	Pos. 5473
(Down and Connor)	Jan 30 1866–Dec 25 1880	Jan 10 1840–July 28 1842			
	(transcript)	Dec 28 1847–Nov 27 1880			
		(transcripts)			
	1848–1881	1840–1842		PRONI	MIC.1D/69A
		1847–1882			
	1836–1900	1836–1842	1852–1887	UHF	
		1847–1900			
Larne	Aug 15 1821–Nov 23 1828	Sept 21 1821–Nov 9 1828		NLI	Pos. 5472
(Down and Connor)	Dec 14 1828–Feb 9 1841	Dec 28 1828–Oct 1 1840			
	Mar 8 1852–May 12 1872	Apr 11 1852–June 3 1872			
	1821–1883	1821–1883		PRONI	MIC.1D/68, 90
	1820–1900	1821–1900		UHF	
Larne: St. Mac Nissi	1807–1900	1828–1900		UHF	
(Down and Connor)					
Layde	Apr 8 1838–Mar 31 1844	July 1 1837–May 26 1844		NLI	Pos. 5472
(Down and Connor)	Kan 12 1858–July 4 1871	Mar 25 1860–Mar 15 1872			
	Apr 23 1871–Nov 28 1880	Apr 27 1872–Nov 14 1880			
	1838–1844	1837–1844		PRONI	MIC.1D/68
	1858–1881	1860–1881			
	1858–1900	1860–1900		UHF	
Loughguile	May 13 1845–June 1 1868	May 4 1845–May 14 1868		NLI	Pos. 5473
(Down and Connor)	June 21 1868–Nov 1 1869	June 5 1868–Nov 2 1869			
	Nov 10 1869–Dec 20 1880				
	1845–1881	1845–1869		PRONI	MIC.1D/69A
	1825–1900	1825–1900		UHF	
Portglenone	Jan 14 1864–Nov 28 1880	Feb 13 1864–Sept 30 1880		NLI	Pos. 5475
(Down and Connor)	1864–1881	1864–1882		PRONI	MIC.1D/71
		1864–1900		UHF	
Portrush	July 7 1844–Dec 23 1880	May 14 1848–Nov 4 1880		NLI	Pos. 5476
(Down and Connor)		(also a transcript)			
	1844–1881	1848–1889		PRONI	MIC.1D/72

Parish (Diocese)	Baptisms	Marriages	Burials	Location	Reference
Ramoan	Oct 21 1838–Dec 14 1880	Oct 13 1838–Sept 16 1880		NLI	Pos. 5476
(Down and Connor)	1838–1881	1838–1883		PRONI	MIC.1D/72
	1838–1900	1838–1900		UHF	
Rasharkin	Aug 16 1848–Nov 13 1880	July 20 1848–Dec 4 1880		NLI	Pos. 5476
(Down and Connor)	1848–1881	1848–1881		PRONI MIC.	1D/72
	1848–1900	1847–1900		UHF	
Rathlin Island	1856–1880	1857–1880		PRONI	MIC.1D/92
(Down and Connor)	1856–1900	1857–1900		UHF	

Armagh

Parish (Diocese)	Baptisms	Marriages	Burials	Location	Reference
Armagh (Armagh)	July 15 1796–Oct 29 1810	Jan 4 1802–May 13 1803		NLI	Pos. 5590;
	Nov 1810–Nov 3 1835	Jan 2 1817–Nov 11 1835			Baptisms
	Nov 3 1835–Dec 7 1843	Nov 17 1835–Dec 25 1880			from 1843
	Dec 6 1843–May 8 1861				Pos. 5591
	May 12 1861–May 17 1870				
	May 15 1870–Dec 30 1880				
	1796–1880	1802–1803		PRONI	MIC.1D/41–42
		1806–1810			
		1816–1881			
	1796–1900	1802–1809		AA	
		1816–1823			
		1835–1900			

Parish (Diocese)	Baptisms	Marriages	Burials	Location	Reference
Ballymacnab (Armagh)	Jan 6 1844–Aug 21 1870 Aug 20 1870–Dec 24 1880	Jan 16 1844–Dec 16 1880		NLI	Pos. 5586
	1844–1881	1944–1880		PRONI	MIC.1D/37–38
	1820–1900	1844–1900		AA	
Ballymore and Mullaghbrack (Armagh)	Oct 9 1843–May 27 1853 Oct 7 1853–Nov 20 1856 June 5 1859–Dec 12 1880	Oct 21 1843–Oct 1853 Oct 16 1853–Nov 23 1856 July 24 1859–Nov 12 1880		NLI	Pos. 5586
	1843–1865	1843–1865		PRONI	MIC.1D/37
	1859–1880	1859–1880			
	1798–1802	1831 1900		AA	
	1831–1900				
	See NLI			LDS	0926031
Clonfeacle (Armagh)	See Tyrone				
Creggan Lower (Armagh)	Feb 14 1845–Dec 30 1880	Feb 13 1845–Nov 27 1880		NLI	Pos. 5589
	1845–1880	1845–1881		PRONI	MIC.1D/40
	1845–1900	1845–1900		AA	
	See NLI			LDS	0926034
Creggan Upper (Armagh)	Aug 5 1796–Jan 19 1803 Sept 23 1812–Mar 28 1822 Apr 2 1822–May 29 1829 May 26 1845–May 31 1871 Jan 2 1870–Dec 28 1880	Aug 8 1796–Feb 16 1803 Dec 18 1812–Mar 22 1822 Apr 8 1822–July 24 1829 May 8 1845–Mar 1 1870 May 13 1871–Nov 26 1880		NLI	Pos. 5592
	1796–1803	1796–1803		PRONI	MIC.1D/43
	1812–1829	1812–1829			
	1845–1881	1845–1881			
	1796–1803	1796–1803		AA	
	1812–1900	1812–1900			
Derrynoose (Armagh)	Feb 1 1835–Jan 29 1837 Dec 1846–Jan 28 1866 Feb 1 1866–Dec 30 1880	July 17 1846–Jan 31–1875 Feb 8 1875–Dec 9 1880	July 22 1846–Apr 1851	NLI	Pos. 5589
	1835–1837	1846–1881	1846–1851	PRONI	MIC.1D/40
	1846–1881				
	1814–1819	1808–1814	1823–1851	AA	
	1823–1830	1823–1833			
	1832–1837	1846–1900			
	1846–1900				
	See NLI			LDS	1279356 item 1
Dromintee (Armagh)	June 7 1853–Aug 31 1879	Nov 8 1853–Dec 13 1877		NLI	Pos. 5590
	1853–1879	1853–1877		PRONI	MIC.1D/41
	1853–1900	1853–1877			
		1883 1884		AA	
		1887–1900			
Drumcree (Armagh)	Jan 1 1844–June 30 1864 June 17 1864–Dec 31 1880	Feb 9 1844–Nov 23 1863 July 23 1864–Nov 27 1880	May 26–Dec 22 1863 June 24 1864–Dec 30 1880	NLI	Pos. 5586
	1844–1881 (some gaps)	1844–1881 (some gaps)	1863–1880	PRONI	MIC.1D/37; C.R.2/8
	1844–1899	1844–1900	1863–1900	AA	
Dungannon (Armagh)	See Tyrone				
Eglish (Armagh)	Jan 21 1862–Nov 4 1880	Jan 27 1862–Nov 5 1880		NLI	Pos. 5585
	1862–1881	1862–1882		PRONI	MIC.1D/36

Parish (Diocese)	Baptisms	Marriages	Burials	Location	Reference
Eglish (Armagh)	1862–1900	1862–1900	1877–1900	AA	
	1862–1900	1862–1900	1877–1900	IW	
Faughart (Armagh)	Apr 16 1851–Dec 23 1880 (indexed)	Apr 21 1851–Nov 24 1880		NLI	Pos. 5596
	1861–1881 (indexed)	1851–1882		PRONI	MIC.1D/47
	1851–1896	indexed 1851–1900			
	1851–1900	1851–1900		AA	
	Apr 16 1851–Dec 23 1880 (indexed)	Apr 21 1851–Nov 24 1880		LDS	0926040 item 1–5
Forkhill (Armagh)	Jan 1 1845–Apr 29 1879	Jan 12 1844–Dec 29 1880		NLI	Pos. 5587
	1845–1879	1844–1878		PRONI	MIC.1D/38
	1845–1900	1844–1900		AA	
	See NLI			LDS	0926041 item 1–2
Killeavy Lower (Armagh)	Jan 4 1835–Jan 27 1860	Jan 6 1835–Jan 26 1860	Aug 1858–Jan 30 1860	NLI	Pos. 5588
	Jan 1 1860–Dec 29 1880	Jan 15 1860–Dec 29 1862	Jan 9 1860–Dec 24 1862		
		May 21 1874–Nov 29 1878			
	1835–1881	1835–1862	1858–1862	PRONI	MIC.1D/39
		1868–1869			
		1874–1878			
	1835–1900	1835–1862			
		1868–1900		AA	
	See NLI			LDS	0926042
Killeavy Upper (Armagh)	Oct 22 1832–Oct 31 1868	Nov 4 1832–Oct 13 1868		NLI	Pos. 5588
	Nov 7 1868–Dec 31 1880	Dec 30 1868–Dec 29 1880			
	1832–1880	1832–1882		PRONI	MIC.1D/39
	1832–1900	1832–1900		AA	
	See NLI	See NLI	See NLI	LDS	0926042
Kilmore (Armagh)	Jan 7 1845–Dec 19 1880	Jan 3 1845–Dec 31 1880		NLI	Pos. 5587
	1845–1881	1845–1881		PRONI	MIC.1D/38
	1845–1900	1845–1900		AA	
Loughgall and Tartaraghan	Jan 1835–Aug 29 1852	Aug 20 1833–Jan 5 1854		NLI	Pos. 5587
	Oct 8 1854–May 2 1858	Feb 8 1860–Nov 22 1880			
	July 12–Dec 27 1857				
	Sept 18 1859–Dec 28 1880				
	1835–1881	1833–1880		PRONI	MIC.1D/38
	1834–1900	1833–1900		AA	
Loughgilly (Armagh)	May 17 1825–Dec 31 1844	Feb 12 1825–Nov 29 1844		NLI	Pos. 5587
	Feb 4 1849–Dec 19 1880	Feb 18 1849–Dec 20 1880			
	1825–1844	1825–1844		PRONI	MIC.1D/38
	1849–1881	1849–1881			
	1825–1900	1825–1900		AA	
Magheralinn (Dromore)	See Down				
Newry (Dromore)	Sept 18 1818–Nov 4 1819	May 16 1820–May 1825	Nov 6 1818–Apr 28 1819	NLI	Pos. 5501
	May 4 1820–July 1825	Aug 21 1825–Oct 23 1826	1820–July 17 1820		1818–26;
	Aug 21 1825–Sept 24 1826	Nov 6 1826–Jan 15 1851	Sept 11 1825–Oct 7 1826		Pos. 5502
	Oct 1826–May 1843	Jan 21 1851–Dec 29 1880	Nov 8 1826–May 31 1862		1826–80;
	May 1843–Dec 1880				Pos. 5503
	Index from 1858				Index
	1818–1884 (indexed from 1858)	1820–1917	1818–1862	PRONI	MIC.1D/26–28

Parish (Diocese)	Baptisms	Marriages	Burials	Location	Reference
Newry (Dromore)	1818–1900	1820–1900	1818–1900	UHF	
	See NLI			LDS	0926087
Seagoe (Dromore)	Sept 1836–Feb 25 1870	Oct 16 1836–Feb 5 1860	Apr 13 1837–Jan 27 1860	NLI	Pos. 5498
	Mar 3 1870–Dec 26 1880	Feb 10 1860–Nov 18 1880	Feb 16 1860–Dec 5 1880		
	1836–1881	18367–1881	1837–1880	PRONI	MIC.1D/23–24
	1836–1900	1836–1900		AA	
	See NLI			LDS	0926088
Shankill (Dromore)	Sept 13 1822–Dec 30 1865 (modern transcript with gaps)	Jan 19 1866–Dec 28 1880	Jan 5 1866–Dec 27 1880	NLI	Pos. 5498
	Jan 1 1866–Dec 31 1880				
	1822–1881	1866–1881	1866–1881	PRONI	MIC.1D/23
	1822–1900	1822–1900	1825–1900	AA	
	See NLI			LDS	0926089
Tynan (Armagh)	June 2 1822–Aug 11 1834	June 6 1822–Oct 26 1834		NLI	Pos. 5589
	Aug 12 1838–July 25 1842	June 22 1845–Oct 18 1877			
	May 17 1845–Sept 2 1880				
	1822–1834	1822–1834		PRONI	MIC.1D/40
	1838–1842	1845–1877			
	1845–1884				
	1822–1900	1822–1834		AA	
		1836			
		1888–1900		AA	
	See NLI			LDS	09799710 item 6–8

Belfast
All Down and Connor diocese

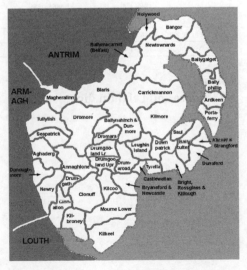

Parish	Baptisms	Marriages	Burials	Location	Reference
Ballymacarrett	Oct 11 1841–Oct 7 1865	Oct 8 1841–May 7 1865		NLI	Pos. 5469
	Nov 5 1865–Dec 29 1880	Oct 12 1865–Dec 30 1880			
	1841–1888	1841–1888		PRONI	MIC.1D/65

Parish	Baptisms	Marriages	Burials	Location	Reference
Holy Cross	Sept 20 1868–Dec 31 1880	Sept 12 1868–Dec 25 1880		NLI	Pos. 5469
	1868–1881	1868–1881		PRONI	MIC.1D/65
	1834–1900	1868–1900		UHF	
Holy Family	1869–1900	1895–1900		UHF	
	1888–1900	1894–1900		UHF	
Sacred Heart	1849–1900	1890–1900		UHF	
St. Brigid's	1809–1900	1891–1900		UHF	
St. Joseph's	Dec 22 1872–Dec 27 1880	Sept 24 1872–Dec 1 1880		NLI	Pos. 5471
	1872–1881	1872–1881		PRONI	MIC.1D/67
	1809–1900	1872–1900		UHF	
St. Malachy's	May 10 1858–Dec 28 1880	June 9 1858–Dec 26 1880		NLI	Pos. 5468
	Jan 1 1870–Dec 28 1880	(many pages mutilated)			
	(transcript)				
	1858–1881	1858–1881		PRONI	MIC.1D/64
	1858–1900	1858–1900		UHF	
St. Mary's	Feb 18 1867–Sept 21 1876	Feb 18 1867–Dec 27 1880		NLI	Pos. 5471
	Sept 22 1876–Dec 31 1880				
	1867–1881	1867–1881		PRONI	MIC.1D/67
	[1774]–1900	1867–1900		UHF	
St. Mathew's	1841–1900	1841–1900		UHF	
St. Paul's	1887–	1887–		LC	
	1824–1900	1887–1900		UHF	
St. Peter's	Oct 31 1866–May 8 1871	Oct 22 1866–Dec 29 1880		NLI	Pos. 5468;
	May 14 1871–Feb 17 1875				Pos. 5469
	Feb 22 1875–Aug 2 1879				
	Aug 2 1879–Dec 29 1880				
	1866–1881	1866–1881		PRONI	MIC.1D/64–65
	[1780]–1900	1866–1900		UHF	
St. Vincent de Paul	1874–1900	1896–1900		UHF	
Union Workhouse	1884–1900			UHF	

Carlow
All Kildare and Leighlin diocese

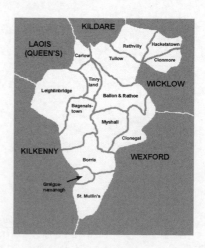

Parish	Baptisms	Marriages	Burials	Location	Reference
Ballon and Rathoe	Jan 2 1785–Sept 10 1795	Aug 10 1782–Dec 10 1795	Aug 9 1825–Dec 6 1834	NLI	Pos. 4189
	July 2 1816–Dec 26 1830	Jan 8 1820–Dec 14 1825	Jan 15 1861–Dec 28 1871		
	Jan 9 1820–Feb 14 1825	Aug 10 1816–Nov 26 1880			
	(not a duplicate)				
	Jan 6 1831–Dec 27 1867				
	1781–1899	1782–1899		CGP	
Borris	May 2 1782–Dec 23 1813	Jan 26 1782–Dec 4 1813		NLI	Pos. 4196
	Feb 2 1825–Mar 15 1840	Feb 8 1825–Mar 3 1840			
	Mar 22 1840–Dec 30 1855	Apr 28 1840–Nov 23 1868			
	Jan 1 1856–Dec 30 1876	Feb 2 1869–Nov 27 1880			
	Jan 7 1877–Dec 25 1880				
	See NLI			LDS	0926107
	1782–1899	1782–1899		CGP	
Carlow	June 1774–Jan 1789 (gaps)	Nov 8 1769–Aug 20 1786		NLI	Pos. 4193
	Dec 7–Dec 17 1793	1791 (some)			
	Jan 19 1794–Dec 17 1795	1794 (some)			
	Jan 1799–May 1804	Jan 1 1820–June 17 1845			
	Jan 10–Apr 15 1806	Jan 22 1845–Apr 14 1856			
	Jan 2–Feb 5 1807	May 10 1856–Nov 22 1880			
	Jan 1–May 8 1809				
	Jan 5–12 1811				
	1820–June 1845				
	Jan 1 1845–1880				
	Index 1834–49				
	1774–1899	1769–1899		CGP	
	See NLI			LDS	0926119
					item 1–2
Clonegal	Jan 7 1833–Nov 27 1842	Feb 14 1833–May 20 1871		NLI	Pos. 4197
	Nov 27 1842–Dec 5 1852	May 25 1871–Nov 16 1880			
	Dec 5 1852–Mar 29 1868				
	Apr 2 1868–Apr 30 1871				
	(all transcripts)				
	June 5 1871–Nov 16 1880				
	(original)				
	See NLI			LDS 0926110	
	1833–1899	1833–1899		CGP	
	1833–1900	1833–1871		WFHC	
Clonmore	Nov 23 1819–Apr 9 1833	Feb 10 1813–Feb 19 1833		NLI	Pos. 4198
	Apr 7 1833–Feb 26 1860	May 4 1833–Feb 19 1860			
	Mar 4 1860–Dec 11 1880	May 16 1860–Dec 11 1880			
	1819–1900	1819–1827			
		1833–1900		WFHC	
	1813–1899	1819–1899	1861–1899	CGP	
Dunleckney	Jan 1 1820–June 27 1841	Jan 8 1820–June 26 1841		NLI	Pos. 4195
	July 1 1841–Dec 25 1857	July 8 1841–Nov 28 1857			
	Jan 3 1858–Nov 27 1880	Jan 19 1858–Nov 27 1880			
	See NLI			LDS	0926113
	1820–1899	1820–1899		CGP	
Graiguenamanagh	See Kilkenny				

Parish	Baptisms	Marriages	Burials	Location	Reference
Hacketstown	1815–20 (a few entries)	Aug 31 1820–Dec 1 1827		NLI	Pos. 4191
	Aug 29 1820–Apr 20 1823	Mar 3 1829–Nov 28 1863			
	July 10 1826–Sept 7 1826	Nov 20 1861–Sept 25 1870			
	Oct 14 1827–Mar 23 1877	Feb 2 1877–Aug 1 1878			
	Jan 4 1862–Mar 23 1878	May 9 1878–Nov 25 1880			
	Mar 10 1878–Dec 26 1879				
	See NLI			LDS	0926115 item 1
	1827–1899	1828–1899		CGP	
	1827–1900	1827–1900		WFHC	
Leighlinbridge	Jan 1 1783–Oct 22 1786	Feb 9 1783–Jan 14 1788		NLI	Pos. 4195
	Dec 1 1819–June 26 1827	Jan 12 1820–Feb 27 1827			
	July 6 1827–Nov 16 1844	July 12 1827–Nov 22 1880			
	Nov 17 1844–Sept 29 1867				
	Jan 2 1859–Dec 26 1880				
	1783–1900	1783–1899	1898–1899	CGP	
	See NLI			LDS	1363869
Myshall	Feb 11 1822–May 3 1846	Sept 17 1822–Jan 30 1845		NLI	Pos. 4198
	Oct 25 1846–Dec 25 1880	(pages missing and mutilated)			
		Feb 17 1846–Nov 27 1880			
	See NLI			LDS	0926123
	1846–1899	1846–1899		CGP	
Rathvilly	Oct 19 1797–Jan 15 1813	Oct 5 1800–Feb 13 1812		NLI	Pos. 4189
	June 29 1813–Apr 25 1842	June 29 1813–Nov 27 1880			
	Apr 25 1842–Dec 12 1880				
	1797–1887	1797–1900		WFHC	
	1797–1899	1800–1899	1844–1899	CGP	
St. Mullins	May 8 1796–Sept 28 1800	June 20 1796–Feb 5 1807		NLI	Pos. 4196
	Feb 1 1801–Apr 16 1807	Jan 8 1808–May 20 1809			
	Sept 4 1807–Mar 3 1810	Jan 24 1820–June 10 1832			
	Jan 19 1812–Apr 16 1814	Oct 25 1807–Mar (?) 8 1813			
	Feb 8 1816–Mar (?) 25 1816	Aug 10 1832–Nov 30 1871			
	Jan 6 1820–July 30 1832	Feb 6 1872–Nov 25 1880			
	Aug 10 1832–Nov 30 1871				
	Jan 4 1872–Dec 30 1880				
	1796–1899	1796–1899	1875–1899	CGP	
Tinryland	Mar 28 1813–May 24 1833	June 20 1813–Feb 28 1843		NLI	Pos. 4192
	June 2 1833–Dec 20 1857	Apr 25 1843–Nov 26 1857			
	Jan 6 1858–Nov 27 1880	Jan 21 1858–Nov 27 1880			
	1813–1899	1813–1899	1898–1899	CGP	
Tullow	Aug 13 1763–Jan 10 1781	May 5 7 1775–Feb 20 1776		NLI	Pos. 4194
	Jan 19 1798–Jan 1 1802	(2 entries for 1777)			
	June 5 1807–July 4 1831 (?)	Jan 18 1799–Feb 27 1800			
	Aug 23 1830–Apr 18 1858	June 19 1807–May 20 1830			
	Apr 22 1858–Oct 9 1876	(transcript many gaps)			
	Oct 10 1876–Dec 21 1880	Nov (?) 20 1830–Feb 20 1860			
		Apr 30 1860–Nov 18 1880			
	1748–1899	1748–1899	1767–1775		
			1861–1899	CGP	

Cavan

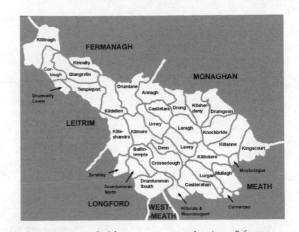

Parish (Diocese)	Baptisms	Marriages	Burials	Location	Reference
Annagh (Kilmore)	Nov 12 1845–Oct 25 1864 (Anna East) Jan 1849–Sept 1875 (Anna West) Oct 3 1875–Dec 29 1880	July 1847–Dec 1880 (Anna East) Nov 1864–Aug 1899 (Anna West)		NLI	Pos. 7505, 5342
	1875–1881			PRONI	MIC.1D/75
	1845–1920	184/–1900		CHGC	
Ballintemple (Kilmore)	Oct 16 1862–Dec 26 1880	Oct 20 1862–Nov 20 1880		NLI	Pos. 5343
	1862–1881	1862–1881		PRONI	MIC.1D/76
	1862–1899	1862–1899		CHGC	
Carnaross (Meath)	See Meath				
Castlerahan and Munterconnaught (Kilmore)	Feb 6 1752–July 1771 Feb 3 1773–Nov 4 1776 Nov 6 1814–Aug 16 1820 Oct 26 1828–May 2 1841 Aug 1854–Feb 17 1879	Sept 5 1751–June 8 1771 Feb 4 1773–Feb 26 1775 Nov 20 1814–June 7 1820 May 17 1832–Nov 27 1841 Aug 7 1855–Nov 26 1878	Sept 1751–June 1758 Dec 1761–July 1769 Feb 1773–Oct 1775 Dec 1814–Oct 1820 May 26 1832–Oct 24 1841	NLI	Pos. 5348
	1752–1771 1773–1776 1814–1820 1828–1841 1854–1879	1751–1771 1773–1775 1814–1820 1832–1841 1855–1878	1751–1758 1761–1769 1773–1775 1814–1820 1832–1841	PRONI	MIC.1D/81
	1752–1920	1752–1920	1752–1899	CHGC	
Castletara (Kilmore)	June 26 1763–June 12 1809 Apr 19 1862–Dec 26 1880	June 12 1763–Apr 29 1793 Oct 28 1808–June 11 1809		NLI	Pos. 5350, 6430
	1763–1809 1862–1881	1763–1793 1808–1809		PRONI	MIC.1D/83–84
	1763–1920	1763–1920		CHGC	
Corlough (Kilmore)	Feb 12 1877–Dec 16 1880	Feb 12 1877–Oct 21 1880	Feb 16 1877–Dec 19 1880	NLI	Pos. 5346
	1877–1881	1877–1882	1877–1881	PRONI	MIC.1D/79
	1877–1911	1877–1911		CHGC	
	See NLI			LDS	0926129 item 3
Crosserlough (Kilmore)	Oct 1843–Feb 17 1876 Dec 1866–Dec 13 1880 Apr 2 1876–Aug 6 1880	Dec 1866–Dec 13 1880 Oct 10 1868–Nov 27 1880	Dec 1866–Dec 13 1880	NLI	Pos. 5344
	1843–1881	1843–1881	1843–1876	PRONI	MIC.1D/77
	1843–1920	1843–1920	1843–1899	CHGC	
	See NLI			LDS	0926130

Parish (Diocese)	Baptisms	Marriages	Burials	Location	Reference
Denn (Kilmore)	Oct 19 1856–Jan 16 1874 (transcript—many gaps)	Oct 20 1856–Oct 28 1858		NLI	Pos. 5350
	1856–1874 (gaps)	1856–1858		PRONI	MIC.1D/83
	1856–1899	1856–1899		CHGC	
Drumgoon (Kilmore)	Feb 22 1829–July 25 1872			NLI	Pos. 5348
	Oct 1 1872–Sept 12 1879				
	1829–1879	1829–1872		PRONI	MIC.1D/81
	1829–1920	1829–1920		CHGC	
Drumlane (Kilmore)	Jan 1836–Nov 20 1867 (out of order)	Sept 1 1870–Dec 8 1880		NLI	Pos. 5342
	Jan 6 1868–Dec 12 1880				
	1836–1881	1870–1880		PRONI	MIC.1D/75
	1835–1920	1835–1920		CHGC	
Drumlumman South (Ardagh and Clonmacnois)	Nov 13 1837–Aug 3 1873	Dec 2 1837–June 18 1873	Dec 21 1837–Sept 17 1869	NLI	Pos. 4236
	May 5 1875–Dec 5 1880	Feb 27 1876–Nov 30 1880	Feb 16 1876–Dec 18 1880		
	See NLI			LDS	1279229 item 7
	1837–1899	1837–1899	1837–1899	CHGC	
Drumreilly Lower (Kilmore)	See Leitrim				
Drung (Kilmore). See also Kilsherdany	1847–1883			PRONI	C.R.2/10
	1847–1920			CHGC	
Glangevlin (Kilmore)	Mar 2 1867–Dec 29 1880	Jan 28 1867–Nov 15 1880		NLI	Pos. 5345
	1867–1881	1867–1881		PRONI	MIC.1D/78
	1867–1899	1867–1920		CHGC	
	See NLI			LDS	0979703 item 5
Kilbride and Mountnugent	See Meath				
Kildallen (Kilmore)	Apr 15 1867–Dec 31 1880	Jan 1 1867–Dec 9 1880		NLI	Pos. 5345
	1867–1881	1867–1881		PRONI	MIC.1D/78
	1867–1900	1867–1900		CHGC	
	Apr 15 1867–Dec 31 1880	Jan 1 1867–Dec 9 1880		LDS	0979703 item 2
Killanne (Kilmore)	Jan 28 1835–Nov 20 1849	Jan 12 1835–Feb 12 1850		NLI	Pos. 5349
	Jan 13 1868–Nov 19 1880	Jan 28 1868–Sept 22 1880			
	1835–1849	1835–1850		PRONI	MIC1D./82
	1868–1880	1868–1880			
	See NLI			LDS	0926132 item 2
	1835–1920	1835–1920		CHGC	
Killeshandra (Kilmore)	Jan 4 1835–Oct 14 1840	Jan 7 1835–Sept 1 1840		NLI	Pos. 5345/6
	Dec 24 1840–Aug 24 1844	Aug 19 1849–May 20 1852			
	Mar 15 1845–July 17 1852	Aug 1 1853–Oct 15 1868			
	Aug 1 1853–Oct 15 1868	Sept 28 1868–Nov 15 1880			
	Oct 3 1868–Dec 31 1880				
	1835–1880	1835–1840		PRONI	MIC.1D/78–79
		1849–1881			
	See NLI			LDS	099703 item 7
	1835–1920	1835–1920	1835–1899	CHGC	
Killinagh (Kilmore)	Apr 1 1869–Dec 31 1880	June 28 1869–Nov 28 1880	Feb 21 1875–Dec 27 1880	NLI	Pos. 5350
	1869–1881	1869–1881	1875–1881	PRONI	MIC.1D/83
	1860–1900	1860–1900	1875–1899	CHGC	

Parish (Diocese)	Baptisms	Marriages	Burials	Location	Reference
Killinkere and Mullagh (Kilmore)	May 27 1766–Oct 19 1790	Dec 23 1766–Aug 29 1789		NLI	Pos. 5349
	Jan 1 1842–Apr 11 1862	Jan 22 1842–Nov 32 1861			
	Mar 5 1864–Dec 12 1880	June 4 1864–Nov 19 1880			
	1766–1790	1766–1789		PRONI	MIC.1D/82
	1842–1861	1842–1861			
	1864–1880	1864–1880			
	1766–1920	1766–1920	1842–1899 Mullagh	CHGC	
Kilmore (Kilmore)	May 1 1859–Dec 31 1880	May 1 1859–Dec 31 1880	May 1 1859–Dec 31 1880	NLI	Pos. 5343
	1859–1881	1859–1881	1859–1881	PRONI	MIC.1D/76
	1859–1909	1859–1909	1859–1909	CHGC	
Kilsherdany (Kilmore)	June 26 1803–Nov 26 1814	July 10 1803–Jan 18 1814		NLI	Pos. 5342
	Nov 19 1826–Apr 29 1849	Jan 12–May 20 1835			
	Oct 4 1855–Jan 10 1860	1843–Apr 29 1849			
	Oct 1 1855–Aug 16 1857				
	1803–1814	1803–1814		PRONI	MIC.1D/48
	1826–1849	1835			
	1855–1860	1843–1849			
	1855–1857				
	1803–1899	1803–1899		CHGC	
Kingscourt (Meath)	Oct 16 1838–Aug 13 1854	Aug 15 1838–May 27 1861	Sept 1846–May 30 1858	NLI	Pos. 4183
	Jan 1 1864–Dec 31 1880				
	Oct 16 1838–Aug 13 1854	Aug 15 1838–May 27 1861	Sept 1846–May 30 1858	LDS	0926175
	Jan 1 1864–Dec 31 1880				
	1838–1920	1838–1920		CHGC	
Kinnally (Kilmore)	Dec 11 1835–Mar 28 1853	Dec 3 1835–Apr 29 1853	Apr 5 1853–Mar 7 1857	NLI	Pos. 5346
	Apr 5 1853–Mar 7 1857	Apr 5 1853–Mar 7 1857			
	Mar 16 1857–Dec 17 1880				
	1835–1881	1835–1857	1853–1857	PRONI	MIC.1D/79
	1835–1899	1835–1900	1852–1857	CHGC	
Knockbride (Kilmore)	May 15 1835–Aug 19 1860	Jan 15 1835–Aug 20 1860	Jan 11 1835–1860	NLI	Pos. 5349
	Sept 7 1860–May 20 1879	Sept 12 1860–Jan 25 1877	Sept 10 1860–Mar 6 1875		
	1835–1879	1835–1879	1835–1875	PRONI	MIC.1D/82
	See NLI			LDS	0926133 item 3
	1835–1920	1835–1920		CHGC	
Laragh (Kilmore)	May 2 1876–Dec 1 1880			NLI	Pos. 5342
	1876–1881			PRONI	MIC.1D/75
	1876–1920	1835–1920		CHGC	
Lavey (Kilmore)	Jan 12 1867–Sept 19 1880			NLI	Pos. 5342
	1867–1881			PRONI	MIC.1D/75
	1867–1899	1867–1899		CHGC	
Lurgan (Kilmore)	Jan 6 1755–Aug 1 1795	Feb 1755–Aug 29 1770	Nov 12 1821–Oct 5 1840	NLI	Pos. 5347
	(very patchy)	Jan 14 1773–Sept 6 1780	Oct 1 1840–Mar 30 1855		
	Nov 1 1821–Sept 30 1840	Nov 21 1821–Sept 23 1840			
	Oct 10 1840–Dec 31 1875	Oct 10 1840–Nov 27 1875			
	Jan 4 1876–Dec 24 1880				
	1755–1795 (gaps)	1855–1770		PRONI	MIC.1D/80–81
	1821–1881	1773–1780			
	1821–1875	1821–1855			
	1755–1899	1755–1920		CHGC	
	See NLI			LDS	0926134

Parish (Diocese)	Baptisms	Marriages	Burials	Location	Reference
Moybologue	See Meath				
Mullagh (Kilmore)	June 29 1842–Feb 78 1872	June 29 1842–July 6 1872	Sept 29 1842–Feb 3 1857	NLI	Pos. 5347
	1760–1790	1766–1789	1842–1857	PRONI	MIC.1D/80, 82
	1842–1872	1842–1872			
Mullahoran (Ardagh and Clonmacnois)	Jan 21 1859–Dec 26 1880	Jan 31 1859–Dec 6 1880	Feb 7 1859–Feb 26 1875	NLI	Pos. 4237
	1859–1902	1859–1902	1859–1875; 1925–1937	LDS	1279229 item 10
	1859–1902	1859–1902	1859–1937	CHGC	
Scrabby (Ardagh and Clonmacnois)	See Longford				
Templeport (Kilmore)	Sept 4 1836–July 14 1870	Nov 18 1836–July 4 1870	Feb 26 1827–Dec 1845	NLI	Pos. 5345
	July 26 1870–Dec 24 1880	Sept 15 1870–Oct 16 1880	July 26 1870–Dec 16 1880		
	1836–1880	1836–1882	1827–1845; 1870–1880	PRONI	MIC.1D/78
	1836–1904	1836–1904	1827–1899	CHGC	
	See NLI			LDS	0979703 item 6
Urney (Kilmore)	July 6 1812–Dec 12 1829	July 19 1812–Feb 23 1830		NLI	Pos. 5342/3
	Dec 1829–July 24 1859	Feb 23 1830–Aug 3 1859			
	Jan 1 1860–Dec 30 1880	Sept 14 1859–Nov 27 1880			
	1812–1881	1812–1880		PRONI	MIC.1D/75–76
	1812–1920	1812–1920		CHGC	

Clare

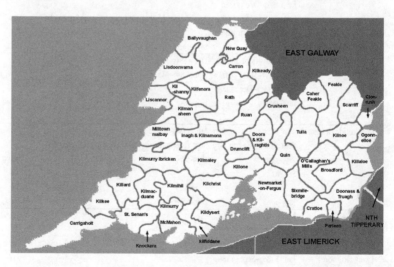

Parish (Diocese)	Baptisms	Marriages	Burials	Location	Reference
Ballyvaughan (Galway)	Sept 1 1854–July 29 1876			NLI	Pos. 2440
	Aug 18 1876–Dec 31 1880				
	1854–1900	Not specified		CHGC	
	1854–1900			online	Clare Co. Library
Broadford (Killaloe)	Jan 19 1844–Dec 19 1880	Feb 10 1844–Nov 27 1880		NLI	Pos. 2476
	1845–1900	Not specified		CHGC	
	1844–1880	1844–1880		LDS	0979694 item 3
Caher Feakle (Killaloe)	Feb 16 1842–Mar 27 1861	Jan 16 1842–Feb 12 1861		NLI	Pos. 2487
	Mar 25 1861–Jan 28 1873	Nov 15 1862–July 28 1880			
	Feb 4 1873–Dec 26 1880				

Parish (Diocese)	Baptisms	Marriages	Burials	Location	Reference
Caher Feakle (Killaloe)	1842–1900	Not specified		CHGC	
Carrigaholt (Killaloe)	Feb 8 1853–Mar 17 1878	Jan 12 1852–Mar 17 1878		NLI	Pos. 2485
	Feb 19 1878–Dec 15 1880	Mar 5 1878–Nov 15 1880			
	1853–1900	Not specified		CHGC	
	Feb 8 1853–Mar 17 1878	Jan 12 1852–Mar 17 1878			
	Feb 19 1878–Dec	Mar 5 1878–Nov		LDS	0926099
Carron (Galway)	Oct 26 1853–Dec 25 1880	Nov 24 1856–June 22 1880		NLI	Pos. 2440
	1854–1900	Not specified		CHGC	
	Oct 26 1853–Dec 25 1880	Nov 24 1856–June 22 1880		LDS	0926063
Clonrush (Killaloe)	July 1846–Mar 3 1880	Jan 22 1846–Feb 10 1880		NLI	Pos. 2476
	1846–1900	Not specified		CHGC	
	July 1846–Mar 3 1880	Jan 22 1846–Feb 10 1880		LDS	0926093 item 1
Cratloe (Limerick)	Nov 26 1802–Dec 30 1856	Jan 15 1822–Dec 10 1856		NLI	Pos. 2410/11
	Jan 16 1857–Nov 19 1877	Feb 3 1857–Sept 8 1877			
	1802–1900	Not specified		CHGC	
Crusheen (Killaloe)	Feb 1860–Dec 29 1880			NLI	Pos. 2472
	1860–1900	Not specified		CHGC	
	Feb 1860–Dec 29 1880			LDS	0926093 item 2
Doonass and Truagh (Killaloe)	July 27 1851–Dec 12 1880	Sept 6 1851–Nov 29 1880		NLI	Pos. 2476
	1851–1900	Not specified		CHGC	
	1851–1880	1851–1880		LDS	09/9694 item 2
Doora and Kilraghtis (Killaloe)	Mar 1 1821–Jan 23 1863	Jan 10 1823–Dec 5 1880		NLI	Pos. 2472 (B.to 1862); remainder 2474
	Mar 1862–Dec 23 1880				
	1821–1900	Not specified		CHGC	
Drumclift (Killaloe)	Mar 19 1841–Oct 1 1879	Apr 3 1837–Dec 1 1880		NLI	Pos. 2472
	1841–1900	Not specified		CHGC	
Feakle (Killaloe)	Apr 22 1860–Dec 25 1880	Sept 21 1860–Aug 17 1880		NLI	Pos. 2476
	1860–1900	Not specified		CHGC	
	1842–1861	1842–1861			
	1860–1880	1860–1880		LDS	0979696 items 5, 7; 0979694 it 5
Inagh and Kilnamona (Killaloe)	Feb 23 1850–Oct 1 1865 (indexed)	Apr 14 1850–July 26 1865 (indexed)		NLI	Pos. 2472
	Oct 6 1865–Dec 25 1880	Oct 9 1865–July 29 1880			
	1850–1900	Not specified		CHGC	
Kilchrist (Killaloe)	Oct 2 1846–Dec 29 1880	Nov 1 1846–June 20 1880		NLI	Pos. 2471
	1846–1900	Not specified		CHGC	
	Oct 2 1846–Dec 29 1880	Nov 1 1846–June 20 1880		LDS	0926092
Kildysart (Killaloe)	July 1829–Nov 1866 (indexed transcript with parish history)	Jan 1867–Dec 22 1880		NLI	Pos. 2475
	Nov 14 1866–Dec 28 1880				
	1829–1900	Not specified		CHGC	
Kilfenora (Galway)	June 1 1836–May 15 1847	Dec 2 1865–Nov 26 1880		NLI	Pos. 2440
	Sept 3 1854–Sept 12 1876				
	Oct 8 1876–Dec 27 1880				
	1836–1900	Not specified		CHGC	
	June 1 1836–May 15 1847	Dec 2 1865–Nov 26 1880		LDS	0926065
	Sept 3 1854–Sept 12 1876				
	Oct 8 1876–Dec 27 1880				

Parish (Diocese)	Baptisms	Marriages	Burials	Location	Reference
Kilfiddane (Killaloe)	Aug 15 1868–Dec 20 1880	Jan 8 1869–Fe 10 1880		NLI	Pos. 2485
	1868–1900	Not specified		CHGC	
Kilkee (Killaloe)	Mar 3 1869–Dec 12 1880			NLI	Pos. 2485
	1836–1900	Not specified		CHGC	
	Mar 3 1869–Dec 12 1880			LDS	0926100
Killaloe (Killaloe)	May 24 1828–June 19 1844	Feb 26 1829–Sept 7 1880		NLI	Pos. 2477
	June 23 1844–Jan 21 1855				
	Feb 1 1855–Dec 8 1880				
	1828–1900	Not specified		CHGC	
Killard (Killaloe)	May 13 1855–Dec 29 1880	Feb 12 1867–Oct 31 1880		NLI	Pos. 2487
	(transcript)				
	1855–1900	Not specified		CHGC	
	1855–1880	1867–1880		LDS	0979696 item 2–3
Killkeady (Killaloe)	Feb 1833–1840	Dec 24 1870–Dec 31 1880		NLI	Pos. 2473
	(transcript)	Feb 20 1871–July 24 1880			
	1840–1855 (transcript)				
	1855–1866 (transcript)				
	1833–1900	Not specified		CHGC	
Killone (Killaloe)	Jan 25 1863–July 21 1880	Feb 17 1853–Dec 15 1880		NLI	Pos. 2471
	(Killone)	(Killone)			
	Dec 10 1853–Dec 15 1880	Jan 21 1854–Nov 19 1880			
	(Clarecastle)	Clarecastle)			
	1834–1900	Not specified		CHGC	
	1853–1880	1854–1880		LDS	0979693 item 1–2
Kilmacduane (Killaloe)	Jan 17 1854–Dec 30 1880	May 1 1853–Nov 29 1867		NLI	Pos. 2485
	1854–1900	Not specified		CHGC	
Kilmaley (Killaloe)	Sept 23 1828–Dec 31 1880			NLI	Pos. 2474
	1829–1900	Not specified		CHGC	
	Sept 23 1828–Dec 31 1880			LDS	0926094
	1882–1900			Online	Rootsweb Clare
Kilmanaheen (Galway)	Jan 15 1870–Sept 8 1880			NLI	Pos. 2440
	1823–1900	Not specified		CHGC	
	Jan 15 1870–Sept 8 1880			LDS	0926067
Kilmihil (Killaloe)	Mar 20 1849–Jan 12 1870	Jan 20 1849–Sept 19 1869		NLI	Pos. 2485
	(indexed)	(indexed)			
	Jan 1 1870–Dec 29 1880	Apr 8 1869–Nov 13 1880			
	1849–1900	Not specified		CHGC	
Kilmurry Ibricken (Killaloe)	Apr 25 1839–Apr 12 1876	Apr 13 1839–Aug 14 1852		NLI	Pos. 2486
	Jan 1 1876–Dec 26 1880	Sept 1855–Aug 2 1863			
	(transcript)	Feb 11 1863–Oct 15 1876			
		Feb 5 1876–Nov 27 1880			
	1839–1900	Not specified		CHGC	
	Apr 25 1839–Apr 12 1876	Apr 13 1839–Aug 14 1852		LDS	0926101
	Jan 1 1876–Dec 26 1880	Sept 1855–Aug 2 1863			
	(transcript)	Feb 11 1863–Oct 15 1876			
		Feb 5 1876–Nov 27 1880			
Kilmurry McMahon (Killaloe)	Nov 1 1845–Dec 19 1880	Sept 20 1837–Oct 16 1880	Nov 5 1844–Apr 1848	NLI	Pos. 2485
	1842–1900	Not specified		CHGC	

Parish (Diocese)	Baptisms	Marriages	Burials	Location	Reference
Kilnoe (Killaloe)	Nov 1 1832–Dec 31 1880	Nov 2 1832–July 4 1880		NLI	Pos. 2477
	1832–1900	Not specified		CHGC	
Kilshanny (Galway)	No records microfilmed			NLI	
See also Lisdoonvarna	1869–1900	Not specified		CHGC	
Knockera (Killaloe)	Jan 23 1859–Dec 30 1880	Feb 10 1859–Nov 23 1880		NLI	Pos. 2485
	1859–1900	Not specified		CHGC	
Limerick city: Parteen	See Limerick				
Liscannor (Galway)	June 15 1843–July 4 1854	Feb 17 1866–Oct 4 1880		NLI	Pos. 2440
	July 3 1854–Feb 27 1873	(transcript)			
	May 25 1873–Oct 4 1880				
	1843–1900	Not specified		CHGC	
Lisdoonvarna Galway)	June 1 1854–Nov 19 1876	Jan 12 1860–Nov 23 1880		NLI	Pos. 2440
	1854–1900	Not specified		CHGC	
Milltownmalbay	Nov 16 1831–July 8 1855	Nov 24 1856–Dec 1 1858		NLI	Pos. 2486
(Killaloe)	May 1 1855–Dec 1 1858	Feb 9 1859–Nov 27 1880			
	Dec 4 1858–Dec 31 1880				
	1831–1900	Not specified		CHGC	
New Quay (Galway)	Oct 4 1847–Aug 31 1854	Oct 3 1854–Dec 30 1880	Feb 5 1848–Apr 20 1863	NLI	Pos. 2441
	(transcript)		(transcript)		
	1836–1900	Not specified		CHGC	
	1847–1880	1848–1863		LDS	0979691 item 1
Newmarket–on–	Apr 29 1828–Feb 25 1866	1828–Aug 13 1865		NLI	Pos. 2471–2
Fergus (Killaloe)	1828–1900	Not specified		CHGC	
	Apr 29 1828–Feb 25 1866	1828–Aug 13 1865		LDS	0926095 item 2
O'Callaghan's Mills	Jan 4 1835–Dec 31 1880	Jan 14 1835–Nov 14 1880		NLI	Pos. 2476
(Killaloe)	1835–1900	Not specified		CHGC	
	1835–1880	1835–1880		LDS	0979694 item 6
Ogonnelloe (Killaloe)	Mar 29 1832–Feb 25 1869	Feb 9 1857–Feb 9 1869		NLI	Pos. 2476
	(transcript)	(transcript)			
	1832–1900	Not specified		CHGC	
	1832–1869	1857–1869		LDS	0979694 item 1
Quin (Killaloe)	Jan 4 1816–Mar 1 1855	Jan 29 1833–Feb 14 1855		NLI	Pos. 2473
	Jan 1855–Dec 31 1880	Jan 10 1855–June 26 1880			
	1815–1900	Not specified		CHGC	
	Jan 4 1816–Mar 1 1855	Jan 29 1833–Feb 14 1855		LDS	0926096
	Jan 1855–Dec 31 1880	Jan 10 1855–June 26 1880			
Rath (Killaloe)	Apr 4 1819–Dec 25 1836	Jan 27 1818–Feb 25 1844		NLI	Pos. 2474
	Feb 216 1837–Nov 15 1862	Feb 27 1859–Nov 26 1862			(B. to 1862);
	Oct 31 1862–Dec 23 1880	Nov 10 1862–June 27 1880			remainder 2475
	1819–1900	Not specified		CHGC	
Ruan (Killaloe)	Aug 18 1845–Dec 23 1880	July 2 1846–June 23 1880		NLI	Pos. 2473
	1845–1900	Not specified		CHGC	
Scarriff (Killaloe)	May 5 1852–Mar 24 1872	Nov 22 1852–Apr 20 1872		NLI	Pos. 2476
	Mar 24 1872–Dec 31 1880	Apr 20 1872–June 15 1880			
	1852–1900	Not specified		CHGC	
	May 5 1852–Mar 24 1872	Nov 22 1852–Apr 20 1872		LDS	0926097
	Mar 24 1872–Dec 31 1880	Apr 20 1872–June 15 1880			
Sixmilebridge	Dec 15 1828–Aug 28 1839	Jan 25 1829–July 29 1839		NLI	Pos. 2474
(Killaloe)	Jan 28 1840–Dec 23 1864	May 1840–Nov 26 1864			
	Jan 6 1865–Dec 26 1880	Feb 12 1865–Oct 12 1880			
	1828–1900	Not specified		CHGC	

Parish (Diocese)	Baptisms	Marriages	Burials	Location	Reference
St. Senan's (Killaloe)	Aug 1 1827–Dec 8 1831	Jan 7 1829–Dec 6 1880		NLI	Pos. 2487
	Jan 14 1833–Sept 29 1863				
	Oct 1 1863–Dec 31 1880				
	1827–1900	Not specified		CHGC	
	1827–1880	1829–1880		LDS item 4	0979696
Tulla (Killaloe)	Jan 1819–Mar 28 1846	Jan 1 1819–Feb 24 1846		NLI	Pos. 2471
	Apr 21 1846–Dec 28 1861	Apr 20 1846–Nov 30 1861			
	(indexed)	(indexed)			
	Jan 1 1862–Dec 29 1880	Jan 21 1862–Oct 21 1880			
	(indexed)				
	1819–1900	Not specified		CHGC	
	1819–1880	1819–1880		LDS	0979693 item 4

Cork East
Cork City: Cork & Ross diocese

Parish (Diocese)	Baptisms	Marriages	Burials	Location	Reference
Aghada	Jan 1 1815–March 26 1837	May 11 1838–Nov 26 1880		NLI	Pos. 4990
(Cloyne)	March 12 1838–Nov 26 1880				
	1792–1895	1785–1897		MHC	
Annakissy	June 16 1806–Dec 28 1829	July 28 1805–Nov 19 1835		NLI	Pos. 5001
(Cloyne)	Jan 3 1830–Dec 26 1880	Jan 21–June 4 1837			
		July 9 1837–Nov 27 1880			
	1805–1895	1806–1875		MHC	
Ballymacoda and	Nov 10 1835–Aug 28 1880	Sept 22 1835–Nov 11 1879		NLI	Pos. 4991
Ladysbridge (Cloyne)	1835–1899	1836–1899		MHC	
Blarney (Cloyne)	Aug 12 1791–June 6 1792	Sept 24 1778–March 2 1813		NLI	Pos. 5006;
	Feb 2 1821–Dec 19 1825				marriages
	Oct 29 1826–May 25 1845	Feb 15 1821–Nov 26 1825			from 1848
	June 1 1845–Dec 22 1880	Dec 17 1826–Aug 26 1849			on Pos. 5007
		Jan 11 1848–Nov 8 1880			
	1820–1896	1779–1813		MHC	
		1821–1895			
Carrigaline	Jan 1 1826–Dec 19 1880	Jan 23 1826–Nov 18 1880		NLI	Pos. 4790
(Cork & Ross)					

Parish (Diocese)	Baptisms	Marriages	Burials	Location	Reference
Carrigaline (Cork & Ross)	1826–1880	1826–1880		Published	Thompson, *Families*
Carrigtohill (Cloyne)	Dec 2 1817–July 18 1873 July 19 1873–Nov 5 1880	Nov 22 1817–Oct 13 1878		NLI	Pos. 4989
	1817–1899	1818–1892		MHC	
Castlelyons (Cloyne)	Aug 12 1791–Dec 28 1828 Jan 3 1830–Dec 22 1880	Jan 17 1830–Nov 19 1880		NLI	Pos. 4994
	1791–1892	1830–1896		MHC	
Castletownroche (Cloyne)	Aug 25 1811–Dec 29 1834 Jan 2 1835–Dec 27 1866	Sept 19 1811– Oct 181845 Nov 29 1845–Oct 13 1880		NLI	Pos. 4995; b. 1835–, m. 1845–, 4996
	1810–1899	1811–1899		MHC	
Cloyne (Cloyne)	Sept 2 1791–Nov 4 1793 Oct 5 1803–July 30 1812 Jan 2 1821–Dec 29 1831 July 1 1833–Dec 29 1878	Feb 3 1786–Feb 17 1801 April 14 1801–Dec 2 1820 Jan 11 1821–Nov 26 1831 Jan 10 1832–May 18 1880		NLI	Pos. 4989 baptisms; Pos. 4990 marriages
	1802–1899	1802–1899		MHC	
Cobh (Cloyne)	1812–Dec 31 1820 Jan 22 1821–May 24 1827 June 5 1827–May 1842 August 1842–May 31 1863 June 4 1863–Dec 30 1877 Jan 3 1878–Dec 19 1880			NLI	Pos. 4986; baptisms from 1821, marriages from 1812 on Pos. 4987
	1812–1891	1812–1899		MHC	
Conna (Cloyne)	Sept 1834–Sept 1844 (some gaps) Dec 16 1845–Dec 26 1880	Oct30 1845–Nov13 1880		NLI	Pos. 4996
	1832–1895	1844–1895		MHC	
Cork city: Blackrock	July 10 1810–May 31 1811 Feb 5 1832–Aug 15 1837 Feb 3 1839–June 17 1839 Jan 6 1841–Aug 16 1847 Jan 13 1848–Dec 5 1880	Sept 16 1810–May 18 1811 Feb 7 1832–Ayg 15 1837 Feb 13 1841–Oct 9 1847 Jan 18 1848–Nov 2 1880		NLI	Pos. 4791
	1848–1899	1848–1899		CCAP	
Cork city: Ss Peter and Paul's	April 24 1766–Oct 22 1766 Nov 14 1780–Jan 21 1798 Jan 21 1798–Sept 23 1803 Jan 1 1809–June 17 1811 April 1834–May 31 1840 Jan 15 1837–Dec 30 1855 Feb 1 1856–Sept 13 1870 Mar 3 1870–Dec 25 1880	April 30 1766–Sept 18 1776 Oct 22 1780–Oct 6 1803 Jan 22 1809–Aug 23 1810 July 22 1814–Aug 30 1817 May 5 1834–May 30 1840 (scraps 1825 & 1827) Jan 17 1838–Dec 3 1853 Jan 3 1856– Nov 27 1880		NLI	Pos. 4785; B. from 1798, M. from 1780, on Pos. 4786; B. from 1870, M. from 1856 on Pos. 4887
Cork city: St Finbarr's (South)	Aug 10 1756–Sept 7 1757 July 5 1760–Sept 17 1763 Mar 22 1772–July 30 1777 Jan 15 1789–Dec 30 1802 Jan 1 1803– Dec 1834 Jan 3 1835–Dec 19 1856 Jan 12 1857–Jan 6 1878 Jan 7 1878–Dec 31 1880	Bans 1753–1774 (many gaps) Apr 22 1775–Sept 3 1789 Jan 7 1789–June 20 1810 June 21 1810–Jan 14 1860 Jan 1 1860–Dec 2 1877 Jan 8 1878–Nov 27 1880		NLI	B. 1776–1856, Pos. 4778; B. 1857–1880, Pos. 4779; M. 1775–1810, Pos. 4779; M. 1810–1880 Pos. 4780l
	1756–1900	1756–1900		CCAP	

Parish (Diocese)	Baptisms	Marriages	Burials	Location	Reference
Cork city: St Mary's	July 1748–May 1764	July 10 1748–May 30 1764		NLI	B.1748–1764,
	Mar 1765–Nov 1788	April 16 1765–Nov 19 1788			Pos. 4780;
	(gaps)	Jan 7 1789–Dec 26 1812			B. 1773–1807,
	Aug 1780–Dec 1788	Jan 7 1813–Nov 25 1845			Pos. 4781;
	(gaps)	Mar 1831–1834 (odd pages)			B. 1789–1834,
	Jan–May 1786	Jan 14 1845–Dec 30 1880			Pos. 4782;
	Jan 1789–Jan 1807 (gaps)	1846–1853 (odd pages)			B. 1833–1859,
	Jan 1808–Mar 1834				Pos. 4783;
	Mar 1831–1834 (gaps)				B. 1869–1880,
	Nov 1833–Oct 1853				Pos. 4874;
	1846–1853 (gaps)				M. 1748–1788,
	1852–1880				Pos 4784;
					M. 1789–1880,
					Pos. 4785
	1748–1899	1748–1899		CCAP	
Cork city: St. Patrick's	Oct 7 1831–Jan 3 1851	July 16 1832–June 29 1851		NLI	Pos. 4788
	Nov 30 1836–Mar 27 1872	(very few for 1831–34)			
	April 1 1872–Dec 29 1880	Nov 19 1836–Dec 20 1880			
	1831–1899	1831–1899		CCAP	
Doneraile(Cloyne)	April 16 1815–Sept 17 1836	Jan 26 1815–May 14 1867		NLI	Pos. 5000
	Dec 21 1836–May 12 1867	March 4 1866–Dec 2 1880			
	March 1 1866–Dec 28 1880				
	1815–1900	1815–1900		MHC	
Douglas (Cork & Ross)	Nov 15 1812–Aug 30 1851	Nov 25 1812–July 25 1851		NLI	Pos. 4790
	Sept 27 1851–Dec 23 1867	Aug 23 1851–Mar 3 1867			
	Feb 26 1867–Dec 17 1880	Mar 2 1867–Nov 13 1880			
Fermoy (Cloyne)	Jan 1 1828–Aug 27 1848	May 18 1828–Dec 21 1880		NLI	Pos. 4993
	Jan 4 1849–Dec 27 1880				baptisms;
	Workhouse: April 28				Pos. 4994
	1854–Sept 17 1880				marriages
	1827–1890	1828–1899		MHC	
Glanmire (Cork & Ross)	May 10 1818–Oct 12 1828	May 29 1818–Oct 6 1828		NLI	Pos. 4789;
	Oct 13 1828–Dec 31 1841	Nov 11 1828–Dec 1841			m. 1871–
		Feb 11 1871–Oct 2 1880			Pos. 4790
	1818–1828	1818–1828			
	1828–1841	1828–1841			
	1842–1871 to date	1842–1871 to date		LC	
Glanworth and Ballindangan (Cloyne)	Jan 1 1836–Dec 12 1880	Glanworth only: Jan 12		NLI	Pos. 4996
	Ballindangan Sept 1870–	1836–Oct 19 1880			
	Dec 29 1880				
	1836–1899	1836–1899		MHC	
Glounthane (Cork & Ross)	Aug 20 1864–Dec 25 1880	Oct 8 1864–Nov 25 1880		NLI	Pos. 4789
Imogeela (Cloyne)	Feb 1 1833–Dec 19 1880	Sept 22 1833–Sept 6 1879		NLI	Pos. 4991
	1835–1899	1834–1899		MHC	
Kildorrery(Cloyne)	May 15 1824–Sept 30 1853	Jan 25 1803–Aug 15 1880		NLI	Pos. 4994
	1824–1899	1803–1895		MHC	
Killeagh (Cloyne)	March 29 1829–Sept 30 1880	Nov 1 1822–July 10 1880		NLI	Pos. 4992
	1829–1896	1823–1897		MHC	

Parish (Diocese)	Baptisms	Marriages	Burials	Location	Reference
Kilpadder (Cloyne)		Feb 12 1858–Nov 20 1869		NLI	Pos. 5008
KIlshannig (Cloyne)	Apr 10 1842–June 23 1850			NLI	Pos. 5008
Kilworth (Cloyne)	Sept 19 1829–Oct 9 1876	Oct 3 1829–Dec 16 1880		NLI	Pos. 4996
Lisgoold (Cloyne)	July 13 1807–July 26 1821	Oct 16 1821–Nov 13 1880		NLI	Pos. 4991
	July 31 1821–April 29 1853				
	May 8 1853–Dec 31 1880				
	1807–1895	1822–1899		MHC	
Lismore	See Waterford				
Mallow (Cloyne)	Jan 1–July 17 1809	April 17 1757–Nov 22 1823		NLI	Pos. 4997; baptisms from 1847, marriages from 1844 on Pos. 4998
	June 28 1817–Feb 19 1818	Oct 6 1805–Sept 6 1820			
	Aug 27 1820–June 23 1828	April 30 1832–Jan 31 1841			
	Jan 2 1825–July 31 1828	Feb 2 1844–Oct 17 1880			
	Jan 2 1825–Dec 28 1828				
	April 13 1832–Dec 14 1840				
	Jan 4 1841–1880				
	1809	1758–1900		MHC	
	1817–1828				
	1832–1899				
Middleton (Cloyne)	Sept 24 1819–Dec 29 1863	Oct 31 1819–April 21 1864		NLI	Pos. 4986
	Jan 3 1864–Dec 30 1880	Jan 16 1864–Dec 31 1880			
	1819–1899	1810–1854		MHC	
		1866–1899			
Mitchelstown (Cloyne)	Jan 1 1792–July 13 1801	Jan 7 1822–Nov 27 1845		NLI	Pos. 4992; from 1845, Pos. 4993
	Sept 11 1814–Aug 1833	July 13 1845–Nov 1 1880			
	Sept 12 1833–Nov 1845				
	July 6 1845–Dec 26 1880				
	1792–1801	1815–1899		MHC	
	1815–1899				
Monkstown (Cork & Ross)	May 2 1875–Dec 26 1880	June 5 1875–Nov 29 1880		NLI	Pos. 4791
Passage West (Cork & Ross)	Apr 5 1795–May 15 1832	Aug 23 1813–Sept 21 1816		NLI	Pos. 4791, 4792
	July 3 1813–Sept 29 1816	May 1 1832–Aug 26 1844			
	May 1 1832–Sept 14 1844	Sept 12 1844–Feb 12 1865			
	Sept 4 1844–Feb 12 1865	Mar 1 1859–Oct 19 1880			
	Mar 6 1859–Dec 30 1880				
Rathcormack (Cloyne)	Jan 10 1792–March 1850	Jan 7 1829–June 2 1866		NLI	Pos. 4995
	March 4 1850–June 7 1866				
	June 12 1866–Dec 28 1880				
	1792–1899	1829–1899		MHC	
Tracton Abbey (Cork & Ross)	Dec 12 1802–Dec 25 1853	June 6 1840–Feb 10 1880		NLI	Pos. 4789
	Jan 24 1853–Dec 10 1880				
Youghal (Cloyne)	Sept 15 1803–Mar 2 1830	Feb 16 1830–June 29 1862		NLI	Pos. 4988; marriages from 1866 on Pos. 4989
	Feb 1 1830–Aug 1846	June 7 1866–Nov 27 1880			
	Sept 4 1846–Aug 21 1875				
	Sept 1 1875–Nov 30 1880				
	1803–1893	1802–1899		MHC	

Cork North-west

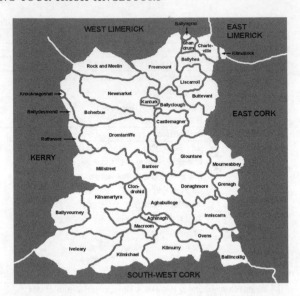

Parish (Diocese)	Baptisms	Marriages	Burials	Location	Reference
Aghabulloge (Cloyne)	Jan 4 1820–April 13 1856	Jan 5 1820–Nov 20 1880		NLI	Pos. 5007
	Jan 5 1856–Dec 19 1880				
	1820–1895	1820–1895		MHC	
Aghinagh (Cloyne)	April 3 1848–Dec 12 1880			NLI	Pos. 5007
	1848–1895	1858–1895		MHC	
Ballincollig (Cork & Ross)	Jan 16 1820–March 19 1828	Jan 12 1825–Feb 19 1828		NLI	Pos. 4791
	Aug 26 1828–Dec 30 1857	Aug 28 1828–Nov 28 1857			
	Jan 3 1858–Dec 24 1880	Oct25 1873–Aug 29 1880			
Ballyagran	See West Limerick				
Ballyclough (Cloyne)	Aug 15 1807–Dec 30 1818	Jan 19 1805–Dec 2 1827		NLI	Pos. 5009
	Jan 3 1819–Dec 14 1845	Feb 3 1828–Aug 18 1867			(b.–5; Pos.
	Jan 4 1846–July 15 1880				5010)
	1807–1896	1805–1896		MHC	
Ballydesmond	No records microfilmed			NLI	
(Kerry)	1888–1900 (Vol. 14)	1888–1900 (Vol. 11)		[Published]	o'k
Ballyhea (Cloyne)	Jan 12 1809–July 24 1873	June 23 1811–July 20–1873		NLI	Pos. 4992
	Nov 12 1871–Dec 2 1880	Nov 8 1871–July 18 1880			
	1809–1899	1811–1899		MHC	
Ballyvourney (Cloyne)	April 11 1825–Dec 29 1829			NLI	Pos. 5007
	1822–1895	1871–1895		MHC	
	1810–1868 (gaps)			LDS	823808
	1810–1868 (Vol. 11)			Published	o'k
	1810–1824			Online	Grogan
Banteer (Cloyne)	Jan 1 1847–Dec 24 1880	Feb 2 1847–Dec 9 1880		NLI	Pos. 5011
	1828–1899	1828–1899		MHC	
Boherbue	See Kerry				
Buttevant (Cloyne)	July 1 1814–Dec 27 1879	July 23 1814–Sept 14 1880		NLI	Pos. 4998
	1814–1895	1820–1896		MHC	
Castlemagner (Cloyne)	May 7 1832–Dec 26 1880	May 8 1832–Oct 12 1880		NLI	Pos. 5009
	1832–1899	1832–1885		MHC	

Parish (Diocese)	Baptisms	Marriages	Burials	Location	Reference
Charleville (Cloyne)	May 2 1827–Dec 31 1880	Aug 10 1774–Nov 15 1792		NLI	Pos. 5001;
		Nov 23 1794–July 3 1822			from 1827,
		June 3 1827–Dec 9 1880			Pos. 5002
	1827–1895	1774–1814			
		1828–1895		MHC	
Clondrohid (Cloyne)	1807–1822	Apr 21 1822–June 1 1847		NLI	Pos. 5002;
	April 11 1822–Oct 22 1843	Jan 18 1848–Nov 21 1880			from 1844,
	June 2 1844–Dec 30 1880				Pos. 5003
	1807–1895	1822–1894		MHC	
Donaghmore (Cloyne)	April 1 1803–Dec 13 1815	Jan 18 1790–Feb 3 1828		NLI	Pos. 5003
	Oct 1 1815–April 3 1828	Feb 7 1828–Jan 7 1835			baptisms to
	April 6 1828–Oct 21 1834	Oct 23 1834–Sept 17 1875			1828; Pos.
	Oct 23 1834–Sept 17 1875	Feb 13 1870–July 8 1880			5004
	Jan 1 1870–July 8 1880				remainder
	1803–1895	1790–1899		MHC	
Dromtarriffe (Kerry)	Feb 6 1832–July 26 1851	Jan 25 1832–July 17 1852		NLI	Pos. 4264
	Aug 1 1851–Dec 26 1880	Jan 25 1852–July 27 1880			
	1832–1875	1832–1880		LDS	0883884 item 5; 0883696 13
	1832–1840 (Vol. 4)	1832–1865 (Vol. 2)		Published	o'k
	1841–1848 (Vol. 3)	1865–1900 (Vol. 14)			
	1851–1865 (Vol. 4)				
	165–1900 (Vol. 6)				
	1832–1884	1832–1884		KGC	
Freemount (Cloyne)	Sept 10 1827–March 22 1840	Oct 15 1827–Oct 2 1880		NLI	Pos. 5008
	July 15–Dec 28 1843				
	Jan 10 1858–Dec 18 1880				
	1827–1843	1823–1895		MHC	
	1859–1896				
Glountane (Cloyne)	May 20 1829–Aug 1844			NLI	Pos. 5008
	May 16 1847–Dec 21 1880				
	1829–1895	1858–1895		MHC	
Inniscarra (Cloyne)	July 3 1814–Sept 29 1844	Aug 7 1814–June 1 1871		NLI	Pos. 5005
	Jan 1 1845–Dec 31 1879	July 15 1871–Nov 25 1880			b.–1844; Pos. 5006 rest
	1814–1895	1814–1899		MHC	
Iveleary (Cork & Ross)	Nov 1 1816–Aug 29 1843	Nov 20 1816–May 9 1880		NLI	Pos. 4794 b.–1843; rest Pos. 4795
	Sept 3 1843–Dec 30 1880				
	1816–1875	1816–1880		LDS	0883696; 0883784
	1816–1863 (Vol. 7)	1816–1899 (Vol. 7)		Published	o'k
	1853–1900 (Vol. 9)				
	1816–1900	1816–1900		Online	Grogan
Kanturk (Cloyne)	July 28 1822–Oct 16 1849	Feb 20 1824–Jan 19 1850		NLI	Pos. 5008
	Sept 21 1849–Dec 26 1880	Sept 29 1849–Dec 26 1880			
	Workhouse: Sept 1 1844–Aug 18 1867				
	1822–1899	1824–1899		MHC	
Kilmallock	See East Limerick				

Parish (Diocese)	Baptisms	Marriages	Burials	Location	Reference
Kilmichael (Cork & Ross)	Oct 6 1819–Feb 23 1847 Mar 10 1847–Dec 23 1880	Jan 9 1819–Feb 12 1850 Jan 23 1851–Aug 7 1880		NLI	Pos. 4797; marriage from 1851 on Pos. 4798
Kilmurry (Cork & Ross)	June 2 1786–Feb 1812 Feb 22 1812–Dec 20 1825 Jan 8 1826–Dec 30 1838 Dec 14 1838–June 29 1872 July 2 1872–Dec 31 1880	1803–1805 (fragmented) Feb 22 1812–Nov 24 1825 Jan 8 1826–Dec 1 1838 Jan 30 1839–Nov 13 1880		NLI	Pos. 4803
Kilnamartyra (Cloyne)	Jan 30 1803–Dec 16 1820 Jan 16 1821–Dec 11 1880 1803–1894	Jan 8 1803–June 4 1833 Sept 1839–Feb 10 1880 1803–1895		NLI MHC	Pos. 5003
Knocknagoshel	See Kerry				
Liscarroll (Cloyne)	March 1 1812–Oct 14 1837 Nov 24 1833–Dec 19 1880 1812–1895	Feb 14 1813–Oct 15 1837 July 6 1831–Oct 28 1880 1813–1895		NLI MHC	Pos. 4999
Macroom (Cloyne)	April 11–18 1803 Sept 28 1805–April 7 1814 Jan 5 1814–June 30 1823 July 1 1823–Oct 26 1843 Dec 21 1843–Dec 31 1880 1805–1817 1824–1898	Jan 20 1808–Aug 14 1813 Sept 19 1813–Nov 7 1880 1864–1866 (*Vol.* 14) 1831–1947 (*Vol.* 14) 1780–1899		NLI Published MHC	Pos. 5004 b. to 1823; Pos. 5005 remainder o'κ
Millstreet (Kerry)	Dec 4 1853–July 14 1865 July 23 1865–Dec 31 1878 Jan 12 1873–Dec 21 1880 1822–1823 1853–1875 1822–1823 (*Vol.* 11) 1859–1900 (*Vol.* 11) 1860–1862 (*Vol.* 11)	Jan 14 1855–Nov 6 1880 1855–1880 1855–1870 (*Vol.* 2) 1870–1900 (*Vol.* 11)		NLI LDS Published	Pos. 4267 0883884 item 6; 0883697 2 o'κ
Mourneabbey (Cloyne)	June 1 1829–Dec 29 1880 1829–1895	Oct 22 1829–Sept 24 1880 1829–1895		NLI MHC	Pos. 4999
Newmarket (Cloyne)	Nov 17 1821–Dec 24 1833 July 8 1833–Oct 8 1865 March 13 1866–Dec 30 1880 1833–1899	Jan 10 1822–Sept 16 1865 March 9 1866–Aug 21 1880 1822–1899		NLI MHC	Pos. 5010 baptisms; Pos. 5011 marriages
Ovens (Cork & Ross)	Sept 24 1816–May 24 1825 Sept 11 1825–Sept 8 1833 Oct 27 1834–Dec 30 1877	Sept 24 1816–May 24 1825 Sept 22 1825–Aug 27 1833 Oct 25 1834–Feb 14 1837 Jan 22 1839–Nov 13 1877		NLI	Pos. 4795
Rathmore	See Kerry				
Rock and Meelin (Cloyne)	March 17 1866–Dec 26 1880 1866–1899	April 14 1866–March 1 1880 1867–1899		NLI MHC	Pos. 5009
Shandrum (Cloyne)	March 1 1829–Dec 26 1880 1793–1895	 1793–1896		NLI MHC	Pos. 5001

Cork (South-west)

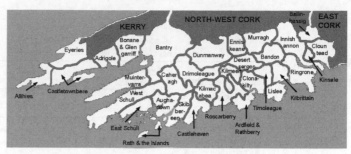

Parish (Diocese)	Baptisms	Marriages	Burials	Location	Reference
Adrigole (Kerry)	Jan 1 1830–Dec 9 1849	Jan 1831–Oct 26 1849		NLI	Pos. 4287
	Aug 12 1855–Jan 20 1879	Sept 1 1855–Aug 10 1878			
Allihies (Kerry)	Oct 6 1822–June 10 1860	Jan 1823–Feb 27 1826		NLI	Pos. 4286
	Sept 10 1859–Dec 29 1874	Jan 10 1832–Feb 12 1861			
	Jan 1 1875–Dec 26 1880	Jan 8 1860–Feb 13 1872			
		Oct 7 1871–Aug 20 1880			
	1822–	1823–		Published	O'Dwyer, Allihies
Ardfield and	Jan 1 1801–April 5 1837	May 1800–July 2 1837		NLI	Pos. 4771
Rathberry (Cork	(1802 missing)	(1812–1816 missing)			
& Ross)	April 7 1832–Dec 27 1876	May 17 1832–May 30 1880			
Aughadown (Cork	June 1822–Oct 12 1838	Oct 15 1822–Feb 28 1865		NLI	Pos. 4775
& Ross)	Oct 20 1838–Jan 28 1864				
	Jan 1 1865–Dec 31 1880				
Ballingarry (Cork	April 27 1836–Dec 27 1878	April 21 1836–Nov 30 1878		NLI	Pos. 4801
& Ross)	1809–1835			LC	
	1836–1880				
Ballinhassig	March 8 1821–Dec 24 1874	July 15 1821–Sept 29 1877		NLI	Pos. 4795;
(Cork & Ross)	Mountain parish:	Feb 6 1875–Nov 23 1880			from 1875
	Oct 10 1858–Dec 20 1877				on Pos. 4796
	Jan 9 1875–Dec 20 1880				
Ballymartle	Nov 20 1841–Dec 12 1859	Aug 28 1841–Jan 12 1860		NLI	Pos. 4801
(Cork & Ross)	1809–1835			LC	
See also Clountead	1836–1880				
Bandon (Cork &	Jan 5 1794–Dec 30 1803	July 29 1794–Dec 1 1803		NLI	Pos. 4793;
Ross)	Jan 2 1804–Oct 25 1811	(some entries for 1790 also)			baptisms from
	Jan 1 1814–Dec 31 1822	Jan 10 1804–Sept 25 1811			1823,
	Jan 1 1823–Dec 30 1835	Jan 9 1814–March 7 1848			marriages
	Jan 1 1836–Jan 27 1855	Jan 9 1848–Nov 27 1880			from 1848 on
	Jan 7 1855–Dec 30 1880				Pos. 4794
Bantry (Cork & Ross)	1788	May 7 1788–May 28 1823		NLI	Pos. 4802;
	1791–2 (parts)	May 1823–Dec 5 1857			baptisms from
	Nov 1794–July 1799 (parts)	Jan 7 1872–Nov 5 1880			1875,
	Jan 1808–May 1809				marriages
	1812–1814 (parts)				from 1872 on
	July 1822–June 11 1824				Pos. 4803
	March 31 1823–Dec 31 1866				
	Jan 1 1867–Sept 28 1875				
	Oct 1 1875–Dec 28 1880				

Parish (Diocese)	Baptisms	Marriages	Burials	Location	Reference
Bonane and Glengarriff (Kerry)	July 22 1846–Dec 25 1856 Jan 3 1857–Dec 21 1877 Jan 9 1878–Dec 26 1880	July 18 1847–Nov 29 1856 Feb 1 1857–Feb 9 1875 Feb 2 1876–Feb 10 1880		NLI	Pos. 4288
Caheragh (Cork & Ross)	June 10 1818–Sept 1858 Oct 1858–Dec 27 1880	June 23 1818–Aug 25 1858 Nov 27 1858–Dec 4 1880		NLI	Pos. 4799
Castlehaven (Cork & Ross)	Oct 14 1842–Dec 30 1880			NLI	Pos. 4774
Castletownbere (Kerry)	Sept 1819–April 25 1854 May 4 1854–Dec 28 1859 Jan 1 1859–Sept 22 1878 1819–	July 1819–Feb 5 1859 Jan 8 1858–Nov 20 1880 1819–		NLI Published	Pos. 4284 O'Dwyer, Castletownbere
Clonakilty (Cork & Ross)	Aug 3 1809–March 1827 Jan 1 1827–Dec 31 1873	Jan 8 1811–Nov 17 1880		NLI	Pos. 4772
Clountead, Ballingarry and Ballymartle (Cork & Ross) See also Ballymarlte	April 27 1836–Dec 27 1878 Jan 1 1879–Dec 26 1880 1809–1835 1836–1880	April 21 1836–Nov 30 1878 Jan 30 1879–Oct 30 1880		NLI LC	Pos. 4801
Desertserges (Cork & Ross)	June 14 1817–May 28 1855 June 11 1855–Dec 17 1880 Confirmations from 1860	(with Enniskeane) Sept 29 1813–Sept 26 1880		NLI Online	Pos. 4798 Swanton
Drimoleague (Cork & Ross)	July 20 1817–Oct 20 1846 Oct 25 1846–June 12 1876 June 4 1876–Dec 26 1880	July 20 1817–Nov 14 1863 Dec 8 1876–Dec 10 1880 (1878 missing)		NLI	Pos. 4801
Dunmanway (Cork & Ross)	June 21 1818–April 24 1838 July 1 1837–Dec 29 1880	June 21 1818–Nov 27 1880		NLI	Pos. 4805
Enniskeane (Cork & Ross)	Nov 24 1813–July 1837 Aug 1 1837–Dec 30 1880 Partial	(with Desertserges) Sept 29 1813–Sept 26 1880 Confirmations from 1860		NLI Online	Pos. 4798 Swanton
Eyeries (Kerry)	April 1843–March 25 1873 Jan 5 1873–Dec 31 1880 1843–	Feb 1824–Feb 23 1873 Feb 6 1873–Aug 28 1880 1824–		NLI Published	Pos. 4286 O'Dwyer, Eyeries
Innishannon (Cork & Ross)	Aug 20 1825–Dec 29 1846 Jan 4 1847–Nov 30 1880	Aug 16 1825–Oct 9 1880		NLI	Pos. 4797
Kilbrittain (Cork & Ross)	Aug 1810–Sept 8 1814 July 9 1811–Feb 1848 Mar 29 1850–Mar 30 1851 April 6 1852–April 23 1863 April 16–1863–Dec 28 1880	Aug 1810–Sept 8 1814 Aug 2 1810–June 7 1863 (with Rathclareen) Nov 7 1863–Sept 12 1880	NLI	Pos. 4796	
Kilmacabea (Cork & Ross)	June 9 1832–Dec 24 1880	July 10 1832–Feb 28 1865 May 28 1865–Sept 14 1880		NLI	Pos. 4771
Kilmeen and Castleventry (Cork & Ross)	Aug 1821–Feb 13 1858 Feb 19 1858–Dec 31 1880			NLI	Pos. 4772
Kinsale (Cork & Ross)	Jan 20 1805–July 20 1806 Jan 1 1815–Sept 4 1821 Sept 3 1817–Dec 28 1829 Aug 29 1828–May 2 1859 May 16 1859–Dec 23 1880	Aug 31 1828–April 26 1859 May 16 1859–Dec 23 1880		NLI	Pos. 4800; b. & m. from 1859 on Pos. 4801

Parish (Diocese)	Baptisms	Marriages	Burials	Location	Reference
Lislee (Cork & Ross)	Aug 1 1804–Oct 1 1836 (Transcript made in 1873) June 23 1835–Aug 27 1873	Nov 12 1771–Aug 31 1873 (Transcript made in 1873) Feb 13 1836–March 16 1873 (Original)		NLI	Pos. 4776; b. & m. from 1835 on Pos. 4777
Muintervarra (Cork & Ross)	May 5 1820–Feb 16 1856 Mar 2 1856–Dec 24 1880	Feb 4 1819–Sept 30 1880		NLI	Pos. 4799
Murragh (Cork & Ross)	Jan 1834–Dec 29 1864	Jan 26 1834–Oct 8 1864 Jan 7 1865–Nov 27 1880		NLI	Pos. 4796
Rath and The Islands (Cork & Ross)	July 21 1818–Sept 15 1851 Oct 4 1851–Dec 28 1880	Jan 31 1819–Aug 18 1851 Feb 5 1852–Nov 25 1880		NLI	Pos. 4773; baptisms and marriages from 1853 on Pos. 4774
Ringrone (Cork & Ross)	Sept 16 1819–Nov 19 1854 Jan 6 1855–Dec 24 1880	Sept 30 1819–June 12 1857 Jan 20 1856–Nov 16 1880		NLI	Pos. 4802
Roscarberry (Cork & Ross)	Nov 13 1814–Dec 28 1880	Jan 12 1820–Oct 20 1880		NLI	Pos. 4773
Schull East (Cork & Ross)	Oct 24 1807–Sept 30 1815 Jan 1816–Dec 27 1839 Jan 1 1840–Dec 31 1870 Jan 1 1871–Dec 27 1880	Feb 1809–Nov 5 1815 Jan 21 1816–Nov 25 1832 Jan 31 1833–Sept 17 1870 Feb 4 1871–Dec 21 1880		NLI	Pos. 4804; baptisms and marriages from 1871 on Pos. 4805
Schull West (Cork & Ross)	Jan 1 1827–Feb 24 1864 Nov 15 1863–Dec 20 1880	Jan 25 1827–Feb 9 1864 (with gaps) Apr 9 1864–Apr 27 1880		NLI	Pos. 4800
Skibbereen (Cork & Ross)	Mar 27 1814–Dec 31 1826 Jan 6 1827–Dec 31 1864 Jan 1 1865–Oct 16 1880	Nov 3 1837–Oct 16 1880		NLI	Pos. 4774; baptisms from 1865, marriages from 1837 on Pos. 4775
Timoleague (Cork & Ross)	Nov 1842–Dec 24 1880	Apr 6 1843–Feb 10 1880		NLI	Pos. 4773
Watergrasshill	Jan 5 1836–Dec 24 1855 Jan 21 1856–Dec 21 1880			NLI	Pos. 4790

Derry/Londonderry

Parish (Diocese)	Baptisms	Marriages	Burials	Location	Reference
Arboe	Nov 9 1827–Dec 30 1860	Nov 12 1827–Dec 12 1861		NLI	Pos. 5583
(Armagh)	Jan 1 1861–Dec 10 1880	Jan 5 1862–Dec 27 1880			
	1827–1880	1827–1881		PRONI	MIC.1D/34
	1827–1900	1827–1900		IW	
	See NLI			LDS	0926029
Ardtrea and	July 1 1832–Mar 28 1834	Apr 14 1830–July 12 1843		NLI	Pos. 5584
Desertlin Armagh)	Jan 20 1838–Feb 16 1843	Nov 12 1854–Feb 6 1869			
	Nov 1 1854–Feb 21 1869				
	Jan 18 1864–June 14 1880				
	1832–1834	1838–19843		PRONI	MIC.1D/35
	1854–1939	1830–1843			
	1854–1837 (gaps)				
	See NLI			LDS	0926030
	1832–1900	1830–1900		IW	
		1830–1843		TGC	
		1854–1871			
		1878			
		1882			
		1884–1886			
		1898–1900			
Ballinascreen	Nov 20 1825–Feb 21 1834	Nov 29 1825–Feb 11 1834		NLI	Pos. 5764
(Derry)	June 5 1836–May 31 1863	Apr 3 1834–May 17 1863			
	June 1 1863–Dec 28 1880	June 3 1863–Oct 17 1880			
	1836	1834–1885	1831–1832	PRONI	MIC.1D/59
	1846–1881		1848–1851		
	1836	1834–1900	1882–1884	TGC	
	1846–1900				
Ballinderry (Armagh)	Dec 19 1826–Oct 30 1838	Jan 10 1827–Nov 7 1880		NLI	Pos. 5581
	Sept 25 1841–Dec 18 1880				
	1826–1839	1827–1880		PRONI	MIC.1D/32
	1841–1881				
	1826–1900	1826–1900		IW	

Parish (Diocese)	Baptisms	Marriages	Burials	Location	Reference
Ballymoney (Down and Connor)	See Antrim				
Ballyscullion (Derry)	Sept 8 1844–Dec 22 1880	Sept 14 1844–Nov 2 1880		NLI	Pos. 5763
	1844–1881	1844–1883		PRONI	MIC.1D/58
	1844–1900	1844–1900		TGC	
Banagher (Derry)	Jan 16 1848–July 21 1878 (incomplete)	Dec 24 1851–Jan 6 1878		NLI	Pos. 5764
	1848–1878 (incomplete)	1857–1878 (incomplete)		PRONI	MIC.1D/59
	1848–1900	1850–1878		TGC	
		1884–1900			
Coleraine (Derry)	Aug 4 1843–Aug 2 1863	Aug 29 1863–Dec 13 1880		NLI	Pos. 5767
	1843–1880			PRONI	MIC.1D/62
	1843–1900	1864–1900		TGC	
Coleraine (Down and Connor)	May 5 1848–Dec 27 1880	May 15 1848–Oct 16 1880		NLI	Pos. 5474
	1848–1881	1848–1881		PRONI	MIC.1D/70
Cumber Upper (Derry)	May 18 1863–Dec 27 1880	Sept 20 1863–Dec 28 1880		NLI	Pos. 5762
	1863–1881	1863–1882		PRONI	MIC.1D/57
	1853–1854			TGC	
	1863–1900	1863–1900			
Derry city: St. Columb's (Derry)	Oct 12 1823–Sept 10 1826	Nov 28 1823–Sept 6 1826	Apr 19 1863–Dec 30 1863	NLI	Pos. 5762
	Sept 3 1836–Dec 1851 (3 sections)	Mar 28 1835–July 20 1836			
		Jan 4 1841–Nov 6 1851			
	Jabn 1 1852–Apr 17 1863	(transcript)			
	Jan 1 1864–July 23 1880	Apr 6 (1854?)–Dec 30 1863 (fragmented)			
	1823–1826	1823–1826		PRONI	MIC.1D/57
	1836–1881	1835–1836			
	1841–1863	1863			
	1823–1826	1823–1826		TGC	
	1833–1900	1835–1837			
	1841–1900				
Derry city: St. Eugene's Cathedral (Derry)	June 11 1873–Dec 30 1880			NLI	Pos. 5762
	1873–1881			PRONI	MIC.1D/57
	1873–1900	1873–1900		TGC	
Derry city: Waterside (Derry)	Jan 6 1864–Nov 29 1874	Jan 7 1864–Nov 30 1880		NLI	Pos. 5761
	Dec 1 1874–Dec 26 1880				
	1864–1881	1864–1880		PRONI	MIC.1D/56
	1864–1900	1864–1900		TGC	
Desertcreight (Armagh)	See Tyrone				
Desertmartin and Kilcronaghan (Derry)	Nov 1 1848–Dec 19 1880	Nov 13 1848–Nov 27 1880	Nov 11 1848–Dec 6 1880	NLI	Pos. 5765
	1848–1881	1848–1880	1848–1882	PRONI	MIC.1D/60
	1848–1900	1848–1900	1848–1900	TGC	
Dungiven (Derry)	July 4 1847–May 4 1853	Sept 29 1864–Dec 26 1880	Mar 4 1870–Dec 31 1871	NLI	Pos. 5764
	Sept 7 1863–Dec 26 1880				
	1825–1834	1825–1834	1825–1832	PRONI	MIC.1D/59
	1847–1881	1864–1882	1870–1871		
	1825–1834	1825–1834	1825–1832	TGC	
	1847–1900	1864–1900	1870–1871		

Parish (Diocese)	Baptisms	Marriages	Burials	Location	Reference
Errigal (Derry)	Apr 26 1846–Dec 15 1880	Feb 25 1873–Dec 23 1880		NLI	Pos. 5764
	1846–1881	1873–1880		PRONI	MIC.1D/59
	1846–1900	1872–1900		TGC	
Faughanvale (Derry)	Nov 4 1860–Nov 2 1880	Sept 1863–Dec 25 1880		NLI	Pos. 5762
	1863–1881	1860–1880		PRONI	MIC.1D/57
	1863–1900	1860–1900		TGC	
Greenlough	Oct 5 1846–Dec 29 1880	June 14 1846–Dec 25 1880	June 21 1846–Aug 18 1870	NLI	Pos. 5763
	1846–1881	1846–1882	1846–1870	PRONI	MIC.1D/58
	1845–1900	1846–1900		TGC	
Kilrea (Derry)	Aug 23 1846–Dec 26 1860	Aug 23 1846–Dec 26 1860	Aug 23 1846–Dec 26 1860	NLI	Pos. 5763 and
	Jan 1861–Aug 1865	Jan 1861–Mar 12 1877	Jan 1861–Mar 12 1877		Pos. 5764
	1846–1865	1846–1877	1846–1877	PRONI	MIC.1D/58–59
	1846–1865	1846–1900	1846–1877	TGC	
	1874–1900				
Limavady (Derry)	Dec 1855–Dec 25 1962	Apr 9 1856–Dec 18 1861	May 2 1859–Dec 10 1869	NLI	Pos. 5761
	Jan 12 1862–Dec 26 1880	Apr 20 1862–Dec 23 1880			
	Jan 3 1862–June 9 1879				
	(Ballykelly)				
	1855–1880	1856–1881	1859–1869	PRONI	MIC.1D/56
	1855–1900	1856–1900	1859–1900	TGC	
Lissan (Armagh)	July 22 1823–Dec 30 1880	Sept 1 1839–Nov 20 1880		NLI	Pos. 5585
	1839–1881	1839–1880		PRONI	MIC.1D/36
	1822–1900	1822–1900		IW	
		1822–1830		TGC	
		1839–1900			
Maghera and	Mar 17 1841–Oct 18 1857	May 13 1841–May 11 1853	May 18 1848–Sept 7 1857	NLI	Pos. 5763
Killylough (Derry)	Oct 25 1857–Dec 28 1880	Oct 25 1857–Nov 16 1880	Oct 29 1857–Sept 15 1880		
	1841–1881	1841–1853	1848–1880	PRONI	MIC.1D/58
		1857–1882	1887–1888		
	1841–1900	1841–1900	1848–1888	TGC	
Magherafelt	Jan 4 1834–July 26 1857	Jan 2 1834–Apr 21 1857		NLI	Pos. 5579
(Armagh)	Jan 10 1858–Dec 26 1880	Feb 10 1858–Dec 16 1880			
	1834–1880	1834–1881		PRONI	MIC.1D/30–31
	1830–1900	1858	TGC		
Tamlaghtard (Derry)	Sept 13 1863–Dec 24 1880	Oct 29 1863–Nov 16 1880	Sept 28 1863–Jan 2 1880	NLI	Pos. 5761
	1863–1881	1863–1881	1863–1880	PRONI	MIC.1D/56
	1833–1900	1833–1900	1863–1880	TGC	
Termoneeny (Derry)	Sept 27 1837–Aug 1839	Sept 27 1837–Aug 1839	Sept 27 1837–Aug 1839	NLI	Pos. 5763
	June 22 1852–Aug 15 1865	Apr 19 1852–Aug 15 1865			
	Oct 27 1867–Aug 18 1871	Jan 12 1868–Feb 12 1871			
	Nov 27 1871–Dec 30 1880	Dec 7 1873–Dec 28 1880			
	1837–1839	1837–1839	1837–1839	PRONI	MIC.1D/58
	1852–1865	1852–1865			
	1867–1881	1868–1871			
		1873–1880			
	1837–1900	1837–1900		Online index	Lavey
	1837–1839	1837–1839	1837–1839	TGC	
	1852–1865	1852–1900	1868–1900		
	1867–1900				

Donegal

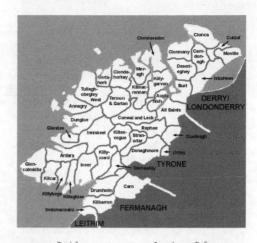

Parish (Diocese)	Baptisms	Marriages	Burials	Location	Reference
All Saints (Raphoe)	Dec 10 1843–Mar 25 1870	Nov 30 1843–Mar 20 1870		NLI	Pos. 4598
	Dec 1 1856–Dec 13 1880				
	Mar 22 1857–Dec 25 1880				
	Apr 30 1870–Nov 7 1880				
	1843–1881	1843–1870		PRONI	MIC.1D/85
	1843–1886	1843–1886		TGC	
	1884–1911	1886–1921		LDS	1279235 items 7–10
Annagry (Raphoe)	1868–			LC	
Ardara (Raphoe)	Jan 6 1869–Nov 18 1877	May 13 1867–Apr 2 1875		NLI	Pos. 4599
	Jan 31 1878–Dec 31 1880				
	1869–1880	1867–1875		PRONI	MIC.1D/86
	1867–1912	1856–1921		LDS	1279234 items 7–10 and others
Aughnish (Raphoe)	Nov 24 1873–Dec 18 1880	Dec 18 1873–Dec 12 1880		NLI	Pos. 4598
	1873–1881	1873–1881		PRONI	MIC.1D/85
	1873–1899	1873–1899		DA	
	Nov 24 1873–Dec 18 1880	Dec 18 1873–Dec 12 1880		LDS	1279234 items 27–29
Burt and Inch (Derry)	Nov 20 1859–Sept 26 1880	Jan 7 1856–Sept 30 1880	Apr 21 1860–July 9 1866	NLI	Pos. 5766
	1859–1880	1856–1880	1860–1866	PRONI	MIC.1D/55
	1859–1900	1850	1860–1866	TGC	
		1856–1900	1898–1899		
Carn (Clogher)	See Fermanagh				
Carndonagh (Derry)	Jan 23 1847–Oct 16 1873	Jan 12 1849–Sept 11 1873		NLI	Pos. 5765
	Nov 23 1873–Dec 26 1880	Nov 23 1873–Nov 7 1880			
	1847–1881	1849–1881		PRONI	MIC.1D/54
	1846–1900	1846–1900	1846–1851	TGC	
Clonca (Derry)	Nov 2 1856–Dec 8 1880	Apr 22 1870–Dec 26 1880	NLI		Pos. 5765
	May 5 1868–Dec 26 1880	Jan 14 1877–Dec 6 1880			
	1856–1881	1870–1885		PRONI	MIC.1D/54
	1856–1900	1870–1900		TGC	
Clondahorkey (Raphoe)	Oct 7 1877–Dec 28 1880	Jan 28 1879–Nov 2 1880		NLI	Pos. 4599
	1877–1881	1877–1882		PRONI	MIC.1D/86
	1856–1899	1856–1899		DA	
	1877–1913	1877–1920		LDS	1279235 item 1–3

Parish (Diocese)	Baptisms	Marriages	Burials	Location	Reference
Clondavadoc (Raphoe)	Feb 21 1847–Jan 29 1871	Feb 24 1847–July 12 1869	Feb 21 1847–Feb 5 1869	NLI	Pos. 4600
	1847–1871	1847–1869	1847–1869	PRONI	MIC.1D/87
	1847–1899	1847–1899	1847–1899	DA	
	Feb 21 1847–Jan 29 1871	Feb 24 1847–July 12 1869	Feb 21 1847–Feb 5 1869	LDS	1279236 items 2
Clonleigh (Derry)	Apr 1 1773–Feb 22 1795	Aug 1788–Sept 14 1781 (sic)		NLI	Pos. 5766
	Jan 10 1836–May 18 1837	1843–1879			
	Mar 3 1853–Sept 7 1879	Nov 14 1853–Apr 20 1870			
	Mar 12 1853–Mar 25 1870	Sept 16 1879–Nov 13 1880			
	May 1 1864–Dec 31 1880				
	1773–1795	1778–1781		PRONI	MIC.1D/61
	1836–1837	1843–1881			
	1853–1880				
	1773–1795	1778–1779		TGC	
	1836–1837	1781, 1785, 1791,			
	1853–1900	1842–1900			
Clonmany (Derry)	Jan 12 1852–Dec 30 1880			NLI	Pos. 5765
	1852–1881			PRONI	MIC.1D/54
	1852–1900	1852–1900		TGC	
Conwal and Leck (Raphoe)	May 15 1853–Mar 13 1862	May 15 1853–Mar 13 1862		NLI	Pos. 4598
	Sept 1854–Jan 41855	Jan 8 1857–Nov 22 1863			
	May 26 1856–Dec 30 1862	Feb 1 1877–Nov 27 1880			
	Mar 29 1868–Dec 31 1880				
	Oct 11 1874–Dec 26 1880				
	1874–1881	1877–1881		PRONI	MIC.1D/85
	1853–1899	1853–1899		DA	
	1851–1950	1854–1962		LDS	1279236 item 22–26 and others
Culdaff	Jan 3 1838–Nov 6 1841	Jan 14 1849–Dec 19 1880		NLI	Pos. 5766
	June 7 1847–Dec 13 1880				
	1838–1841	1849–1880		PRONI	MIC.1D/55
	1847–1880				
	1838–1900	1838–1843		TGC	
	1848–1900	1867–1887			
Desertegney (Derry)	Dec 3 1864–Dec 21 1880	Nov 9 1871–Dec 30 1880		NLI	Pos. 5765
	1864–1881	1871–1872		PRONI	MIC.1D/54
	1864–1900	1871–1900		TGC	
Donaghmore (Derry)	Nov 16 1840–Dec 20 1863	Apr 16 1846–Nov 28 186		NLI	Pos. 5767
	Jan 1 1864–Dec 18 1880	Jan 1 1864–Nov 14 1880			
	1840–1880	1846–1883		PRONI	MIC.1D/62
	1840–1900	1846–1900		TGC	
Drumholm (Raphoe)	June 17 1866–Dec 28 1880	Aug 12 1866–Sept 28 1880		NLI	Pos. 4599
	1866–1881	1866–1881		PRONI	MIC.1D/86
	1866–1912	1866–1947		LDS	1279237 item 10–11
Dungloe (Raphoe)	Nov 1 1876–Dec 31 1880			NLI	Pos. 4600
	1876–1881			PRONI	MIC.1D/87
	1876–1921	1878–1921		LDS	1279236 items 14–19 and others

Parish (Diocese)	Baptisms	Marriages	Burials	Location	Reference
Glencolmkille	1879 earliest			LC	
(Raphoe)	1879–1949	1879–1949		LDS	1279235 items 6, 11
Glenties (Raphoe)	Nov 30 1866–Nov 6 1880			NLI	Pos. 4599
Gortahork (Raphoe)	Nov 11 1849–Apr 14 1861	Aug 20 1861–Dec 3 1880	Nov 2 1849–Aug 6 1869	NLI	Pos. 4600
	Nov23 1871–Dec 26 1880				
	1849–1861	1861–1880	1849–1869	PRONI	MIC.1D/87
	1871–1880				
	1856–1896				
	1887–1959	1856–1880			
	1900–1939			LDS	1279234 items 4, 5
Inniskeel (Raphoe)	Oct 11 1866–Dec 29 1880			NLI	Pos. 4599
	1866–1881			PRONI	MIC.1D/86
	1866–1917	1866–1923		LDS	1279237, items 4–7 and others
Innismacsaint	July 25 1848–Nov 22 1880	Sept 5 1847–Oct 21 1880		NLI	Pos. 5569
(Clogher)	1847–1880	1847–1880		PRONI	MIC.1D/12
	July 25 1848–Nov 22 1880	Sept 5 1847–Oct 21 1880		LDS	979704 item 6
Inver (Raphoe)	Jan 30 1861–Dec 25 1880	Feb 3 1861–June 27 1867		NLI	Pos. 4599
	Nov 26 1875–Dec 27 1880				
	1861–1881	1861–1867		PRONI	MIC.1D/86
		1875–1881			
	Jan 30 1861–Dec 25 1880	Feb 3 1861–June 27 1867			
		Nov 26 1875–Dec 27 1880		LDS	0926210
	1861–1877	1861–1899		DA	
Iskaheen (Derry)	Sept 19 1858–Dec 26 1880			NLI	Pos. 5766
	1858–1880			PRONI	MIC.1D/55
	1858–1900			TGC	
	1858–1923	1858–1921		LDS	1279235 item 17–20
Kilbarron (Raphoe)	Nov 19 1854–Jan 4 1858	Jan 7 1858–Nov 20 1880		NLI	Pos. 4601
	Jan 1 1858–Oct 11 1866				
	Oct 14 1866–Dec 8 1880				
	1854–1881	1858–1881		PRONI	MIC.1D/88
KIlcar (Raphoe)	Jan 4 1848–Dec 29 1880			NLI	Pos. 4599
	1848–1881			PRONI	MIC.1D/86
	1848–1911	1901–1921	1906–1958	LDS	1279236 items 4–7
Killaghtee (Raphoe)	Jan 12 1845–Apr 18 1847	Sept 20 1857–Nov 7 1880		NLI	Pos. 4601
	Oct 10 1850–Oct 9 1853				
	July 26 1857–Nov 24 1880				
	1845–1847	1857–1881		PRONI	MIC.1D/88
	1850–1853				
	1857–1881				
	1857–1886	1857–1886		LDS	1279234 item 6
Killybegs (Raphoe)	Oct 12 1850–Dec 29 1880			NLI	Pos. 4601
	1850–1881			PRONI	MIC.1D/88
	1850–1911	1850–1914		LDS	1279234 items 24–26

Parish (Diocese)	Baptisms	Marriages	Burials	Location	Reference
Killygarvan (Raphoe)	Oct 11 1868–Dec 26 1880	Feb 2 1873–Jan 15 1879		NLI	Pos. 4598
	1868–1880	1873–1879		PRONI	MIC.1D/85
	1859–1899	1872–1899		DA	
Killymard (Raphoe)	Sept 20 1874–Dec 25 1880			NLI	4599
	1874–1881			PRONI	MIC.1D/86
	Sept 20 1874–Dec 25 1880			LDS	
Kilmacrennan (Raphoe)	Nov 2 1862–Sept 26 1880			NLI	Pos. 4598
	1862–1880			PRONI	MIC.1D/85
	1862–1899	1877–1899		DA	
	1862–1912	1863–1973		LDS	1279235 items 24–28
Kilteevogue (Raphoe)	Dec 2 1855–Apr 8 1862	Nov 8 1855–Mar 23 1862		NLI	Pos. 4598
	Apr 1 1870–Dec 8 1880	May 5 1870–Dec 1880			
	1855–1862	1855–1862		PRONI	MIC.1D/85
	1870–1880	1870–1882			
	1855–1910	1855–1913		LDS	1279234 items 22–23 and others
Mevagh (Raphoe)	Jan 1 1871–July 28 1878 (transcript)			NLI	Pos. 4600
	1871–1878			PRONI	MIC.1D/87
	1853–1859				
	1871–1927	1878–1921		LDS	1279234 items 11–16
Moville (Derry)	Nov 7 1847–Dec 28 1880	Nov 4 1847–Dec 12 1880	Nov 2 1847–July 23 1854	NLI	Pos. 5762
	1847–1880	1847–1880	1847–1854	PRONI	MIC.1D/55
	1847–1900	1847–1900	1847–1854	TGC	
	1852–1854 (part?)	1850–1867	1850–1854 (part)	Online	Palmer
Raphoe (Raphoe)	Feb 13 1876–Dec 11 1880	Feb 10 1876–Nov 7 1880		NLI	Pos. 4598
	1876–1881	1876–1881		PRONI	MIC.1D/85
	1876–1899	1876–1899		DA	
	1876–1949	1876–1936 (gaps)		LDS	1279235 item 14–16
Stranorlar (Raphoe)	1860 earliest			LC	
	1877–1899	1877–1899		DA	
	1877–1926	1877–1921	1905–1935	LDS	1279235 items 21–3
Tawnawilly (Raphoe)	Dec 12 1872–Dec 30 1880	Jan 9 1873–Oct 2 1880		NLI	Pos. 4599
	1872–1881	1873–1882		PRONI	MIC.1D/86
	1872–1932	1873–1911		LDS	1279234 items 17–19 and others
Termon and Gartan (Raphoe)	1862 earliest			LC	
	1882–1949	1880–1928		LDS	1279237
Tullaghobegley West (Raphoe)	Jan 6 1868–Mar 17 1871			NLI	Pos. 4600
	May 11 1873–Dec 29 1880				
	1868–1871				
	1873–1881			PRONI	MIC.1D/87
	1868–1935	1866–1943		LDS	1279234 items 8–13 and others

Parish (Diocese)	Baptisms	Marriages	Burials	Location	Reference
Urney (Derry)	See Tyrone				

Down

An index to all UHF records is searchable online,
at *www.ancestryireland. co.uk.*

Parish (Diocese)	Baptisms	Marriages	Burials	Location	Reference
Aghaderg (Dromore)	Jan 5 1816–Aug 20 1840	Feb 1 1816–Sept 5 1839	Sept 22 1838–Nov 1840	NLI	Pos. 5504
	Sept 11 1840–Aug 25 1876	Oct 4 1839–Aug 17 1876	Jan 30 1843–Aug 9 1876		
	1816–1876	1816–1876	1816–1876	PRONI	MIC.1D/29
	1840–1900	1839–1900		UHF	
Annaghlone (Dromore)	Sept 21 1834–Mar 4 1851	May 22 1851–Nov 18 1880	Apr 13 1851–Nov 28 1880	NLI	Pos. 5499
	Mar 29 1851–Nov 15 1880				
	1834–1881	1851–1881	1851–1882	PRONI	MIC.1D/24
	See NLI			LDS	0926074 item 1–2
	1851–1900 (Magheral)	1834–1900 (Drumballyroney)		UHF	
	1851–1900 (Magheral)	1851–1900 (Magheral)			
Ardkeen (Down and Connor)	Jan 11 1828–Nov26 1838	Jan 13 1828–June 3 1839		NLI	Pos. 5478
	June 2 1852–Dec 22 1880	June 9 1852–Dec 24 1880			
	1828–1838	1828–1839		PRONI	MIC.1D/74
	1852–1882	1852–1889			
	1828–1900	1828–1837		UHF	
		1853–1900			
Ballyculter (Down and Connor)	Jan 17 1844–May 21 1864	Aug 27 1843–Apr 15 1880		NLI	Pos. 5477
	Nov 19 1870–Dec 1 1880 (transcript)				
	1844–1864	1843–1882		PRONI	MIC.1D/73
	1870–1881				
Ballygalget (Down and Connor)	Jan 11 1828–Apr 18 1835	June 9 1852–Sept 5 1866		NLI	Pos. 5478
	June 18 1852–Feb 20 1853 (transcript)	Mar 4 1867–Oct 20 1880			
	June 2 1852–Feb 28 1864				
	Nov 10 1866–Dec 19 1880				

Parish (Diocese)	Baptisms	Marriages	Burials	Location	Reference
Ballygalget (Down and Connor)	1828–1835 1872–1864 1866–1881	1852–1882		PRONI	MIC.1D/74
	1828–1899	1852–1899	1894–1899	UHF	
Ballynahinch and Dunmore (Dromore)	May 1 1827–July 1 1836 Apr 14 1836–July 28 1864 July 1 1863–Dec 31 1880	Mar 3 1829–July 25 1864		NLI	Pos. 5500
	1827–1881	1829–1864		PRONI	MIC.1D/25
	See NLI			LDS	0926075 item 1–2
	1827–1900	1826–1900		UHF	
Ballyphillip and Portaferry (Down and Connor)	Mar 20 1843–Dec 31 1880 (transcript)	Mar 20 1843–Dec 31 1880 (transcript)		NLI	Pos. 5478
	1843–1881	1843–1881	1843–1881 (partial)	PRONI	MIC.1D/74
	1843–1900	1843–1900	1843–1900	UHF	
Bangor (Down and Connor)	1855–			LC	
	1844–1900	1855–1900		UHF	
Blaris (Down and Connor)			Subscriptions in Holy Trinity cemetery	PRONI	T.1602
	1840–	1840–		LC	
	1840–1900	1840–1900	1840–1900	UHF	
Bright, Rossglass and Killough (Down and Connor)	Nov 10 1856–Nov 26 1880 (also a transcript)	Nov 22 1856–Sept 17 1880		NLI	Pos. 5478
	1856–1881	1856–1881		PRONI	MIC.1D/74
	1856–1900	1856–1900		UHF	
Bryansford and Newcastle (Down and Connor)	Feb 24 1845–Dec 30 1880	Mar 25 1845–Dec 28 1880	Apr 18 1860–Nov 8 1880	NLI	Pos. 5477
	1845–1881	1845–1885	1860–1882	PRONI	MIC.1D/73
	1845–1900	1845–1900	1860–1900	UHF	
Carrickmannon and Saintfield (Down and Connor)	Oct 1 1837–Dec 4 1880	Oct 18 1845–Nov 17 1880		NLI	Pos. 5467
	1837–1881	1845–1883		PRONI	MIC.1D/63
	1837–1900	1845–1900		UHF	
Castlewellan (Down and Connor)	Nov 18 1859–Dec 25 1880	Nov 18 1859–Dec 25 1880		NLI	Pos. 5477
	1859–1881			PRONI	MIC.1D/73
	1859–1899	1859–1899	1866–1868	UHF	
Clonallon (Dromore)	Nov 28 1826–Nov 17 1838 Nov 19 1838–Jan 9 1869	Nov 23 1826–Dec 30 1880		NLI	Pos. 5497
	1826–1869	1826–1882		PRONI	MIC.1D/22
	See NLI			LDS	0926077 item 1–2
	1826–1900			UHF	
Clonuff (Dromore)	Sept 15 1850–Dec 26 1880	Aug 4 1850–Dec 30 1880	July 3 1850–Dec 6 1880	NLI	Pos. 5504
	1850–1880	1850–1880	1850–1881	PRONI	MIC.1D/29
	See NLI			LDS	0926078
	1850–1900	1850–1900	1850–1900	UHF	
Donoughmore (Dromore)	May 30 1835–July 22 1874 Sept 30 1871–Dec 20 1880	Sept 2 1825–Sept 25 1880	Oct 17 1840–1871	NLI	Pos. 5497
	1835–1880	1825–1882	1840–1871	PRONI	MIC.1D/22
	See NLI			LDS	0926079
	1828–1900			UHF	

Parish (Diocese)	Baptisms	Marriages	Burials	Location	Reference
Downpatrick (Down and Connor)	Oct 6 1851–Dec 29 1880	Feb 16 1853–Nov 8 1880	Aug 22 1851–Dec 31 1880	NLI	Pos. 5478
	1851–1882	1853–1882	1851–1882	PRONI	MIC.1D/74
	1851–1900	1852–1900		UHF	
Dromara (Dromore)	Jan 14 1844–Dec 19 1880	Jan 14 1844–Dec 18 1880	Jan 10 1844–Sept 12 1880	NLI	Pos. 5499
	1844–1880	1844–1880	1844–1880	PRONI	MIC.1D/24; CR.2/3
	See NLI			LDS	0926080
	1844–1900	1844–1900	1844–1900	UHF	
Dromore (Dromore)	Mar 3 1823–Jan 17 1845	Sept 8 1821–Dc 31 1844	Nov 9 1821–Jan 5 1845	NLI	Pos. 5504
	Jan 1 1845–Dec 30 1880	Feb 4 1845–Nov 17 1880	Nov 15 1847–Dec 27 1880		
	1823–1881	1821–1882	1821–1882	PRONI	MIC.1D/29
	1823–1881			LDS	Film 926081
	1823–1900	1821–1900	1847–1900	UHF	
Drumaroad (Down and Connor)	Jan 20 1853–Oct 24 1880	May 22 1853–Nov 3 1880		NLI	Pos. 5476
	1853–1881	1853–1880		PRONI	MIC.1D/72
	1853–1900	1853–1900		UHF	
Drumgath (Dromore)	Apr 13 1829–Dec 10 1880	July 6 1837–Nov 14 1880	June 5 1837–Nov 24 1880	NLI	Pos. 5499
	1829–1881	1837–1880	1837–1880	PRONI	MIC.1D/24
	See NLI			LDS	0926084 item 1–2
	1829–1900	1837–1900	1837–1900	UHF	
Drumgooland Lower (Dromore)	Mar 24 1832–Dec 3 1880	Apr 27 1832–Nov 18 1880	Mar 11 1832–Nov 14 1880	NLI	Pos. 5497
	1832–1881	1832–1880	1832–1881	PRONI	MIC.1D/22
	See NLI			LDS	0926083
	1832–1900	1832–1900	1832–1900	UHF	
Drumgooland Upper (Dromore)	May 26 1827–Dec 28 1880	Aug 9 1827–Dec 28 1880	May 6 1828–Nov 2 1880	NLI	Pos. 5497
	1827–1880	1827–1880	1828–1881	PRONI	MIC.1D/22
	1827–1946	1827–		LDS	0990108 item 4; 0994208 item1
	1827–1900	1827–1900		UHF	
Dunsford (Down and Connor)	April 1845	April 1845	Feb 22 1848–Feb 28 1868	NLI	Pos. 5476
	Feb 27 1848–Dec 19 1880	Feb 28 1848–Nov 24 1880			
	1845–1881	1845–1880	1848–1868	PRONI	MIC.1D/72
	1880–1900			UHF	
Holywood (Down and Connor)	Nov 18 1866–Dec 25 1880	May 3 1867–Nov 4 1880		NLI	Pos. 5471
	1866–1880	1867–1883		PRONI	MIC.1D/67
	1866–1900	1867–1900		UHF	
Kilbroney (Dromore)	Jan 1 1808–Jan 22 1843	Jan 29 1808–Dec 6 1853	Jan 1 1808–Jan 7 1843	NLI	Pos. 5499
	Jan 2 1843–Dec 19 1880	Mar 22 1848–Dec 30 1880	Jan 4 1843–Dec 30 1880		
	1808–1881	1808–1881	1808–1881	PRONI	MIC.1D/24–25
	See NLI			LDS	0990108 item 4; 0926085 item1–3
	1808–1900	1808–1900	1808–1900	UHF	
Kilclief and Strangford (Down and Connor)	Jan 14 1866–July 26 1867	Nov 25 1865–Oct 26 1868		NLI	Pos. 5476
	Oct 9 1870–Nov 19 1880	Jan 8 1871–Jan 13 1881			
	1866–1881	1865–1881		PRONI	MIC.1D/72
	1898–1900	1898–1900		UHF	

Parish (Diocese)	Baptisms	Marriages	Burials	Location	Reference
Kilcoo (Down and Connor)	Oct 22 1832–Dec 1 1880			NLI	Pos. 5476
	1832–1880			PRONI	MIC.1D/72
	1832–1899	1899–1899		UHF	
Kilkeel (Down and Connor)	July 1839–Sept 12 1877	May 9 1838–Apr 18 1876		NLI	Pos. 5477
	May 26 1845–Dec 27 1880 (transcript)	Oct 30 1867–Apr 19 1869			
	May 3 1857–Aug 9 1878				
	1839–1881	1839–1876		PRONI	MIC.1D/73
	1845–1900	1883–1900		UHF	
Kilmore (Down and Connor)	1837–1900	1896–1900	1891–1897	UHF	
Loughinisland (Down and Connor)	1806–Oct 24 1852	Nov 1 1805–Oct 23 1852	Nov 10 1805–Oct 5 1852 (some pages missing]	NLI	Pos. 5477
	1806–1852	1805–1852	1805–1852	PRONI	MIC.1D/73
	1886–1900	1805–1900	1805–1899	UHF	
Magheralinn (Dromore)	1815–1816	1815–1816	Jan 1 1817–Oct 4 1845	NLI	Pos. 5501
	Jan 1 1817–Dec 20 1845	Jan 5 1817–Dec 27 1845	Jan 10 1846–May 11 1871		
	Dec 6 1845–June 4 1871	Dec 26 1845–May 12 1871	Oct 3 1871–Dec 6 1880		
	July 17 1871–Dec 9 1880	July 10 1871–Dec 18 1880			
	1815–1881	1815–1882	1815– 1880	PRONI	MIC.1D/26
	See NLI			LDS	0926086
	1815–1900	1815–1900	1815–1900	UHF	
Mourne Lower (Down and Connor)	Aug 28 1842–Dec 18 1867	Sept 11 1839–Nov 21 1866		NLI	Pos. 5478
	Jan 11 1868–Dec 14 1880	Aug 25 1867–Oct 10 1880			
	1842–1881	1839–1880		PRONI	MIC.1D/74
	1845–1900	1883–1900		UHF	
Newry (Dromore)	See Armagh				
Newtownards (Down and Connor)	June 17 1864–Dec 23 1880			NLI	Pos. 5467
	1864–1881			PRONI	MIC.1D/63
	1844–1900	1855–1900		UHF	
Saul (Down and Connor)	May 17 1868–Dec 10 1880	May 1 1868–Dec 21 1880		NLI	Pos. 5478
	1868–1880	1868–1881		PRONI	MIC.1D/74
	1785–1900	1785–1900		UHF	
Seapatrick (Dromore)	Jan 24 1843–Dec 14 1880	July 10 1850–Oct 4 1880	July 31 1850–Dec 16 1880	NLI	Pos. 5501
	1843–1881	1850–1882	1833–1880	PRONI	MIC.1D/26
	See NLI			LDS	0926076
	1843–1900	1850–1900	1833–1900	UHF	
Tullylish (Dromore)	Jan 1 1833–Apr 14 1844	Jan 10 1833–Apr 8 1844	Jan 18 1833–Apr 17 1844	NLI	Pos. 5500
	May 7 1844–Aug 13 1844	Feb 4 1845–Dec 31 1880	May 1 1844–Dec 30 1880		
	Apr 26 1846–Feb 5 1856 (Clare and Gilford)	Apr 26 1846–Nov 25 1853 (Clare and Gilford)	Apr 26 1846–Nov 25 1853 (Clare and Gilford)		
	Jan 21 1843–Dec 31 1880				
	1833–1881	1833–1881	1833–1881	PRONI	MIC.1D/25
	See NLI			LDS	0926090 item 1–3
	1853–1900	1853–1900	1853–1900	UHF	
Tyrella (Down and Connor)	Apr 21 1854–Dec 26 1880	July 10 1854–Dec 5 1880		NLI	Pos. 5476
	1854–1881	1854–1881		PRONI	MIC.1D/72
	1854–1900	1854–1900		UHF	

Dublin
All Dublin archdiocese

Parish (Diocese)	Baptisms	Marriages	Burials	Location	Reference
Artane. (See also Coolock)	No registers microfilmed			NLI	
	1774–	1774–		LC	
	1771–1899	1771–1899		FHP	
Balbriggan	July 17 1770–Feb 15 1778	July 17 1770–Feb 15 1778		NLI	Pos. 9209
	Aug 22 1796–Oct 5 1813	Aug 29 1796–June 17 1810			
	Oct 27 1816–May 22 1860	Feb 12 1817–Nov 25 1856			
	Jan 1 1856–July 19 1893	Jan 12 1856–Nov 28 1900			
	May 21 1861–Feb 26 1871	Nov 25 1861–Feb 14 1871			
	July 23 1893–Oct 14 1901				
	1770–1899	1796–1899		FHP	
Ballybrack	–	Jan 9 1860–Nov 15 1908 (with index)		NLI	Pos. 9211
	1841–	1860–		LC	
	1841–1900	1860–1900		DLRHS	
Blackrock	July 23 1854–Oct 28 1900			NLI	Pos. 9212
	1850–	1922–		LC	
	1854–1900			DLRHS	
Blanchardstown	Dec 3 1774–Dec 8 1824	Jan 1775–Nov 7 1824		NLI	Pos. 6613, 6617
	Jan 5 1824–Dec 28 1856	Aug 8 1824–Nov 11 1856			
	Apr 25 1852–Dec 26 1880	Jan 18 1857–Nov 25 1880			
	1771–1878	1771–1899		FHP	
Bohernabreena	1868–1901			DCLA	
	1868–			LDS	
Booterstown	1755–1900	1755–1900		DLRHS	
	Oct 13 1755–Dec 20 1790	June 4 1756–Dec 20 1794		NLI	Pos. 9084 (b.); 9085 (m)
	Jan 1 1791–Oct 20 1816	Jan 1 1791–Sept 31 (sic) 1816			
	Jan 3 1817–Dec 29 1845	Oct 5 1816–Dec 26 1845			
	Jan 4 1846–July 2 1854	Jan 11 1846–Feb 11 1856			
	July 2 1854–Mar 7 1902	Jan 13 1856–Oct 34 1899			
Cabinteely	Sept 25 1863–Sept 13 1903	Apr 30 1866–Nov 22 1910		NLI	Pos. 9211
	1859–	1859–		LC	
	1862–1900			DLRHS	

Parish (Diocese)	Baptisms	Marriages	Burials	Location	Reference
Chapelizod	Oct 7 1849–Dec 15 1901	Nov 1849–July 29 1901		NLI	Pos. 9199
	1846–	1846–		LC	
	1850–1900			DCLA	
Clondalkin	1778–1800	June 11 1778–Feb 24 1800		NLI	Pos. 6612
	June 1812–May 1822	Aug 23 1812–Feb 19 1822			
	1823–1826	Aug 3 1835–Aug 28 1842			
	Jan 1837	Apr 20 1856–Nov 28 1880			
	Aug 1809–Feb 1813				
	June 1813–June 1818				
	June 1822–Aug 1830				
	Dec 1830–Aug 1833				
	1834–1837				
	July 1848				
	Apr 1849–Aug 1852				
	Transcript 1809–1852				
	1853– 188				
	1778–1896	1778–1900		DCLA	
Coolock	No registers microfilmed			NLI	
	1879–	1879–		LC	
Dalkey	Jan 13 1861–Dec 7 1899	Apr 13 1894–Oct 25 1910		NLI	Pos 9212
	1861–	1894–		LC	
	1861–1900			DLRHS	
Donabate	Nov 3 1760–Dec 27 1807	Feb 1 1761–June 6 1805		NLI	Pos. 6618
	July 4 1824–Oct 5 1869	Feb 9 1865–Nov 29 1880			
	Feb 28 1869–Oct 17 1880				
	1760–1899	1761–1899		FHP	
Donnybrook See also	Apr 15 1871–Feb 24 1902	Jan 21 1877–Nov 19 1905		NLI	
Haddington Road					Pos. 9309
	1865–	1865–		LC	
Dundrum	July 2 1854–Dec 1 1901	Sept 26 1865–Nov 17 1901		NLI	Pos. 9309
	Separate Index				
	1854–1900	1865–1900		DLRHS	
Fairview	June 18 1879–Dec 23 1880	June 10 1879–Nov 27 1880		NLI	Pos. 6609
Finglas	Mar 4 1788–July 31 1788	Nov 20 1757–July 11 1760		NLI	Pos. 6613
	Dec 6 1784–oct 161823	Dec 12 1784–July 17 1794			
	Nov 5 1823–Nov 18 1827	Oct 11 1821–Aug 10 1823			
	Jan 61828–Nov 27 1828	Nov 5 1823–Nov 18 1827			
	Dec 7 1828–May 30 1841	Jan 61828–Nov 27 1828			
	June 1 1841–Feb 20 1854	Jan 8 1829–June 1 1841			
	Jan 3 1854–Dec 12 1880	June 1 1841–Feb 20 1854			
		Jan 24 1854–Nov 24 1880			
	1812–1899	1812–1899		FHP	
Garristown	Jan 4 1857–Dec 27 1874	July 27 1857–Oct 29 1880		NLI	Pos. 6617
	Jan 1 1875–Nov 25 1880				
	1857–1899	1857–1899		FHP	
Glasthule	May 27 1865–Dec 24 1902			NLI	Pos 9211
	Separate index				
	1865–1900	1860–1900 (Ballybrack)		DLRHS	
Haddington Road	Apr 16 1798–Aug 16 1829	Apr 16 1798–Aug 16 1829			
	Jan 1 1830–Feb 13 1845	Jan 1 1830–Feb 13 1845			
	Jan 21 1845–July 16 1849	Jan 21 1845–July 16 1849			

Parish (Diocese)	Baptisms	Marriages	Burials	Location	Reference
Haddington Road	Jul 17 1849–Mar 5 1866	Jul 17 1849–Dec 26 1876		NLI	Pos. 9214
	Mar 12 1866–Dec 26 1876	Jan 7 1877–Dec 1 1905			
	Jan 1 1877–Mar 19 1907				See also Pos. 9215 for miscellaneous indexes
		1798–1916			
	1798–1876	1798–1876		DCLA	
Howth	Dec 24 1784–Dec 26 1800	Jan 9 1785–Dec 1 1800		NLI	Pos. 6618
	Aug 6 1806–Aug 31 1831	Aug 5 1806–Nov 16 1815			
	Aug 26 1831–Dec 28 1853	May 13 1818–Nov 25 1824			
	Jan 6 1854–Dec 25 1880	Jan 1 1826–July 13 1831			
		Sept 2 1831–Dec 30 1856			
		Jan 6 1857–Nov 14 1880			
	1784–1899	1784–1899		FHP	
Kingstown	Dec 4 1768–July 31 1861 (Indexed)	Jan 27 1769–Mar 27 1932 (Indexed to 1861)		NLI	Pos. 9071 (B. to 1861); Pos. 9072 (B. to 1914); Pos. 9073 (M)
	Aug 9 1861–Mar 22 1914 (Indexed)				
	1755–1900	1755–1900		DLRHS	
	1790–1859	1790–1859		WFHC	
Lucan	Sept 1818–July 1834	Sept 5 1818–July 13 1835		NLI	Pos. 6612.
	Aug 23 1835–Aug 28 1842	Jan 11 1831–Nov 22 1834			Pos 9310
	Feb 4 1849–Jan 26 1862	Aug 3 1835–Sept 18 1842			from 1885
	Mar 3 1885–Oct 27 1907	Feb 18 1849–Nov 1861			
		Sept 15 1887–Oct 28 1908			
	1818–1901	1818–1900		DCLA	
Lusk	Sept 1757–Aug 6 1801	Nov 20 1757–Jan 12 1801 (poor condition)		NLI	Pos. 6616
	Mar 11 1802–Dec 27 1835 (early years very faint)	Mar 11 1802–Dec 27 1835 (early years very faint)			
	Aug 3 1856–Dec 21 1880	Mar 6 1856–Nov 22 1880			
	1701–1900	1701–1900		FHP	
Malahide	Apr 20 1856–Apr 13 1901 Index	May 7 1856–June 24 1901		NLI	Pos. 9310
	1856–1900	[See also Swords]		FHP	
Maynooth	See Kildare				
Monkstown	No registers microfilmed			NLI	
	1865–	1881–		LC	
	1855–1900	1865–1900		DLRHS	
Naul	No registers microfilmed			NLI	
	1832–1899	1833–1899		FHP	
Newcastle–Lyons	No records microfilmed			NLI	
	1773–	1773–		LC	
Palmerstown	Aug 26 1798–Dec 31 1799	Sept 24 1837–Sept 27 1857		NLI	Pos. 6612
	Sept 3 1837–Apr 24 1864				
	1798–1862	1838–1858		DCLA	
Rathfarnham	Jan 1 1777–May 1781	Feb 5 1777–May 19 1781	Newscuttings,	NLI	Pos. 8972
	May 1781–Nov 14 1781	May 26 1781–Nov 18 1781	Parochial notes		
	Nov 18 1781–Dec 1 1788	Sept 22 1807–Jan 9 1832			

Parish (Diocese)	Baptisms	Marriages	Burials	Location	Reference
Rathfarnham	Sept 18 1807–Jan 15 1832	Jan 23 1832–Jan 8 1852			
	Jan 22 1832–Feb 1 1852	Jan 5 1852–Nov 21 1858			
	Jan 1 1852–Feb 7 1857	Nov 19 1862–Nov 3 1864			
	Jan 7 1861– 1917	Nov 12 1864–Mar 4 1787			
		Feb 12 1878–July 24 1933			
	1777–1857	1777–1864		DCLA	
Rathgar	No records microfilmed			NLI	
	1874–	1874–		LC	
Rathmines	Nov 23 1823–Feb 12 1840	Nov 23 1823–Feb 12 1840		NLI	Pos. 9200
	Mar 22 1840–Dec 10 1850	Mar 22 1840–Dec 10 1850			(bapt to 1886,
	Dec 9 1848–Aug 26 1860	Dec 9 1848–Aug 26 1860			marr. To 1881)
	Dec 9 1848–Nov 28 1881	Dec 17 1848–Dec 10 1881			Pos. 9201
	Dec 15 1881–Jun 26 1886	Jan 7 1882–Aug 1 1886			
	Aug 8 1886–Feb 13 1899	Aug 10 1886–Jan 21 1901			
	Feb 15 1899–Oct 9 1906	All with indexes			
	All with indexes				
	1823–	1823–		LC	
Rush	July 12 1785–Dec 27 1828	Sept 22 1785–Dec 27 1796		NLI	Pos. 6617
	Mar 13 1829–Dec 27 1856	July 14 1799–Apr 28 1810			
	Dec 31 1856–Dec 28 1880	Aug 16 1813–Dec 3 1828			
		1829–Sept 29 1856			
		Jan 1 1857–Nov 27 1880			
	1785–1826	1785–1826		FHP	
Saggart	Oct 4 1832–Feb 1862	May 21 1832–Aug 14 1878		NLI	Pos. 6483
	May 13 1878				
	Jan 12 1862–Dec 26 1880				
	1832–1899	1832–1878		DCLA	
Sandyford	Mar 8 1841–Dec 28 1856	Nov 16 1823–Nov 24 1856		NLI	Pos 9308
	Jan 22 1857–Dec 18 1904	Mar 8 1841–Dec 28 1856			
	Jan 4 1857–Oct 22 1905	Jan 13 1857–Nov 21 1909			
		Jun 1 1876–Nov 17 1901			
	1823–	1823–		LC	
	1823–1900	1823–1856		DCLA	
Sandymount	No registers microfilmed			NLI	
	1865–	1865–		LC	
Skerries	Oct 12 1751–Dec 31 1781	June 22 1751–Nov 17 1781		NLI	Pos. 6614
	Jan 6 1872–June 23 1814	Jan 10 1782–July 5 1814			
	July 12 1814–Dec 23 1853	(poorly filmed)			
	Jan 1 1854–Dec 23 1880	Aug 15 1814–Mar 25 1856			
		Apr 24 1856–Nov 6 1880			
	1751–1899	1751–1899		FHP	
Swords	Dec 26 1763–July 7 1777	Oct 3 1763–June 7 1777		NLI	Pos. 6616
	June 2 1802–Nov 29 1819	June 24 1802–Nov 25 1819			
	Dec 3 1819–Sept 15 1828	Dec 26 1819–Dec 15 1828			
	Sept 15 1828–Dec 4 1845	Jan 19 1829–Dec 3 1845			
	Dec 2 1845–Mar 23 1856	Jan 12 1846–Nov 26 1856			
	(Indexed)	Feb 2 1857–Nov 7 1880			
	Mar 28 1858–Dec 21 1880				
	1763–1899	1751–1899		FHP	
Terenure	No registers microfilmed			NLI	
	1870–	1894–		LC	

Dublin City
All Dublin archdiocese

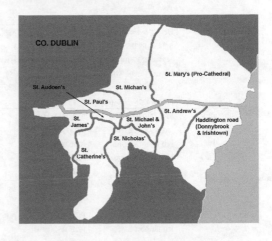

Parish (Diocese)	Baptisms	Marriages	Burials	Location	Reference
Aughrim St.	No registers microfilmed			NLI	
	1888–	1888–		LC	
Berkeley Road	No registers microfilmed			NLI	
	1890–	1890–		LC	
Cabra	No registers microfilmed			NLI	
	1909–	1856–		LC	
Harrington St. (St. Kevin's)	May 8 1865–Apr 21 1873	Feb 1865–Jan 10 1893		NLI	Pos 9312
	Apr 22 1873–Feb 17 1880	Jan 16 1893–Nov 17 1912			(bapt. To
	Feb 17 1880–Jun 16 1885	Index on Pos. 9314			1890)
	Jun 19 1885–Jun 27 1890				Pos. 9313
	Jun 27 1890–Nov 23 1897				(bapt. To
	Nov 23 1897–Dec 24 1901				1901)
	Index on Pos. 9311				Pos. 9314
					(marr.)
St. Agatha's	Dec 15 1852–Dec 31 1800	Jan 7 1853–Dec 16 1880		NLI	Pos. 6611
	Dec 29 1879–Dec 31 1880				
	1852–1900	1853–1900		DCLA	
St. Andrew's	Jan 1741/2–July 1752	Jan 1741/2–July 1751	NLI	Pos. 6605–6610	
	July 1750–June 1773	Oct 1751–June 1773			
	Sept 1751–June 1776	June–Oct 1756			
	Feb 1777–Sept 1787	Mar 1759–May 1776			
	Oct 1772–Sept 1790	June 1792–May 1793			
	Aug 1779–May 1793	July 1773–Dec 1778			
	Aug 1790–Jan 1801	July 1776–Oct 1777			
	Jan 1792–1801	Apr 1789–May 1793			
	Mar–Apr 1802	Sept 1790–Oct 1801			
	Jan 1801–1812	Apr–Aug 1804			
	Jan 1811–July 1822	Jan 1801–Dec 1880			
	June 1810–Dec 1880				
	1742–1776	1741–1777		DCLA	
	1780–1787	1780–1787			
	1799–1804	1799–1804			
	1849–1858				

Parish (Diocese)	Baptisms	Marriages	Burials	Location	Reference
St. Audoen's	Dec 1778–Dec 1799	Feb 8 1747–Aug 13 1785		NLI	Pos. 6778
	June 22 1800–Aug 19 1825	Jan 1800–Aug 30 1825			
	Sept 22 1825–July 14 1833	Oct 3 1825–June 14 1833			
	July 1833–Sept 19 1856	Aug 4 1833–June 21 1859			
	(poor condition)	Oct 14 1856–Dec 12 1880			
	June 11 1878–Dec 31 1880				
St. Catherine's	May 1740–Dec 1749	May 1740–Dec 1749		NLI	Pos. 7138–7141
	Jan 1750–Aug 1765	Jan 1750–Aug 1765			
	Feb 1761–Oct 1766	June 1765–Dec 1792			
	June 1765–Feb 1794	Feb–July 1794			
	Dec 10 1797	1799 (scraps)			
	Nov 1799–Dec 1805	1800–1818			
	Nov 1799–Dec 1810	1811–1821			
	Feb 1806–Nov 1819	1823–1828			
	Jan 1811–Sept 1821	1822–1851 (gaps)			
	Mar–Dec 1820	1849–1863 (John's Lane)			
	June 1821– Dec 1880	1852–Nov 1856			
	(gaps)	1857–1880			
St. James'	Sept 1752–1784	1754–1755		NLI	Pos. 7228–7232
	Apr 1785–Aug 1798/9	Oct 8 1804–Dec 13 1833			
	Apr 1800–1880	1856–1858			
	Multiple registers for	Mar 4 1832–Nov 26 1856			
	all periods	June 3 1859–May 1868			
	Many registers poorly	Aug 23 1868–Dec 29 1880			
	legible many	Many entries are not			
	entries out of	in chronological order			
	chronological order				
	1803–1882	1806–1896		DCLA	
St. Laurence O'Toole's	July 20 1853–June 4 1875	June 19 1856–Dec 26 1880		NLI	Pos. 6611
	June 7 1875–Dec 31 1880				
St. Mary's (Pro–Cathedral)	1741–	1741–		LC	
	1741–1900				
	Index 1810–1939 on	1741–1900		NLI	Pos. 9148–9167
	Pos. 9162				
St. Michael and John's	Jan 1 1768–Jan 1857	Jan 8 1784–Dec 1851		NLI	Pos. 7358–7360
	Mar 2 1856–Dec 30 1880	Jan 11 1852–Nov 28 1880			
	Indexed 1876–1880	Indexed c 1743–1842			
	1743–1792	1742–1792		DCLA	
St. Michan's	Feb 1726–Jan 1734	Feb 25 1726–July 19 1730		NLI	Pos. 8829–8831
	Jan 1735–Dec 1739	June 1730–Jan 1734			
	Sept 1739–Oct 1744	Jan 1735–Dec 1739			
	June 1755–Sept 1763	Dec 1739–Sept 1744			
	Oct 1744–Mar 1768	Oct 1744–May 29 1763			
	Sept 1770	Mar 18 1756–Oct 26 1763			
	Aug 1795– June 1854	Aug 16 1795–Aug 23 1823			
	May 1830–June 1850	Sept 1823–Mar 1856			
	May 1850–July 1854	Mar 31 1856–1884 Indexed			
	July 9 1854–Dec 7 1869				
	Nov 2 1868–Nov 20 1869				

Parish (Diocese)	Baptisms	Marriages	Burials	Location	Reference
St. Nicholas'	Jan 3 1742–Aug 21 1752	Sept 29 1767–Dec 13 1801	Apr 7 1829–May 2 1856	NLI	Pos.
(Without)	Jan 11 1767–Dec 26 1801	Dec 21 1783–Dec 22 1796	Dec 3 1857–May 22 1905		7267–7270;
	Aug 15 1772–Nov 26 1780	Mar–Oct 1791			7275; 7277;
	Dec 1 1782–Jan 2 1785	Jan–Feb 1793			7368
	Mar 22 1788–Sept 20 1790	Jan 2 1802–Aug 16 1828			
	1781–1794 (scraps)	Jan 1 1807–June 1 1807			
	1823 (fragment)	Nov 20 1814			
	Nov 21 1824– 1857	1824–1827			
	1858– 1880 (index)	1822–July 29 1866			
		Sept 14 1856–Sept 13 1865			
St. Paul's	1731–1882 (indexed)	1731–1889 (indexed)		NLI	Pos. 8828 8838
	1731–1898	1732–1900		FHP	

Fermanagh

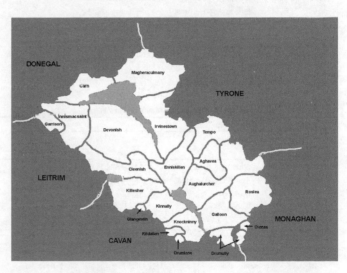

Parish (Diocese)	Baptisms	Marriages	Burials	Location	Reference
Aghavea (Clogher)	Mar 31 1862–Dec 26 1880	May 11 1866–June 15 1880		NLI	Pos. 5572
	1862–1882	1866–1881		PRONI	MIC.1D/15
		1896–1897			
Aughalurcher	Oct 19 1835–Dec 28 1880			NLI	Pos. 5569
(Clogher)	1835–1883			PRONI	MIC.1D/12;
					CR.2/12
	See NLI			LDS	979704 item 6
Carn (Clogher)	Mar 19 1851–Oct 28 1877	Jan 9 1836–Nov 23 1880		NLI	Pos. 5569
	Nov 18 1877–Dec 30 1880				
	1851–1881	1836–1881		PRONI	MIC.1D/12–13
	See NLI			LDS	0926049 item 1
Cleenish (Clogher)	Dec 28 1835–Sept 8 1839	Apr 8 1866–Nov 14 1880		NLI	Pos. 5571
	Feb 8 1859–Jan 25 1868				
	Aor 8 1866–Dec 3 1880				
	1835–1839	1866–1881		PRONI	MIC.1D/14
	1859–1881				
	See NLI			LDS	979705 item 1–4

Parish (Diocese)	Baptisms	Marriages	Burials	Location	Reference
Clones (Clogher)	See Monaghan				
Devonish (Clogher)	Feb 12 1853–Aug 1879			NLI	Pos. 5567
	Arrnaged chronologically by letter				
	1853–1879			PRONI	MIC.1D/10
	See NLI			LDS	926050
Drumlane (Kilmore)	See Cavan				
Drumully (Clogher)	Jan 6 1845–Apr 2 1866	July 14 1864–Oct 31 1880		NLI	Pos. 5572
	July 7 1864–Dec 26 1880				
	1845–1881	1864–1881		PRONI	MIC.1D/15
Enniskillen (Clogher)	1838–Sept 27 1868	Feb 10 1818–Dec 26 1880		NLI	Pos. 5567 to
	Sept 30 1868–Dec 26 1880				1868; remainder
					on Pos. 5568
	1838–1881	1817–1880		PRONI	MIC.1D/10–11
Galloon (Clogher)	Jan 1 1853–Feb 27 1859	May 10 1847–July 24 1879		NLI	Pos. 5572
	June 14 1863–Dec 30 1880				
	1853–1859	1847–1879		PRONI	MIC.1D/15
	1863–1881				
Garrison (Clogher)	July 12 1860–Apr 14 1874	Jan 12 1860–May 19 1873			
	Oct 31 1871–Dec 23 1880				
	Oct 2 1871–Oct 4 1880			NLI	Pos. 5569
	1860–1881	1860–1880		PRONI	MIC.1D/12
	See NLI			LDS	979704 item 3–5
Glangevlin (Kilmore)	See Cavan				
Innismacsaint (Clogher)	See Donegal				
Irvinestown Clogher)	(Nov 29 1846–July 3 1874	Dec 22 1851–Aug 28 1874		NLI	Pos. 5571
	Aug 18 1874–Dec 21 1880	Aug 7 1874–Aug 7 1880			
	1846–1881	1851–1882		PRONI	MIC.1D/14
	See NLI			LDS	979705 item 7–10
Kildallen (Kilmore)	See Cavan				
Killesher (Kilmore)	Sept 2 1855–Dec 16 1880	Sept 2 1855–Dec 16 1880	Sept 2 1855–Dec 16 1880	NLI	Pos. 5345
	1855–1881	1855–1881	1855–1881	PRONI	MIC.1D/78
	See NLI		Sept 2 1855–Dec 16 1880	LDS	0926133 item 1
Kinnally (Kilmore)	See Cavan				
Knoc+ninny (Kilmore)	May 21 1855–Nov 27 1870	Jan 1855–Nov 24 1870		NLI	Pos. 5349
	1855–1870	1855–1870		PRONI	MIC.1D/78
	See NLI			LDS	979703 item 1
Magheraculmany (Clogher)	Aug 24 1836–Jan 11 1857	Nov 13 1837–Nov 1 1844		NLI	Pos. 5571
	Mar 22 1857–Dec 26 1869	Apr 24 1857–Dec 6 1869			
	Jan 2 1870–Dec 29 1880	Nov 12 1844–Apr 13 1857			
		Jan 15 1870–Dec 27 1880			
	1836–1881	1837–1881		PRONI	MIC.1D/14; C.R.2/1
	See NLI			LDS	979705 item 11–14
Roslea (Clogher)	Jan 6 1862–Dec 26 1880	Jan 19 1862– Nov 26 1880		NLI	Pos. 5577
	1862–1881	1862–1881		PRONI	MIC.1D/20
	See NLI			LDS	0926057
Tempo (Clogher)	Nov 1 1845–Oct 13 1870	Oct 11 1845–Nov 23 1870			
	Aug 2 1871–Dec 18 1880	Jan 3 1871–Nov 8 1880		NLI	Pos. 5570

Galway West

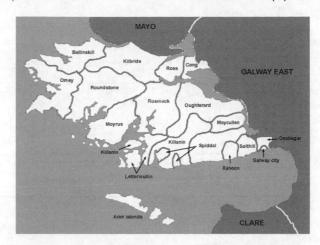

Parish (Diocese)	Baptisms	Marriages	Burials	Location	Reference
Aran Islands (Tuam)	Nov 7 1874–Dec 23 1880	Feb 20 1872–Dec 21 1880		NLI	Pos. 4219
	1872–1905	1872–1905		LDS	1279214 item 8
	1872–1900	1872–1900		GFHSW	
Ballinakill (Tuam)	1869–1900	1869–1900		GFHSW	
	1869–1903	1870–1903		LDS	1279212
	July 23 1869–Dec 26 1880	July 25 1869–Dec 5 1880		NLI	Pos. 4218
	May 14 1876–Dec 26 1880	Jan 12 1875–Nov 17 1880			
	(separate register)	(separate register)			
Castlegar (Galway)	Mar 8 1827–Dec 31 1841	Mar 8 1827–Dec 15 1841	Mar 25 1827–Oct 28 1841	NLI	Pos. 2438
	Jan 2 1842–July 31 1863	Jan 8 1842–Oct 24 1864	Jan 9 1842–July 31 1864		
	Nov 3 1864–Nov 21 1880	Nov 3 1864–Nov 21 1880	Nov 13 1864–Nov 21 1880		
	1827–1908	1827–1912	1828–1908	GFHSW	
	See NLI			LDS	0979690 item 2
Cong	See Mayo				
Galway city:	Apr 21 1690–Dec 28 1690			NLI	Pos. 2436
St. Nicholas (Galway)	Mar 31 1723–Mar 10 1726				
	See NLI			LDS	0926070
Galway city:	Nov 15 1810–Dec 30 1821	Jan 7 1789–Nov 29 1824	Sept 1 1788–Dec 17 1809	NLI	Pos. 2436
St. Nicholas East	Oct 1 1831–Dec 1858	Oct 17 1831–Dec 23 1858	Oct 16 1831–Dec 26 1858		& 2437
	1810–1858	1789–1858	1789–1858	GFHSW	
	See NLI			LDS	0926070
Galway city:	Apr 5 1818–Mar 30 1835	Apr 12 1818–Aug 22 1868	Apr 5 1818–Mar 31 1861	NLI	Pos. 2436 &
St. Nicholas North	Apr 7 1835–Oct 28 1867		1866–8 (2 pages only)		2437
	1818–1867	1818–1868	1818–1868	GFHSW	
	See NLI			LDS	0926070
Galway city:	Feb 2 1859–Dec 26 1880	Feb 3 1859–Nov 30 1880	Feb 20 1859–Dec 31 1880	NLI	Pos. 2437
St. Nicholas North	1859–1900	1859–1900	1859–1900	GFHSW	
& East	See NLI			LDS	0926070
Galway city:	Apr 21 1690–Dec 28 1690	1809–1821 (3 pages only)	1811–1869 (5 pages only)	NLI	Pos. 2436
St. Nicholas South	Mar 31 1723–Mar 10 1726	Mar 12 1814– Dec 26 1826	Mar 5 1814–Nov 16 1826		
and West	1805–1821 (2 pages only)	Feb 13 1822–Sept 29 1859	Aug 15 1847–July 3 1859		
	Feb 27 1814–Dec 13 1826	Aug 13 1828–Oct 13 1845	Aug 13 1828–Oct 13 1845		
	Oct 16 1822–Aug 20 1866	Jan 9 1846–Jan 31 1852	Feb 7 1846–Dec 21 1851		
	Aug 13 1828–Oct 13 1845	Nov 4 1959–Oct 8 1868	Nov 8 1859 Sept 8 1868		
	Jan 6 1846–Apr 12 1853	Nov 9 1872–Dec 31 1880	Nov 25 1872–Dec 5 1880		

Parish (Diocese)	Baptisms	Marriages	Burials	Location	Reference
Galway city:	1859–1868				
St. Nicholas South		1872–1880			
and West	1814–1900	1809–1900	1810–1900	GFHSW	
	See NLI			LDS	0926070
Kilbride (Tuam)	Dec 11 1853–Nov 12 1880 (transcript)			NLI	Pos. 4214
	Ross			LC	
	1853–1900	1853–1900		MSFHC	
	See NLI			LDS	0926221 item 2
Killanin (Galway)	Jan 1 1875–Dec 26 1880	Jan 26 1875–Dec 6 1880		NLI	Pos. 2439
	1875–1900	1875–1900	1881–1888	GFHSW	
	See NLI			LDS	0926228 item 2
Lettermullin (Tuam)	Aug 17 1853–May 16 1880	July 18 1853–Nov 1 1880		NLI	Pos. 4218
	Aug 18 1872–Nov 21 1880 (KIlleen)				
	1861–1900	1853–1895		LDS	127921 item 11–13
	1853–1900	1853–1900		GFHSW	
Moycullen (Galway)	Jan 2 1786–Mar 9 1823	Jan 8 1786–Jan 13 1823	Jan 4 1786–Mar 13 1823	NLI	Pos. 2441
	Jan 4 1837–May 3 1841	Oct 1 1843–Oct 3 1848	Nov 1848–Dec 21 1880		
	Oct 6 1843–Oct 3 1848	Feb 18 1849–Nov 16 1880			
	Nov 4 1848–Dec 26 1880	Jan 8 1786–Jan 13 1823	Jan 4 1786–Mar 13 1823	LDS	0926071
	Jan 2 1786–Mar 9 1823	Oct 1 1843–Oct 3 1848	Nov 1848–Dec 21 1880		
	Jan 4 1837–May 3 1841	Feb 18 1849–Nov 16 1880			
	Oct 6 1843–Oct 3 1848				
	Nov 4 1848–Dec 26 1880				
	1793–1812	1793–1812		Published	AH No 14 pp 126–134
	1848–1900	1849–1900	1848–1900	GFHSW	
Moyrus (Tuam)	Dec 8 1853–Sept 20 1873	Sept 9 1852–Sept 6 1874		NLI	Pos. 4218
	Oct 18m 1874–Nov 7 1880	Nov 1 1874–Nov 20 1880			
	1853–1900	1854–1900		GFHSW	
	1852–1903	1852–1903		LDS	1279212 items 8–10
Omey (Tuam)	Jan 7 1838–Oct 7 1855	Sept 15 1839–May 6 1855 (assorted entries for different dates)		NLI	Pos. 4218
	July 1856–Oct 26 1874				
	Oct 2 1864–Aug 7 1880 (Ballyconneely)				
		Aug 19 1858–Feb 27 1874 (assorted entries for different dates)			
		Oct 29 1864–Dec 18 1873			
		June 26 1874–Dec 14 1880			
	1838–1900 (Clifden)	1838–1900 (Clifden)	1869–1877 (Ballyconeely)	GFHSW	
	1864–1900 (Ballyconeely)	1864–1900 (Ballyconeely)			
	1881–1900 (Omey/Ballindoon)	1885–1900 (Omey/Ballindoon)			
	1838–1924	1839–1938	1869–1872	LDS	1279213 item 1–7; 1279213 1;
Oughterard (Galway)	June 27 1809–Aug 18 1821	July 27 1809–Feb 23 1816	Mar 8 1827–Feb 4 1874	NLI	Pos. 2438
	Mar 9 1827–Dec 30 1880	Mar 20 1827–Dec 28 1880			
	1809–1900	1809–1900	1827–1874	GFHSW	

Parish (Diocese)	Baptisms	Marriages	Burials	Location	Reference
Oughterard (Galway)	1809–1821	1809–1816	1827–1874	LDS	0979690 item 3
	1827–1880	1827–1880			
Rahoon (Galway)	Jan 3 1819–Dec 31 1832	Jan 3 1819–Dec 27 1832	Jan 3 1819–July 23 1826	NLI	Pos. 2437
	Jan 1 1833–Jan 28 1845		2 pages for 1830		
	Apr 17 1845–Mar 25 1877				
	1806–1913	1806–1913	1806–1913	GFHSW	
	Jan 3 1819–Dec 31 1832	Jan 3 1819–Dec 27 1832	Jan 3 1819–July 23 1826	LDS	0926069
	Jan 1 1833–Jan 28 1845		2 pages for 1830		
	Apr 17 1845–Mar 25 1877				
Rosmuck (Galway)	Aug 11 1840–Dec 27 1880			NLI	Pos. 2439
	1840–1900		1863	GFHSW	
Ross (Tuam)	Dec 25 1853–Apr 29 1871				
	Jan 10 1873–Dec 19 1880			NLI	Pos. 4216
	Kilbride			LC	
	1853–1900	1853–1900		GFHSW	
	1853–1919	1883–1903		LDS	1279259 item 6–10
Roundstone (Tuam)	Aug 3 1872–Dec 26 1880	Aug 4 1872–Dec 19 1880		NLI	Pos. 4218
	1872–1900	1872–1900		GFHSW	
	1872–1910	1872–1900		LDS	1279212 items 8–10
Salthill (Galway)	No records microfilmed			NLI	
Spiddal (Galway)	Feb 7 1861–Mar 25 1873	Apr 29 1873–Nov 3 1880	Apr 22 1873–Dec 8 1880	NLI	Pos. 2438
	Apr 13 1873–Dec 25 1880				
	1861–1900	1873–1900	1873–1900	GFHSW	
	See NLI			LDS	0979690 item 4

Galway East

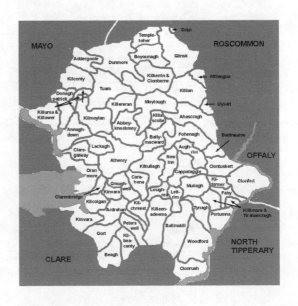

Parish (Diocese)	Baptisms	Marriages	Burials	Location	Reference
Abbeyknockmoy (Tuam)	No records microfilmed			NLI	
	1821–1900	1844–1900	1847–1848	GFHSW	
	1821–1832	1837–1844	1847–1848	LDS	1279210 item 9–14
	1837–1858	1894–1901			
	1841–1854				
	1894–1915				
Addergoole (Tuam)	Aug 7 1858–Nov 18 1877	Jan 10 1859–Dec 11 1880		NLI	Pos. 4210
	Jan 8 1878–Dec 31 1880				
	1858–1900	1859–1900		GFHSW	
	1858–1891	1859–1884		LDS	1279208 item 1–2
	1878–1918				
Ahascragh (Elphin)	Jan 10 1840–May 6 1880	Jan 29 1866–Nov 26 1880		NLI	Pos. 4616, 4617
	Aug 15 1870–Dec 31 1880 (Ahascragh only)	(Ahascragh only)			
	1840–1899	1866–1899		RHGC	
	See NLI			LDS	09899751
				Online	Familysearch
Annaghdown (Tuam)	Sept 1834–Sept 12 1869	Mar 15 1834–Nov 29 1868		NLI	Pos. 4219
	Feb 2 1875–Jan 4 1880	Feb 6 1875–June 12m 1880			
	1834–1900	1834–1900		GFHSW	
	1834–1909 (gaps)	1834–1909 (gaps)		LDS	1279206 item 1–2
Ardrahan (Galway)	May 30 1839–Mar 221846	Mar 26 1845–Feb 20 1850		NLI	Pos. 2442
	Nov 18 1866–Nov 15 1880	Feb 3 1867–Sept 13 1887			
	1839–1900	1845–1900	1878	GFHSW	
	See NLI			LDS	0926062
Athenry (Tuam)	Aug 3 1858–Sept 21 1878			NLI	Pos. 4219
	Aug 15 1858–Oct 1 1878				
	1858–1900	1858–1900		GFHSW	
	1858–1919	1858–1901		LDS	1279207 item 6–7; 1279209 4–5
Athleague	See Roscommon				Pos. 4613
Aughrim (Clonfert)	Mar 27 1828–Dec 28 1880			NLI	Pos. 2431
	1828–1900	1829–1900	1825–1830	EGFHS	
	1828–1901	1828–1921	1892–1901	LDS	1279215
Ballinakill (East Galway) (Clonfert)	Apr 15 1839–Oct 22 1851			NLI	Pos. 2434
	Feb 5 1859–Dec 24 1880				
	Nov 20 1858–Dec 26 1859				
	1839–1850	1870–1900		EGFHS	
	1860–1900	1891–1903		LDS	0979689 item 12, 14; 1279216 22/
	1839–1851				
	1858–1859				
	1859–1880				
	1890–1902				
Ballinasloe (Clonfert)	Sept 23 1820–July 27 1832	Sept 23 1820–July 27 1832	Sept 23 1820–July 27 1832	NLI	Pos. 2432
	July 19 1832–Feb 21 1841	July 19 1832–Feb 21 1841	July 19 1832–Feb 21 1841		
	June 7 1841–June 14 1847				
	July 6 1847–May 30 1862				
	June 6 1862–Dec 31 1880				
	1820–1900	1820–1900	1825–1830	EGFHS	
	1820–1900	1853–1902		LDS	1279217

Parish (Diocese)	Baptisms	Marriages	Burials	Location	Reference
Ballymacward (Clonfert)	Oct 1 1841– Nov 15 1843			NLI	Pos. 2431
	May 2 1855–Feb 15 1874				
	May 12 1855–Dec 30 1880				
	1856–1890	1885–1900		EGFHS	
	1855–1901	1885–1902		LDS	1279226
Beagh (Galway)	Feb 5 1851–June 25 1851	Mar 1849–Feb 23 1850		NLI	Pos. 2442
	Jan 14 1855–Apr 3 1881	May 19 1860–Oct 18 1881			
	1855–1900			EGFHS	
	See NLI			LDS	0979692
	1855–1856			Online	Celtic Cousins
Boyounagh (Tuam)	Oct 5 1838–June 11 1858	Oct 9 1838–July 17 1865		NLI	Pos. 4211
	Dec 11 1859–Oct 25 1863				
	Oct 8 1865–Dec 26 1880				
	1838–1900	1838–1865		EGFHS	
	1859–1908			LDS	1279211 item 9
Cappataggle (Clonfert)	Jan 6 1809–Mar 10 1814	Jan 6 1809–Mar 10 1814	Jan 6 1809–Mar 10 1814	NLI	Pos. 2431
	Jan 1 1814–May 29 1827	Jan 1 1814–May 29 1827	Jan 1 1814–May 29 1827		
	Sept 23 1827–June 24 1844	Sept 23 1827–June 24 1844	Sept 23 1827–June 24 1844		
	June 26 1844–Sept 15 1869	Nov 1 1831–June 25 1844	June 26 1844–Sept 15 1869		
		July 18 1844–July 30 1863			
	1799–1900	1806–1863	1806–1849	EGFHS	
		1893–1900			
	1809–1844	1831–1844	1827–1844	LDS	1279215,
	1844–1917	1844–1865	1844–1869		1279216
Carabane (Clonfert)	July 14 1831–Mar 6 1878	July 24 1831–Jan 29 1878		NLI	Pos. 2434
	1831–1900	1834–1900		EGFHS	
	1831–1902	1832–1912		LDS	0979689;
					1279216
Claregalway (Galway)	Nov 11 1849–Dec 29 1880	Nov 12 1849–Nov 23 1880	Nov 11 1849–Nov 1876	NLI	Pos. 2429
	1849–1902	1849–1908	1849–1876	GFHSW	
Clarenbridge (Galway)	Aug 7 1854–Mar 29 1881	June 13 1837–Feb 18 1882		NLI	Pos. 2442
	Aug 7 1854–Mar 29 1881	June 13 1837–Feb 18 1882		LDS	0979690
	1854–1900	1837–1900		GFHSW	
Clonfert (Clonfert)	No records microfilmed			NLI	
	1884–1900			EGFHS	
	1893–1901	1894–1904		LDS	1279215
Clonrush	See Clare				
Clontuskert (Clonfert)	Oct 2 1827–Dec 20 1880	Oct 2 1827–Oct 4 1868	Oct 2 1827–Oct 4 1868	NLI	Pos. 2431
	(modern transcript)	Mar 2 1870–Dec 5 1880			
	Oct 2 1827–Oct 4 1868				
	Mar 2 1870–Dec 5 1880				
	1827–1900			EGFHS	
	1827–1901	1827–1901		LDS	1279215
Craughwell (Galway)	Nov 20 1847–Mar 28 1881	July 6 1856–Nov 25 1876		NLI	Pos. 2442
	1847–1894	1847–1858	1847–1850	EGFHS	
		1869–1876			
	Nov 20 1847–Mar 28 1881	July 6 1856–Nov 25 1876		LDS	0979692
Donaghpatrick (Tuam)	Apr 8 1844–June 30 1844	Apr 8 1844–Dec 6 1846		NLI	Pos. 4219
	Nov 12 1849–June 9 1861	Dec 8 1849–June 15 1861			
	Aug 1 1863–Dec 27 1880	Sept 12 1863–Nov 18 1880			
	1844–1900	1844–1900		GFHSW	
	1857–1901	1857–1905		LDS	1279206 item 12

Parish (Diocese)	Baptisms	Marriages	Burials	Location	Reference
Dunmore (Tuam)	Mar 2 1833–Mar 1 1846	Mar 17 1833–Sept 6 1860		NLI	Pos. 4211
	Dec 12 1853–Oct 21 1859	Jan 13 1861–Sept 9 1877			
	(two sections 1856–59)				
	Dec 14 1847–Jan 20 1854				
	Sept 16 1877–Dec 30 1880				
	1833–1900	1833–1900		GFHSW	
	1833–1860	1833–1860		LDS	1279210 item
	1877–1910				4–8
Dysart	See Roscommon				
Fahy (Clonfert)	No records microfilmed			NLI	
	1873–1900	1876–1900		EGFHS	
	1893–1903	1894–908		LDS	1279216
Fohenagh (Clonfert)	Aug 1 1827–Apr 4 1877	Aug 1 1827–Apr 4 1877	Aug 1 1827–Apr 4 1877	NLI	Pos. 2431
	1828–1900	1828–1885		EGFHS	
	1827–1877	1827–1877		LDS	1279215 4–8;
	1889–1902	1890–1905			0926058
Glinsk (Elphin)	Sept 5 1836–Jan 28 1846	Nov 1 1836–Apr 24 1865	Sept 14 1836–Sept 20 1839	NLI	Pos. 4620
	Nov 2 1846 (?)–June 22 1848	July 6 1865–Nov 1 1880			
	Mar 15 1849–Sept 23 1866				
	Oct 6 1866–Dec 26 1880				
	1836–1900	1836–1900	1836–1839	RHGC	
Gort (Galway)	Feb 14 1848–Feb 13 1862	Dec 6 1853–Feb 20 1862		NLI	B. to 1872:,
	July 17 1854–Dec 28 1872	Feb 23 1862–Feb 17 1863			M. to 1862
	Feb 18 1862–Feb 17 1863				Pos. 2441;
	Jan 5 1873–Mar 2 1881				remainder 2442
	See NLI			LDS	0979691
	1848–1880			EGFHS	
Kilbeacanty (Galway)	Aug 6 1854–Jan 7 1881			NLI	Pos. 2442
	See NLI			LDS	0979692
	1855–1900	1881–1900		EGFHS	
Kilchreest (Galway)	Feb 1 1855–June 25 1881	Feb 2 1865–Feb 23 1886		NLI	Pos. 2442
	1855–1900	1865–1897		EGFHS	
	See NLI			LDS	0926064
Kilcolgan (Galway)	Nov12 1854–July 21 1881	Jan 29 1871–Sept 6 1884		NLI	Pos. 2442
	See NLI			LDS	0979691
	1854–1900	1871–1900		GFHSW	
Kilconly (Tuam)	Mar 3 1872–Dec 29 1880			NLI	Pos. 4212
	1872–1900	1872–1900		GFHSW	
	1872–1913			LDS	1279214 item 4
Kilkerrin and	No records microfilmed			NLI	
Clonberne (Tuam)	1892–1900	1884–1893		EGFHS	
	1892–1903	1893–1935	1920–1926	LDS	1279213
					item 8–9
KIllascobe (Tuam)	July 13 1867–Dec 24 1880	May 7 1807–July 20 1819		NLI	Pos. 4220
		Nov 25 1825–June 8 1847			
		July 25 1849–Dec 15 1880			
	1806–1902	1806–1902		LDS	1279259 item 13
Killeenadeema	May 1 1836–Dec 12 1880	Apr 24 1836–Oct 2 1880		NLI	Pos. 2434
(Clonfert)	1836–1900	1836–1900		EGFHS	
	1836–1932	1837–1915		LDS	1279216

Parish (Diocese)	Baptisms	Marriages	Burials	Location	Reference
Killereran (Tuam)	June 12 1870–Dec 26 1880	Feb 26 1851–Aug 8 1858		NLI	Pos. 4220
	Oct 24 1870–July 1 1879				
	1870–1900	1851–1900		GFHSW	
	1870–1900	1851–1879			
	1888–1900		LDS	1279214 item 1–2	
Killian (Elphin)	Apr 22 1804–July 26 1833	Apr 21 1804–Feb 28 1843	Oct 21 1844–Dec 5 1859	NLI	Pos. 4613, 4614
	Oct 19 1844–Dec 29 1863	Oct 13 1844–Mar 31 1863			
	Dec 13 1859–Mar 23 1861	Jan 16 1860–Oct 5 1865			
	May 12 1860–Nov 21 1880	(Newbridge)			
	(Newbridge)	Jan 24 1864–Nov 18 1880			
	Jan 14 1864–Nov 21 1879				
	1804–1900	1804–1900	1804–1900	EGFHS	
	See NLI			LDS	0989748
	1860–1880	1860–1880		BIVRI	
				Online	Familysearch
	1804–1900	1804–1900	1844–1859	RHGC	
Killimore and	Oct 8 1831–Dec 29 1846	Nov 7 1831–July 27 1880		NLI	Pos. 2433
Tiranascragh	Jan 1 1847–Sept 10 1879				
(Clonfert)	1831–1891	1831–1841			
	1851–1897		EGFHS		
	1831–1901	1831–1902		LDS	1279215
Killursa and	No records microfilmed			NLI	
Killower (Tuam)	1880–1912	1880–1916		LDS	1279207 items 13–14
	1880–1916	1880–1920		GFHSW	
Kilmoylan (Tuam)	Dec 18 1835–Aug 5 1860	Oct 14 1813–July 20 1872	NLI	Pos. 4220	
	Aug 4 1872–July 9 1879	Aug 1 1871–Nov 26 1880			
	1835–1906	1813–1894	1835–1868	LDS	1279207 item 1–5
	1835–1900	1813–1900		GFHSW	
		1813–1816		Online	Bishop
Kiltormer (Clonfert)	Mar 12 1834–July 15 1860	Feb 9 1834–May 20 1860		NLI	Pos. 2433
	May 22 1862–Dec 20 1880	Sept 30 1860–Sept 28 1873			
	1834–1900	1834–1900		EGFHS	
	1834–1903	1834–1926	1834–1836	LDS	1279217
Kiltullagh (Clonfert)	June 25 1844–Jan 15 1854	Jan 30 1830–Aug 4 1880	Sept 5 1830–May 23 1837	NLI	Pos. 243434
	Dec 21 1862–Oct 12 1872				
	1844–1881	1826–1900	1830–1841	EGFHS	
	1844–1901	1826–1902	1830–1841	LDS	1279216
Kinvara (Galway)	June 28 1831–May 15 1837	July 9 1831–May 13 1837	List of the inhabitants 1834,	NLI	B. and M. to
	June 23 1843–Aug 29 1853	June 26 1843–Aug 12 1853	Easter dues, and		1853: Pos. 2442;
	July 31 1854–Sept 29 1867	Nov 17 1867–Jan 18 1881	remembrance masses 1835/7–		remainder
	Oct 11 1867–Mar 27 1881		May 13 1837. Certificates		2443
			issued 1844–1855		
	1831–1853			LDS	0926068
	1831–1900	1831–1900		GFHSW	
Lackagh (Tuam)	July 1842–Sept 24 1847	Sept 10 1841–Dec 20 1847		NLI	Pos. 4220
	Apr 1 1848–Sept 25 1853	Sept 25 1853–Mar 1 1880			
	Sept 5 1853–Dec 26 1880				
	1842–1900	1841–1900	1858–1876	GFHSW	
	See NLI			LDS	0976227

Parish (Diocese)	Baptisms	Marriages	Burials	Location	Reference
Leitrim (Clonfert)	May 22 1815–Aug 3 1819	May 22 1815–Aug 3 1819	May 22 1815–Aug 3 1819	NLI	Pos. 2434
	Oct 13 1819–Dec 28 1822	Oct 13 1819–Dec 28 1822	Oct 13 1819–Dec 28 1822		
	Jan 4 1823–June 1 1829	Jan 4 1823–June 1 1829	Jan 4 1823–June 1 1829		
	Sept 30 1850–Dec 17 1880	Dec 9 1846–Nov 28 1880	Dec 16 1846–Sept 18 1880		
	1815–1840	1816–1830	1816–1830	EGFHS	
	1846–1929	1842–1850	1847–1887		
		1887–1900			
	See NLI			LDS	1279215
Loughrea (Clonfert)	Apr 29 1827–Dec 27 1848	May 12 1827–Nov 24 1880		NLI	Pos. 2435
	Jan 1 1849–July 27 1863	July 21 1868–Dec 21 1880			
	July 21 1863–Aug 8 1871				
	July 21 1868–Dec 21 1880				
	1810–1900	1786–1900	1817–1826	EGFHS	
	1810–1901	1810–1901	1817–1826	LDS	1279216/7
Moylough (Tuam)	Jan 16 1848–Oct 28 1863	Nov 20 1848–Sept 29 1863		NLI	Pos. 4220
	Sept 20 1860–July 1870	Dec 17 1860–Dec 7 1870			
	Jan 11 1871–Dec 8 1880	Jan 12 1871–Oct 23 1880			
	Jan 2 1873–Dec 31 1880	Feb 17 1873–Oct 18 1880			
	1848–1900	1837–1900		EGFHS	
	1848–1903	1848–1903		LDS	1279210
Mullagh (Clonfert)	Feb 11 1859–Dec 24 1880	Apr 26 1863–Oct 22 1880		NLI	Pos. 2434
	1846–1885 (incomplete)	1846–1885 (incomplete)			
	Jan 3 1863–Sept 13 1880	Jan 3 1863–Sept 13 1880			
	1863–1900			EGFHS	
	1863–1903	1846–1920		LDS	1279218
New Inn (Clonfert)	Oct 17 1827–Apr 23 1840	Oct 28 1827–May 15 1842		NLI	Pos. 2431
	Aug 11 1841–Dec 5 1880	July 29 1839–Nov 15 1880			
	1827–1900	1827–1900		EGFHS	
	1827–1903	1827–1908	1893–1930	LDS	1279216
Oran	See Roscommon				
Oranmore (Galway)	Mar 11 1833–Apr 29 1839	May 2 1833–July 18 1838	Jan 7 1833–Dec 24 1837	NLI	Pos. 2438
	May 25 1833–Dec 28 1843	Aug 24 1843–Nov 8 1880			
	Dec 28 1843–Dec 25 1880				
	See NLI			LDS	0979690
	1833–1900	1833–1900	1833–1837	GFHSW	
Peterswell (Galway)	Jan 27 1854–Jan 15 1881	Jan 28 1856–July 24 1886		NLI	Pos. 2442
	See NLI			LDS	0979692
	1854–1900	1856–1900		EGFHS	
Portumna (Clonfert)	Oct 6 1830–Feb 1 1878	Oct 27 1830–Nov 1 1876		NLI	Pos. 2433
	Feb 22 1878–Dec 24 1880	Feb 6 1878–Oct 14 1880			
	1830–1891	1832–1864		EGFHS	
	1830–1891	1830–1890		LDS	1279216
Templetoher (Tuam)	Aug 25 1858–Jan 25 1872	Sept 11 1858–Feb 11 1872		NLI	Pos. 4213
	1856–1900	1859–1872	1858–1870	EGFHS	
	1856–1900	1858–1889		LDS	1279259
Tuam (Tuam)	Mar 3 1790–July 2 1804	Jan 26 1799 (?)–Mar 6 1832		NLI	Pos. 4221, 4222
	Oct 14 1811–Oct 5 1829	Oct 17 1832–Dec 26 1880			
	Nov 1 1829–Apr 12 1845				
	May 1 1845–Oct 1 1857				
	Oct 3 1858–July 13 1873				
	1790–1900	1790–1900		GFHSW	
	1790–1929	1795–1901		LDS	1279208/9

Parish (Diocese)	Baptisms	Marriages	Burials	Location	Reference
Tynagh (Clonfert)	May 1 1816–Dec 31 1842	May 22 1809–Dec 10 1842		NLI	Pos. 2433
	Sept 25 1846–Dec 31 1880	Sept 26 1846–Feb 10 1863			
	1816–1842	1809–1842		EGFHS	
	1846–1864	1846–1864			
	1874–1900				
Woodford (Clonfert)	Apr 20 1821–Nov 25 1843	Apr 22 1821–Nov 25 1843		NLI	Pos. 2433
	Mar 6 1851–Aug 4 1861	Mar 1 1851–July 23 1861			
	Apr 22 1865–Sept 13 1868	July 27 1865–Feb 9 1869			
	Feb 20 1869–Oct 16 1880	Feb 18 1871–Feb 19 1880			
	1821–1900	1821–1900		EGFHS	
	1821–1860	1821–1866		LDS	1279217/8
	1865–1908	1881–1889			
	1865–1889			Online	Egan

Kerry
All Kerry diocese

Parish (Diocese)	Baptisms	Marriages	Burials	Location	Reference
Abbeydorney	Oct 2 1835–Sept 10 1844	Jan 24 1837–July 20 1859		NLI	Pos. 4274
	Feb 27 1851–Sept 6 1859	Nov 2 1859–Nov 10 1880			
	Nov 7 1880–Dec 6 1880				
	1835–1900	1835–1900		KGC	
Ardfert	Mar 1819–Nov 1819	Feb 15 1825–Jan 25 1826		NLI	Pos. 4272
	July–Sept 1824	Jan 10 1835–Feb 24 1846			
	Feb 8 1835–Oct 2 1846	Nov 4 1859–Nov 30 1880			
	Oct 1 1859–Dec 20 1874				
	Dec 24 1984–Dec 26 1880				
	1859–1900	1860–1900		KGC	
	1818–1846	1825–1846		LDS	0883784 item 6; 0883740 item 3
	1818–1839	1825–1843 (Vol. 8)		O'K	
	1839–1846 (Vol. 8)				

Parish (Diocese)	Baptisms	Marriages	Burials	Location	Reference
Ballanvohir	Apr 2 1829–Mar 12 1834	May 1 1829–June 3 1835		NLI	Pos. 4274
	Mar 23 1837–Mar 19 1839	May–Oct 1837			
	Oct 2 1851–Dec 26 1880	Sept 1855–Nov 14 1880			
	(transcript)	(transcript)			
	1829–1834	1829–1899		KGC	
	1837–1839				
	1851–1899				
Ballybunion	Nov 1 1831–Jan 4 1870	Feb 7 1837–Nov 13 1869		NLI	Pos. 4280
	Jan 2 1870–Dec 27 1880	Jan 15 1870–Nov 21 1880			
	1831–1900	1860–1900		KGC	
Ballyheigue	Dec 1 1857–Dec 17 1880	Jan 13 1858–Feb 10 1880		NLI	Pos. 4273
	1867–1900	1857–1900		KGC	
Ballylongford	Mar 20 1823–May 12 1838	June 1826–Jan 1827		NLI	Pos. 4284
	(very fragmented)	Feb 1828–Aug 1828			
	Oct 1869–Dec 31 1880	Jan 1832–Nov 1837			
		(very fragmented)			
	1823–1900	1823–1900		KGC	
Ballymacelligot	Oct 4 1868–Dec 19 1880	Nov 14 1868–July 30 1880		NLI	Pos. 4273
	1868–1900	1859–1900		KGC	
Beaufort	Mar 10 1844–Jan (?) 1880	Jan 7 1843–Feb 25 1879		NLI	Pos. 4265
	1844–1880	1846–1896		KGC	
Boherbue	July 22 1833–Dec 7 1860	March 22 1863–Nov 25 1880		NLI	B. to 1865, Pos.
	Feb 8 1863–Dec 29 1873				4265;
	Jan 6 1873–Dec 24 1880				remainder
					4266
	1833–1875	1863–1880		LDS	0883696 item
					12; 0883884
					item 4
	1833–1864 (Vol. 2)	1863–1870 (Vol. 3)		O'K	
	163–1900 (Vol. 11)	1863–1900 (Vol. 11)			
		1903–1947 (Vol. 14)			
Bonane and	July 22 1846–Dec 25 1856	July 18 1847–Nov 29 1856		NLI	Pos. 4288
Glengarriff	Jan 3 1857–Dec 21 1877	Feb 1 1857–Feb 9 1875			
	Jan 9 1878–Dec 26 1880	Feb 2 1876–Feb 10 1880			
Brosna	Mar 15 1868–May 14 1878			NLI	Pos. 4283
	1866–1900	1880–1900		KGC	
	1866–1875			LDS	1238660 item 3
	1866–1900 (Vol. 8)	1872–1900 (Vol. 8)		O'K	
Cahirciveen	Nov 11 1846–June 24 1863			NLI	Pos. 4285
	(some pages mutilated)				
	Apr 16 1863–Jan 18 1879				
	(transcript)				
	1863–1900	1863–1900		KGC	
Cahirdaniel	Feb 1831–July 29 1867	May 1831–Feb 18 1868		NLI	B., Pos. 4287;
	(mutilated)	(many pages mutilated)			M. 4288
	1831–1893	1831–1893		KGC	
Castleisland	Apr 1823–Dec 29 1859	Oct 10 1822–Aug 10 1858		NLI	M. and B. to
	Jan 1 1859–Aug 29 1869	Feb 8 1859–May 6 1880			1869, Pos. 4276;
	Feb 15 1870–Dec 18 1880				remainder
					4277
	1823–1899	1823–1899		KGC	

Parish (Diocese)	Baptisms	Marriages	Burials	Location	Reference
Castleisland	1829–1913	1825–1918		LDS	1279379
	1823–1858 (*Vol. 6*)	1822–1891 (*Vol. 7*)		O'K	
	1859–1869 (*Vol. 4*)	1878–1900 (*Vol. 7*)			
	1870–1872 (*Vol. 6*)				
Dingle	Feb 25 1825–Apr 20 1837	May 1 1821–Dec 30 1859		NLI	Pos. 4277 to
	Sept 30 1837–Dec 6 1859	Jan 28 1860–Oct 13 1880			1859; remainder
	Jan 1 1860–Sept 15 1869				4278
	Sept 11 1869–Jan 12 1880				
	1824–1899	1860–1900		KGC	
Dromod	Feb 1850–Aug 5 1867	Jan 29 1850–Mar 5 1867		NLI	Pos. 4288
	Apr 13 1867–Dec 31 1880	Apr 13 1867–Dec 31 1880			
Duagh	Jan 1 1819–Dec 2 1833	Jan 24 1832–Nov 10 1833	May 9 1844–Dec 6 1846	NLI	Pos. 4282
	Dec 2 1833–Nov 27 1852	Jan 26 1834–Aug 14 1852			
	1853–Sept 28 1871	1853–June 18 1871			
	(some early pages missing)	(some early pages missing)			
	Oct 1 1871–Dec 27 1880	Jan 18 1872–Oct 19 1880			
	1819–1906	1827–1911		KGC	
Fossa	Jan 11 1857–Dec 17 1880	Jan 21 1858–Sept 26 1880		NLI	Pos. 4265
	1857–1900			KGC	
Glenbeigh	Mar 17 1830–Aug 1837	Mar 1830–Feb 1835		NLI	Pos. 4285
	(fragmented)	(fragmented)			
	June 21 1841–Mar 25 1870				
	(fragmented pages missing)				
	Apr 9 1870–Dec 30 1880				
	1825–1837	1829–1837		KGC	
	1885–1900	1843–1898			
Glenflesk	Sept 1821–Mar 12 1873	Feb 13 1831–Feb 25 1873		NLI	Pos.4266
	1820–1873	1831–1848		KGC	
	1852–1873				
	1820–1875	1831–1880 (gaps)		LDS	0883747 item 2,19
	1820–1832 (*Vol. 7*)		1831–1900 (*Vol. 6*)		O'K
	1832–1862 (*Vol. 7*)				
	1862–1894 (*Vol. 8*)				
Keel	Feb 5 1804–July 8 1813	Feb 4 1804–Mar 15 1818		NLI	Pos. 4273
	Jan 9 1815–Oct 1817	May 1818–June 18 1834			
	Apr 7 1818–June 30 1834	Aug 28 1834–Feb 4 1845			
	July 6 1834–Mar 1845	Apr 9 1845–July 31 1880			
	Feb 29 1845–Nov 1 1880				
	1804–1820			Online	Genweb, Kerry
Kilcummin	Jan 10 1821–Aug 31 1859	Jan 31 1823–Sept 23 1859		NLI	Pos. 4265
	Feb 8 1873–May 11 1880	Feb 8 1873–May 11 1880			
	1821–1875	1823–1859		LDS	0883784 item
		1873–1880			5, 0883740 item 5
	1821–1900 (*Vol. 5*)	1823–1859 (*Vol. 5*)		O'K	
		1873–1900 (*Vol. 5*)			
	1821–1900	1823–1859		KGC	
	1873–1900				

Parish (Diocese)	Baptisms	Marriages	Burials	Location	Reference
Kilgarvan	Apr 15 1818–Aug 23 1846	Nov 4 1818–Aug 1 1846		NLI	Pos. 4290
	Aug 10 1846–Nov 30 1853	Sept 23 1846–Apr 16 1864			
	Dec 2 1863–Dec 31 1880	Sept 6 1864–May 1880			
	1841–1895	1818–1895		KGC	
Killarney	Aug 5 1792–June 24 1803	Aug 15 1792–June 27 1803		NLI	Pos. 4262 to
	June 27 1803–July 12 1809	June 29 1803–July 18 1809			1830; B. to
	July 16 1809–Sept 5 1816	July 16 1809–Sept 1 1816			1865. M. to
	Sept 3 1816–Apr 15 1824	Sept 2 1816–May 23 1824			1857, 4263;
	Apr 16 1824–Jan 17 1830	June 11 1824–Jan 28 1830			remainder
	Jan 3 1830–Dec 25 1880	Feb 1 1830–May 24 1857			4264
		Jan 7 1858–Nov 9 1880			
	1785–1839	1792–1880		LDS	0883697
					item 4,5;
					0883851 1
	1785–1803 (Vol. 5)	1792–1839 (Vol. 5)		O'K	
	1803–1833 (Vol. 6)	1839–1890 (Vol. 7)			
	1833–1840 (Vol. 7)	1891–1900 (Vol. 7)			
	1840–1865 (Vol. 8)				
	1865–1900 (Vol. 14)				
	1786–1900	1796–1900		KGC	
Killeentierna	June 14 1801–Dec 24 1809	June 12 1803–Feb 28 1828		NLI	Pos. 4272
	July 24 1823–Nov 14 1880	Jan 8 1830–July 10 1880			
		(transcript)			
Killeentierna	1801–1809	1803–1812		KGC	
	1823–1920	1815–1828			
		1830–1860			
		1864–1884			
	1801–1875	1803–1880		LDS	0883740 item
					4, 0883818
					item 18
	1801–1809 (Vol. 4 & 6)	1803–1900 (Vol. 6)		O'K	
	1823–1870 (Vol. 4 & 6)				
	1871–1900 (Vol. 6)				
	1801–1805			Online	Grogan
Killiny	Dec 7 1828–Dec 31 1864	Feb 28 1829–Nov 13 1864		NLI	Pos. 4275 to
	Jan 3165–June 16 1879	Jan 18 1865–Sept 11 1880			1864;
					remainder 4276
	1828–1899	1829–1899		KGC	
Killorglin	1798–1802	1798–1802		KGC	
	1806–1851	1806–1850			
	1881–1917	1884–1946			
Killury	Dec 10 1782–July 1786	Feb 13 1809–Feb 16 1836		NLI	Pos. 4278, 4279
	Nov 4 1806–Nov 29 1819	(many pages illegible)			
	July 18 1820–Apr 29 1835				
	Sept 4 1831–June 29 1845				
	Aug 31 1845–Apr 20 1858				
	May 8 1858–Dec 25 1880				
	1782–1900	1809–1900		KGC	

Parish (Diocese)	Baptisms	Marriages	Burials	Location	Reference
Kilmelchidar	Jan 14 1807–Jan 19 1808	Jan 1808–Aug 5 1808		NLI	Pos. 4274 to
	Jan 1 1808–June 29 1828	Feb 5 1808–May 31 1828			1828;
	July 1 1828–July 30 1871	July 24 1828–Nov 1880			remainder
	Aug 24 1871–Dec 19 1880				4275
Kilnaughten	Oct 1 1859–Dec 26 1880	July 26 1859–May 29 1880		NLI	Pos. 4280
	1859–1900	1859–1900		KGC	
Knocknagoshel	1866–1900			KGC	
Listowel	Aug 1802–June 1826	Jan 8 1837–May 26 1828		NLI	Pos. 4281
	Oct 1826–Dec 1833	Nov 10 1842–Feb 28 1842			
	Jan 1837–May 1838	Sept 2 1843–Feb 12 1844			
	Nov 1842–May 1843	Mar 9 1846–July 10 1846			
	Scpt 1843–Feb 1844	June 25 1850–Jan 1851			
	Mar 1846–July 1846	Feb 6 1851–May 5 1853			
	May 1850–Jan 1851	June 7 1855–May 30 1855			
	Mar 1852–May 1853	June 18 1855–Nov 21 1880			
	May 1855–July 1855				
	Jan–July 1841				
	May 1856–1880				
	1802–1906	1837–1906		KGC	
Lixnaw	Aug 4 1810–Mar 27 1843	Jan 15 1810–June 6 1852		NLI	B. to 1849 Pos.
	Apr 2 1843–Feb 20 1845	Aug 17 1856–Nov 27 1875			4281;
	June 4 1848–Dec 25 1875	Jan 17 1876–Dec 1 1880			remainder
	Feb 14 1876–Dec 1 1880				4282
	1810–1901	1810–1900		KGC	
Milltown	Oct 9 1825–Sept 20 1840	Oct 7 1821–Nov 1832		NLI	Pos. 4266
	Oct 1 18841–Aug 21 1859	Oct 17 1841–June 6 1861			
	1825–1859	1821–1829		KGC	
	1886–1895	1841–1861			
		1887–1894			
Molahiff	Jan 1 1830–Sept 22 1872	Jan 13 1830–Mar 13 1872		NLI	Pos. 4267
	(very poor condition)	(very poor condition)			
	Sept 29 1859–June 8 1871				
	(Aglis)				
	Jan 20 1871–Aug 10 1872				
	Oct 1872–Oct 23 1880				
	(damaged)				
	1830–1894	1830–1894		KGC	
	1872–1900 (Vol. 8)	1881–1900 (Vol. 8)		o'k	
Moyvane	July 21 1855–Oct 7 1877	Oct 4 1855–Nov 27 1880		NLI	Pos. 4283
	1830–1917	1831–1917		KGC	
Prior	No records microfilmed			NLI	
	1851–1900	1853–1900		KGC	
Rathmore	Sept 19 1837–March 14 1841	Jan 26 1839–May 3 1874		NLI	Pos. 4268
	Jan 14 1844–Dec 20 1874				
	1837–1875	1839–1880		LDS	0883875
					0883698
	1837–1846 (Vol. 1)	1839–1874 (Vol. 1)		o'k	
	1846–1874 (Vol. 1)	1875–1900 (Vol. 5)			
	1875–1900 (Vol. 5)				
	1837–1900	1839–1874		KGC	

Parish (Diocese)	Baptisms	Marriages	Burials	Location	Reference
Sneem	Aug 17 1845–Nov 26 1848	Feb 2 1858–Nov 27 1880		NLI	Pos. 4288
	Nov 1 1857–Dec 25 1880				
	1833–1848	1858–1868		KGC	
	1857–1900	1882–1900			
	Aug 1845–Sept 1848			NLI	Ms 2729
Spa	Nov 11 1866–Dec 31 1880	Jan 27 1867–Nov 11 1880		NLI	Pos. 4274
Templenoe	Jan 1 1819–Dec 24 1838	Jan 26 1819–Mar 2 1824		NLI	Pos. 4289
	Jan 2 1839–Dec 30 1858	Jan 17 1826–June 30 1838			
	Jan 2 1859–Dec 19 1870	Jan 23 1839–Nov 27 1858			
	Jan 1 1871–Aug 1 1876	Jan 9 1859–Oct 24 1880			
	Aug 6 1876–Feb 16 1879				
	1819–1846	1819–1900		KGC	
	1848–1876				
	1887–1900				
Tralee	Jan 1 1772–Feb 24 1795	May 1 1832–Nov 26 1853		NLI	B. to 1845,
	Mar 1 1795–Dec 28 1813	Nov 18 1853–June 21 1856			Pos. 4269; B.
	Jan 14 1818–July 30 1832	June 24 1856–Feb 1 1876			to 1874, M. to
	Aug 1 1832–July 30 1843				1832, 4270;
	Aug 1 1843–June 22 1856				remainder
	June 24 1856–Dec 22 1867				4271
	Jan 1 1868–June 4 1874				
	1772–1900	1875–1900		KGC	
Tuosist	Apr 22 1844–May 26 1880			NLI	Pos. 4287
	(some pages missing)				
Valentia	Mar 7 1825–July 5 1864	Feb 5 1827–April 1856		NLI	Pos. 4287
	May 15 1867–Dec 14 1880				
	1825–1864				
	1867–1902	1827–1855		KGC	

Kildare

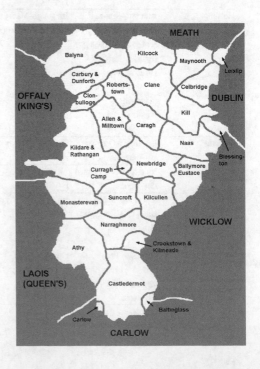

Parish (Diocese)	Baptisms	Marriages	Burials	Location	Reference
Allen and Milltown	Oct 15 1820–Oct 31 1852	Oct 17 1820–Oct 26 1876		NLI	Pos. 4206
(Kildare and Leighlin)	1820–1899	1820–1899		KHGS	
Athy (Dublin)	Dec 7 1779–Mar 21 1797	Jan 14 1780–Feb 12 1797		NLI	Pos. 6479/80
	Sept 11 1803–Aug 21 1807	Sept 21 1803–Feb 2 1810			
	Aug 23 1807–Nov 26 1816	Feb 9 1812–June 25 1812			
	Dec 10 1821–Mar 5 1837	July 17 1815–Mar 7 1816			
	Mar 17 1837–Aug 14 1853	June 24 1822–Jan 25 1837			
	Aug 21 1853–Apr 7 1873	Apr 6 1837–Nov 22 1853			
	Apr 9 1873–Dec 31 1880	Jan 10 1854–Nov 26 1880			
	1753–1899	1753–1899		KHGS	
Ballymore Eustace	Mar 8 1779–Apr 27 1792	Oct 18 1779–Nov 27 1794		NLI	Pos. 6481
(Dublin)	Jan 10 1787–Mar 1 1790	Feb 21 1787–June 11 1796			
	May 3 1792–Apr 6 1796	May 15 1797–July 19 1830			
	Jan 5 1797–Oct 28 1830	Apr 22 1826–Dec 1 1838			
	Apr 23 1826–Dec 26 1838	Jan 27 1839–Nov 26 1863			
	Jan 1 1839–Apr 27 1854	Jan 25 1864–Oct 25 1880			
	May 7 1854–Dec 31 1880				
	1779–1900	1779–1900		WFHC	
	1779–1899	1779–1899		KHGS	
Baltinglass See Wicklow					
Balyna (Kildare	Oct 17 1785–Oct 27 1801	Nov 5 1797–May 23 1799		NLI	Pos. 4206
and Leighlin)	Nov 6 1801–July 17 1803	Jan 27 1866–Dec 23 1880			
	Aug 24 1807–Oct 21 1811	Nov 13 1801–Jan 31 1802			
	Jan 15 1815–Feb 22 1815	Oct 1 1807–Oct 26 1811			
	Feb 1 1818–Apr 12 1829	Jan 25 1815–Feb 7 1815			
	Feb 1 1818–Dec 21 1865	Apr 7 1817–Aug 21 1830			
	(1818–1829 duplicate	Mar 23 1818–Nov 15 1880			
	entries)	(1818–1830 duplicate entries)			
	1785–1899	1797–1899		KHGS	
	1785–1899	1785–1899		Published	Index, 1988
Blessington	See Wicklow				
Caragh (Kildare and	June 19 1849–Aug 12 1866	Feb 7 1850–Nov 23 1859		NLI	Pos. 4206
Leighlin)	Aug 6 1849–July 4 1875	Feb 7 1850–June 30 1875			
	June 17 1866–Apr 19 1874	(transcript)			
	(transcript)				
	1849–1899	1850–1899		KHGS	
Carbury and	Oct 1 1821–May 22 1850	Nov 2 1821–Oct 27 1850	Feb 18 1869–June 9 1879	NLI	Pos. 4206
Dunforth	June 9 1850–Dec 5 1880	Oct 6 1850–Nov 14 1880			
(Kildare and Leighlin)					
Carlow	See Carlow				
Castledermot	Nov 5 1789–Feb 3 1821	Nov 5 1789–Feb 3 1821		NLI	Pos. 6480/81
(Dublin)	1822–Oct 18 1829	May 1822–Dec 14 1829			
	1829–Nov 9 1842	Jan 18 1830–Nov 2 1842			
	Dec 4 1842–Dec 10 1856	Jan 10 1843–Dec 27 1856			
	(index 1854–80)	Feb 15 1857–Dec 19 1880			
	Jan 18 1857–Dec 26 1880				
	1789–1899	1789–1899		KHGS	
Celbridge (Dublin)	Jan 4 1857–Dec 19 1880			NLI	Pos. 6613
	1857–1882			KHGS	

Parish (Diocese)	Baptisms	Marriages	Burials	Location	Reference
Clane (Kildare and Leighlin)	Mar 17 1785–Sept 4 1785	Apr 10 1825–June 2 1828		NLI	Pos. 4206
	Feb 1 1786–July 3 1786	Nov 15 1829–June 5 1840			
	Dec 8 1788–Apr 8 1789	July 19 1840–Nov 23 1880			
	Feb 28 1825–Feb 28 1827				
	Sept 6 1829–May 31 1840				
	June 2 1840–Dec 26 1880				
	1821–1899	1821–1899		KHGS	
Clonbulloge	See Offaly				
Crookstown and Kilmeade (Dublin)	Apr 28 1837–Aug 17 1840	July 1 1837–Aug 8 1840		NLI	Pos. 6485
	Aug 1840–Aug 7 1843	July 1 1842–July 25 1846			
	Apr 28 1843–July 7 1846	Jan 16 1853–Feb 5 1856			
	Aug 9 1849–May 5 1853				
	May 5 1853–Mar 17 1856				
	1853–1856	1853–1856		KHGS	
Curragh Camp (Kildare and Leighlin)	Aug 5 1855–July 9 1871	Sept 15 1855–Jan 15 1871		NLI	Pos. 4207
	Nov 12 1871–Dec 19 1880	Dec 3 1871–Sept 13 1880			
	1855–1899	1855–1899	1877–1890	KHGS	
Kilcock (Kildare and Leighlin)	July 6 1771–Dec 4 1786	Jan 28 1770–May 28 1787		NLI	Pos. 4207
	Aug 14 1816–Dec 23 1826	Feb 27 1791–May 1 1791			
	Oct 9 1831–June 28 1834	Aug 7 1816–Sept 29 1822			
	July 8 1834–Dec 19 1880	July 8 1834–Nov 16 1880			
	1770–1791	1770–1791		LDS	0926117 item 1
	1771–1899	1770–1899	1889–1897	KHGS	
Kilcullen (Dublin)	Oct 22 1777–Sept 1818	May 11 1786–Nov 20 1806		NLI	Pos. 6484
	Apr 25 1829–Sept 13 1840	Apr 24 1810–Oct 27 1816			
	Jan 11 1857–Dec 14 1880	May 11 1829–Nov 14 1831			
		Apr 11 1836–June 23 1840			
		Jan 25 1857–Nov 26 1880			
	1777–1899	1786–1899		KHGS	
Kildare and Rathangan (Kildare and Leighlin)	Nov 1 1815–Dec 31 1837	Nov 1 1815–Nov 30 1837		NLI	Pos. 4208
	Jan 6 1838–Mar 28 1864	Jan 17 1838–Feb 7 1864			
	Apr 3 1864–Nov 28 1880	Apr 18 1864–Nov 28 1880			
	1815–1899	1815–1899		KHGS	
Kill (Kildare and Leighlin)	Nov 9 1840–June 30 1872	Feb 27 1843–Apr 8 1872		NLI	Pos. 4208
	June 23 1872–Dec 19 1880				
	1813–1899	1813–1899		KHGS	
	Nov 9 1840–June 30 1872	Feb 27 1843–Apr 8 1872		LDS	0926115 item 2
	June 23 1872–Dec 19 1880				
Leixlip	1844–1899	1845–1899		KHGS	
Maynooth (Dublin)	Aug 24 1814–Sept 10 1827	Jan 12 1806–Aug 27 1827		NLI	Pos. 6615
	Sept 15 1827–Feb 1 1857	Sept 16 1827–Nov 24 1856			
	Jan 4 1857–Dec 24 1880				
	1814–1899	1806–1899		KHGS	
Monasterevan (Kildare and Leighlin)	Jan 1 1819–Feb 22 1835	Sept 11 1819–Feb 26 1835		NLI	Pos. 4203
	Mar 28 1829–Aug 15 1835	Jan 15 1835–July 17 1855			
	Jan 4 1835–June 24 1855	July 10 1855–Nov 25 1880			
	June 29 1855–Dec 26 1880				
	1819–1899	1819–1900		KHGS	
Naas (Kildare and Leighlin)	Mar 1 1813–Jan 24 1865	Feb 28 1813–Aug 15 1877	Mar 14 1861–Dec 30 1868	NLI	Pos. 4208
	Feb 5 1865–Dec 28 1880	June 5 1876–Oct 26 1880			
	1813–1899	1813–1899		KHGS	

Parish (Diocese)	Baptisms	Marriages	Burials	Location	Reference
Narraghmore (Dublin)	Apr 27 1827–Apr 26 1837 Mar 23 1856–Dec 30 1880 Feb 8 1868–Dec 27 1880	Oct 26 1827–June 11 1837 Apr 3 1856–Nov 23 1880		NLI	Pos. 6485
Newbridge (Kildare and Leighlin)	Aug 2 1786–Jan 18 1795 Jan 14 1820–Aug 18 1832 Jan 1 1834–Oct 1 1846 Oct 23 1836–Dec 31 1843 Sept 20 1846–Aug 5 1860 (index to 1861) Mar 4 1849–Sept 22 1861 Oct 5 1861–Nov 24 1867 May 12 1867–Dec 27 1880 1786–1899	Aug 6 1786–Jan 20 1795 Jan 17 1820–Aug 15 1846 Oct 25 1849–Sept 25 1861 Sept 21 1846–Sept 25 1862 Oct 1 1861–Nov 24 1880 1786–1899	 1889–1894	NLI KHGS	Pos. 4209
Rathangan (Kildare and Leighlin)	1880–1899	1880–1899	1888–1892	KHGS	
Robertstown (Kildare and Leighlin)	No records microfilmed			NLI	
Suncroft (Kildare and Leighlin)	Mar 29 1805–Dec 26 1880 1805–1899	May 15 1805–July 29 1880 1805–1899	 1892–1899	NLI KHGS	Pos. 4209

Kilkenny

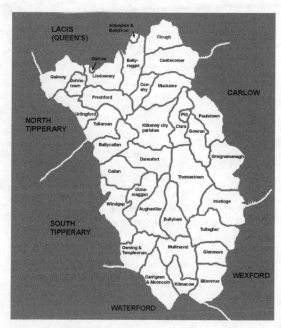

Parish (Diocese)	Baptisms	Marriages	Burials	Location	Reference
Abbeyleix and Ballyroan (Kildare and Leighlin)	June 6 1824–Aug 23 1830 Jan 19 1838–Dec (?) 26 1849 Apr 6 1850–Jan 5 1879 Jan 6 1878–Dec 5 1880 Index 1850–1878 1824–1899	July 2 1824–July 28 1830 Jan 30 1838–Nov 22 1880 1824–1899		NLI IMA	Pos. 4199

Parish (Diocese)	Baptisms	Marriages	Burials	Location	Reference
Aughaviller (Ossory)	Oct 22 1847–Dec 14 1880	Feb 24 1848–Nov 2 1880		NLI	Pos. 5022
	1848–1900	1848–1879		KA	
Ballycallan (Ossory)	May 26 1845–Dec 30 1880	July 22 1845–Nov 25 1880		NLI	Pos. 5027
	1820–1900	1820–1900		KA	
	See NLI			LDS	0926187
Ballyhale (Ossory)	Aug 26 1823–Apr 4 1876			NLI	Pos. 5021
	1823–1900	1876–1910		KA	
Ballyragget (Ossory)	Aug 31 1856–Dec 31 1880	Apr 10 1856–Nov 18 1880		NLI	Pos. 5017
	1856–1900	1856–1900		KA	
	See NLI			LDS	0979702 item 4
Callan (Ossory)	Jan 27 1821–Oct 29 1844	Jan 28 1821–Oct 16 1844		NLI	Pos. 5025
	Nov 14 1844–June 11 1875	Nov 4 1844–Feb 15 1874			
	Nov 28 1871–Dec 28 1880	Jan 28 1871–Nov 25 1880			
	See NLI			LDS	0926189
	1821–1900	1821–1900		KA	
Carrigeen and Mooncoin (Ossory)	Sept 12 1779–Nov 19 1780	Jan 26 1772–Mar 4 1783		NLI	Pos. 5018
	Oct 21 1781–Feb 7 1782	Jan 16 1789–Feb 21 1814			
	Feb 8 1782–Oct 14 1797	Feb 21 1816–Sept 27 1836			
	Dec 3 1797–Feb 13 1816	Jan 16 1837–May 12 1879			
	Feb 20 1816–Dec 29 1836				
	Jan 5 1837–Dec 29 1878				
	1779–1900	1772–1900		KA	
Castlecomer (Ossory)	Jan 1 1812–Oct 2 1818	Aug 13 1831–June 6 1847		NLI	Pos. 5019
	Dec 24 1828–June 3 1847	July 15 1847–Nov 24 1880			
	Apr 12 1847–Dec 7 1880				
	1812–1818	1835–1900		KA	
	1828–1900				
	See NLI			LDS	0926190; 0979702 item 1–3
Clara (Ossory)	No records microfilmed			NLI	
	1778–1808	1835–1900		KA	
	1835–1900				
Clough (Ossory)	Jan 1 1812–Oct 2 1818	Aug 13 1831–June 6 1847		NLI	Pos. 5017
	Dec 24 1828–June 3 1847	Aug 3 1859–Nov 11 1880			
	Jan 3 1858–Nov 21 1880				
	1833–1900	1833–1911		KA	
	See NLI			LDS	0926190; 0979702 item 1–3
Conahy (Ossory)	June 2 1832–Dec 22 1876	June 17 1832–Nov 22 1880		NLI	Pos. 5016
	Jan 8 1877–Dec 28 1880				
	1832–1900	1832–1900		KA	
	June 2 1832–Dec 22 1876	June 17 1832–Nov 22 1880		LDS	0926191
	Jan 8 1877–Dec 28 1880				item 2–3
Danesfort (Ossory)	Jan 1819–Feb 13 1869	Jan 8 1824–June 3 1868		NLI	Pos. 5025
	(many pages missing)	(many pages missing)			
	See NLI			LDS	0926193
	1819–1900 (gaps in 1870's)	1823–1863		KA	
		1874–1900			

Parish (Diocese)	Baptisms	Marriages	Burials	Location	Reference
Dunamaggan (Ossory)	Sept 25 1826–June 7 1840	Oct 20 1826–June 16 1842		NLI	Pos. 5022
	Apr 25 1843–May 12 1845	Feb 25 1843–Apr 29 1844			
	May 17 1844–Dec 20 1880	Feb 24 1870–Nov 25 1880			
	1826–1900	1826–1844		KA	
		1876–1900			
Durrow (Ossory)	Jan 1 1789–Mar 30 1792	July 29 1811–Mar 27 1820		NLI	Pos. 5013
	Jan 2 1801–Feb 28 1805	May 23 1822–Sept 18 1827			
	(also a transcript)	July 17 18342–May 28 1860			
	June 9 1811–Jan 27 1820	June 9 1861–Nov 18 1880			
	May 19 1822–Feb 18 1827				
	May 26 1832–Feb 15 1857				
	Mar 8 1857–Dec 28 1880				
	1789–1900	1811–1899		IMA	
Freshford (Ossory)	Jan 12 1773–Aug 31 1797	Aug 13 1775–Nov 11 1779		NLI	Pos. 5015
	Mar 27 1800–Feb 9 1825	Feb 1 1801–Nov 28 1877			
	Jan 21825–Dec 28 1847	Jan 7 1878–Nov 24 1880			
	Jan 2 1848–Jan 3 1878				
	Jan 5 1878–Dec 25 1880				
	1772–1797	1775–1900 (patchy)		KA	
	1800–1900				
	See NLI			LDS	0926192 item 1–7
Galmoy (Ossory)	Sept 10 1805–May 2 1807	Sept 16 1861–Jan 29 1880		NLI	Pos. 5017, 6955
	June 6 1861–Dec 15 1880				
	See NLI			LDS	0979701 item 4–5
	1861–1900	1861–1900		KA	
Glenmore (Ossory)	Mar 28 1831–Dec 11 1880	Jan 17 1831–Aug 31 1880		NLI	Pos. 5022
	1801–1900	1802–1900		KA	
Gowran (Ossory)	Jan 1 1809–July 20 1828	Jan 11 1810–Nov 28 1828		NLI	Pos. 5026, 5027
	July 1 1828–May 4 1852	July 17 1828–Apr 28 1852			
	May 8 1852–Dec 20 1880	July 1 1852–Feb 24 1879			
	1809–1911	1810–1900		KA	
	See NLI			LDS	0926194 item 1–5
Graignamanagh	Apr 22 1838–Dec 27 1868	July 5 1818–Nov 26 1868		NLI	Pos. 4198
(Kildare and Leighlin)	Jan 1 1869–Dec 24 1880	Jan 17 1869–Nov 3 1880			
	1818–1900	1818–1900		KA	
Inistioge (Ossory)	Dec 2 1810–Feb 2 1829	Jan 22 1827–Oct 9 1876		NLI	Pos. 5021, 5022
	Feb 3 1829–Dec 22 1876	Oct 27 1840–Feb 1 1877			
	Oct 20 1840–Feb 4 1877				
	1810–1900	1758–1777		KA	
		1827–1900			
Johnstown (Ossory)	Aug 16 1814–Jan 26 1845	Feb 2 1851–Nov 13 1880		NLI	Pos. 5012
	Mar 1 1845–Dec 18 1880				
	1815–1880	1851–1880		LDS	0979700 item 2
	1815–1900	1850–1900		KA	
Kilkenny: St.	Apr 6 1768–Jan 15 1785	June 12 1768–Nov 27 1810		NLI	Pos. 5029, 5030
Canice's (Ossory)	Jan 18 1785–Dec 30 1810	Jan 10 1811–Nov 26 1844			
	Jan 71811–Dec 22 1844	Jan 7 1845–Nov 24 1880			
	Jan 3 1845–Dec 30 1880				

Parish (Diocese)	Baptisms	Marriages	Burials	Location	Reference
Kilkenny: St. Canice's (Ossory)	1768–1810 1768–1900	1768–1810 1768–1900	1777–1779	LDS KA	0926195
Kilkenny: St. John's (Ossory)	Jan 1809–July 8 1830 Feb 1 1842–Feb 17 1877 1789–1900	June 24 1809–July 5 1830 Apr 11 1842–May 30 1872 1789–1900		NLI KA	Pos. 5030
Kilkenny: St. Mary's (Ossory)	Jan 1 1754–Aug 23 1782 Aug 6 1784–Dec 1810 Oct 5 1762–Aug 21 1766 Feb 4 1811–Oct 7 1816 Oct 12 1816–May 7 1833 May 2 1833–Oct 13 1858 Oct 28 1858–Dec 27 1880 1754–1900 1754–1833	Jan 1754–Sept 3 1809 Oct 23 1762–Apr 26 1766 Jan 9 1798–Aug 27 1799 Jan 24 1801–Feb 7 1842 Feb 4 1811–Oct 7 1816 Nov 3 1816–Oct 13 1858 Nov 8 1858–Nov 18 1880 1754–1900 1754–1858	1754–1786 1754–1787	NLI KA LDS	Pos. 5028, 5029 0926196 item 1–3; 0926197 1–5
Kilkenny: St. Patrick's (Ossory)	Aug 11 1800–Mar 31 1867 Apr 2 1867–Dec 31 1880 1800–1900	July 19 1801–Jan 26 1868 1800–1900		NLI KA	Pos. 5027, 5028
Kilkenny city: Workhouse (Ossory)	Apr 30 1876–Dec 6 1880 1876–1899			NLI KA	Pos. 5030
Kilmacow (Ossory)	July 2 1858–Dec 31 1880 See NLI 1858–1880 1836–1900	Aug 9 1858–Nov 18 1880 1798–1853 (gap 1858–1900)	June 30 1858–Dec 24 1880	NLI LDS Online: Genweb, Kilkenny KA	Pos. 5023, 5024 0926198
Lisdowney (Ossory)	May 26 1817–Oct 2 1853 Apr 15 1854–Aug 20 1877 Oct 30 1853–Dec 29 1880 See NLI 1817–1900	Sept 12 1771–Apr 28 1778 Nov 26 1828–Aug 13 1853 Nov 17 1853–Oct 27 1880 1817–1900		NLI LDS KA	Pos. 5017 0979701 item 1–3; 0926199 1–3
Muckalee (Ossory)	Oct 30 1801–Sept 1806 (very damaged) June 15 1840–Jan 8 1854 May 1 1853–Dec 28 1857 Jan 5 1858–Jan 28 1873 May 12 1871–Jan 28 1873 Aug 3 1873–Dec 5 1880 1801–1806 1840–1900 See NLI	Apr 19 1809–June 25 1853 Apr 28 1853–Nov 28 1857 Jan 28 1858–Feb 19 1873 1809–1911		NLI KA LDS	Pos. 5026 0926200 item 1–5
Mullinavat (Ossory)	Feb 21 1843–Dec 15 1880 See NLI 1836–1900	May 18 1843–Mar 1 1880 1842–1883 1887–1900		NLI LDS KA	Pos. 5021 0926201
Owning and Templeorum (Ossory)	Oct 7 1803–June 21 1815 Sept 15 1815–May 8 1846 May 10 1846–1851 1851–1854 (many large gaps) Jan 31 1851–Dec 27 1864 Jan 3 1865–Dec 29 1880 1803–1900	Aug 5 1815–Nov 29 1849 Nov 25 1851–Oct 24 1864 Jan 19 1851–Nov 22 1864 Jan 30 1865–Nov 6 1880 1815–1900	Sept 12 1803–March 1806 Apr 29 1808–June 17 1815	NLI KA	Pos. 5019, 5020

Parish (Diocese)	Baptisms	Marriages	Burials	Location	Reference
Paulstown (Kildare and Leighlin)	July 9 1824–Apr 19 1846	Jan 21 1824–Nov 28 1840		NLI	Pos. 4198
	May 20 1852–May 30 1869	Jan 21 1841–Feb 11 1861			
	June 3 1855–Mar 4 1860	Jan 22 1861–Nov 25 1869			
	Mar 11 1860–May 1 1870	Feb 28 1870–Nov 27 1880			
	Jan 2 1870–Dec 12 1880				
	See NLI			LDS	0926124
	1840's (sporadic)	1824–1900		KA	
	1824–1900				
Pitt (Ossory)	July 8 1855–Dec 31 1880	Aug 13 1855–Oct 14 1880		NLI	Pos. 5028
Slieverue (Ossory)	Nov 26 1766–Apr 14 1778	Feb 2 1766–May 23 1778	Dec 1766 Feb 21 1778	NLI	Pos. 5031
	Feb 27 1781–June 25 1799	May 26 1791–July 9 1801			
	Apr 1777–Sept 18 1801	Oct 1 1801–Nov 25 1836			
	Oct 4 1801–Dec 31 1836	Jan 1837–Nov 16 1880			
	Dec 26 1836–Dec 26 1880				
	1766–1900	1766–1900		KA	
Thomastown (Ossory)	June 23 1782–Sept 27 1809	Jan 1786–Aug 10 1806		NLI	Pos. 5024,
	Jan 9 1810–Mar 28 1834	May 27 1810–Aug 8 1833			
	Mar 17 1834–Dec 23 1880	Aug 7 1833–Nov 22 1880			
	1782–1900	1785–1806		KA	
	1847–1900 (Tullaherin)	1810–1900			
		1847–1900 (Tullaherin)			
	See NLI			LDS	0926202
Tullagher (Ossory)	Apr 6 1817–June 28 1819	Jan 27 1835–Nov 3 1877		NLI	Pos. 5020, 5021
	Jan 26–Mar 17 1825				
	Jan 6 1830–July 12 1840				
	July 12 1840–Dec 29 1877				
	Feb 1 1834–Dec 31 1877				
	1817–1819	1830–1910		KA	
	1825–1910				
	1820–1900	1830–1900		KA	
Tullaroan (Ossory)	Mar 5 1843–Apr 15 1876	Apr 27 1843–Feb 7 1880		NLI	Pos. 5026
	See NLI			LDS	0926204
	1843–1900	1843–1900		KA	
Urlingford (Ossory)	May 5 1805–Feb 15 1844	May 9 1805 Nov 7 18843		NLI	Pos. 5016
	May 5 1805–July 11 1823 (transcript)	Aug 5 1843–Sept 1870			
	Feb 16 1844–Oct 18 1857	Feb 20 1871–July 20 1880			
	Feb 15 1846–Dec 3 1870				
	Aug 21 1869 Dec 26 1880				
	Dec 16 1870–Dec 18 1880				
	1805–1900	1805–1900		KA	
Windgap (Ossory)	Aug 18 1822–Feb 27 1852 (transcript)	Sept 14 1822–Mar 1 1880 (transcript)		NLI	Pos. 5023
	Mar 10 1852–Dec 27 1869 (transcript)				
	Jan 5 1870–Dec 10 1880				
	See NLI			LDS	0926205
	1822–1900	1822 1875		KA	
		1989–1900			

Laois (Queen's)

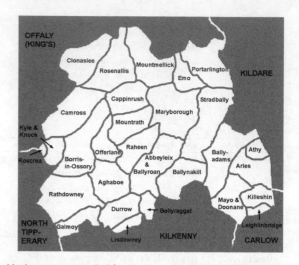

Parish (Diocese)	Baptisms	Marriages	Burials	Location	Reference
Abbeyleix and Ballyroan (Kildare and Leighlin)	June 6 1824–Aug 23 1830 Jan 19 1838–Dec (?) 26 1849 Apr 6 1850–Jan 5 1879 Jan 6 1878–Dec 5 1880 Index 1850–1878	July 2 1824–July 28 1830 Jan 30 1838–Nov 22 1880		NLI	Pos. 4199
	1824–1899	1824–1899		IMA	
Aghaboe (Ossory)	1795–1825 (some large gaps) June 18 1826–Dec 19 1850 Jan 28 1849–Dec 12 1880	July 4 1794–Feb 1807 Nov 1 1816–Aug 10 1824 Aug 2 1825–Aug 4 1846 June 25 1850–May 20 1880		NLI	Pos. 5012
	1796–1880	1794–1880		LDS	0979700 item 1
	1795–1899	1794–1910		IMA	
	1795–1799			Online	Connors
Arles (Kildare and Leighlin)	1821–1856 (arranged by townland possibly some missing) Mar 20 1831–Jan 22 1843 Jan 6 1843–Aug 15 1861 Jan 1 1849–Dec 27 1858 (not a duplicate) Jan 9 1859–Dec 26 1880	1821–1856 (arranged by townland possibly some missing) Sept 28 1831–Feb 27 1843 Aug 30 1843–July 24 1861 June 19 1850–Nov 25 1858 (not a duplicate) Jan 17 1859–Nov 24 1880	1821–1856 (arranged by townland, possibly some missing)	NLI	Pos. 4190
	1821–1899	1821–1899		IMA	
Athy	See Kildare				
Ballyadams (Kildare and Leighlin)	Jan 3 1820–Feb 28 1847 Feb 9 1845–June 14 1874 (transcript) June 14 1874–Dec 20 1880	Jan 12 1820–Nov 24 1853 Mar 341 1845–Apr 25 1874 (transcript)		NLI	Pos. 4200
	1820–1899	1820–1899		IMA	
Ballynakill (Kildare and Leighlin)	Oct 14 1794–Mar 19 1815 Jan 16 1820–May 26 1820 Nov 4 1820–Sept 19 1872 Sept 29 1872–June 11 1876 Apr 1 1877–Nov 3 1880	Oct 27 1794–Feb 7 1815 Jan 15 1820–July 7 1820 Nov 3 1820–Nov25 1875 May 22 1877–Nov 3 1880		NLI	Pos. 4200
	1794–1899	1800–1899	1794–1815	IMA	

Parish (Diocese)	Baptisms	Marriages	Burials	Location	Reference
Ballyragget	See Kilkenny				
Borris-in-Ossory (Ossory)	May 4 1840–Mar 12 1878	July 20 1840–Sept 23 1880		NLI	Pos. 5014
	Nov 17 1855–Nov 25 1879	Nov 17 1855–Nov 25 1879			
	See NLI			LDS	0926188
	1840– 1926	1840–1926		IMA	
Camross (Ossory)	May 12 1816–Sept 1 1829	Jan 21 1820–Mar 1830		NLI	Pos. 5014
	Mar 12 1821–Dec 27 1829	Aug 18 1839–Feb 8 1842			
	May 1818–Oct 6 1820	Aug 30 1846–1851			
	July 12 1823–Mar 18 1830	Aug 9 1855–Sept 17 1865			
	Oct 14 1838–Sept 11 1865	Oct 26 1865–Nov 25 1880			
	(many pages missing 1838–50)				
	Oct 8 1865–Dec 26 1880				
	1816–1899	1820–1899		IMA	
Cappinrush (Kildare and Leighlin)	Oct 20 1824–Aug 3 1862	Aug 1 1819–July 27 1862		NLI	Pos. 4201
	July 6 1862–Dec 26 1880	July 24 1862–Oct 19 1880			
	1824–1899	1819–1899		IMA	
Clonaslee (Kildare and Leighlin)	Jan 15 1849–Dec 20 1880	Feb 20 1849–Oct 14 1880		NLI	Pos. 4202
	1849–1906	1849–1899	1892–1970	IMA	
Durrow (Ossory)	Jan 1 1789–Mar 30 1792	July 29 1811–Mar 27 1820		NLI	Pos. 5013
	Jan 2 1801–Feb 28 1805	May 23 1822–Sept 18 1827			
	(also a transcript)	July 17 1834?–May 28 1860			
	June 9 1811–Jan 27 1820	June 9 1861–Nov 18 1880			
	May 19 1822–Feb 18 1827				
	May 26 1832–Feb 15 1857				
	Mar 8 1857–Dec 28 1880				
	1789–1900	1811–1899		IMA	
Emo (Kildare and Leighlin)	July 4 1875–Dec 19 1880	Apr 26 1875–Nov 25 1880		NLI	Pos. 4203
	1875–1899	1875–1899		IMA	
Galmoy	See Kilkenny				
Killeshin (Kildare and Leighlin)	Nov 23 1819–Oct 16 1843	Jan 20 1822–Nov 24 1846		NLI	Pos. 4190
	Feb 12 1840–June 2 1844	Jan 26 1840–May 19 1844			
	Aug 16 1846–Aug 5 1849	Nov 27 1846–Aug 5 1849			
	Oct 10 1846–Dec 28 1856	Nov 27 1846–Nov 27 1856			
	Jan 4 1857–Dec 19 1880	Jan 27 1857–Nov 21 1880			
	1820–1899	1822–1899		CGP	
Kyle and Knock (Killaloe)	Jan 26 1845–Dec 23 1880	Feb 13 1846–Sept 8 1880		NLI	Pos. 2479
	See NLI			LDS	0979695 item 6
	1845–1911	1846–1911		TNFHF	
Leighlinbridge	See Carlow				
Lisdowney	See Kilkenny				
Maryborough (Kildare and Leighlin)	May 14 1826–Feb 4 1838	Apr 27 1826–Jan 30 1838		NLI	Pos. 4201
	Feb 4 1838–Nov 16 1851	Feb 14 1838–Jan 8 1855			
	1845–1873 (alphabetical transcript)	1850–1940 (alphabetical transcript)			
	Apr 28 1873–Dec 27 1880	Jan 10 1858–Nov 25 1880			
	1826–1909	1828–1899	1876–1916	IMA	
Mayo and Doonane (Kildare and Leighlin)	June 21 1843–Sept 17 1877	May 1843–Sept 2 1877		NLI	Pos. 4190
	Sept 24 1877–Dec 12 1880	Feb 14 1878–Nov 27 1880			
	1814–1899	1815–1899		IMA	
	See NLI			LDS	0926112

Parish (Diocese)	Baptisms	Marriages	Burials	Location	Reference
Mountmellick (Kildare and Leighlin)	Jan 1 1814–Dec 23 1837	Feb 2 1814–Apr 27 1843		NLI	Pos. 4204
	Aug 6 1837–May 27 1860	July 7 1843–Nov 21 1872			
	1837–1859 (alphabetical transcript)	Jan 19 1873–Aug 29 1880			
	Apr 19 1860–Dec 26 1880				
	Feb 26 1864–Feb 4 1879				
	1860–1886 (alphabetical transcript)				
	1814–1899	1814–1899	1890–1948	IMA	
	See NLI			LDS	0926121
Mountrath (Kildare and Leighlin)	Oct 12 1823–Apr 21 1867	Oct 12 1823–Apr 21 1867		NLI	Pos. 4201
	May 13 1867–Dec 26 1880	May 13 1867–Dec 26 1880			
	1823–1902	1827–1899	1882–1899	IMA	
	See NLI			LDS	0926122
Offerlane (Ossory)	May 8 1782–Sept 8 1816	Sept 21 1784–May 9 1816		NLI	Pos. 5018
	May 4 1831–May 27 1880	Feb 9 1831–Feb 11 1855			
		Sept 17 1857–May 4 1880			
	1772–1900	1784–1900		IMA	
Portarlington	See Offaly				
Raheen (Kildare and Leighlin)	Apr 5 1819–Dec 19 1880	Jan 20 1820–Sept 30 1880		NLI	Pos. 4202, 4205
	Jan 1 1843–Aug 27 1875	Nov 30 1866–May 30 1868			
	Feb 4 1844–Sept 10 1875	Aug 15 1844–Feb 13 1855			
		July 4 1860–May 24 1866			
		Jan 20 1870–Jan 10 1875			
	1819–1899	1819–1899	1884–1925	IMA	
Rathdowney (Ossory)	July 13 1763–Nov 28 1781	May 18 1769–Nov 7 1781		NLI	Pos. 5013, 5014
	Sept 14 1782–July 20 1789	Sept 7 1782–July 15 1789			
	May 6 1790–Nov 20 1791	Sept 15 1789–Nov 22 1791			
	Apr 14 Sept 1 1810	Jan 14–May 3 1808			
	June 2 1839–Jan 29 1840	Oct 6 1839–Mar 3 1840			
	Apr 26 1840–Dec 31 1880	May 27 1840–Nov 9 1880			
	1763–1900	1764–1895		IMA	
Roscrea	See North Tipperary				
Rosenallis (Kildare and Leighlin)	Oct 21 1765–Jan 19 1777	Oct 12 1765–June 10 1777	Oct 14 1824–Sept 21 1827	NLI	Pos. 4205
	Feb 1 1782–Aug 13 1782	Feb 7 1782–June 10 1782			
	Aug 3 1823–Dec 27 1879	July 1823–July 24 1859			
		Jan 18 1865–Oct 26 1880			
	1766–1901	1765–1899	1921–1987	IMA	
Stradbally (Kildare and Leighlin)	Jan 21820–May 18 1855	Jan 20 1820–June 24 1849		NLI	Pos. 4202
	Jan 26 1851–Dec 26 1880	Feb 24 1851–Nov 4 1880			
	1820–1899	1820–1899	1893–1983	IMA	

Leitrim

Parish (Diocese)	Baptisms	Marriages	Burials	Location	Reference
Annaduff (Ardagh and Clonmacnois)	Feb 29 1849–Dec 31 1880	Feb 12 1849–Feb 10 1880	Feb 5 1849–Dec 21 1880	NLI	Pos. 4236
	1849–1900	1849–1900	1849–1887	LHC	
	1849–1984	1849–1983	1849–1886	LDS	1279224 item
			1930–1984		18–20; 1279225
					1–3
Aughavas (Ardagh and Clonmacnois)	May 19 1845–Feb 4 1876	Aug 28 1845–July 4 1879	May 11 1845–July 2 1880	NLI	Pos. 4240
	Jan 1 1876–Dec 23 1880	Jan 10 1876–Nov 14 1880	May 5 1876–Nov 18 1880		
	1845–1900	1845–1900	1845–1900	LHC	
	1845–1968	1845–1920	1845–1899	LDS	1279224
					item 15–17
Ballinaglera (Kilmore)	1883–			LC	
	1883–1900	1887–1900		LHC	
Bornacoola (Ardagh and Clonmacnois)	Jan 4 1871–Dec 31 1880	June 13 1836–Sept 28 1837		NLI	Pos. 4234
		May 9 1850–Nov 1 1880			
	1824–1837	1824 1837	1853–1900	LHC	
	1850–1900	1850–1900			
	1824–1897	1824–1838			
	1850–1897	1833–1892		LDS	1279224 item
					13–14
Carrigallen (Kilmore)	Nov 2 1829–Feb 7 1830	Jan 27 1841–Apr 24 1848	Mar 12 1842–June 25 1860	NLI	Pos. 5350
	Dec 30 1838–Dec 12 1880	1854–Dec 10 1875			
	(many pages missing)	(some pages missing)			
	1829–1891 (gaps)	1841–1890 (gaps)	1841–1860	PRONI	MIC.1D/7, 83
	1829–1900 (Many gaps)	1841–1900 (Many gaps)	1841–1860	LHC	

Parish (Diocese)	Baptisms	Marriages	Burials	Location	Reference
Clooneclare (Kilmore)	Apr 29 1841–Dec 1885	Nov 12 1850–Sept 9 1884		NLI	Pos. 7505
	1841–1900	1850–1900		LHC	
Cloone–Conmaicne (Ardagh and Clonmacnois)	Feb 1 1820–Mar 12 1820	Jan 6 1823–Jan 6 1839		NLI	Pos. 4241
	Jan 1 1834–May 27 1834	Jan 6 1823–Feb 17 1845			
	Nov 13 1834–Jan 13 1841				
	Jan 2 1843–Oct 4 1849				
	Jan 6 1850–Nov 20 1880				
	Jan 12 1843–Feb 14 1879				
	Jan 13 1850–Feb 25 1878				
	1823–1900	1823–1900	1823–1878	LHC	
	1820–1927	1823–1921	1850–1878	LDS	1279223 item
			1919–1921		12–14
Drumlease (Kilmore)	Aug 21 1859–Apr 12 1879	Sept 15 1859–Oct 31 1880		NLI	Pos. 5344
	1859–1879	1859–1881		PRONI	MIC.1D/77
	1859–1900	1859–1900		LHC	
Drumreilly Lower (Kilmore)	Mar 4 1867–Dec 26 1880			NLI	Pos. 5345
	1867–1880			PRONI	MIC.1D/78
	1867–1900	1893–1900		LHC	
	See NLI			LDS	0926129 item 4
Drumreilly Upper (Kilmore)	1878–1900	1870–1900		LHC	
Ennismagrath (Kilmore)	Jan 1835–July 1839	1830–1839	1833–1839	NLI	Pos. 7505
	1834				
	1834–1839	1834–1839	1834–1839	LHC	
	1881–1900	1881–1900			
Fenagh (Ardagh and Clonmacnois)	June 5 1825–Oct 13 1829	Oct 4 1826–Feb 18 1832	June 1825–Feb 21 1834	NLI	Pos. 4239
	Nov 24 1834–Apr 12 1843	Juna 15 1835–Mar 22 1842	Nov 24 1834–Dec 21 1841		
	June 5 1843–Nov 4 1852	Jan 17 1844–Feb 9 1880			
	Nov 22 1852–Dec 9 1880 (indexed)				
	1825–1900	1826–1900	1825–1894	LHC	
	1825–1829	1825–1899	1825–1894	LDS	1279223 item
	1843–1849				1–3
	1852–1883				
Glenade (Kilmore)	Nov 10 1867–Dec 16 1880	Nov 10 1867–June 15 1880		NLI	Pos. 5344
	1867–1881	1873–1880		PRONI	MIC.1D/77
	1867–1900	1866–1900		LHC	
	1867–1899	1867–1899		SHGC	
Gortletteragh (Ardagh and Clonmacnois)	Apr 4 1830–Aug 1 1840	Jan 6 1826–Sept 12 1827	Jan 10 1826–Sept 15 1826	NLI	Pos. 4238
	July 16 1848–Mar 6 1874	Feb 16 1830–Apr 30 1835	Mar 29 1830–Feb 17 1831		
	Mar 30 1874–Dec 31 1880	May 22 1848–Feb 17 1874 (disordered)	Mar 9 1839–July 29 1839		
			Aug 1 1851–July 29 1869		
	1830–1839	1826	1852–1868	LHC	
	1849–1900 (sic)	1831–1834			
		1849–1900			
	1830–1840	1826–1835	1826–1839 (gaps)	LDS	1279224 item
	1848–1895	1852–1895	1851–1869		4–6
Killargue (Kilmore)	Sept 26 1852–Dec 26 1880	Nov 2 1852–Feb 4 1880		NLI	Pos. 5344
	1852–1881	1852–1881		PRONI	MIC.1D/77
	1853–1900	1852–1900		LHC	

Parish (Diocese)	Baptisms	Marriages	Burials	Location	Reference
Killasnet (Kilmore)	Mar 28 1852–Apr 1868	Mar 28 1852–Apr 1868	Mar 28 1852–Apr 1868	NLI	Pos. 5350
	Feb 23 1868–Jan 31 1869	Jan 30 1868–May 21 1871			
	Nov 29 1878–Nov 23 1880	Nov 11 1878–Nov 15 1880			
	1852–1869	1852–1871		PRONI	MIC.1D/83
	1878–1881	1878–1881			
	1852–1900	1852–1900	1852–1866	LHC	
	1879–1897 (sic)	1879–1897 (sic)			
Killenummery	May 8 1828–Aug 7 1846	June 22 1827–Aug 16 1846	May 18 1838–Apr 15 1846	NLI	Pos. 4241
(Ardagh and	Nov 1 1848–Dec 30 1880	Nov 10 1848–Dec 28 1880			
Clonmacnois)	1828–1845	1827–1845	1829–1845	LHC	
	1849–1900	1849–1900			
	1828–1920	1828–1883	1838–1846	LDS	1279223 item
		1908–1910			6–7
		1922–1923			
	1828–1899	1827–1899		SHGC	
Kiltoghart (Ardagh	Aug 16 1826–Apr 23 1854	July 19 1832–May 3 1854	Aug 10 1832–Apr 10 1854	NLI	Pos. 4240
and Clonmacnois)	May 7 1854–Dec 30 1880	July 30 1854–Nov 24 1880	May 31 1854–Aug 11 1874		
	(Gowel) Mar 4 1866–	(Gowel) May 13 1866–	(Gowel) Apr 11 1866–		
	Dec 26 1880	Feb 29 1876	Sept 10 1877		
	1826–1900	1832–1900	1832–1853		
			1867–1889	LHC	
	1826–1891	1841–1891	1841–1879	LDS	1279223
					item 4–5
Kiltubrid (Ardagh	Jan 6 1841–Apr 27 1874	Jan 7 1841–May 22 1873	Jan 15 1847–May 1 1873	NLI	Pos. 4234
and Clonmacnois)	1841	1841	1847–1872	LHC	
	1847–1900	1847–1900			
	1841–1874	1841–1873	1847–1873	LDS	1279223 item
	1880–1924	1883–1922			9–11
Kinlough (Kilmore)	July 12 1835–Mar 1860	Nov 26 1840–Dec 16 1880		NLI	Pos. 5344
	Apr 8 1860–Dec 24 1880				
	1835–1881	1840–1881		PRONI	MIC.1D/77
	1835–1900	1840–1900			
		1855, 1853 missing	1867–1900	LHC	
Mohill (Ardagh	Aug 4 1836–May 7 1854	July 14 1836–May 18 1854	July 3 1836–May 9 1854	NLI	Pos. 4239
and Clonmacnois)	June 11 1854–Dec 23 1880	Aug 28 1854–July 19 1879	May 22 1854–July 27 1879		
	Including workhouse				
	baptisms 1846–55				
	1836–1900	1836–1900	1836–1900	LHC	
	1836–1905	1836–1905	1836–1883	LDS	1279224 item
		1910–1916			1–3
Murhan (Ardagh	May 18 1861–Dec 21 1880	June 10 1868–Nov 20 1880		NLI	Pos. 4240
and Clonmacnois)	1861–1900	1867–1900		LHC	
	1861–1895			LDS	1279223 item8
Oughteragh	Nov 9 1869–Dec 28 1880	Jan 17 1870–Nov 20 1880		NLI	Pos. 5346/7
(Kilmore)	May 26 1871–Dec 16 1880				
	1869–1881	1787–1881		PRONI	MIC.1D/79–80
	1841–1900	1841–1900		LHC	
Rossinver (Kilmore)	Aug 17 1851–Jan 29 1875	Aug 28 1844–Sept 8 1870		NLI	Pos. 5350
	(many gaps)				
	1851–1875	1844–1870		PRONI	MIC.1D/83
	very poor condition	very poor condition			
	1851–1900	1844–1869		LHC	
		1875–1900			

Limerick East

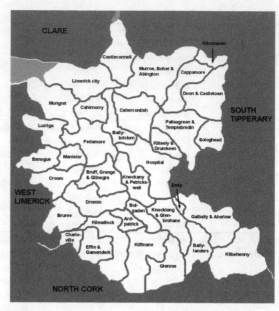

Parish (Diocese)	Baptisms	Marriages	Burials	Location	Reference
Ardpatrick (Limerick)	No records microfilmed			NLI	
	1861–1900	1861–1900		LA	
Ballybricken and	Nov 9 1800–July 25 1841	Aug 10 1805–Oct 27 1841		NLI	Pos. 2509
Bohermore (Cashel	Aug 2 1841–Dec 26 1880	Nov 6 1841–Oct 23 1880			
and Emly)	1800–1900	1801–1900		TFHR	
	1801–1841	1801–1841	1801–1841 (scraps)	LDS	1279253
	1800–1900	1805–1900		LA	
Ballylanders	Mar 6 1849–Dec 25 1877	Jan 3 1857–Nov 25 1877 (modern transcript)		NLI	Pos. 2500
(Cashel and Emly)	1842–1899	1841–1900		TFHR	
	1849–1900	1857–1900		LA	
Banogue (Limerick)	Sept 21 1861–Dec 21 1880	Oct 6 1861–Apr 27 1880		NLI	Pos. 2427
	1861–1900	1861–1900		LA	
Bruff, Grange and	Jan 6 1808–July 30 1827	Jan 27 1808–July 8 1827		NLI	B & M to 1827
Gilnogra (Limerick)	Aug 10 1827–Nov 10 1845	Sept 20 1827–Oct 22 1845			Pos. 2428;
	Nov 2 1845–Dec 23 1880	Nov 17 1845–Nov 23 1880			remainder 2429
	1781–1900	1781–1900		LA	
Bruree (Limerick)	Jan 6 1842–Mar 11 1868	July (?)28 1861–Oct 13 1880		NLI	Pos. 2428
	Mar 22 1868–Dec 23 1880				
	1826–1900	1826–1900		LA	
Bulgaden (Limerick)	Mar 22 1812–Sept 27 1832	June 4 1812–Jan 27 1833		NLI	Pos. 2428
	Oct 6 1832–Jan 5 1854	Feb 5 1833–Nov 30 1853			
	Jan 23 1854–Dec 31 1880	Feb 2 1854–Nov 27 1880			
	1812–1900	1812–1900		LA	
Caherconlish (Cashel	Jan 19 1841–Dec 30 1880	Feb 6 1841–Oct 8 1880		NLI	Pos. 2508
and Emly)	1841–1900	1841–1900		TFHR	
	1841–1900	1841–1900		LA	
Cahirnorry	Jan 3 1830–Jan 2 1840	July 12 1827–Dec 2 1843		NLI	Pos. 2419
(Limerick)	Jan 4 1840–Dec 15 1880	Jan 11 1844–Nov 8 1880			
	1830–1900	1827–1900		LA	

Parish (Diocese)	Baptisms	Marriages	Burials	Location	Reference
Cappamore (Cashel and Emly)	1842–1900	1843–1900		TFHR	
	1845–1900	1843–1900		LA	
	Apr 4 1845–Dec 31 1880	Feb 25 1845–Nov 14 1880		NLI	Pos. 2508
Castleconnell (Killaloe)	Feb 5 1850–Jan 10 1864	Aug 10 1863–Nov 27 1880		NLI	Pos. 2477
	Aug 10 1863–Dec 31 1880				
	1850–1900	1863–1900		LA	
Charleville	See North Cork				
Croom (Limerick)	Oct 29 1828–Oct 30 1844	Dec 1770–July 23 1794	Dec 1770–July 23 1794	NLI	Pos. 2427
	Oct 4 1844–Dec 30 1880	Aug 23 1807–Feb 26 1810			
		May 6 1806–Mar 3 1829			
		May 2 1829–Sept 28 1844			
		Sept 29 1844–Nov 27 1880			
	1828–1900	1770–1900		LA	
Doon and Castletown (Cashel and Emly)	Mar 25 1824–Dec 27 1874	Jan 20 1839–Feb 17 1874		NLI	Pos. 2497
	1824–1900	1839–1900		TFHR	
	1824–1900	1839–1900		LA	
Dromin (Limerick)	May 19 1817–Sept 19 1837	June 23 1817–Dec 1 1837		NLI	Pos. 2426
	Mar 21 1849–Dec 16 1880	Mar 21 1849–Nov 14 1880			
	1817–1900	1817–1900		LA	
Effin and Gamenderk (Limerick)	Mar 1843–Dec 31 1880	Apr 24 1843–Nov 1880		NLI	Pos. 2427
	1843–1900	1843–1900		LA	
Emly	See South Tipperary				
Fedamore (Limerick)	Oct 29 1806–July 16 1813	Jan 9 1814–Nov 26 1825		NLI	Pos. 2409,
	Jan 1 1814–Jan 29 1822	Aug 1854–Dec 27 1880			2429, 2430
	July 30 1854–Dec 25 1880	Oct 29 1806–July 16 1813			
	Jan 4 1826–May 31 1833 (Manister)	Jan 7 1826–June 12 1833 (Manister)			
	June 2 1833–Dec 26 1880 (Manister)	June 20 1833–Aug 6 1880 (Manister)			
	1806–1900	1806–1900		LA	
Galbally and Aherlow (Cashel and Emly)	Mar 9 1810–June 23 1828 (July 1820–1821 missing)	Oct 1809–Aug 34 1880 (Mar 1820–July 1821 missing)		NLI	Pos. 2499
	December 1828–June 1871				
	1810–1900	1809–1900		TFHR	
	1810–1900	1809–1900		LA	
Glenroe (Limerick)	June 27 1853–Dec 26 1880	Aug 2 1853–Mar 19 1880		NLI	Pos. 2428
	1853–1900	1853–1900		LA	
Hospital (Cashel and Emly)	Jan 11 1810–Jan 10 1842	Feb 10 1812–Jan 16 1842	NLI	Pos. 2507	
	Jan 20 1842–Dec 29 1880	Jan 22 1842–Nov 6 1880			
	1810–1899	1812–1899		TFHR	
	1810–1900	1812–1900		LA	
Kilbehenny (Cashel and Emly)	Dec 17 1824–Apr 30 1843	Jan 30 1825–Feb 28 1843	NLI	Pos. 2500	
	May 4 1843–Jan 23 1870	May 1 1843–Jan 20 1870			
	1824–1899	1825–1899		TFHR	
	1824–1900	1825–1900		LA	
Kilcommon	See North Tipperary				
Kilfinane (Limerick)	June 1832–July 30 1856	Aug 20 1832–July 39 1856		NLI	Pos. 2429; B &
	Aug 14 1856–Apr 22 1859	Sept 5 1856–Mar/ 8 1859			M 1861–1880,
	Mar 231859–Mar 8 1880	May 4 1859–Aug 18 1880			2423
	July 1 1861–Dec 28 1880 (Ardpatrick)	Aug 18 1861–Sept 13 1880 (Ardpatrick)			
	1832–1900	1832–1900		LA	

Parish (Diocese)	Baptisms	Marriages	Burials	Location	Reference
Kilmallock	Oct 22 1837–Dec 19 1880	Nov 2 1837–Nov 24 1880		NLI	Pos. 2427
(Limerick)	1837–1900	1837–1900		LA	
Kilteely and (Cashel	Dec 3 1815–Apr 5 1829	Nov 14 1832–Nov 17 1880		NLI	Pos. 2506
and Emly) Drumkeen	Sept 3 1832–Dec 20 1880				
	1810–1899	1815–1899		TFHR	
	1815–1900	1832–1900		LA	
Knockany and	Mar 14 1808–Nov 24 1821	Apr 25 1808–Oct 21 1821	June 1 1819–Mar 29 1821	NLI	Pos. 2505
Patrickswell (Cashel	Dec 3 1921–Nov 22 1841	Jan 20 1822–Feb 23 1841			
and Emly)	May 3 1841–Dec 22 1880	May 3 1841–Oct 188 1880			
	1808–1899	1808–1899		TFHR	
	1808–1900	1808–1900	1819–1821	LA	
Knocklong and	Apr 26 1809–June 5 1819	Apr 12 1809–Oct 17 1819		NLI	Pos. 2509
Glenbrohane (Cashel	Sept 14 1823–June 11 1830	Jan 28 1824–Oct 1 1831			
and Emly)	Jan 30 1832–July 30 1854	Jan 7 1832–Feb 4 1854			
	Nov 30 1854–Jan 15 1878	Aug 20 1854–Jan 15 1878			
	1809–1899	1809–1899		TFHR	
	1809–1900	1809–1900		LA	
Limerick city:	Sept 26 1831–Feb 14 1877	July 1 1814–Nov 9 1819		NLI	Pos. 2410
Parteen (Limerick)		Feb 4 1821–Jan 10 1836			
		Feb 9 1847–Jan 22 1877			
	1831–1900	Not specified		CHGC	
Limerick city:	May 2 1788–Dec 30 1797	July 21 1821–Dec 15 1850		NLI	Pos. 2411 to
St. John's (Limerick)	Jan 1 1825–Jan 26 1829	Jan 11 1851–June 23 1877			1850;
	Jan 26 1829–Oct 31 1841				remainder
	Nov 1 1841–Dec 31 1849				2412
	Jan 5 1850–June 30 1877				
	1788–1900	1821–1900		LA	
Limerick city:	Jan 2 1745–Apr 13 1795	Oct 29 1745–Apr 13 1795		NLI	Pos. 2412 to
St. Mary's (Limerick)	Mar 2 1795–Oct 13 1816	Apr 13 1795–Oct 3 1816			1816;
	Nov 1 1816–Dec 31 1836	Aug 30 1816–Nov 30 1836			remainder
	Jan 6 1837–June 24 1862	Jan 7 1837–June 19 1862			2413
	1745–1900	1745–1900		LA	
	1745–1900	Not specified		CHGC	
Limerick city: St.	Aug 16 1776–Oct 18 1801	Feb 3 1772–Sept 12 1802		NLI	Pos. 2415 to
Michael's (Limerick)	Jan 12 1803–Feb 23 1807	Mar 28 1803–July 28 1804			1838; 2416 to
	Oct 14 1807–Apr 12 1813	Oct 18 1807–Aug 21 1808			1861;
	Jan 3 1814–Sept 13 1819	June 3 1810–May 6 1813			remainder
	Jan 19 1820–Mar 28 1824	May 6 1821–Mar 2 1824			2417
	May 13 1824–Dec 8 1838	June 6 1814–Nov 26 1819			
	Feb 14 1825–Oct 1 1830	May 13 1824–Dec 4 1838			
	Dec 9 1838–Dec 27 1852	Feb 6 1826–Nov 14 1828			
	Dec 27 1852–Feb 8 1876	Dec 26 1838–June 30 1877			
	1776–1900	1772–1900		LA	
Limerick city: St.	Nov 1 1764–Apr 4 1784	Nov 4 1764–Feb 24 1784		NLI	Pos. 2413 to
Munchin's (Limerick)	Apr 8 1784–June 30 1792	May 11 1784–May 25 1792			1819;
	Oct 3 1798–Aug 30 1819	Oct 2 1798–May 12 1819			remainder
	Sept 4 1819–Oct 31 1835	Sept 2 1819–Nov 10 1835			2414
	Nov 16 1824–June 19 1828	Jan 24 1825–May 21 1828			
	Feb 15 1836–Sept 29 1877	Dec 3 1837–Aug 5 1877			
	1764–1900	1764–1900		LA	

Parish (Diocese)	Baptisms	Marriages	Burials	Location	Reference
Limerick city: St. Patrick's (Limerick)	Jan 7 1812–Apr 30 1844	Jan 15 1812–Sept 17 1740		NLI	Pos. 2410
	May 8 1844–Apr 30 1830	Feb 11 1841–Oct 24 1880			
	May 8 1834–Dec 27 1875				
	1805–1900	1806–1900		LA	
Manister	See Fedamore				
Mungret (Limerick)	Nov 3 1844–Dec 19 1880	Nov 27 1844–Nov 12 1880		NLI	Pos. 2409/10
	1844–1900	1844–1900		LA	
Murroe, Boher and Abington (Cashel and Emly)	June 15 1814–Nov 3 1845	Nov 29 1815–Nov 2 1845		NLI	Pos. 2508
	Nov 3 1845–Dec 25 1880	Nov 16 1845–Sept 1 1880			
	1814–1899	1815–1899		TFHR	
	1814–1900	1815–1900		LA	
Pallasgreen and Templebredin (Cashel and Emly)	Jan 2 1811–Dec 29 1833	Jan 9 1811–Jan 29 1838		NLI	Pos. 2498
	Jan 1 1934–Oct 13 1861	Feb 8 1838–Oct 13 1861			
	Oct 20 1861–Dec 26 1880	Oct 26 1861–Dec 11 1880			
	1811–1899	1811–1899		TFHR	
	1811–1900	1811–1900		LA	
Sologhead (Cashel and Emly)	Oct 18 1809–Feb 27 1823	Jan 7 1810–Nov 24 1828		NLI	Pos. 2498 to
	Mar 2 1823–Apr 30 1828	Oct 14 1832–Jan 30 1854			1828;
	Feb 25 1837–Jan 23 1854	Feb 7 1854–Nov 27 1880			remainder on
	Feb 12 1854–Dec 31 1880				Pos. 2499
	1809–1900	1810–1900		TFHR	
	1809–1880	1810–1880		LA	

Limerick West
All diocese of Limerick

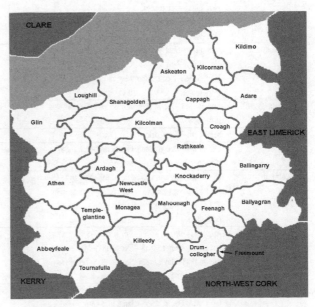

Parish (Diocese)	Baptisms	Marriages	Burials	Location	Reference
Abbeyfeale	Feb 11 1829–Oct 1843	Nov 5 1856–Nov 1880		NLI	B. 1829–43,
	Aug 4 1856–Dec 30 1880				Pos. 6779;
					remainder
					2426
	1829–1900	1825–1900		LA	

Parish (Diocese)	Baptisms	Marriages	Burials	Location	Reference
Adare	July 7 1832–Dec 25 1848	July 4 1832–Dec 2 1848		NLI	Pos. 2420
	Jan 4 1849–May 29 1865	Feb 17 1849–Feb 21 1865			
	1832–1900	1832–1900		LA	
Ardagh	Mar 24 1845–Dec 31 1869	Oct 25 1841–Nov 13 1869		NLI	Pos. 2424
	1845–1900	1841–1900		LA	
Askeaton	Jan 9 1829–Sept 1 1861	Jan 2 1829–July 21 1861		NLI	Pos. 2419
	Sept 1 1861–Dec 26 1880	Oct 3 1861–July 18 1880			
	1829–1900	1829–1900		LA	
	1829–1881	1829–1881		Online	Familysearch
Athea	Apr 16 1830–July 20 1856	Nov 1 1827–Feb 5 1856		NLI	Pos. 2424
	Dec 10 1850–July 26 1879	Feb 23 1851–July 19 1879			
	1830–1900	1827–1900		LA	
Ballingarry	Jan 21 1825–May 29 1828	Jan 23 1825–Feb 16 1836		NLI	Pos. 2421
	Dec 17 1849–Dec 18 1880	Jan 12 1850–Oct 16 1880			
	1825–1900	1825–1900		LA	
Ballyagran	Sept 10 1841–Nov 17 1844	Sept 16 1841–Sept 21 1844		NLI	Pos. 2430
	Jan 4 1847–Aug 30 1847	Jan 15 1847–Oct 1 1847			
	Sept 22 1850–May 21 1860	Jan 4 1851–Nov 4 1859			
	Sept 14 1860–Oct 30 1880	June 19 1860–Dec 25 1879			
	June 2 1861–Nov 8 1880	Jan 15 1861–Nov 8 1880			
	1841–1900	1841–1900		LA	
Cappagh	Jan 1 1841–Nov 3 1880	Jan 14 1841–Apr 20 1880		NLI	Pos. 2421
	1841–1900	1841–1900		LA	
Croagh	Aug 10 1836–June 11 1843	Jan 9 1844–Oct 16 1880		NLI	Pos. 2420
	Nov 3 1843–Oct 31 1859				
	Nov 13 1859–Dec 15 1880				
	1836–1900	1744 (?sic)–1900		LA	
Drumcollogher	Mar 4 1830–Sept 30 1850	Jan 24 1830–Sept 14 1850		NLI	Pos. 2423
	Nov 11 1851–Nov 10 1864	Oct 1 1851–Oct 17 1864			
	Nov 16 1864–Dec 27 1880	May 26 1866–Oct 12 1880			
	1830–1900	1830–1900		LA	
Feenagh	Aug 29 1854–Dec 28 1880	July 27 1854–Dec 18 1880		NLI	Pos. 2424
	1833–1900	1833–1900		LA	
Freemount	See North–West Cork				
Glin	Oct 30 1851–Dec 31 1880	Oct 18 1851–Oct 4 1881		NLI	Pos. 2426
	1851–1900	1851–1900		LA	
Kilcolman	Oct 28 1827–Dec 30 1843	Jan 13 1828–Nov 10 1843		NLI	Pos. 2421
	Jan 8 1844–Sept 26 1859	Jan 13 1844–Nov 21 1880			
	Oct 22 1859–Aug5 1877				
	1827–1900	1828–1900		LA	
Kilcornan	Apr 9 1825–1833	Apr 11 1825–1833		NLI	Pos. 2420
	Jan 26 1834–July 26 1848	Dec 22 1833–Mar 7 1848			
	July 30 1848–May 27 1883	Sept 10 1848–Feb 6 1883			
	1825–1900	1825–1900		LA	
Kildimo	Jan 1 1831–Nov 21 1845	Jan 14 1831–Nov 30 1845		NLI	Pos. 2419 (B.
	Jan 7 1846–Dec 31 1880	Jan 8 1846–Aug 1 1880			1846–80);
					Pos 2420
	1831–1900	1831–1900		LA	
Killeedy	Aug 11 1840–Mar 1 1874	Dec 13 1840–Feb 14 1874		NLI	Pos. 2423
	1840–1900	1840–1900		LA	
Knockaderry	Feb 24 1838–Dec 27 1880	Feb 24 1838–Dec 15 1880		NLI	Pos. 2421
	1838–1900	1838–1900		LA	

Parish (Diocese)	Baptisms	Marriages	Burials	Location	Reference
Loughill	Oct 28 1855–Dec 26 1880	Nov 1 1855–July 4 1880		NLI	Pos. 2420
	1855–1900	1855–1900		LA	
Lurriga	Oct 2 1801–Mar 13 1826	Apr 26 1802–Nov 26 1825		NLI	Pos. 2409
	Mar 16 1826–Dec 30 1843	Jan 10 1826–Dec 2 1843			
	Jan 5 1844–Dec 20 1880	Jan 20 1844–Dec 14 1880			
	1801–1900	1802–1900		LA	
Mahoonagh	Mar 24 1812–Aug 30 1830	Aug 31 1810–Feb (?) 1826		NLI	Pos. 2424/25
	June 14 1832–July 5 1838	Jan 1826–May 1 1839			
	Nov 14 1839–June 19 1869	Feb 9 1840–Aug 10 1869			
	1812–1900	1810–1900		LA	
Monagea	Jan11 1809–July 21 1813	Jan 8 1777–Feb 29 1792		NLI	Pos. 2423
	Mar 25 1829–Dec 19 1831	Feb 1 1829–Dec 27 1880			
	Aug 19 1833–Nov 30 1841				
	Dec 31 1841–Nov 3 1880				
	1776–1900	1777–1900		LA	
Newcastle Union Workhouse	Nov 14 1852–July 4 1869			NLI	Pos. 2425
	June 17 1869–Dec 16 1880				
Newcastle West	May 28 1815–Oct 27 1831	Apr 20 1815–Nov 19 1831		NLI	Pos. 2425
	Nov 3 1831–Dec 28 1851	Nov 3 1831–Dec 28 1851			
	Jan 2 1852–Nov 29 1874	Jan 25 1852–Feb 2 1871			
	1815–1900	1815–1900		LA	
Rathkeale	Jan 1 1811–July 12 1823	Jan 1 1811–Feb 7 1825		NLI	Pos. 2422
	Sept 23 1831–May 12 1839	Jan 7 1811–May 7 1839			
	June 1 1839–Dec 27 1846	(duplicates included)			
	Jan 4 1847–Feb 15 1861	May 7 1839–Feb 12 1861			
	Feb 20 1861–Dec 26 1875	Apr 13 1861–Jan 1 1876			
	1811–1900	1811–1900		LA	
Shanagolden	Apr 28 1824–July 23 1835	Apr 27 1824–Oct 6 1877		NLI	Pos. 2418/19
	Aug 3 1835–Aug 29 1842				
	Sept 3 1842–Sept 20 1862				
	Oct 2 1862–Nov 7 1877				
1824–1900	1824–1900			LA	
Templeglantine	Dec 4 1864–July 15 1879	Jan 14 1865–June 8 1879		NLI	Pos. 2426
	1864–1900	1864–1900		LA	
Tournafulla	Jan 13 1867–Apr 3 1875	July 31 1867–Aug 31 1880		NLI	Pos. 2424
	1867–1900	1867–1900		LA	

Longford

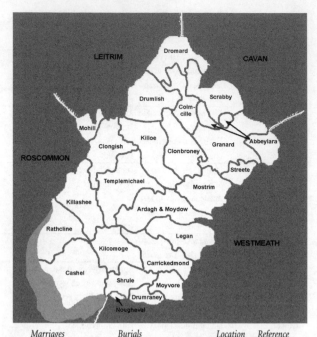

Parish (Diocese)	Baptisms	Marriages	Burials	Location	Reference
Abbeylara (Ardagh and Clonmacnois)	July 9 1854–Dec 28 1880	July 12 1854–Dec 2 1879	Aug 9 1854–Dec 29 1880	NLI	Pos. 4236
	1854–1897	1855–1899	1884–1882	LGC	
	1854–1984	1854–1984	1854–1984	LDS	1279229 item 3–5
Ardagh and Moydow (Ardagh and Clonmacnois)	Feb 12 1793–Jan 6 1816	Feb 12 1793–Oct 29 1842	Nov 26 1822–Oct 24 1842	NLI	Pos. 4235
	Oct 6 1822–Oct 28 1842	Nov 10 1842–Nov 10 1880	Nov 1 1842–Mar 13 1876		
	Nov 1 1842–Nov 11 1880				
	1793–1895	1792–1895	1822–1895	LGC	
	1793–1815	1793–1984	1822–1984	LDS	1279220; 1279270
	1823–1977				
	1793–1895	1792–1895	1822–1895	Online	Genweb Longford
Carrickedmond (Ardagh and Clonmacnois)	Apr 8 1835–Mar 30 1844	Jan 18 1835–Aug 19 1842	Jan 28 1835–Nov 17 1842	NLI	Pos. 4239
	May 30 1848–Dec 3 1880	May 31 1848–June 14 1880	May 26 1848–Jan 2 1869		
	1835–1901	1835–1887	1835–1869	LDS	1279222 item 1–3
		1890–1901			
	1835–1887	1835–1888	1835–1899	LGC	
Cashel (Ardagh and Clonmacnois)	May 15 1830–Apr 21 1910	May 15 1830–Apr 21 1910	June 22 1830–Mar 27 1831	NLI	Pos 9359
			Apr 13 1867–May 10 1880		
	1850–1899	1850–1899	1850–1880	LGC	
	1830–1910	1830–1910	1830–1831	LDS	1279221 item 3–4
			1839–1880		
Clonbroney (Ardagh and Clonmacnois)	Jan 25 1849–Mar 2 1862	Jan 8 1854–Feb 27 1862	Jan 8 1854–Feb 27 1862	NLI	Pos. 4233
	Mar 13 1862–Nov 9 1880	Feb 16 1863–July 1880	Mar 5 1862–Jan 10 1878		
	1828–1901	1849–1899	1828–1892	LGC	
	1848–1911	1853–1911	1853–1892	LDS	1279229 item 11–13; 1279270 7–9
	1828–1901	1828–1899	1828–1892	Online	Genweb Longford

Parish (Diocese)	Baptisms	Marriages	Burials	Location	Reference
Clongish (Ardagh and Clonmacnois)	Oct 25 1829–Mar 12 1857 Aug 3 1829–Sept 23 1879 Mar 15 1857–Dec 26 1880	Aug 3 1829–Sept 23–1879	Aug 22 1829–Dec 15 1880	NLI	Pos. 4233
	1829–1888	1829–1880	1829–1879	LGC	
	1829–1887	1829–1879	1829–1881	LDS	1279219 item 11–12
	1829–1841			Online	Genweb Longford
Colmcille (Ardagh and Clonmacnois)	July 1845–Feb 11 1873	Aug 3 1845–May 22 1871	July 22 1845–Dec 21 1858	NLI	Pos. 4238
	1833–1899	1833–1858	1836–1858	LGC	
	1833–1984	1833–1871 1876–1983	1932–1971	LDS	1279229 item 1–2, 14–15; 1279228
Dromard (Ardagh and Clonmacnois)	Jan 14 1838–July 15 1845 Jan 10 1852–June 18 1855 May 22 1853–Dec 26 1880 Jan 3 1872–Dec 26 1880	Feb 13 1835–Apr 15 1855 Oct 5 1853–Nov 2 1868 Nov 26 1874–Nov 22 1880	Dec 11 1853–Oct 15 1868 July 26 1874–Dec 20 1880	NLI	Pos. 4241
	1840–1899	1853–1884	1853–1881	LGC	
	1854–1910	1853–1885	1853–1881	LDS	1279229 item 8–9
Drumlish (Ardagh and Clonmacnois)	Jan 1 1834–Mar 13 1868 Mar 4 1874–Dec 30 1880	Jan 12 1834–Feb 25 1868 Jan 1 1870–June 16 1872 Jan 15 1877–Nov 8 1880	Jan 2 1834–Mar 13 1868 Feb 16 1870 July 10 1872 Aug 13 1876–Dec 13 1880	NLI	Pos. 4234
	1834–1899	1834–1899	1834–1888	LGC	
	1834–1889	1834–1889	1834–1889	LDS	1279221 item 5
Drumraney	See Westmeath				
Granard (Ardagh and Clonmacnois)	Jan 1 1779–Apr 2 1811 1812–1818 (fragments) Oct 20 1816–Feb 26 1832 Jan 1832–June 2 1869 Jan 2 1820–Dec 26 1880	Dec 3 1782–May 25 1815 Sept 10 1816–July 14 1836 July 18 1836–May 6 1869 June 30 1869–Dec 8 1880	Dec 18 1782–Aug 8 1816 Apr 29 1818–Apr 28 1820 Sept 16 1816–Dec 27 1847 Jan 3 1848–May 24 1865	NLI	Pos. 4237
	1779–1894	1782–1869	1811–1818	LGC	
	1779–1928	1782–1900	1782–1862	LDS	12792298 item 1–6; 1279270, 13–
	1778–1894	1811–1865	1811–1865	Online	Genweb Longford
Kilcomoge (Ardagh and Clonmacnois)	Sept 7 1859–Dec 19 1880	Sept 13 1859–Feb 4 1880	Nov 13 1859–Nov 18 1880	NLI	Pos. 4234
	1859–1880	1859–1880	1859–1880	LGC	
	1859–1984	1859–1981	1859–1880	LDS	12792222 item 5–7; 12879270 4–6
	1859–1880	1859–1880	1859–1880	Online	Genweb Longford
Killashee (Ardagh and Clonmacnois)	Nov 1 1826–Nov 4 1843 Apr 9 1848–July 4 1868 June 4 1865–Nov 24 1880	Nov 19 1826–Oct 23 1843 June 18 1848–Apr 5 1868 May 18 1864–Oct 9 1880	Nov 15 1826–Aug 3 1843 Nov 20 1858–May 11 1868	NLI	Pos. 4235
	1826–1898	1828–1898	1841–1865	LGC	
Killoe (Ardagh and Clonmacnois)	Jan 1 1826–July 21 1832 Jan 1 1826–Aug 31 1852 Feb 4 1853–Oct 7 1868 Apr 11 1869–Dec 18 1880	May 29 1826–July 18 1832 Jan 2 1826–Oct 21 1852 Sept 5 1854–Dec 16 1868 Jan 31 1869–Nov 1 1880	Jan 2 1826–June 10 1853 Aug 23 1853–Dec 29 1868 Jan 20 1869–Dec 26 1880	NLI	Pos. 4238

Parish (Diocese)	Baptisms	Marriages	Burials	Location	Reference
Killoe (Ardagh	1826–1917	1826–1917	1826–1884	LGC	
and Clonmacnois)	1826–1917	1826–1868	1826–1868	LDS	1279221 item 6–14
	1826–1917	1826–1917	1826–1884	Online	Genweb Longford
Legan (Ardagh and	Jan 5 1855–Dec 29 1880	Jan 7 1855–Dec 11 1880	Jan 20 1855–Dec 25 1880	NLI	Pos. 4234
Clonmacnois)	1855–1899	1855–1896	1855–1890	LGC	
	1855–1905	1855–1905	1855–1890	LDS	1279221 item 15
Mohill	See Leitrim				
Mostrim	June 8 1838–Dec 29 1880	June 11 1838–Oct 29 1880	May 23 1838–Dec 9 1880	NLI	Pos. 4233
	1838–1895	1838–1891	1838–1888	LGC	
	1838–1895	1838–1894	1838–1888	LDS	1279219 item 10
Moyvore (Meath)	Sept 5 1831–Feb 8 1862	Feb 12 1832–Spr 28 1862	Aug 6 1831–Apr 1863	NLI	Pos. 4171
	Feb 18 1862–Dec 25 1880	Mar 21862–Dec 25 1880	May 1863–Sept 5 1865		
	Sept 5 1831–Feb 8 1862	Feb 12 1832–Spr 28 1862	Aug 6 1831–Apr 1863	LDS	0926167 item 1–2
	Feb 18 1862–Dec 25 1880	Mar 21862–Dec 25 1880	May 1863–Sept 5 1865		
	1832–1900	1832–1900	1831–1865	DSHC	
Nougheval	See Westmeath				
Rathcline (Ardagh	Jan 12 1840–March 9 1904	Jan 12 1840–March 9 1904	Dec 10 1839–March 17 1899	NLI	Pos. 9539
and Clonmacnois)	1840–1899	1840–1898	1841–1899	LGC	
	1840–1889	1840–1903	1835–1869	LDS	1279222 item 4
			1839–1899		
Scrabby (Ardagh	Feb 12 1833–Mar 15 1854	Feb 17 1833–Feb 22 1855	Sept 9 1835–Mar 1854	NLI	Pos. 4237
and Clonmacnois)	Mar 4 1855–10 Dec 28 1867	Apr 15 1855–June 29 1871	Apr 7 1856–Aug 20 1860		
	Apr 4 1870–Sept 29 1880	June 11 1877–Nov 13 1880			
	1833–1899	1845–1867	1836–1860	LGC	
	1833–1920	1833–1871		LDS	1279228 item 10–13
		1877–1906	1833–1860		
	1836–1899	1836–1899		CHGC	
Shrule (Ardagh	Mar 26 1820–Oct 26 1830	May 12 1829–Oct 25 1830	Mar 14 1820–Sept 12 1830	NLI	Pos. 4235
and Clonmacnois)	Nov 1 1830–Dec 24 1874	Dec 26 1830–Nov 8 1874	Nov 8 1830–Aug 17 1876		
	1820–1887	1820–1888	1820–1899	LGC	
	1820–1874	1820–1874	1830–1876	LDS	1279219 item 13–14; 1279221 1–2
	1875–1902	1875–1903			
Streete (Ardagh and Clonmacnois)	See Westmeath				
Templemichael (Ardagh and Clonmacnois)	Jan 5 1802–Jan 3 1808	Jan 20 1802–Feb 26 1829	Jan 30 1802–Feb 19 1829	NLI	Pos. 4232
	June 6 1808–Jan 28 1829	Mar 1 1829–June 9 1868	Mar 1 1829–Oct 4 1865		
	Mar 1 1829–June 11 1862	June 4 1868–Dec 13 1880			
	June 12 1862–July 7 1868				
	June 3 1868–Dec 31 1880				
	1802–1885	1802–1897	1802–1829	LGC	
	1802–1920	1820–1900	1802–1869	LDS	1279219 item 1–9

Louth

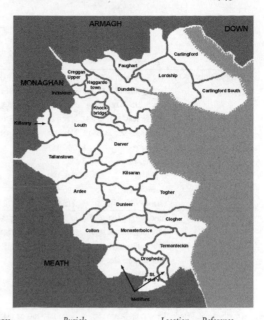

Parish (Diocese)	Baptisms	Marriages	Burials	Location	Reference
Ardee (Armagh)	Apr 10 1763–June 24 1802	Aug 8 1769–June 10 1802	July 1 1802–Oct 31 1810	NLI	Pos. 5601
	July 20 1802–Oct 25 1810	Aug 10 1802–Oct 29 1810	Mar 7 1821–Feb 7 1825		
	Mar 4 1821–Dec 11 1880	Mar 5 1821–Feb 9 1826			
	1763–1810	1769–1800	1765–1810	PRONI	MIC.1D/52
	1821–1881	1821–1826	1821–1825		
	1763–1900	1763–1900	1810–1921	AA	
Carlingford	Apr 2 1835–Aug 13 1848	Apr 23 1838–Aug 12 1848	Apr 7 1835–Aug 12 1848	NLI	Pos. 5594
(Armagh)	Aug 13 1848–Dec 22 1880	Sept 13 1848–Dec 30 1880	Oct 29 1867–Dec 30 1880		
	1835–1881	1835–1881	1835–1848	PRONI	MIC.1D/45
			1869–1882		
	1835–1900	1835–1900		AA	
Carlingford South	June 4 1811–Aug 13 1838	Feb 19 1811–July 17 1838		NLI	Pos. 5593
(Armagh)	Aug 14 1838–Dec 29 1880	Sept 19 1838–Dec 11 1880			
	1811–1881	1811–1882		PRONI	MIC.1D/44
	1811–1900	1811–1900	1811–1877	AA	
	See NLI			LDS	0926033
Clogher (Armagh)	Nov 2 1744–Oct 17 1777	Feb 12 1742–Aug 25 1771	Nov 30 1744–July 21 1772	NLI	Pos. 5599
	Apr 4 1780–Dec 30 1799	Apr 4 1780–Sept 18 1799	Mar 20 1780–1799		
	Mar 9 1833–Oct 23 1836	Apr 11 1833–Oct 27 1836	(incomplete)		
	Aug 5 1837–Dec 21 1880	Aug 18 1837–Nov 21 1880			
	1744–1777	1742–1771	1744–1772	PRONI	MIC.1D/53
	1780–1799	1780–1799	1780–1799 (gaps)		
	1833–1881	1833–1881			
	1744–1799	1742–1799	1742–1799	AA	
	1833–1900	1833–1900			
Collon (Armagh)	Apr 2 1789–Mar 1807	Jan 1789–Feb 1807		NLI	Pos. 5597
	Aug 15 1819–Dec 29 1836	Dec 2 1817–Dec 21 1835			
	Jan 6 1836–Dec 14 1880	(fragmented and disordered)			
		Feb 7 1836–Sept 19 1845			
		Mar 11 1848–Nov 27 1880			

Parish (Diocese)	Baptisms	Marriages	Burials	Location	Reference
Collon (Armagh)	1789–1807	1789–1807		PRONI	MIC.1D/48
	1819–1881	1817–1845			
	1848–1881				
Creggan Upper (Armagh)	Aug 5 1796–Jan 19 1803	Aug 8 1796–Feb 16 1803		NLI	Pos. 5592
	Sept 23 1812–Mar 28 1822	Dec 18 1812–mar 22 1822			
	Apr 2 1822–May 29 1829	Apr 8 1822–July 24 1829			
	May 26 1845–May 31 1871	May 8 1845–Mar 1 1870			
	Jan 2 1870–Dec 28 1880	May 13 1871–Nov 26 1880			
	1796–1803	1796–1803		PRONI	MIC.1D/43
	1812–1829	1812–1829			
	1845–1881	1845–1881			
	1796–1803	1796–1803		AA	
	1812–1900	1812–1900			
Darver (Armagh)	June 29 1787–Oct 26 1819	July 27 1787–June 23 1836		NLI	Pos. 5596
	Nov 1819–Mar 30 1836	May 3 1837–Feb 29 1848			
	Nov 23 1833–1846	Feb 4 1847–Nov 17 1880			
	June 18 1846–Dec 31 1880				
	1787–1880	1837–1883	1871–1879	PRONI	MIC.1D/47
	1787–1900	1787–1900	1871–1879	AA	
	See NLI			LDS	0926035
Drogheda: St. Peter's (Armagh)	Jan 9 1744–May 2 1757	Nov 1 1815–July 24 1842		NLI	Pos. 5597; From 1815 Pos. 5598
	Aug 25 1764–Oct 27 1771	(very poor)			
	Apr 7 1777–Feb 26 1778	July 26 1842–Jan 4 1866			
	June 14 1781–Oct 1 1783	Jan 3 1866–Dec 26 1880			
	Nov 28 1783–Apr 1795				
	Oct 1803–Dec 19 1804				
	Nov 1815–July 24 1842				
	(very poor)				
	July 29 1842–Dec 1880				
	1744–1757	1815–1880		PRONI	MIC.1D/48–49
	1764–1771				
	1777–1778				
	1781–1795				
	1803–1804				
	1815–1881				
	1744–1804	1804		AA	
	1815–1899	1819–1900			
	See NLI			LDS	0926036/7
Dundalk (Armagh)	Aug 4 1790–Sept 30 1802	Aug 15 1790–Nov 19 1802	Aug 17 1790–Nov 27 1802	NLI	Pos. 5595
	May 25 1814–Aug 30 1831	Oct 27 1817–Aug 20 1831			
	Aug 29 1831–Dec 31 1844				
	Jan 25 1845–Jan 18 1868				
	Jan 21 1868–Dec 31 1880				
	1790–1802	1790–1802	1790–1802	PRONI	MIC.1D/46
	1814–1881	1817–1831			
	1790–1802	1790–1802	1790–1802	AA	
	1814–1900	1817–1900			
	See NLI			LDS	0979711 item 1–4
		1790–1802		Online	Hall

Parish (Diocese)	Baptisms	Marriages	Burials	Location	Reference
Dunleer (Armagh)	Oct 29 1847–Dec 26 1880	Nov 13 1772–Feb 21 1798	Dec 3 1847–Dec 7 1858	NLI	Pos. 5602
		Jan 28 1848–Nov 24 1880	Jan 1 1877 Dec 6 1880		
	1847–1881	1772–1798	1847–1858	PRONI	MIC.1D/50
		1848–1882	1877–1882		
	1798–1900	1772–1900	1832–1900	AA	
	See NLI			LDS	0926039
Faughart (Armagh)	Apr 16 1851–Dec 23 1880 (indexed)	Apr 21 1851–Nov 24 1880		NLI	Pos. 5596
	1861–1881 (indexed)	1851–1882		PRONI	MIC.1D/47
	1851–1896	indexed 1851–1900		AA	
	1851–1900	1851–1900		AA	
	See NLI			LDS	0926040 item 1–5
Haggardstown (Armagh)	Jan 12 1752–May 28 1789	Jan 21 1752–Oct 17 1789	Jan 8 1752–Sept 12 1789	NLI	Pos. 5594
	May 29 1789–Aug 21 1838	June 11 1789–Aug 27 1838	Sept 4 1789–Mar 11 1806		
	July 5 1838–Nov 27 1880	Nov 1 1838–Nov25 1880	Sept 9 1831–Aug 27 1838		
	1752–1880	1752–1880	1752–1806	PRONI	
			1831–1838		MIC.1D/45
	1752–1900	1752–1900	1752–1838	AA	
Inniskeen (Clogher)	See Monaghan				
Killanny	See Monaghan				
Kilsaran (Armagh)	Jan 1 1809–May 8 1824	Jan 23 1809–Oct 228 1826		NLI	Pos. 5599
	Aug 3 1831–June 28 1836	Aug 30 1831–Nov 14 1836			
	Juny 19 1853–Dec 27 1880	Sept 11 1853–Nov 27 1880		PRONI	
	1809–1824	1809–1826			53
	1831–1836	1831–1836			
	1853–1881	1853–1882			
	1809–1900	1809–1900		AA	
Knockbridge (Armagh)	Nov 3 1858–1869	Scpt 19 1858–1869		NLI	Pos. 5594
	1858–1869	1858–1869		PRONI	MIC.1D/45
	1851	1858–1869		AA	
	1858–1869	1889–1900			
	1881–1900				
	Nov 3 1858–1869	Sept 19 1858–1869		LDS	0926043
Lordship (Armagh)	Jan 7 1838–Aug 27 1864	Jan 21 1838–Aug 28 1864		NLI	Pos. 5595
	Sept 4 1864–Dec 30 1880	Sept 1 1864–Nov 25 1880			
	1838–1881	1838–1880		PRONI	MIC.1D/46–47
	1833–1900	1833–1900		AA	
	See NLI			LDS	0926044/5
Louth (Armagh)	Mar 12 1833–Sept 25 1871	Apr 8 1833–Dec 18 1873		NLI	Pos. 5593
	Oct 14 1873–Dec 4 1880	Jan 23 1874 Dec 7 1880			
	1833–1871	1833–1881		PRONI	MIC.1D/44
	1873–1881				
	1833–1900	1835–1900		AA	
Mellifont (Armagh)	Dec 2 1821–Dec 29 1848	Dec 14 1821–Dec 9 1848		NLI	Pos. 5599
	1821–1881	1821–1882		PRONI	MIC.1D/53
	1821–1900	1821–1900		AA	
Monasterboice (Armagh)	Nov 1 1814–Oct 30 1830	Nov 2 1814–Sept 28 1830	Nov 5 1814–Nov 30 1815	NLI	Pos. 5600
	Jan 9 1834–Dec 23 1859	Oct 21 1830–Nov 20 1872	Jan 4 1820–Dec 8 1822		
	Jan 6 1860–Dec 19 1880	Jan 20 1870–Nov 20 1872	Sept 12 1830–Jan 10 1850		

Parish (Diocese)	Baptisms	Marriages	Burials	Location	Reference
Monasterboice (Armagh)	1814–1830	1814–1872	1814–1850 (gaps)	PRONI	MIC.1D/51–52
	1834–1881		1857–1858		
			1876–1877		
	1814–1830	1814–1872	1814–1822	AA	
	1834–1900				
Tallanstown (Armagh)	Nov 9 1817–Apr 13 1825	Apr 4 1804–Mar 16 1816		NLI	Pos. 5602
	Sept 25 1830–Nov 6 1835	Apr 17 1816–June 1 1863			
	Nov 9 1835–Sept 28 1875	Aug 31 1867–Nov 25 1880			
	Oct 12 1875–Dec 27 1880				
	1817–1825	1804–1863		PRONI	MIC.1D/50
	1830–1881	1867–1884			
	1817–1825	1804–1900		AA	
	1835–1900				
	See NLI			LDS	0979712 item 4–9
Termonfeckin (Armagh)	Apr 3 1823–Feb 3 1853	Apr 14 1823–Nov 27 1852	Jan 1 1827–Oct 11 1833	NLI	Pos. 5600
	Jan 6 1853–Dec 17 1880	Apr 12 1853–Nov 9 1880			
	1823–1881	1823–1881	1827–1833	PRONI	MIC.1D/51
	1823–1900	1799–1900	1799–1833	AA	
	See NLI			LDS	0926044/5
Togher (Armagh)	Nov 1 1791–Apr 24 1828	July 31 1791–Mar 17 1828	June 3 1791–May 8 1817	NLI	Pos. 5597
	Aug 8 1869–Dec 31 1880	Feb 24 1873–Nov 13 1880			
	1791–1828	1873–1881	1791–1817	PRONI	MIC.1D/48
	1869–1881				
	1791–1900	1791–1900	1791–1817	AA	

Mayo

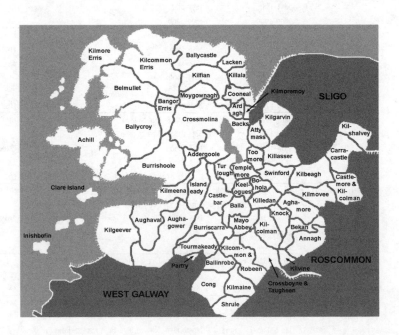

Parish (Diocese)	Baptisms	Marriages	Burials	Location	Reference
Achill (Tuam)	Dec 29 1867–Dec 26 1880	Oct 18 1867–June 25 1880		NLI	Pos. 4222
	1868–1900	1867–1900		MNFHRC	
	1868–1911	1867–1813		LDS	1279259 item 3–5
Addergoole (Killala)	Jan 15 1840–Mar 2 1866	Jan 13 1840–Mar 10 1878		NLI	Pos. 4229
	Mar 2 1866–June 11 1878				
	June 16 1878–Dec 26 1880				
	1840–1900	1840–1900		MNFHRC	
	1840–1880	1840–1878		LDS	1279205 item 9–11
		1842–1862		Online	Dees
Aghamore (Tuam)	Feb 2 1864–Dec 26 1880 (transcript)	Dec 22 1864–Sept 22 1880		NLI	Pos. 4217
	1864–1900	1864–1900		MSFHC	
	1864–1901	1864–1921		LDS	1279206 item 13–15
Annagh (Tuam)	Nov 17 1851–Dec 30 1870	June 14 1852–June 30 1870		NLI	Pos. 4217
	Jan 6 1871–Dec 26 1880	Nov 20 1870–Dec 1 1880			
	1851–1900	1852–1900		MSFHC	
	1854–1924	1852–1902		LDS	1279208 item 3–6
Ardagh (Killala)	Feb 5 1870–July 14 1880			NLI	Pos. 4230
	1866–1900	1882–1900		MNFHRC	
		1870–1880		LDS	1279204 item 23
Attymass (Achonry)	June 16 1875–Aug 22 1880	Feb 1 1874–Oct 15 1880		NLI	Pos. 4224
	1875–1900	1874–1897		MNFHRC	
	June 16 1875–Aug 22 1880	Feb 1 1874–Oct 15 1880		LDS	0926002 item 1–2
Aughagower (Tuam)	Apr 9 1828–May 17 1836	Nov 16 1854–Dec 7 1880		NLI	Pos. 4210
	Mar 17 1842–Aug 20 1854				
	Sept 24 1854–Dec 18 1880				
	1828–1900	1828–1900		MSFHC	
	1828–1836	1854–1903		LDS	1279209 item 19–20; 1279210,
	1842–1854				1–3
	1854–1903				
	1828–1836	1857–1868		Online	Dees
	1842–1846				
Aughaval (Tuam)	July 9 1845–Nov 14 1858 (Not precisely ordered)	Apr 9 1823–Oct 6 1837 (Not precisely ordered)		NLI	Pos. 4210
	Jan 18 1859–Mar 24 1872	Aug 10 1834–May 25 1857			
	Jan 19 1862–Mar 11 1874	(Not precisely ordered)			
	Apr 7 1872–Dec 26 1880	Feb 4 1857–Feb 1 1861			
	Mar 151874–Dec 29 1880	Jan 15 1862–Dec 20 1880			
	1845–1900	1823–1900		MSFHC	
	1845–1905	1823–1905		LDS	12792210/1 item 17–22, 1–4; More
	1848–1873	1825–1860		Online	Dees
Backs (Killala)	Aug 28 1848–Dec 11 1859 (Rathduff)	Dec 1 1848–Apr 14 1860 (Rathduff)		NLI	Pos. 4230

Parish (Diocese)	Baptisms	Marriages	Burials	Location	Reference
Backs (Killala)	Jan 2 1861–Sept 14 1879 (Rathduff)	Jan 27 1865–Dec 2 1869 (Rathduff)		NLI	Pos. 4230
	Oct 12 1854–Oct 2 1856 (Knockmore)	Feb 24 1874–Sept 1879 (Rathduff)			
	Mar 4 1858–Aug 16 1879 (Knockmore)	Sept 25 1860–Nov 21 1861 (Knockmore)			
		Jan 13 1869–July 13 1879 (Knockmore)			
	1829–1900	1815–1897		MNFHRC	
	1830–1851	1829–1850		LDS	1279205 item
	1854–1879	1848–1864			5–8
	1848–1879	1865–1880			
	1865–1880				
	1854–1863			Online	Dees
Balla (Tuam)	May 28 1837–Dec 27 1880	July 3 1837–Oct 3 1880		NLI	Pos. 4213
	1837–1900	1837–1900		MSFHC	
	1837–1905	1837–1905		LDS	1279209 item 2–3
	1837–1841			Online	Dees
Ballinrobe (Tuam)	Aug 20 1843–Dec 20 1851 (Inc some marriages)	Oct 24 1850–Apr 30 1856		NLI	Pos. 4215
	Nov 7 1850–Apr 17 1856	Jan 14 1861–Nov 7 1880			
	Jan18 1861–Nov 7 1880				
	June 19 1871–Dec 29 1880				
	1843–1900	1850–1900		MSFHC	
	1843–1903	1850–1911		LDS	1279209 item 8–10; 0926219
Ballycastle (Killala)	Aug 8 1864–Dec 15 1880	Jan 15 1869–Sept 3 1880		NLI	Pos. 4229
	1853–1900	1869–1900		MNFHRC	
	1853–1880	1869–1880		LDS	1279204 item 20–21
Ballycroy (Killala)	No records microfilmed			NLI	
	1885–1900	1869–1900		MNFHRC	
Bangor Erris(Killala)	Aug 1 1860–Dec 26 1880	Sept 4 1860–Mar 28 1880		NLI	Pos. 4231
	1860–1901	1860–1914		MNFHRC	
	1860–1881	1860–1881		LDS	1279205 item 12, 16
Bekan (Tuam)	Aug 3 1832–Feb 2 1844 (some missing)	May 7 1832–Aug 6 1844 (some missing)		NLI	Pos. 4219
	Dec 15 1844–May 20 1861 (some missing)	Aug 8 1844–May 22 1872 (some missing)			
	Sept 15 1851–May 7 1871				
	1832–1900	1832–1900		MSFHC	
Belmullet (Killala)	Feb 15 1841–Dec 19 1872	Jan 8 1836–May 11 1845		NLI	Pos. 4231
	Dec 21 1872–Dec 26 1880				
	1841–1900	1836–1900		MNFHRC	
	1842–1880	1836–1880		LDS	1279205 item 13–15
Bohola (Achonry)	Oct 1857–Dec 26 1880	Oct 29 1857–May 30 1880		NLI	Pos. 4224
	1857–1900	1857–1900		MNFHRC	

Parish (Diocese)	Baptisms	Marriages	Burials	Location	Reference
Burriscarra (Tuam)	Sept 1 1839–Dec 24 1880	Sept 29 1839–Mar 1 1880		NLI	Pos. 4213
	1839–1900	1839–1900		MSFHC	
	1839–1895	1839–1903		LDS	1279210 item 15–16; 0979699 1–2
	1839–1881 (extracts?)	1839–1849 (part?)		Online	Dees
Burrishoole (Tuam)	Jan 30 1872–Nov 27 1880			NLI	Pos. 4222
	1872–1900	1872–1900		MNFHRC	
	1872–1920	1872–1911		LDS	1279207 item 9–11
Carracastle (Achonry)	Jan 17 1853–Dec 26 1880	July 1 1847–Nov 21 1880		NLI	Pos. 4223
	1853–1900	1847–1900		MNFHRC	
	1853–1908	1847–1903		LDS	1279233 item 1–2
Castlebar (Tuam)	Jan 2 1838–Apr 17 1855 (in disorder) Feb 25 1855–June 16 1872 June 22 1872–Dec 28 1880	June 16 1824–Apr 17 1843 June 27 1843–Dec 9 1880		NLI	Pos. 4214
	1838–1900	1824–1900		MSFHC	
	1838–1984	1824–1982		LDS	1279260/1
	Extracts	1828–1831, 1883–1896		Online	Dees
Castlemore and Kilcolman (Achonry)	Nov 1851–Nov 17 1861 Jan 25 1864–June 2 1872 Jan 5 1860–Feb 6 1876 1861 1864–1872 (transcript) Feb 13 1876–Dec 31 1880	Aug 10 1830–Oct 2 1867 Feb 4 1868–Nov 10 1880		NLI	Pos. 4226
	1851–1900	1830–1900		RHGC	
	1851–1911	1830–1963		LDS	1279232 item 1–9
	1851–1900			SHGC	
Clare Island (Tuam)	Oct 14 1851–Nov 21 1880			NLI	Pos. 4211
	Oct 14 1851–Nov 21 1880			LDS	0926220 item 3
	1851–1853			Online	Dees
Cong and The Neale (Tuam)	Feb 28 1870–Dec 20 1880 (transcript)			NLI	Pos. 4214
	1870–1900	1870–1900		MSFHC	
	1870–1924	1870–1900		LDS	1279214 item 6–7
Cooneal (Killala)	Nov 26 1843–Dec 19 1880	Oct 10 1843–Dec 21 1880		NLI	Pos. 4230
	1844–1881	1843–1881		MNFHRC	
	c 1830–c 1870	c 1830–c 1870		LDS	1279204 item 24
Crossboyne and Taugheen (Tuam)	July 7 1862–Feb 3 1877 May 10 1877–Dec 26 1880	Jan 9 1877–July 29 1880		NLI	Pos. 4217
	1825–1900	1794–1900		MSFHC	
	1825–1913	1791–1876		LDS	1279211 item 5–8
Crossmolina (Killala)	Aug 27 1831–Aug 8 1841 Apr 23 1845–Dec 28 1880	Nov 18 1832–Feb 10 1841 Mar 10 1846–Dec 27 1880		NLI	Pos. 4230
	1831–1900	1832–1900		MNFHRC	

Parish (Diocese)	Baptisms	Marriages	Burials	Location	Reference
Crossmolina (Killala)	1831–1880	1832–1880		LDS	1279204 item 22
	1831–1838?,			Online	Dees
	1865–1875				
Inishbofin (Tuam)	Oct 14 1867–Dec 15 1880	Nov 18 1867–Oct 25 1880		NLI	Pos. 4219
	1867–1900	1867–1900		GFHSW	
	1867–1903	1877–1878		LDS	1279213 item 10
Islandeady (Tuam)	Sept 7 1839–Dec 30 1866	Sept 17 1839–Sept 2 1880		NLI	Pos. 4212
	Jan 6 1867–May 14 1876				
	1839–1900	1839–1900		MSFHC	
	1839–1913	1839–1898		LDS	1279213
					item 11–14
		1839–1903 (part)		Online	Dees
Keelogues (Tuam)	Aug 15 1847–Dec 24 1880	Aug 10 1847–Sept 4 1880		NLI	Pos. 4215
	1847–1909	1847–1909		MNFHRC	
	1847–1909	1872–1909		LDS	1279259
					item 1–2
Kilbeagh (Achonry)	Jan 1 1855–Dec 26 1880	May 18 1845–Mar 13 1866		NLI	Pos. 4224
		Jan 22 1855–Sept 12 1880			
	1847–1900	1844–1900		MNFHRC	
	1855–1924	1845–1902		LDS	1279230
					item 1–6
Kilcolman (Tuam)	Apr 7 1835–Jan 29 1838	June 8 1806–Feb 4 1830		NLI	Pos. 4217
	Mar 26 1839–May 16 1858	Jan 7 1835–Mar 7 1836			
	May 16 1858–May 28 1873	Dec 29 1838–June 25 1871			
	1835–1900	1805–1900		MSFHC	
	1835–1913	1806–1898		LDS	1279207
					item 15–20
Kilcommon and	Oct 5 1857–Dec 24 1880	Oct 10 1857–June 24 1880		NLI	Pos. 4216
Robeen (Tuam)	Dec 8 1865–Dec 24 1880	Nov 25 1865–Apr 24 1880			
	(Roundfort)	(Roundfort)			
	1857–1900	1857–1900		MSFHC	
	1857–1880	1857–1880		LDS	1279209 item
	1896–1924	8165–1899			11–12; 0926223
		1896–1924			
Kilcommon Erris	No records microfilmed			NLI	
(Killala)	1883–1910	1843–1848		MNFHRC	
Kilfian (Killala)	Oct 1 1826–Apr 7 1836	July 2 1826–Oct 2 1844	Oct 6 1826–Feb 6 1832	NLI	Pos. 4230
	1826–1836	1826–1836	1826–1836	MNFHRC	
	1826–1836	1826–1836	1826–1832	LDS	1279205 item 2
		1843–1844			
Kilgarvin (Achonry)	Mar 15 1870–Dec 31 1880	Nov 16 1844–May 4 1880		NLI	Pos. 4224
	1870–1900	1844–1900		MNFHRC	
	Mar 15 1870–Dec 31 1880	Nov 16 1844–May 4 1880		LDS	
Kilgeever (Tuam)	Feb 20 1850–Mar 7 1869			NLI	Pos. 4212
	(transcript)				
	Aug 1 1872–Dec 12 1880				
	1850–1900	1850–1900		MSFHC	
	1850–1872	1844–1845		·LDS	1279224 item
	1894–1922	1906–1922			2; 0926224 1;
	1872–1880 Louisburgh	1872–1880 Louisburgh			&more
		1844–1878		Online	Dees

Parish (Diocese)	Baptisms	Marriages	Burials	Location	Reference
Killala (Killala)	Apr 6 1852–Aug 25 1873 Sept 21 1873–Dec 23 1880	Dec 14 1873–Nov 3 1880		NLI	Pos. 4231
	1852–1900	1873–1900		MNFHRC	
	1852–1880	1873–1880		LDS	1279204 item 17–19
Killasser (Achonry)	Nov 1 1847–Dec 31 1880	Dec 13 1847–June 5 1880	Nov 1 1847–Apr 3 1862	NLI	Pos. 4223
	1848–1900	1847–1900	1847–1848	MNFHRC	
	1847–1902	1847–1921		LDS	1279232 item 16–17
Killedan (Achonry)	Feb 2 1861–Dec 29 1880	May 22 1834–Apr 3 1862 Nov 6 1861–Aug 8 1880		NLI	Pos. 4224
	1861–1900	1835–1900		MSFHC	
	1860–1909	1834–1909		LDS	1279231 item 3–6
	1860–1882?	1835–1900 (?part?)		Online	Celtic cousins
Kilmaine (Tuam)	June 30 1854–Dec 31 1877 Jan 20 1878–Dec 24 1880	May 19 1855–Oct 20 1877		NLI	Pos. 4216
	1854–1900	1854–1900		MSFHC	
	1854–1909	1855–1909		LDS	1279214 item 3–4; 0926225 2–4
Kilmeena (Tuam)	No records microfilmed			NLI	
	1858–	1858–		LC	
	1870–1900	1870–1900		MSFHC	
Kilmore Erris (Killala)	June 24 1860–Dec 27 1880	Sept 1 1860–Nov 4 1880		NLI	Pos. 4231
	1859–1900	1860–1900		MNFHRC	
	1860–1881	1860–1881		LDS	1279205 item 17–18
Kilmoremoy (Killala)	See Sligo				
Kilmovee (Achonry)	Feb 21 1854–Dec 21 1880 June 18 1854–Dec 19 1880	Nov 3 1824–Aug 28 1848 Oct 12 1854–Dec 21 1880		NLI	Pos. 4224
	1854–1900	1824–1900		MSFHC	
	1854–1913	1824–1848 1855–1925		LDS	1279230 item 7–9; 0926017
Kilshalvey (Achonry)	See Sligo				
Kilvine (Tuam)	No records microfilmed			NLI	
	1872–1911	1872–1908		LDS	1279206 item 10
	1870–1900	1870–1900		MSFHC	
Knock (Tuam)	Dec 17 1868–Dec 29 1880	Sept 7 1875–Dec 5 1880		NLI	Pos. 4218
	1868–1900	1874–1900		MSFHC	
	1868–1913	1875–1943		LDS	1279206 item 3–5
Lacken (Killala)	Aug 19 1852–Nov 24 1874 (transcript–many gaps)	Mar 29 1854–Feb 7 1869 (transcript–many gaps)		NLI	Pos. 4230
	1852–1900	1881–1900		MNFHRC	
	1852–1874	1854–1869		LDS	1279205 item 4
Mayo Abbey (Tuam)	Apr 4 1841–Dec 20 1880	Sept 10 1841–June 5 1880		NLI	Pos. 4215
	1841–1900	1841–1900		MSFHC	
	1841–1899	1841–1906		LDS	1279209 item 6–7

Parish (Diocese)	Baptisms	Marriages	Burials	Location	Reference
Moygownagh	No records microfilmed			NLI	
(Killala)	1887–1900	1881–1900		MNFHRC	
Partry (Tuam)	Oct 23 1869–July 15 1868	Jan 7 1870–July 11 1878		NLI	Pos. 4216
Shrule (Galway)	July 7 1831–Aug 12 1864	July 1 1831–June 23 1848		NLI	Pos. 2438
		Oct 26 1855–May 10 1864			
	1831–1900	1831–1900		MSFHC	
Swineford (Achonry)	Mar 19 1822–June 26 1826	June 7 1808–July 3 1846		NLI	Pos. 4225
	May 12 1841–Aug 23 1850	July 3 1846–Mar 31 1878			
	Sept 1 1850–May 7 1859	Apr 24 1878–Nov 23 1915			
	July 2 1859–Sept 29 1875				
	Oct 2 1875–Dec 31 1900				
	1822–1826	1808–1878		MNFHRC	
	1841–1900				
	1822–1915	1808–1915		LDS	1279233 item 5–9; 0926020
Templemore		May 20 1872–Mar 11 1880		NLI	Pos. 4224
(Achonry)	1888–1900	1872–1900		MNFHRC	
		May 20 1872–Mar 11 1880		LDS	0926021
Toomore (Achonry)	Dec 30 1871–Jan 6 1880	Apr 30 1833–Mar 17 1840		NLI	Pos. 4223
		Jan 20 1870–Dec 22 1880			
	1871–1900	1872–1900		MNFHRC	
	1871–1893	1833–1911		LDS	12792031 item 18–19; 0926022
	1872–1879			Online	Glanduff
Tourmakeady	Aug 26 1869–Dec 26 1880	1869–Sept 5 1880		NLI	Pos. 4216
(Tuam)	(transcript)				
	1869–1900	1847–1900		MSFHC	
	1862–1885	1870–1878		LDS	1279206 item 16
		1883–1903			
Turlough (Tuam)	Aug 1 1847–Dec 7 1865	Aug 8 1847–June 8 1880		NLI	Pos. 4213
	Dec 8 1865–Dec 25 1880				
	1847–1900	1849–1900		MNFHRC	
	1847–1911	1847–1909		LDS	1279212 item 5–7

Meath
All Meath
diocese,
except where
noted

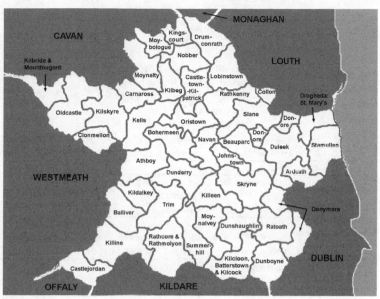

Parish (Diocese)	Baptisms	Marriages	Burials	Location	Reference
Ardcath	Oct 25 1795–June 29 1879	June 18 1797–June 30 1879		NLI	Pos. 4180
	1795–1900	1797–1900		MHC	
Athboy	Apr 18 1794–Nov 15 1799	May 5 1794–Nov 7 1799	Apr 23 1794–Mar 27 1798	NLI	Pos. 4173
	Mar 3 1807–May 16 1826	Apr 9 1807–Oct 24 1864	Mar 18 1807–Feb 23 1826		
	Jan 14 1827–Jan 12 1858	Feb 6 1865–Nov 25 1880	Jan 2 1865–Sept 23 1873		
	Jan 1 1858–Dec 29 1880				
	1794–1900	1794–1900	1794–1847	MHC	
Balliver	Feb 12 1837–Dec 9 1880	Apr 7 1837–July 12 1880	Feb 12 1837–Nov 16 1880	NLI	Pos. 4179
	1837–1901			MHC	
	See NLI			LDS	0926163
Beauparc	Dec 17 1815–Sept 8 1880	Jan 10 1816–July 22 1881		NLI	Pos. 4180
	1815–1900	1816–1900	1816–1839	MHC	
Bohermeen	June 2 1832–Dec 31 1880	Apr 22 1831–May 30 1881	Jan 5 1833–May 5 1842	NLI	Pos. 4182
			Jan 15 1865–Mar 13 1868		
	1832–1900	1831–1900	1833–1868	MHC	
	See NLI			LDS	0926164
Carnaross	Aug 25 1806–Oct 14 1807	June 1805–Feb 12 1820	June 9 1805–Sept 13 1856	NLI	Pos. 4184
	May 21 1808–Sept 28 1815	Feb 16 1823–Feb 24 1825			
	June 2 1827–Feb 6 1859	Jan 27 1828–Apr 12 1861			
	Feb 27 1859–Apr 2 1881	July 12 1861–May 11 1882			
	1806–1900	1805–1900	1805–1856	MHC	
	See NLI			LDS	0926165
Castlejordan	See Offaly				
Castletown–Kilpatrick	Dec 18 1805–Jan 22 1821	May 22 1816–May 19 1822		NLI	Pos. 4184
	Apr 12 1821–May 28 1822	Jan 24 1824–Apr 18 1841			
	Jan 7 1826–Sept 26 1832	Nov 10 1842–Nov 13 1873			
	Oct 3 1832–May 11 1841	Nov 13 1873–Nov 27 1880			
	Apr 1 1841–Nov 27 1873				
	Nov 27 1873–Nov 27 1880				
	1805–1900	1816–1900		MHC	

Parish (Diocese)	Baptisms	Marriages	Burials	Location	Reference
Clonmellon	Jan 6 1759–Sept 18 1784 (some gaps)	Jan 17 1857–Aug 20 1784 (some gaps)	Jan 30 1757–Sept 17 1784 (some gaps)	NLI	Pos. 4187
	Feb 3 1785–Apr 29 1791	Aug 16 1784–Sept 4 1809	Dec 25 1878–Oct 29 1809		
	Jan 3 1815–Mar 24 1815	Jan 19 1815–Feb 21 1815	Nov 7 1819–July (15?) 1850		
	May 1 1791–Mar 10 1809	July 19 1819–July 29 1845			
	Apr 5 1809–Nov 2 1809	Jan 10 1846–June 19 1872			
	Jun 18 1819–July 10 1845				
	July 11 1845–Aug 25 1872				
	1759–1901	1757–1901	1757–1993	DSHC	
	1759–1900	1757–1900	1759–1849	MHC	
Collon	See Louth				
Donore	Jan 1 1840–Feb 5 1881	Apr 27 1840–Sept 7 1881 (1841–1850 missing)		NLI	Pos. 4181
	1840–1900	1840–1900	1840–1841	MHC	
Donymore	Apr 30 1802–June 23 1823	June 17 1802–June 7 1823	June 7 1802–Apr 14 1823	NLI	Pos. 4179
	Aug 14 1823–Nov 16 1880	July 23 1823–Nov 16 1880	Nov 2 1833–Apr 11 1863		
	1836–1900	1836–1900	1833–1863	MHC	
Drogheda: St Mary's	Apr 30 1835–June 9 1867	Apr 24 1870–Feb 2 1881		NLI	Pos. 4180
	June 9 1867–Nov 23 1875				
	Jan 2 1872–Jan 11 1881				
	1835–1900	1870–1900	1870–1871	MHC	
	See NLI			LDS	0926169
Drumconrath	Oct 1811–Aug 25 1861	Sept 31 [sic] 1811– Sept 22 1861	Aug 11 1861–Mar 25 1872	NLI	Pos. 4184
	Sept 15 1861–Feb 9 1881	Oct 4 1861–Feb 7 1881			
	1811–1900	1811–1900	1861–1872	MHC	
Duleek	Feb 2 1852–Mar 7 1880	Feb 24 1852–June 21 1881		NLI	Pos. 4181
	1852–1901	1852–1911		MHC	
	See NLI			LDS	0926168
Dunboyne	Sept 2 1798–Apr 19 1823	June 31 [sic] 1787– Nov 22 1863	June 7 1787–Oct 31 1877	NLI	Pos. 4176
	May 1 1823–Aug 11 1844	Feb 2 1834–Aug 26 1836			
	Sept 6 1844–Dec 16 1877	Jan 12 1864–Dec 29 1877			
	1798–1900	1787–1900	1787–1877	MHC	
Dunderry	Oct 11 1837–Oct 24 1857	Oct 15 1841–May 31 1869		NLI	Pos. 4187
	Aug 10 1841–July 17 1869	May 10 1871–Oct 7 1883			
	May 3 1870–Mar 20 1881				
	1837–1900	1841–1901		MHC	
Dunshaughlin	Jan 1 1789–Oct 9 1791	Oct 25 1800–July 26 1801	Oct 9 1791–Jan 24 1828	NLI	Pos. 4177
	Jan 8 1849–Apr 14 1880	Aug 2 1801–Feb 11 1834	Jan 7 1863–Dec 23 1872		
		Feb 13 1849–Apr 1880			
	1789–1880	1801–1880	1789–1872	MHC	
	See NLI			LDS	0926166
Johnstown	Jan 12 1839–Apr 24 1881	Jan 21839–Aug 29 1881		NLI	Pos. 4182
	1839–1900	1839–1900		MHC	
	See NLI			LDS	0926170
Kells	July 12 1791–Dec 2 1827	Aug 1 1791–Dec 26 1873	June 13 1794–Mar 30 1824	NLI	Pos. 4185
	July 17 1828–Nov 28 1831				
	Jan 27 1832–Dec 31 1873				
	(some for 1830)				
	1791–1900	1791–1900	1784–1828	MHC	

Parish (Diocese)	Baptisms	Marriages	Burials	Location	Reference
Kilbeg	Dec 1817–Jan 8 1852	Jan 15 1810–June 16 1813		NLI	Pos. 4184
	Mar 17 1858–Dec 24 1869	Jan 15 1830–May 21 1852			
		May 23 1858–Oct 10 1869			
	1815–1900	1829–1900	1830–1870	MHC	
	See NLI			LDS	0926173
Kilbride and	Jan 1 1832–Jan 27 1864	Jan 1 1832–Nov 22 1863		NLI	Pos. 4172
Mountnugent	Jan 13 1864–Nov 27 1880	Feb 4 1864–Nov 27 1880			
	1830–1900	1830–1863	1906–1983	DSHC	
	See NLI	See NLI		LDS	0926174
	1832–1900	1832–1899		CHGC	
Kilcloon, Batterstown	Feb 21 1836–Dec 12 1880	Apr 14 1836–June 14 1880		NLI	Pos. 4177
and Kilcock. See	Feb 21 1836–Dec 12 1880	Apr 14 1836–June 14 1880			
also Kilcock (Kildare)	(transcript)	(transcript)			
	1836–1900	1836–1900		MHC	
Kildalkey	No records microfilmed			NLI	
	1782–1901	1782–1901	1782–1901	MHC	
Killeen	July 2 1742–Aug 26 1750	Feb 2 1865–Aug 26 1880	July 2 1742–Aug 26 1750	NLI	Pos. 4178
	Jan 2 1791–Mar 25 1832	(Kilmessan)	Jan 2 1791–Mar 25 1832		
	Apr 10 1832–Dec 30 1864		Apr 10 1832–Oct 24 1871		
	(Killmessan)		(Killmessan)		
	Mar 25 1832–Dec 6 1880		Mar 25 1832–Dec 6 1880		
	(Dunsany Killeen)		(Dunsany, Killeen)		
	Jan 21 1865–Nov 26 1880				
	(Kilmessan				
	1790–1896	1790–1896	1790–1896	MHC	
	1742–1900 (Kilmessan)	1742–1900 (Kilmessan)	1756–1900 (Kilmessan)	MHC	
Killine	Jan 29 1829–Jan 15 1833	Jan 29 1829–Jan 15 1833	Jan 29 1829–Jan 15 1833	NLI	Pos. 4179
	Feb 4 1833–Mar 4 1878	Mar 1833–Nov 29 1877	Feb 3 1833–Feb 9 1855		
	1829–1877	1829–1877	1829–1855	MHC	
Kilskyre	Apr 22 1784–Dec 30 1838	Jan 22 1784–Nov 2 1790	Jan 9 1784–Aug 29 1790	NLI	Pos. 4186
	Jan 1 1839–Oct 19 1841	June 12 1808–July 31 1841	Nov 29 1859–Oct 27 1873		
	(Ballinlough separately)	Jan 28 1842–Feb 16 1874			
	Nov 10 1841–Mar 4 1873	Apr 13 1874–Oct 30 1880			
	1784–1901	1784–1900	1784–1921	MHC	
	See NLI			LDS	0926173
Kingscourt	Oct 16 1838–Aug 13 1854	Aug 15 1838–May 27 1861	Sept 1846–May 30 1858	NLI	Pos. 4183
	Jan 1 1864–Dec 31 1880				
	See NLI			LDS	0926175
	1838–1920	1838–1920		CHGC	
Lobinstown	Oct 8 1823–Apr 5 1881	Sept 28 1823–May 19 1881		NLI	Pos. 4183
	1823–1900	1823–1900		MHC	
Moybologue	Feb 28 1867–Dec 18 1880	May 12 1868–Oct 14 1880		NLI	Pos. 5349
(Kilmore)	1867–1881	1868–1882		PRONI	MIC.1D/82
Moynalty	July 25 1830–Apr 4 1880	Dec 1 1829–Jan 31 1883	Mar 2 1830–Jan 10 1880	NLI	Pos. 4187
	1830–1900	1829–1900	1830–1879	MHC	
	See NLI			LDS	0926176
Moynalvey	Oct 4 1811–Oct 5 1828	Nov 4 1783–Nov 6 1786	Oct 15 1811–Sept 29 1828	NLI	Pos. 4178
	Mar 25 1831–Dec 24 1877	Oct 7 1811–Sept 29 1828	Oct 28 1877–Dec 18 1880		
	Jan 13 1878–Dec 26 1880	Apr 24 1831–Nov 1 1880			
	See NLI			LDS	0926177
	1811–1900	1783–1900	1811–1881	MHC	

Parish (Diocese)	Baptisms	Marriages	Burials	Location	Reference
Navan	Jan 14 1782–May 20 1813	Apr 4 1853–Oct 21 1868	June 18 1868–July 4 1880	NLI	Pos. 4181
	Sept 7 1842–Jan 1881	Oct 25 1868–Nov 19 1881			
	Oct 22 1868–Dec 29 1880				
	1782–1901	1853–1901		MHC	
Nobber	July 22 1754–Feb 10 1821	Jan 17 1757–Feb 7 1821	Feb 6 1757–Jan 23 1821	NLI	Pos. 4183
	Jan 6 1821–July 12 1865	Mar 5 1821–May 11 1865	Jan 23 1821–Feb 10 1866		
	1754–1900	1757–1900	1757–1866	MHC	
	See NLI			LDS	0926179
Oldcastle	Jan 5 1789–Feb 9 1807	Apr 28 1789–Feb 10 1807	Mar 27 1789–Feb 4 1807	NLI	Pos. 4188
	Nov 6 1808–Mar (?) 28 1834	Nov 7 1808–Nov 28 1840	Nov 3 1808–Jan 2 1809		
	Feb 18 1834–Nov 14 1877	Jan 9 1841–June 29 1846			
		July 12 1846–Nov 17 1877			
	1789–1900	1789–1900		MHC	
	See NLI			LDS	0926180
Oristown	Dec 25 1757–July 25 1784	Nov 1 1763–May 27 1780		NLI	Pos. 4186
	(some gaps)	Jan 27 1783–June 7 1784			
	1774–1778 (various dates)	Apr 24 1797–Apr 17 1801			
	Apr 30 1797–May 16 1814	Sept 15 1801–Aug 3 1842			
	(some gaps)	Mar 7 1848–Sept 19 1880			
	Feb 14 1831–Dec 22 1840				
	(some gaps)				
	Nov 14 1847–Dec 26 1880				
	1774–1900	1763–1900	1771–1831	MHC	
	See NLI			LDS	0926181
Rathcore and	No records microfilmed			NLI	
Rathmolyon	1878–1911	1879–1912		MHC	
Rathkenny	Nov 30 1784–Dec 6 1815	Nov 27 1784–Sept 10 1788		NLI	Pos. 4182
	Nov 30 1784–Dec 6 1815	1785–1816 (some entries only)			
	July 12 1818–Feb 22 1861	Aug 3 1818–Dec 5 1844			
	Aug 5 1866–Mar 1 1876	May 21 1846–Nov 22 1857			
		Oct 1 1866–Feb 10 1876			
	1784–1900	1867–1900	1796–1816	MHC	
Ratoath	May 10 1781–Jan 23 1818	Jan 1780–May 7 1818	June 26 1789–Apr 15 1818	NLI	Pos. 4177
	Aug 1 1818–Dec 29 1880	Aug 17 1818–Dec 13 1880			
	1781–1900	1780–1900	1789–1814	MHC	
	See NLI			LDS	0926182
Skryne	Nov 28 1841–Dec 12 1880	Jan 16 1842–May 19 1880		NLI	Pos. 4179
	1841–1900	1842–1900		MHC	
Slane	Jan 1 1851–May 29 1881	Jan 7 1851–Nov 26 1881		NLI	Pos. 4187
	Jan 1 1851–May 29 1881	Jan 7 1851–Nov 26 1881		LDS	0926183
	1851–1900	1851–1900		MHC	
Stamullen	Jan 1 1831–Dec 22 1879	May 3 1830–Nov 29 1879	Jan 3 1834–Dec 27 1877	NLI	Pos. 4182
	1831–1901	1830–1901		MHC	
	See NLI			LDS	0926183
Summerhill	Apr 13 1812–Apr 26 1854	Apr 16 1812–Feb 26 1854	Apr 14 1812–Nov 11 1836	NLI	Pos. 4178
	May 10 1854–Dec 12 1880	July 13 1854–Sept 30 1880			
	1812–1900	1812–1900	1812–1836	MHC	
	See NLI			LDS	0926184
Trim	July 25 1829–Dec 29 1880	July 30 1829–Nov 27 1880	Jan 7 1831–Apr 12 1841	NLI	Pos. 4179
	1829–1901	1829–1901	1831–1841	MHC	
	See NLI			LDS	0926185

Monaghan
All Clogher diocese

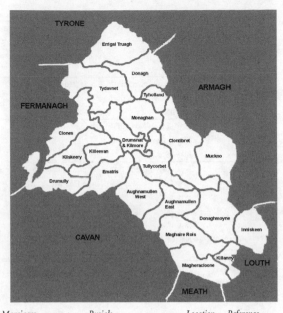

Parish (Diocese)	Baptisms	Marriages	Burials	Location	Reference
Aughnamullen East	July 26 1857–Oct 26 1876	July 26 1857–Oct 26 1876	July 26 1857–Oct 26 1876	NLI	Pos. 5576
	Aug 3 1878–Dec 9 1880	Aug 20 1878–Nov 1 1880			
	1857–1881	1857–1881	1857–1881	PRONI	MIC.1D/19
	1878–1900			MA	
	July 26 1857–Oct 26 1876	July 26 1857–Oct 26 1876	July 26 1857–Oct 26 1876	LDS	0979707
	Aug 3 1878–Dec 9 1880	Aug 20 1878–Nov 1 1880			
Aughnamullen West	Feb 14 1841–Dec 23 1867	Feb 2 1841–Nov 30 1867		NLI	Pos. 5575
	Jan 3 1868–Nov 14 1880	Jan 9 1868–Nov 27 1880			
	1841–1881	1841–1881		PRONI	MIC.1D/18
	1868–1880			MA	
Clones	July 23 1848–Apr 30 1854	May 30 1821–Mar 3 1840		NLI	Pos. 5577;
	Apr 22 1855–Feb 18 1866	Oct 1 1840–Feb 9 1866			marr. 1878–
	Feb 25 1866–Dec 29 1880	Apr 17 1866–Nov 21 1880			Pos. 5578
	1848–1881	1821–1881		PRONI	MIC.1D/20–21
	1848–1880	1821–1866		MA	
Clontibret	Feb 12 1861–July 4 1874	Aug 27 1861–Dec 21 1880		NLI	Pos. 5573
	Sept 2 1872–Dec 24 1880				
	July 4 1874–Dec 31 1880				
	1860–1881	1861–1881		PRONI	MIC.1D/16
	1861–1880			MA	
Donagh	May 2 1836–Feb 28 1878	May 2 1836–Feb 28 1878		NLI	Pos. 5574
	(illegible in many parts)	(illegible in many parts)			
	Jan 14 1861–Dec 30 1880	Sept 30 1860–Nov 25 1880			
	1836–1881	1836–1882		PRONI	MIC.1D/17;
					C.R.2/11
	1835–1880	1836–1860		MA	
Donaghmoyne	Jan 19 1863–Jan 28 1878	Oct 11 1872–Oct 7 1880		NLI	Pos. 5572
	Jan 15 1869–Dec 10 1880				
	1863–1880	1872–1880		PRONI	MIC.1D/15
	1841–1900			MA	

Parish (Diocese)	Baptisms	Marriages	Burials	Location	Reference
Drumsnat and Kilmore	Feb 16 1836–June 13 1872	Feb 16 1836–June 13 1872	Feb 16 1836–June 13 1872	NLI	Pos. 5575
	1875–1880	1875–1880	1875–1880		
	1875–1881	1836–1872	1875–1883	PRONI	MIC.1D/18; C.R.2/13
Drumully	Jan 6 1845–Apr 2 1866	July 14 1864–Oct 31 1880		NLI	Pos. 5572
	July 7 1864–Dec 26 1880				
	1845–1881	1864–1881		PRONI	MIC.1D/15
Ematris	May 14 1848–Mar 22 1860	Feb 2 1850–Nov 2 1861		NLI	Pos. 5578
	Mar 15 1861–Mar 9 1876				
	1848–1876	1850–1861		PRONI	MIC.1D/21
Errigal Truagh	Nov 1 1835–June 20 1852	Dec 1 1837–July 28 28 1849		NLI	Pos. 5576
	Mar 24 1861–Dec 29 1880	Jan 28 1862–May 27 1880			
	1835–1852	1837–1849		PRONI	MIC.1D/19
	1861–1881	1862–1881			
	1835–1880			MA	
	See NLI			LDS	0979706 item 1–3
Inniskeen	July 3 1837–Oct 27 1862	Apr 7 1839–Nov 26 1850		NLI	Pos. 5575
	July 12 1863–Dec 29 1880				
	1837–1881	1839–1850		PRONI	MIC.1D/5; C.R.2/2
	1836–1848			MA	
	See NLI			LDS	0926053
Killanny	Jan 9 1857–Dec 26 1880	Jan 20 1862–Dec 28 1880		NLI	Pos. 5574
	1857–1881	1862–1882		PRONI	MIC.1D/17
Killeevan	Jan 29 1871–Dec 1880	Jan 29 1871–Aug 25 1880		NLI	Pos. 5577
	1871–1881	1871–1881		PRONI	MIC.1D/20
	1841–1842			MA	
Kilskeery	Oct 3 1840–June 15 1862	Aug 30 1840–May 27 1862		NLI	Pos. 5568
	June 19 1862–Feb 18 1870	July 17 1862–Feb 27 1870			
	Jan 27 1870–Dec 24 1880	Feb 3 1870–Mar 1 1880			
	1840–1881	1940–1882		PRONI	MIC.1D/11
	See NLI			LDS	0926054 item 1–4
	Jan 27 1870–Dec 24 1880	Feb 3 1870–Mar 1 1880			
Maghaire Rois	Jan 6 1858–Apr 19 1870	Feb 21 1838–Jan 31 1844		NLI	Pos. 5578
	Jan 1 1878–Dec 31 1880	Jan 17 1858–Apr 19 1870			
	1858–1870	1838–1844		PRONI	MIC.1D/21
	1878–1880	1858–1881			
	See NLI			LDS	0926055 item 1–2
Magheracloone	May 2 1836–Nov 8 1863	Oct 9 1826–Mar 8 1859		NLI	Pos. 5574
	Jan 16 1865–0 Dec 10 1880	Apr 9 1866–Nov21 1880			
	1836–1863	1826–1859		PRONI	MIC.1D/17; C.R.2/17
	1865–1881	1866–1880			
Monaghan	Nov 6 1835–Dec 21 1847	Feb 6 1827–June 7 1850		NLI	Pos. 5570
	June 12 1849–Apr 21 1850 (indexed)	Jan 12 1857–Nov 16 1880			
	Jan 4 1857–May 27 1875				
	May 29 1875–Dec 26 1880				

Parish (Diocese)	Baptisms	Marriages	Burials	Location	Reference
Monaghan	1835–1847	1827–1880		PRONI	MIC.1D/13;
	1849–1881 (indexed)				C.R.2/6
	1835–1900	1827–1850		MA	
Muckno	Nov 1 1835–Apr 15 1862	Oct 31 1835–Apr 8 1862		NLI	Pos. 5576; 5577
	Apr 21 1862–Jan 12 1869	Apr 28 1862–Oct 20 1868			
	Dec 4 1868–Dec 31 1880	Nov 15 1868–Dec 9 1880			
	1835–1881	1835–1881		PRONI	MIC.1D/19–20
	See NLI			LDS	0979707 item 4–6
Tullycorbet	Apr 1862–July 22 1876 (indexed)	May 27 1862–June 15 1876		NLI	Pos. 5573
	July 3 1876–Dec 13 1880				
	1862–1881	1862–1876		PRONI	MIC.1D/16
	1862–1875	1862–1876		MA	
	1876–1900 (Ballybay)				
Tydavnet	Nov 1 1835–Dec 12 1862	Apr 18 1825–Oct 19 1865		NLI	Pos. 5573; 5574
	Jan 1 1863–Nov 24 1871	Jan 9 1876–Nov 26 1880			
	Nov 22 1871–Dec 31 1880				
	1835–1881	1825–1865		PRONI	MIC.1D/2, 16–17
		1876–1881			
	1835–1880			MA	
Tyholland	May 1 1835–Jan 12 1851	Jan 1 1827 July 26 1851	Jan 19 1851–Dec 19 1863	NLI	Pos. 5572
	Jan 19 1851–Dec 19 1863	Jan 19 1851–Dec 19 1863			
	Dec 18 18865–Dec 14 1876	Feb 1 1866–Nov 28 1872			
	Dec 12 1877–Dec 27 1880	Dec 3 1877–Nov 5 1880			
	1835–1881	1827–1882		PRONI	MIC.1D/3, 15
	1835–1880			MA	

Offaly (King's)

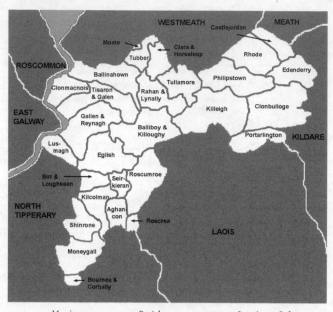

Parish (Diocese)	Baptisms	Marriages	Burials	Location	Reference
Aghancon (Killaloe)	Nov 5 1870–Dec 14 1880	Jan 27 1870–Oct 1 1880		NLI	Pos. 2479
	1830–1899	1830–1899		IMA	
Balliboy and	Jan 5 1821–Dec 30 1833	June 29 1821–Dec 5 1833	Feb 1 1826–Dec 30 1880	NLI	Pos. 4175
Killoughy (Meath)	Jan 5 1834–Dec 27 1880	Jan 10 1834–Oct 28 1880			
	See NLI			LDS	0926171
	1821–1899	1821–1899	1828–1881	IMA	
Ballinahown (Ardagh	Aug 12 1821–Dec 21 1824	Jan 7 1830–Aug 29 1845	Nov 21 1829–Sept 9 1845	NLI	Pos. 4235
and Clonmacnois)	Feb 12 1826–Feb 25 1839	Oct 15 1854–Dec 26 1880	Sept 2 1854–Dec 26 1880		
	Feb 6 1841–Sept 21 1845				
	July 23 1854–Dec 24 1880				
	1821–1899	1822–1900	1821–1846	IMA	
	1821–1905 (some gaps)	1823–1974	1821–1828	LDS	1279227 item
			1829–1845		1–6
			1854–1881		
			1882–1894		
Birr and Loughkeen	May 5 1838–Jan 6 1847	May 5 1838–Nov 28 1846		NLI	Pos. 2478
(Killaloe)	Jan 3 1847–Dec 30 1880	Jan 7 1847–Nov 27 1880			
	1838–1913	1838–1905	1869–1970	IMA	
	See NLI			LDS	0926091
	1838–1913	1838–1913		TNFHF	
Bournea and Corbally	See North Tipperary				
Castlejordan (Meath)	Nov 5 1826–Aug 28 1870	Nov 9 1826–Aug 21 1870	Nov 15 1848–July 31 1849	NLI	Pos. 4173
	Sept 4 1870–Dec 29 1880	Sept 5 1870–Oct 8 1880			
	1826–1900	1826–1870	1919–1993	DSHC	
Clara & Horseleap	See Westmeath				
Clonbulloge (Kildare	Nov 7 1819–June 14 1869	Jan 2 1808–June 14 1869		NLI	Pos. 4202
and Leighlin)	June 20 1869–Dec 26 1880	July 1 1869–Oct 30 1880			
	1819–1899	1808–1899		IMA	

Parish (Diocese)	Baptisms	Marriages	Burials	Location	Reference
Clonmacnois (Ardagh and Clonmacnois)	Apr 19 1826–Feb 28 1846 Jan 6 1841–July 31 1842 Feb 1 1848–Dec 21 1880 Jan 16 1876–Nov 14 1880 1826–1908 1826–1908	Apr 24 1826–Dec 14 1840 Feb 2 1841–Feb 8 1842 Feb 21 1848–Nov 25 1880 Feb 17 1876–Sept 12 1880 1826–1899 1826–1908	Jan 2 1841–Feb 18 1842 Feb 3 1848–Sept 29 1880 1892–1906	NLI IMA LDS	Pos. 4243 1279227
Edenderry (Kildare and Leighlin)	Jan 2 1820–Dec 29 1838 Jan 6 1839–Jan 2 1880 1820–1899	Jan 9 1820–Nov 20 18837 Sept 17 1838–Jan 7 1880 1820–1899	 1935–1981	NLI IMA	Pos. 4207
Eglish (Meath)	Jan 1 1809–Dec 23 1810 Feb 13 1819–May 16 1852 May 23 1852–Dec 18 1880 1809–1899	Feb 21 1819–Mar 3 1829 June 4 1829–Nov 27 1880 1819–1899	Feb 26 1819–Apr 18 1829 June 15 1837–May 12 1846 Jan 8 1848–Mar 16 1849 Jan 1851 1807–1899	NLI IMA	Pos. 4175
Gallen and Reynagh (Ardagh and Clonmacnois)	Nov 16 1811–Sept 4 1812 Sept 28 1816–July 6 1817 Oct 2 1816–Mar 29 1822 July 13 1818–Sept 12 1827 Aug 25 1822–June 15 1825 Mar 6 1829–Oct 2 1837 Feb 18 1838–Dec 31 1880 1811–1899 1816–1973	Oct 16 1797–July 23 1837 Oct 13 1816–Apr 20 1822 Aug 25 1822–June 15 1825 Feb 18 1838–Dec 31 1880 1797–1899 1797–1983	Nov 15 1803–Nov 28 1804 Nov 13 1819–Apr 30 1820 Aug 25 1822–June 15 1825 Jan 2 1827–Sept 7 1827 Apr 24 1829–Sept 27 1831 1807, 1809, 1811 (a few deaths recorded) 1803–1832 1893–1980	NLI IMA LDS	Pos. 4242 1279226
Kilcolman (Killaloe)	Mar 7 1830–Nov 27 1869 See NLI	Apr 29 1830–Feb 24 1868		NLI LDS	Pos. 2479 0979695
Killeigh (Kildare and Leighlin)	Apr 23 1844–Dec 11 1875 Jan 1 1876–Nov 19 1880 1844–1899	1859–July 30 1875 Feb 17 1876–Nov 19 1880 1843–1899		NLI IMA	Pos. 4203
Lusmagh (Clonfert)	Dec 5 1827–May 3 1829 Apr 22 1833–Dec 29 1880 1833–1899 1833–1925	July 8 1832–Nov 25 1880 1832–1899 1832–1925	Jan 5 1837–Dec 15 1880 1837–1882 1833–1925	NLI IMA LDS	Pos. 2433 1279215 item 28–30
Moate	See Westmeath				
Moneygall (Killaloe)	Jan 8 1820–Aug 21 1873 1820–1911 See NLI 1820–1900	Jan 24 1820–June 14 1873 1820–1899 1820–1900		NLI IMA LDS TNFHF	Pos. 2479 0979695
Philipstown (Kildare and Leighlin)	Aug 12 1795–Sept 23 1798 Jan 6 1820–Feb 18 1855 Nov 4 1850–Dec 30 1866 Jan 1 1867–Dec 26 1880 1795–1899	Jan 7 1820–May 3 1855 Jan 27 1851–Dec 2 1866 Feb 1 1867–Nov 24 1880 1820–1899	 1880–1919	NLI IMA	Pos. 4202
Portarlington (Kildare and Leighlin)	Jan 1 1820–Nov 22 1846 (indexed) Nov 25 1846–Feb 27 1876 (indexed) Mar 5 1876–Dec 26 1880 (indexed) 1820–1899	Nov 24 1822–July 16 1845 July 21 1845–June 21 1876 Jan 14 1876–Nov 27 1880 1820–1899	 1904–1960	NLI IMA	Pos. 4205

Parish (Diocese)	Baptisms	Marriages	Burials	Location	Reference
Rahan and Lynally (Meath)	July 6 1810–Apr 28 1816	July 31 1810–Feb 28 1816		NLI	Pos. 4174
	Jan 2 1822–Dec 27 1835	Jan 9 1822–Jan 29 1880			
	Jan 1 1836–Mar 31 1845				
	Apr 5 1845–Feb 7 1880				
	1810–1899	1810–1899		IMA	
Rhode (Kildare and Leighlin)	Jan 29 1829–June 16 1879	Aug 4 1829–Feb 23 1878		NLI	Pos. 4205
	June 22 1879–Dec 14 1880	(gaps)			
	Jan 3 1866–Dec 14 1880				
	1829–1899	1829–1899		IMA	
Roscrea	See North Tipperary				
Roscumroe (Killaloe)	Feb 13 1833–Dec 21 1880	Jan 9 1833–Nov 1 1871		NLI	Pos. 2479
	Jan 28 1872–June 26 1880				
	1833–1899	1833–1899	1936–1983	IMA	
	See NLI			LDS	0979695
Seirkieran (Ossory)	Apr 11 1830–May 3 1857	July 4 1830–June 14 1857	NLI		Pos. 5013
	June 19 1857–Dec 17 1880	July 9 1857–Nov 27 1880			
	1830–1901	1830–1899	1877–1902	IMA	
	1870–1880	1870–1880		LDS	0979695
Shinrone (Killaloe)	Feb 21 1842–Feb 7 1876	Apr 10 1842–Feb 7 1876		NLI	Pos. 2480
	Jan 4 1875–Dec 13 1880				
	(most of 1875 missing)				
	1842–1899	1842–1899		IMA	
Tisaron and Galen (Ardagh and Clonmacnois)	Oct 17 1819–July 24 1865	Nov 26 1819–Nov 26 1833	Dec 19 1821–Aug 9 1835	NLI	Pos. 4243
	June 21 1876–Apr 28 1877	Mar 6 1855–Jan 24 1876			
	1819–1899	1819–1899	1821–1960	IMA	
	1819–1984	1819–1833	1821–1877	LDS	1279226
		1877–1984	1883–1889		
			1929–1984		
Tubber	See Westmeath				
Tullamore (Meath)	June 14 1809–Feb 20 1810	Apr 26 1801–Sept 29 1807		NLI	Pos. 4174
	Nov 1 1820–Feb 24 1822	Apr 9–10 1809			
	Feb 1 1827–Jan 31 1836	Nov 2 1820–Feb 19 1822			
	Mar 1 1836–Dec 26 1880	Feb 1 1827–Dec 29 1880			
	1819–1899	1801–1899		IMA	
	See NLI			LDS	0926186

Roscommon

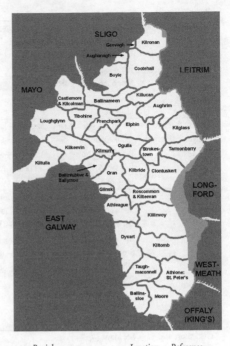

Parish (Diocese)	Baptisms	Marriages	Burials	Location	Reference
Athleague (Elphin)	Jan 4 1808–May 10 1828	June 23 1808–Feb 11 1834	Jan 3 1807–1837	NLI	Pos. 4613
	Aug 20 1834–Sept 1835	Mar 15 1836–Aug 25 1865			
	Oct 12 1835–July 25 1864	Jan 26 1865–Mar 5 1878			
	Jan 8 1865–Dec 23 1880				
	1808– 1900	1808–1900	1808–1837	RHGC	
Athlone: St. Peter's (Elphin)	Jan 4 1798–Feb 24 1810	Jan 7 1789–Jan 12 1817	Jan 3 1789–Dec 15 1816	NLI	Pos. 4603, 4604
	Feb 25 1810–Jan 31 1845	Jan 14 1817–Feb 4 1845	Jan 5 1817–May 25 1854		
	Feb 1 1845–Sept 30 1864	Mar 28 1845–Sept 18 1864	July 16 1845–Oct 26 1880		
	Oct 2 1864–Aug 12 1877	Oct 3 1864–Nov 22 1880			
	Aug 12 1877–Dec 31 1880				
	1789–1900	1789–1900	1789–1880	RHGC	
	See NLI			LDS	0989750/
				Online	Familysearch
Aughanagh	See Sligo				
Aughrim (Elphin)	Aug 13 1816–Dec 23 1837	Aug 21 1816–Dec 9 1837		NLI	Pos. 4610, 4611
	Feb 27 1825–Feb 2 1860	Mar 18 1825–Nov 19 1859			
	Jan 18 1865–Dec 27 1880	Jan 9 1865–Sept 13 1880			
	Jan 21 1865–Dec 31 1880	Feb 12 1865–Oct 4 1880			
	(Kilmore and Clonaff)	(Kilmore)			
	1816–1900	1816–1900		RHGC	
Ballinameen (Elphin)	Nov 20 1859–July 22 1871	Feb 5 1860–Oct 31 1880		NLI	Pos. 4605
	Sept 3 1871–Dec 14 1880				
	1859–1900	1860–1900		RHGC	
	See NLI			LDS BIVRI,	0989738/
				Online	Familysearch

Parish (Diocese)	Baptisms	Marriages	Burials	Location	Reference
Ballinasloe (Clonfert)	Sept 23 1820–July 27 1832	Sept 23 1820–July 27 1832	Sept 23 1820–July 27 1832	NLI	Pos. 2432
	July 19 1832–Feb 21 1841	July 19 1832–Feb 21 1841	July 19 1832–Feb 21 1841		
	June 7 1841–June 14 1847				
	July 6 1847–May 30 1862				
	June 6 1862–Dec 31 1880				
	1820–1900	1820–1900	1825–1830	EGFHS	
	1820–1900	1853–1902		LDS	1279217
Ballintubber and Balllymoe (Elphin)	Dec 21 1831–Dec 26 1863	Aug 7 1831–Jan 17 1864		NLI	Pos. 4618
	(poor condition)	Feb 15 1840–Oct 14 1850			
	Feb 18 1840–Nov 12 1865	Apr 23 1855–Sept 16 1862			
	Feb 26 1864–Nov 25 1880	Jan 12 1863–Aug 5 1880			
	1821–1900	1821–1900		RHGC	
Boyle (Elphin)	Feb 13 1793–May 13 1796	Nov 13 1792–Jan 23 1797	July 2 1848–Sept 18 1964	NLI	Pos. 4607,
	Mar 13 1803–Mar 1806	July 1803–June 1804			4608
	Jan 4–Mar 9 1811	July 4 1808–Dec 30 1827			
	Apr 18 1814–Sept 30 1827	Sept 24 1828–June 16 1848			
	Sept 2 1827–June 27 1848	July 3 1848–June 30 1864			
	July 1 1848–Sept 18 1864	Oct 6 1864–Set 25 1880			
	Sept 30 1864–Dec 29 1880				
	1793–1900	1792–1900	1848–1864	RHGC	
	See NLI			LDS	0989743 /
				Online	Familysearch
Castlemore and Kilcolman	See Mayo				
Clontuskert (Elphin)	Jan 3 1865–Nov 7 1880	Feb 9 1865–Feb 22 1879		NLI	Pos. 4612
	Aug 23 1874–Nov 16 1878	Jan 18 1875–Feb 6 1879			
	(Kilgefin)				
	1865–1900	1865–1900		RHGC	
	See NLI			LDS	0989747
Cootehall (Elphin)	Mar 26 1843–Mar 25 1861	Apr 6 1843–June 3 1860		NLI	Pos. 4612
	Apr 7 1861–Aug 4 1869	Apr 14 1861–Sept 23 1880			
	Apr 29 1869–Dec 24 1880				
	1843–1900	1843–1900		RHGC	
	See NLI			LDS	0989746
	1843–1881	1843–1880 (Online only)		BIVRI	Online,
					Familysearch
Dysart (Elphin)	July 6 1850–Oct 26 1862	Dec 23 1862–Aug 31 1880		NLI	Pos. 4616
	Dec 7 1862–Dec 30 1880	Feb 2 1865–July 9 1870			
	Jan 6 1865–Dec 18 1871	(Tisara)			
	1850–1900	1862–1900	1862–1865	RHGC	
	See NLI			LDS, BIVRI	0989755/
					Familysearch
Elphin (Elphin)	June 11 1807–Dec 23 1808	May 6 1807–Sept 11 1808		NLI	Pos. 4609,
	Dec 10 1808–Feb 16 1810	Dec 10 1808–Dec 21 1824			4610
	Jan 1 1809–July 21 1815	May 3 1824–Oct 4 1830			
	May 23 1810–Apr 29 1818	Mar 31 1864–Dec 20 1880			
	Aug 1 1818–Sept 26 1825				
	Mar 9 1825–Oct 13 1843				
	Nov 12 1841–July 28 1860				
	Jan 13 1866–Nov 19 1880				
	1808–1900	1807–1900	1807–1838	RHGC	

Parish (Diocese)	Baptisms	Marriages	Burials	Location	Reference
Frenchpark (Elphin)	Jan 7 1865–Dec 27 1880			NLI	Pos. 4618
	1865–1900	1865–1900		RHGC	
Geevagh	See Sligo				
Glinsk (Elphin)	Sept 5 1836–Jan 28 1846	Nov 1 1836–Apr 24 1865	Sept 14 1836–Sept 20 1839	NLI	Pos. 4620
	Nov 2 1846 (?)–June 22 1848	July 6 1865–Nov 1 1880			
	Mar 15 1849–Sept 23 1866				
	Oct 6 1866–Dec 26 1880				
	1836–1900	1836–1900	1836–1839	RHGC	
Kilbride (Elphin)	July 12 1835–Sept 6 1849	Sept 10 1838–Oct 15 1846		NLI	Pos. 4614
	Apr 12 1868–Dec 12 1880				
	1835–1900	1838–1900		RHGC	
	See NLI			LDS	0989749
Kilglass (Elphin)	Oct 20 1865–Dec 24 1880			NLI	Pos. 4611
	1865–1900	1865–1900		RHGC	
		pre–1850 (reconstructed)		Online	Williams
Kilkeevin (Elphin)	Nov 15 1804–May 15 1809	Nov 17 1804–July 31 1809	Feb 20 1805–May 6 1809	NLI	Pos. 4619
	Jan 17 1816–Aug 31 1819	Jan 15 1816–Apr 27 1820	Jan 26 1816–Oct 4 1819		
	Jan 6 1826–Jan 23 1840	Oct 28 1838–Dec 29 1839	Jan 1 1852–1855		
	Jan 4 1840–Jan 28 1860	May 20 1839–Jan 23 1860			
	Jan 1 1860–Dec 31 1864	Jan 11 1860–Nov 15 1864			
	Jan 1 1865–Jan 27 1878				
	Jan 1878–Dec 27 1880				
	1804–1900	1804–1900	1805–1855	RHGC	
Killinvoy (Elphin)	July 26 1841–July 7 1859	July 17 1841–Feb 15 1858	1854–1880	NLI	Pos. 4617
	Jan 8– Feb 19 1860	Nov 9 1854–Sept 24 1864			
	May 25 1854–Sept 25 1864	Nov 8 1864–Nov 7 1880			
	Oct 1 1864–Dec 20 1880				
	1841–1900	1841–1900	1854–1881	RHGC	
	See NLI			LDS	0989752
Killucan (Elphin)	June 24 1811–June 27 1833	Apr 7 1825–June 17 1833	Oct 11 1820–Mar 4 1826	NLI	Pos. 4606
	July 4 1833–June 24 1850	July 11 1833–Dec 5 1850			
	June 24 1850–Nov 27 1864	Jan 16 1851–Oct 9 1864			
	Dec 4 1864–Dec 26 1880	Nov 24 1864–Nov 13 1880			
	1811–1900	1825–1900	1820–1826	RHGC	
	See NLI			LDS	0989741
Kilmurry (Elphin)	Jan 15 1865–Sept 7 1880	Feb 8 1869–Feb 9 1880 (?)		NLI	Pos. 4611
	1865–1900	1865–1900		RHGC	
Kilronan (Ardagh and Clonmacnois)	Jan 1 1824–July 27 1829	Oct 24 1823–June 10 1829	Jan 16 1835–July 18 1872	NLI	Pos. 4242
	Jan 1 1835–Mar 25 1876	Jan 7 1835–Sept 16 1872			
	1824–1900	1823–1900	1835–1872	RHGC	
	1824–1829	1823–1829	1835–1872	LDS	1279224 item
	1835–1976	1835–1872			7–12
		1877–1984			
Kiltomb (Elphin)	Oct 11 1835–May 26 1845	Oct 20 1835–July 2 1846	June 24 1837–Mar 31 1845	NLI	Pos. 4617
	Apr 1 1848–Dec 26 1864	Jan 16 1848–Dec 27 1864	Jan 15 1857–May 17 1862		
		Jan 9 1865–Nov 19 1880	Jan 6–Nov 23 1865		
	1835–1900	1835–1900	1837–1865	RHGC	
	See NLI	See NLI		LDS	0989751/
				Online	Familysearch
Kiltulla (Tuam)	Sept 11 1839–Oct 27 1860	Aug 25 1839–Oct 7 1860		NLI	Pos. 4212
	Nov 11 1860–Nov 21 1880	Nov 19 1860–Apr 16 1874			
		Jan 3 1877–Dec 26 1880			

Parish (Diocese)	Baptisms	Marriages	Burials	Location	Reference
Kiltulla (Tuam)	See NLI			LDS	0926226
	1839–1900	1839–1900		RHGC	
Loughglynn (Elphin)	Mar 10 1817–Nov 20 1826	Apr 10 1817–Mar 24 1827	Jan 14 1850–June 18 1854	NLI	Pos. 4617, 4618
	Dec 15 1829–July 30 1835	Feb 10 1836–Apr 24 1840	1868–1880		
	July 6 1835–Nov 24 1840	Dec 23 1849–Feb 16 1858			
	Dec 17 1849–Apr 17 1863	Jan 11 1865–Oct 18 1880			
	Jan 1 1865–Mar 10 1878	Jan 30 1865–May 5 1867			
	Jan 10 1865–May 19 1867				
	(Lisacul & Erritt)				
	Feb 10 1878–Dec 19 1880				
	(Lisacul & Erritt)				
	1817–1900	1817–1900	1850–1880	RHGC	
	See NLI		1849–1900	LDS. Part	0989753 item
				BIVRI/	1–3/
				Online	Familysearch
Moore (Tuam)	Sept 17 1876–Dec 26 1880	Jan 22 1877–Nov 19 1880		NLI	Pos. 4220
	1872–1900	1872–1900		RHGC	
	1876–1938	1877–1907		LDS	1279214 item 9–10
Ogulla (Elphin)	Jan 7 1865–Dec 26 1880	Jan 28 1864–May 6 1880		NLI	Pos. 4611
	1865–1900	1864–1900		RHGC	
Oran (Elphin)	No registers microfilmed			NLI	
	1864–1900	1864–1900		RHGC	
Roscommon and Kilteevan (Elphin)	Oct 1 1837–Sept 22 1864	Jan 10 1820–Aug 27 1864		NLI	Pos. 4614
	Mar 26 1864–Dec 30 1880				
	1820–1900	1820–1900	1821–1824	RHGC	
	See NLI			LDS	0989748/
				Online	Familysearch
Strokestown (Elphin)	Oct 1830–May 1835	Oct 24 1830–June 15 1835		NLI	Pos. 4608, 4609
	July 1835–Jan 1846	June 17 1833–Oct 30 1864			
	Jan 1831–Feb 1833	Oct 18 1830–May 30 1833			
	(Lisonuffy &	(Lisonuffy and			
	Cloonfinlough)	Cloonfinlough)			
	June 1842–Dec 1842	July 6 1835–Sept 27 1849			
	Dec 1851–Nov 1852	(Lisonuffy and			
	Nov 1853–Dec 1864	Cloonfinlough)			
	May 1857–Nov 1862	Jan 9 1965–Nov 11 1880			
	Apr 1865–Nov 1866				
	Jan 1865–Dec 1880				
	1830–1900	1830–1900		RHGC	
	See NLI	See NLI		LDS	0989745
				Online	Familysearch
Tarmonbarry (Elphin)	Jan 22 1865–Dec 23 1880	Jan 26 1865–Dec 31 1880		NLI	Pos. 4611
	Jan 6 1865–Dec 19 1880				
	(Lisonuffy and Bumlin)				
	1865–1900	1865–1900		RHGC	
Taughmaconnell (Clonfert)	July 31 1842–Dec 15 1880	Jan 13 1863–Aug 19 1880		NLI	Pos. 2432
	1842–1900	1842 (sic)– 1900		RHGC	
	See NLI			LDS	0926061
	1842–1900	1863–1900		EGFHS	

Parish (Diocese)	Baptisms	Marriages	Burials	Location	Reference
Tibohine (Elphin)	Jan 1 1833–Sept 24 1864	Jan 7 1833–June 11 1864		NLI	Pos. 6955
	May 5 1875–Dec 18 1880	Feb 7 1865–Apr 25 1880			(1864).
					Pos 4619
	1833–1900	1833–1900		RHGC	

Sligo

Parish (Diocese)	Baptisms	Marriages	Burials	Location	Reference
Achonry (Achonry)	1878–Oct 8 1880	Aug 3 1865–Aug 16 1880		NLI	Pos. 4227
	1878–1899	1865–1905		SHGC	
	1878–1908	1864–1942		LDS	1279231
Ahamlish (Elphin)	Nov 27 1796–May 28 1829	Dec 3 1796–Dec 27 1830	Nov 26 1796–Oct 1822	NLI	Pos. 4602
	Jan 4 1831–Nov 29 1835	Jan 22 1831–Sept 22 1857	Jan 13 1827–Sept 24 1830		
	Sept 9 1836–Nov 25 1845	Nov 2 1857–Dec 29 1863	Jan 3 1831–July 24 1845		
	Jan 2 1846–Dec 31 1863	Jan 18 1864–June 3 1880			
	Jan 8 1864–Mar 19 1879				
	1796–1900	1796–1899	1796–1845	SHGC	
Aughanagh (Elphin)	May 9 1803–Jan 19 1808	Jan 11 1800–June 15 1802	Mar 3 1800–Mar 12 1802	NLI	Pos. 4606
	(trans)	Apr 7 1829–Mar 8 1850	July 12–Sept 16 1816		
	Oct 13 1816–Dec 22 1818	Nov 1858–Feb 27 1863	Nov 30 1822–Sept 20 1846		
	(trans)	Nov 20 1864–Oct 10 1880	Nov 10 1858–Oct 17 1874		
	Jan 3 1821–Sept 20 1825				
	(trans)				
	Nov 1803–Nov 1807				
	1817–Nov 1818				
	Jan 1821–1841				
	Jan 1844–1846				
	1848–1852				
	1856–1864				
	1864–1880				

Parish (Diocese)	Baptisms	Marriages	Burials	Location	Reference
Aughanagh (Elphin)	1803–1899	1841–1899		SHGC	
	See NLI			LDS	0989739,
				BIVRI,	0989740 /
				Online	Familysearch
	1803–1900			RHGC	
Ballysodare and Kilvarnet (Achonry)	Apr 25 1842–Aug 14 1853 Feb 28 1858–Dec 26 1880	Jan 14 1858–Dec 5 1880		NLI	Pos. 4227
	1842–1899	1858–1899		SHGC	
	1842–1897	1858–1933		LDS	1279230
Castleconnor (Killala)	Jan 14 1855–Dec 26 1880	Oct 26 1854–Nov 2 1880		NLI	Pos. 4230
	1835–1905	1835–1899	1847–1896	SHGC	
	1835–1880	1835–1880	1855–1880	LDS	1279204 item 1–2
	1835–1880	1836–1876	1854–1880	Online	Genweb, Sligo
Castlemore and Kilcolman	See Mayo				
Cloonacool (Achonry)	Oct 27 1859–Nov9 1880	Oct 9 1859–Nov 9 1880		NLI	Pos. 4227
	1859–1899	1859–1914		SHGC	
	1859–1908	1859–1921		LDS	1279230/1
Curry (Achonry)	Oct 6 1867–Dec 25 1880	Nov 3 1867–Dec 15 1880		NLI	Pos. 4227
	1867–1906	1867–1899		SHGC	
	1867–1923	1867–1903		LDS	1279231
Dromard and Skreen (Killala)	Jan 1 1823–Aug9 1859 July 17 1848–Sept 29 1877 Sept 27 1877–Dec 31 1880	Nov13 1817–Feb 16 1860 Feb 12 1878–Dec 11 1880 July 12 1848–Aug 18 1869	Sept 25 1825–Feb 29 1828	NLI	Pos. 4229
	1823–1892	1817–1899	1825–1828	SHGC	
	1817–1892	1835–1880	1853–1880	LDS	1279204 0926025
	1823–1868 (?)	1818–1859 (?)		Online	Williams
Drumcliff (Elphin)	May 2 1841–Dec 31 1864 (transcript) Jan 1 1865–May 2 1880	Jan 15 1865–Nov 28 1880		NLI	Pos. 4603
	1841–1899	1865–1899		SHGC	
	See NLI			LDS	0989735
				Online	Familysearch
Drumrat (Achonry)	Nov 12 1843–June 24 1847 Sept 25 1842–Mar 6 1855 Jan 10 1874–July 3 1880	Jan 12 1842–May 5 1851 Dec 1872–May 15 1881		NLI	Pos. 4228
	1843–1900	1833–1890		SHGC	
Easkey (Killala)	June 1864–Dec 28 1880			NLI	Pos. 4230
	1864–1899	1898–1939		SHGC	
	1864–1899			Online	Williams
Emlefad and Kilmorgan (Achonry)	July 4 1856–Oct 7 1877 Nov 27 1874–Dec 26 1880	Aug 12 1824–Jan 7 1866 Feb 11 1866–Feb 22 1875		NLI	Pos. 4228
	1856–1899	1824–1899		SHGC	
Geevagh (Elphin)	Feb 25 1873–May 20 1880	Jan 13 1851–Nov 25 1880		NLI	Pos. 4607
	1851–1899	1851–1899		SHGC	
	1873–1880	1851–1880		LDS	989742
				Online	Familysearch
Glenade (Kilmore)	See Leitrim				

Parish (Diocese)	Baptisms	Marriages	Burials	Location	Reference
Kilfree and Killaraght (Achonry)	May 4 1873–Nov 27 1880	Feb 19 1844–Dec 11 1868 May 22 1868–Nov 20 1880		NLI	Pos. 4227
	1873–1899	1844–1899		SHGC	
Kilglass (Killala)	Oct 17 1825–July 7 1867 Aug 15 1867–Dec 28 1880	Nov 2 1825–May 2–30 1867 Nov 21 1867–Dec 22 1880	Nov 2 1825–June 15 1867	NLI	Pos. 4229
	1825–1900	1825–1900	1825–1867	SHGC	
	1825–1876 ?	1826–1867	March 1825–June 1867	Online	Williams
Killenummery (Ardagh and Clonmacnois)	See Leitrim				
Killoran (Achonry)	Apr 19 1878–Dec 24 1880	Apr 22 1846–Nov 11 1880		NLI	Pos. 4228
	1878–1899	1846–1912		SHGC	
Kilmactigue (Achonry)	Apr 8 1845–Dec 27 1856 Jan 5 1857–June 18 1864 July 1 1864–July 24 1880	Jan 23 1848–Sept 4 1880		NLI	Pos. 4226
	1845–1899	1848–1899		SHGC	
Kilmoremoy (Killala)	May 15 1823–Oct 14 1836 May 9 1849–July 16 1849 July 23 1851–Sept 8 1867 Feb 2 1868–Dec 31 1880	May 15 1823–Oct 4 1842 Oct 22 1850–Feb 4 1868 Feb 2 1868–Dec 31 1880	Apr 29 1823–Aug 12 1836 Sept 12 1840–May 3 1844	NLI	Pos. 4231
	1823–1900	1823–1900	1823–1931	MNFHRC	
	1823–1852	1823–1842		LDS	1279205;
	1850–1867	1849–1868			1279205, 3
	1868–1879	1823–1842			
Kilshalvey (Achonry)	Jan 3 1842–Dec 22 1877 Mar 31 1860–Aug 12 1877	Apr 30 1833–Apr 18 1876		NLI	Pos. 4228
	1842–1899	1840–1899		SHGC	
	1840–1908	1833–1930 (gaps)		LDS	1279233 09260018
Kinlough (Kilmore)	July 12 1835–Mar 1860 Apr 8 1860–Dec 24 1880	Nov 26 1840–Dec 16 1880		NLI	Pos. 5344
	1835–1881	1840–1881		PRONI	MIC.1D/77
	1835–1900	1840–1900 1855, 1853 missing	1867–1900	LHC	
Rossinver (Kilmore)	Aug 17 1851–Jan 29 1875 (many gaps)	Aug 28 1844–Sept 8 1870		NLI	Pos. 5350
	1851–1875 very poor condition	1844–1870 very poor condition		PRONI	MIC.1D/83
	1851–1900	1844–1869 1875–1900		LHC	
Sligo: St John's (Elphin)	Oct 3 1858–Feb 6 1854 Feb 7 1864–May 24 1870 June 23 1870–Apr 1 1877	Oct 7 1858–Dec 21 1880		NLI	Pos. 4615, 4616
	1831–1899	1831–1899	1831–1848	SHGC	
	See NLI			LDS	0989736
				Online	Familysearch
Taunagh (Elphin)	Nov 1 1803–Dec 28 1834 May 3 1836–Dec 27 1864 Jan 3 1865–Dec 29 1880	Nov 28 1803–Jan 25 1809 May 12 1836–Dec 12 1862 Jan 29 1865–Dec 29 1880	June 15 1836–Jan 21 1843 June 15 1836–Jan 21 1843	NLI	Pos. 4604
	1803–1900	1803–1899	1836–1843	SHGC	
	See NLI			LDS, BIVRI, Online	0989737 / Familysearch

Parish (Diocese)	Baptisms	Marriages	Burials	Location	Reference
Templeboy (Killala)	Sept 5 1815–Nov 26 1816	Oct 22 1815–Dec 28 1837		NLI	Pos. 4230
	May 30 1826–Nov 13 1838	Jan 20 1868–Oct 23 1880			
	June 21 1868–Dec 26 1880	(Kilmacshalgan)			
	(Kilmacshalgan)	Dec 2 1875–Sept 5 1880			
	Nov 1 1875–Dec 15 1880	(Templeboy)			
	(Templeboy)				
	1815–1899	1815–1899	1815–1833	SHGC	
	1868–1903	1868–1891			
	(Kilmacshalgan)	(Kilmacshalgan)			
	1815–1838	1815–1838	LDS	1279204 item	
	1875–1880			13, 14	

Tipperary North

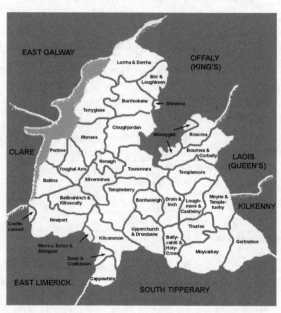

Parish (Diocese)	Baptisms	Marriages	Burials	Location	Reference
Ballina (Cashel and	Mar 1832–Nov 25 1871	May 1832–Feb6 1872		NLI	Pos. 2507
Emly)	1832–1911	1832–1872		TFHR	
	1832–1903	1832–1903		TNFHF	
Ballinahinch and	July 7 1839–Feb 7 1874	Jan 26 1853–Feb 4 1874		NLI	Pos. 2503
Killoscully (Cashel	1839–1899	1853–1899		TFHR	
and Emly)	1839–1899	1853–1899		TNFHF	
Ballycahill and	Jan 2 1835–Oct 16 1878	Jan 1 1835–Dec 29 1878		NLI	Pos. 2493
Holy–Cross (Cashel	1835–1900	1835–1900		TFHR	
and Emly)	1835–1900	1835–1900		TNFHF	
Birr and Loughkeen	See Offaly				
(Killaloe)					
Borrisokane	June 24 1821–Dec 29 1835	July 30 1821–Nov 28 1835	NLI		Pos. 2483
(Killaloe)	Jan 1 1836–Sept 3 1844	(many pages illegible)			
	Sept 8 1844–Dec 30 1880	Jan 21 1836–Jan 21 1844			
		Oct 2 1844–Nov 16 1880			
	1821–1911	1821–1911		TNFHF	

Parish (Diocese)	Baptisms	Marriages	Burials	Location	Reference
Borrisoleigh (Cashel and Emly)	Nov 9 1814–Dec 31 1826	Nov 24 1814–Dec 2 1826		NLI	Pos. 2488 to
	Jan 2 1827–July 31 1843	Jan 17 1827–July 31 1843			1826; Pos. 2489
	Aug 1 1843–Dec 24 1880	Aug 1843–Nov 15 1880			
	1814–1900	1814–1898		TFHR	
	1814–1900	1814–1900		TNFHF	
Bournea and Corbally (Killaloe)	July 10 1836–Dec 1 1866	June 28 1836–Dec 1 1866		NLI	Pos. 2478
	Jan 27 1867–Dec 30 1880	Jan 27 1867–May 30 1880			
	(1873 missing)	(1873 missing)			
	1836–1866	1836–1866		TNFHF	
Castleconnell	See Limerick				
Cloughjordan (Killaloe)	Aug 25 1833–Nov 3 1858	May 22 1833–Nov 17 1858		NLI	To 1858, Pos.
	Nov 8 1858–Dec 26 1880	Jan 7 1859–Nov 25 1880			2481; 2482
	1833–1911	1833–1911		TNFHF	
Drom and Inch (Cashel and Emly)	Mar 25 1827–Aug 24 1840	May 5 1827–Oct 16 1880		NLI	Pos. 2491
	Aug 18 1840–Dec 26 1880				
	1809–1900	1807–1880		TFHR	
	1807–1900	1807–1900		TNFHF	
Gortnahoe (Cashel and Emly)	Sept 10 1805–Dec 20 1830	Oct 3 1805–Nov 27 1830		NLI	Pos. 2493
	Apr 1 1831–Nov 28 1843	Oct 30 1831–Dec 31 1843			
	Jan 28 1844–Aug 27 1878	Jan 15 1844–Oct 7 1880			
	1805–1900	1805–1900		TFHR	
Kilcommon (Cashel and Emly)	Mar 7 1813–Jan 30 1840	June 12 1813–Jan 26 1840		NLI	Pos. 2506 to
	Feb 1 1840–Apr 23 1847	May 30 1840–Apr 28			1846; Pos. 2507
	May 1 1847–Dec 31 1880	1847–May 2 1847–Nov 25 1880			
	1813–1895	1813–1899		TFHR	
	1813–1900	1813–1900		TNFHF	
Lorrha and Dorrha (Killaloe)	Oct 4 1829–Dec 8 1844	Oct 18 1829–Nov 24 1844		NLI	Pos. 2480
	Jan 1 1845–Sept 4 1880	Jan 20 1845–Nov 27 1880			
	1829–1911	1829–1903		TNFHF	
		1908–1911			
Loughmore and Castleiny (Cashel and Emly)	Mar 25 1798–July 28 1840	Apr 16 1798–June 26 1840		NLI	Pos. 2490
	Aug 1 1840–Dec 29 1880	Sept 6 1840–Oct 20 1880			
	1798–1899	1798–1899		TFHR	
	1798–1900	1798–1900		TNFHF	
Moneygall (Killaloe)	See Offaly				
Monsea (Killaloe)	Feb 1 1834–Dec 9 1865	Feb 2 1834–Nov 13 1870		NLI	Pos. 2481
	1834–1911	1834–1911		TNFHF	
Moycarkey (Cashel and Emly)	Oct 13 1793–Nov 19 1796	Oct 6 1793–Oct 16 1796		NLI	Pos. 2488
	Jan 1 1800–Feb 3 1800	Jan 12 1810–Nov 8 1817			
	1801 (scraps)	Jan 17 1830–Feb 3 1822			
	Jan 2 1801–Oct 22 1809	Feb 5 1833–May 2 1854			
	June 7 1810–Nov 22 1810	Sept 13 1854–Oct 26 1880			
	Jan 12 1817–Apr 11 1818				
	Jan 2 1830–Jan 24 1833				
	Feb 4 1833–June 22 1854				
	July 1854–Dec 1880				
	1793–1900	1793–1900		TFHR	
	1793–1796	1793–1796		TNFHF	
	1800–1810	1810–1817			
	1817–1818	1818–1900			
	1830–1900				

Parish (Diocese)	Baptisms	Marriages	Burials	Location	Reference
Moyne and Templetuohy (Cashel and Emly)	Jan 4 1809–Mar 28 1848 Apr 2 1848–Dec 31 1880 1809–1900 1809–1900	Feb 1804–Nov 8 1880 1804–1900 1804–1900		NLI TFHR TNFHF	Pos. 2491
Nenagh (Killaloe)	Jan 1 1792–Nov 1809 Nov 22 1830–Nov 1842 Fjan 1845–Apr 19 1858 Jan 3 1859–Dec 27 1880 1792–1809 1830–1842 1845–1911	Jan 8 1792–Feb 26 1797 Sep7 1818–Sept 28 1840 Sept 30 1840–Mar 4 1851 July 7 1850–Nov 27 1880 1792–1797 1818–1911		NLI TNFHF	Pos. 2483 (B. to 1809); 2484
Newport (Cashel and Emly)	Oct 18 1795–Sept 30 1809 July 16 1812–Mar 18 1830 Feb 28 1813–May20 1839 Mar 20 1830–May 25 1847 May 27 1847–July 17 1859 Nov 1 1859–Dec 31 1880 1795–1900 1795–1809 1812–1900	Apr 20 1795–Feb 8 1809 July 26 1812–Nov 28 1829 Feb 28 1813–May 20 1839 Jan 15 1830–May 23 1847 June 5 1847–Feb 24 1859 Nov 2 1859–Dec 9 1880 1795–1900 1795–1809 1812–1900	Mar 24 1795–May 18 1844 Feb 28 1813–May 20 1839	NLI TFHR TNFHF	Pos. 2505 to 1847; remainder on Pos. 3506
Portroe (Killaloe)	Nov 11 1849–Dec 13 1880 (transcript) 1849–1911	Nov 18 1849–Nov 14 1880 (transcript) 1849–1911		NLI TNFHF	Pos. 2483
Roscrea (Killaloe)	Jan 1 1810–June 13 1822 June 17 1822–July 31 1832 Aug 5 1832–Dec 26 1863 Jan 1 1864–Dec 24 1880 1810–1832 1810–1900	Feb 10 1810–Aug 4 1822 Apr 30 1823–Aug 4 1832 Aug 14 1832–Nov 27 1842 Jan 20 1842–Nov 13 1880 1810–1832 1810–1900		NLI LDS TNFHF	Pos. 2479 (B. & M. to 1832; remainder 2480 0979696 item 1
Shinrone	See Offaly				
Silvermines (Killaloe)	Nov 29 1840–Dec 16 1880 1840–1911 See NLI	Jan 28 1841–Oct 2 1880 1841–1911		NLI TNFHF LDS	Pos. 2481 0926098
Templederry (Killaloe)	Sept 13 1840–Feb 13 1850 1842–Apr 4 1869 Mar 25 1869–Dec 30 1880 1840–1911	Feb 11 1839–Feb 12 1850 Dec 13 1846 (?)–Feb 9 1869 1839–1911		NLI TNFHF	Pos. 2482
Templemore (Cashel and Emly)	Aug 16 1807–Nov 30 1821 Aug 16 1807–Nov 25 1821 (transcript) Nov 16 1809–Jan 31 1829 Nov 28 1821–Nov 19 1835 Jan 10 1836–Oct 28 1849 Nov 4 1849–Dec 27 1880 1809–1900 1807–1900	Nov 15 1807–Apr 10 1825 Nov 30 1809–Jan 13 1820 Feb 11 1834–Oct 23 1849 Nov 10 1849–Sept 12 1880 1809–1900 1807–1825 1834–1900		NLI TFHR TNFHF	Pos. 2491 bap to 1835, marr to 1825; rest Pos. 2492
Terryglass (Killaloe)	July 1 1827–May 4 1837 May 6 1837–July 7 1846 July 12 1846–Dec 10 1880 (transcripts)	Sept 11 1827–Nov 20 1880		NLI	Pos. 2482

Parish (Diocese)	Baptisms	Marriages	Burials	Location	Reference
Terryglass (Killaloe)	1827–1911	1827–1911		TNFHF	
	Scc NLI			LDS	0926102
Thurles (Cashel and Emly)	Mar 9 1795–Jan 19 1810	Apr 13 1795–Nov 18 1804		NLI	Pos. 2489 to
	July 9 1805–Nov 17 1821	Jan/ 7 1805–Feb 15 1820			1833; Pos. 2490
	Aug 10 1822–Dec 29 1833	Aug 13 1822–Dec 30 1833			
	Jan 1 1834–Apr 28 1870	Jan 13 1834–Feb 14 1870			
	1795–1924	1795–1924		TFHR	
	1795–1900	1795–1900		TNFHF	
Toomevara Killaloe)	Mar 10 1831–June 6 1856	Aug 31 1830–Sept 16 1836		NLI	Pos. 2481
	May 25 1861–Dec 27 1880	June 18 1861–Nov 12 1880			
	1831–1856	1830–1836		TNFHF	
	1861–1911	1861–1911			
	See NLI			LDS	0926103
Upperchurch and Drombane (Cashel and Emly)	Oct 27 1829–Dec 15 1846	Feb 12 1829–Nov 15 1846		NLI	Pos. 2495
	Dec 8 1846–Feb 29 1876	Jan 24 1847–Feb 29 1876			
	1829–1900	1829–1900		TFHR	
	1829–1900	1829–1900		TNFHF	
Youghal Arra (Killaloe)	Oct 26 1828–Dec 31 1846	Oct (?)1 1820–May 16 1880		NLI	Pos. 2483–4
	Jan 16 1847–Dec 21 1880				
	1828–1911	1820–1911		TNFHF	

Tipperary South

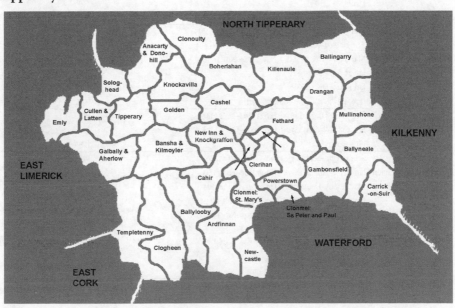

Parish (Diocese)	Baptisms	Marriages	Burials	Location	Reference
Anacarty and	May 13 1821–Oct 1835	May 13 1821–Feb 11 1839		NLI	Pos. 2496
Donohill (Cashel and	Oct 2 1835–Dec 20 1880	Feb 11 1839–Oct 28 1880			
Emly)	1804–1899	1805–1899		TFHR	

Parish (Diocese)	Baptisms	Marriages	Burials	Location	Reference
Ardfinnan (Waterford & Lismore)	Dec 8 1809–Nov 30 1826 (some pages missing) Jan 4 1827–June 30 1845 July 2 1845–Dec 31 1880	Apr 20 1814–Feb 18 1822 Jan 24 1827–June 26 1845 Aug 3 1845–Oct 26 1880		NLI	Pos. 2457
	1810–1911	1817–1911		WHL	
Ballingarry (Cashel and Emly)	June 15 1814–May 24 1827 Aug 30 1827–Mar 12 1839 Mar 12 1839–Dec 31 1880	Apr 19 1814–Feb 19 1822 Jan 8 1826–July 16 1837 Aug 20 1837–Nov 25 1880		NLI	Pos. 2492
	1814–1900	1814–1900		TFHR	
	1842–1911	1842–1911		TNFHF	
Ballylooby (Waterford & Lismore)	May 25 1828–Mar 16 1843 Mar 18 1843–Jan 14 1862 Jan 1 1862–Dec 27 1880	May 25 1828–July 14 1880		NLI	Pos. 2457, 2458
	1828–1911	1828–1911		WHL	
Ballyneale (Waterford & Lismore)	Jan 2 1839–Dec 2 1880			NLI	Pos. 2453
	1839–1911	1839–1911		WHL	
Bansha and Kilmoyler (Cashel and Emly)	Nov 5 1820–Jan 13 1855 (modern transcript) Jan 15 1855–Dec 25 1880	Jan 22 1822–Oct 24 1880 (modern transcript)		NLI	Pos. 2497
	1820–1899	1821–1899		TFHR	
Boherlahan (Cashel and Emly)	Apr 27 1810–Dec 20 1823 Dec 21 1823–Dec 28 1839 Dec 29 1839–May 17 1868	May 16 1810–Jan 21 1824 Feb 2 1824–Jan 30 1840 Feb 1 1840–Feb 24 1868		NLI	Pos. 2504
	1736–1740 1810–1900	1736–740 1810–1900		TFHR	
Cahir (Waterford & Lismore)	Junr 9 1776–Mar 10 1793 Aug 29 1809–Mar 3 1823 Mar 9 1823–Dec 28 1831 Jan 25 1832–Jan 13 1845 Jan 1 1845–Dec 28 1880	July 14 1776–Nov 28 1835 Jan 8 1836–Oct 1866 Nov 3 1864–Nov 20 1880		NLI	Pos. 2459, 2460
	1776–1911	1776–1911		WHL	
Cappawhite (Cashel and Emly)	Oct 5 1815–Jan 29 1846 Feb 4 1846–Nov 13 1878	Feb 13 1804–Jan 25 1846 Feb 3 1846–Oct 6 1878		NLI	Pos. 2497
	1815–1900	1803–1900		TFHR	
Carrick-on-Suir (Waterford & Lismore)	Sept 12 1784–Sept 30 1787 Jan 2 1788–Apr 24 1803 May 31 1805–Dec 29 1805 Jan 3 1806–July 2 1819 Jan 3 1823–Oct 10 1826 Apr 7 1834–Apr 6 1845 Apr 7 1845–Dec 23 1864 Dec 28 1869–Dec 26 1880	Jan 7 1788–Oct 15 1803 Jan 10 1806–Feb 7 1815 Jan 7 1823–Oct 14 1825 Jan 8 1826–Feb 3 1845 Jan 30 1845–Nov 13 1880		NLI	Pos. 2455, 2456, 2457
	1788–1911	1788–1911		WHL	
Cashel (Cashel and Emly)	Nov 11 1793–July 19 1831 July 24 1831–Dec 23 1839 Aug 21 1839–Mar 31 1866 Apr 1 1866–Dec 16 1880	Jan 5 1793–May 16 1831 July 27 1831–Nov 22 1880		NLI	Pos. 2501
	1793–1903	1793–1896		TFHR	
Clerihan (Cashel and Emly)	Apr 27 1852–Dec 25 1880 1852–1900	Aug 1 1852–Aug 7 1880 1852–1900		NLI TFHR	Pos. 2501

Parish (Diocese)	Baptisms	Marriages	Burials	Location	Reference
Clogheen (Waterford & Lismore)	Jan 4 1778–May 18 1789 (some gaps)	July 11 1814–Apr 21 1867		NLI	Pos. 2453, 2454
	Mar 17 1809–June 5 1814				
	June 1 1815–July 20 1851				
	Aug 29 1851–June 4 1868				
	Apr 12 1868–Dec 27 1880				
	1778–1911	1814–1911		WHL	
Clonmel: Ss Peter and Paul (Waterford & Lismore)	Feb 11 1836–Sept 21 1859	Feb 11 1836–Nov 22 1880		NLI	Pos. 2463
	Sept 21 1859–Dec 29 1880				
	1836–1911	1836–1911		WHL	
Clonmel: St. Mary's (Waterford & Lismore)	Feb 4 1790–Dec 26 1790	Apr 24 1797–Feb 10 1836		NLI	Pos. 2460, 2461. 2462
	Mar 1 1793–Dec 31 1793				
	Jan 11 1795–Mar 28 1797				
	Apr 5 1797–Aug 5 1823				
	Aug 5 1823–Dec 28 1842				
	Jan 1 1843–Jan 7 1874				
	Jan 1 1864–Sept 20 1878				
	1790–1911	1798–1911		WHL	
Clonoulty (Cashel and Emly)	Oct 1 1804–June 7 1809	Oct 7 1804–June 7 1809	June 2 1818–Apr 25 1821	NLI	Pos. 2502 to 1855; remainder on Pos. 2503
	July 1809–June 10 1821	Oct 1 1809–May 27 1821			
	June 20 1821–Jan 1 1837	June 12 1821–Nov 4 1836			
	Jan 2 1837–Nov 11 1855	Jan 10 1837–Nov 11 1855			
	Jan 9 1856–Dec 28 1880	Jan 11 1856–Oct 13 1880			
	1804–1900	1804–1898		TFHR	
Cullen and Latten (Cashel and Emly)	Dec 4 1846–Dec 26 1880	Sept 10 1846–Nov 28 1880		NLI	Pos. 2498
	1846–1899	1846–1899		TFHR	
Doon & Castletown	See East Limerick				
Drangan (Cashel and Emly)	1811–1847	1812–1886		NLI	Pos. 2492 to 1846; remainder on Pos. 2493
	May 13 1847–Dec 28 1880	Jan 3 1847–June 13 1880			
	1811–1898	1804–1898		TFHR	
Emly (Cashel and Emly)	July 31 1810–May 4 1839	Apr 27 1809–Oct 20 1838		NLI	Pos. 2500
	May 10 1839–Dec 24 1880	Jan 26 1839 Nov 25 1880			
	1810–1899	1809–1898		TFHR	
Fethard (Cashel and Emly)	Jan 2 1806–June 30 1828	Jan 12 1806–Apr 27 1820		NLI	Pos. 2504
	June 1 1828–Feb 27 1835	Jan 18 1824–Jan 9 1838			
	Mar 1 1835–Jan 30 1847	Jan14 1838–Nov 11 1880			
	Dec 1 1847–Dec 25 1880				
	1806–1900	1806–1900		TFHR	
Galbally and Aherlow	See East Limerick				
Gambonsfield and Kilcash (Waterford & Lismore)	Jan 1 1840–Feb 1 1856	Jan 11 1840–Jan 11 1856		NLI	Pos. 2452, 2453
	Feb 16 1856–Dec 27 1880	Jan 14 1856–Dec 29 1880			
	1840–1911	1840–1911		WHL	
Golden (Cashel and Emly)	May 20 1833–Dec 14 1880	May 20 1833–Nov 7 1880		NLI	Pos. 2503
	1833–1899	1833–1899		TFHR	
Killenaule (Cashel and Emly)	Dec 25 1742–Jan 6 1802	Aug 20 1812–Sept 19 1827		NLI	Pos. 2494
	Jan 2 1814–Aug 10 1827	Oct 14 1827–Nov 29 1851			
	Augg 10 1827–Feb 29 1852	Feb 1 1852–Nov 25 1880			
	Mar 1 1852–Dec 28 1880				
	1742–1900	1741 1900		TFHR	

Parish (Diocese)	Baptisms	Marriages	Burials	Location	Reference
Knockavilla (Cashel and Emly)	May 10 1834–Dec 26 1880	July 10 1834–Nov 15 1880		NLI	Pos. 2503
	1834–1905	1834–1905		TFHR	
Mullinahone (Cashel and Emly)	July 3 1809–Apr 27 1835	Feb 26 1810–Mar 3 1835		NLI	Pos. 2488
	Apr 30 1835–Dec 25 1880	(transcript)			
		May 18 1835–Sept 23 1880			
	1810–1899	1810–1867		TFHR	
Murroe, Boher & Abington	See East Limerick				
New Inn and Knockgraffon (Cashel and Emly)	Mar 14 1820– Mar 31 1847	June 10 1798–Nov 26 1834		NLI	Pos. 2502
	Apr 3 1847–Dec 22 1880	Jan 8 1835–Oct 2 1880			
	1820–1896	1798–1900		TFHR	
Newcastle	See Waterford				
Pallasgreen and Templebredin	See East Limerick				
Powerstown (Waterford & Lismore)	Sept 8 1808–Oct 18 1845	Aug 11 1808–Nov 27 1880		NLI	Pos. 2455
	Oct 20 1845–Nov 16 1880				
	1808–1911	1808–1911		WHL	
Sologhead	See East Limerick				
Templetenny (Waterford and Lismore)	Nov 9 1817–June 2 1872	Jan 25 1818–Nov 13 1875		NLI	Pos. 24
	June 20 1872–Dec 24 1880	Feb 7 1876–Nov 28 1880			
	1817–1911	1818–1911		WHL	
Tipperary (Cashel and Emly)	Jan 1 1810–Sept 30 1822	Feb 11 1793–May 20 1809		NLI	Pos. 2495 to 1848; remainder on Pos. 2496
	Oct 1 1822–Oct 6 1833	Jan 10 1810–Nov 30 1844			
	Jan 1 1833–Dec 31 1848	Jan 8 1845–Nov 25 1880			
	(transcript)				
	Jan 1849–Dec 28 1868				
	Jan 11 1869–Dec 31 1880				
	1780–1899	1793–1900		TFHR	

Tyrone

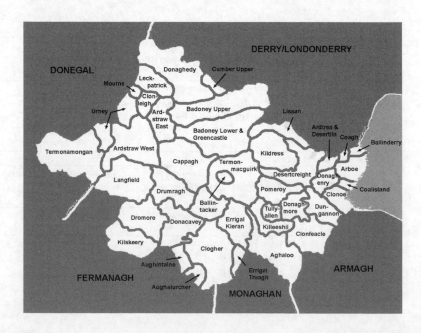

Parish (Diocese)	Baptisms	Marriages	Burials	Location	Reference
Aghaloo (Armagh)	Jan 1 1846–Dec 31 1880	Jan 2 1832–May 29 1834			
		Oct 2 1837–Nov 21 1880		NLI	Pos. 5585
	1846–1881	1832–1880		PRONI	MIC.1D/36
	1846–1900	1826–1900	1868–1900	IW	
Arboe (Armagh)	See Derry/Londonderry				
Ardstraw East (Derry)	Dec 18 1861–Dec 24 1880	Dec(?) 8 1860–Oct 13 1880		NLI	Pos. 5765
	1860–1880	1860–1881		PRONI	MIC.1D/60
Ardstraw West (Derry)	June 3 1846–Mar 10 1850	May 15 1843–Apr 7 1878		NLI	Pos. 5767
	Jan 18 1852–Jan 30 1877	Feb 10–Oct 27 1880			
	Nov 23 1873 Dec 19 1880				
	Dec 25 1877–Dec 26 1880				
	1846–1881	1843–1878		PRONI	MIC.1D/62
		1880			
Ardtrea and Desertlin (Armagh)	See Derry/Londonderry				
Aughalurcher (Clogher)	See Fermanagh				
Aughintaine (Clogher)	Nov 14 1870–Dec 28 1880	Nov 18 1870–Jan 13 1880		NLI	Pos. 5569
	1870–1881	1870–1883		PRONI	MIC.1D/12
	See NLI			LDS	0979704
Badoney Lower and Greencastle (Derry)	Oct 31 1866–Dec 24 1880			NLI	Pos. 5765
	1865–1881	1865–1880		PRONI	MIC.1D/60
	1865–1900	1865–1893		TGC	
Badoney Upper (Derry)	Oct 31 1866–Dec 24 1880			NLI	Pos. 5765
	1866–1881			PRONI	MIC.1D/60
	1866–1881	1865–1881 (Plumbridge)		IW	
	1865–1881 (Plumbridge)				
Ballinderry (Armagh)	See Derry/Londonderry				
Ballintacker (Armagh)	Sept 26 1832–Dec 26 1880	July 11 1834–Dec 3 1880		NLI	Pos. 5584
	1832–1881	1834–1882		PRONI	MIC.1D/35
	1832–1900	1834–1900		IW	
Cappagh (Derry)	July 16 1843–Dec 6 1880	July 24 1843–Nov 20 1880	July 21 1843–Jan 13 1865	NLI	Pos. 5766; baptisms from 1846 on Pos. 5765
	June 12 1846–Oct 1863 (1 page only)				
	1843–1883	1843–1883	1843–1865	PRONI	MIC.1D/60–61
	1843–1900	1843 1900	1843–1965	TGC	
Carrickmore (Armagh)	No records microfilmed			NLI	
	1881–1900	1881–1900		IW	
Clogher (Clogher)	Apr 12 1856–Apr 13 1857	Sept 28 1825–Nov 10 1835		NLI	Pos. 5567
	Apr 18 1857–Dec 23 1880	Mar 1940–Feb 19 1857			
		Apr 22 1857–Oct 21 1880			
	1856–1881	1825–1835	1840–1881	PRONI	MIC.1D/10; C.R.2/14
	1856–1881	1825–1881		IW	
Clonfeacle (Armagh)	Oct 16 1814–Mar 22 1840	Nov 9 1814–Mar 19 1840		NLI	Pos. 5580
	Aug 25 1840–Dec 26 1880	Apr 23 1840–Oct 14 1880			
	1814–1881	1814–1881		PRONI	MIC.1D/31
	1814–1900	1814–1900		AA	
	See NLI			LDS	0979708
	1814–1900	1814–1900		IW	

Parish (Diocese)	Baptisms	Marriages	Burials	Location	Reference
Clonleigh (Derry)	See Donegal				
Clonoe (Armagh)	Feb 15 1810–May 23 1816	Dec 3 1806–June 25 1816	Dec 11 1806–May 31 1816	NLI	Pos. 5579
	July 21 1810–Feb 13 1812	Jan 6 1823–Jan 11 1850			
	Oct 2 1822–Apr 16 1850	Apr 26 1850–Nov 27 1880			
	Apr 14 1850–Dec 21 1880				
	1810–1816	1806–1816	1806–1816	PRONI	MIC.1D/30
	1822–1881	1823–1881			
	1810–1900	1806–1816		IW	
		1823–1900			
Coagh (Armagh)	Dec 21 1865–Oct 17 1880	Dec 25 1865–Nov 26 1879		NLI	Pos. 5582
	1865–1882	1865–1881		PRONI	MIC.1D/33
		1884–1891			
	1865–1900	1865–1900		IW	
Coalisland (Armagh)	Dec 24 1861–Aug 18 1880	May 9 1862–Feb 6 1879	Nov 15 1861–Mar 4 1868	NLI	Pos. 5583
	1861–1880	1862–1879	1861–1868	PRONI	MIC.1D/34
	1822–1900	1822–1900		IW	
	1861–1877	1862–1877	1861–1868	LDS	0979709 item 3
Cumber Upper (Derry)	See Derry/Londonderry				
Desertcreight (Armagh)	Jan 2 1827–Dec 28 1851	Jan 23 1827–Sept 8 1858		NLI	Pos. 5585
	Jan 1 1852–Sept 10 1858	Jan 23 1859–Dec 4 1880			
	Oct 17 1858–Dec 19 1880				
	1827–1881	1827–1881		PRONI	MIC.1D/36
	1814–1900	1811–1900		IW	
Donacavey (Clogher)	Nov 24 1857–Dec 14 1880	Oct 26 1857–Nov 25 1880		NLI	Pos. 5571
	1857–1881	1857–1880		PRONI	MIC.1D/14
	See NLI			LDS	0926051
Donaghedy (Derry)	Apr 1 1854–June 28 1863 (Dunamanagh)	Nov 11 1857–July 11 1859 (Dunamanagh)	Dec 4 1857–July 15 1859	NLI	Pos. 5761, 5466
	Sept 1 1853–Dec 11 1880	(Dec?) 13 1862–1 May 31 1863			
	1854–1880	1857–1859	1857–1859	PRONI	MIC.1D/55–56
		1862–1863			
	1854–1900	1858–1859	1857–1859	TGC	
		1862–1900			
Donaghenry (Armagh)	Jan 1 1822–Dec 22 1840	Jan 1 1822–Dec 26 1840	Jan 1 1822–Jan 27 1839	NLI	Pos. 5583
	Feb 16 1849–Dec 23 1880	May 28 1853–Nov 16 1880	Jan 15 1854–May 18 1868		
	1822–1840	1822–1841	1854–1869	PRONI	MIC.1D/8, 34
	1849–1881	1853–1880			
	See NLI			LDS	0979709 item 2
Donaghmore (Armagh)	Feb 24 1837–Dec 24 1870	Mar 7 1837–July 30 1868		NLI	Pos. 5582
	Jan 11 1871–Dec 31 1880				
	1837–1880	1837–1860		PRONI	MIC.1D/33–34
	1837–1900	1837–1900		IW	
	1871–1880			LDS	0979709
Dromore (Clogher)	Nov 1 1835–Dec 30 1864	Oct 21 1833–Nov 23 1864		NLI	Pos. 5568
	Jan 1 1865–Dec 19 1880	Jan 10 1865–Nov 23 1880			
	1835–1881	1833–1881		PRONI	MIC.1D/11
	See NLI			LDS	0926052
	1835–1880 ?			Online	Genweb, Tyrone

Parish (Diocese)	Baptisms	Marriages	Burials	Location	Reference
Drumragh (Derry)	May–Nov 1846	June–Aug 1846	May–Sept 1846	NLI	Pos. 5765
	Nov 13 1853–Dec 22 1880	Nov 7 1853–Dec 26 1880	Nov 23 1853–Dec 11 1880		
	Indexed				
	1846	1846	1846	PRONI	MIC.1D/60;
	1853–1881	1853–1881	1853–1881		C.R.2/9
	Baptisms Indexed				
	1846–1879				
Dungannon	Oct 14 1821–Oct 30 1826	Oct 6 1821–Oct 30 1826	Oct 11 1821–June 7 1826	NLI	Pos. 5580;
(Armagh)	Oct 25 1826–Dec 2 1829	Oct 30 1826–Dec 10 1829	Nov 7 1826–Nov 24 1829		Baptisms and
	Apr 24 1830–July 9 1833	May 2 1831–May 26 1833	Apr 26 1831–May 30 1833		marriages
	Aug 11 1833–June 10 1834	Aug 23 1833–Nov 12 1834	Aug 13 1833–June 1 1834		from 1834,
	Aug 3 1834–Dec 30 1851	June 16 1834–Dec 29 1851	July 3 1834–Dec 29 1854		5581
	Jan 4 1852–Dec 31 1880	Jan 3 1854–Nov 20 1880	Jan 4 1852–Dec 31 1880		
	1821–1881	1821–1881	1821–1881	PRONI	MIC.1D/31–32
	1783–1790	1783–1788	1821–1900	1821–1900	IW
	1821–1900				
	See NLI			LDS	0926038
Errigal Kieran	Jan 3 1847–Dec 28 1880	Jan 14 1864–Dec 16 1880		NLI	Pos. 5584
(Armagh)	1847–1881 (Ballygawley)			PRONI	MIC.1D/35
	1864–1881 (Ballymacelroy)				
1834–1897		1864–1900		IW	
Errigal Truagh	See Monaghan				
(Clogher)					
Kildress (Armagh)	Jan 4 1835–Dec 6 1852	Mar 15 1835–Jan 29 1876	Mar 6 1835–Dec 24 1842	NLI	Pos. 5586
	Jan 11 1857–Aug 10 1859	Jan 7 1840–Feb 19 1851			
	Jan 6 1861–Feb 17 1865	Jan 10 1878–Dec 4 1880			
	Jan 2 1878–Dec 6 1880				
	1835–1881 (gaps)		1835–1842	PRONI	MIC.1D/37
	1835–1900	1835–1900	1835–1842	AA	
	1835–1900	1835–1900	1835–1842	IW	
	1835–1900 (part?)			Online	Genweb, Tyrone
Killeeshil (Armagh)	Aug 10 1845–Dec 27 1856	Sept 3 1845–Dec 31 1856	Aug 13 1845–Dec 16 1856	NLI	Pos. 5582
	Jan 14 1857–Dec 21 1880	Jan 14 1857–Dec 14 1880	Jan 14 1857–Jan 27 1875		
			Nov 4 to Dec 1880		
	1816–1880	1816–1883	1816–1875	PRONI	MIC.1D/33
			1880–1881		
	1816–1900	1816–1900		IW	
Kilskeery (Clogher)	Oct 3 1840–June 15 1862	Aug 30 1840–May 27 1862		NLI	Pos. 5568
	June 19 1862–Feb 18 1870	July 17 1862–Feb 27 1870			
	Jan 27 1870–Dec 24 1880	Feb 3 1870–Mar 1 1880			
	1840–1881	1940–1882		PRONI	MIC.1D/11
	See NLI			LDS	0926054
Langfield (Derry)	Sept 6 1846–Dec 18 1880	Sept 17 1846–Oct 18 1880	July 18 1853–Feb 2 1856	NLI	Pos. 5765
	1846–1880		1853–1856	PRONI	MIC.1D/60
Leckpatrick (Derry)	Sept 13 1863–Dec 12 1880	Oct 25 1863–Nov 16 1880		NLI	Pos. 5767
	1863–1881	1863–1884		PRONI	MIC.1D/62
	1863–1900	1863–1900		TGC	
Lissan (Armagh)	See Derry/Londonderry				
Mourne (Derry)	Jan 6 1866–Dec 29 1880	Apr 1 1866–Dec 3 1880		NLI	Pos. 5766
		(transcript)			
	1866–1881	1866–1883		PRONI	MIC.1D/62

Parish (Diocese)	Baptisms	Marriages	Burials	Location	Reference
Pomeroy (Armagh)	Feb 26 1837–Nov 24 1840	Mar 5 1837–Dec 11 1840	Mar 7 1837–Dec 5 1840	NLI	Pos. 5585
	Dec 5 1841–May 2 1852	Dec 5 1841–June 10 1865	Apr 20 1857–Apr 12 1861		
	Apr 21 1857–Aug 3 1865	July 11 1869–Dec 25 1880	July 27 1871–Dec 30 1880		
	Feb 1 1869–Dec 9 1880				
	1837–1852	1837–1865	1837–1840	PRONI	MIC.1D/36
	1857–1865	1869–1882	1857–1861		
	1869–1881		1871–1881		
	1837–1900	1819–1900		IW	
Termonamongan	Mar 28 1863–Dec 29 1880	Sept 12 1863–Nov 13 1880		NLI	Pos. 5765
(Derry)	1863–1881	1863–1880		PRONI	MIC.1D/60
Termonmacguirk	Dec 7 1834–Feb 9 1857	Oct 23 1834–Dec 31 1857		NLI	Pos. 5582
(Armagh)	1834–1857	1834–1857		PRONI	MIC.1D/33
	1834–1857	1834–1857		IW	
Tullyallen (Armagh)	Jan 1 1816–Jan 2 1834	Jan 3 1816–Jan 2 1834	Jan 2 1816–May 29 1834	NLI	Pos. 5582; from
	Mar 2 1837–Aug 24 1844	Apr 3 1837–July 29 1844	Mar 5 1837–Aug 22 1844		1849, Pos.
	Jan 14 1849–Dec 25 1880	Jan 9 1849–Nov 14 1880			5599
Urney (Derry)	No records microfilmed			NLI	
	No records microfilmed			PRONI	
	From 1866	From 1866		LC	
	1856–1900	1856–1900		TGC	

Waterford
All Waterford and Lismore diocese, except where indicated

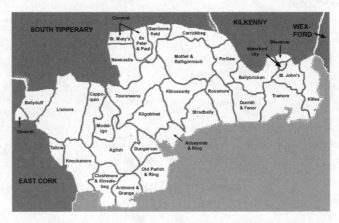

Parish (Diocese)	Baptisms	Marriages	Burials	Location	Reference
Abbeyside and Ring	July 6 1828–Dec 26 1842	July 24 1828–Feb 8 1842		NLI	Pos. 2469
	May 21 1842–Dec 29 1880	May 26 1842–Nov 18 1880			
	1828–1911	1828–1911		WHL	
Aglish	May 17 1838–Dec 31 1880	Jan 25 1877–Nov 20 1880		NLI	Pos. 2464
	1831–1911	1833–1911		WHL	
Ardmore and Grange	Oct 17 1823–Jan 19 1833	Nov 24 1857–Set 23 1880	Jan 8 1826–Jan 11 1827	NLI	Pos. 2465
	Jan 1 1857–Dec 31 1880				
	1816–1911	1857–1911		WHL	
Ballyduff	June 23 1849–Feb 6 1861	Nov 8 1853–Feb 12 1861		NLI	Pos. 2469,
	Apr 14 18761–June 4 1878	June 8 1861–Nov 18 1880			2470
	Jan 26 1879–Dec 21 1880				
	1849–1911	1853–1911		WHL	

Parish (Diocese)	Baptisms	Marriages	Burials	Location	Reference
Cappoquin	Apr 14 1810–June 16 1870 (indexed transcript) June 19 1870–Dec 21 1880	Jan 7 1807–Aug 8 1871 July 23 1870–Oct 2 1880		NLI	Pos. 2467
	1819–1911	1807–1911		WHL	
Carrickbeg	Jan 1 1842–Oct 30 1846 Feb 27 1847–Dec 28 1876	Jan 11 1807–Jan 8 1867 Nov 23 1866–Jan 9 1881		NLI	Pos. 2450
	1842–1911	1807–1911		WHL	
Clashmore and Kinsalebeg	Jan 6 1811–Oct 1 1845 Oct 12 1845– Aug 23 1879	Jan 23 1810–Aug 23 1879		NLI	Pos. 2462, 2464
	1811–1911	1810–1911		WHL	
Clonmel: Ss Peter and Paul	See South Tipperary				
Clonmel: St. Mary's	See South Tipperary				
Dungarvan	Feb 17 1787–Apr 27 1787 Sept 3 1811–May 17 1823 July 27 1823–Apr 30 1830 May 1 1830–July 13 1839 Jan 7 1838–July 26 1877 Sept 1 1877–Dec 28 1880	May 14 1809–Nov 29 1828 Jan 8 1829–Dec 2 1838 Feb 21 1838–Sept 1 1877 Sept 24 1877–Nov 12 1880		NLI	Pos. 2468, 2469
	1787–1911	1809–1911		WHL	
Dunhill and Fenor	Apr 4 1829–Nov 18 1843 Jan 5 1844–June 12 1881 Nov 16 1852–Feb 6 1876	Nov 26 1836 Feb 17 1874 Jan 14 1853–Nov 18 1880 (Fenor)	Jan 1 1879–Nov 24 1881	NLI	Pos. 2448, 2449
	1829–1911	1837–1911		WHL	
Gambonsfield and Kilcash	See South Tipperary				
Kilgobinet	Ap 7 1848–Oct 24 1872 Mar 14 1873–Dec 25 1880	Oct 10 1848–Apr 6 1880		NLI	Pos. 2464
	1848–1911	1848–1911		WHL	
Killea	May 7 1815–July 20 1820 Oct 10 1845–Dec 13 1863 (transcript) Feb 17 1874–Dec 19 1880 (transcript) Dec 24 1863–Mar 17 1881 (transcript)	Jan 8 1780–Oct 9 1791 Jan 13 1793–Feb 18 1798 (transcript) Apr 3 1815–July 20 1820 Aug 29 1837–Aug 3 1838 Oct 5 1845–Apr 27 1882		NLI	Pos. 2450
	1809–1911	1780–1911		WHL	
Kilrossanty	July 4 1822–Aug 4 1858 Jan 9 1859–Dec 27 1880	Jan 16 1859–Sept 8 1880		NLI	Pos. 2465
	1822–1911	1859–1911		WHL	
Kilworth	See East Cork				
Knockanore	May 4 1816–Apr 24 1823 Sept 1833–June 25 1872 Jan 17 1872–Dec 27 1880	Feb 7 1854–June 12 180		NLI	Pos. 2462
	1816–1911	1803–1911		WHL	
Lismore	Mar 13 1820–Feb 14 1831 July 11 1840–June 19 1848 Feb 21 1849–Apr 16 1858 Aug 27 1866–Dec 28 1880	Nov 24 1822–Oct 8 1839 Feb 27 1840–Nov 4 1866 May 1849–Feb 20 1857 Sept 1866–Nov 6 1880		NLI	Pos. 2467, 2468
	1820–1911	1822–1911		WHL	

Parish (Diocese)	Baptisms	Marriages	Burials	Location	Reference
Modeligo	July 28 1846–Dec 22 1880			NLI	Pos. 2470
	1815–1911	1820–1911		WHL	
Mothel and	Mar 23 1831–June 17 1852	Mar 4 1845–Oct 16 1880		NLI	Pos. 2449
Rathgormack	June 20 1852–Jan 13 1881				
	1831–1911	1852–1911		WHL	
Newcastle	July 1 1814–Dec 31 1845	Jan 7 1822–Oct 23 1880		NLI	Pos. 2454
	Jan 1 1846–Oct 31 1862				
	Nov 2 1862–Dec 29 1880				
	1814–1911	1822–1911		WHL	
Old Parish and Ring	Jan 5 1813–Apr 24 1840	Jan 17 1813–Feb 13 1840		NLI	Pos. 2465
	Aug 12 1840–Aug 15 1859	Jan 24 1841–Mar 8 1859			
	1813–1911	1813–1911		WHL	
Portlaw	Jan 26 1809–Oct 3 1825	Jan 15 1805–Feb 27 1881		NLI	Pos. 2449, 2450
	Dec 16 1825–Oct 24 1860	Feb 14 1814–Nov 19 1862			
	June 1 1858–Jan 23 1881	Nov 6 1860–Feb 21 1882			
	1809–1911	1805–1911		WHL	
Rossmore	Mar 27 1797–Aug 1830	Apr 27 1797–Feb 11 1880		NLI	Pos. 2452
	Feb 1831–Feb 21 1869				
	1798–1911	1797–1911		WHL	
Slieverue (Ossory)	See Kilkenny				
Stradbally	Nov 3 1806–May 30 1814	Aug 4 1805–Nov 28 1840		NLI	Pos. 2465,
	June 1 1814–Sept 22 1828	Sept 20 1840–Aug 2 1863		2466, 2467	
	Sept 30 1828–July 29 1835	Sept 13 1863–Oct 13 1880			
	Aug 1 1835–Oct 13 1850				
	Oct 19 1850–Aug 28 1863				
	Aug 20 1863–Dec 9 1880				
	1797–1911	1805–1911		WHL	
Tallow	Apr 19 1797–Mar 11 1831	Apr 20 1798–Apr 25 1803		NLI	Pos. 24
	Apr 9 1831–Sept 19 1842	Oct 11 1808–Nov 13 1853			
	Jan 19 1856–Dec 31 1880				
	1797–1911	1799–1911		WHL	
Touraneena	July 8 1852–Dec 11 1880	June 20 1852–Nov 14 1880		NLI	Pos. 24
	1852–1911	1852–1911		WHL	
Tramore	Jan 7 1798–Oct 24 1831			NLI	Pos. 24
	Jan 29 1786–July 29 1840				
	1798–1911	1785–1911		WHL	
Waterford city:	Jan 4 1795–Oct 13 1816	Jan 7 1797–Sept 6 1832		NLI	Pos. 2450, 2451
Ballybricken	Dec 1 1816–Apr 30 1832	Sept 10 1832–Sept 9 1843			(B.); 2452 (M.)
	May 1 1832–Apr 5 1841	Jan 8 1843–Nov 17 1874			
	Apr 6 1841–Jan 8 1844	Jan 7 1875–Nov 22 1880			
	Jan 8 1844–Jan 3 1875				
	Jan 3 1875–Dec 30 1880				
	1797–1911	1797–1911		WHL	
Waterford city:	1729–1752	Nov 26 1743–Jan 8 1787		NLI	Pos. 2444, 2445
Holy Trinity	1731–1749 St Stephen's	St Peter's			
	1732–1796 St Michael's	Sept 5 1747–Dec 20 1756			
	(gaps)	Feb 3 1761–Aug 30 1777			
	Nov 1737–Aug 1746	Jan 5 1791–June 28 1795			
	St Peter's	June 26 1796–Nov 24 1796			
	July 1752–Dec 1767	St Michael's			
	Jan 1768–July 1775	Jan 9 1797–Feb 20 1820			

Parish (Diocese)	Baptisms	Marriages	Burials	Location	Reference
Waterford city: Holy Trinity	Feb 1793–Dec 1805	Aug 2 1819–Sept 9 1838			
	Jan 1806–July 1819	Sept 25 1838–Nov 1863			
	Dec 1809–Sept 1815				
	July 1819–Dec 1863				
	1729–1911	1747–1911		WHL	
Waterford city: St. John's	Apr 7 1706–Mar 26 1730	Apr 7 1706–Mar 26 1730		NLI	Pos. 2446
	Mar 5 1759–Mar 29 1787	Feb 10 1760–Feb 2 1808			
	Oct 1795–Aug 10 1807	Feb 2 1808–June 1 1817			
	Aug 2 1807–Mar 31 1816	Sept 12 1828–Nov 28 1856			
	June 1 1818–July 24 1828				
	Aug 17 1828–July 17 1837				
	1759–1911	1760–1911		WHL	
Waterford city: St. Patrick's and St. Olaf's	Apr 11 1731–Feb 10 1743	May 24 1743–Oct 29 1752		NLI	Pos. 2447
	Feb 13 1743–Oct 29 1752	Oct 30 1752–June 3 1772			
	Oct 30 1752–June 3 1772	Oct 10 1772–May 22 1783			
	June 6 1772–Sept 8 1791	Nov 23 1783–May 8 1791			
	May 9 1795–Mar 27 1798	Jan 25 1799–Dec 9 1800			
	Nov 18 1798–Mar 2 1801	Sept 12 1826–Sept 19 1839			
	Apr 9 1798–Jan 8 1799				
	Apr 3 1827–Oct 11 1839				
	1706–1911	1706–1911		WHL	

Westmcath

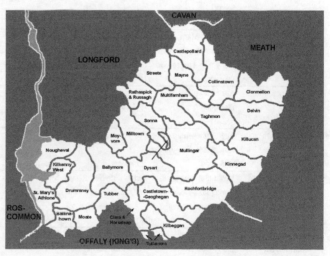

Parish (Diocese)	Baptisms	Marriages	Burials	Location	Reference
Ballinahown	See Offaly				
Ballymore (Meath)	Sept 22 1824–Sept 2 1841	April 1839–Sept 10 1870		NLI	Pos. 4171
	Mar 18 1839–Dec 30 1871 (some duplicates)	Feb 4 1872–Nov 27 1880			
	Sept 22 1824–Sept 2 1841				
	Mar 18 1839–Dec 30 18771				
	Jan 9 1872–Dec 31 1880				
	1824–1900	1872–1900		DSHC	
	See NLI			LDS	0926163

Parish (Diocese)	Baptisms	Marriages	Burials	Location	Reference
Castlepollard (Meath)	Jan 4 1763–Mar 25 1765	1763–June 10 1790	Mar 10 1764–June 22 1790	NLI	Pos. 4164, 4165
	Oct 9 1771–June 30 1790	Mar 21 1793–Aug 15 1793	Jan 19 1793–June 13 1825		
	Jan 4 1795–Feb 16 1796	Jan 7 1795–June 16 1825			
	Feb 21 1796–Aug 19 1805	Nov 21 1825–Sept 14 1875			
	Aug 23 1805–June 24 1825				
	Nov 15 1825–Mar 20 1837				
	Mar 24 1837–Oct 17 1875				
	Oct 22 1875–Dec 22 1880				
Castletown–	Aug 2 1829–May 2 1835	Feb 8 1829–Mar 3 1835		NLI	Pos. 4169
Geoghegan (Meath)	May 8 1835–Mar 29 1850	July 26 1835–Feb 10 1850			
	Mar 2 1846–Dec 12 1880	Oct 9 1846–May 27 1880			
	June 23 1861–Dec 26 1880	Jan 7 1862–Nov 26 1880			
	1829–1900	1829–1900	1829–1844	DSHC	
Clara and Horseleap	Feb 16 1845–Dec 26 1880	Nov 16 1821–Nov 25 1880	Jan 9 1825–Feb 23 1854	NLI	Pos. 4174
(Meath)	Sept 2 1878–Dec 14 1880		Oct 2 1864–Oct 4 1868		
	(transcript)				
	1845–1910	1821–1899	1825–1868	IMA	
Clonmellon (Meath)	See Meath				
Collinstown (Meath)	Feb 24 1807–Apr 29 1815	June 21 1784–June 6 1837	Apr 24 1784–Oct 1949	NLI	Pos. 4168, 4169
	Mar 13 1821–Nov 18 1843	June 15 1837–Nov 26 1880			
	Mar 4 1844–June 6 1844				
	May 12 1844–Dec 24 1880				
	1807–1901	1784–1901	1784–1849	MHC	
	See NLI			LDS	0926165
	1807–1900	1784–1844	1809–1926	DSHC	
Delvin (Meath)	Jan 1 1785–Mar 17 1789	Feb 7 1785–Mar 16 1789	Feb 7 1785–Mar 5 1789	NLI	Pos. 4172
	July 23 1792–July 20 1812	July 30 1792–July 1812	July 7 1792–July 26 1812		
	July 5 1830–Dec 29 1880	Sept 30 1830–Oct 4 1880	Jan 3 1849–Apr 1 1855		
	1783–1900	1785–1900	1785–1985	DSHC	
Drumraney (Meath)	Apr 26 1834–Dec 22 1880	May 2 1834–Sept 29 1880		NLI	Pos. 4171
	1834–1900	1834–1900		DSHC	
	See NLI			LDS	0926167
Dysart (Meath)	Aug 10 1836–Aug 24 1862	Feb 5 1825–Feb 24 1862		NLI	Pos. 4168
	Apr 28 1861–Dec 30 1880				
	1836–1900	1825–1900	1862–1900	DSHC	
Kilbeggan (Meath)	Nov 4 1818–Aug 28 182	Oct 23 1818–Nov 26 1859	Sept 28 1818–Dec 17 1843	NLI	Pos. 4176
	Apr 24 1825–Dec 9 1859	Jan 7 1860–Nov 16 1880			
	Jan 8 1860–Dec 5 1880				
	1818–1900	1821–1900	1818–1884	DSHC	
Kilbride and	Jan 1 1832–Jan 27 1864	Jan 1 1832–Nov 22 1863		NLI	Pos. 4172
Mountnugent	Jan 13 1864–Nov 27 1880	Feb 4 1864–Nov 27 1880			
(Meath)	1830–1900	1830–1863	1906–1983	DSHC	
	See NLI			LDS	0926174
	1832–1900	1832–1899		CHGC	
Kilkenny West	Aug 5 1829–Dec 15 1880			NLI	Pos. 4171
(Meath)	1829–1900	1829–1900	1829–1993	DSHC	
Killucan (Meath)	May 7 1821–July 28 1838	May 11 1821–Sept 30 1847		NLI	Pos. 4166
	July 26 1838–Dec 27 1865	Oct 26 1847–Nov 27 1874			
	Jan 6 1866–Jan 19 1875	Jan 18 1875–Nov 26 1880			
	Jan 20 1875–Dec 28 1880				
	1866–1900	1821–1900		DSHC	
	See NLI			LDS	0926172

Parish (Diocese)	Baptisms	Marriages	Burials	Location	Reference
Kinnegad (Meath)	June 22 1827–Jan 31 1869	July 18 1844–Jan 25 1869	Feb 7 1869–Dec 23 1880	NLI	Pos. 4170
	Jan 29 1869–Dec 29 1880	Feb 6 1869–Sept 8 1880			
	1827–1890	1844–1899	1833–1975	DSHC	
Mayne (Meath)	Aug 1777–May 29 1796	Nov 17 1777–Apr 24 1796	Aug 7 1777–Nov 27 1796	NLI	Pos. 4167
	Jan 22 1798–Nov 29 1820	Jan 7 1798–Dec 1 1820	Feb 2 1803–Sept 9 1820		
	Apr 2 1824–Apr 5 1835	May 9 1824–July 4 1843	Apr 2 1824–Aug 9 1844		
	Feb 21 1847–Aug 22 1863	Aug 20 1846–July 21 1850	Jan 1864–Oct 27 1869		
	(some pages missing)	Nov 2 1864–July 19 1880	Jan 4 1846–July 31 1850		
	1777–1820	1777–1820	1777–1797	DSHC	
	1824–1835	1824–1843	1824–1869		
	1847–1900	1864–1900	1919–1993		
	See NLI			LDS	0926176
Milltown (Meath)	Jan 1 1781–Sept 12 1808	Apr 2 1809–Oct 3 1825	Jan 12 1781–Nov 17 1808	NLI	Pos. 4167
	Apr 2 1809–Oct 3 1825	Mar 1 1826–Nov 15 1849	Apr 2 1809–Oct 3 1825		
	Mar 1 1826–Nov 15 1849	Feb 18 1850–May 3 1860	Mar 1 1826–Nov 15 1849		
	Feb 18 1850–May 3 1860	May 3 1860–Oct 16 1869	Feb 18 1850–May 3 1860		
	May 3 1860–Oct 16 1869	Nov 15 1869–Nov 3 1872	May 3 1860–Oct 16 1869		
	Sept 21 1869–Nov 18 1872	Jan 14 1781–Feb 11 1805			
	Dec 10 1872–Dec 22 1880	Jan 13 1873–Oct 16 1880			
	1791–1900	1781–1913	1781–1899	DSHC	
Moate (Ardagh and Clonmacnois)	Jan2 1830–Nov 30 1836	Jan2 1830–Nov 30 1836	Feb 2 1837–May 13 1883	NLI	Pos. 9358
	Feb 2 1837–May 13 1883	Feb 2 1837–May 13 1883			
	May 17 1883–Aug 3 1911				
	1820–1900	1830–1900	1830–1900	DSHC	
	1811–1900	1824–1900	1811–1900		
	(Ballyloughloe)	(Ballyloughloe)	(Ballyloughloe)		
	1830–1910	1830–1915	1830–1836	LDS	1279227
		1835–1916			
Moyvore	See Longford				
Mullingar (Meath)	1741/2 (fragment)	Oct 26 1737–July 20 1754	May 6 1757–Oct 31 1797	NLI	Pos. 4161, 4162,
	July 15 1742– Dec 19 1796	Jan 10 1779–Apr 21 1824	Jan 4 1833–May 26 1838		4163
	Jan 13 1797–May 2 1800	Jan 8 1833–Apr 9 1859	Feb 28 1843–1880		
	Jan 1 1800–Apr 13 1816	May 18 1860–July 12 1879			
	May 1 1825– Nov 23 1842	July 10 1879–Nov 27 1880			
	Nov 13 1843–Jan 24 1863				
	Jan 22 1863–Mar 12 1872				
	Mar 13 1872–Dec 31 1880				
	1742–1900	1737–1754	1830–1940	DSHC	
		1779–1782			
		1783–1824			
		1833 1859			
		1860–1900			
	See NLI			LDS	0926178
Multifarnham (Meath)	Feb 6 1824–Dec 28 1841	Feb 15 1824–Dec 9 1841	Jan 28 1831–July 16 1844	NLI	Pos. 4168
	Jan 1 1842–Dec 26 1880	Jan 7 1842–June 4 1880			
	1824–1900	1824–1900	1830–1848	DSHC	
Nougheval (Meath)	No records microfilmed			NLI	
	1857–1908	1857 1908	1920–1993	DSHC	
Rathaspick and Russagh (Ardagh and Clonmacnois)	Mar 16 1822–Sept 9 1826	Dec 31 1819–Feb 7 1826	Mar 11 1822–Feb 20 1826	NLI	Pos. 4236
	July 24 1832–Apr 21 1833	Oct 27 18322–Oct 4 1833	Aug 2 1832–Nov 1833		
	May 1 1836–Dec 9 1843	Jan 11 1838–Nov 23 1843	Aug 15 1837–Oct 10 1843		
	Dec 17 1843–Oct 18 1846	Jan 7 1844–Nov 20 1880	Feb 8 1844–Dec 19 1880		
	Mar 28 1847–Dec 30 1880				

Parish (Diocese)	Baptisms	Marriages	Burials	Location	Reference
Rathaspick and Russagh (Ardagh and Clonmacnois)	1826–1900	1821–1842 1844–1900	1828–1993	DSHC	
	1822–1984	1825–1983	1822–1909 1928–1984	LDS	1279229
Rochfortbridge (Meath)	Jun 1 1823–Apr 9 1847 Apr 11 1847–Dec 28 1856 Jan 9 1857–Dec 27 1880	Dec 26 1816–Dec 1 1855 Jan 20 1856–Nov 26 1880		NLI	Pos. 4172
Sonna (Meath)	Sept 23 1837–Dec 31 1880	Nov 26 1838–July 20 1880		NLI	Pos. 4168
	1837–1900	1838–1900	1859–1993	DSHC	
St. Mary's, Athlone (Ardagh and Clonmacnois)	Jan 1 1813–Sept 24 1826 Feb 4 1827–Mar 17 1827 May 3 1839–Apr 30 1852 Feb 1 1853–Dec 28 1855 Jan 1 1856–Feb 26 1868	Jan 1 1813–Sept 24 1826 Feb 4 1827–Mar 17 1827 June 5 1819–Apr 17 1827 (some deaths and baptisms included) Jan 24 1834–Dec 26 1851 Feb 9 1854–Feb 5 1863	Jan 1 1813–Sept 24 1826 Feb 4 1827–Mar 17 1827 June 4 1819–Dec 29 1826 (some marriages and baptisms included)	NLI	Pos. 4242
	1813–1827 1834–1984 1813–1900	1813–1827 1834–1984 1813–1900	1813–1827 1813–1900	LDS DSHC	1279224 1279226
Streete (Ardagh and Clonmacnois)	July 6 1820–July 14 1827 Nov 21 1831–Dec 20 1831 Dec 15 1834–Dec 29 1880	Aug 10 1820–Jan 22 1828 Jan 4 1835–Nov 19 1880	Sept 27 1823–Aug 13 1829 Dec 14 1834–Jan 8 1841 July 19 1842–Dec 29 1880	NLI	Pos. 4236
	1820–1901	1820–1826 1835–1881 1887–1902	1834–1881 1887–1913	LDS	1279228
	1821–1863	1820–1900	1772–1995	DSHC	
Taghmon (Meath)	Sept 22 1781–Mar 7 1790 June 8 1800–June 30 1800 Mar 24 1809–Dec 28 1840 Jan 1 1841–Dec 29 1850 Jan 2 1864–Dec 30 1880	Jan 12 1782–July 16 1791 Aug 7 1809–May 14 1848 Sept 2 1868–Nov 3 1880	Sept 1 1809–Feb 25 1848	NLI	Pos. 4165
Tubber (Meath)	Nov 2 1821–Dec 25 1880	Nov 6 1824–Dec 13 1880		NLI	Pos. 4176
	1820–1899	1820–1899	1832–1845	IMA	
	See NLI			LDS	0926185
	1820–1900	1824–1900	1824–1873	DSHC	
Tullamore (Meath)	See Offaly				

Wexford
All Ferns diocese
Copies of all NLI Wexford
microfilms are also available
at Wexford County Library

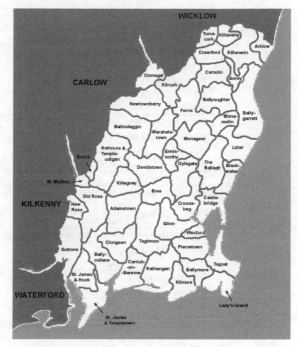

Parish (Diocese)	Baptisms	Marriages	Burials	Location	Reference
Adamstown	Jan 13 1807–Dec 30 1836	Dec 8 1849–Feb 13 1865	Sept 27 1823–Jan 30 1832	NLI	Pos. 4258
	Jan 7 1837–Oct 7 1848	Nov 26 1864–Oct 19 1880	(ages given)		
	Nov 10 1850–Sept 11 1864				
	Apr 13 1849–Mar 27 1861				
	Nov 20 1864–Oct 30 1880				
	1837–1900	1892–1900		WGC	
	(gaps 1864–1892)				
Arklow	See Wicklow				
Ballindaggin	July 18 1871–Dec 30 1880	July 2 1871–Nov 11 1880		NLI	Pos. 4251
Ballycullane	Sept 13 1827–Sept 3 1880	Oct 7 1827–Sept 12 1880	Oct 10 1828–Jan 31 1832	NLI	Pos. 4259
	(very poor condition)				
	1827–1900	1827–1896	1828–1832	WGC	
Ballygarrett	Nov 10 1828–Feb 19 1863	Aug 30 1828–Nov 13 1865	Aug 7 1830–Apr 18 1857	NLI	Pos. 4255
			Oct 28 1865–Apr 19 1867		
			(ages given)		
	1828–1900	1830–1900	1830–1869	WGC	
Ballymore	May 22 1840–Dec 24 1880	Feb 13 1840–Oct 23 1880		NLI	Pos. 4246
	1821–1900	1802–1899		WGC	
Ballyoughter	Sept 30 1810–Dec 31 1811	Aug 20 1815–Feb 10 1868		NLI	Pos. 4255
	Aug 5 1815–Nov 28 1832	July 13 1871–Dec 27 1880			
	Aug 18 1844–Apr 19 1871				
	July 5 1871–Dec 27 1880				
Blackwater	1815–Dec 28 1839 (early	Jan 8 1815–Dec 10 1839	Jan 5 1843–Dec 20 1880	NLI	Pos. 4245
	years barely legible)	Jan 13 1840–Nov 27 1880			
	Jan 4 1840–Dec 21 1880				
	1825–1900	1815–1881	1840–1883	WGC	

Parish (Diocese)	Baptisms	Marriages	Burials	Location	Reference
Borris	See Carlow				
Bree	Jan 3 1837–Dec 26 1880	Jan 23 1837–Nov 27 1880		NLI	Pos. 4251
Camolin	June 1 1853–Dec 10 1880	Mar 10 1853–Nov 7 1880	Jan 3 1858–Feb 7 1879	NLI	Pos. 4257
Carrick–on–Bannow	Aug 29 1832–Nov 9 1873 (some missing) Aug 10 1873–Dec 31 1880	Sept 11 1830–Sept 23 1873 July 16 1873–Nov 27 1880		NLI	Pos. 4244
	1873–1900			WGC	
Castlebridge	Oct 30 1832–Dec 31 1880 July 17 1871–Dec 24 1880 (Screen)	Dec 1 1832–Oct 27 1880 Oct 6 1871–Oct 20 1880 (Screen)		NLI	Pos. 4247
	1832–1900	1832–1892		WGC	
Clonegal	See Carlow				
Clongeen	Jan 29 1847–Dec 30 1880	Apr 25 1847–Nov 25 1880	Jan 30 1856–Dec 3 1880 (ages given)	NLI	Pos. 4261
	1847–1900	1847–1900		WGC	
Craanford	Jan 8 1856–Dec 3 1880 Aug 26 1871–Oct 28 1880	Nov 30 1871–Nov 28 1880		NLI	Pos. 4257
	1871–1900	1871–1900		WGC	
Crossabeg	Jan 8 1856–Dec 3 1880			NLI	Pos. 4251
	1794–1900	1794–1900	1899–1900	WGC	
Davidstown	1805–Dec 24 1880	June 1808–Nov 27 1880		NLI	Pos. 4251
	1806–1900	1829–1889		WGC	
Enniscorthy	May 16 1794–June 10 1804 (also in transcript) Mar 1 1806–May 23 1816 (also in transcript) June 2 1816–Dec 31 1835 (also in transcript) Jan 1 1836–Dec 30 1861 Jan 1 1836–Nov 6 1841 Jan 2 1862–Dec 23 1880	May 3 1794–Sept 25 1805 (also in transcript) Sept 17 1805–May 12 1816 (also in transcript) July 20 1816–Nov 28 1835 (also in transcript) Jan 1 1836–Nov 30 1861 Mar 6 1821–Oct 28 1835		NLI	Pos. 4249
	1794–1900	1794–1900		WGC	
Ferns	May 16 1819–Feb 14 1840 Sept 6 1840–Dec 24 1880	May 14 1819–Jan 10 1840 Nov 2 1840–Nov 18 1880		NLI	Pos. 4254
	1819–1900	1840–1900	1840–1859	WGC	
Glinn	Jan 23 1817–Feb 3 1867 Feb 7 1867–Dec 20 1880	Jan 26 1817–Jan 17 1867 Feb 5 1867–Nov 27 1880	Jan 6 1823–Dec 21 1880 (ages given)	NLI	Pos. 4247
	1817–1900	1817–1883	1867–1883	WGC	
Gorey	May 26 1845–Nov 10 1880	June 5 1845–July 3 1847 Aug 4 1847–May 2 1880		NLI	Pos. 4256
Killanerin	Jan 1 1852–Oct 31 1880	Jan 25 1852–Oct 14 1880		NLI	Pos. 4255
Killaveny	Nov 20 1800–Dec 20 1836 Jan 13 1837–Apr 29 1875 Ovt 15 1857–Apr 10 1864 (Anacorra)	Nov 14 1800–Sept 10 1836 Jan 7 1837–May 4 1875 Aug 5 1860–Feb 6 1864 (Anacorra)	Oct 19 1862–Mar 13 1867 (Anacorra)	NLI	Pos. 4257
	1800–1900	1800–1900		WFHC	
Killegney	Mar 17 1816–Sept 20 1850 (part of 1824 missing) Jan 20 1853–Oct 24 1880	Mar 17 1816–Sept 20 1850 (part of 1824 missing) Feb 7 1853–Dec 2 1880	Mar 17 1816–Sept 20 1850 (part of 1824 missing); Feb 3 1861–Sept 12 1880 (ages given);	NLI	Pos. 4250
	1816–1900	1816–1900	1816–1900	WGC	

Parish (Diocese)	Baptisms	Marriages	Burials	Location	Reference
Kilmore	Apr 6 1752–Mar 30 1785	Apr 6 1752–Mar 30 1785	Apr 6 1752–Mar 30 1785	NLI	Pos. 4246
	June 24 1790–Nov 3 1794	June 24 1790–Nov 3 1794	June 24 1790–Nov 3 1794		
	Jan 2 1798–Mar 12 1826	Jan 2 1798–Mar 12 1826	Jan 2 1798–Mar 12 1826		
	(Some pages missing)	(Some pages missing)	(Some pages missing)		
	July 7 1828–Sept 29 1854	Nov 4 1827–Sept 10 1856			
	Jan 11850–Dec 28 1880	Jan 26 1850–Oct 20 1880			
	1768–1900	1768–1850	1768–1850	WGC	
Kilrush	May 29 1841–Nov 16 1846			NLI	Pos. 4251
	Mar 6 1855–Dec 26 1880				
Lady's Island	Aug 1737–May 24 1740	Feb 17 1753–Dec 2 1759		NLI	Pos. 4244
	May 16 1752–Mar 1763	Feb 16 1754–May 1800			
	Jan 1766–Dec 22 1802	(1798/99 missing,			
	Jan 18 1807–Feb 1 1818	Jan 18 1807–Feb 1 1818			
	Apr 26 1838–Dec 20 1880				
	1737–1900	1838–1900	1868–1900	WGC	
Litter	Oct 2 1798–Sept 8 1816	Jan 20 1788–Apr 14 1798		NLI	Pos. 4255
	Sept 13 1816–Dec 18 1853	Sept 25 1806–Oct 3 1880			
	Jan 3 1844–Dec 11 1880				
	1818–1900	1768–1898		WGC	
Marshalstown	May 16 1854–Dec 22 1880	Nov 28 1854–May 1 1880	Oct 10 1854–Nov 18 1856	NLI	Pos. 4248
			Feb 15 1860–Aug 2 1862		
			Oct 28 1876–Jan 16 1878		
Monageer	Nov 18 1838–Dec 13 1880	Nov 12 1838–Nov 3 1880	Aug 1 1838–Dec 22 1880	NLI	Pos. 4248
	(Monageer)	(Monageer)	(ages given–Monageer)		
	May 12 1842–Mar 18 1853	Jan16 1847–Nov 23 1852	Oct 25 1847–Jan 25 1872		
	Oct 26 1869–Oct 10 1872	Oct 7 1869–Nov 2 1872	(Boolavogue)		
	May 5 1879–Dec 13 1880	July 1879–Nov 27 1880			
	(all Boolavogue)	(all Boolavogue)			
Monamolin	Feb 23 1839–Sept 24 1856	Nov 23 1834–Apr 1 1856		NLI	Pos. 4255
	Mar 15 1858–Oct 13 1880	Oct 20 1859–Aug 13 1880			
New Ross	Nov 22 1789–Aug 23 1809	Feb 22 1859–Nov 30 1880	May 14 1794–July 22 1809	NLI	Pos. 4259, 4260
	Aug 27 1809–Aug 7 1841		Aug 2 1809–Nov 17 1814		
	Aug 1841–Apr 6 1870		Apr 9 1822–Feb 15 1859		
	Apr 10 1870–Dec 12 1880				
	1789–1900	1817–1900		WGC	
Newtownbarry	1834–Nov 1 1851	May 20 1834–June 29 1880	1834	NLI	Pos. 425
	Apr 26 1857–Dec 29 1880		1857–8		
			1872–3		
Old Ross	Jan 9 1759–Aug 9 1759	Nov 3 1752–Feb 27 1759	May 16 1794–July 12 1808	NLI	Pos. 4259
	Jan 27 1778–Jan 29 1830	Jan 17 1778–Feb 29 1824	(ages given)		
	July 10 1851–Mar 8 1863	Aug 4 1851–Sept 21 1862	May 1863–Dec 27 1880		
	Feb 26 1863–Dec 19 1880	Apr 15 1863–Oct 28 1880			
Oylegate	Mar 4 1804–Dec 3 1820	Apr 18 1803– Oct 13 1820	Apr 7 1865–Dec 6 1870	NLI	Pos. 4254
	Aug 10 1832–Nov 30 1853	Oct 14 1832–Nov 19 1853	(ages given)		
	Sept 8 1848–Dec 23 1880	Sept 28 1848–Aug 12 1880	Oct 27 1860–Dec 16 1880		
	Nov 20 1860–Dec 24 1880	Nov 18 1860–Dec 16 1880	(Glenbrien–ages given)		
	(Glenbryan)	(Glenbryan)			
	1804–1900	1803–1900	1865–1870	WGC	
	(gap 1820–1832)	(gap 1820–1832)			
Piercetown	Dec 18 1811–July 30 1854	Jan 10 1812–July 26 1854		NLI	Pos. 4250
	Jan 18 1839–July 28 1854	Jan 29 1839–Nov 27 1852			
	(Murrintown)	(Murrintown)			

Parish (Diocese)	Baptisms	Marriages	Burials	Location	Reference
Piercetown	Aug 8 1854–Nov 13 1880	Aug 12 1854–Nov 13 1880			
	1811–1900	1812–1900		WGC	
Rathangan	Jan 27 1803–Aug 28 1805	June 25 1803–June 15 1806		NLI	Pos. 4244
	Jan 19 1813–Feb 9 1853	Jan 7 1813–Nov 27 1852			
	June 19 1845–June 10 1850	Nov 26 1846–July 29 1854			
	Mar 30 1844–Oct 31 1854	Feb 15 1854–Aug 24 1880			
	Apr 2 1853–Dec 30 1880				
	1803–1850	1805–1850		WGC	
	1846–1854 (Cleariestown)	1844–1854 (Cleariestown)			
Rathnure and	Oct 3 1846–Jan 25 1853	Oct 17 1846–Jan 29 1853	Oct 18 1846–Jan 28 1853	NLI	Pos. 4248
Templeudigan	Feb 7 1853–Jan 23 1878	Feb 7 1853–Jan 31 1878	(ages given);		
	June 17 1877–Nov 30 1880	July 18 1877–July 13 1880	Feb 24 1853–Feb 9 1878		
	Mar 18 1878–Dec 31 1880	Mar 4 1878–Aug 28 1880	(ages given);		
			Feb 18 1878–Oct 16 1880		
			(ages given);		
	1846–1878	1847–1853	1846–1853	WGC	
St James and Hook	Nov 29 1835–Aug 10 1840	Nov 7 1875–Nov 29 1880	Oct 17 1835–May 28 1854	NLI	Pos. 4258
	Mar 28 1844–Sept 17 1873		(ages given)		
	Sept 23 1873–Dec 29 1880				
	1835–1873			WGC	
St James and	Dec 23 1792–Oct6 27 1793	Nov 18 1792–June 11 1815	Jan 2 1816–Apr 21 1879	NLI	Pos. 4245
Templetown	Jan 7 1795–Nov 8 1798	Jan 8 1812–Nov 26 1842			
	Apr 6 1805–Mar 28 1815	Jan 18 1843–Nov 30 1860			
	Jan 5 1812–Dec 22 1815	Sept 17 1870–Nov 24 1880			
	Jan 1816–Oct 13 1880	Feb 9 1861–Nov 1880			
	Mar 6 1870–Dec 23 1880	June 18 1843–Nov 3 1880			
		(transcript)			
	1793–1894 (gaps 1798–	1792–1859	1816–1879	WGC	
	1805, 1814–1816)	(gap 1815–1843)			
St Mullins	See Carlow				
Suttons	Nov 3 1824–Nov 7 1879	Feb 12 1825–Sept 26 1879	May 17 1827–Nov 26 1836	NLI °	Pos. 4261
	Feb 19 1862–Dec 15 1880	Feb 22 1862–Nov 27 1880	Jan 13 1858–Dec 19 1880		
	(Ballykelly)	(Ballykelly)			
	1826–1900	1825–1894	1827–1884	WGC	
Taghmon	May 26 1801–July 8 1832	May 29 1801–Mar 7 1835	Jan 3 1828–Dec 3 1846	NLI	Pos. 4247
	July 11 1832–Dec 21 1865	Apr 6 1866–Nov 27 1880	(ages given)		
	Mar 3 1866–Dec 19 1880		Feb 20 1866–Dec 23 1880		
			(ages given)		
	1801–1900			WGC	
Tagoat	Jan 16 1853–Dec 8 1875	Feb 8 1853–Nov 27 1875	Oct 16 1875–Aug 3 1880	NLI	Pos. 4245
	Nov 16 1875–Dec 30 1880	Oct 31 1875–Nov 21 1880			
	1853–1900	1853–1900	1853–1881	WGC	
The Ballagh	Oct 29 1837–Jan 27 1853	Nov 4 1837–Nov 26 1852		NLI	Pos. 4248
	Feb 25 1875–Dec 26 1880	Nov 10 1874–July 20 1878			
	Oct 1863–Dec 17 1880				
Tomacork	Jan 1785–May 20 1786	June 18 1793–Feb 23 1797	May 12 1794–Dec 30 1797	NLI	Pos. 4256
	Feb 8 1791–Nov 24 1797	Jan 19 1807–Mar 1845	May 1 1847–Nov 13 1856		
	Jan 5 1807–May 6 1836	June 2 1847–Sept 12 1880	May 18 1864–Jan 11 1871		
	Nov 15 1832–May 27 1847		Apr 20 1873–Dec 24 1880		
	May 31 1847–Dec 28 1880				
	1785–1900	1793–1900		WFHC	

Parish (Diocese)	Baptisms	Marriages	Burials	Location	Reference
Wexford	May 1671–1685 (poorly legible)	May 1671–1685 (poorly legible)		NLI	Pos. 4252 (baptisms to 1851); 4253
	Dec 13 1686–Jan 29 1689	Apr 4 1724–Dec 10 1822			(baptisms to
	Jan 13 1694–Mar 19 1710	Jan 9 1823–Nov 25 1867			1880); 4254
	Feb 19 1723–Aug 7 1787	Nov 26 1867–Nov 27 1880			(marriages)
	June 2 1815–June 26 1838				
	June 27 1838–Aug 25 1851				
	Aug 28 1851–Feb 15 1869				
	Mar 1 1869–Dec 31 1880				
	1686–1900	1671–1900		WGC	

Wicklow
All Dublin diocese,
except where noted

Parish (Diocese)	Baptisms	Marriages	Burials	Location	Reference
Arklow (Dublin)	May 25 1809–June 4 1809	Jan 7 1818–Nov 27 1843		NLI	Pos. 6474/75
	Dec 21 1817–Dec 31 1843	Jan 7 1844–Oct 27 1856			
	Jan 2 1844–Oct 27 1856	Jan 12 1857–Nov 26 1880			
	Jan 1 1857–Oct 2 1868				
	Oct 4 1868–Dec 29 1880				
	1809–1880	1813–1880		WFHC	
	1818–1961 (part?)			Online	CMC Wicklow
Ashford	Sept 18 1864–Dec 31 1880	Oct 6 1864–Nov 5 1880		NLI	Pos. 6477/8
	1864–1900	1864–1900		WFHC	
Aughrim	No records microfilmed			NLI	
	1879–1900	1879–1900		WFHC	
Avoca	June 15 1791–Feb 26 1805	June 15 1791–Feb 26 1805		NLI	Pos. 6476/77
	May 27 1809–Dec 21 1825	Oct 23 1778–Jan 26 1797			
	Oct 3 1825–June 5 1836	Nov 6 1812–Oct 25 1825			

Parish (Diocese)	Baptisms	Marriages	Burials	Location	Reference
Avoca	June 2 1836–Apr 23 1867	Oct 10 1825–Feb 6 1843			
	Mar 5 1843–Apr 18 1867	Apr 22 1844–Feb 28 1867			
	Apr 21 1867–Dec 25 1880	Apr 15 1844–Feb 3 1867			
		May 1 1867–Nov 2 1880			
	1778–1900	1778–1900		WFHC	
Ballymore Eustace	See Kildare				
Baltinglass (Kildare and Leighlin)	May 31 1807–Feb 18 1810	Feb 2 1810–Apr 16 1811	Aug 12 1824–Sept 11 1830	NLI	Pos. 4192
	July 8 1810–Apr 4 1811	Nov 20 1813–Sept 12 1815			
	Oct 4 1813–Jan 19 1830	Apr (?) 25 1816–Apr 25 1831			
	Mar 7 1830–July12 1857	Jan 28 1830–May 19 1857			
	May 12 1857–Nov 5 1865	July 23 1857–Feb 12 1866			
	Nov 12 1865–Dec 19 1880	May 3 1866–Dec 18 1880			
	See NLI			LDS	0926104 item 2
	1807–1800	1807–1880		WFHC	
Blackditches	June 9 1810–Aug 1825	June 18 1810–Aug 1825		NLI	Pos. 6483, 6615
	May 4 1830–June 10 1830	Aug 6 1826–June 7 1833			
	June 9 1826–Apr 25 1830	Feb 2 1833–Jan 25 1845			
	Feb 15 1833–Mar 4 1844	Apr 8 1844–May 8 1862			
	Mar 10 1844–May 8 1862	1862–1880			
	1860–1880				
	1810–1825	1810–1900		WFHC	
	1833–1898				
Blessington	Apr 4 1852–Nov 14 1880	Feb 22 1852–Dec 4 1880		NLI	Pos. 6483, 6615
	1852–1880 (Church of Kilbride)	1877–1880 (Church of Kilbride)			
	1821–1900	1834–1900		WFHC	
Bray	Bray, Little Bray, Shankill, Old Connaught and Shanganagh baptisms from St. Michael's, (Kingstown) 1768–1861.	Feb 19 1792–March 4 1821		NLI	Pos. 9371
		Sept 8 1822–June 16 1856 (indexed)			
		July 22 1856–Nov 11 1901			
	Aug 19 1792–Mar 4 1821				
	July 7 1822–Mar 9 1856 (indexed)				
	Mar 16 1856–May 18 1886				
	May 16 1886–Mar 2 1905				
	1790–1900	1790–1900		WFHC	
Clonegal	See Carlow				
Clonmore	See Carlow				
Dunlavin	Oct 1 1815–Sept 29 1839	Feb 14 1831–Oct 19 1839 (Ink badly faded)		NLI	Pos. 6484
	Oct13 1839–Sept 8 1857	Nov 12 1839–Nov 20 1857 (Ink badly faded)			
	1857–Dec 15 1880 (Ink badly faded)	Feb 12 1857–Nov 22 1880			
	1815–1900	1815–1900		WFHC	
Enniskerry	Oct 7 1825–Sept 22 1861	Nov 1 1825–Sept 29 1861		NLI	Pos. 6478
	Sept 11 1859–Dec 5 1880	Mar 6 1859–Nov 18 1880			
	1825–1900	1825–1900		WFHC	

Parish (Diocese)	Baptisms	Marriages	Burials	Location	Reference
Glendalough	June 20 1807–Jan 18 1838	Jan 6 1808–June 27 1838		NLI	Pos. 6474
	Aug 24 1839–May 1 1866	May 14 1840–July 24 1866.			
	Apr 17 1857–Dec 24 1880	May 2 1857–Oct 6 1880			
	1807–1837	1807–1837		WFHC	
	1840–1881	1840–1881			
Hacketstown	See Carlow				
KIlbride	Jan 1858–1880	Feb 1858–1880		NLI	Pos. 6615
	1821–1835	1858–1900		WFHC	
	1858–1900				
Killaveny	Sec Wexford			NLI	
Kilquade	Aug 23 1826–June 29 1855	Aug 12 1826–Sept 29 1862		NLI	Pos. 6478
	Dec 17 1861–Feb 7 1863	Nov 4 1862–Nov 8 1880			
	1826–1900	1826–1900		WFHC	
Little Bray	Dec 27 1891–May 25, 1898	Feb 10 1866–Feb 13 1901		NLI	Pos. 9372
	1863–1891	1863–1891		WFHC	
Rathdown Union	No registers microfilmed			NLI	
Workhouse	1841–1900	1876–1894		DLRHS	
Rathdrum	Jan 6 1795–Jan 29 1799	Nov 7 1816–Aug 5 1835		NLI	Pos. 6476
	Ocyt 1 1816–July 29 1835	Aug 3 1835–Sept 22 1854			
	Aug 2 1835–Oct 3 1854	Nov 14 1854–Nov 3 1880			
	Sept 27 1854–June 12 1875				
	June 12 1875–Dec 21 1880				
	1795–1797	1810–1833		WFHC	
	1816–1900	1854–1880			
Rathvilly	See Carlow				
Roundwood	Jun 5 1881–Oct 11 1900	May 2 1857–Aug 4 1902		NLI	Pos. 9372
	1881–1900	1857–1900		WFHC	
Wicklow	Jan 7 1747/8–Oct 9 1754	Jan 7 1747/8–Sept 1 1754		NLI	Pos. 6482
	Sept 9 1753–Dec 9 1775	Jan 19 1753–Nov 25 1761			
	Sept 27 1761–Dec 1762	Dec 19 1761–May 13 1777			
	Jan 1776–June 9 1781	Jan 11 1762–Feb 22 1778			
	1784/5 (4 entries)	Jan 22 1779–Oct 2 1780			
	May 15 1796–Dec 29 1830	Nov 20 1795–Feb 15 1874			
	Nov 29 1829–Dec 28 1862	June 23 1874–Nov 27 1880			
	Oct 17 1861–June 7 1874				
	July 1874–Dec 1880				
	1747–1791	1747–1900		WFHC	
	1829–1900				

Variant names of Roman Catholic parishes

Variant Name	Map Name	County
Abbey	Ballinakill (East Galway)	Galway
Abbeygormacan	Mullagh	Galway
Abbeymahon	Lislee	Cork
Abbeyshrule	Carrickedmond	Longford
Abington	Murroe, Boher and Abington	Limerick Tipperary
Aghabog	Killeevan	Monaghan
Aghagower	Aughagower	Mayo
Aghalurcher	Aughalurcher	Fermanagh Tyrone
Aghanagh	Aughanagh	Sligo
Aghanishin	Aughnish	Donegal
Aghanlo	Limavady	Derry
Aghanloo	Tamlaghtard	Derry
Aghavas	Aughavas	Leitrim
Aghintaine	Aughintaine	Tyrone
Aghyaran	Termonamongan	Tyrone
Aglis	Molahiff	Kerry
Aglish	Ovens	Cork
Aglish	Castlebar	Mayo
Aglish	Borrisokane	Tipperary
Ahane	Castleconnell	Limerick Tipperary
Aherlow	Galbally and Aherlow	Limerick Tipperary
Aille	Killeenadeema	Galway
Alfred Street	St. Malachy's	Belfast city
Anacorra	Killaveny	Wexford Wicklow
Annaclone	Annaghlone	Down
Annacurra	Killaveny	Wexford Wicklow
Annascaul	Ballanvohir	Kerry
Annegelliffe	Urney	Cavan
Ardagh	Killeagh	Cork
Ardboe	Arboe	Tyrone Derry
Ardbraccan	Bohermeen	Meath
Ardcarn	Cootehall	Roscommon
Ardclinis	Layde	Antrim
Ardcroney	Cloughjordan	Tipperary
Ardfield	Ardfield and Rathberry	Cork
Ardglass	Dunsford	Down
Ardnageesha	Watergrasshill	Cork
Ardoyne	Holy Cross	Belfast city
Arigna	Kilronan	Roscommon
Arney	Cleenish	Fermanagh
Arra	Youghal Arra	Tipperary
Arran Quay	St. Paul's	Dublin city
Artrea	Ardtrea and Desertlin	Derry Tyrone
Ashbourne	Ratoath	Meath
Ashford	Killeedy	Limerick
Askamore	Kilrush	Wexford
Athlacca	Dromin	Limerick

Variant Name	Map Name	County
Athnowen	Ovens	Cork
Aughadowey	Coleraine	Antrim Derry
Aughalee	Magheralinn	Armagh Down
Aughaloe	Aghaloo	Tyrone
Aughmacart	Durrow	Kilkenny Laois
Aughnacloy	Aghaloo	Tyrone
Aughnasheelin	Oughteragh	Leitrim
Bagenalstown	Dunleckney	Carlow
Bailieboro	Killanne	Cavan
Baldoyle	Howth	Dublin
Ballagh	Clontuskert	Roscommon
Ballaghaderreen	Castlemore and Kilcolman	Mayo, Sligo Rosc
Ballaghameehan	Rossinver	Leitrim Sligo
Ballee	Saul	Down
Ballee	Ballyculter	Down
Ballina	Kilmoremoy	Sligo Mayo
Ballinabrackey	Castlejordan	Meath Offaly
Ballinacargy	Sonna	Westmeath
Ballinaclough	Silvermines	Tipperary
Ballinacourty	Ballanvohir	Kerry
Ballinadee	Ringrone	Cork
Ballinafad	Aughanagh	Sligo
Ballinagar	Killeigh	Offaly Laois
Ballinakill and Kilcrone	Ballintubber and Balllymoe	Roscommon
Ballinakill Upper	Woodford	Galway
Ballinameen	Killucan	Roscommon
Ballinamona	Grenagh	Cork
Ballinamona	Mourneabbey	Cork
Ballinamore	Oughteragh	Leitrim
Ballindereen	Kilcolgan	Galway
Ballinderry	Aghagallon	Antrim
Ballindine	Kilvine	Mayo
Ballindoon	Omey	Galway
Ballinlough	Kilskyre	Meath
Ballinora	Ballincollig	Cork
Ballinskelligs	Prior	Kerry
Ballinspittal	Ringrone	Cork
Ballintra	Drumholm	Donegal
Ballintubber	Burriscarra	Mayo
Ballisodare	Ballysodare and Kilvarnet	Sligo
Ballivana	Bulgaden	Limerick
Ballonkillen	Dunleckney	Carlow
Ballyanne	Old Ross	Wexford
Ballybay	Tullycorbet	Monaghan
Ballybay	Kiltomb	Roscommon
Ballybeg	Sneem	Kerry
Ballyboggan	Castlejordan	Meath Offaly
Ballyboy	Balliboy and Killoughy	Offaly
Ballybrown	Lurriga	Limerick

Variant Name	Map Name	County
Ballycastle	Ramoan	Antrim
Ballyclog	Donaghenry	Tyrone
Ballyclogan	Legan	Longford
Ballycommon	Philipstown	Offaly
Ballyconneely	Omey	Galway
Ballyconnell	Clonmore	Carlow
Ballyconnell	Clonmore	Wicklow
Ballyconnell	Kildallen	Cavan Fermanagh
Ballydonoghue	Ballybunion	Kerry
Ballyduggan	Leitrim	Galway
Ballyea	Killone	Clare
Ballyfarnon, Keadue	Kilronan	Roscommon
Ballyferriter	Kilmelchidar	Kerry
Ballyfin	Cappinrush	Laois
Ballyforan	Dysart	Galway Roscommon
Ballygar	Killian and Killeroran	Galway
Ballygarvan	Ballinhassig	Cork
Ballygarvan	Douglas	Cork
Ballygawley	Errigal Kieran	Tyrone
Ballygovey	Tourmakeady	Mayo
Ballygowan	Larne	Antrim
Ballygunner	Waterford city: St. John's	Waterford
Ballyhaunis	Annagh	Mayo
Ballyhean	Castlebar	Mayo
Ballyheedy	Ballinhassig	Cork
Ballyhooly	Castletownroche	Cork
Ballykelly	Limavady	Derry
Ballykelly	Suttons	Wexford
Ballykinlar	Tyrella	Down
Ballylaneen	Stradbally	Waterford
Ballyloughloe	Moate	Westmeath Offaly
Ballymacelroy	Errigal Kieran	Tyrone
Ballymachugh	Drumlumman South	Cavan
Ballymackenny	Monasterboice	Louth
Ballymacormack	Templemichael	Longford
Ballymadun	Garristown	Dublin
Ballymagleeson	Dunboyne	Meath
Ballymahon	Shrule	Longford
Ballymascanlan	Lordship	Louth
Ballymena	Kirkinriola	Antrim
Ballymodan	Bandon	Cork
Ballymoe	Ballinakill and Kilcrone	Roscommon
Ballymore	Ballymore and Mullabrack	Armagh
Ballymote	Emlefad and Kilmorgan	Sligo
Ballymurrin	Crossabeg	Wexford
Ballynacourty	Oranmore	Galway
Ballynahaglish	Backs	Mayo
Ballynahaglish	Spa	Kerry
Ballynahill	Loughill	Limerick

Variant Name	Map Name	County
Ballynahill	Shanagolden	Limerick
Ballyorgan	Glenroe	Limerick
Ballyovey	Tourmakeady	Mayo
Ballyphillip	Portaferry	Down
Ballyporeen	Templetenny	Tipperary
Ballyseedy	Ballymacelligot	Kerry
Ballyshannon	Kilbarron	Donegal
Ballysheehan	Clogheen	Tipperary
Ballysokeery	Cooneal	Mayo
Ballysteen	Askeaton	Limerick
Ballyvoige	Kilnamartyra	Cork
Balnahown	Ballinahown	Offaly Westmeath
Balrothery	Balbriggan	Dublin
Balscadden	Balbriggan	Dublin
Balydonohoe	Ballybunion	Kerry
Banagher	Gallen and Reynagh	Offaly
Banagher	Tisaron and Galen	Offaly
Banbridge	Tullylish	Down
Banbridge	Seapatrick	Down
Bandon	Desertserges	Cork
Bannow	Carrick on Bannow	Wexford
Bansha	Bansha and Kilmoyler	Tipperary
Barefield	Doora and Kilraghtis	Clare
Barna	Moneygall	Offaly Tipperary
Barnderrig	Kilbride	Wicklow
Barntown	Glinn	Wexford
Barryroe	Lislee	Cork
Baslic	Ogulla	Roscommon
Batterstown	Kilcock	Meath
Belenagare	Frenchpark	Roscommon
Belgooly	Ballingarry	Cork
Belgooly	Ballymartle	Cork
Belgooly	Clountead, Ballingarry and Ballymartle	Cork
Bellaghy	Ballyscullion	Derry
Belleek	Carn	Donegal Fermanagh
Belturbet	Annagh	Cavan
Benown	Kilkenny West	Westmeath
Beragh	Ballintacker	Tyrone
Bessbrook	Killeavy Lower	Armagh
Birdhill	Newport	Tipperary
Blackditches	Boystown	Wicklow
Blacklion	Beauparc	Meath
Blackrock	Haggardstown	Louth
Bodyke	Kilnoe	Clare
Boher	Murroe, Boher and Abington	Limerick Tipperary
Bohermore	Ballybricken and Bohermore	Limerick
Bohermore	St. Nicholas East	Galway
Bonniconlon	Kilgarvin	Mayo

Variant Name	Map Name	County
Boolavogue	Monageer	Wexford
Borris	Moycarkey	Tipperary
Botha	Devonish	Fermanagh
Bournea	Bournea and Corbally	Offaly Tipperary
Boyertown	Bohermeen	Meath
Boystown	Blackditches	Wicklow
Breaghwy	Castlebar	Mayo
Breedogue	Ballinameen	Roscommon
Brigown	Mitchelstown	Cork
Broadford	Drumcollogher	Limerick
Brookeborough	Aghavea	Fermanagh
Bruckless	Killaghtee	Donegal
Bulgadine	Bulgaden	Limerick
Bullaun	NewInn	Galway
Bumlin	Tarmonbarry	Roscommon
Bunclody	Newtownbarry	Wexford
Buncrana	Desertegney	Donegal
Bundoran	Innismacsaint	Donegal Fermanagh
Bunninadden	Kilshalvey	Mayo Sligo
Burgess	Youghal Arra	Tipperary
Bushmills	Portrush	Antrim
Caharagh	Caheragh	Cork
Caherlistrane	Donaghpatrick	Galway
Cahirivahalla	Cahirnorry	Limerick
Callen	Millstreet	Cork
Calry	Sligo: St. John's	Sligo
Caltra	Aughanagh	Sligo
Cam	Kiltomb	Roscommon
Camp	Ballanvohir	Kerry
Camus	Clonleigh	Donegal Tyrone
Cannavee	Kilmurry	Cork
Cape Clear	Rath and The Islands	Cork
Cappah	Kilcornan	Limerick
Capppagh	Modeligo	Waterford
Carigdonan	Kildorrery	Cork
Carn	Lady's Island	Wexford
Carna	Moyrus	Galway
Carnacon	Burriscarra	Mayo
Carnagh	Old Ross	Wexford
Carnew	Tomacork	Wicklow Wexford
Carolanstown	Kilbeg	Meath
Carrabane	Carabane	Galway
Carrabrown	Castlegar	Galway
Carrah	Ballyvaughan	Clare
Carraroe	Lettermullin	Galway
Carraroe	Sligo: St. John's	Sligo
Carrick	Glencolmkille	Donegal
Carrickerry	Ardagh	Limerick
Carrick–finea	Drumlumman South	Cavan

Variant Name	Map Name	County
Carrickmacross	Maghaire Rois	Louth Monaghan
Carrickmacross	Magheracloone	Monaghan
Carrickmore	Termonmacguirk	Tyrone
Carrick–on–Shannon	Kiltoghart	Leitrim
Carrigart	Mevagh	Donegal
Castleblayney	Muckno	Monaghan
Castlecarberry	Carbury and Dunforth	Kildare
Castlederg	Ardstraw West	Tyrone
Castlegregory	Killiny	Kerry
Castleiny	Loughmore and Castleiny	Tipperary
Castlemahon	Mahoonagh	Limerick
Castlemaine	Keel	Kerry
Castlerea	Kilkeevin	Roscommon
Castletown	Offerlane	Laois
Castletownarra	Portroe	Tipperary
Castletowndelvin	Delvin	Westmeath
Castleventry	Kilmeen	Cork S–W
Castlewarren	Pitt	Kilkenny
Cathedral parish	Waterford city: Holy Trinity	Waterford
Causeway	Killury	Kerry
Cavan	Urney	Cavan
Chapel	Killegney	Wexford
Chapel Lane	St. Mary's	Belfast city
Chapel–Russel	Kildimo	Limerick
Charlestown	Kilbeagh	Mayo
Christ Church	St Finbarr's (South)	Cork city
Chuchtown	Dysart	Westmeath
Churchtown	Liscarroll	Cork
Churchtown	Cloyne	Cork
Cilcornan	Kilcornan	Limerick
Clanvaraghan	Drumaroad	Down
Claragh	Pitt	Kilkenny
Clare	Tullylish	Down
Clare Abbey	Killone	Clare
Clarecastle	Killone	Clare
Claremorris	Kilcolman	Mayo
Claudy	Cumber Upper	Tyrone Derry
Cleariestown	Rathangan	Wexford
Clenor	Annakissy	Cork
Clifden	Omey	Galway
Cliffoney	Ahamlish	Sligo
Clodiagh	Inistioge	Kilkenny
Clogagh	Timoleague	Cork
Clogh	Clough	Kilkenny
Cloghan	Kilteevogue	Donegal
Cloghan	Gallen and Reynagh	Offaly
Clogher	Clonoulty	Tipperary
Clogherhead	Clogher	Louth
Clogherny	Carlingford	Louth

Variant Name	Map Name	County
Cloghogue	Killeavy Upper	Armagh
Cloghue	Killeavy Upper	Armagh
Clohanes	Killiny	Kerry
Clonaff	Aughrim	Roscommon
Clonaghdoo	Mountmellick	Laois
Clonaliz	Ardcath	Meath
Clonalvey	Ardcath	Meath
Clonbur	Ross	Galway
Cloncue	Woodford	Galway
Clondegad	Kilchrist	Clare
Clonduff	Clonuff	Down
Clonea	Mothel and Rathgormack	Waterford
Clonea	O'Callaghan's Mills	Clare
Cloneen	Drangan	Tipperary
Clonkeen Kyrie	Ballymacward	Galway
Clonkeenkerrill	Ballymacward	Galway
Clonlara	Doonass and Truagh	Clare
Clonmeen	Banteer	Cork
Clonmore	Templemore	Tipperary
Clontarf	Artane	Dublin
Cloonclare	Clooneclare	Leitrim
Clooney	Kilmanaheen	Clare
Clooney	Quin	Clare
Cloonfinlough	Strokestown	Roscommon
Cloonoghill	Kilshalvey	Mayo Sligo
Clostaken	Carabane	Galway
Cloughbawn	Killegney	Wexford
Cloughmills	Dunloy	Antrim
Clouncagh	Knockaderry	Limerick
Clouney	Quin	Clare
Clountead	Ballingarry	Cork
Clountead	Ballymartle	Cork
Cloverhill	Oran	Galway Roscommon
Cluan–a–Donald	Killashee	Longford
Coachford	Aghabulloge	Cork
Colmanswell	Ballyagran	Cork Limerick
Colmcille East	Scrabby	Cavan Longford
Comber	Newtownards	Down
Connor	Drumaul	Antrim
Cookstown	Desertcreight	Derry Tyrone
Coolaney	Killoran	Sligo
Coolcappa	Kilcolman	Limerick
Coolderry	Aghancon	Offaly
Coole	Mayne	Westmeath
Cooleavota	Kanturk	Cork
Coolera	Sligo: St. John's	Sligo
Cooley	Carlingford South	Louth
Cooline	Ballyhea	Cork
Coolmeen	Kilfiddane	Clare

Variant Name	Map Name	County
Coolock	Artane	Dublin
Cooraclare	Kilmacduane	Clare
Cootehill	Drumgoon	Cavan
Corbally	Bournea and Corbally	Tipperary Offaly
Corbally	Roscrea	Tipperary Offaly
Corlough	Drumreilly Lower	Cavan Leitrim
Corofin	Rath	Clare
Cortown	Bohermeen	Meath
Couraganeen	Bournea and Corbally	Tipperary Offaly
Courcey's Country	Ringrone	Cork
Craiga	Culfeightrin	Antrim
Craiga	Cushendun	Antrim
Cranagh	Badoney Upper	Tyrone
Creagh	Skibbereen	Cork
Creagh and Kilclooney	Ballinasloe	Galway Roscommon
Crecora	Mungret	Limerick
Creeve	Elphin	Roscommon
Creggan	Faughanvale	Derry
Creggs	Glinsk	Galway Roscommon
Croghan	Killucan	Roscommon
Crooke	Killea	Waterford
Crookstown	Narraghmore	Kildare
Crosgar	Kilmore	Down
Crossmaglen	Creggan Upper	Armagh Louth
Crowinstown	Delvin	Westmeath
Cruisetown	Nobber	Meath
Cuffe's Grange	Danesfort	Kilkenny
Cúl Máine	Magheraculmany	Fermanagh
Culallen	Dunshaughlin	Meath
Culduff	Culdaff	Donegal
Culfreightrin	Culfeightrin	Antrim
Cullen	Millstreet	Cork
Cullyhanna	Creggan Lower	Armagh
Culmaine	Magheraculmany	Fermanagh
Cumber Lower	Faughanvale	Derry
Cummer	Kilmoylan (and Kilcummer)	Galway
Curragha	Donymore	Meath
Curraghroe	Clontuskert	Roscommon
Currens	Killeentierna	Kerry
Currin	Drumully	Fermanagh Monaghan
Cushendall	Layde	Antrim
Cushinstown	Old Ross	Wexford
Cushleak	Cushendun	Antrim
Daingean	Philipstown	Offaly
Damastown	Naul	Dublin
Danaghcloney	Tullylish	Down
Dangan	Killeagh	Cork
Darara	Clonakilty	Cork
Derby Street, Belfast	St. Peter's	Belfast city

Variant Name	Map Name	County
Derriaghy	Hannastown, Rock and Derriaghy	Antrim
Derry city	St. Columb's	Derry
Derrybrien	Ballinakill (East Galway)	Galway
Derrygonnelly	Devonish	Fermanagh
Derrykeighan	Ballymoney	Antrim Derry
Derrylin	Knockninny	Fermanagh
Derryloran	Desertcreight	Derry Tyrone
Derrymacash	Seagoe	Armagh
Derryvullen	Irvinestown	Fermanagh
Desertlin	Ardtrea and Desertlin	Derry Tyrone
Desertmore	Ovens	Cork
Desertoghill	Kilrea	Derry
Devenish	Devonish	Fermanagh
Devenish West	Carn	Donegal Fermanagh
Doe	Clondahorkey	Donegal
Donagh	Carndonagh	Donegal
Donaghcavey	Donacavey	Tyrone
Donaghmore	Donoughmore	Down
Donaghmore	Cahirnorry	Limerick
Donanaghta	Clonfert	Galway
Donapatrick	Oristown	Meath
Donard	Dunlavin	Wicklow
Donegal	Killymard	Donegal
Donegall Street	St. Patrick's	Belfast city
Donemagan	Dunamaggan	Kilkenny
Donemana	Donaghedy	Tyrone
Donfort	Carbury and Dunforth	Kildare
Donfort	Carbury and Dunforth	Kildare
Doniry	Ballinakill (East Galway)	Galway
Donoghmore	Donymore	Meath
Donoghmore	Tullyallen	Tyrone
Donohill	Anacarty and Donohill	Tipperary
Donoughmore	Cahirnorry	Limerick
Donoughmore	Donaghmore	Cork
Donoughmore	Lislee	Cork
Donoughpatrick	Donaghpatrick	Galway
Doonbeg	Killard	Clare
Doonfeeny	Ballycastle	Mayo
Dourus	Templenoe	Kerry
Douth	Rathkenny	Meath
Down	Downpatrick	Down
Downings	Caragh	Kildare
Draperstown	Ballinascreen	Derry
Drimacoo	Ballindereen	Galway
Drinagh	Drimoleague	Cork
Drogheda	Drogheda: St. Peter's	Louth
Dromahaire	Drumlease	Leitrim
Dromiskin	Darver	Louth
Drum	Athlone: St. Peter's	Roscommon

Variant Name	Map Name	County
Drum	Balla	Mayo
Drumachose	Limavady	Derry
Drumacoo	Ballindereen	Galway
Drumall	Drumaul	Antrim
Drumballyroney	Annaghlone	Down
Drumcondrath	Drumconrath	Meath
Drumconra	Drumconrath	Meath
Drumcullen	Eglish	Offaly
Drumglass	Dungannon	Armagh Tyrone
Drumhome	Drumholm	Donegal
Drumkeen	Newport	Tipperary
Drumkeerin	Ennismagrath	Leitrim
Drumlumman North	Mullahoran	Cavan
Drummin	Aughaval	Mayo
Drumoghill	All Saints	Donegal
Drumquin	Langfield	Tyrone
Drumshanbo	Murhan	Leitrim
Dualla	Boherlahan	Tipperary Sth
Duhill	Ballylooby	Tipperary Sth
Dun Laoghaire	Kingstown	Dublin
Dunamanagh	Donaghedy	Tyrone
Dunamon	Glinsk	Galway Roscommon
Dunbin	Haggardstown	Louth
Dunboe	Coleraine	Antrim Derry
Duncormuck	Rathangan	Wexford
Dundrum	Tyrella	Down
Dunfanaghy	Clondahorkey	Donegal
Duniry	Ballinakill (East Galway)	Galway
Dunkerrin	Moneygall	Offaly Tipperary
Dunmore East	Killea	Waterford
Dunnelin	Kilmelchidar	Kerry
Dunquin	Kilmelchidar	Kerry
Dunsany	Killeen	Meath
Durrow	Lorrha and Dorrha	Tipperary
Durrow	Tullamore	Westmeath Offaly
Durrus	Muintervarra	Cork
Dury	Doora and Kilraghtis	Clare
Dysart	Ruan	Clare
Dysart Galen	Ballynakill	Laois
Eadestown	Naas	Kildare
Ederney	Magheraculmany	Fermanagh
Edgeworthstown	Mostrim	Longford
Eglish	Borrisokane	Tipperary
Emphrick	Ballyhea	Cork
Ennis	Drumclift	Clare
Enniskeen	Kingscourt	Cavan Meath
Ennispollen	Cushendun	Antrim
Ennistymon	Kilmanaheen	Clare
Errigal Trough	Errigal Truagh	Monaghan Tyrone

Variant Name	Map Name	County
Erris	Bangor Erris	Mayo
Erritt	Loughglynn	Roscommon
Estersnow	Ballinameen	Roscommon
Eveleary	Iveleary	Cork
Eyrecourt	Clonfert	Galway
Fahan	Burt	Donegal
Fairymount	Tibohine	Roscommon
Falls Road	St. Paul's	Belfast city
Fanad	Clondavadoc	Donegal
Farrihy	Kildorrery	Cork
Faughalstown	Mayne	Westmeath
Feeny	Banagher	Derry
Fehonagh	Mahoonagh	Limerick
Ferbane	Tisaron and Galen	Offaly
Finlagan	Limavady	Derry
Finney	Kilbride	Galway
Fintona	Donacavey	Tyrone
Fintown	Inniskeel	Donegal
Firies	Molahiff	Kerry
Fivemiletown	Aughintaine	Tyrone
Flagmount	Caher Feakle	Clare
Fletcherstown	Castletown–Kilpatrick	Meath
Fore	Collinstown	Westmeath
Fourmilehouse	Kilbride	Roscommon
Fourmilewater	Newcastle	Tipperary Waterford
Foxford	Toomore	Mayo
Foynes	Shanagolden	Limerick
Francis St.	St. Nicholas' (Without)	Dublin city
Frenchpark	Belenagare	Roscommon
Fuerty	Athleague	Roscommon Galway
Fuithre	Tisaron and Galen	Offaly
Galen	Tisaron and Galen	Offaly
Gallow	Summerhill	Meath
Galtrim	Moynalvey	Meath
Gargory	Drumgooland Lower	Down
Garrycloyne	Blarney	Cork
Garvagh	Errigal	Derry
Garvaghey	Dromore	Down
Garvaghy	Annaghlone	Down
Gaynstown	Mullingar	Westmeath
Geesala	Bangor Erris	Mayo
Gilford	Tullylish	Down
Glanamanagh	New Quay	Clare
Glantane	Glountane	Cork
Glasdrummond	Mourne Lower	Down
Glasslough	Donagh	Monaghan
Glasson	Nougheval	Westmeath
Glenamaddy	Boyounagh	Galway
Glenaragh	Ballyvaughan	Clare

Variant Name	Map Name	County
Glenavy	Glenavy and Killead	Antrim
Glenbrien	Oylegate	Wexford
Glenbrohane	Knocklong and Glenbrohane	Limerick
Glenbryan	Oylegate	Wexford
Glendermott	Derry city: Waterside	Derry
Glenfin	Kilteevogue	Donegal
Glengoole	Gortnahoe	Tipperary
Glenisland	Islandeady	Mayo
Glenswilly	Conwal and Leck	Donegal
Glynn	Glinn	Wexford
Goggins	Ballinhassig	Cork
Goleen	Schull West	Cork
Goresbridge	Paulstown	Kilkenny
Gorteen	Ballymacward and Clonkeenkerrill	Galway
Gorthlethra	Gortletteragh	Leitrim
Gortin	Badoney Lower and Greencastle	Tyrone
Gortroe	Rathcormack	Cork
Gowel	Kiltoghart	Leitrim
Grague	Carlow	Carlow Kildare
Graig	Graignamanagh	Carlow Kilkenny
Graigue	Killeshin	Laois
Graiguecullen	Killeshin	Laois
Graine	Urlingford	Kilkenny
Granagh	Ballingarry	Limerick
Grane	Urlingford	Kilkenny
Grange	Carlingford South	Louth
Grange	New Inn	Galway
Grangegeeth	Rathkenny	Meath
Grangemockler	Ballyneale	Tipperary Sth
Grenagh	Mourneabbey	Cork
Gurteen	Kilfree and Killaraght	Sligo
Gweedore	Tullaghobegley West	Donegal
Hagerstown	Haggardstown	Louth
Halston St.	St. Nicholas Without	Dublin city
Hannastown	Hannastown, Rock and Derriaghy	Antrim
Headford	Killursa and Killower	Galway
Herbertstown	Hospital	Limerick
Hilltown	Clonuff	Down
Hollyford	Kilcommon	Tipperary
Hollymount	Kilcommon and Robeen	Mayo
Holmpatrick	Skerries	Dublin
Holy Family	Dublin city: Aughrim St.	Dublin city
Horeswood	Suttons	Wexford
Imolagga	Kildorrery	Cork
Inch	Burt	Donegal
Inch	Drom and Inch	Tipperary
Inch	Kilmaley	Clare
Inch	Burt	Donegal
Inchicronan	Crusheen	Clare

Variant Name	Map Name	County
Inchigeelagh	Iveleary	Cork
Inis Caoin Locha Eirne	Enniskillen	Fermanagh
Inis Muighe Saimh	Garrison	Fermanagh
Innishargy	Ardkeen	Down
Innismagrath	Ennismagrath	Leitrim
Irremore	Lixnaw	Kerry
Island	Lady's Island	Wexford
James' St.	Dublin city: St. James'	Dublin city
Johnstown	Balyna	Kildare
Keadue	Kilronan	Roscommon
Keady	Derrynoose	Armagh
Keash	Drumrat	Sligo
Keelgarrylauder	Keel	Kerry
Kenmare	Templenoe	Kerry
Kilawalla	Burriscarra	Mayo
Kilballyowen	Carrigaholt	Clare
Kilbannon	Kilconly	Galway
Kilbarrack	Baldoyle	Dublin
Kilbarron	Terryglass	Galway Tipperary
Kilbarry	Oristown	Meath
Kilbarrymeeden	Rossmore	Waterford
Kilbegnet	Glinsk	Galway Roscommon
Kilbonane	Kilmurry	Cork
Kilbraghtis	Doora and Kilraghtis	Clare
Kilbride	Clara and Horseleap	Offaly Westmeath
Kilbride	Donymore	Meath
Kilbride	Dunboyne	Meath
Kilbrin	Ballyclough	Cork
Kilbrogan	Bandon	Cork
Kilbryan	Boyle	Roscommon
Kilcameen	Oranmore	Galway
Kilcash	Gambonsfield	Tipperary Sth
Kilcleagh	Moate	Offaly Westmeath
Kilcloon	Kilcock	Meath
Kilclooney	Ballinasloe	Galway Roscommon
Kilcluney	Ballymacnab	Armagh
Kilcolman	Aghancon	Offaly
Kilcolman	Castlemore and Kilcolman	Sligo, Mayo Roscommon
Kilcommuck	Kilcomoge	Longford
Kilconduff and Meelick	Swineford	Mayo
Kilconickny	Carabane	Galway
Kilconieran	Carabane	Galway
Kilconnell	Aughrim	Galway
Kilcooley	Leitrim	Galway
Kilcooly	Ogulla	Roscommon
Kilcoony	Donaghpatrick	Galway
Kilcorkey	Belenagare and Frenchpark	Roscommon
Kilcormac	Balliboy and Killoughy	Offaly
Kilcornan	Clarenbridge	Galway

Variant Name	Map Name	County
Kilcorny	Carron	Clare
Kilcreehy	Liscannor	Clare
Kilcrohane	Muintervarra	Cork
Kilcrone	Ballintubber and Balllymoe	Roscommon
Kilcronin	Carron	Clare
Kilcummer	Kilmoylan	
Kilcummin	Oughterard	Galway
Kilcurley	Haggardstown	Louth
Kildrumsherdan	Kilsherdany	Cavan
Kilfarboy	Milltownmalbay	Clare
Kilfaughnabeg	Kilmacabea	Cork
Kilfeacle	Golden	Tipperary Sth
Kilfearagh	Kilkee	Clare
Kilfeary	Kilkee	Clare
Kilfinny	Croagh	Limerick
Kilgarvan	Kilgarvin	Mayo
Kilgefin	Clontuskert	Roscommon
Kilgerrill	Fohenagh	Galway
Kilglass	Legan	Longford
Kilimy	Knockera	Clare
Kilkeranmore	Roscarberry	Cork
Kilkerley	Haggardstown	Louth
Kill	Philipstown	Offaly
Kill	Rossmore	Waterford
Kill	Tubber	Offaly Westmeath
Killaan	New Inn	Galway
Killabin	Arles	Laois
Killaderry	Philipstown	Offaly
Killalaghtan	Cappataggle	Galway
Killalon	Clonmellon	Meath Westmeath
Killaloo	Ballycallan	Kilkenny
Killan	Clonmellon	Meath Westmeath
Killanena	Caher Feakle	Clare
Killann	Killegney	Wexford
Killann	Rathnure and Templeudigan	Wexford
Killannin	Killanin	Galway
Killany	Killanny	Monaghan
Killaraght	Kilfree and Killaraght	Sligo
Killavullen	Annakissy	Cork
Killea	All Saints	Donegal
Killea	Templemore	Tipperary
Killead	Glenavy and Killead	Antrim
Killeagh	Delvin	Westmeath
Killeagha	Kilbride and Mountnugent	Westmeath, Cavan, Meath
Killeany	Lisdoonvarna	Clare
Killeen	Lettermullin	Galway
Killeenavara	Ballindereen	Galway
Killeroran	Killian	Galway
Killery	Killenummery	Leitrim Sligo

Variant Name	Map Name	County
Killichel	Tullyallen	Tyrone
Killilagh	Lisdoonvarna	Clare
Killilla	Blackwater	Wexford
Killimer	Knockera	Clare
Killimorbologe	Killimore and Tiranascragh	Galway
Killimoredaly	Kiltullagh	Galway
Killina	Ogulla	Roscommon
Killira	Craughwell	Galway
Killishall	Tullyallen	Tyrone
Killodiernan	Monsea	Tipperary
Killofin	Kilmurry McMahon	Clare
Killogileen	Craughwell	Galway
Killokennedy	Broadford	Clare
Killora	Craughwell	Galway
Killoran	Mullagh	Galway
Killoscully	Ballinahinch and Killoscully	Tipperary
Killoscully	Newport	Tipperary
Killosolan	Ahascragh	Galway
Killoughter	Annagh	Cavan
Killoughy	Balliboy and Killoughy	Offaly
Killowen	Coleraine	Antrim Derry
Killsha	Glenflesk	Kerry
Killukin	Ogulla	Roscommon
Killulagh	Delvin	Westmeath
Killumod	Killucan	Roscommon
Killusty	Fethard	Tipperary Sth
Killygordon	Cappagh	Tyrone
Killygordon	Donaghmore	Donegal
Killyman	Dungannon	Armagh Tyrone
Killyon	Killine	Meath
Kilmacduagh	Gort	Galway
Kilmacshalgan	Templeboy	Sligo
Kilmain	Killinvoy	Roscommon
Kilmainham Wood	Moybologue	Cavan Meath
Kilmalinoge	Portumna	Galway
Kilmanagh	Ballycallan	Kilkenny
Kilmanahan	Tubber	Offaly Westmeath
Kilmannon	Rathangan	Wexford
Kilmarshal	Marshalstown	Wexford
Kilmeague	Allen and Milltown	Kildare
Kilmeedy	Feenagh	Limerick
Kilmeen	Boherbue	Cork Kerry
Kilmeen	Leitrim	Galway
Kilmegan	Drumaroad	Down
Kilmessan	Killeen	Meath
Kilmoe	Schull West	Cork
Kilmoon	Lisdoonvarna	Clare
Kilmore	Aughrim	Roscommon
Kilmore	Silvermines	Tipperary

Variant Name	Map Name	County
Kilmoyler	Bansha and Kilmoyler	Tipperary
Kilmoyley	Ardfert	Kerry
KIlmuckridge	Litter	Wexford
Kilmurry	See also Ogulla	Roscommon
Kilmurry	Baslick	Roscommon
Kilmurry	Kilquade	Wicklow
Kilnabionogue	Portumna	Galway
Kilnaboy	Rath	Clare
Kilnadeema	Killeenadeema	Galway
Kilnamanach	Ballinameen	Roscommon
Kilnancavc	Templederry	Tipperary
Kilnelehan	Ballinakill (East Galway)	Galway
Kilpatrick	Castletown–Kilpatrick	Meath
Kilquain	Fahy (& Kilquain)	Galway
Kilrane	Tagoat	Wexford
Kilreaghtis	Doora and Kilraghtis	Clare
Kilrickill	Cappataggle	Galway
Kilronan	Killian and Killeroran	Galway
Kilronan	Newcastle	Tipperary Waterford
Kilrooskey	Clontuskert	Roscommon
Kilrush	St. Senan's	Clare
Kilseily	Broadford	Clare
Kilshanny	Lisdoonvarna	Clare
Kilsheelan	Gambonsfield and Kilcash	Tipperary Waterford
Kilskerry	Kilskeery	Monaghan Tyrone
Kiltalla	Keel	Kerry
Kiltane	Bangor Erris	Mayo
Kiltartan	Gort	Galway
Kilteskil	Killeenadeema	Galway
Kilteskin	Cloyne	Cork
Kilthomas	Peterswell	Galway
Kiltimagh	Killedan	Mayo
KIltoom	Kiltomb	Roscommon
Kiltoraght	Kilfenora	Clare
Kiltoraghta	Kilfenora	Clare
Kiltrustan	Strokestown	Roscommon
Kiltullagh	Kiltulla	Roscommon
Kilturra	Kilshalvey	Mayo Sligo
Kilure	Fohenagh	Galway
Kilvarnet	Ballysodare and Kilvarnet	Sligo
Kilvenogue	Templemore	Tipperary
Kilwarlin	Magheralinn	Armagh Down
Kinalea	Tracton Abbey	Cork
Kinawley	Kinnally	Cavan Fermanagh
Kingwilliamstown	Ballydesmond	Cork
Kinnitty	Roscumroe	Offaly
Kinsealy	Baldoyle	Dublin
Kircubbin	Ardkeen	Down
Knockanure	Moyane	Kerry

Variant Name	Map Name	County
Knockcroghery	Killinvoy	Roscommon
Knockea	Cahirnorry	Limerick
Knockeany	Knockany and Patrickswell	Limerick
Knockgordegur	Abbeyleix and Ballyroan	Kilkenny Laois
Knockgraffon	New Inn and Knockgraffon	Tipperary
Kyle	Roscrea	Tipperary Offaly Laois
Lack	Ballanvohir	Kerry
Lackaroe	Roscumroe	Offaly
Lanesboro	Rathcline	Longford
Lattin	Cullen and Latten	Tipperary
Latton	Aughnamullen West	Monaghan
Laurencetown	Kiltormer	Galway
Lavey	Termoneeny	Derry
Leany	Multifarnham	Westmeath
Leap	Kilmacabea	Cork
Learmount	Cumber Upper	Derry Tyrone
Lecanvey	Aughaval	Mayo
Leck	Ballanvohir	Kerry
Leenane	Kilbride	Galway
Leenane	Ross	Galway
Leighlin	Leighlinbridge	Carlow
Leitrim	Drumgooland Upper	Down
Leixlip	Maynooth	Dublin Kildare
Leixnaw	Lixnaw	Kerry
Lemanaghan	Ballinahown	Offaly Westmeath
Letterfrack	Ballinakill	Galway
Letterkenny	Conwal and Leck	Donegal
Lettermacaward	Dungloe	Donegal
Lickblea	Castlepollard	Westmeath
Lickerrig	Carabane	Galway
Lickmolassy	Portumna	Galway
Lifford	Clonleigh	Donegal Tyrone
Lisacul	Loughglynn	Roscommon
Lisbouny	Nenagh	Tipperary
Lisburn	Blaris	Antrim Down
Liskeevy	Addergoole	Galway
Lisnaskea	Aughalurcher	Fermanagh Tyrone
Lisonuffy	Strokestown	Roscommon
Lisronagh	Powerstown	Tipperary
Lissevard	Roscarberry	Cork
Litter	Roscumroe	Offaly
Long Tower	Derry city: St. Columb's	Derry
Longford	Templemichael	Longford
Longwood	Killine	Meath
Lough Egish	Aughnamullen East	Monaghan
Lough Gowna	Scrabby	Cavan Longford
Loughbracken	Drumconrath	Meath
Loughcrew	Oldcastle	Meath
Loughduff	Mullahoran	Cavan

Variant Name	Map Name	County
Loughilly	Loughgilly	Armagh
Loughkeen	Birr	Offaly
Louisburg	Kilgeever	Mayo
Lower Exchange St.	Dublin city: St. Michael and John's	Dublin city
Lower Fahan	Desertegney	Donegal
Lurgan	Shankill	Armagh
Lynally	Rahan	Offaly
Lyons	Kill	Kildare
Macosquin	Coleraine	Antrim Derry
Maghene	Innismacsaint	Donegal Fermanagh
Maghera	Bryansford and Newcastle	Down
Magheradroll	Ballynahinch and Dunmore	Down
Magherally	Tullylish	Down
Magherow	Drumcliff	Sligo
Magilligan	Tamlaghtard	Derry
Maguiresbridge	Aughalurcher	Fermanagh Tyrone
Malin	Clonca	Donegal
Malin	Clonca	Donegal
Manister	Fedamore	Limerick
Manorhamilton	Clooneclare	Leitrim
Manulla	Balla	Mayo
Marhin	Kilmelchidar	Kerry
Market St.	Galway city: St. Nicholas North	Galway
Marshallstown	Mitchelstown	Cork
Mayglass	Ballymore	Wexford
Meath St.	Dublin city: St. Catherine's	Dublin city
Meelick	Clonfert	Galway
Meelick	Limerick city: Parteen	Limerick city Clare
Meelick	Swineford	Mayo
Menlough	KIllascobe	Galway
Middle St.	St. Nicholas South and West	Galway
Middletown	Tynan	Armagh
Milford	Freemount	Cork Limerick
Milltown	Addergoole	Galway
Minolla	Balla	Mayo
Mohill–Manachain	Mohill	Leitrim Longford
Moilough	Oldcastle	Meath
Moira	Magheralinn	Armagh Down
Monanimy	Annakissy	Cork
Monegay	Monagea	Limerick
Moneymore	Ardtrea and Desertlin	Derry Tyrone
Monivea	Abbeyknockmoy	Galway
Monknewtown	Rathkenny	Meath
Mount Collins	Tournafulla	Limerick
Mountbellew	Moylough	Galway
Mountshannon	Clonrush	Clare Galway
Mourintown	Piercetown	Wexford
Mourneabbey	Grenagh	Cork
Moviddy	Kilmurry	Cork

Variant Name	Map Name	County
Moville Upper	Iskaheen	Donegal
Moy	Clonfeacle	Armagh Tyrone
Moydow	Ardagh and Moydow	Longford
Moyglass	Ballymore	Wexford
Moyglass	Killenaule	Tipperary Sth
Moyloughy	Oldcastle	Meath
Moynalvy	Moynalvey	Meath
Moynoe	Scarriff	Clare
Muckarky	Moycarkey	Tipperary
Muinbheag	Bagenalstown	Carlow
Mulavilly	Kilmore	Armagh
Mullagh	Kilmurry Ibricken	Clare
Mullaghbawn	Forkhill	Armagh
Mullaghbrac	Ballymore and Mullabrack	Armagh
Mullinalaghta	Scrabby	Cavan Longford
Mulogh	Newcastle	Tipperary Waterford
Murhaun	Murhan	Leitrim
Murrinstown	Piercetown	Wexford
Myross	Castlehaven	Cork
Nalnagar	Killeigh	Offaly
New Glanmire	Glounthane	Cork
Newbawn	Adamstown	Wexford
Newbliss	Killeevan	Monaghan
Newbridge	Avoca	Wicklow
Newbridge	Killian and Killeroran	Galway
Newport	Burrishoole	Mayo
Newtonwbutler	Galloon	Fermanagh
Newtown	Rossmore	Waterford
Newtown	Kilcock	Kildare
Newtown	Dunleckney	Carlow
Newtowncashel	Cashel	Longford
Newtowncunningham	All Saints	Donegal
Newtownforbes	Clongish	Longford
Newtownhamilton	Creggan Lower	Armagh
Newtownsandes	Moyvane	Kerry
Newtownstewart	Ardstraw East	Tyrone
Nohaval	Ballymacelligot	Kerry
Nohill	Kilkenny West	Westmeath
North Anne St.	St. Michan's	Dublin city
North William St.	St. Agatha's	Dublin city
Nurney	Monasterevan	Kildare
O'Brennan	Ballymacelligot	Kerry
Oghill	Laurencetown	Galway
Oilgate	Oylegate	Wexford
Old Glasnevin	Dublin city: St. Paul's	Dublin city
Omagh	Drumragh	Tyrone
Oning	Owning and Templeorum	Kilkenny
Oola	Sologhead	Limerick Tipperary
Oughavall	Aughaval	Mayo

Variant Name	Map Name	County
Oulart	The Ballagh	Wexford
Pallaskenry	Kildimo	Limerick
Patrick's Well	Knockany and Patrickswell	Limerick
Patrick's Well	Lurriga	Limerick
Pettigo	Carn	Donegal Fermanagh
Piltown	Owning and Templeorum	Kilkenny
Plumbridge	Badoney Upper	Tyrone
Pobal	Tempo	Fermanagh
Pollough	Ballinahown	Offaly Westmeath
Portadown	Drumcree	Armagh
Portaferry	Ballyphillip	Down
Portglenone	Greenlough	Derry
Portlaoise	Maryborough	Laois
Portrane	Donabate	Dublin
Prince's Dock	St. Joseph's	Belfast city
Pubblebrien	Lurriga	Limerick
Puckane	Monsea	Tipperary
Queenstown	Cobh	Cork
Rackwallis	Monaghan	Monaghan
Rahara	Killinvoy	Roscommon
Raharney	Killucan	Westmeath
Raheen	Killeigh	Offaly
Raheenagh	Killeedy	Limerick
Ramelton	Aughnish	Donegal
Ramsgrange	St. James and Hook	Wexford
Randalstown	Drumaul	Antrim
Rathaspick	Rathaspick and Russagh	Westmeath
Rathberry	Ardfield and Rathberry	Cork
Rathclareen	Kilbrittain	Cork
Rathcoffey	Clane	Kildare
Rathfeigh	Skryne	Meath
Rathgarraf	Castlepollard	Westmeath
Rathkyran	Carrigeen and Mooncoin	Kilkenny
Rathmullen	Killygarvan	Donegal
Rathowen	Rathaspick and Russagh	Westmeath
Rathregan	Dunboyne	Meath
Rathwine	Killucan	Westmeath
Ratoo	Killury	Kerry
Ravensdale	Lordship	Louth
Raymoghey or St. Johnston	All Saints	Donegal
Raymunterdoney	Gortahork	Donegal
Redcross	Avoca	Wicklow
Richhill	Kilmore	Armagh
Riverstown	Taunagh	Sligo
Robertstown	Shanagolden	Limerick
Rock	Hannastown, Rock and Derriaghy	Antrim
Rockcorry	Ematris	Monaghan
Rockhill	Bruree	Limerick
Rooskey	Tarmonbarry	Roscommon

Variant Name	Map Name	County
Ros Muc	Rosmuck	Galway
Rosbercon	Tullagher	Kilkenny
Roscomroe	Roscumroe	Offaly
Rosemount	Tubber	Offaly
Rosemount	Tubber	Westmeath
Roslea	Balla	Mayo
Roslee	Mayo Abbey	Mayo
Rosnaree	Donore	Meath
Ross	Roscarberry	Cork
Rosscahill	Killanin	Galway
Rosselettery	Roscarberry	Cork
Rosse's Point	Sligo: St. John's	Sligo
Rossmore	Clonoulty	Tipperary
Rostrevor	Kilbroney	Down
Roundfort	Kilcommon and Robeen	Mayo
Rowlestown	Rolestown	Dublin
Rushivee	Rathkenny	Meath
Rushivee	Slane	Meath
Russagh	Rathaspick and Russagh	Westmeath
Saintfield	Carrickmannon	
Santry	Artane	Dublin
Scotshouse	Drumully	Monaghan Fermanagh
Scramogue	Tarmonbarry	Roscommon
Screen	Castlebridge	Wexford
Seville Place	St. Laurence O'Toole's	Dublin city
Shanaglish	Beagh	Clare Galway
Shannonbridge	Clonmacnois	Offaly
Shanrahan	Clogheen	Tipperary
Sherkin	Rath and The Islands	Cork
Skerries	Holmpatrick	Dublin
Skerry	Glenravel	Antrim
St. Brendan's	Loughrea	Galway
St. Ibare,	Lady's Island	Wexford
St. John of Jerusalem	Cork city: St Finbarr's (South)	Cork city
St. John's	Killinvoy	Roscommon
St. John's	Coleraine	Derry Antrim
St. Joseph's	Berkeley Road	Dublin city
St. Kevin's	Harrington St.	Dublin city
St. Kyran	Seirkieran	Offaly
St. Margaret's	Lady's Island	Wexford
St. Margaret's	Finglas	Dublin
St. Mary's	Haddington Road	Dublin
St. Michael's	Ballinasloe	Roscommon Galway
St. Michael's and Stephen's	Holy Trinity	Waterford
St. Nicholas	St Finbarr's (South)	Cork city
St. Nicholas	Kildorrery	Cork
St. Patrick's	Tagoat	Wexford
St. Sylvester's	Malahide	Dublin
Staghall	Drumlane	Cavan Fermanagh

Variant Name	Map Name	County
Staholmock	Kilbeg	Meath
Staplestown	Rathcoffey	Kildare
Stewartstown	Coalisland	Tyrone
Stonehall	Kilcornan	Limerick
Strabane	Clonleigh	Donegal Tyrone
Strabane	Leckpatrick	Tyrone
Straide	Templemore	Mayo
Strandhill	Sligo: St. John's	Sligo
Sullon	Skibbereen	Cork
Swanlinbar	Kinnally	Cavan Fermanagh
Tacumshan	Lady's Island	Wexford
Taghshiney	Carrickedmond	Longford
Taghshinod	Carrickedmond	Longford
Tamlaght	Limavady	Derry
Tamlaght O'Crilly	Greenlough	Derry
Tamney	Clondavadoc	Donegal
Tandragee	Ballymore and Mullaghbrack	Armagh
Tang	Nougheval	Longford Westmeath
Tarbert	Kilnaughten	Kerry
Taughboyne	All Saints	Donegal
Templebredon	Pallasgreen and Templebredin	Limerick Tipperary
Templebrigid	Carrigaline	Cork
Templecrone Upper	Dungloe	Donegal
Templeganton	Templeglantine	Limerick
Templemaly	Doora and Kilraghtis	Clare
Templemartin	Murragh	Cork
Templemore	St. Columb's	Derry
Templemore	St. Eugene's Cathedral	Derry
Templeodigan	Killegney	Wexford
Templetenny	Clogheen	Tipperary
Templetown	St. James and Templetown	Wexford
Templetrine	Ringrone	Cork
Templetuohy	Moyne and Templetuohy	Tipperary
Termonmaguirk	Carrickmore	Tyrone
The Naule	Naul	Dublin
The Rower	Inistioge	Kilkenny
Threemilehouse	Drumsnat and Kilmore	Monaghan
Tickmacreevan	Glenarm	Antrim
Tintern	Ballycullane	Wexford
Tisrara	Dysart	Galway Roscommon
Toem	Cappawhite	Tipperary Nth
Tolerton	Mayo and Doonane	Laois
Tomgrany	Kilnoe	Clare
Tomregan	Kildallen	Cavan
Tomregan	Kildallen	Fermanagh
Tory Island	Gortahork	Donegal
Touclea, Towvahara	Lisdoonvarna	Clare
Touheran	Liscannor	Clare
Trillick	Kilskeery	Tyrone Monaghan

Variant Name	Map Name	County
Tritonville Road	Sandymount	Dublin
Tuagh	Beaufort	Kerry
Tuahnadroman	Kilnamartyra	Cork
Tuamgrany	Kilnoe	Clare
Tubber	Kilkeady	Clare
Tubber	Killkeady	Clare
Tubberclaire	Kilkenny West	Westmeath
Tullaghobegley East	Gortahork	Donegal
Tullaher	Tullagher	Kilkenny
Tullaherin	Thomastown	Kilkenny
Tullycross	Ballinakill	Galway
Tullyfern	Killygarvan	Donegal
Tullyniskin	Dungannon	Armagh Tyrone
Tullyorier	Annaghlone	Down
Tulsk	Kilmurry	Roscommon
Tulsk	Ogulla	Roscommon
Tumna	Cootehall	Roscommon
Tuogh	Beaufort	Kerry
Turanascragh	Killimore and Tiranascragh	Galway
Turbotstown	Mayne	Westmeath
Turin	Taghmon	Westmeath
Union	Moynalvey	Meath
Uskane	Borrisokane	Tipperary
Valleymount	Boystown	Wicklow
Virginia	Lurgan	Cavan
Walshestown	Clogher	Louth
Warrenpoint	Clonallon	Down
Washestown	Mullingar	Westmeath
Waterville	Dromod	Kerry
Westland Row	St. Andrew's	Dublin city
Westport	Aughaval	Mayo
Wheeragh	Tisaron and Galen	Offaly
Wheran	Castlepollard	Westmeath
Whitechurch	Blarney	Cork
Whitecross	Loughgilly	Armagh
Whitegate	Clonrush	Clare Galway
Whitehall	Irvinestown	Fermanagh
Whitehill	Irvinestown	Fermanagh
Whitehouse (Belfast city)	Greencastle	Antrim
Williamstown	Templetoher	Galway
Yellow Furze	Beauparc	Meath

Chapter 15 ~

RESEARCH SERVICES, SOCIETIES, REPOSITORIES AND PUBLISHERS

RESEARCH SERVICES

A. Professional Associations

Two associations of professional researchers exist: the Association of Ulster Genealogists and Record Agents (AUGRA), based exclusively in Northern Ireland; and the Association of Professional Genealogists in Ireland (APGI), with members north and south. Both bodies are principally concerned with upholding research standards rather than undertaking commercial research in their own right. The secretaries of both associations will supply a list of members on request.

- The Secretary, AUGRA, Glen Cottage, Glenmachan Road, Belfast BT4 2NP, Northern Ireland.
- The Secretary, APGI, c/o The Genealogical Office, 2 Kildare St, Dublin 2. *www.apgi.ie*

B. The Irish Genealogical Project (IGP)

In the early 1980s, as part of a series of government-sponsored youth employment and training schemes in the Republic of Ireland, local history and heritage societies and other interested bodies began to organise the indexing of local parish records. With some exceptions, at the outset little thought was given to the potential value of these records. In the mid-1980s the number of areas covered by the indexing projects grew, and their efforts were co-ordinated by an umbrella body, the Irish Family History Council, later to become the Irish Family History Foundation. An ambitious plan was drawn up under the aegis of this body to transcribe and computerise not only all of the parish records of all denominations for the entire country but also all other sources of major genealogical interest: the Tithe Books, Griffith's Valuation, the civil records of births, marriages and deaths, the 1901 and 1911 census returns and local gravestone inscriptions. Increased government funding was secured for this plan, known as The Irish Genealogical Project. In 1990 four centres in Northern Ireland were added and the International Fund for Ireland also became involved.

The overall aim of the Project was to realise the tourist potential of Irish genealogy by creating a single organisation that could combine the experience and expertise of professional genealogists with the speed and accuracy of the local databases to provide a comprehensive, affordable, Ireland-wide research service. Unfortunately, this aim is unlikely to be achieved in the foreseeable future. The very strengths that made the local centres possible—their voluntary ethos, diversity of funding and structure and solid local roots—have made it virtually impossible to co-ordinate their activities into a single service.

An umbrella body, Irish Genealogy Ltd, has made some progress in creating a single signposting index online at *www.irishgenealogy.ie*, allowing users who do not know an Irish county of origin to identify which centre holds the relevant records. As of May 2005 the index holds almost three million records, from ten centres. Unfortunately, though perhaps not surprisingly, not all of the remaining centres have agreed to co-operate with it.

That said, the local centres continue to index and to provide research services, and some of these services are excellent. None of the centres allows direct access to its records. Instead, all research is carried out by the centre, for a fee.

The list below also includes some centres that have not been directly involved in the IGP.

Area	Address	Comment
Antrim	Ulster Historical Foundation 12 College Square East Belfast BT1 6DD Northern Ireland Tel: +44 028 90 332288 Fax +44 028 90 239885 *www.ancestryireland.co.uk*	Full commissioned research service. The UHF is a long-established, highly reputable research and publishing agency. The website offers paying access to most of their records, including parish and GRO databases.
Armagh	Armagh Ancestry 42 English Street Armagh BT60 7BA Northern Ireland Tel: + 44 2837 521802 Fax: + 44 2837 510180	Full commissioned research service. Originally part of the archives of the Catholic Archdiocese of Armagh.
Carlow	Carlow Genealogy Project Old School College Street Carlow Tel: + 353 (503) 30850 *carlowgenealogy@iolfree.ie*	Partial commissioned research service. Status unclear.

- National Library of Ireland, Kildare St, Dublin 2, Tel: +353 (0) 661881.
  www.nli.ie. Open 10am–9pm, Mon.–Wed.; 10am–5pm, Thurs. and Fri.;
  10am–1pm, Sat.
- Registry of Deeds, Henrietta St, Dublin 1, Tel: +353 (0)1 6707500.
  www.landregistry.ie. Open 10am–4.30pm, Mon.–Fri.
- Society of Friends Library, Quaker House, Stocking Lane, Rathfarnham,
  Dublin 16, Tel: +353 (0)1 4956890. *www.quakers-in-ireland.org*. Open
  Thursdays, 11am–1pm.
- Representative Church Body Library, Braemor Park, Rathgar, Dublin 14, Tel:
  +353 +353 (0)1 4923979. *ireland.anglican.org/library*. Open 9am–1pm and
  2pm–5pm, Mon.–Fri.

C. United Kingdom

England

- The National Archives, Kew, Richmond, Surrey, TW9 4DU, Tel: +44 (0) 20
  8876 3444. *www.nationalarchives.gov.uk*.
- The Family Records Centre, 1 Myddelton Street, Islington, EC1R 1UW,
  London, Tel: +44 (0)845 603 7788. *www.familyrecords.gov.uk*.
- The British Postal Museum & Archive, Freeling House, Phoenix Place,
  London, WC1X 0DL, Tel: +44 (0)20 7239 2570. *www.postalheritage.org.uk*.

Scotland

- General Register Office for Scotland, New Register House, Edinburgh,
  Scotland, EH1 3YT, Tel: +44 (0) 131 314 4411. *www.gro-scotland.gov.uk*. See
  also *www.scotlandspeople.gov.uk* for online records.

Wales

- Llyfrgell Genedlaethol Cymru/National Library of Wales, Aberystwyth,
  Ceredigion, Cymru/Wales, SY23 3BU, Tel: +44 (0)1970 632 800.
  www.llgc.org.uk.

PUBLISHERS

- Belgrave Publications, Belgrave Avenue, Cork, Ireland (*Irish Roots*).
  www.irishrootsmagazine.com.
- Eneclann, Unit 1b, Trinity College Enterprise Centre, Pearse Street, Dublin 2,
  Ireland, Tel: + 353 1 6710338. *www.eneclann.ie*.
- Flyleaf Press, 4 Spencer Villas, Glenageary, Co. Dublin, Ireland, Tel: +353 1
  2845906. *www.flyleaf.ie*.
- Genealogical Publishing Company, Inc., 3600 Clipper Mill Road, Suite 260
  Baltimore, Maryland 2121, USA, Tel: 1-800-296-6687. *www.genealogical.com*.
- Geography Publications, 24 Kennington Road, Templeogue, Dublin 6W,
  Ireland, Tel: + 353 1 4566085. *www.geographypublications.com*.

General Repositories

- Church of Jesus Christ of Latter-Day Saints Family History Centre, 403 Hollywood Road, Belfast BT4 2GU, Tel: +44 (0) 28 9076825O. Open Wednesday, Thursday, Saturday.
- General Register Office, Oxford House, 49–55 Chichester St, Belfast BT1 4HL, Tel: +44 (0) 9025200O. *www.groni.gov.uk.* The indexes are now computerised. Appointment advisable.
- Linen Hall Library, 17 Donegall Square North, Belfast BT1 5GD, Northern Ireland, Tel: +44 (0)28 9032 1707. *www.linenhall.com.* Open 9.30am–5.30pm, Mon.–Fri.; 9.30am–4.00pm, Sat.
- Presbyterian Historical Society, Church House, Fisherwick Place, Belfast BT1 6DW, Tel: +44 028 9032 2284. *www.presbyterianireland.org/phsi.* Open 10am–12.30pm, Mon.–Fri.
- Public Record Office of Northern Ireland, 66 Balmoral Avenue, Belfast BT9 6 NY, Tel: (0232) 661621. *www.proni.gov.uk.* Open 9.15am–4.45pm, Mon.–Fri.
- Society of Friends Library, Meeting House, Railway Street, Lisburn, Co., Antrim. Postal queries only.

B. Republic of Ireland

County Libraries

See *www.library.ie:* many county libraries have online catalogues.

General Repositories

- Church of Jesus Christ of Latter-Day Saints Family History Centre, *The Willows,* Finglas Road, Glasnevin, Dublin 11, Tel: (01) 8306684. Open evenings and Saturday morning.
- Cork Archives Institute, Christ Church, South Main St, Cork, Tel: +353 (0) 21 4277809. *www.corkcorp.ie/ourservices/rac/archives.* Open 10am–1pm and 2.30pm–5pm, Mon.–Fri.
- Dublin City Library and Archive, 138–142 Pearse St, Dublin 2, Tel: +353 (0)1 6744999. *www.dublincity.ie.* Open 10am–8pm, Mon.–Thurs. and 10am–5pm, Fri. and Sat.
- The Genealogical Office: 2 Kildare St, Dublin 2, Tel: +353 (0)1 6618811. Open 10am–4.30pm, Mon.–Fri.
- The General Register Office, Joyce House, 8–11 Lombard St East, Dublin 2, Tel: +353 (0)1 6711000. *www.groireland.ie.* Research room open 9.30am–4.30pm, Mon.–Fri.
- Land Valuation Office, Irish Life Centre, Abbey Street, Dublin 1, Tel: +353 (0)1 6763211. *www.valoff.ie.* Open 9.30am–12.30pm and 2pm–4.30pm, Mon.–Fri.
- National Archives of Ireland, Bishop Street, Dublin 8, Tel: +353 (0)1 4072300. *www.nationalarchives.ie.* Open 10am–5pm, Mon.–Fri.

- Huguenot Society of Great Britain and Ireland, The Hon. Secretary, Sunhaven, Dublin Road, Celbridge, Co. Kildare. www.huguenotsociety.org.uk
- Irish Family History Society, po Box 36, Naas, Co. Kildare: publishes Irish Family History homepage.eircom.net/~ifhs
- Irish Genealogical Research Society, 82, currently (2005) without premises: publishes The Irish Genealogist. www.igrsoc.org
- Kerry Genealogical Society, 119/120 Rock Street, Tralee, Co. Kerry.
- North of Ireland Family History Society, c/o School of Education, Queen's University, 69 University Street, Belfast BT7 1HL: publishes North Irish Roots. www.nifhs.org
- Raheny Heritage Society, 68 Raheny Park, Raheny, Dublin 5: members' facilities only.
- Roscommon Family History Society, Bealnamullia, Athlone, Co. Roscommon: annual Journal since 2001. www.geocities.com/corofahiso
- Ulster Historical and Genealogical Guild, Ulster Historical Foundation, 12 College Square East, Belfast BT1 6DD, Northern Ireland: publishes Familia: Ulster Genealogical Review. www.ancestryireland.co.uk
- Wexford Family History Society, Carraig Mór, Mauldintown, Wexford: members' facilities only.
- Wicklow County Genealogical Society, Summerhill, Wicklow Town, Co. Wicklow.

B. Abroad

- Canadian Genealogy Centre, Library and Archives Canada, 395 Wellington Street, Ottawa, ON K1A 0N4, Canada. www.genealogy.gc.ca
- Federation of Family History Societies, po Box 2425, Coventry CV5 6YX, England. www.ffhs.org.uk
- Federation of Genealogical Societies, po Box 200940, Austin, TX 78720-0940, USA. www.fgs.org
- Irish Family Names Society, po Box 2095, La Mesa, CA 92044, USA.
- Irish Genealogical Society International, po Box 16585, St Paul MN 55116, USA: publishes Septs. www.rootsweb.com/~irish/
- National Genealogical Society, 3108 Columbia Pike, Suite 300, Arlington, Virginia 22204-4304, USA. www.ngsgenealogy.org
- New Zealand Society of Genealogists, Po Box 8785, Auckland 3, New Zealand
- The Society of Australian Genealogists, Richmond Villa, 120 Kent St., Sydney, NSW 2000, Australia: publishes Descent.

REPOSITORIES

A. Northern Ireland

Area Libraries:
See online catalogue at www.ni-libraries.net.

Area	Address	Comment
Laois/Offaly	Irish Midlands Ancestry, Bury Quay, Tullamore, Co. Offaly, Tel: +353 (0) 506 21421, ohas@iol.ie, www.irishmidlandsancestry.com	Full commissioned research service. Almost all church records, as well as a wide range of other sources.
Leitrim	Leitrim Genealogy Centre, c/o Leitrim County Library, Ballinamore, Co. Leitrim, Tel: +353 (0) 71 964012, Fax: +353 (0) 71 964425, leitrimgenealogy@eircom.net	Full commissioned research service. Virtually all major records for the area.
Limerick	Limerick Archives, The Granary, Michael Street, Limerick, Tel: +353 (0) 61 410777, Fax: +353 (0) 61 415125, www.limerickancestry.com	Closed at present (2005). All church records, and a wide range of other sources.
Longford	Longford Genealogy Centre, 1 Church Street, Longford, Tel: +353 (0) 43 41235, Fax: +353 (0) 43 41279, email: longroot@iol.ie	Partial commissioned research service.
Mayo North	Mayo North Family Heritage Centre, Enniscoe, Castlehill, Ballina, Co. Mayo, Tel: +353 (0) 96 31809, Fax: +353 (0) 96 31885, normayo@iol.ie, mayo.irish-roots.net	Full commissioned research service. All church records, along with a wide range of other sources.
Mayo South	Mayo South Family Heritage Centre, Main Street, Ballinrobe, Co. Mayo, Tel: +353 (0) 94 954214, soumayo@iol.ie, mayo.irish-roots.net	Full commissioned research service. Virtually all major records for the area.
Meath	Meath Heritage Centre, Castle Street, Trim, Co. Meath, Tel: +353 (0) 46 943633, meathhc@iol.ie	Partial commissioned research service. Almost all church records.

Area	Address	Comment
Monaghan	Monaghan Ancestry 6 Tully Monaghan Tel: +353 (0) 87 6310360/ + 353 (0) 47 82304 email: theoemcmahon@eircom.net	Partial commissioned research service. Limited range of sources.
Offaly	See Laois	
Roscommon	Roscommon Heritage and Genealogy Centre Church Street Strokestown Co. Roscommon Tel: +353 (0) 71 9633380 Fax: +353 (0) 71 9633398 www.roscommonroots.com	Full commissioned research service. Almost all church records for the area.
Sligo	Aras Reddan, Temple Street Sligo Tel: +353 (0) 71 9143728 heritagesligo@eircom.net www.sligoroots.com	Full commissioned research service. Virtually all major sources for the area.
Tipperary	Tipperary Family History Research The Excel Heritage Centre Mitchell Street Tipperary town Tel: +353 (0) 62 80555/80556 Fax: +353 (0) 62 80552 research@tfhr.org www.tfhr.org	Partial commissioned research service. Roman Catholic registers for Cashel and Emly diocese only.
Tipperary North	Tipperary North Family History Research Centre Governor's House, Kickham Street Nenagh Co. Tipperary Tel: +353 (0) 67 33850 tipperarynorthgenealogy@eircom.net	Full commissioned research service. Catholic records for part of North Tipperary. A wide range of other sources.
Tipperary South	Bru Boru Heritage Centre Cashel Co. Tipperary Tel: +353 (0) 62 61122 Fax: +353 (0) 62 62700	Full commissioned research service. A wide range of non-Church sources, including gravestone inscriptions and civil records
Tyrone	See Fermanagh	

Area	Address	Comment
Waterford	Waterford Heritage Services Jenkin's Lane Waterford Tel: +353 (0) 51 876123 Fax: +353 (0) 50645 mnoc@iol.ie www.waterford-heritage.ie	Full commissioned research service. Almost all Catholic records for Waterford and Lismore diocese.
Westmeath	Dún na Sí Heritage Centre Moate Co. Westmeath Tel: +353 (0) 90 648183 Fax: +353 (0) 90 6481661 dunnasimoate@eircom.net	Partial commissioned research service. A large proportion of church records for the area.
Wexford	Wexford Heritage & Genealogy Society Yola Farmstead Folk Park, Tagoat Rosslare Co. Wexford Tel: +353 (0) 53 32611 Fax: +353 (0) 53 32612 wexgen@eircom.net homepage.eircom.net/~yolawexford	Partial commissioned research service. Virtually all Catholic records for the area.
Wicklow	Wicklow Family History Centre Wicklow's Historic Gaol Kilmantin Hill Wicklow Tel: +353 (0) 404 20126 Fax: +353 (0) 404 61612 whfc@eircom.net www.wicklow.ie	Full research service. Virtually all major sources for the area.

SOCIETIES

A. Ireland

- Ballinteer Family History Society, 29 The View, Woodpark, Ballinteer, Dundrum, Dublin 16: publishes *Gateway to the Past* annually. Members' facilities. www.iol.ie/~ryan/

- Cork Genealogical Society, 22 Elm Drive, Shamrock Lawn, Douglas, Cork: annual *Journal* since 2001. Members' facilities only. homepage.tinet.ie/~aocleman

- Federation of Local History Societies (Conascadh na gCumann Staire Aitiula), c/o Dermot Ryan, Winter's Hill, Kinsale, Co. Cork. homepage.eircom.net/~localhist

- Genealogical Society of Ireland, 11 Desmond Avenue, Dun Laoghaire, Co. Dublin: publishes *The Genie Gazette*. Members' facilities only. www.familyhistory.ie